Statistical Methods of Quality Assurance

Statistical Methods of Quality Assurance

H.-J. Mittag

FernUniversität, Hagen
Germany

and

H. Rinne

Justus-Liebig-Universität, Giessen
Germany

CRC Press is an imprint of the
Taylor & Francis Group, an **informa** business
A CHAPMAN & HALL BOOK

First published 1993 by Chapman & Hall

First English language edition 1993

Published 2019 by CRC Press
Taylor & Francis Group
6000 Broken Sound Parkway NW, Suite 300
Boca Raton, FL 33487-2742

Original German language edition – *Statistische Methoden der Qualitätssicherung* – © 1991 Carl Hanser Verlag, Munich. Translated by **Bernard Schreck**, Iowa State University, USA

CRC Press is an imprint of Taylor & Francis Group, an Informa business

First issued in paperback 2019

ISBN 13: 978-0-367-44990-2 (pbk)
ISBN 13: 978-0-412-55980-8 (hbk)

Visit the Taylor & Francis Web site at
http://www.taylorandfrancis.com

and the CRC Press Web site at
http://www.crcpress.com

A catalogue record for this book is available from the British Library

Library of Congress Cataloging-in-Publication data available

Table of Contents

Preface

During the last decade industry has placed increasing emphasis on the issue of quality. Intensified competition in the marketplace has forced companies all over the world to focus on improving product quality. At the same time advances in computer technology have allowed the use of relatively inexpensive but powerful soft- and hardware for quality control. More and more enterprises realize that a high standard of quality is an essential requirement for long term success and are investing large amounts of money in the development of in-house quality assurance departments. Consequently, the number of people working in the field of quality assurance is increasing. Since most of them do not have any prior knowledge in this area, neither from their undergraduate or graduate education nor from any other source, they need to acquire a basic understanding of quality assurance while practising their profession. Hence, there is a large demand for continuing education and professional training. Well-designed textbooks for self-study are therefore appropriate to fill this noticeable gap.

Under these circumstances we decided to develop a textbook in statistical quality assurance designed to satisfy the following general guidelines:

▷ **Suitability for self-study**

The book had to be a complete introduction to statistical quality control. This objective required the material to be self-contained, to emphasize visual presentations, to avoid any unnecessary abstraction and to offer opportunities for solving exercises in order to ensure adequate understanding. A special feature of this text is that it contains many carefully elaborated figures, tables, examples and completely solved problems.

▷ **Combining academic standards with suitability for practioners**

The book needed to be close to industrial practice without merely having the characteristics of a recipe collection. Nowadays, anyone who is responsible for quality assurance should know more than mere descriptions of procedures that omit the theoretical background. Technical details become outdated rapidly and long numerical derivations fade into the background, losing their previous importance. Hence, this text provides a solid overall picture of a broad range of quality assurance procedures and a sound understanding of the basic statistical theory involved.

▷ **Transmission of new research developments into practice**

In addition to standard procedures, the book should also present results of recent research in order to encourage their practical application. In order to meet this goal a detailed presentation of selected results from recent research and references to up-to-date journal articles have been included.

For example, this text deals in greater detail with the effects of counting or measurement errors in acceptance sampling and control charting than many other available textbooks.

This textbook is based on a German correspondence study course "Statistical Methods in Quality Assurance" which was developed by the authors between 1987 and 1989 at the suggestion of Prof. Dr. Dr. Josef Gruber, chair of the department of Statistics and Econometrics at the FernUniversität Hagen, Germany. In 1991 this course appeared in its second edition as a textbook at Hanser in Munich, Germany. As a response to the ongoing demand for this text, the Hanser Verlag is currently working on publishing a revised and considerably improved third edition. A Russian translation is to appear in 1993. This English text corresponds to the scheduled third German edition.

The authors want to thank Prof. Dr. Dr. Gruber for his continuing support, encouragement and helpful advice in the development of this book. We also highly appreciate the support of R. Bartz, Chancellor of the FernUniversität, financing a first translation of the correspondence study course. For their helpful suggestions and corrections regarding the presentation of the material we want to thank Dr. L. Bauer, Prof. Dr. E. v. Collani, Dr. Dr. W. Gohout, Dr. H. Webersinke, Dipl.-Kfm. T. Holl, Dipl.-Kfm. M. Schüppel as well as Dipl.-Ök. K. Straube. Especially, we are obliged to Mr. B. Schreck, MA Statistics (University of Michigan, Ann Arbor), for preparing the English translation of the text, and to Dipl.-Kfm. I. Kuhnert who edited the LaTeX-files for this book. For the – hopefully few – remaining errors we take, of course, full responsibility. We are also very grateful to those companies who gave permission to reproduce graphics and photos.

January 1993

Hans-Joachim Mittag, University of Hagen, Germany
Horst Rinne, University of Giessen, Germany

A Guide to this Book

This textbook is designed to be a self-instructional introduction to statistical quality assurance. After working through this book the reader will

Goals of this textbook

- be familiar with the basic concepts of quality assurance (QA) and be able to differentiate between the various fields of QA (Chapter 1);
- have obtained a general view of the most important probability distributions of quality characteristics and test statistics (Chapter 2);
- have learned the theoretical background of hypothesis testing in statistical quality assurance (SQA);
- be able to design sampling plans for attributes and for variables (Chapter 3);
- be familiar with the procedures of the most common sampling schemes, in particular the ISO 2859 and ISO 3951 (Chapter 3);
- have learned to design and evaluate classical and modified SHEWHART control charts for attributes and for variables (Chapter 4);
- understand the principles of non-SHEWHART charts like CUSUM and EWMA charts and be able to make an appreciative comparison between SHEWHART- and non-SHEWHART-type charts (Chapter 4).

Readership of the book

This book intends to address students and scientists (e.g. in the areas of engineering, economics, statistics, computer science, etc.) as well as professionals, who are involved in quality assurance (i.e. engineers, technicians, managers, etc.). To respond to these circumstances the presentation takes into account that the readers will have differing levels of background statistical knowledge.

Contents of the book

The book 'Statistical Methods of Quality Assurance' is divided into four chapters, that are supplemented by an appendix of tables (Chapter 5), a separate section with solutions to exercises (Chapter 6) and various index lists (Chapter 7):

- Chapter 1: **Introduction**

  In Chapter 1 we will describe the technical and industrial environment of QA and discuss the basic terminology of QA. The presentation will be supplemented by a background of the historical development as well as an outlook towards future trends.

- Chapter 2: **Foundations of Statistical Quality Assurance**

  In Chapter 2 we will introduce the statistical tools which are commonly used in SQA and which will then be applied in Chapters 3 and 4. First, we will present the most important discrete and continuous distributions. Then, we will give a brief general view of the theory of hypothesis testing and finally we will discuss in detail the testtheoretical background of SQA.

- Chapter 3: **Acceptance Sampling**

  Chapter 3 gives a description of procedures for testing and rating finite populations. Acceptance control can be applied to incoming as well as outgoing goods (acceptance inspection/final inspection), and also during the manufacturing process, e.g., between two stages or when components are transferred from one department of a plant to another. We will discuss attribute as well as variable acceptance sampling and present all the various types of sampling plans (single, double, multiple and sequential). In addition, various sampling systems will be introduced. We will especially consider the consequences that can result from errors made by the inspection personnel, when good units are classified defective and vice versa. At the end there will be an introductory treatment of how to design economic sampling plans.

- Chapter 4: **Statistical Process Control**

  The issue of statistical process control (SPC) is to monitor an ongoing production process, which is a population with a potentially infinite number of elements. A typical aspect of SPC is that the product units reach the inspection as a continuous stream of output. We will first consider continuous sampling plans which monitor the production process with varying inspection intensity (i.e., switching between screening every unit and sampling). Following this we will outline the basic concepts of monitoring a process with the help of quality control charts and introduce the most commonly used control charts for both attribute and variable inspection. Besides the SHEWHART control charts we will also discuss the previously mentioned CUSUM and EWMA charts. The latter are not yet widely used.

- Chapter 5: **Statistical Tables**

  The statistical tables which are necessary for studying this text (especially distributions and percentiles of distributions) are presented separately in this chapter. In order to facilitate their use, we have added a short introduction at the beginning of each table. The reader will find the formulas that are used to obtain the tabulated values as well as numerical examples for working with the tables.

- Chapter 6: **Solutions to exercises**

  We have learned from past experience that the described statistical methods and procedures cannot be learned by reading alone, but rather through "learning-by-doing". Thus we have included more than 100 problems in Chapters 2 - 4. Since this book is designed for self-study, detailed solutions to all the problems are presented in this chapter.

- Chapter 7: **Index Lists**

  At the end of the book the reader will find several useful index lists. For the sake of a clear structure, these are combined into a separate chapter. We want to mention the annotated bibliography (textbooks, journals and reference books) and provide a detailed subject index.

How do I use this text?

The core of this book are chapters 3 and 4. In spite of some cross connections between them they can be studied independently of each other. Chapter 1 is very easy to read and intends to give an informative view and a broader context. Readers who are familiar with the practice of quality control could omit this chapter. If the text is studied in chronological order, then the discussion of all the distributions in Chapter 2 may be a little dry. However, in this chapter we deliberately give detailed presentations in order to enable readers with little or no statistical background to work through this book without having to refer to additional literature. A person with a thorough background in the theory of statistics can immediately start with chapter 3 or 4 and can use chapter 2 for reference purposes. Chapters 5 and 6 have the character of appendices. If one does not intend to work through the examples and problems in the text, then those chapters are not needed. Chapter 7 is especially useful for readers who are also using this text as a reference book.

The following figure presents an overview of the structure and use of this book. The bold arrows show the principal flow of reading, the thin arrows indicate how one may jump forward and backward between the individual chapters. The chapters are presented in blocks of different size, where the height of the block is proportional to the size of the chapter. The blocks with the central Chapters 3 and 4 are printed boldface.

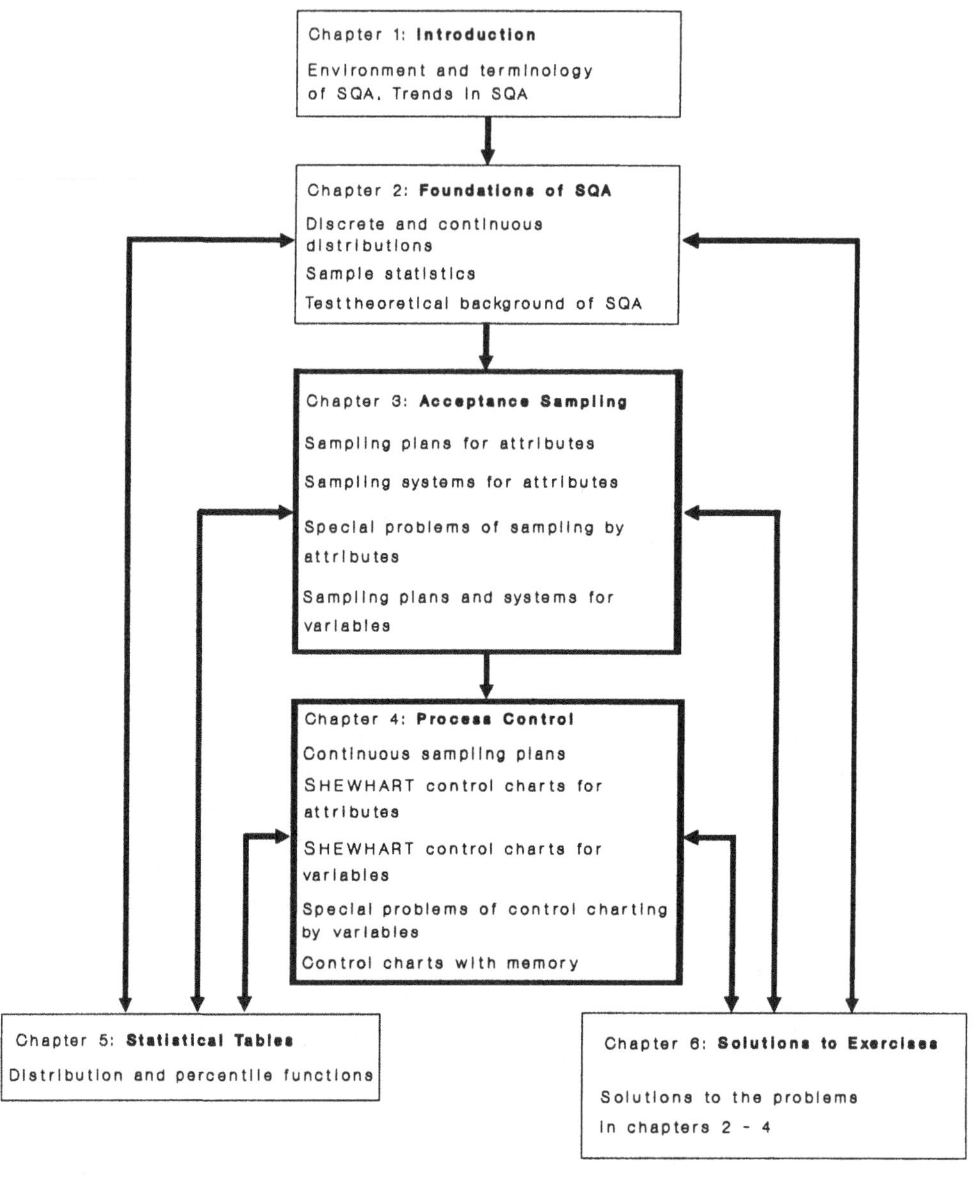
Chapter 1: Introduction
Environment and terminology of SQA, Trends in SQA
Chapter 2: Foundations of SQA
Discrete and continuous distributions
Sample statistics
Testtheoretical background of SQA
Chapter 3: Acceptance Sampling
Sampling plans for attributes
Sampling systems for attributes
Special problems of sampling by attributes
Sampling plans and systems for variables
Chapter 4: Process Control
Continuous sampling plans
SHEWHART control charts for attributes
SHEWHART control charts for variables
Special problems of control charting by variables
Control charts with memory
Chapter 5: Statistical Tables
Distribution and percentile functions
Chapter 6: Solutions to Exercises
Solutions to the problems in chapters 2 - 4
Chapter 7: Registers
Bibliography and index registers

1 Introduction

In this introductory chapter we will present the basic ideas and the historical development of quality assurance, without getting into mathematical-statistical issues at this point. In sections 1.1 and 1.2 we will explain what is meant by quality, quality control and statistical quality control and how statistical quality control can be systematically divided into different areas. In section 1.3 we will outline the historical development of quality assurance, beginning with the introduction of the control chart method in the 1920's to the computer aided quality control methods, which can be seen as a module in computer integrated manufacturing. The presentation of recent trends in the development of quality assurance will also be based on a few examples from practice.

Figure on the title page of this chapter (page before): Inspection sampling of semifinished products. (We express our thanks to the Co. Dr. BONGARDS (Systeme für technische EDV-Anwendungen, Wilnsdorf, Germany) for their permission to reproduce this graphic.

1.1 Quality and Quality Assurance

1.1.1 Quality as an Entrepreneurial Strategy

Determining factors for the success of an enterprise:

The success of an enterprise significantly depends on its innovative strength, its productivity and the quality of the produced goods or services.

- Innovative strength

The **innovative strength** of a company, i.e. its ability to bring new goods or processes onto the market and to maintain them there, is a major factor contributing to its chances of survival. Presently more and more markets are buyer's markets, because the supply exceeds the demand. As a consequence, the competition between price and quality is intensified. In order not to lose out in the marketplace, companies have to develop strategies for gaining or defending advantages over the competition. Since more and more industries are subject to fast technological change, innovative products have become an increasingly important element of marketing. They allow a company to distinguish itself in profile against its competitors and to guard against losing its advantages in the market. The innovative potential of an enterprise is an indicator of its ability to adapt to a changing market situation.

- Productivity

Productivity, i.e., the relation between output and input, has dramatically increased in almost all industrial sectors during the last decades. Contributory causes for this development were the introduction of more effective manufacturing processes and the technological advances in the area of data processing. One just has to think of computer aided manufacturing (**CAM**). The increase in productivity of manufacturing facilities is already reaching its limits in many areas as the potential of rationalization becomes exhausted.

- Quality

Product innovation and assurance of **quality** are examples of influential parameters that are not directly price-related, but with which a company can strengthen its position in the market and relieve the pressure of competition. Products with an unsatisfactory quality level cannot maintain their market position, at least in the medium and high price range. The basis of the success of Japanese products was their combination of high technological sophistication (technological innovation) with a high level of quality and a comparatively low price. This shows that quality assurance is a powerful tool in the quest for competitiveness.

Increasing importance of quality for consumer and producer

Companies are beginning to pay more attention to quality as a strategic goal, because buyers increasingly base their decision to buy a product on its quality aspects. A company with a good reputation for its quality has the advantage of a 'confidence bonus' and can thus establish higher prices than its competitors (provided they don't have a similar image). This can even apply on a higher level to the entire economy of a country. The label

"Made in Japan" triggers different quality associations in a buyer than, for example, the label "Made in Hongkong".

Quality and productivity

As a result, many companies are increasing their efforts to improve quality, because their managements realize that an efficient quality assurance can increase the productivity. Through improving quality one can reduce the costs that are related to low-quality goods and rejects, and hence lower the cost per unit. In the long run a higher level of quality improves the quality image and hence increases the market share of a company. The resulting increased share of the market makes it possible to produce larger runs and thus lower the unit costs even further.

Striving for quality improvements as well as increasing productivity do not exclude each other, but can be realized at the same time through effectively applied quality control. An efficient handling of quality assurance is however complicated by dynamic developments of technology and the resulting trend towards short-lived products and processes.

Remark

We will not go into the details of the competing strategies for securing one's competitiveness, but will rather concentrate on the success factor quality and, in particular, on its statistical aspect. Readers with an interest in quality from the marketing point of view are referred to a special issue of the German journal *Absatzwirtschaft* (October 1991).

1.1.2 The Concept of Quality

Colloquial use of the word "quality":

quality
=
quality of design

What is meant by the term **quality**? An analysis of this word shows that it is not uniquely defined. This becomes very evident in the comparison of its meaning in common language and the technical language of professionals or researchers in the field of quality assurance[1]. In the colloquial use the word quality creates the association of an especially good and excellent product. In this sense a car X may be a quality product, but not a car Y. However, in the eyes of an expert of quality assurance, who is performing a quality inspection of the two different types of automobile, both sampled products can be quality products. The inspector may even come to the conclusion that car X is qualitatively worse than car Y if, for example, an equal amount of noise due to wind and rattling was noticed whilst driving both cars. In car X one might not have expected this to happen, whereas in car Y one may have been surprised if there were no draft and rattling.

Consequently, one needs to distinguish between a **quality of design** and a **quality of conformity to specifications**. For the first we will also

[1]The word **quality** will in the following be abbreviated by **Q**, **quality assurance** by **QA** and **statistical quality assurance** by **SQA**.

use the term **design quality** and for the latter the term **product quality**. One usually means design quality when talking of quality *per se*, i.e., quality differences, quality improvements and quality deterioration. For example, the quality differences between car X and car Y may be deliberately designed by their manufacturers in order to satisfy the different expectations of customers. In quality assurance the meaning of the term quality is, in general, different than in the colloquial use of the word.

The term quality in technical terminology:

quality
=
quality of workmanship

Quality assurance professionals use the term quality to describe the extent of conformance between the specified characteristics of a product and its actual characteristic. The German Society for Quality (DGQ) for example gives the definition (DGQ 1979, p.13):

> *"Quality: All those characteristics of a product or service that are related to its fitness to fulfill given requirements."*

In the following pages the word **quality** will be used almost exclusively in this sense, i.e., as a **measure of conformance of design and workmanship**. Differences between the design and the actual product are unwanted and one in fact wants to prevent them. This is one of the main goals of quality assurance.

Presentation of the different quality aspects in a quality cycle

The quality of a product is determined by all the different quality aspects in the following **quality cycle**. This describes (DGQ 1979, p.14)

> *"the uninterupted sequence of all quality influential measures and results during the manufacturing process and the application of a product or service."*

Figure 1.1/1 gives an example of a quality cycle. The following diagram could, for example, apply to the generator of a power station. One can assign a different quality aspect to each stage of the cycle.

Quality circle
=
internal committees with the purpose of maintaining and improving quality

This circle should not be confused with a different kind of **quality circle**. In most companies there is a loosely organized quality committee, which is usually a group of volunteers from the different departments, who have set themselves the goal to explore technical and economical possibilities to improve quality and especially to detect and correct deficiencies in quality. In Japan there is a quality circle movement with several million members. The fact that in Europe and other places similar organizations have evolved shows that this movement is not a result of the special circumstances of Japan.

Complexity of the concept of quality

The concept of quality is complex in two ways. On the one side almost all the departments of an enterprise influence the quality of conformance in some way or the other and are responsible for certain quality aspects. On

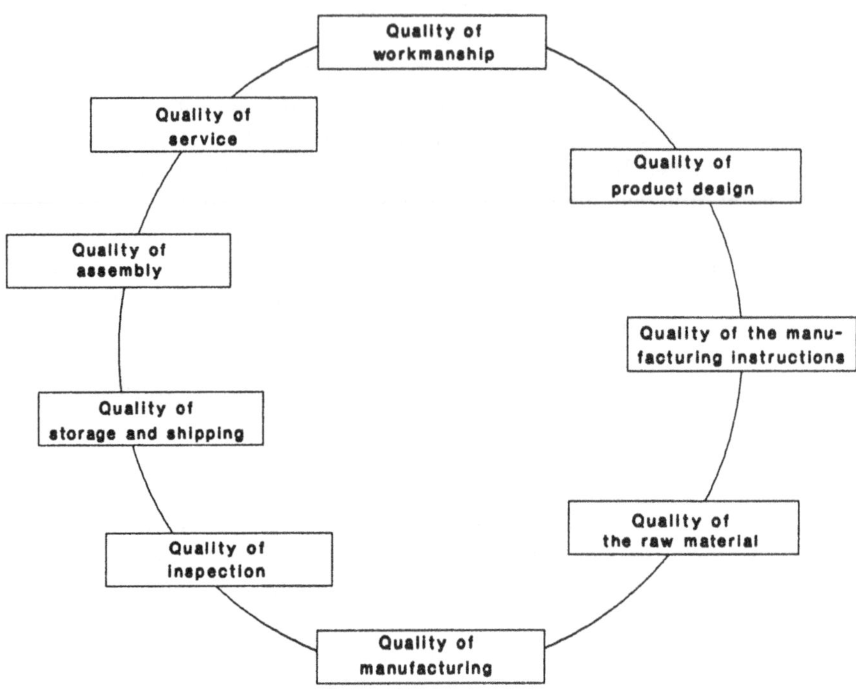

Figure 1.1/1: Quality cycle (based on DGQ 1979, p.14)

the other side a product has in general a vast number of quality characteristics, which are measurable or inspectable and which can be attributed to specific quality aspects. For each of these **quality characteristics** one can theoretically administer a quality inspection. We would obviously expect different kinds of deviations between the nominal and observed values. The quality of a product with a variety of quality characteristics could then be given by a suitably weighted sum of the individual quality characteristics.

Differentiation between quality and reliability

Although the concept of quality is not the same as the concept of **reliability**, the two terms are used almost as synonyms. Reliability is quality over time and we could define

> *"Reliability is quality under specified conditions before and after a given time period" (DGQ 1979).*

Measures for the reliability of a product

There are many parameters or measures for the reliability of a product, e.g., the **survival probability** (=probability that the product does not break down during a given time), the **probability to readiness** (=probability that a product will function at a random or specified time) or the **efficiency** (=proportion of life time that the product is working).

The issue of reliability is outside the scope of this book. In order to discuss this subject we would need to introduce the fairly demanding theory of **statistical life testing**. We decided not to include this subject, because the statistical procedures of life testing belong to a different field of statistics than those which are traditionally related to quality assurance and which are presented in this text.

Remarks

1. The definition of the term "quality" in section 1.1.2 includes the quality of products as well as of services. In this text we will exclusively discuss the quality of products (series production). The evaluation of services is usually concerned with different quality characteristics than that of industrial production, i.e., the time between placement and execution of an order (waiting/delivery time), the length of service (service time) or the kind or quality of advice that the customer receives (quality characteristic "information"). So far the quality control of services has not been sufficiently researched in a scientific way. Some attempts can, for example, be found in PARASURAMAN/ZEITHAML/BERRY (1985) and GRANT/LEAVENWORTH (1988).

2. A good survey of the present attempts to standardize central terminology of quality assurance on an international level can be found in FREUND (1985). Most active in these attempts are the standards committee of the **ASQC** (American Society for Quality Control), the **EOQ** (European Organization for Quality, head of all the European quality assurance associations) and the Technical Committee of the **ISO** (International Organization for Standardization).

3. The interested reader, who would like to get an idea of the rapid development in the field of reliability theory, will find references in the appended bibliography; for example refer to BANKS (1989), BEICHELT/FRANKEN (1984), KALBFLEISCH/PRENTICE (1980), O'CONNOR (1985), MILLER (1981), NELSON (1982) or RINNE (1979).

1.1.3 Quality Differences and their Causes

Experience in manufacturing tells us that no two production units of a product are exactly identical. Similar to the law of nature which states that two individuals of a species are never completely equal, we find the same holds for products and services. The deviations are sometimes very big and easy to recognize, as, for example, the height difference of two persons, but they can also be very subtle and difficult to spot. Sometimes it requires sophisticated precision instruments to determine differences. This shows that if two units of a product apparently have the same value of a quality characteristic, then it is due to the limitations of the measuring instrument, e.g., the power of a microscope. In spite of the development of modern manufacturing methods and measuring instruments there are still deviations, only their magnitude has changed. As a first requirement of being able to control these deviations one must be able to measure them. The following statement of an advertisement of the German company Osram in the German magazine "Stern" (issue 42, October 1980, p.39) gives a practical example of the order of magnitude of deviations and their consequences in an everyday product:

> *" 1/1000 mm deviation in the filament and a light bulb lasts 200 hours less."*

Classifications of product deviations

We distinguish between three **types of deviations** in a product:

▷ **Deviations within a unit**

An example of this kind of deviation would be the quality of a surface with varying roughness or the diameter of a piston which is larger at the top than at the bottom.

▷ **Deviations between units**

These are deviations between different product units from the same manufacturing process. For example the intensity of light can vary between several consecutively produced light bulbs.

▷ **Deviations over time**

By this we mean deviations between product units, that are produced at a different time of day or on a different day of the week. Just think of "monday products" or "end of day quality".

Classification of the deviations in a product according to their source

There are four main causes for these deviations. They are called the four **M**'s, i.e., man, machine, method, and material:

- Probably the largest source of deviations is **man**, i.e. the people who participate in the manufacturing process or monitor it.
- Sources of deviation in a **machine** are, for example, the wear and tear in tools, the play of bearings, vibrations, positioning of tool and work piece or instabilities in the supply of electricity, water and air, oil or steam pressure. All those variations superpose each other and determine in which tolerance range a machine is running.
- The **method** of production determines the interplay of man, machine and inflow as well as outflow of material and is consequently also a source of deviation in the resulting product.
- We have already learned that every product has deviations and since the raw **material** of a manufacturing process is itself a previously produced product, it follows that we also have to expect deviations in it. Its quality characteristics, like its ultimate strength, flexibility, porosity, content of humidity, chemical consistency, etc. vary and lead to deviations in the final product.

Besides these "four M's" another source of variation is **environmental influences**, e.g., temperature, noise, light intensity, humidity, dust, radiation. Whether the detected deviations can be ascribed to one or the other of the sources listed above has to be determined through an analysis of variance in each case.

We will now focus on the aspect of product quality in the cyclic quality diagram of figure 1.1/1. When determining the product quality we have to keep in mind that all manufacturing is fundamentally subject to the above influences and that production without tolerance is not possible. Already at the stage of design and planning one has to therefore allow for **tolerance ranges** around the nominal values of the quality characteristics. The task of QA is now to ensure that the manufacturing process stays within this range.

Classification of the causes of variation according to their influentiability

In order to control the quality of a production one needs to distinguish between tolerable and intolerable variations. For this purpose it has been found helpful to classify the sources of deviations from the nominal value of a quality characteristic into two categories: variation due to random and to systematic causes.

Random or **non-assignable causes** of variation in a product are inherent in the production process and, in principle, cannot be eliminated. The magnitude and effect of these causes cannot be calculated in the sense of prediction. The effects of the individual sources on the resulting product are very small and can hardly be detected, since the observed random variation is caused by the superposition and interaction of all these simultaneously occurring causes. Random causes, like the vibration or the play in a bearing of a machine lead to a natural spread in the values of the quality characteristic, e.g. the variation in the filling weight of a product, the lifetime of a neon tube or the diameter of screws.

Figure 1.1/2 graphs the densities of two normally distributed quality characteristics of the same product for two different manufacturing processes. The normal distributions have the same expectation μ, i.e., the quality characteristics of the two processes have the same average value. Hence, the processes differ only in the spread of their values. Process I with distribution I has a naturally wider spread than process II with distribution II. If we would require that the values of the quality characteristic lie within a tolerance region, which is centered at μ and has lower and upper boundaries G_l and G_u respectively, then it would follow that we expect a larger proportion of defectives in process I. The probability of the occurrence of defective units is represented by the cross-hatched areas in figure 1.1/2.

If the natural spread is too big compared to the required tolerance range, then there are only two solutions: one either has to sort out the defectives

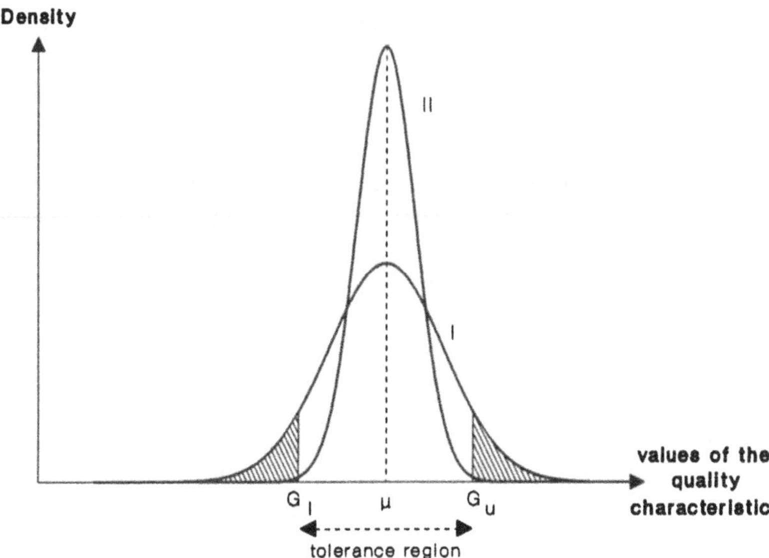

Figure 1.1/2: Proportion of defectives of two manufacturing processes with different spread of the quality characteristic

of the entire production or one has to find a manufacturing process with a smaller natural spread.

Systematic or **assignable causes** of deviation from the norm have the characteristic that they are detectable and can be at least influenced if not corrected. If they are occurring, one observes gradual or sudden changes in the distribution of the quality characteristic. Examples of these detectable causes can be given for all the afore-mentioned sources of deviations. A slow shift of a distribution parameter can, for example, be caused by wear and tear in a tool, an increase in temperature or fatigue of the personnel. A sudden change in quality can be caused by the damage of a tool or machine, a new supplier of raw materials, a change in the manufacturing process or a new shift of workers.

Figure 1.1/3 shows how the present expectation $\mu = \mu_I$ of the values of a quality characteristic with distribution I can shift to the right, for example, as a result of a different supplier of raw materials. Since the tolerance region remains constant the shift from μ_I to μ_{II} causes an increase in the fraction defective. The probability that the quality characteristic has a value outside of the tolerance region $[G_l, G_u]$ is again represented by the shaded and cross-hatched areas in figure 1.1/3.

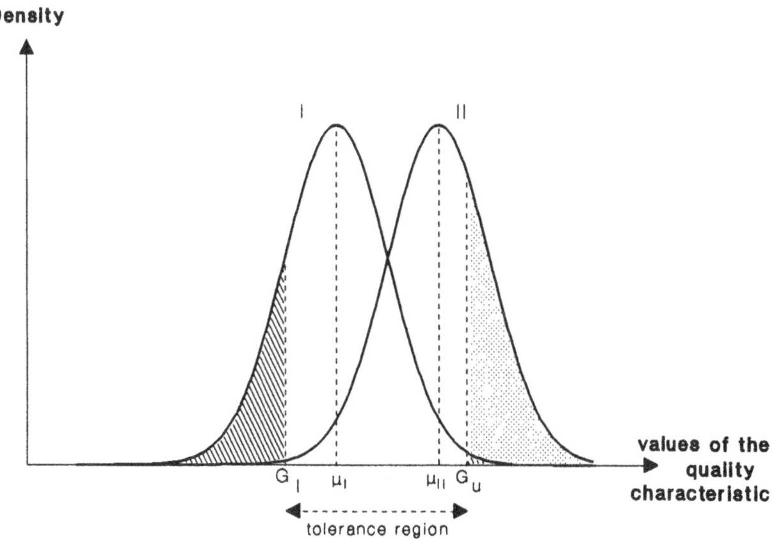

Figure 1.1/3: Fraction defective of two manufacturing processes with a different level of the quality characteristic

1.1.4 Quality Assurance

Quality assurance i.w.s.: All measures that are taken to achieve quality

Quality assurance in a wider sense (QA i.w.s.) includes all measures that are taken in order to achieve quality. It concerns most functional units of a company, from the provision of supplies to financing and organization. It is concerned with technical, economical, mathematical-statistical and in case of product liability, even legal aspects. Ergonomical and psychological considerations may also play a role in QA. This is why some managers consider it to be a separate operational field. In practice this is also documented by the fact that the issue of quality assurance appears as a separate entity on the organizational plan of an enterprise or as a separate sphere of responsibility of the board of directors. Sometimes it is directly put under the responsibility of the executive board.

Aspects of quality assurance

The different aspects of quality assurance are:

- **quality planning**
- **quality inspection**
- **quality supervision**

Quality planning: determination of quality design (product design)

In **quality planning** one is mainly concerned with the selection of important quality characteristics of a product or a service (e.g., power input, light intensity or lifetime of a light bulb) and also the tolerance regions of these characteristics. The latter may be determined by practical requirements or given norms (e.g., power input 40 Watt/h, light intensity of 30 candela and minimum lifetime 1000 hours in the case of a light bulb). The starting point for the design of a marketable product – regardless of whether it is an innovation or already existing in similar form – is an analysis of the market situation (among other aspects, detection of a niche in the market) and the expected use for the potential buyer. This is an issue of marketing. The result is a specification of the quality characteristics of the product (**product design**) that takes into account the specific market situation.

Another aspect of quality planning: process design (incl. experimental design)

Quality planning also includes the design of the manufacturing process by quality engineers (**process design**). The choice of manufacturing process not only effects the production costs, but also determines the magnitudes of the tolerance regions of the quality characteristics. The method of measuring the quality characteristic has to be chosen depending on the order of these magnitudes. A remote photo-electronic measurement involves, for example, less measurement errors than a measurement with a sliding gauge.

In the context of process design one also often runs an experiment before starting the production in order to find out how variation in selected process parameters such as pressure, temperature and consistency of the raw material effects the quality characteristics of interest (process optimization through **experimental design**). In most cases this is less expensive than the later modification of an unsatisfactory manufacturing process.

Quality inspection: comparison of actual and nominal values

The goal of **quality inspection** is then to determine whether and to what extent a product or service satisfies the desired quality requirements. To do this one inspects selected characteristics (usually the quality characteristics) and compares their realizations to the nominal values previously determined in quality planning. This aspect of quality inspection is also called **quality assurance in a restricted sense (QA i.r.s)** and is often associated with the word **quality control**.

Quality supervision: analysis of the inspection results for the purpose of quality control

Quality supervision plans, monitors and inspects the development of a product or a service. It follows after quality planning and is based on the results of quality inspection.

Figure 1.1/4 gives a summary of these relations. From now on we will use the term quality assurance to denote quality assurance i.r.s., i.e., quality inspection as discussed above.

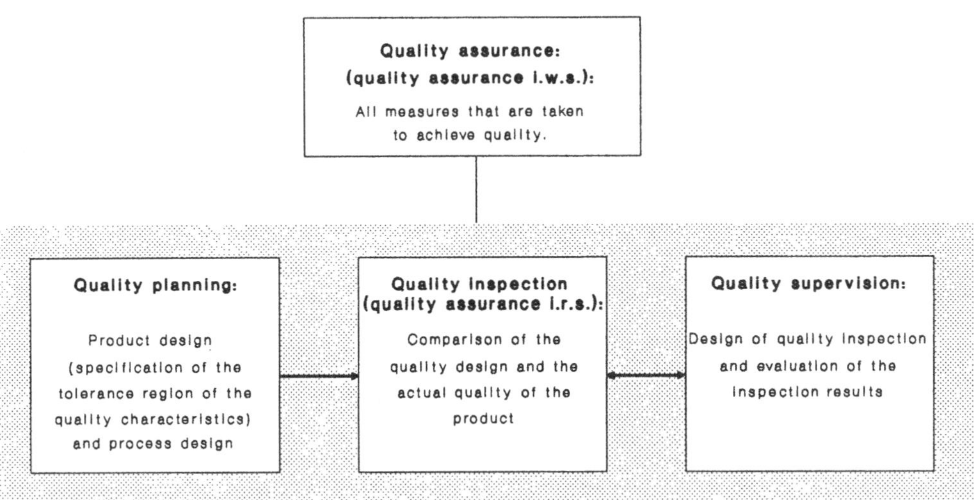

Figure 1.1/4: Quality assurance and its functions

Remarks

1. In the last few years product and process design have also gained importance in Europe, in particular under the name **Taguchi-method**, after having been widely accepted in Japan for about thirty years and in the USA since the mid-eighties. The Taguchi method groups variables with influence on a particular quality characteristic into **controllable factors and disturbance** or **noise factors**. Instead of trying to find and monitor the noise factors in the ongoing production process (online-control) Taguchi proposes a three-stage-design based on the concept of what he calls offline-control (preline control in our terminology).

   In the first stage, the stage of system design, the process is designed in a way to ensure that it is able to fulfill the given task. In the second step, the stage of parameter design, one then tries to find those levels of the controllable factors for which the quality characteristic of interest is least influenced by noise factors. In the approach of the Taguchi-method the parameter design has the key role. Its goal is to design systems (products and processes) which are robust against noise and disturbances. Finally, at the third stage of tolerance design one determines whether the tolerance ranges of the involved factors need to be tightened. Taguchi's method goes back to the statistical theory of experimental design, which was developed in the twenties and thirties by R.A. FISHER (see figure 1.3/5). A modern presentation of this theory is for example given by BOX/HUNTER/HUNTER (1978) or MASON/GUNST/HESS (1989). In the anglosaxon literature the Taguchi-method was first presented in TAGUCHI/WU (1979). A didactically revised presentation is given by ROSS (1988) and RYAN (1989, chapter 14). We further want to mention the works of BENDELL/DISNEY/PRIDMORE (1989) and DEHNAD (1989) because they contain many case studies.

2. Since 1987 international standards (ISO 9000 to ISO 9004) recommend what the system of quality assurance of an enterprise should look like. These standards have been accepted without modification by almost all leading nations in the world. In Germany we have DIN ISO 9000 etc., in the USA they are called ANSI/ASQC Q90 (up to Q94) whereas in Great Britain they are called BS 5750.

1.2 Statistical Quality Assurance

Definition of "statistical quality assurance"

Statistical Quality Assurance, often abbreviated by **SQA**, denotes the area of statistics which is concerned with the application of statistical methods for the purpose of quality assurance. Since we are only intending to discuss quality assurance i.r.s. we will use the term SQA to denote the application of statistical methods for this purpose, i.e., to quality inspection.

1.2.1 Two Examples from Practice

We will start with two examples which will give an idea of how quality assurance is applied in practice, and then present a description of its goals and a classification into different fields of SQA.

Example 1.2/1: Inspection of the filling weight of sugar packets

A filling machine is supposed to fill 1 kg packets of sugar (net weight). The machine runs at a very high speed, it fills about 2000 packets per hour. The crucial quality characteristic here is the filling weight. If it is too high, then too much sugar is used. If it is too low the company has to fear complaints from consumers and maybe even from official authorities, because of a violation of the applicable laws. It would be impossible to weigh and check every individual packet. The reasons against **100% inspection** or **screening** are:

Arguments in favour of sampling inspection

- The inspection costs for the necessary personnel and machinery would be very high, possibly more than the production costs.
- Even such a thorough inspection would not be free of errors.
- Neither the customer nor the law can require that every packet contains exactly 1 kg of sugar. A certain spread in the sense of randomly falling short of or exceeding the nominal weight stated on the packet is always tolerated and also does not violate the law.

Consequently one will administer **partial** or **sampling inspection** and, for example, take a sample of twenty packets every hour and draw inference about the state of the process based on these twenty observations. We will, at the moment, leave it open as to how this is done. The task of quality control is to decide whether the process is in control, i.e. runs within the given tolerance range, or not. In the first case one would not want to take any action, but in the latter one would have to take corrective actions, such as readjusting the machine. Regardless of how one decides, it is possible that one commits an error. Due to the natural spread of the process it can happen just by chance that we draw an 'unlucky sample', which deceives us about the 'true' state of the process.

In example 1.2/1 it is possible that the packets of the sample just happen to have the right weight, although the machine fills with a wrong weight. We then would not initiate an alarm and continue to produce at an undesired level (**neglected alarm**). As a consequence, we would risk either using too much sugar or complaints by the consumer and government inspector. The other possible error, a **false alarm**, would be committed if the weights of the twenty packets of the sample happen to have incorrect weights although the process runs at a desirable level. Then one would correct a non-existent defect.

Statistical errors that can occur in example 1.2/1:

- neglected alarm (type II error)
- false alarm (type I error)

The theory of statistics gives us the tools and methods to make statements about the probabilities of these two types of errors and to control the magnitudes of these errors, especially of the one with the more dangerous consequences. If one is able to financially evaluate the effects of making a wrong decision and if one would know according to which probability law the machine changes its filling weight, then one could attempt to determine the interval between samples, the sample size and the tolerance limits in such a way that the total loss through inspection costs and decision errors is minimized (**economic process control**).

Example 1.2/2: Fraction of safety fuses defective

A manufacturer of domestic electrical appliances equips their products with safety fuses from a certain supplier. The fuses are delivered in shipments of 1000 units and the buyer does not want to accept the shipment without inspection. An inspection of each unit is principally not possible because the fuse is destroyed during the process (**destructive inspection**). Supplier and buyer agree on the following **inspection plan**: A sample of 30 units is randomly taken from each delivery of 1000 fuses. In case of no or only one defective fuse (a fuse that does not fulfill the requirements) the buyer has to accept the entire shipment. In case of two or more defective fuses the buyer has the right to complain about the delivery and, as a result, pay a reduced price. If the procedure were not a destroying inspection, then a complaint could have different consequences. For example, defective units might be sorted out (and reimbursements made by the supplier) or the entire delivery could be returned.

The contract further specifies that a delivery is allowed to contain up to 1% defective units. The appliance manufacturer also knows that a shipment with more than 10% defective units is critical in the sense that the resulting loss would be too high.

Statistical errors that can occur in example 1.2/2:

- Producer's risk (type I error)

- Consumer's risk (type II error)

With the help of mathematical-statistical methods, which will be presented in chapters 2 and 3 of this book, one can determine how well the above inspection plan protects the interests of both the supplier and buyer. Conversely, one can also construct plans, that provide a specified level of protection. In the inspection plan of example 1.2/2 the maximal probability that deliveries with not more than 1% defective units are wrongly rejected is 3.4%. This is called the **producer's** or **supplier's risk**. The **consumer's** or **buyer's risk** is given by the probability that deliveries with 10% or more defective units are accepted. Here its maximum value is 18%.

As before one can try to find an inspection procedure based on a cost model with an inspection cost parameter and loss parameters related to decision errors. Then, two decision parameters would have to be determined so that the costs are minimized: the sample size and the critical number of defective units that lead to rejection.

1.2.2 Goals of Statistical Quality Assurance

Three characteristics of SQA:

- Sampling instead of screening

The two preceeding examples demonstrate that the goal of SQA is to ensure that the actual product agrees with the product design, i.e., the nominal values of the quality characteristics and their tolerance ranges. Both examples illustrate three typical characteristics of SQA:

SQA is never a census, but a sampling inspection.

However, it can happen that the outcome of a sampling inspection results in taking the action of screening. There are also situations where a screening of certain quality characteristics is absolutely necessary (e.g., a function test of a heart pace maker or of car brakes). Then there are also quality characteristics which can absolutely not be screened, because the inspection either destroys or significantly reduces its fitness for use. Whenever sampling is possible it has, in general, three advantages over screening:

- Sampling results are obtained very fast.
- Sampling is cheaper.
- Sampling can be performed more thoroughly and carefully.

Through the increasingly more powerful technology of automated data processing these arguments may lose some weight. We could also give examples where, after the introduction of modern electronic data processing technology, sampling inspection was switched to screening (see section 1.3).

The goal of SQA is not to make statements about individual product units, but to make statements about a population of product units.

- Statements about a population

This tells us that the main point of interest of SQA, and statistical analysis in general, is a population of elements with a certain characteristic and not the individual element. In example 1.2/1 the observed weights of the sampled packets were used to draw inference about the process level of the machine, i.e., about the potentially infinite population of all the packets that could be filled by the machine in this state. In example 1.2/2 the goal was to evaluate the quality of a finite population of a product, i.e., the 1000 safety fuses in the shipment.

In SQA there is always the risk that the conclusions resulting from the outcome of the sample are wrong.

- Possibility of decision errors

We saw in example 1.2/1 that a blind as well as a neglected alarm could happen and in example 1.2/2 we had a consumer's as well as a producer's risk. Decision errors can even occur when every unit is screened, but this is due to different causes, i.e., lack of diligence or existence of measurement errors during the inspection. In sampling inspection decision errors are mainly due to the randomness in the selection of the sample.

Characteristics of a random sample

One obviously would like to calculate the probability of occurrence of such decision errors. Provided that the sample has the characteristics of a **random sample** this is possible with the help of mathematical-statistical methods. By random sample we mean a sample which selects the sample units according to a random mechanism. This means the following: Every product unit of the population of interest has a known, but not necessary equal, probability of selection. Further, there should be no interaction between the selection mechanism and the inspected quality characteristic.

In summary we can say:

Goal of SQA

The goal of statistical quality assurance is to use sampling results in order to draw conclusions about the quality of a population of product units by means of mathematical-statistical methods.

1.2.3 Classification of Statistical Quality Assurance

The procedures of SQA can be classified according to several, not necessary exclusive, criteria. We will only introduce the two criteria which determine the structure of this text. Our first criterion is the time of inspection and the second, how the quality characteristic is measured.

Classification of SQA according to the time of inspection:

According to the time of inspection we distinguish between **process control** and **acceptance sampling**.

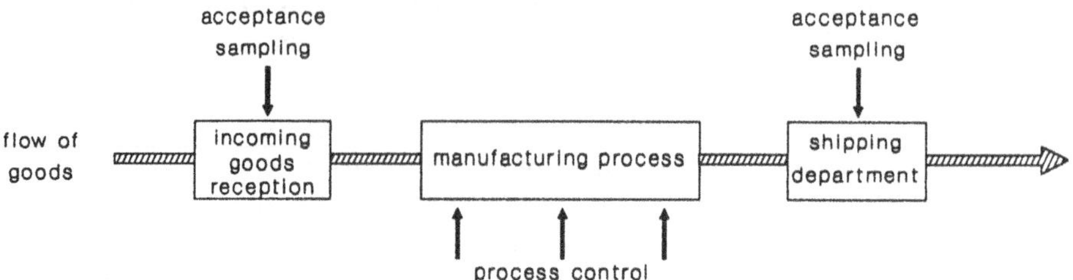

Figure 1.2/1: Acceptance sampling and process control

- Process control

By **process control** we mean all the inspection procedures administered during the process of manufacturing which are suitable to give information about the state of the process, and thus make it possible to intervene in the process with the intention to maintain the quality characteristic of the product within the specified tolerance limits. Example 1.2/1 belongs to this category. The area of statistical quality assurance that is concerned with this issue has been given the name statistical process control, usually abbreviated by **SPC**. In this area of process inspection one generally deals with a population of potentially infinite size, i.e., its underlying statistical theory is about sampling from populations of infinite size.

The most important statistical tool of process control is the **quality control chart**, also called **control chart**. The classical version, the control chart designed by SHEWHART (**SHEWHART chart**), is a graphical device into which the inspection results are entered in chronological order (directly or in condensed form). The chart contains certain critical boundaries and if a sampling result is found to be outside these limits, then well defined measures to influence the manufacturing process are taken. Sometimes such an event also affects consecutive inspections. In process control via electronic data processing the critical boundaries and the inspection results are often only displayed on a monitor to avoid paperwork for the inspection personnel. Besides the SHEWHART chart other recently introduced charts are the **CUSUM chart** (cumulative sum chart) and the **EWMA chart** (exponentially weighted moving average chart) which are more sensitive to small and slow changes of certain process parameters (i.e., location and spread). Whereas in the SHEWHART chart one only intervenes in the process when *individual observations* of a sampling statistic are outside certain (parallel) critical lines, the method of the CUSUM chart for example is to continually sum the deviations of consecutive observations from their nominal values. The decision to intervene with the process is then based on this sum, i.e., whether the ***sum of the observed deviations from the nominal values*** intersects certain (not necessarily parallel) critical lines.

- Final inspection/ acceptance control

The purpose of **acceptance sampling** is to investigate whether a particular **lot** of a semifinished or final product satisfies the quality standard expressed by the percentage of defectives. Example 1.2/2 belongs to this category. The statistical tool of acceptance sampling is the **sampling plan**. It contains instructions about the **sample size** corresponding to a particular lot size and the conditions for accepting the lot. In acceptance control one always deals with a lot of finite size, and thus this area is an application of the statistical theory of sampling from finite populations. Provided that the sample size is very small compared to the lot size it is possible to work with the more simple theory of sampling from populations with infinite size.

- Continuous sampling inspection: inspection with varying intensity

In between acceptance control and process control there is the intermediary category of **continuous sampling inspection**. Its corresponding sampling plans, called continuous sampling plans (**CSP**), can be applied to the same situations as quality control charts, i.e., when the output does not naturally divide into separate lots (continuous production, potentially infinite lot size). Different to process control with control charts one does not perform the inspection by continually taking samples, but according to the observed level of quality, the plan switches between partial inspection and screening. Another difference is that the primary goal is not to intervene in the ongoing production (recall that inspection with control charts plans to intervene in the manufacturing process whenever the critical boundaries are exceeded), but to primarily keep the **average outgoing quality**, i.e., the proportion of defectives after inspection, below a specified limit.

Classification of SQA according to how the quality characteristic is measured:

- inspection by variables

Another approach to classifying the procedures of SQA is to distinguish between **inspection by variables and inspection by attributes**. The analysis of the product quality in inspection by variables is based on measurements or on an index which is obtained as the result of measurements. Example 1.2/1 was a case of inspection by variables (variable: filling weight).

- inspection by attributes

In inspection by attributes the produced units are only classified into one of the two categories "good" (fit to use) and "bad" (not fit to use). This is why attribute inspection is sometimes called **good-bad inspection**. Example 1.2/2 belongs to this category. The case where one counts the number of nonconformities or defects per sample unit also belongs to the category of attribute inspection. The determined intensity of nonconformities per unit can then be used in two ways: one way would be to determine whether the unit is good (no or few defects) or bad (large number of defects) and the other way would be to rate an entire lot or process as either good or bad. In the latter case one would use the total number of nonconformities in the sample as a criterion.

The differentiation between **measured** and **counted** characteristics is not the same as distinguishing between **measurable** and **non-measurable** characteristics. A non-measurable characteristic can only occur in counting inspection. Counting or attribute inspection can, however, also be applied to measurable characteristics, by simply considering the unit to be good if the value of the characteristic lies within specified tolerance limits, or to be bad if not. In this case one either does not make use of the available exact information of the measurement or does not even make an exact measurement.

Criteria for the choice of inspection procedure

The choice of inspection procedure very much depends on the technological and economical circumstances and also on the available human resources, unless the type of characteristic does not allow a particular choice. When inspection happens manually, counting inspection has the definite advantage over measuring inspection, in that it can be performed by less skilled personnel with technologically less sophisticated instruments. As a result of this and also the shorter time needed for inspection and analysis, the inspection costs per unit are usually lower. However, since attribute quantities have a lower content of information than measured quantities, a good-bad inspection may need a larger sample size than a variable inspection procedure with an equivalent discriminatory power. In a concrete situation one can use a comparison of costs to determine the best choice of procedure.

Figure 1.2/2 summarizes the above classification of SQA.

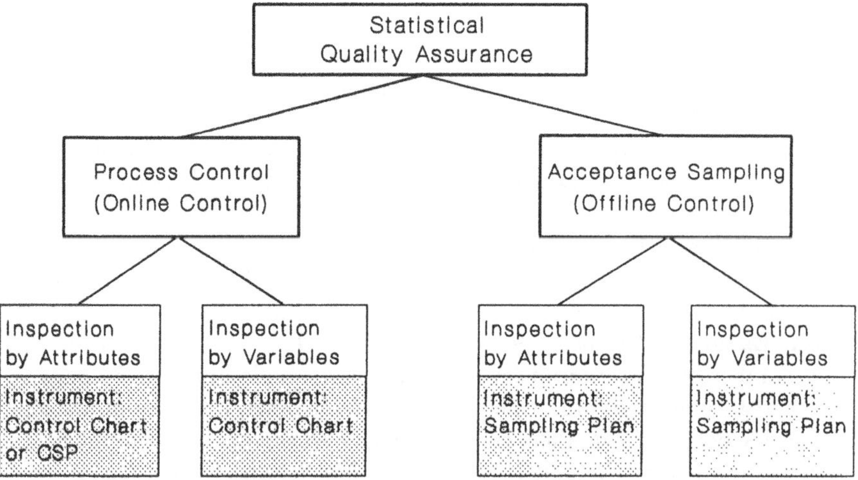

Figure 1.2/2: Classifaction of statistical quality assurance

1.3 Evolution of Quality Assurance

In recent times quality assurance has experienced rapid changes. New possibilities in information technology and electronic data processing, as well as computerized manufacturing processes and inspection procedures, are changing the old structures of quality assurance. In section 1.3.1 we will first sketch the history of QA from the beginnings to the development of a solid scientific foundation. In section 1.3.2 we will then describe the recent trends of development in QA and illustrate them with examples of practical applications. In section 1.3.3 we will show how computer aided quality assurance can be seen as a module in the wider concept of computer integrated manufacturing.

1.3.1 Historical Development of Quality Assurance

Beginnings of QA

We can assume that since men began to produce goods the production of these goods was also supervised and their quality evaluated. An indication that sampling inspection is not an invention of this or the last century can, for example, be found in the German term for sample "Stichprobe". The term describes the act of stabbing into a sack of grain with a dagger in order to sample its content. This is how even many centuries ago buyers of grain and cotton took a sample from the bag or bundle in order to get an idea of the quality of the goods. How many such samples to draw and how to conclude about the quality of the entire lot was a custom and not a result of scientific reasoning. From the first appearance of manufacturing in the 17th century until the start of the industrial revolution at the beginning of the 19th century, the manufacturing and the inspection of the product were both in the hands of the artisan. These were trained through a long apprenticeship and journeyman's years of service. The tradition and method of manufacturing remained almost unchanged over generations. With the introduction of the division of labour this all changed. The unskilled factory worker, who only performed a few motions, was not able to carry the responsibility for the entire product. Thus quality control became a separate task.

A scientific foundation of QA with respect to how many sample units to inspect and what conclusions to draw from the result and the eventual extension to SQA took place relatively late. One usually dates the beginning of SQA back to the year 1924, when W. A. SHEWHART introduced his first control chart. Figure 1.3/1 shows the first control chart by SHEWHART, a control chart for the fraction of nonconforming units. It monitors whether the nonconforming fraction of the product remains within the control limits during the time of observation.

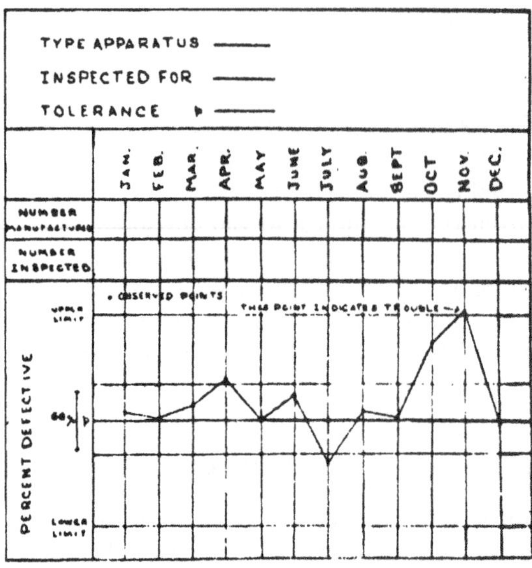

Figure 1.3/1:
SHEWHART's first design of a control chart

WALTER ANDREW SHEWHART (3/18/1891 - 3/11/1967) – figure 1.3/2 shows a portrait of him – was employed as an engineer in the Western Electric Company from 1918-1924. After the company was converted to the Bell Telephone Laboratories, he worked there as a research engineer and statistician until his retirement in 1956. In 1954 he was appointed a

Figure 1.3/2:
WALTER ANDREW SHEWHART (1891-1967)

honorary professor at Rutgers University. His first book 'Economic Control of Manufactured Product' appeared in 1931 and in 1939 his second book 'Statistical Methods from the Viewpoint of Quality Control' was edited by W. E. DEMING. Because of his extraordinary merit in the development and introduction of statistical methods of quality assurance the American Society for Quality Control (ASQC) founded the SHEWHART-Medal in 1947, which is awarded every year to an outstanding professional in the field of quality assurance.

The second pioneer in the area of SQA is H. F. DODGE. He, too, worked in the Bell Telephone Laboratories, where he developed the theory of acceptance sampling in the late 1920's. HAROLD FRENCH DODGE (1/23/1893 - 12/10/1976) was employed as a developmental engineer at Western Electric Company, respectively, Bell Laboratories, from 1917 to 1958. In 1958 he became Professor of Applied and Mathematical Statistics at Rutgers University. Figure 1.3/3 shows a portrait of him.

Figure 1.3/3:
HAROLD FRENCH DODGE
(1893 -1976)

DODGE made many contributions to the theory of acceptance sampling. Some of these will be mentioned in chapter 3. In 1944 he published, together with H. G. ROMIG, his probably most famous work "Sampling Inspection Tables – Single and Double Sampling".

The beginnings of SQA coincided with the development of the statistical theory of hypothesis testing by JERZY NEYMAN (4/16/1894 - 8/5/1981),

Close relationship between SQA and testing theory:

figure 1.3/4a, EGON S. PEARSON (8/11/1895 - 6/12/1980), figure 1.3/4b, and R. A. FISHER (2/17/1890 - 7/29/1962), figure 1.3/5. SQA and testing theory are closely interrelated. SQA is basically an application of testing theory and both areas have mutually stimulated each others development in the last fifty years. We will illustrate this with three examples:

- Operating characteristic and power function

Without knowledge of the theory of type I and type II errors , which is based on the work of NEYMAN and PEARSON, it would not be possible to rationally evaluate a proposed sampling procedure. Testing theory developed, for example, the concept of the **power function**, which determines the rejection probability of a test dependent of the tested parameter. An important tool for the design and evaluation of sampling plans in acceptance control is the **operating characteristic function**, often abbreviated to **OC function**, the complement function of the power function. It gives the probability that the test does not reject the null hypothesis.

Figure 1.3/4a:
JERZY NEYMAN (1894-1981)

Figure 1.3/4b:
EGON S. PEARSON (1895-1980)

- Sequential tests and statistical decision theory

When the shortage of material during the last world war forced SQA to develop inspection procedures utilizing as few sample units as possible (especially in the case of destructive inspection) ABRAHAM WALD (10/31/1902 - 12/13/1950), figure 1.3/6, developed the **sequential test procedures** and the **statistical decision theory** in the US. The application of WALD's theory, an emigrated Austrian, was so efficient (it reduced the amount of inspection by as much as 60% compared to non-sequential procedures with the same error probabilities) that the US declared his theory a national secret and did not allow its publication until the end of the war.

Figure 1.3/5:
R. A. FISHER (1890-1962)

Figure 1.3/6:
ABRAHAM WALD
(1902-1950)

- Bayesian statistics

In order to also give a recent example of the close relationship between SQA and the theory of statistics we want to mention the subject of empirical Bayesian inference. This area attempts to make a bridge between the subjective school of Bayesian statistics and the objective classical theory by combining the advantages of both statistical philosophies. The price is a fairly demanding mathematical model. Through the opportunity of testing this new approach in acceptance sampling, especially for the objective estimation of prior distributions, SQA provides an important empirical context for this new theory.

Quality as an economic philosophy

Today quality assurance is seen as an issue which concerns the entire enterprise and which has to be taken into account by every employee and especially the mangement. The statistician W. EDWARDS DEMING (1900) shown in figure 1.3/7 has contributed significantly to the development of the concept of quality as an economic philosophy.

Figure 1.3/7:
W. EDWARDS DEMING (1900)

At the invitation of the **JUSE** (**J**apanese **U**nion of **S**cientists and **E**ngineers) in the beginning of the fifties he held seminars and training courses for technicians and managers in Japan, in order to assist the languished Japanese industry in statistical questions during its process of reconstruction. DEMING gave the issue of quality the importance of a strategic economic goal of an enterprise and showed the way to accomplish this. His activities in Japan were so successful that the industry of the US, which had a leading position in almost all world markets, began to lose market shares against the Japanese during the 1960's. In the 1970's the crisis of American industry, which did not assign an equal importantance to the issue of quality, became more and more apparent. Then it was again DEMING, who woke up his countrymen with the slogan "If Japan can, why can't we" in an

NBC television series with the same title, and thus helped to re-establish the idea of quality in the US.

National and international organizations in quality assurance

One can definitely say that today SQA has reached a high level of development and possesses a sophisticated methodological body. However, it is not necessarily true that anybody who has learnt to apply the methods of SQA is also automatically an expert in quality assurance. For this one needs to have additional knowledge, i.e., of the relevant technical, legal and management aspects. In most industrialized economies of the East and West there are organizations for quality assurance with the goal of presenting a complete picture of all issues in quality control. In the US the **ASQC** (American Society for Quality Control) was founded in 1946. In Europe there is the **EOQ** (European Organization for Quality). Suborganizations of the EOQ exist in almost all European countries and offer a wide range of publications (refer to the literature index in chapter 7) and training courses in all areas of quality assurance. To give an idea of the activities of these organizations we will mention the situation in the United Kingdom. During the postwar period a quality movement was growing, particularly within the automotive industry and the defence area. In 1960 a National Council for Quality and Reliability was founded and in 1972 a national **Institute of Quality Assurance** (**IQA**) emerged. The British Association for Quality Assurance (**BQA**) which was formed in 1981 and is a member of the EOQ is an integral part of the IQA. The IQA supports national activities in improving quality and represents a forum for tackling issues around quality. The Institute regularly offers training courses in diverse quality related subjects. Without having successfully passed such courses employees hardly have a chance in finding an attractive position in the quality assurance department of British companies.

Remarks

1. A description of the life, work, and significance of W. A. SHEWHART can be found in OLMSTEAD (1956) and DEMING (1967). In 1967 the journal *Industrial Quality Control* published a special issue in commemoration of his death (Issue 24, 1967, p.81ff).
2. The contribution of DODGE to the development of statistical quality assurance was also given appreciation in various trade journals. For example, in the *Journal of Quality Technology* (issue 9, 1977, p.95ff) appeared a special edition in commemoration of DODGE, that reprinted, besides his biography, all his most important publications.

1.3.2 The Present Situation and Trends in Quality Assurance

On a national level most companies, even entire branches, are exposed to an increasingly intense competition for the market. A determining factor for the survival and long term success of a company is, as previously described, the quality of its products and services. Hence, it is not surprising that the issue of quality assurance is gaining in importance. In the current practice of quality assurance one can observe four main developing tendencies. They are all related to the issue of quality and its process of becoming an economic strategy and marketing tool of a company:

- development of quality assurance towards a customer-oriented strategy of the company comprising all activities (**TQM** = total quality management),
- increasing **application of statistical procedures** already at the level of **quality planning** (e.g., applying methods of experimental design in product and process design),
- a tendency to **administer quality inspection at an earlier stage** of the process with the goal of avoiding defective units or a neccessary mending of nonconformities,
- increasing **automatization of QA** and introducing computer aided measurement and evaluation technology (quality assurance based on electronic data processing systems is replacing the traditional quality inspector).

Trend towards quality inspection during the manufacturing process (online inspection)

We will now illustrate the latter two topics and their consequences in more detail. Let us first consider the trend towards an active quality control procedure during the manufacturing process. Whereas in former times companies administered quality inspection mainly at the end of the manufacturing process (**acceptance control**), the inspection is now happening during the manufacturing process (**process control**). For example, in the field of Computer Science electronic information processing is classified into online and offline processing according to whether the input terminal and the main computer are connected or not. In the same way one speaks of **online inspection** and **offline inspection**, depending on whether the inspection procedure influences the ongoing production or not. Thus online and offline inspection are nothing but modern synonyms for the terms process control and acceptance control respectively.

Computerization started the trend towards online inspection

The observed trend from offline to online control is very appropriately expressed by the slogan 'make it right the first time'. Quality inspection at an earlier stage of the manufacturing process makes it possible to quickly detect unwanted changes in the process and thus to correct them. A requirement for such a direct feedback is, of course, that the measured data are quickly analysed and evaluated, for example, through automized electronic data processing. The trend from a *static* quality inspection (inspection after the manufacturing process) to a *dynamic* quality control (inspection during the process with the possibility to intervene) has been made possible, if not initiated, by the possibilities of modern data processing. Companies that follow this strategy can significantly reduce their production costs through avoiding defective output and later mending of defects. The ultimate goal is a "controlled production", where ideally there would not be any defective output.

Delegating the responsibility for quality to the supplier

Especially in large enterprises an element in the strategy of "controlled production" through active quality assurance is a transfer of quality assurance measures from one's own premises to the supplier. The purpose of this is to ensure the quality of the manufacturing materials (raw materials, parts) through suitable arrangements with the supplier. In the automotive industry it is, for example, now quite common to require a supplier to carefully and completely keep record of its internal quality assurance and to keep quality inspection records (computerized control charts, statistical analysis) for eventual later inspection. Suppliers who are not able to keep up with these requirements have to fear losing the buyer to more efficient competitors. This agreement about quality assurance measures with the supplier enables a company to dispense with the inspection of incoming goods and restrict itself to an occasional inspection of the supplier's quality assurance, so-called **quality audits**.

Trend towards automized quality inspection

Related to the development of a dynamic quality control is the automization of quality assurance. In many branches of industry electronic data processing has been commonly used for a long time. Even in smaller companies accounting and pay-roll have been widely computerized. In the area of quality assurance the introduction of automized information processing is happening quite slowly. This may be due to the fact that in the area of accounting and pay-roll administration, for example, it is possible to design widely applicable procedures (PC with standard software), whereas the design of quality assurance in a company depends very much on the specific circumstances (arrangements with suppliers, human resources, etc.) and the quality requirements on the final product. Today even small and medium sized companies participate in automized quality assurance. For them the appropriate technology is that of the **personal computer (PC)**. PCs are becoming more and more powerful and at the same time less expensive. It is also possible to link PCs to **local area networks (LAN)** and in-house-systems, which can also be connected to public communication networks. Present problems are incompatibility of hardware and software and an insufficient supply of software (for many quality control tasks there are no standard packages).

It was not until the automization of quality assurance that the goal of controlled production became a real possibility. At least in big corporations, the current trend is to not consider quality assurance (i.e., obtaining and evaluating data) as an isolated data processing task, but to embed it in the all-encompassing concept of **computer integrated manufacturing**. Production integrated quality assurance at an advanced level means that a manufacturing stage is directly coupled with the inspection of relevant quality characteristics. An example given by KIRSTEIN (1984) is the grinding of pieces of a certain material, which is performed in such a way so that the procedure stops automatically as soon as a photo-electronic measuring device signals that a specified nominal value has been reached. Here inspection is not performed between two manufacturing stages, but integrated into the process.

Production integrated quality inspection

Use of process integrated measuring systems

The advances in the area of electronic information processing have also revolutionized measuring technology. Manual measurements are increasingly replaced by **computer controlled measuring machines (process integrated measuring systems)**. The modern quality inspector no longer keeps count-lists, but rather monitors the functioning of automatic machines or the output of a data processing system (i.e., computer-generated tables or graphs and statistical analysis). Examples of such computerized numerically controlled measurement machines, abbreviated **CNC-measuring machines** are:

- precision instruments for measuring of work pieces;
- test systems for the analysis of the tensile, compressive or bending strength of work pieces;
- photoanalytic instruments for the measuring or counting two dimensional objects;
- test systems for the inspection of the hardness and structural characteristics of surfaces;
- radiation sensitive thermometers for remote measurement of the temperature on a surface.

Examples from practice

We will now illustrate the first two points with three photos from applications. The first photo shows a microprocessor controlled laser micrometer in action. This machine can perform various measuring procedures (e.g., remote determination of a diameter, deviations in concentric running, distances between edges). The program of a specific application is accessed through an input keyboard. In figure 1.3/8 the diameters of lathe workpieces of a series production are determined and evaluated (e.g., control of the tolerance limits with alarm in case of exceeding these limits, calculation of mean value and standard deviation, construction of histograms, and output of requested information via terminal or printer). For inspection,

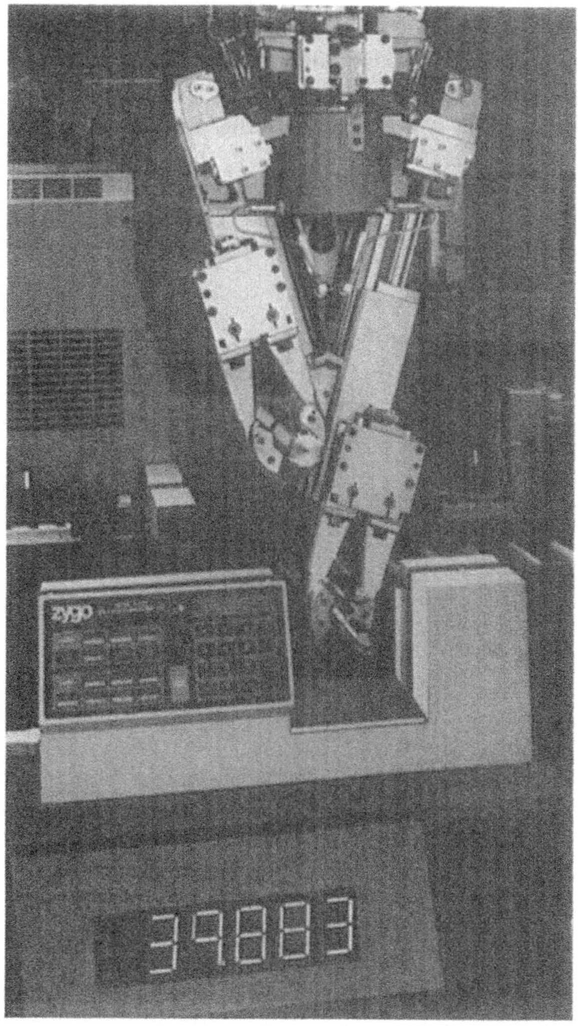

Figure 1.3/8: Measuring inspection of lathe work pieces with a laser scanner (source: L.O.T. GmbH, Darmstadt, Germany)

the work pieces are held into a laser beam with the help of a mechanical device. The inserted pieces cause an interruption of the light signal (shadow casting). These interruptions are automatically analysed and result in the output of geometric data.

Figure 1.3/9 shows a multiple coordinate measuring machine, which can inspect the form and size of three dimensional work pieces with complex geometry. The measurements are taken with the help of an inductive sensor system. The moveable probe of the machine touches the work piece point by point. After every measurement the three coordinates are recorded by the system and evaluated as well as documented either on screen or by a plotter or printer.

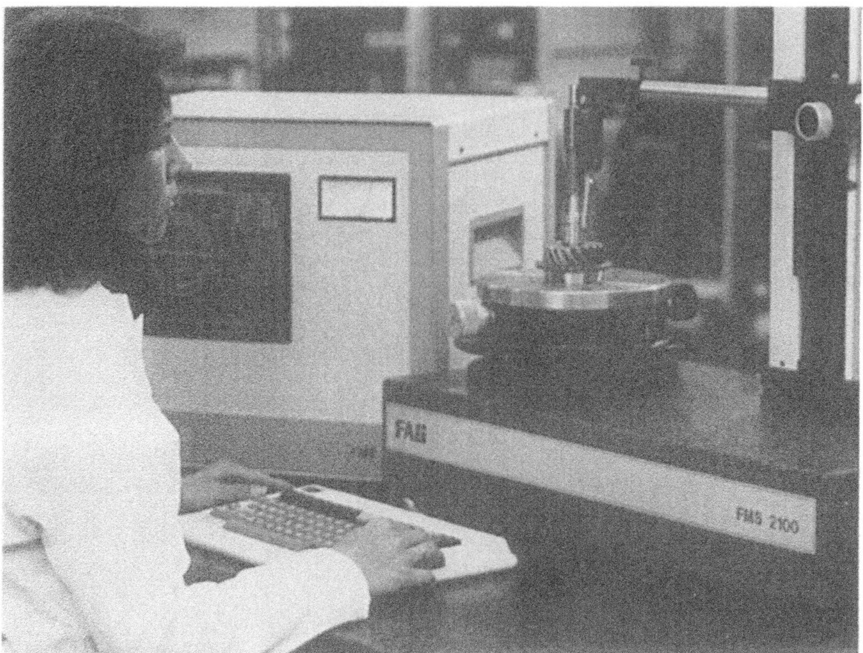

Figure 1.3/9: Measuring inspection of lathe work with an inductive sensor system (source: FAG Kugelfischer, Schweinfurt, Germany)

CNC-measuring technology allows not only the precise determination of geometric data, but also the determination of other quality characteristics, such as testing the behaviour under the influence of test forces or measuring other similar characteristic quantities. Figure 1.3/10 shows a CNC-test device for the determination of the tensile strength of a sample of synthetic material. The inspection personnel first enters all relevant parameters for the test procedure via an input terminal and then starts the test. All characteristics which describe the observed force-deformation reaction of the sample are automatically recorded. From these data the characteristics of the material are immediately determined and clearly displayed.

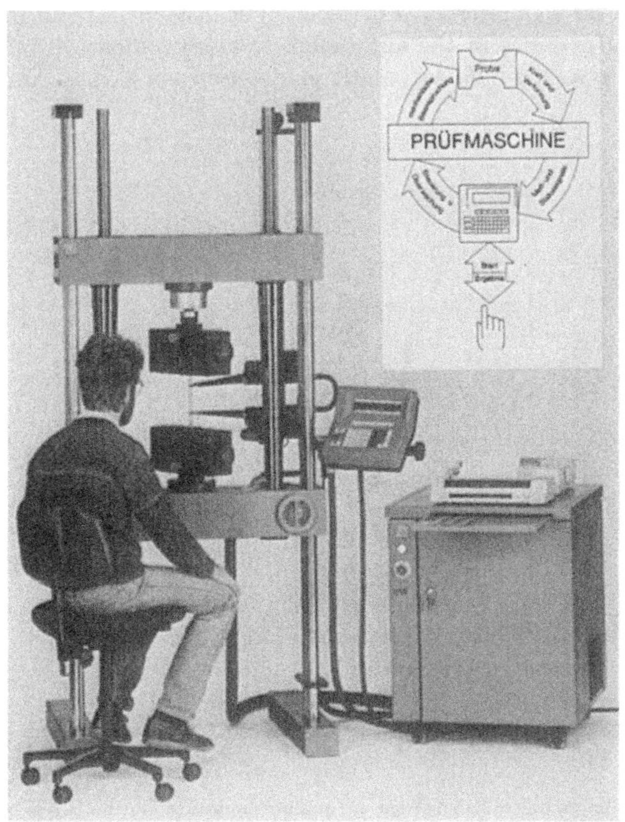

Figure 1.3/10: Testing the tensile strength of synthetic materials with an all-purpose measuring machine (source: UTS Testsysteme, Ulm, Germany)

Advantages of computer aided quality assurance

The application of modern computer based measuring machines in quality assurance brings several obvious advantages. It makes it possible to

- reduce the tolerance range ("quality control in micro-dimensions") and also almost abolish measurement errors which naturally occur in non-automatic measuring due to unavoidable fatigue of the inspection personnel;
- record quality characteristics which could not be measured before the invention of this technology or which would otherwise require an unrealistic amount of inspection;
- sometimes replace a sampling procedure through complete screening without increasing, and maybe even decreasing, inspection costs.

Examples of the latter two points are, respectively, the analysis of pulverous raw material through interactive photoanalytic instruments and the screening of even large series in the automobile industry. Figure 1.3/11 presents the model of such a fully automatic photo-electronic inspection.

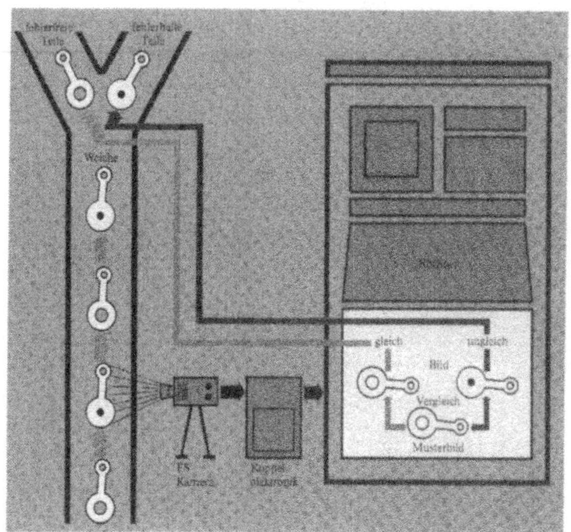

Figure 1.3/11: Photo-electronic screening with a video camera (source VW, Germany)

Remark

A good survey of the technical innovations in quality assurance can be obtained by regularily reading the trade journal *Quality Progress*. SCHEER (1988) describes the general effects of the increasing introduction of electronic data processing on the entire operation of companies. The monograph of KEATS/HUBELE (1989) describes the feedback of proceeding automization in manufacturing and process control.

1.3.3 Computer Aided Quality Assurance - A Module of Computer Integrated Manufacturing

Definition and list of CAx-systems

It is not only in quality assurance, but also in many other areas of enterprises, that in recent years many processes were automized in order to rationalize and achieve a more consumer oriented flexibility. These applications of information technology in the various technical fields of a company are spoken of as **CAx-systems**. In this term "CA" means "computer aided" and "x" stands for the specific application. The most common systems are:

- **CAD:** computer aided development and design (**D**=**design**), e.g., the drawing and altering of three dimensional objects on a screen;
- **CAM:** computer aided control of transport, storage, and manufacturing units (**M**=**manufacturing**), e.g., automatic control of manufacturing systems;
- **CAE:** computer aided engineering, especially in the area of project design (**E**= **engineering**), e.g., analysis of wiring diagrams with the help of simulation software;
- **CAP:** computer aided planning of work (**P**=**planning**), e.g., the programming of machine tools;
- **CAQ:** computer aided quality assurance (**Q** =**quality assurance**), e.g. the automatic control of nominal specifications for product series including statistical analysis.

Systems for application in management and planning

Outside the technical field of a company there are also many management and planning tasks which can be performed with the help of electronic data processing. These activities are increasingly taken over by so-called **PPC-systems**. The latter means **software systems for production planning and control**. On the left side of figure 1.3/12 is a list of the standard functions of PPC-systems. The previously described functions of CAx-systems are on the right side.

Presentation of the CIM concept

Since about 1985 hardware and software designers are publicizing under the slogan **computer integrated manufacturing (CIM)** that all the processor controlled subsystems of a company should be integrated into one big system. This would, for example, mean the connection of the individual components, i.e., PPC, CAD, CAM, etc. into a larger system. The CIM approach sees a company as one big unit and aims at coordinating all the activities from market oriented product specification to the shipping of the products by taking advantage of the possibilities of modern information technology (integration of data transfer and production stages).

The differentiation between PPC-systems and the individual components of CAx-systems is not standard in all literature. For example, internal data management is sometimes assigned to PPC (as in figure 1.3/12), sometimes to CAM.

A characteristic of CIM is that data which are generated at one stage of the manufacturing sequence can be immediately used in other stages of the process. This saves the multiple recording of the same data. In addition, it avoids shortages of information and speeds up the whole process. In a factory that is consistently organized according to the CIM system,

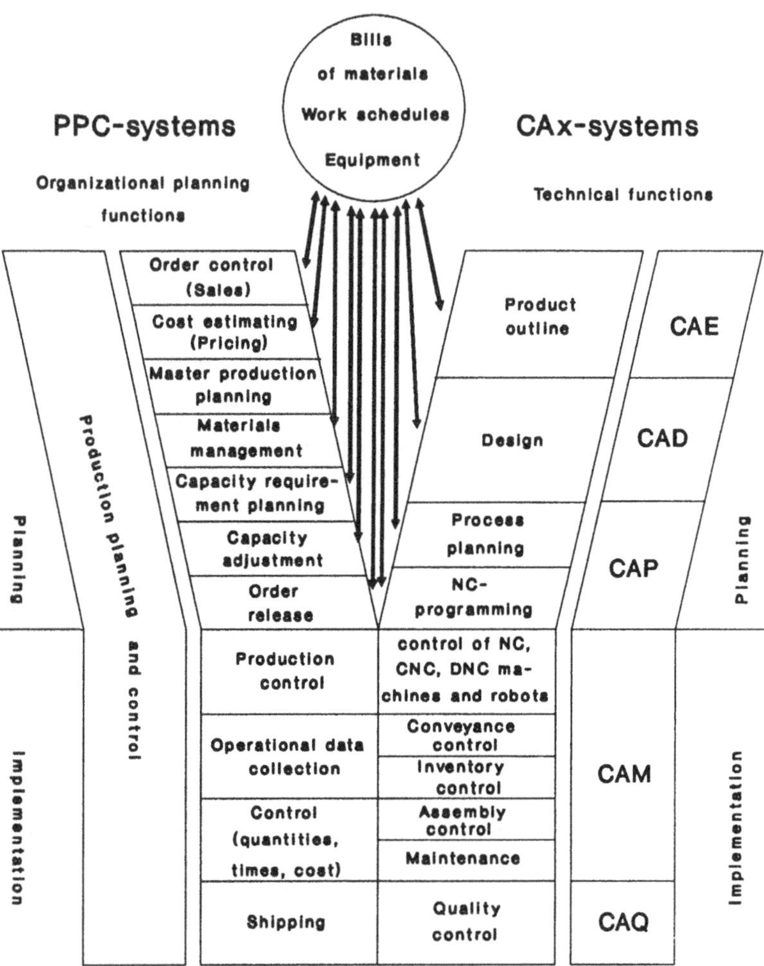

Figure 1.3/12: Information systems for a manufacturing process (based on SCHEER 1988)

it is possible to enter product specifications at an input interface and to thus generate the desired output without having to manually interfere in the fully automatic manufacturing process. Production planning and manufacturing is controlled in the style of cybernetic control circuits and, if necessary, immediately adjusted. In the context of CIM the component CAQ is part of a control circuit that, among other functions, controls modern manufacturing and measuring machines (e.g., robots and mechanical devices, photo-electronic test systems).

In practice the realization of such a **factory of the future** is still far away, especially as the technical requirements for combining presently existing isolated solutions of automization like CAD and CAM are not yet given. There are compatibility problems of the hard- and software of different manufacturers. The future of CIM will depend on how the problem of connecting into and between systems is solved. On a national and international level the introduction of standards has already begun. We only want to mention the **manufacturing automation protocols**, abbreviated **MAP**, of GENERAL MOTORS that have the goal of creating a standard communication structure in the area of manufacturing and to make it possible to connect different companies through an information network.

Many experts are predicting that CIM will be a dominating data processing theme of the 1990's. Most of the larger companies have already begun to take the first steps towards CIM, i.e., through connecting individual CAx-modules. According to the following prognosis (fig. 1.3/13) it will surely take many years until CIM will be completely realized on a wide scale.

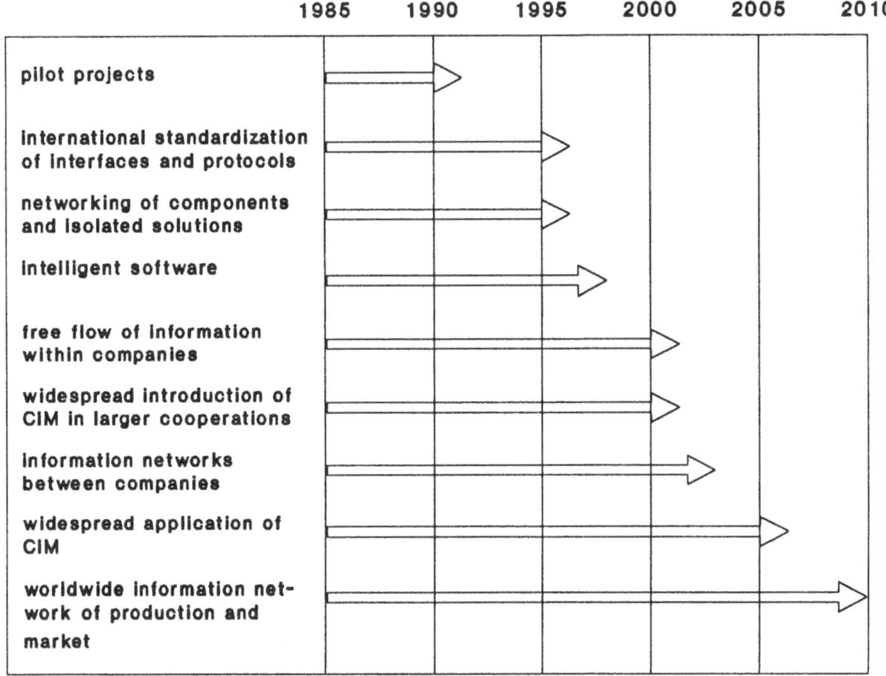

Figure 1.3/13: Prognosis for the world wide development of CIM (source: Siemens-Nixdorf, Germany)

The long time for the development of CIM depends not only on the above problems of hard- and software compatibility. It is also due to the fact that the decision to introduce a CIM system is a far-reaching strategic decision requiring an enormous amount of investment, especially since its benefit is, at the moment, almost impossible to quantify.

Remarks

1. A modern CAQ software system has to be connectable to the existing automated islands and be integratable into a later CIM system. So far there is very little software for the area of quality assurance. Packages like AQUA (IBM), SPCplus (Hewlett Packard) or moQuiss (SCS) have found limited acceptance, but they only cover the most standard inspection procedures. In addition to specialized CAQ-systems the industry has recently also started to work with user friendly all-round statistical software packages, which contain powerful programs for quality assurance applications. The more popular ones of these are STATGRAPHICS, SAS, STATISTICA or SYSTAT. These packages do sometimes even allow the application of less established test procedures, like control charting with CUSUM or EWMA charts. A good overview of the available software for quality assurance on the American market is published yearly in the "Directory of Software for Quality Assurance and Quality Control" in the journal *Quality Progress*.
2. Due to the present popularity of the issue of CIM there is an immense flood of literature and journals, which exclusively devote themselves to this subject. We only want to mention the journal *Computer Integrated Manufacturing*.

2 Foundations of Statistical Quality Assurance

Before we can introduce the most important procedures of acceptance sampling and process control we need to cover the fundamental statistical theory that is necessary to understand these procedures. Since this book intends to address a wide audience the material is presented in a way that will also enable readers without a strong statistical background to work through it. For those readers this chapter is intended as a compact presentation of the missing prerequisite knowledge from the viewpoint of statistical quality control.

Preview of chapter 2

In sections 2.1 and 2.2 we will introduce the probability distributions which are relevant for the theory of quality control, among them the Bernoulli distribution, the Poisson distribution, the normal distribution, the binomial distribution and the hypergeometric distribution. In this context terms like "distribution function", "expectation", "percentile" and various terms used in sampling theory are going to be defined. Section 2.3 will present the idea of statistical testing and will cover in depth the risks and errors involved in testing hypotheses. Practical examples will illustrate the terms "power function" and "operating characteristic function", which are of central importance in testing theory.

Figure on the title page of this chapter: Graph of OC function and OC percentiles

2.1 Distributions of Quality Characteristics

Our definition of **quality** is, as discussed in section 1.2, the entity of those characteristics of a product or a service that relate to its fitness to fulfill given requirements. We will call such characteristics **quality characteristics**. The possible values or categories that such a characteristic can take are called **outcomes** or **realizations** of the characteristic. Which particular outcome will be observed is random. Such variables, which take on values according to a random mechanism, are called **random variables** or stochastic variables. Section 2.1.1 describes the measurement of these realizations of quality characteristics. After this, in sections 2.1.2 – 2.1.4, we will present models for distributions which describe the behaviour of random variables.

Example 2.1/1

The following list contains five different random variables (quality characteristics) and their possible realizations:

Quality characteristic 1:	Fit of a seat cover
Realizations:	good fit, too small, too big
Quality characteristic 2:	Taste of a food item
Realizations:	very good, good, satisfactory, unsatisfactory
Quality characteristic 3:	Exhaust gas temperature of a car engine
Realizations:	degrees in Celsius
Quality characteristic 4:	Length of a workpiece
Realizations:	measurement in cm, mm or more exact, depending on the precision of the measuring instrument
Quality characteristic 5:	Errors per page of a manuscript
Realizations:	0, 1, 2, 3, etc.

2.1.1 Measuring Quality Characteristics

The determination of the outcome of a quality characteristic is called **measurement.** Depending on the type of the characteristic different **measuring scales** are used. We distinguish between the following scales: Types of measuring scales:

▷ **Nominal Scale** - Nominal scale

On a nominal scale the outcomes of a characteristic are names or categories. There is no order among different outcomes, we can only say they are "equal" or "not equal". The measurement of a nominal characteristic determines whether the characteristic of the object equals a particular realization or whether it differs. The scale of the first quality characteristic in example 2.1/1 is nominal.

- Ordinal or rank scale

▷ Ordinal or Rank Scale

On an ordinal or rank scale the outcomes of a quality characteristic are not only sorted by means of the criterion 'equal or not equal' but are also put in a natural increasing or decreasing order (smaller/bigger, worse/better, more/less). It is common to use the natural numbers to express the order of the outcomes. In this context they are called ranks. The second quality characteristic in example 2.1/1 has an ordinal scale, and we can also order it by ranks as follows: very good = 1, good = 2, satisfactory = 3, unsatisfactory = 4. An ordinal measurement is unique , except for monotone increasing transformations. For example, the above characteristic could be rescaled in the following way: very good = 10, good = 20, satisfactory = 30, unsatisfactory = 40. This would equally describe the natural order of the four outcomes. In general a monotone increasing transformation preserves the order.

- Cardinal or metric scale (interval, proportional and absolute scale)

▷ Cardinal or Metric Scale

On a cardinal or metric scale we can, in addition to the natural order, determine the differences and/or proportions of the outcomes of the characteristic of interest. In this case outcomes are real numbers that are given in units of specified dimension. The measurement of a cardinal or metric variable is unique up to linear transformations. The last three characteristics in example 2.1/1 are on a cardinal scale. There are three different types of cardinal scales:

- **Interval Scale**
  In addition to the order the difference between outcomes is measured in units, e.g., degree celsius in the temperature measurement of the third characteristic (example 2.1/1).

- **Proportional Scale**
  For characteristic four, the length of the work piece, the interval scale starts at the natural origin 0 and the measurement of the interval is proportional to the actual length. Scales of this kind are called proportional scales. It is also possible to measure the ratio of outcomes, i.e., the ratio of the length of two pieces.

- **Absolute Scale**
  If the proportional scale has a natural unit, e.g., the number of errata measured by characteristic five, we call it an absolute scale.

In general we distinguish between two types of characteristics. First, characteristics with outcomes on a nominal and ordinal scale are called **qualitative characteristics**, because their outcomes are not of numerical nature even if they are coded by numbers or ranks. Second, characteristics that take on values on a cardinal or metric scale are called **quantitative characteristics**. This second type of characteristic is **discrete** if the set of possible outcomes is countable. The natural numbers or integers are examples of this, but the outcome set is not restricted to those. If the outcome can be any real number in a given range which is an uncountable set, we call the characteristic **continuous**.

Types of characteristics:

- Qualitative characteristics
- Quantitative characteristics (discrete or continuous)

For the statistician it is important to know the type of the characteristic since it determines which procedure is appropriate for the analysis. This will become evident again and again in the following sections. Table 2.1/1 gives an overview of all the different types of characteristics.

Problem 2.1/1

List at least one more example for each type of characteristic.

2.1.2 Distributions of Qualitative Characteristics

A **theoretical distribution** or **distribution model** describes the probability of occurrence of outcomes of a characteristic within a population of units. An **empirical distribution** or **frequency distribution** describes the – relative or absolute – frequency of the different outcomes of a characteristic during a specific observation or in a sample from the population.

Let A denote a qualitative characteristic and let A_i denote a specific outcome. Then

$$Pr(A = A_i) =: Pr(A_i) =: P_i \qquad \text{with} \quad 0 \leq P_i \leq 1 \tag{2.1}$$

means the probability of the occurrence of the event $A = A_i$ (say "Prob" of "$A = A_i$")[1]. We think of P_i as the probability that a randomly selected element from the population (the lot or the process) has the characteristic A_i. In a population with a finite number of elements, e.g., a shipment or a lot out of the production, we can calculate P_i by

Interpreting the probability P_i of the event A_i

$$P_i = \frac{N_i}{N} \qquad \text{with} \quad 0 \leq N_i \leq N \tag{2.2}$$

where N denotes the total number of units in the population and N_i denotes the number of units for which the characteristic has outcome A_i.

[1] When numbering formulas we only use a one-level approach to keep these numbers small, whereas for tables, figures, examples and problems we have chosen a two-level approach.

	Nominal Scale	Ordinal Scale Rank Scale	Cardinal Scale / Metric Scale	
			Interval Scale	Proportional Scale and Absolute Scale
Characteristics that can be measured	qualitative characteristics (nominally or ordinally scaled)		quantitative characteristics (continuous or discrete)	
Defined relations between outcomes	$=, \neq$	$=, \neq, <, >$	$=, \neq, <, >, +, -$	$=, \neq, <, >, +, -, \cdot, :$
Interpretations	Differentiation "equal - not equal" possible	Differentiation "smaller - bigger" possible*	differences have empirical meaning*	proportions have empirical meaning*
Admissible transformations	unique invertable (bijective)	monotone increasing (isotone)	linear $y = ax + b$ $(a > 0)$	stretching $y = ax$ $(a > 0)$
Examples of appropriate statistics	mode, frequency	median, quartile*	arithmetic mean, standard deviation*	geometric mean, coefficient of variation*
Examples	product names, numberplates, zipcodes, marital status, area of study	school grades, army rank, grade category (agricultural products), earthquake scale (Mercalli), wind strength (Beaufort), evaluations, sensory characteristics	temperature (C), temperature (F), calendar date	temperature (K), income, age, measurements on cm-gramm-sec-scale system, earthquake scale (Richter), wind strength (m/sec), time (production, standstill), counts mistakes, broken threads, standstills)
Content of information	low . . . . increasing to . . . . high			
Sensitivity to measurement errors	low . . . . increasing to . . . . high			

* including all statements on the left of this line.

Table 2.1/1: Common types of scales and characteristics (as presented by PADBERG/WILRICH 1981, p.180)

Outcomes and partitions

In order to construct the theoretical distribution of a qualitative characteristic we need to define $k \geq 2$ outcomes A_i $, i = 1 \ldots k$, so that they form a **partition** of the outcome set. Formally this means

$$Pr(A_i \cap A_j) = 0 \qquad \text{for all } i \neq j \tag{2.3 a}$$

$$\sum_{i=1}^{k} P_i = 1. \tag{2.3 b}$$

The outcomes have to be mutually exclusive and cover all possible events.

It is possible that the outcomes of a nominally scaled characteristic are not mutually exclusive, which means that this specific characteristic can simultaneously have two or more outcomes. In this case the outcomes do not form a partition, but it is possible to redefine them so that (2.3a) and (2.3b) hold.

Case of not mutually exclusive outcomes

Example 2.1/2

The production control of a car manufacturer's paintshop classifies the finished bodies in the following way:

A_1^* - without fault	with	$Pr(A_1^*)= 0.85$
A_2^* - runs	with	$Pr(A_2^*)= 0.12$
A_3^* - bubbles	with	$Pr(A_3^*)= 0.08$.

Some bodies have runs and bubbles at the same time. Since these cases are counted twice, i.e., once under the category A_2^* and the second time under the category A_3^*, the above events do not form a partition of the outcome set. However, the following outcomes of the characteristic "paint quality" form a partition:

$A_1 := A_1^*$	- without fault	$A_2 := A_2^* \setminus A_3^*$	- runs only
$A_3 := A_3^* \setminus A_2^*$	- bubbles only	$A_4 := A_2^* \cap A_3^*$	- runs and bubbles

The symbols $\cup$, $\cap$, $\setminus$ denote the set operations union, intersection and difference.

Problem 2.1/2

a) Find the probabilities of the redefined outcomes $A_i, i = 1, \ldots, 4$, in example 2.1/2. Are the outcomes A_2^* and A_3^* independent events? What are the conditional probabilities $Pr(A_2^*|A_3^*)$ and $Pr(A_3^*|A_2^*)$?

b) Suppose a characteristic B has three outcomes B_1^*, B_2^*, B_3^* that can simultaneously occur in any combination. How many classes B_i need to be created in order to define a characteristic with mutually exclusive outcomes? Illustrate the problem and its solution using a Venn diagram. Express the B_i's using the set operations $\cup$, $\cap$, $\setminus$.

c) Give another example of a characteristic in quality control which does not have mutually exclusive outcomes.

2.1.3 Discrete Distributions

a) The Uniform Distribution and Basic Concepts of Statistical Distribution Theory

Equidistant uniform distribution

The simplest model of the distribution of a discrete random variable with a finite number of outcomes is the **equidistant uniform distribution** . It has the property that all outcomes occur with equal probability and that the distance between outcomes is constant. Although there are very few quality characteristics which can be seen as a random variable with such a distribution, we are presenting this model in order to illustrate the basic concepts of distribution theory in a simple and clear way.

Let X be a random variable with $L+1$ outcomes (values, realizations). Let a be the smallest value and let the rest of the values follow with fixed distance $b: a, a+b, a+2b, a+3b, \ldots, a+Lb$. Unless there is some specific knowledge about the probability of occurrence of the $L+1$ possible realizations, one will assume, since there is no sufficient reason to do otherwise, that these $L+1$ probabilities are equal and assign each of them the value $1/(L+1)$. The function which relates the outcomes x of a discrete random variable X to their probability of occurrence $Pr(X = x)$ is called the **probability massfunction** of X. In this example of an equidistant uniform distribution we redefine $Pr(X = x) =: un(x|a; b; L)$, using an obvious, easy to remember notation, where

Concept of massfunction

Massfunction of the uniform distribution

$$un(x|a;b;L) = \begin{cases} \frac{1}{L+1} & \text{for } x = a + k \cdot b \quad (k = 0, 1, \ldots, L) \\ 0 & \text{elsewhere.} \end{cases} \tag{2.4}$$

The function depends on the parameters a, b and L where $a \in \mathbb{R}; b \in \mathbb{R}^+$; $L \in \mathbb{N}$. Massfunctions are graphically displayed as stick diagrams (see figure 2.1/1a). The length of the sticks above the values of the domain of (2.4) corresponds to the probability $Pr(X = x)$.

The introduction of a probability function $Pr(X = x)$ - read "Probability of $X = x$" - only makes sense for discrete random variables. Because in the case of a continuous random variable, say X, the probability that X takes on a particular value is zero. The **cumulative distribution function** $F(x)$ defined by

$$F(x) := Pr(X \leq x)$$

Concept of distribution function

is a sensible concept for discrete as well as continuous quality characteristics X and is used to describe both types of distributions. By definition it gives the probability that X takes values smaller or equal to x (the probability to reach the realization x).

The distribution function of a discrete random variable is obtained by summing the massfunction over all values smaller or equal to x:

$$F(x) = \sum_{u \le x} Pr(X = u).$$

The graph of the distribution function of a discrete random variable always looks like a step function with jumps at the possible realizations. The size of the jump gives the probability that this specific realization occurs. It follows that this function is discontinuous, but by definition, right continuous. This means, if you approach a discontinuity point from the right, the function takes on the upper and not the lower value at this point.

Using the notation $F(x) =: Un(x|a;b;L)$, the distribution function of the equidistant uniform distribution can be written

$$Un(x|a;b;L) = \begin{cases} 0 & \text{for } x < a \\ \frac{k}{L+1} & \text{for } a + (k-1)b \le x < a + kb \ (k = 1, ..., L) \\ 1 & \text{for } x \ge a + bL \ . \end{cases} \quad (2.5)$$

Distribution function of the uniform distribution

The graph of the above is a step function with jumps of constant size $1/(L+1)$ at $a, a+b, \ldots, a+bL$. In figure 2.1/1b the right continuity at the jumping points is indicated by the full black dots at the upper value. To indicate that a discrete random variable is distributed according to (2.4) and (2.5), we will use the notation $X \sim un(a;b;L)$.

Example 2.1/3

The outcomes of the toss of a fair die have an equidistant uniform distribution with parameters $a = 1, b = 1, L = 5$. The corresponding massfunction and distribution function are as follows:

$$un(x|1;1;5) = \begin{cases} \frac{1}{6} & \text{for } x = 1, 2, \ldots, 6 \\ 0 & \text{else} \end{cases}$$

$$Un(x|1;1;5) = \begin{cases} 0 & \text{for } x < 1 \\ \frac{k}{6} & \text{for } k \le x < k+1 \quad (k = 1, \ldots, 5) \\ 1 & \text{for } x \ge 6. \end{cases}$$

The graph of this massfunction is a stick diagram and the graph of the distribution function is a step function.

a. Massfunction

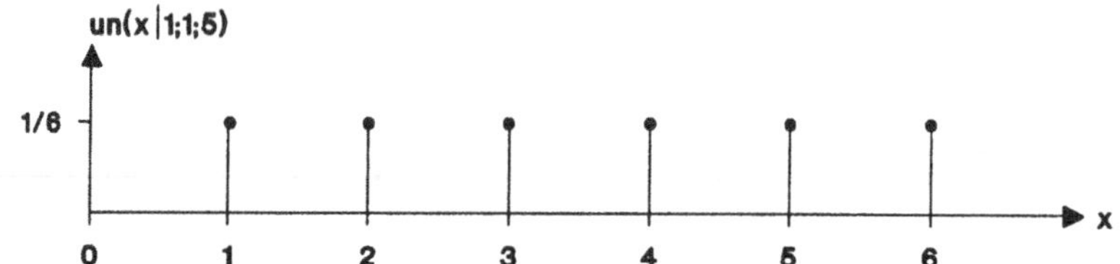

b. Distribution function

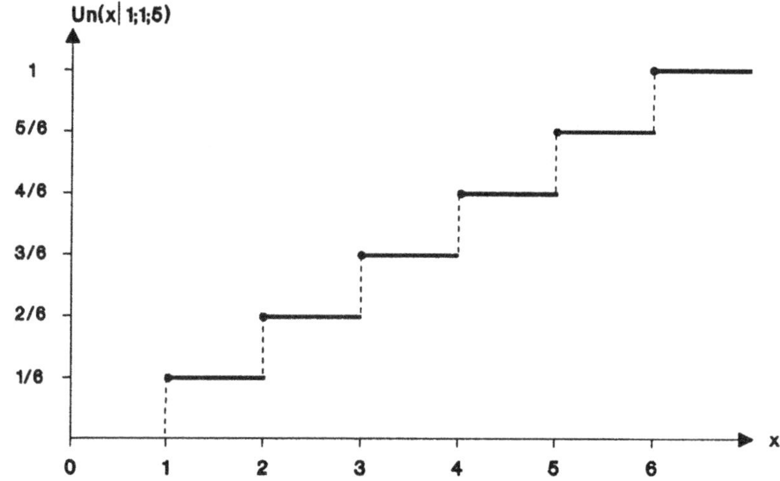

Figure 2.1/1: Uniform distribution (Tossing a fair die)

Excursion: Properties of the distribution function

A distribution function has the following properties:

1. $0 \leq F(x) \leq 1$.

2. $F(x)$ is weakly monotonously increasing: $F(x_1) \geq F(x_2)$ if $x_1 > x_2$.

3. $\lim\limits_{n \to -\infty} F(x) = 0, \quad \lim\limits_{n \to \infty} F(x) = 1$.

The first property is clear since $F(x)$ is defined to be a probability and consequently takes a value between 0 and 1. The monotonous property follows from the fact that $F(x)$ sums probabilities which are nonnegative and that $F(x_1)$ contains at least as many terms as $F(x_2)$ if $x_1 > x_2$. From these two we can deduce the third asymptotic property.

For a given x, the distribution function gives us the probability that the random variable X takes on values smaller or equal to x. However, we are often interested in the inverse question: For a given probability, say $y = F(x) = \omega$, we are interested in the realization x_ω, so that the probability that X takes on values smaller or equal to x_ω is exactly ω, i.e., $F(x_\omega) = \omega$. To answer this question we define the inverse of the distribution function:

$$x := F^{-1}(y) \quad \text{for } 0 \leq y \leq 1.$$

This function is called the **percentile function** of a particular distribution. For a given ω it gives the corresponding **percentile** x_ω of the theoretical distribution.

Percentile function and percentiles of a distribution

$$\left.\begin{array}{l} x_\omega \text{ is the } 100 \cdot \omega\% \text{ percentile of a} \\ \text{distribution determined by } F(x) \end{array}\right\} \quad \Leftrightarrow \quad F(x_\omega) = \omega. \qquad (2.6)$$

Percentiles are functional parameters that numerically describe the position of a distribution on the x-axis. According to (2.6) x_ω is that number for which $Pr(X \leq x_\omega) = \omega$ holds. In other words, $100 \cdot \omega$ percent of all realizations of X are smaller or equal to x_ω, i.e., lie to the left of x_ω. The most commonly used percentiles have their own names:

Special percentiles

$x_{0.5}$ – **median**

$x_{0.25}$ – **first quartile**

$x_{0.75}$ – **third quartile**

Determination of percentiles

The value of the percentile x_ω can be obtained either by putting $y = \omega$ into the percentile function $F^{-1}(y)$, or graphically from the graph of the distribution function $y = F(x)$. The graphical method gives x_ω as the value on the x-axis that corresponds to the value $y = \omega$ on the y-axis. For example, in figure 2.1/8b we can see that the median of the standard normal distribution, which will be introduced later, has the value zero ($x_{0.5} = 0$).

In the case of discrete random variables the distribution function is a step function which does not have an inverse. However, we can define [2]

Generalized percentile function

$$F^{-1}(y) := \inf\{x|F(x) \geq y\}$$

to be the **generalized percentile function** (see, for example, HARTUNG 1987, p.114). In the case of the uniform distribution over the values $a + kb$

[2]The largest lower bound of a non empty set of real numbers, if it exists, is called infimum and is abbreviated as "inf".

$(k = 0, 1, \ldots, L)$ we can write the percentile function as

$$Un^{-1}(y|a;b;L) = \begin{cases} a & \text{for} \quad 0 < y \leq \frac{1}{L+1} \\ a+b & \text{for} \quad \frac{1}{L+1} < y \leq \frac{2}{L+1} \\ \vdots & \vdots \quad \vdots \quad \vdots \quad \vdots \\ a+Lb & \text{for} \quad \frac{L}{L+1} < y \leq 1. \end{cases}$$

Mode (discrete case)

If the massfunction of a discrete random variable has a unique maximum, we call the realization x_M at which the maximum is attained the **mode** of the distribution. Such a distribution is called **unimodal**. If a distribution has several relative maxima, it is said to be **multimodal** (i.e., a distribution with several modes). For the uniform distribution the mode is not defined since its massfunction (2.4) does not attain a maximum (see figure 2.1/1a).

Expectation (discrete case)

Another location parameter of a distribution is the expected value or **expectation** $\mu := E(X)$. For a discrete random variable this is defined by

$$E(X) := \sum_x x \cdot Pr(X = x).$$

In the discrete case the expected value is the average realization of X. We can see it as the arithmetic mean of the realizations weighted by their respective probabilities of occurrence.

Expectation of the uniform distribution

The expectation of the uniform distribution function (2.4) is

$$\mu = \frac{1}{L+1} \sum_{k=0}^{L} (a + kb) = \frac{1}{L+1} \left[a(L+1) + \frac{bL(L+1)}{2} \right] = a + \frac{bL}{2} \quad (2.7)$$

The expectation increases as a, b or L increase.

The **variance** σ^2 of a random variable with expectation μ is defined to be

$$V(X) := E[(X - \mu)^2].$$

Variance and standard deviation

In the discrete case it takes the form

$$V(X) = \sum_x (x - \mu)^2 \cdot Pr(X = x).$$

The variance is a quadratic measure, whereas the **standard deviation**

$$\sigma := +\sqrt{V(X)}$$

is a linear measure of the spread of a distribution. This results from the following property, which holds for all $c \in \mathbb{R}$:

$$V(cX) = c^2 \cdot V(X), \qquad \sigma(cX) = |c| \cdot \sigma(X).$$

The definition of σ, $\sigma := \sqrt{V(X)}$, explains why the variance has the notation σ^2. One can obtain the variance by using the shifting theorem

$$\sigma^2 = E(X^2) - \mu^2.$$

We demonstrate this by calculating the variance of the uniform distribution. Using the result

$$E(X^2) = \frac{1}{L+1}\sum_{k=0}^{L}(a+kb)^2 = a^2 + abL + \frac{b^2L(2L+1)}{6}$$

it follows that

Variance of the uniform distribution

$$\sigma^2 = a^2 + abL + \frac{b^2L(2L+1)}{6} - \left(a + \frac{bL}{2}\right)^2 = \frac{b^2L(L+2)}{12}. \qquad (2.8)$$

The variance of the uniform distribution increases as b or L increase.

Sometimes we are interested in measuring the skewness (asymmetry) of a distribution. We can use the location parameters μ, x_M and $x_{0.5}$ to distinguish between different types of skewness:

Measure of symmetry of a distribution

$x_M = x_{0.5} = \mu \Rightarrow$ distribution is **symmetric**

$x_M < x_{0.5} < \mu \Rightarrow$ distribution is **skewed to the right** or **positively skewed**

$x_M > x_{0.5} > \mu \Rightarrow$ distribution is **skewed to the left** or **negatively skewed**.

Another measure of skewness is the functional parameter

$$a_3 := \frac{E[(X-\mu)^3]}{\sigma^3} = \frac{E(X^3) - 3\mu E(X^2) + 2\mu^3}{\sigma^3}$$

For this measure it holds:

$a_3 = 0 \Rightarrow$ distribution is **symmetric**

$a_3 > 0 \Rightarrow$ distribution is **skewed to the right** or **positively skewed**

$a_3 < 0 \Rightarrow$ distribution is **skewed to the left** or **negatively skewed**.

Interpretation of skewness

In a positively (negatively) skewed distribution, smaller (bigger) outcomes have a higher probability of occurrence, i.e. a positively (negatively) skewed distribution has a mass function respectively a density function that flattens to the right (to the left).

Symmetry of the uniform distribution

In the example of the uniform distribution, the possible realizations have equal probabilities. It is easily verified that $a_3 = 0$.

Example 2.1/4

The equidistant uniform distribution with function parameters $a = 1, b = 1$ and $L = 5$, which models the outcomes of tosses of a fair die (example 2.1/3), has the following functional parameters:

$$\mu = 1 + 0.5 \cdot 5 = 3.5$$

$$\sigma^2 = \frac{1^2 \cdot 5 \cdot 7}{12} = \tfrac{35}{12} \approx 2.9167 \quad \sigma \approx \sqrt{2.9167} \approx 1.7078$$

$$a_3 = \frac{E[(X-\mu)^3]}{\sigma^3} = E[(X-3.5)^3] \cdot \left(\tfrac{35}{12}\right)^{-1.5} = 0.$$

Problem 2.1/3

a) Two fair dice are tossed independently. What is the massfunction of the sum of the two outcomes? Also, find the distribution function as well as the functional parameters $\mu, \sigma, x_{0.5}$ and a_3, which were introduced in this section.

b) In order to produce random digits $0, 1, 2, \ldots, 9$ we can roll a symmetric prisma that has one digit on each surface. For this experiment, write down the massfunction, the distribution function, the percentile function and all functional parameters.

b) The Bernoulli Distribution

The simplest way to classify outcomes of a qualitative characteristic is to assign them to one of two groups. This approach is called a dichotomous classification. The two different outcomes are complementary, e.g., faulty /without fault, conforming/nonconforming, right dimension /wrong dimension. Each type of characteristic can be brought into this form. We will code the two outcomes of interest by "1" and "0" respectively, where we will talk of "1" as a success and of "0" as a failure. The following defines a dichotomous random variable X with massfunction $Pr(X = x) =: be(x|P)$:

Massfunction of the Bernoulli distribution

$$be(x|P) = \begin{cases} 1 - P =: Q & \text{for } x = 0 \\ P & \text{for } x = 1 \\ 0 & \text{else.} \end{cases} \tag{2.9}$$

This two-valued distribution is called **Bernoulli distribution** (named after JACOB BERNOULLI, 1654-1705) or – because of its two realizations – the Zero–One distribution. The only parameter P $(0 < P < 1)$ is called the probability of success. In the case of $P = 0$ or $P = 1$ the random variable becomes single-valued, a **degenerate distribution**, at $x = 0$ or $x = 1$. To indicate that a random variable X has a Bernoulli distribution with parameter P we will write $X \sim be(P)$.

If the population is finite and contains N elements, among which M $(0 < M < N)$ are successes, we get

$$P = \frac{M}{N} \tag{2.10 a}$$

$$Q = \frac{N - M}{N}. \tag{2.10 b}$$

The distribution function $F(x) = Pr(X \leq x) =: Be(x|P)$ of the Bernoulli distribution is

Distribution function of the Bernoulli distribution

$$Be(x|P) = \begin{cases} 0 & \text{for } x < 0, \\ 1 - P = Q & \text{for } 0 \leq x < 1, \\ 1 & \text{for } x \geq 1. \end{cases} \tag{2.11}$$

Figure 2.1/2 shows the mass and distribution functions of the Bernoulli distribution, the simplest case of a discrete distribution, for $P = 0.2$.

The percentile function of the Bernoulli distribution is found to be

$$Be^{-1}(y|P) = \begin{cases} 0 & \text{for } 0 \leq y \leq 1 - P \\ 1 & \text{for } 1 - P < y \leq 1 \end{cases} \tag{2.12}$$

and the mode is given by

Mode of the Bernoulli distribution

$$x_M = \begin{cases} 0 & \text{if } 0 \leq P < 0.5 \\ 1 & \text{if } 0.5 < P \leq 1. \end{cases} \tag{2.13}$$

For $P = 0.5$ the mode is not defined.

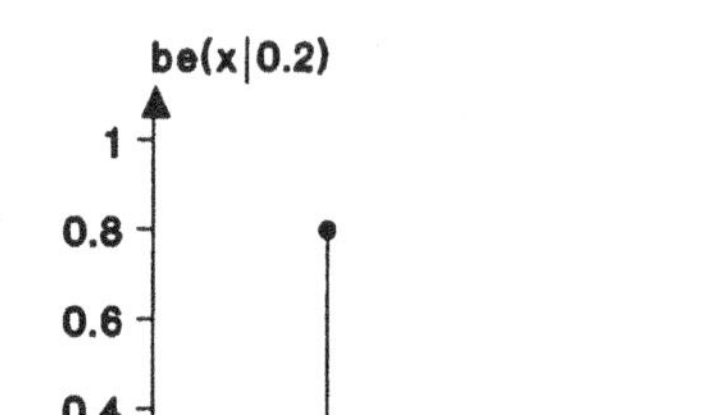

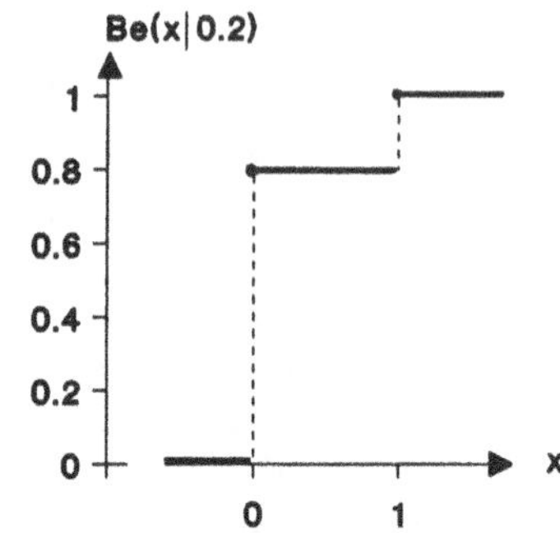

Figure 2.1/2: Bernoulli distribution with P=0.2

Expectation and variance of the Bernoulli distribution

The expectation $\mu = E(X)$ of the Bernoulli distribution is found to be

$$\mu = \sum_{x=0}^{1} x \cdot be(x|P) = 0 \cdot Q + 1 \cdot P = P. \tag{2.14}$$

The variance $\sigma^2 := V(X) = E[(X-\mu)^2]$ is found by using the shifting theorem $\sigma^2 = E(X^2) - \mu^2$ and

$$E(X^2) = \sum_{x=0}^{1} x^2 \cdot be(x|P) = 0^2 \cdot Q + 1^2 \cdot P = P.$$

It results to be

$$\sigma^2 = P - P^2 = P(1-P) = PQ. \tag{2.15}$$

Several of the distributions that are presented in this book evolve from the Bernoulli distribution.

Problem 2.1/4

a) In example 2.1/2 a car body with faults in the paint finish was called "success"[3]. Evaluate formulas (2.9), (2.11) - (2.15) for this example and draw the graphs of $be(x|P)$ and $Be(x|P)$. Calculate $Be^{-1}(0.5|P), \mu, \sigma^2$ and $x_{0.5}$.

b) Which value of P maximises σ^2 in (2.15)? Give the maximal value of σ^2.

c) Calculate the measure of skewness a_3 for the Bernoulli distribution. When is it zero, positive or negative?

[3] In quality control we take a sample to determine the proportion of nonconforming units and in this context success always means that a nonconforming product has been observed. Per se a nonconforming product is of course a failure.

c) The Poisson Distribution

The **Poisson distribution** (SIMEON DENIS POISSON, 1781-1840) occurs in statistical quality control in two different roles. Under certain conditions, which will be discussed later, it is the distribution of a discrete quality characteristic, e.g., the number of faults or nonconformities per production unit. Its main significance, however, is that it can approximate the binomial and hypergeometric distributions.

A random variable (quality characteristic) X is said to have a Poisson distribution if its massfunction $Pr(X = x) =: po(x|\lambda)$ is of the form

Massfunction of the Poisson distribution

$$po(x|\lambda) = \begin{cases} \dfrac{\lambda^x}{x!}e^{-\lambda} & \text{for } x = 0, 1, 2, \ldots \\ 0 & \text{else} \end{cases} \tag{2.16}$$

where $\lambda > 0$. We write $X \sim po(\lambda)$. The function parameter λ is called the **rate** of the Poisson distribution. The distribution function $Po(x|\lambda) := Pr(X \leq x)$ is given by [4]

Distribution function of the Poisson distribution

$$Po(x|\lambda) = \begin{cases} 0 & \text{for } x < 0 \\ \displaystyle\sum_{i=0}^{[x]} \frac{\lambda^i}{i!}e^{-\lambda} & \text{for } x \geq 0. \end{cases} \tag{2.17}$$

Table 5.1/4 gives the values of this function for some values of λ. Using formula (2.17) we can find the massfunction (2.16) by taking differences:

$$po(x|\lambda) = Po(x|\lambda) - Po(x-1|\lambda), \qquad x = 0, 1, 2, \ldots$$

where we define $Po(-1|\lambda) := 0$.

Figure 2.1/3 gives the massfunction and the distribution function of the Poisson distribution with $\lambda = 0.5$.

The Poisson distribution has the following properties:

Expectation, variance and other characteristics of the Poisson distribution

$$\mu = E(X) = \lambda \qquad \text{expectation} \tag{2.18 a}$$

$$\sigma^2 = V(X) = \lambda \qquad \text{variance} \tag{2.18 b}$$

$$x_{M_1} = \lambda - 1, \quad x_{M_2} = \lambda \qquad \text{two modes for } \lambda \in \mathbb{N} \tag{2.19 a}$$

$$x_M = [\lambda] \qquad \text{one mode for } \lambda \notin \mathbb{N} \tag{2.19 b}$$

$$a_3 = 1/\sqrt{\lambda} \qquad \text{skewness.} \tag{2.20}$$

[4] $[x]$ denotes the greatest integer smaller or equal to x (Gauss-bracket function). For example, $[3.1] = 3, [3] = 3, [-3.2] = -4, [-3] = -3$. $[x]$ always rounds a non-integer towards negative infinity. In some computer languages this function is called **floor**.

a. Massfunction

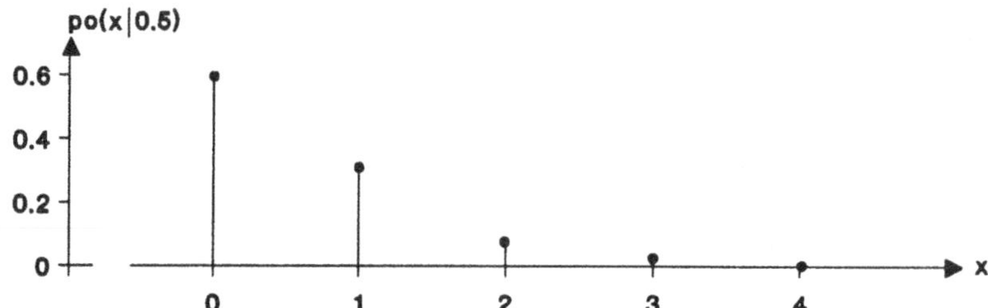

b. Distribution function

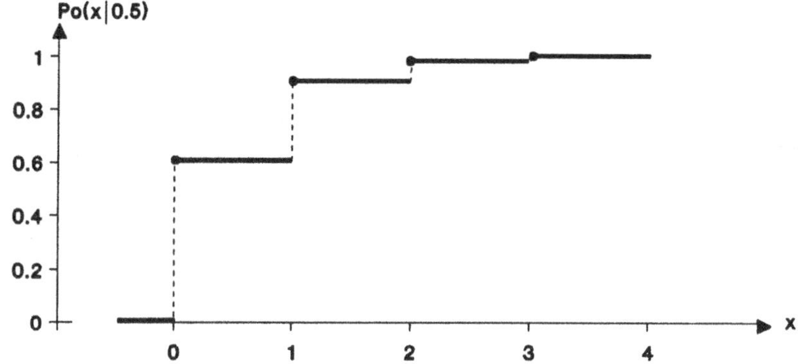

Figure 2.1/3: Poisson distribution with $\lambda = 0.5$

Increasing and decreasing recursion

Since $\lambda > 0$ it follows that $a_3 > 0$, what implies that the Poisson distribution is always skewed to the right (see figure 2.1/3). We have the following recursion formulae for the massfunction:[5]

$$po(x+1|\lambda) = \frac{\lambda}{x+1}\, po(x|\lambda) \tag{2.21 a}$$

$$po(x-1|\lambda) = \frac{x}{\lambda}\, po(x|\lambda) \tag{2.21 b}$$

The Poisson distribution is **reproductive** under summation. This means that the sum of two Poisson distributed random variables also has a Poisson distribution:[6]

[5]With a recursion formula an unknown element of a sequence (here the sequence of probabilities) can be obtained from the preceding or following elements (increasing or decreasing recursion respectively). In order to apply recursion for the calculation of discrete probabilities it is best to determine $Pr(X = x_M)$ and to apply the decreasing recursion $Pr(X = k)$ for $k < x_M$, and the increasing recursion for $k > x_M$. This way the rounding errors are kept small.

[6]The symbol $\sim$ is read as "is distributed".

$$X_1 \sim po(\lambda_1), X_2 \sim po(\lambda_2) \Rightarrow Y := X_1 + X_2 \sim po(\lambda_1 + \lambda_2) \qquad (2.22)$$

The Poisson distribution is often used in acceptance sampling for approximating less handy discrete distributions. Relationships of this kind between the Poisson distribution and other distributions can be grasped from figure 2.2/2 which is following later.

Statistical model behind the Poisson distribution

The Poisson distribution is an appropriate stochastic model for many random processes. It is generally used to describe relatively rare events. In quality control that could be for example an event like a knot in the thread of a sewing machine, a piece of dust on a painted surface or an air bubble in an optical lense. We can observe such events in one, two or three dimensions, i.e., along a line, an area or in a space. Without effecting the generality of our conclusions we can consider the occurrence of events in time. Figure 2.1/4 describes a series of events; in this example five events occurred randomly in the interval [t, t+Δt].

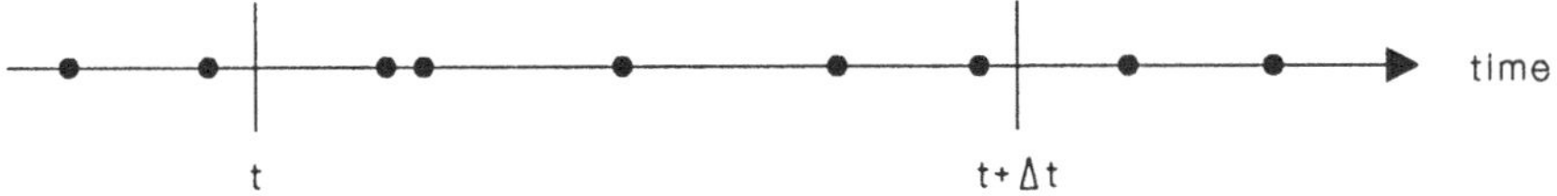

Figure 2.1/4: Events occurring randomly in time

Properties of a Poisson process:

A random process or **stochastic process** is called a **Poisson process** if the following three conditions hold:

- The probability that exactly one event occurs in an interval of length Δt (Δt small) is proportional, up to an error of higher order, to the length of that interval: (- Stationarity)

$$Pr(X = 1|\Delta t) = c \cdot \Delta t + o(\Delta t), \quad c > 0.^7$$

- The probability that more than one event occurs in Δt goes, as $\Delta t \to 0$, faster to zero than Δt itself: (- Ordinarity)

$$Pr(X > 1|\Delta t) = o(\Delta t).$$

- The occurrence of events in mutually exclusive time intervals is stochastically independent.[8] (- No-memory property)

[7] With o(Δt) - say little "oh" of Δt - we will denote, according to LANDAU, a function for which the sequence $|f(\Delta t)|$ / Δt converges to zero as Δt approaches the particular limit (here $\Delta t \to 0$).

[8] Two *events* are **stochastically independent** if the occurrence of one is not influenced by the occurrence of the other. This concept can be naturally extended to *random variables*.

It follows from the first property that the number of events in the interval $[t, t + \Delta t]$ approximately depends on the length of the interval, but not on the starting point t. A stochastic process with this property (translation invariance respective to t) is called a **stationary process**. The second property, often called **ordinarity**, implies that we can neglect the probability of more than one event, provided Δt is of small length. The third condition, called the **no-memory-property**, says that the frequency of events in preceding intervals does not effect the occurrence probability of events in future intervals.

From these three properties we can deduce a system of difference equations for X, the number of events in an interval of fixed length Δt, which has a Poisson distribution with rate $\lambda = c \cdot \Delta t$ (e.g., see MOOD/GRAYBILL/BOES 1983, p. 95-96).

Problem 2.1/5

a) A process in the production of window glass is known to produce, under desirable conditions, on average one impurity (i.e., an air bubble) per 500 cm^2 and past experience suggests that the number of impurities is Poisson distributed. Describe the distribution of the number of impurities on a glass of dimension 0.5 m × 1.0 m ? (Consider an area of 500 cm^2 as a standard unit, comparable to the unit interval.)

b) Glass pieces of size 0.5 m × 1.0 m with up to ten impurities are called grade 1, with 11 to 15 impurities, grade 2, and with more than 15, are considered rejects. What are the probabilities that a randomly selected piece of glass falls in the above categories? Use table 5.1/4.

c) Use equation (2.16) to calculate $po(0|1/3)$ and obtain $po(x|1/3)$ for $x = 1, 2, 3, 4$ using the recursion formula (2.21a). Make a table of these values and compare them to the tabulated values for $po(x|0.3)$ and $po(x|0.35)$ from table 5.1/4. Also find $Pr(1 \leq X \leq 3)$.

2.1.4 Continuous Distributions

a) Rectangular Distribution, Beta Distribution and Basic Concepts of Statistical Distribution Theory

In this section we will look at the distributions of continuous quality characteristics. By definition a continuous random variable can take on any value in a given interval. Further, its distribution function $F(x) = Pr(X \leq x)$ is, in mathematical terms, continuous, which means that it does not have any discontinuities or jumps.

The simplest, in quality control, however, the rarest, form of a continuous distribution is the **rectangular distribution**. It is the continuous analogue of the discrete uniform distribution and is usually called the **continuous uniform distribution**. Let a be the smallest and b the largest possible values of a continuous quality characteristic. If we assume that the probability of observing an event in any subinterval $[x_L, x_U]$ of $[a, b]$ is proportional to its length $x_U - x_L$, then the corresponding random variable X has a rectangular distribution on the interval $[a, b]$:

$$Pr(x_L \leq X \leq x_U) = c \cdot (x_U - x_L) \text{ for all } [x_L, x_U] \subset [a, b]. \qquad (2.23)$$

The distribution function $F(x) =: Re(x|a;b)$ of the rectangular distribution is

Distribution function of the rectangular distribution

$$Re(x|a;b) = \begin{cases} 0 & \text{for } x < a, \\ \dfrac{x-a}{b-a} & \text{for } a \leq x \leq b, \\ 1 & \text{for } x > b. \end{cases} \qquad (2.24)$$

If the distribution function of a continuous random variable is differentiable we will call its derivative

Concept of density function

$$f(x) := F'(x)$$

the **density function** or - shorter - the **density** of the distribution of X. A density function has the following properties:

Excursion: Properties of a density

a) $f(x) \geq 0$

b) $\int_{-\infty}^{x} f(t)dt = F(x)$

c) $\int_{-\infty}^{\infty} f(x)dx = 1$

d) $\int_{a}^{b} f(x)dx = F(b) - F(a) = Pr(a \leq x \leq b)$.

The first property follows from the definition $f(x) = F'(x)$ and the monotony property of $F(x)$. The second property is obtained from the definition by integration. We see that the distribution function of a continuous random variable can no longer be written as a sum of single probabilities of the form $Pr(X = x)$ as in the discrete case, but is an integral over the density with upper limit x. It can be shown that, in the case of a continuous X, the probability $Pr(X = x)$ for the occurrence of a specific outcome is always zero. The third property results from the second by letting $x \rightarrow \infty$. To prove the last property we use the definition of the distribution function. Properties (b) and (d) can be illustrated by figure 2.1/5.

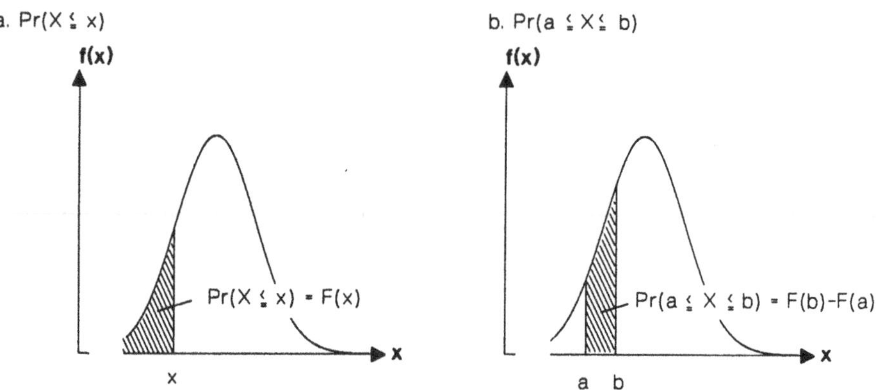

Figure 2.1/5: Relationship between distribution and density function

The density function of a continuous random variable corresponds to the massfunction of the discrete case. Before, the mode of a discrete random variable was defined to be the realization with maximum probability of occurrence. Now, in the continuous case, the mode maximizes the density function. For example, the density of a continuous unimodal distribution has one peak.

Mode (continuous case)

For the rectangular distribution we derive the density $f(x) =: re(x|a;b)$ to be

Density of the rectangular distribution

$$re(x|a;b) = \begin{cases} \dfrac{1}{b-a} & \text{for } a \leq x \leq b \\ 0 & \text{else} \end{cases} \tag{2.25}$$

where $a, b \in \mathbb{R}$. If X is a continuous random variable with density (2.25), then we will write $X \sim re(a;b)$. Figure 2.1/6 shows the density and distribution functions of a rectangular distribution with $a = 1$ and $b = 4$.

The inverse of function (2.24), i.e., the percentile function of the rectangular distribution, is given by

$$Re^{-1}(y|a;b) = a + (b-a)y \quad \text{with } 0 \leq y \leq 1.$$

Looking at figure 2.1/6 a it soon comes clear why this distribution is called 'rectangular'. When the graph of the density of a continuous random variable has the form of a triangle lying on the horizontal (x) axis we talk about a **triangular distribution** (cf. example 2.1/5).

Concept of a triangular distribution

For a *continuous* random variable with density $f(x)$ the expectation $\mu := E(X)$ is defined by

Expectation (continuous case)

$$E(X) := \int_{-\infty}^{\infty} x \cdot f(x)\, dx. \tag{2.26}$$

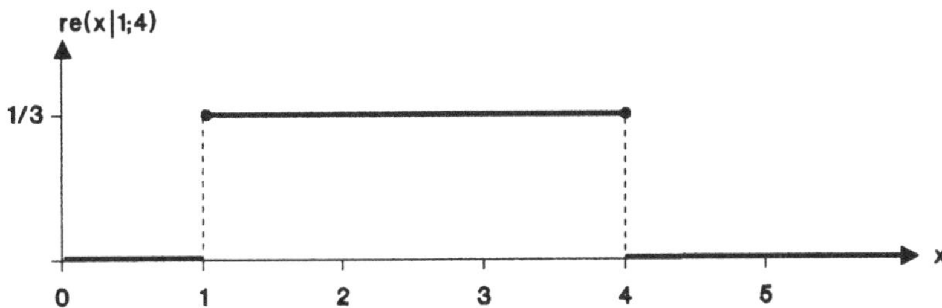

Distribution function

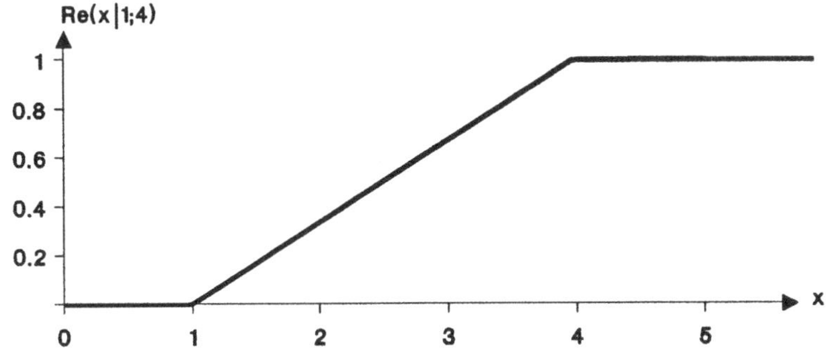

Figure 2.1/6: Rectangular distribution on $[1, 4]$

Note that the existence of this integral cannot be taken for granted. As previously mentioned, the variance $\sigma^2 := V(X)$ is calculated by $V(X) = E[(x-\mu)^2]$, and the standard deviation σ is given by $\sigma = \sqrt{V(X)}$.

The rectangular distribution has the following functional parameters:

Expectation, variance and skewness of the rectangular distribution

$$\mu = \frac{a+b}{2} \qquad \text{expectation} \tag{2.27 a}$$

$$\sigma^2 = \frac{(b-a)^2}{12} \qquad \text{variance} \tag{2.27 b}$$

$$\alpha_3 = 0 \qquad \text{skewness} \tag{2.27 c}$$

The rectangular distribution is not reproductive under summation. For example, the sum of two independent random variables with a rectangular distribution has a triangular distribution.

An important special case of this kind of distribution is the rectangular distribution on [0;1]. It can be used for the generation of random numbers from any specified distribution by simply putting the generated random numbers into the percentile function of the specific distribution.

A generalization of the rectangular distribution on [0;1] is the beta distribution. We say that a random variable has a **beta distribution** if its density $f(x) =: bt(x|\gamma;\delta)$ is of the form

Density of the beta distribution

$$bt(x|\gamma;\delta) := \begin{cases} \frac{1}{B(\gamma;\delta)} x^{\gamma-1}(1-x)^{\delta-1} & \text{for } 0 \le x \le 1, \\ 0 & \text{else.} \end{cases} \tag{2.28 a}$$

The parameters are required to satisfy $\gamma > 0$ and $\delta > 0$. The distribution function $F(X) =: Bt(x|\gamma;\delta)$ of the beta distribution is

Distribution function of the beta distribution

$$Bt(x|\gamma;\delta) := \begin{cases} 0 & \text{for } x < 0 \\ \frac{B_x(\gamma;\delta)}{B(\gamma;\delta)} & \text{for } 0 \le x < 1 \\ 1 & \text{for } x \ge 1 \end{cases} \tag{2.28 b}$$

where

$$B(\gamma;\delta) := \int_0^1 u^{\gamma-1}(1-u)^{\delta-1}du \tag{2.29 a}$$

is called the **beta function**. We also define

$$B_x(\gamma;\delta) := \int_0^x u^{\gamma-1}(1-u)^{\delta-1}du \tag{2.29 b}$$

to be the **incomplete beta function**. It can be shown that $B(1;1) = 1$. From this it follows by (2.25) and (2.28a) that

$$bt(x|1;1) = re(x|0;1),$$

in other words, the beta distribution with parameters $\gamma = 1$ and $\delta = 1$ is the rectangular distribution on [0;1].

We also want to introduce the following functional parameters of the beta distribution:

Expectation and variance of the beta distribution

$$\mu = \frac{\gamma}{\gamma+\delta} \tag{2.30 a}$$

$$\sigma^2 = \frac{\gamma\delta}{(\gamma+\delta)^2(\gamma+\delta+1)}. \tag{2.30 b}$$

Problem 2.1/6

a) What is the value of the constant c in (2.23) ?

b) Verify (2.27a).

c) Show that the mean absolute deviation, i.e., the expectation of the absolute deviation $|X - \mu|$, of a quality characteristic with a rectangular distribution on $[a; b]$ and expectation μ is given by $E(|X - \mu|) = (b - a)/4$.

d) Calculate the percentiles $x_{0.95}$ and $x_{0.05}$ of the rectangular distribution. Also determine the percentile range $x_{0.95} - x_{0.05}$ (inner 90% width).

e) Suppose we want to work with the parameters $c := (a + b)/2$, the interval midpoint, and $d := (a - b)/2$, the half-width of the interval, instead of the parameters a and b. Rewrite formulas (2.24)-(2.27) using the new parameters.

f) Determine (2.24)-(2.27) for the rectangular distribution on [0;1].

b) Exponential, Gamma and other Lifetime Distributions

Derivation of the exponential distribution from the Poisson distribution

We will now consider independent Poisson distributed events that occur with intensity λ per unit time (e.g., per minute). Since the Poisson distribution is reproductive under summation, it follows that the number of events that occur in a time interval of t units is again Poisson distributed, with parameter λt. Hence, the probability that there is no event during the next t time units following the last event is given by

$$po(0|\lambda t) = \frac{(\lambda t)^0}{0!} e^{-\lambda t} = e^{-\lambda t}. \tag{2.31}$$

The statement "there is no event during the first t time units after the last event" is equivalent to "the length of the interarrival time between two consecutive events is at least t time units". This interarrival time is a continuous random variable, say X, and has realizations x. If we set $t = x$, we can express (2.31) by

$$Pr(X > x) = e^{-\lambda x}; x \geq 0.$$

The above probability statement about the occurrence of the next event is monotone decreasing in x. The complementary probability $Pr(X \leq x) = 1 - Pr(X > x)$ is monotone increasing. It is called the distribution function $F(x) =: Ex(x|\lambda)$ of the **exponential distribution**:

Distribution function of the exponential distribution

$$Ex(x|\lambda) = \begin{cases} 0 & \text{for } x < 0, \\ 1 - e^{-\lambda x} & \text{for } x \geq 0. \end{cases} \tag{2.32 a}$$

Density of the exponential distribution

The derivative of (2.32a) gives us the density $f(x) =: ex(x|\lambda)$ of the exponential distribution:

$$ex(x|\lambda) = \begin{cases} 0 & \text{for } x < 0, \\ \lambda e^{-\lambda x} & \text{for } x \geq 0. \end{cases} \tag{2.32 b}$$

For a continuous random variable X with distribution characterised by (2.32) we will use the notation $X \sim ex(\lambda)$. Figure 2.1/7 shows the density and distribution function of an ex(0.5)-distributed random variable.

Percentile function of the exponential distribution

Inverting (2.32a) yields the percentile function of the exponential distribution:

$$Ex^{-1}(y|\lambda) = -\frac{ln(1-y)}{\lambda}; \quad 0 \leq y \leq 1.$$

The functional parameters of the exponential distribution are:

Expectation, variance and other characteristics of the exponential distribution

$$\mu = 1/\lambda \qquad \text{expectation,} \tag{2.33 a}$$

$$\sigma^2 = 1/\lambda^2 \qquad \text{variance,} \tag{2.33 b}$$

$$x_M = 0 \qquad \text{mode,} \tag{2.34 a}$$

$$\alpha_3 = 2 \qquad \text{skewness (skewed to the left)} \tag{2.34 b}$$

Note that the mode and the skewness are independent of the parameter λ.

The derivation of the exponential distribution illustrates its close relationship to the Poisson distribution. The Poisson distribution allows us to make statements about the *number* of events in a given time interval. With the exponential distribution one can make statements about the *interarrival* time between a given event and the next following event. Both distributions are based on the Poisson process. We have already discussed the characteristics "stationarity", "ordinarity" and the "no-memory property" of this process. Relationships between the exponential distribution and other distributions may be taken from figure 2.2/2.

The exponential distribution can be used as a lifetime distribution.

In quality assurance and technical statistics, the exponential distribution is used as a lifetime distribution. For example, if the breakdown times of a machine are Poisson distributed, then the time interval between two consecutive breakdowns can be seen as the lifetime of this machine run. In general, the **lifetime** X of an object or a process is considered to be the

a. Density function

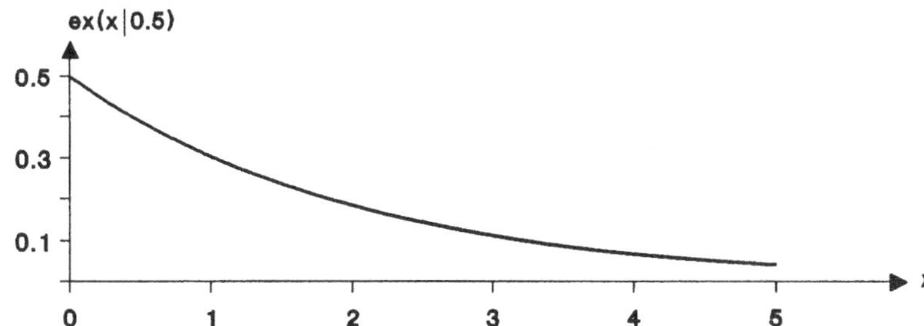

b. Distribution function

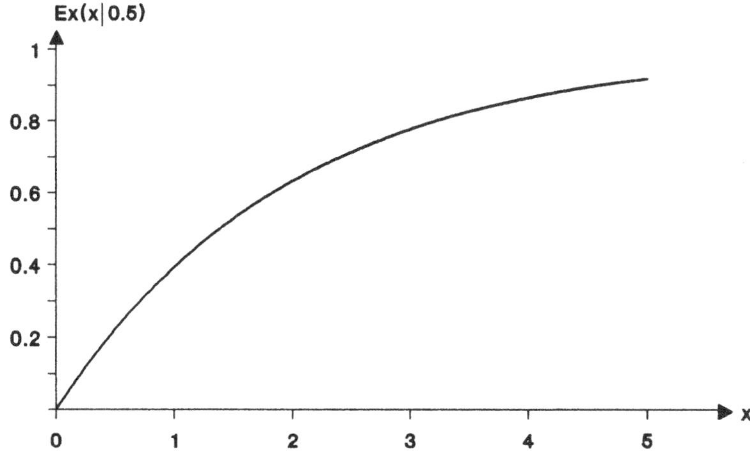

Figure 2.1/7: Exponential distribution with $\lambda = 0.5$

time span between the start of the process, and the failure, or end, of the process. The corresponding distribution function $F(x) = Pr(X \leq x)$ is called the **failure distribution** or **lifetime distribution**. The complementary function

$$R(x) := Pr(X > x) = 1 - F(x)$$

is called the **survival function** or **reliability function** and the density $f(x) = F'(x)$ is called the **failure density**. The ratio

Basic concepts in the theory of lifetime distributions

$$h(x) := \frac{f(x)}{R(x)}; \ x \geq 0;$$

is defined to be the **hazard rate** or **failure rate**. It denotes the approximate probability that a unit that has survived x time units will fail within a very short time. A lifetime distribution is completely characterized by its distribution function $F(x)$, by the reliability function $R(x) = 1 - F(x)$ or by the failure rate $h(x)$. For a given $F(x)$ the failure rate is calculated by $h(x) = F^{'}(x)/(1 - F(x))$. Conversely, for a given failure rate the distribution function is determined by

$$F(x) = 1 - exp\left[-\int_0^x h(r)dr\right]$$

A detailed discussion can, for example, be found in BANKS (1989, sec. 16.3) or WADSWORTH/STEPHENS/GODFREY (1986, sec. 18-1).

Failure rate of the exponential distribution

In the case of the exponential distribution it follows by (2.32) that the failure rate is constant:

$$h(x) = \frac{\lambda e^{-\lambda x}}{1 - (1 - e^{-\lambda x})} = \lambda; \qquad x \geq 0.$$

The failure rate of an object or a process with an exponentially distributed lifetime at time $t = x$ is independent of the lifespan x. This explains why the exponential distribution is sometimes called a "memoryless distribution".

The gamma distribution as a generalization of the exponential distribution

A generalization of the exponential distribution is the gamma distribution. A continuous random variable is said to have a **gamma distribution** if it has a density $f(x) =: ga(x|b;\delta)$ of the form

$$ga(x|b;\delta) := \begin{cases} 0 & \text{for } x < 0 \\ \dfrac{\left(\frac{x}{b}\right)^{\delta-1} e^{-x/b}}{b \cdot \Gamma(\delta)} & \text{for } x \geq 0 \end{cases} \tag{2.35 a}$$

with the parameters $b > 0$ and $\delta > 0$. The distribution function $F(x) =: Ga(x|b;\delta)$ of the gamma distribution is given by

$$Ga(x|b;\delta) := \begin{cases} 0 & \text{for } x < 0 \\ \dfrac{\Gamma_{x/b}(\delta)}{\Gamma(\delta)} & \text{for } x \geq 0. \end{cases} \tag{2.35 b}$$

$$\Gamma(\delta) := \int_0^\infty u^{\delta-1}e^{-u}du \tag{2.36 a}$$

denotes the **gamma function** and

$$\Gamma_y(\delta) := \int_0^y u^{\delta-1}e^{-u}du$$

is the so-called **incomplete gamma function**. The integral cannot be written in a closed form for any $\delta > 0$ and has to be evaluated by numerical integration. For $\delta \in \mathbb{N}$, the gamma function has the representation

$$\Gamma(\delta) = 1 \cdot 2 \cdot \ldots \cdot (\delta - 1) =: (\delta - 1)!\ ^{9} \tag{2.36 b}$$

We want to introduce two functional parameters of the gamma distribution:

Expectation and variance of the gamma distribution

$$\mu = b\delta \tag{2.37 a}$$

$$\sigma^2 = b^2\delta. \tag{2.37 b}$$

The exponential distribution is a special case of the gamma distribution. For $b = 1/\lambda$ and $\delta = 1$ in (2.35a) and using $\Gamma(1) = 1$ we get (2.32b):

Relationship of the gamma distribution to other distributions:

- exponential distribution

$$ga\left(x \middle| \frac{1}{\lambda}; 1\right) = ex(x|\lambda). \tag{2.38 a}$$

The gamma distribution with $b = 1$ and the Poisson distribution are related by

- Poisson distribution

$$Ga(x|1;\delta) = 1 - Po(\delta - 1|x) \quad \text{for } \delta = 1, 2, \ldots \tag{2.38 b}$$

The failure rate $h(x)$ of the gamma distribution is only constant in the case that $\delta = 1$. For $\delta > 0$ it has an increasing failure rate (IFR), and for $\delta < 0$, a decreasing failure rate (DFR). One sometimes speaks of **IFR-** and **DFR-distributions** in this context.

In addition to the exponential and gamma distributions, there are various others which are used as lifetime distributions. They have in common that they are only defined for positive values of a random variable X (lifetime) and their densities are all skewed to the right. We will only mention two typical lifetime distributions and list their densities and – as far as they can be written in closed form – their distribution functions. The interested reader is referred to other textbooks on life testing and reliability theory (see section 1.1.2, especially remark 3).

Further lifetime distributions

Lognormal distribution

$$f(x) = \frac{1}{xb\sqrt{2\pi}} \exp\left[-\frac{(\ln x - a)^2}{2b^2}\right]; \; x \geq 0, a \in \mathbb{R}, b > 0.$$

Weibull distribution

$$f(x) = \frac{c}{b}\left(\frac{x}{b}\right)^{c-1} \exp\left[-\left(\frac{x}{b}\right)^{c}\right]; \; x \geq 0, b > 0, c > 0$$

$$F(x) = 1 - exp\left[-\left(\frac{x}{b}\right)^{c}\right].$$

[9] In mathematics, $x!$ denotes the product of all integers from 1 up to x and is called x factorial.

Problem 2.1/7

a) Let X be a quality characteristic with $X \sim ex(2)$. Determine $\mu = E(X)$, $\sigma^2 = V(X)$ and the probabilities $Pr(X < 1)$, $Pr(X > 2)$, $Pr(0.5 < X < 1.5)$, $Pr(\mu - 3\sigma < X < \mu + 3\sigma)$. Also find the median $x_{0.5}$ and the percentile range $x_{0.975} - x_{0.025}$.

b) Calculate the value of the distribution function (2.32) at the point $x = \mu$ and interpret the result.

c) Suppose the lifetime X of lightbulbs is exponentially distributed. The average burning-time is 2000 hours, and lightbulbs that fail after less than 250 hours are considered nonconforming to specifications. What is the fraction defective, $Pr(X < 250)$?

c) The Normal Distribution

The normal distribution is considered to be the most important distribution in the theory of statistics. It also plays a central role in statistical quality assurance. It is not surprising that the normal distribution is applied on such a wide scope if one considers that under fairly weak assumptions a random variable is already approximately normally distributed. The normal distribution was first derived in 1733 by ABRAHAM DE MOIVRE (1667 - 1754) as the limiting distribution of the binomial distribution (see figure 2.2/2) and was rediscovered by CARL FRIEDRICH GAUSS (1777 - 1855) as a distribution of measurement and observation errors.

Density of the normal distribution

We say that a random variable (quality characteristic) follows a **normal distribution** if its density $f(x) =: no(x|\mu;\sigma^2)$ is given by

$$no(x|\mu;\sigma^2) = \frac{1}{\sigma\sqrt{2\pi}} \exp\left[-\frac{(x-\mu)^2}{2\sigma^2}\right] \tag{2.39}$$

Distribution function of the normal distribution

where $x \in \mathbb{R}$, $\mu \in \mathbb{R}$ and $\sigma^2 > 0$. The cumulative distribution function $F(x) =: No(x|\mu;\sigma^2)$ is of the form

$$No(x|\mu;\sigma^2) = \int_{-\infty}^{x} no(u|\mu;\sigma^2)du. \tag{2.40}$$

The integral in (2.40) cannot be written in closed form and has to be evaluated using a table (see table 5.1/1). Figure 2.1/8 shows the graphs of (2.39) and (2.40) for various values of the parameters μ and σ^2.

For a random variable with probability density (2.39) we use the notation $X \sim no(\mu; \sigma^2)$. The parameters of the normal distribution are, as the notation suggests, its expectation and its variance:

Expectation, variance and further characteristics of the normal distribution

$$E(X) = \mu \quad \text{expectation} \tag{2.41}$$

$$V(X) = \sigma^2 \quad \text{variance.} \tag{2.42}$$

Figure 2.1/8 illustrates the effect of variation of the parameters μ and σ^2 on the curves of the density and distribution functions. As the expectation μ increases the density and the distribution function are both shifted to the right. For decreasing variance σ^2 the density is more condensed and also has higher values around μ, whereas the distribution function becomes steeper.

Since the normal distribution is unimodal and symmetric (see figure 2.1/8a) its median, mode and expectation all have the same value:

$$x_M = x_{0.5} = \mu. \tag{2.43}$$

The density has two turning points

$$x_{W_{1,2}} = \mu \pm \sigma,$$

but the distribution function only one (see figure 2.1/8b)

$$x_{W_3} = \mu.$$

Because of the symmetry of the density it holds that $E[(X-\mu)^3] = 0$ and this implies that the skewness a_3 of the normal distribution is also zero:

$$\alpha_3 = \frac{E[(X-\mu)^3]}{\sigma^3} = 0. \tag{2.44}$$

Relationships between the normal distribution and other distributions are summarized later in figure 2.2/2.

If X is normally distributed then so is any linear transformation of X:

Reproductivity of the normal distribution

$$X \sim no(\mu; \sigma^2) \Rightarrow Y := aX + b \sim no(a\mu + b; a^2\sigma^2). \tag{2.45}$$

Further, the normal distribution is reproductive under linear combination of several independent normally distributed random variables X_i:

$$X_i \sim no\left(\mu_i; \sigma_i^2\right); i = 1, \ldots, n \Rightarrow Y := \sum_{i=1}^{n} a_i X_i \sim no\left(\sum_{i=1}^{n} a_i\mu_i; \sum_{i=1}^{n} a_i^2\sigma_i^2\right). \tag{2.46}$$

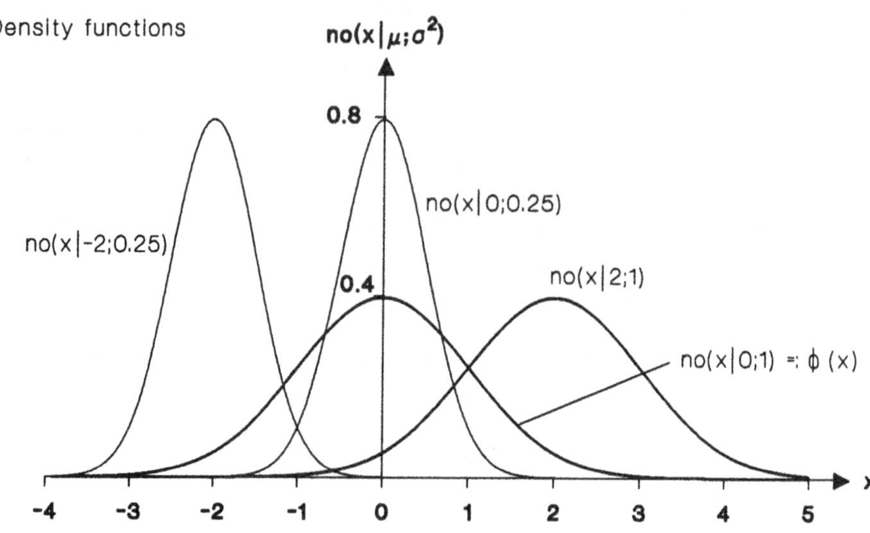

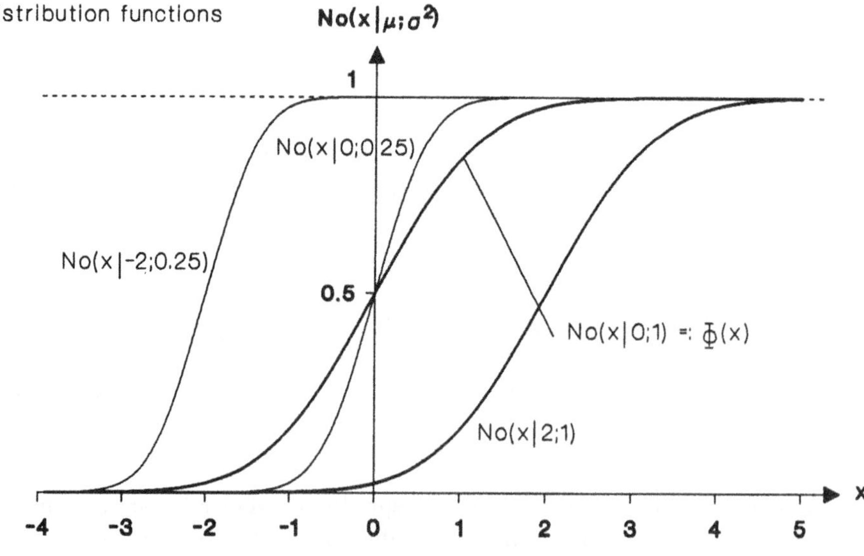

Figure 2.1/8: Normal distribution for four sets of parameter values

Of special importance is the specific linear transformation that transforms a normally distributed random variable into one with $\mu = 0$ and $\sigma^2 = 1$. We know by (2.46) that

$$X \sim no(\mu;\sigma^2) \;\Rightarrow\; Z := \frac{X-\mu}{\sigma} \sim no(0;1). \tag{2.47}$$

The transformation $Z = [X - E(X)]/\sqrt{V(X)}$ can be applied to any random variable with finite variance. It is called **standardization**. Standardizing is a very important method for normal distributions, because any normally distributed random variable can thus be reduced to the standard normal case $Z \sim no(0;1)$. The standardized normal distribution is called the **standard normal distribution**. Realizations

$$z := \frac{x-\mu}{\sigma} \tag{2.48}$$

of standard normally distributed quantities will occur frequently in the following discussion. The density of the standard normal distribution is given by (2.39) with $\mu = 0$ and $\sigma = 1$:

Density of the standard normal distribution

$$\phi(z) := no(z|0;1) = \frac{1}{\sqrt{2\pi}} \exp\left(-\frac{z^2}{2}\right). \tag{2.49}$$

Accordingly, its distribution function is given by

Distribution function of the standard normal distribution

$$\Phi(z) := No(z|0;1) = \int_{-\infty}^{z} \phi(u)du. \tag{2.50}$$

The graphs of the functions (2.49) and (2.50) are already in figure 2.1/8.

The distribution function (2.50) is tabulated in table 5.1/1. As this function is symmetric around (0; 0.5),

$$\Phi(z) = 1 - \Phi(-z), \tag{2.51}$$

it suffices to tabulate $\Phi(z)$ for positive values of z. Table 5.1/1 not only gives the values of the function (2.50), but can also be used to obtain the values of any normal distribution function. It holds that:

Relationship between any normal distribution function and the standard normal distribution function

$$No\left(x|\mu;\sigma^2\right) = \Phi\left(\frac{x-\mu}{\sigma}\right) \tag{2.52 a}$$

$$no\left(x|\mu;\sigma^2\right) = \frac{1}{\sigma}\,\phi\left(\frac{x-\mu}{\sigma}\right). \tag{2.52 b}$$

With (2.52a) and table 5.1/1 we can, for example, calculate

$$No(3|1;16) = \Phi\left(\frac{3-1}{4}\right) = \Phi(0.5) \approx 0.691463$$

$$No(-1|1;16) = \Phi\left(\frac{-1-1}{4}\right) = \Phi(-0.5) \approx 0.308537.$$

The percentile functions $x := No^{-1}(y|\mu;\sigma^2)$ and $z := \Phi^{-1}(y)$ with $y \in (0;1)$ also cannot be written in closed form. The values

$$x_\omega := No^{-1}\left(\omega|\mu;\sigma^2\right), \tag{2.53}$$

$$z_\omega := \Phi^{-1}(\omega) \tag{2.54}$$

are called the percentiles of order ω or the $100\cdot\omega$-th percentiles. We see that the percentiles (2.53) and (2.54) satisfy $No(x_\omega|\mu;\sigma^2) = \omega$ and $\Phi(z_\omega) = \omega$, respectively.

The following table lists a selection of percentiles of the standard normal distribution. Usually "nice" values of ω correspond to "unnice" values of z and vice versa:

ω	0.8413	0.90	0.95	0.975	0.9773	0.99	0.995	0.99865
z_ω	1	1.282	1.645	1.960	2	2.326	2.576	3

Table 2.1/2: Selected percentiles of the standard normal distribution

More percentiles can be found in table 5.2/1. For various ω, $0 \leq \omega < 1$, the corresponding percentiles z_ω of the standard normal distribution function are tabulated. It would suffice to only list a table for $\omega \geq 0.5$, because the function $y = \Phi(z)$ and its inverse, $z = \Phi^{-1}(y)$, are point symmetric. In analogy to (2.51) we have the relationship

$$z_{1-\omega} = -z_\omega. \tag{2.55}$$

With table 5.2/1 one cannot only obtain the percentiles of the standard normal distribution, but with (2.48) one can verify the relationship

Relationship between percentiles of the standard normal and a general normal distribution

$$x_\omega = \mu + z_\omega \cdot \sigma \tag{2.56}$$

between the standard normal and any normal percentile. Thus we can determine any percentile of a general normal distribution.

Concept of variation intervals

We now introduce the concept of variation intervals. An interval that contains $100\cdot(1-\alpha)\%$ of the realizations of a random variable X is called a $100\cdot(1-\alpha)\%$ **variation interval**. Usually α is chosen to be a small number, i.e., $\alpha = 0.1, 0.05, 0.01, 0.001$. We distinguish between **onesided** and **twosided variation intervals**. The latter are also called **central variation intervals**. There are two cases of onesided variation intervals. One gives a *lower bound* and contains the range of the biggest $100 \cdot (1-\alpha)\%$ realizations. In other words, the smallest $\alpha \cdot 100\%$ realizations are excluded. We use the percentile x_α to write the interval $[x_\alpha, +\infty)$. The corresponding probability statement is

$$Pr(X \geq x_\alpha) = 1 - \alpha. \tag{2.57 a}$$

The other case of a onesided variation interval gives an *upper bound*, i.e., the interval is written $(-\infty, x_{1-\alpha}]$, and the analogous probability statement is

$$Pr(X \leq x_{1-\alpha}) = 1 - \alpha. \tag{2.57 b}$$

A twosided $100 \cdot (1-\alpha)\%$ variation interval obviously excludes the smallest $100 \cdot (\alpha/2)\%$ and the largest $100 \cdot (\alpha/2)\%$ realizations. The interval is given by $[x_{\alpha/2}, x_{1-\alpha/2}]$ and the corresponding probability statement is

$$Pr\left(x_{\alpha/2} \leq X \leq x_{1-\alpha/2}\right) = 1 - \alpha. \tag{2.58}$$

If $X \sim no(\mu; \sigma^2)$ we can, according to (2.55 - 2.56), rewrite the statements (2.57) and (2.58) as:

Variation intervals for normally distributed random variables

$$Pr(X \geq \mu - z_{1-\alpha} \cdot \sigma) = 1 - \alpha \tag{2.59 a}$$

$$Pr(X \leq \mu + z_{1-\alpha} \cdot \sigma) = 1 - \alpha \tag{2.59 b}$$

$$Pr(\mu - z_{1-\alpha/2} \cdot \sigma \leq X \leq \mu + z_{1-\alpha/2} \cdot \sigma) = 1 - \alpha. \tag{2.59 c}$$

The relationships in (2.59a-c) are illustrated in the following figure 2.1/9.

a. Twosided (central) variation interval

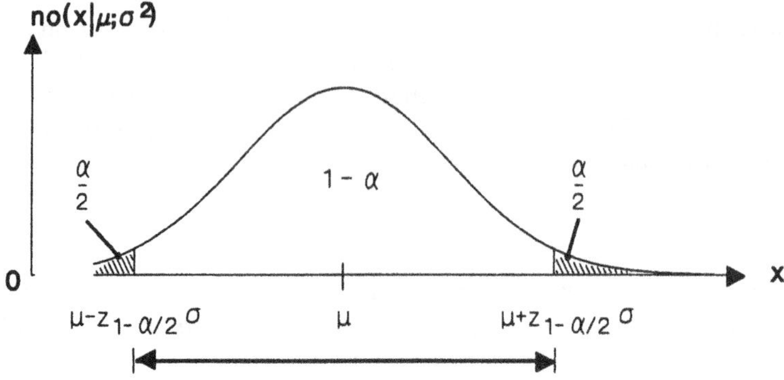

b. Onesided variation interval with lower bound

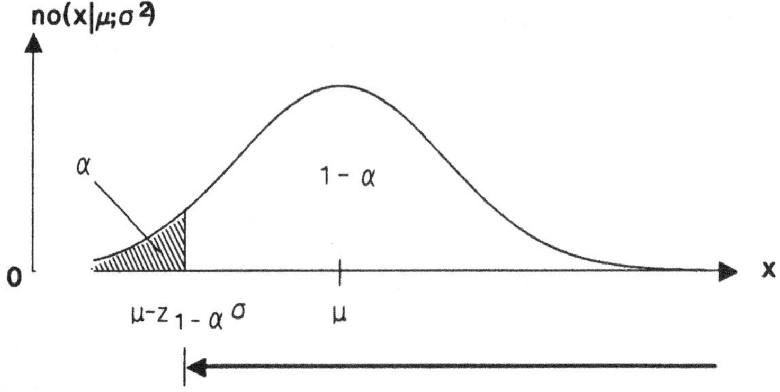

c. Onesided variation interval with upper bound

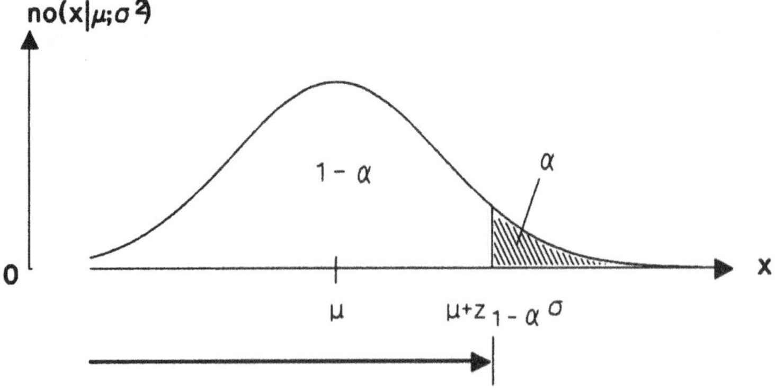

Figure 2.1/9: $100 \cdot (1-\alpha)\%$ variation intervals for a normal distribution

Problem 2.1/8

Suppose that the random variable X is $no(2;25)$-distributed. Calculate the probabilities $Pr(X \geq 10)$, $Pr(-3 \leq X \leq 7)$ and $Pr(X \leq -13)$.

Problem 2.1/9

What is the effect on the density curve, if

a) the expectation μ is increased or decreased while the variance remains constant,

b) the variance σ^2 is increased or decreased while the expectation remains constant ?

Problem 2.1/10

A machine fills sugar in packets with average weight μ and standard deviation $\sigma = 0.5\ g$. The fill-weight of the packets is supposed to be 1 kg with a tolerance region of $[998.5\ g, 1001.5\ g]$. Packets of sugar with weight outside of the tolerance region are considered "nonconforming". We also know that the weights are normally distributed.

a) What percentage of the production has to be scrapped, if the machine is set to $\mu = 1001\ g$?

b) Write the fraction nonconforming P as a function of μ and draw the figure of the function $P = P(\mu)$.

c) What is the optimal setting of the machine so that the fraction nonconforming is minimized? What is this minimum fraction?

d) Suppose the machine is set to $\mu = 1000\ g$. Determine the fraction nonconforming P as a function of σ and draw the graph of $P = P(\sigma)$.

e) When the machine is set to $\mu = 1000\ g$ and $\sigma = 0.5\ g$, what is more dangerous, in the sense that the fraction nonconforming is expected to increase more: a shift of μ by $\pm 0.5\ g$ or an increase of $0.5\ g$ in σ?

Problem 2.1/11

Bullet proof glass is manufactured by glueing together three layers of glass like a sandwich. The thickness of the two outer layers is normally distributed with parameters $\mu = 3\ mm$ and $\sigma = 0.2\ mm$ and that of the inner layer is also normally distributed with parameters $\mu = 6\ mm$ and $\sigma = 0.3\ mm$. The thickness of both transparent glue layers is normally distributed with $\mu = 0.1\ mm$ and $\sigma = 0.1\ mm$.

a) What is the distribution of the total thickness of the glass?

b) Give the twosided and both onesided 99%-variation intervals for the thickness of this bullet proof glass.

d) Approximations with the Normal Distribution

We can see from formula (2.20) for the skewness a_3 of the Poisson distribution that

$$\lim_{\lambda\to\infty} \alpha_3 = \lim_{\lambda\to\infty} \frac{1}{\sqrt{\lambda}} = 0$$

and consequently that the Poisson distribution becomes more and more symmetric as λ increases. The convergence to a symmetric distribution is a necessary but not sufficient condition for convergence of a distribution to a normal distribution, since by (2.44) the normal distribution was found to be symmetric. We see from (2.34b) that, for example, the exponential distribution does not satisfy this necessary condition of asymptotic symmetry for $\lambda \to \infty$. Therefore it cannot converge to a normal distribution. For the Poisson distribution the following rule applies for using the normal approximation:

Normal approximation of the Poisson distribution

$$X \sim po(\lambda);\quad \lambda \geq 9 \quad \Rightarrow\quad X \sim no(\lambda;\lambda) \quad \text{holds approximately.}$$

We will omit the illustration of this rule. In general, when approximating a discrete distribution by a continuous distribution, it is advisable to use a **continuity correction** in order to keep the approximation errors as small as possible. We will illustrate this with the example of the Poisson distribution.

The expression $Pr(X = x) = po(x|\lambda)$ gives, for fixed x, the probability that the discrete random variable X takes the realization x. Putting this x into the density $no(x|\lambda;\lambda)$ of the normal approximation does not result in a probability, but only in a density value. In order to obtain a probability, one has to integrate the density over an interval. The length of this interval has to correspond to the spacing of the discrete random variable. In this case the distance between the discrete realizations is one unit, and, consequently, at every x, one has to integrate the density over a unit interval. The best approximation is obtained if one takes x to be the midpoint of this unit interval, i.e., if one works with $[x - 0.5, x + 0.5]$. With this approach the Poisson massfunction is, for $\lambda \geq 9$, approximated by

Normal approximation of the Poisson distribution with continuity correction

$$\begin{aligned} po(x|\lambda) &= \frac{\lambda^x}{x!}e^{-\lambda} \\ &\approx \int_{x-0.5}^{x+0.5} \frac{1}{\sqrt{2\pi\lambda}} \exp\left[-\frac{(u-\lambda)^2}{2\lambda}\right] du \end{aligned} \qquad (2.60\text{ a})$$

$$= No(x+0.5|\lambda;\lambda) - No(x-0.5|\lambda;\lambda)$$

$$= \Phi\left(\frac{x+0.5-\lambda}{\sqrt{\lambda}}\right) - \Phi\left(\frac{x-0.5-\lambda}{\sqrt{\lambda}}\right).$$

Hence, the approximation of its distribution function is given by

$$Po(x|\lambda) \approx No(x+0.5|\lambda;\lambda) = \Phi\left(\frac{x+0.5-\lambda}{\sqrt{\lambda}}\right). \tag{2.60 b}$$

Table 2.1/3 gives the normal approximation of the Poisson distribution, with and without continuity correction, for $\lambda = 4$. Since $\lambda < 9$, the approximation is not very satisfactory. Column 2 contains the values of the exact distribution function $Po(x|4)$ for $x = 1, \ldots, 9$. The corresponding values of the distribution functions $No(x|4;4) = \Phi[(x-4)/2]$ and $No(x+0.5|4;4) = \Phi[(x-3.5)/2]$ of the normal approximations (without and with a continuity correction) can be found in columns 3 and 4. The approximation errors are listed in columns 5 and 6:

x	$Po(x\|4)$	$\Phi[(x-4)/2]$	$\Phi[(x-3.5)/2]$	(2) – (3)	(2) – (4)
(1)	(2)	(3)	(4)	(5)	(6)
0	0.0183	0.0228	0.0401	-0.0045	-0.0218
1	0.0916	0.0668	0.1057	0.0248	-0.0141
2	0.2381	0.1587	0.2266	0.0794	0.0115
3	0.4335	0.3085	0.4013	0.1250	0.0322
4	0.6288	0.5000	0.5987	0.1288	0.0301
5	0.7851	0.6915	0.7734	0.0936	0.0117
6	0.8893	0.8413	0.8944	0.0480	-0.0051
7	0.9489	0.9332	0.9599	0.0157	-0.0110
8	0.9786	0.9773	0.9878	0.0013	-0.0092
9	0.9919	0.9938	0.9970	-0.0019	-0.0051

Table 2.1/3: Normal approximation of the Poisson distribution with and without continuity correction

Comparison of columns 5 and 6 shows that the approximation errors lie, in the case of the continuity correction, within a smaller range: the maximal absolute error is 0.0322 with and 0.1288 without continuity correction. The advantage of the normal approximation with continuity correction is also illustrated in figure 2.1/10. It contains the curves of the function $Po(x|\lambda)$ and its approximations $\Phi[(x-4)/2]$ and $\Phi[(x-3.5)/2]$.

We already mentioned that fairly weak conditions suffice for a random variable to be approximately normally distributed. These conditions are

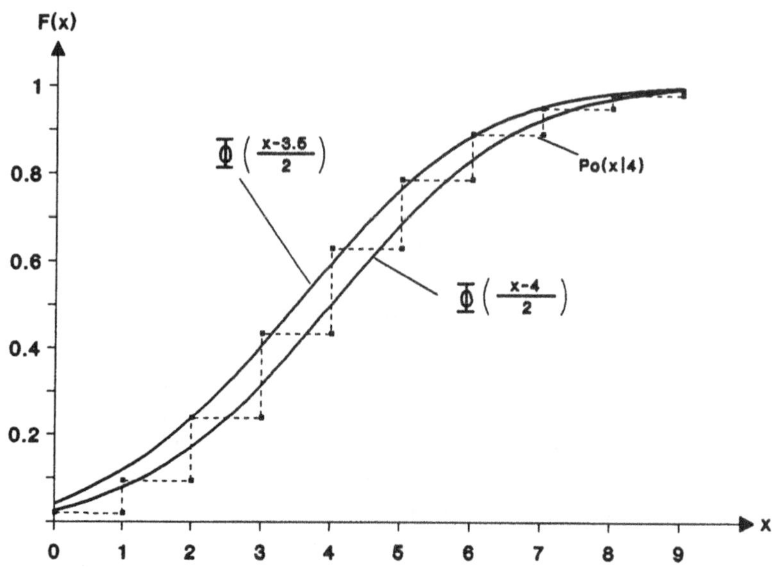

Figure 2.1/10: Normal approximation of the distribution function $Po(x|4)$ with and without continuity correction

expressed in **central limit theorems**. The most general form of the central limit theorem is that of LINDEBERG and FELLER. It states necessary and sufficient conditions for the convergence of sequences of distributions to a normal distribution:

▷ The LINDEBERG/FELLER **central limit theorem**

Let $X_1, X_2, \ldots, X_n$ be arbitrary, but independently distributed random variables with finite expectations $\mu_i := E(X_i)$ and finite variances $\sigma_i^2 := V(X_i)$. Let $f_n(z)$ denote the density of the standardized random variable

$$Z_n := \frac{\sum X_i - \sum \mu_i}{\sqrt{\sum \sigma_i^2}} \tag{2.61}$$

with mean 0 and variance 1 (summation from $i = 1$ to n). Suppose that the series $\{X_i\}$ is uniformly bounded with probability 1, this means that there exists a real number $a > 0$, such that

$$Pr(|X_i| \leq a) = 1 \quad \text{for all } i = 1, \ldots, n.$$

Further, suppose that as $n \to \infty$, $\sum_{i=1}^{n} \sigma_i^2 \to \infty$. Then the sequence of the density functions $f_n(z)$ converges, as $n \to \infty$, to the density of the standard normal distribution:

$$\lim_{n\to\infty} f_n(z) = \frac{1}{\sqrt{2\pi}} \exp\left\{-\frac{z^2}{2}\right\}. \tag{2.62}$$

We also say that the variable Z_n is asymptotically standard normal distributed. For sufficiently large n – usually one requires $n > 30$ – one can, in good approximation, replace $\lim f_n(z)$ by $f_n(z)$, in other words Z_n can be considered to be approximately normally distributed. The LINDEBERG/FELLER theorem can be interpreted as follows: If a random variable Z_n is a sum of the effects of many independent influential quantities $X_1, \ldots, X_n$, then, for sufficiently large n, Z_n is approximately normally distributed, provided that none of the X_i's dominates the others. (If, under the same conditions, the X_i's have a multiplicative relationship, then the product has a lognormal distribution.)

Example 2.1/5

Suppose that the two random variables X_1 and X_2 are independently and identically $re(0;1)$-distributed. One can show analytically that the sum $X := X_1 + X_2$ has, in this case, the density

$$f(x) = \begin{cases} x & \text{for } 0 \le x < 1 \\ 2 - x & \text{for } 1 \le x \le 2 \\ 0 & \text{else.} \end{cases}$$

Since we know by (2.27) that $E(X_1) = E(X_2) = 0.5$ it follows that the expectation of X is $E(X) = 1$. Also since $V(X_1) = V(X_2) = 1/12$, the variance is $V(X) = 1/6$. The graph of the density $f(x)$ is symmetric (as is the normal density), but triangular instead of bell shaped. We call this distribution a triangular distribution.

We now want to construct the twosided variation interval $[x_{0.025}, x_{0.975}]$, i.e., the twosided 95% variation interval. We will first calculate the exact variation interval and then compare it to the one that arises from applying the normal approximation. In the first case $x_{0.025}$ and $x_{0.975}$ are percentiles of the triangular distribution, and in the second case, of the approximating normal distribution.

The percentiles of the above triangular distribution are calculated with the percentile function $F^{-1}(y)$. This function can be obtained from the distribution function $F(x)$. We first get

$$F(x) = \begin{cases} 0 & \text{for } x < 0 \\ x^2/2 & \text{for } 0 \le x < 1 \\ 2x - x^2/2 - 1 & \text{for } 1 \le x < 2 \\ 1 & \text{for } x \ge 2. \end{cases}$$

and then

$$x_y = F^{-1}(y) = \begin{cases} \sqrt{2y} & \text{for } 0 \le y < 0.5 \\ 2 - \sqrt{2 - 2y} & \text{for } 0.5 \le y < 1. \end{cases}$$

This determines the upper and lower bounds of the exact twosided variation interval to be $x_{0.025} = \sqrt{0.05} \approx 0.2236$ and $x_{0.975} = 2 - \sqrt{0.05} \approx 1.7764$.

If one would, in spite of the small number $n = 2$, use the LINDEBERG/FELLER central limit theorem, then $Z_2 := \sqrt{6}\,(X_1 + X_2 - 1)$ would have an approximate standard normal distribution. In particular, it would approximately hold that $X \sim no(1; 1/6)$ with $X = 1 + Z_2/\sqrt{6}$. Thus the percentiles, of $x_{0.025}$ and $x_{0.975}$ are determined by table 5.2/1 and (2.56). Using (2.55) we find the endpoints of the twosided variation interval under the normal approximation to be:

$$x_{0.025} = 1 - z_{0.975} \cdot \sqrt{\tfrac{1}{6}} \approx 1 - 1.96 \cdot \sqrt{\tfrac{1}{6}} \approx 0.1998$$

$$x_{0.975} = 1 + z_{0.975} \cdot \sqrt{\tfrac{1}{6}} \approx 1 + 1.96 \cdot \sqrt{\tfrac{1}{6}} \approx 1.8002.$$

This is a surprisingly good approximation to the exact solution.

Problem 2.1/12

The probabilities in problem 2.1/5b were calculated using the Poisson distribution. Calculate the approximate probabilities under the normal approximation (with continuity correction).

Problem 2.1/13

The most important special case of the LINDEBERG/FELLER central limit theorem is the case where the random variables $X_1, \dots, X_n$ are independently identically distributed (i.i.d.). Then they all have the same expectation $E(X_i) = \mu$ and variance $V(X_i) = \sigma^2$ $(i = 1, \dots, n)$. What form does the variable Z_n of (2.61) take in this case? How can the statement of the central limit theorem be reformulated?

2.2 Sampling and Sampling Distributions

2.2.1 Basic Concepts

a) Quality Characteristics and Quality Standards

We have already introduced various distributions that are used to describe the occurrence of the different realizations of a quality characteristic in a population. All these distributions were one-dimensional, i.e., we only considered one quality characteristic per product. In the following we will also only present the univariate case and omit the multivariate theory.

So far we have made the assumption that the distribution of the quality characteristic in the population is completely known. This implies two things:

- The function that characterizes the distribution (e.g., the cumulative distribution function, massfunction or density function) is known.
- The specific values of the parameters of this function are known.

With this knowledge one can exactly determine whether the population satisfies a given quality standard or not. For example, one can decide whether the fraction nonconforming of a population lies below an acceptable limit, or whether the average lifetime of a series of light bulbs lies above a specified minimum. We need to distinguish between the **quality standard of a unit** and the **quality standard of a population**, i.e., an individual element with a quality characteristic and the overall standard in a collection of elements. Clearly, the quality standard of the population depends on the quality standards of the individual units. The primary goal of statistical quality assurance is to draw inference about the fulfillment of a quality standard in a population based on information about the individual units. From a statistical point of view, the quality standard of an individual unit is related to the specific realization of its quality characteristic, and the quality standard of the population is related to a function parameter, or a functional parameter, of the distribution of the quality characteristic.

Function parameters and functional parameters

At this point we want to further clarify the difference between the terms function parameter and functional parameter, that were introduced. A **function parameter** specifies a distribution and occurs explicitly in the distribution function, massfunction or density. A **functional parameter** is a quantity that depends on the underlying distribution and its function parameters. The most important functional parameters of a distribution are its expectation, its variance and its percentiles. Probabilities, that a quality characteristic satisfies certain properties, are also important functional parameters (e.g., fraction nonconforming).

If the distribution of the population is known, then the only problem in answering the question of whether the population satisfied a required quality standard is to perform the necessary numerical calculations (see problem 2.2/1b). In practice, however, the distribution of the quality characteristic in the population is usually not completely given. One either knows, or at least assumes, that the distribution is of a certain type, e.g., Poisson or normal, but one rarely has information about the magnitudes of its function parameters. However, we can obtain information about them by taking a sample from the population.

Example 2.2/1

A quality standard for a "piston" could, for example, require that its diameter does not lie outside the range 100 $mm \pm 0.2\ mm$, and outside this range it is considered to be nonconforming. The corresponding quality standard for the machine that produces the piston could, for example, require that the fraction nonconforming of the production is at most 5%.

If one thinks of the population as an infinite collection of pistons, one can describe the quality standard of the population in terms of the quality standard of the individual units. Seeing the piston diameter as a random variable X, one can express the quality standard of the population in the form:

$$P = Pr(X \notin [99.8; 100.2]) \leq 0.05.$$

Problem 2.2/1

a) Write down the function parameters of the distributions, that were described in section 2.1.
b) For each of the three cases $X \sim no(100\ mm; 0.01\ mm^2)$, $X \sim no(100\ mm; 0.04\ mm^2)$ and $X \sim no(99.9\ mm; 0.01\ mm^2)$ determine whether the quality standard $Pr(X \notin [99.8; 100.2]) \leq 0.05$ is fulfilled.

b) Basic Terminology of Sampling Theory

We stated in the beginning that the goal of statistical quality assurance is to draw inference about the realization of a quality parameter in a population. The population consisted of a finite or infinite collection of elements (product units or services). In the case of acceptance sampling one usually has a finite size N, whereas in process control one ideally considers the population to be of infinite size.

In quality assurance a sample is taken from this population. However, it is not necessary that the collection from which the sample is taken, the so-called **sample population**, contains the complete underlying population (the **target population**). In this case, the **sample units** are not identical with the **target population units**.

Sample unit: unit selected by the sampling procedure

Population unit: any target unit with quality characteristic of interest

A random mechanism that selects a finite number of units from a population is called a **random sampling procedure**. Such a procedure can have several stages. If it has only one stage we speak of a **one-stage random sample**. If it has several stages, and at every stage the sample is a true subset of the sample of the previous stage, we speak of a **multi-stage sample**.

An example of a two-stage random sample would be a procedure that first divides the population into subpopulations and then takes a random sample of **each** subpopulation. The subpopulations are called **strata**. The resulting sample consists of the individual subsamples of the strata and is called a **stratified sample**. Strictly speaking, this two-stage procedure does not consist of two stages, since on the first stage one selects all the strata of the population and only takes samples at the second stage.

We also do not have a true two-stage procedure if we divide the population into subgroups, then randomly select a number of subgroups and take all units in those subgroups (**clusters**) to be the desired sample. Here one actually only samples at the first stage. This procedure is called **cluster sampling**.

In chapters 3 and 4 we will only discuss procedures that are based on one-stage samples. Since the target and sample population, or respectively, the target and sample units, are identical we will (after example 2.2/2) not further distinguish between them. In other words by sample we will simply understand a finite subset of the population.

One-stage sample: identity of sample population and target population

---

Example 2.2/2

We will now illustrate the previously introduced terms (multi-stage sample, cluster sample and stratified sample) by means of two examples:

(a) In a coal power station, the amount of water in the 10,000 tons of coal that are used per month is determined with the help of a three-stage random sample. The sample units of the first stage are the 500 train loads of 20 tons each. The sample units of the second stage are bulks of 10 kg that are from each goods wagon. The sample units of the third stage are portions of 1 g for the final laboratory test.

(b) A shipment of 5,000 transistors, 20 packets with 250 units each, arrives at the receiving inspection department. Suppose, at the first stage, several of the packets (= sample units) are randomly chosen, and at the second stage, a random sample of transistors is taken from these packets. Then this procedure is a true two stage sample. Whereas, if one chooses several packets at the first stage as before, but submits those packets to 100% inspection, then this procedure is a cluster sample and no longer constitutes a true two stage random sample. In this case, the packets are the clusters. Another approach is to randomly sample 5 transistors from each of the 20 packets. This procedure is an example of a stratified random sample with the packets representing the strata. Since a constant proportion of 2% is sampled from each stratum, we call this a proportional stratified sample.

Sampling without replacement: dependence between sample units

Regardless of the number of stages, a **sample** can be taken **with or without replacement** of the sampled units. In the case of sampling with replacement, an element of the population can be chosen repeatedly in one sample, whereas in the case of sampling without replacement this cannot happen. If a sample is taken without replacement from a finite population – for example the drawing of numbers in a lottery – then the results of the draws are dependent on the previous outcomes. After every draw the population size decreases and the structure of the remaining population also changes with the specific outcome. However, if the **sampling fraction** n/N, i.e., the proportion of the population that is sampled, is small, say $n/N < 0.1$, then the effect can be neglected and one can in approximation work with the simpler theory of sampling with replacement. In quality assurance, samples are exclusively taken without replacement, but, in general, the mentioned requirement is fulfilled and one can use the easier formulas of the case of sampling with replacement. In process control, this is always the case if the population of produced units is considered to be of infinite size. Also, in acceptance control the population size is usually large enough so that $n/N < 0.1$ is satisfied.

Samples can be taken with either **equal or unequal selection probabilities**. If each potential sample unit has the same probability of being selected we speak of a **simple random sample**. In the following, we will assume that the random sample mechanism works with equal selection probabilities. In practice, this needs to be carefully verified in each specific application. Working with unequal selection probabilities will lead to biased samples if not cared for in the process of drawing inference on the population. As the following example demonstrates, sampling with unequal selection probabilities can occasionally occur in the practice of quality assurance.

Example 2.2/3

To determine the average length of fibres in a yarn one randomly marks the yarn at one point, and then measures the length of all fibres that go through this specific point. This procedure is illustrated in figure 2.2/1. The broken line marks the observation point and the crosses on the horizontal lines indicate the beginning and end of a fibre. It is apparent that in such a procedure long fibres have a higher probability of being selected than short ones. In fact it can be shown that the selection probability is proportional to the length of the fibre. The same phenomenon occurs when one observes life times at a fixed time point.

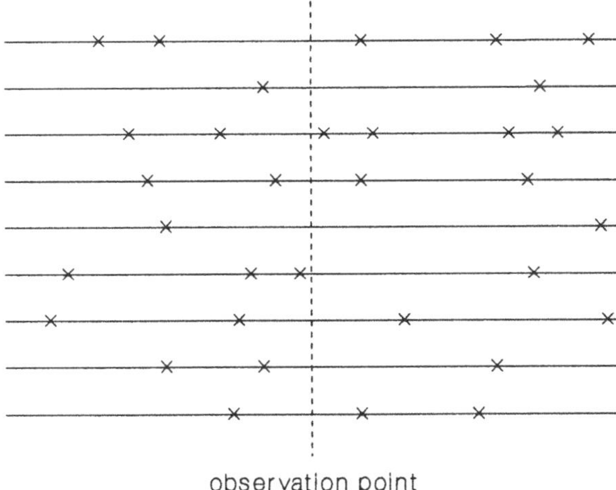

Figure 2.2/1: Measuring the length of fibres in a yarn

c) Realization of Random Samples

The decision on how to select the sample units of a simple random sample usually depends on external circumstances. A simple random sample can, for example, be taken by numbering all the units of the population and drawing a sample of n of those numbers randomly from an urn (sampling with or without replacement). In practice however, one usually does not use mechanical procedures like drawing balls from an urn, but works with random numbers. For a population size of, say, $N = 600$, one can take a sample by reading three consecutive numbers of a table of random numbers and then selecting the unit that has been uniquely assigned to that number. Any random number that exceeds the population size N is simply omitted. Also, in the case of sampling without replacement, any number can only be considered once.

Generation of random numbers

Random numbers can be generated by randomly drawing a series of numbers from an urn that contains the 10 digits $0, 1, \ldots, 9$ with replacement. A property of such a **table of random numbers** is that on the average any of the digits $0, 1, \ldots, 9$ occurs with the same frequency and that the process does not have any specific pattern. Today, random numbers are often generated with the help of computers using deterministic procedures. Such "false" random numbers are called **pseudo random numbers**. The algorithms that produce them are called **random number generators**. Good random number generators have the characteristic that their pseudo random numbers have approximately the same statistical properties as their counterparts, the true random numbers.

The following table 2.2/1 shows a collection of random numbers. The ten digits $0, 1, \ldots, 9$ occur in a random order (digital random numbers). In order to facilitate their handling they are displayed in blocks of 5×5 digits. Almost any pocket calculator can generate random numbers, but one has to be certain about the type of random numbers that are produced. In most cases the random numbers have a rectangular distribution on [0,1], which means that they need to be transformed into digital random numbers (for the transformation of continuously distributed random variables into discrete ones, see problem 2.2/2a).

52294	85023	90382	02622	07838
44562	52628	88687	99741	33192
39650	93119	51042	71259	23902
12918	03693	38021	16723	32969
94313	68582	75019	47178	66094
78498	26973	25295	66186	12088
73496	22521	31881	92913	51860
88111	31372	08242	52906	62388
98434	63860	55582	12470	19164
42444	09420	60215	81995	07320
76263	46375	30795	90705	82773
97587	42555	43025	86449	84997
88829	95740	49839	08343	63983
51261	37891	73161	40957	76758
17280	94401	15504	69670	46008

Table 2.2/1: Digital random numbers

Motivation of pseudo random samples

The use of digital random numbers for the selection of a random sample requires that the units of the population are numbered. For a sample of size n one also has to go to the table random numbers at least n times. Often more than n numbers need to be looked up, because some of them have to be omitted (see example 2.2/4). This procedure can be simplified by selecting the first sample unit with the help of a random digit and then selecting the consecutive units in a fixed **sampling distance** N/n. Such systematic samples that randomly select a starting point are called **pseudo random samples**.

Example 2.2/4

We want to take a sample of size $n = 10$ from a shipment of $N = 500$ units. The following presentation sketches several approaches to taking this random sample.

Case 1: *The units of the population are numbered*

The elements of the shipment have a serial number S. In this particular case, the serial numbers go from 701 to 1200, and consequently the units can be identified by these numbers. Three successive digits are read from the random digits table 2.2/1 and combined to a number Z. Only numbers with values in the range $000 \leq Z \leq 499$ are considered, and the sample is taken to be the units with serial numbers $S_i = 701 + Z_i$ $(i = 1, \ldots, 10)$. Since the sample is drawn without replacement, only the first occurrence of a serial number S_i is included in the sample and the repeated outcomes are omitted. If one starts in the left top corner of the table, and, for example, reads the numbers of the first column in downward direction, then the first first two random numbers are $Z_1 = 197$ and $Z_2 = 479$. Thus the first two units in the sample are those with the serial numbers 898 and 1180.

One could also select the sample units as follows:

$$S_i = \begin{cases} 701 + Z_i & \text{if } 000 \leq Z_i \leq 499 \\ 701 + (Z_i - 500) & \text{if } 500 \leq Z_i \leq 999. \end{cases}$$

In this approach, all possible random numbers Z are included. If one uses table 2.2/1 in the same way as before, the first two sample units result to be those with serial numbers 744 and 898.

Case 2: *Random selection from a box*

The 500 units are packed without a serial number in a box in 5 layers of 10 by 10 units. We want to avoid exclusively sampling units of the top layer, because this layer may, for example, contain selected good units or have suffered the worst transport damages. One solution is to work with a three digit random number. The first digit specifies the layer, i.e., 1 and 6 are assigned to layer 1, 2 and 7 to layer 2, ..., 5 and 0 to layer 5. The second digit specifies the row number and the third the column number. The number 522 would correspond to the unit in row 2 and column 2 of the 5th layer.

Case 3: *Systematic selection with a randomly selected starting point*

At the reception of the goods, the 500 units are put onto a conveyer belt for transportation to their destination. Since the sampling distance is $N/n = 50$ in this case one specifies a starting point between 1 and 50 and then selects every 50-th unit. The two digit random number 52 from the top left corner of table 2.2/1 would lead us to take unit 2 as the starting point and to sample the 2nd, 52nd, 102nd, ... unit of the lot.

Sampling from a population of infinite size (e.g., in process control) is somehow more complicated than the drawing of samples from a finite population (acceptance control). In most cases, one works with a systematic selection procedure and samples periodically over time. It is important to make sure that the selection rhythm does not coincide with some production rhythm (e.g., of a rotating machine) because this would lead to a selection bias in the sample. The general rule for drawing a random sample may sound paradoxical: Randomness has to be carefully planned, because a subjective and arbitrary selection of sample units often does not result in a sample that is representative of the population.

Problem 2.2/2

a) Let $X \sim re(0;1)$, i.e., X is continuously uniformly distributed on the interval [0;1]. How can X be transformed to a random variable Y with $Y \sim un(0;1;9)$, i.e., a discrete uniformly distributed random variable with the realizations $0, 1, \ldots, 9$ and $Pr(Y = 0) = \ldots = Pr(Y = 9) = 0.1$?

b) Suppose that a sample of size $n = 10$ is to be taken from a shipment of 300 units. The units arrive in a box with 6 layers of 5 by 10 units and carry the serial numbers 852 to 1151. In analogy to example 2.2/4, describe three approaches to taking this sample.

2.2.2 Sample Statistics and their Properties

a) Common Sample Statistics

All the elements $x_1, \ldots, x_n$ of a random sample are the realizations of the corresponding random variables $X_1, \ldots, X_n$. The latter constitute the **sample vector**

$$\mathbf{X} = (X_1, X_2, \ldots, X_n). \tag{2.63 a}$$

The components of this n-dimensional random variable, i.e., the **sample variables** X_i, are arranged in the order of their observation. After the sample is drawn one can, instead of $x_1, \ldots, x_n$, also use the vector notation

$$\mathbf{x} = (x_1, x_2, \ldots, x_n). \tag{2.63 b}$$

In other words $\mathbf{x}$ is the realization of the sample vector $\mathbf{X}$.

Similar to one-dimensional random variables, the distribution of a multidimensional random variable can be completely characterized by its distribution function or its massfunction or density. These functions are however multivariate (functions of several variables) and no longer scalar functions (functions of one variable) as in the univariate case.

Example 2.2/5

A shipment of N units contains M nonconforming units (M is unknown; $0 \leq M \leq N$). A sample of size $n = 3$ is taken. The dichotomous variable X_i (possible realizations: 0, 1) describes the state of the unit; $i = 1, 2, 3$. The realization $x_i = 0$ means "conforming" and $x_i = 1$ means "nonconforming". If the sample is drawn *with* replacement, then the joint distribution of the three-dimensional sample vector $\mathbf{X}= (X_1, X_2, X_3)$ of the components of the sample is given by

$$\begin{aligned} Pr(\mathbf{X} = \mathbf{x}) &= Pr(X_1 = x_1, X_2 = x_2, X_3 = x_3) \\ &= P^{x_1+x_2+x_3}(1-P)^{3-(x_1+x_2+x_3)} \end{aligned}$$

where $P := M/N$ denotes the unknown fraction nonconforming.

Definition of the term "statistic"

We can see in example 2.2/5 that working with sample vectors can be fairly complicated. It is much easier to use a scalar function, called a **statistic** $g(\mathbf{X})$. A statistic can be seen as a function that condenses the n variables of the sample vector to one single scalar variable. If the statistic is used to estimate characteristics of the population it is called an **estimator**. If it is used to test a hypothesis about the population it is called **test statistic**. In general, a statistic can be simultaneously used for testing hypotheses and estimation. We will now introduce the statistics that are most commonly used in statistical quality assurance.

Examples of statistics

In acceptance sampling by attributes one uses in general the **sample sum**

$$X_n^T := \sum_{i=1}^{n} X_i \tag{2.64}$$

as a counting variable. The superscript "T" stands for "Total". If the elements X_i of the sample vector have a 0–1 distribution, i.e., if $X_i \sim be(x|P)$ holds, then X_n^T denotes the *number* of "successes" in the sample.

The most frequent statistics used in sampling by variables are the **sample mean**

$$\bar{X}_n := \frac{1}{n}\sum_{i=1}^{n} X_i, \tag{2.65}$$

the **sample variance**

$$S_n^2 := \frac{1}{n-1}\sum_{i=1}^{n}(X_i - \bar{X}_n)^2 = \frac{1}{n-1}\left(\sum_{i=1}^{n} X_i^2 - n\bar{X}_n^2\right) \tag{2.66}$$

and the **sample standard deviation**

$$S_n := +\sqrt{S_n^2}. \tag{2.67}$$

In the case $X_i \sim be(x|P)$, the statistic $\bar{X}_n$ represents the *proportion* of "successes" in the sample.

Further statistics that are occasionally used in variable sampling are the extreme values, the median and the sample range. If the elements of the sample vector are ranked by their values and if $X_{<i,n>}$ denotes the i-th element of the resulting vector, then the **sample extreme values** are defined by

$$X_{<1;n>} := \min_{1\leq i\leq n} X_i \quad \text{sample minimum} \tag{2.68 a}$$

$$X_{<n;n>} := \max_{1\leq i\leq n} X_i \quad \text{sample maximum} \tag{2.68 b}$$

the **sample median** by

$$\tilde{X}_n := \begin{cases} X_{<k+1;n>} & \text{if } n = 2k+1 \\ \frac{1}{2}\cdot(X_{<k;n>} + X_{<k+1;n>}) & \text{if } n = 2k \end{cases} \tag{2.69}$$

and the **sample range** by

$$R_n := X_{<n;n>} - X_{<1;n>}. \tag{2.70}$$

Note that all these statistics are functions of random variables and thus they are again random variables. This is emphasized by the use of capital letters. Capital letters are generally used for random variables, whereas lower case letters are used for their realizations. In section 2.2/3 we will discuss the stochastic properties and the distributions of these statistics. The use of statistics instead of the sample vector serves two purposes:

Notation agreement: random variables - capital letters realizations - small letters

- **Reduction of the dimension of the data**
  The sample vector has dimension $n > 1$, but each of the derived sample statistics $g(\mathbf{x})$ has dimension $m = 1$.

- **Inference about the unknown distribution of the population**
  In statistical quality assurance the sample statistics give us information about the unknown value of the quality standard of the population, i.e., the sample statistic is used for estimation or testing.

Example 2.2/6

The following table 2.2/2 lists the sample results from the process control of the fill weight of 1000 mg vials of a chemical substance. Every half hour a sample of $n = 4$ vials is taken. The results of $m = 20$ such inspections are given below. The observed weights are given in mg and each line contains the data of one sample.

The result of a sample is here described by the four dimensional vector $\mathbf{x}_i$ $(i = 1, \ldots, 20)$. The components of the vector $\mathbf{x}_1$ for example are the four numbers of the first row of the table. Instead of these vectors one can also use the sample statistics (2.65) - (2.70). It is easily verified that for the first sample we get

$$\bar{x}_4 \approx 1000.055; \qquad s_4^2 \approx 0.082; \qquad s_4 \approx 0.286$$

$$x_{<1;4>} = 999.77 \qquad x_{<4,4>} = 1000.43$$

$$\tilde{x}_4 = \frac{1}{2}(1000.11 + 999.91) = 1000.01; \quad r_4 = 1000.43 - 999.77 = 0.66.$$

Number	Sample results			
of sample	1	2	3	4
1	1000.43	999.77	999.91	1000.11
2	1000.05	999.92	1000.44	999.42
3	999.95	1000.12	999.88	999.03
4	1000.16	999.43	999.81	1000.21
5	999.63	999.94	1000.25	999.99
6	999.77	1000.32	999.94	1000.00
7	999.96	1000.03	1000.14	998.89
8	1000.28	999.28	1000.28	1000.36
9	999.31	999.92	999.90	999.59
10	999.18	999.80	1000.54	1000.18
11	999.81	999.23	999.40	999.47
12	999.96	1000.57	999.60	1000.37
13	1000.40	1000.00	999.34	999.92
14	1000.28	1000.57	999.41	998.99
15	1000.25	1000.64	1000.70	999.64
16	1001.13	999.94	999.57	999.84
17	1000.08	999.79	999.00	999.57
18	1000.28	1000.52	1000.82	999.64
19	999.84	1000.24	999.00	999.13
20	1000.26	1000.30	1000.16	1000.51

Table 2.2/2: Sample results of the fill weight inspection of 1000 mg vials

---

Problem 2.2/3

a) What are the possible values of the massfunction in example 2.2/5 with $N = 100$ and $M = 5$?

b) What are the values of the mentioned massfunction if the sample is taken without replacement?

c) Which factors influence, in general, the distribution of a sample vector?

Problem 2.2/4

Which of the introduced statistics can be used to estimate the function parameters of the Bernoulli, Poisson, rectangular and normal distribution?

b) Desirable Properties

Let Θ denote a function or functional parameter of the population and $\hat{\Theta}_n$ denote the sample statistic that is used to estimate Θ on the basis of a sample $X_1, \ldots, X_n$. We will not go into the details of constructing such estimators. They can, for example, be constructed by the **method of moments**, the **maximum likelihood method** or the **least square method** (refer to textbooks e.g., by BAMBERG/BAUR 1989, HARTUNG 1987 or MOOD/GRAYBILL/BOES 1983). In the following we will only describe those properties that are desirable for a sample statistic, regardless of whether it is used for testing or estimation.

Sufficiency: preservation of all the available information

A sample statistic $\hat{\Theta}_n = g(X_1, \ldots, X_n)$ is called **sufficient** if all the information about the parameter Θ that is contained in the n sample variables X_i, $i = 1, \ldots, n$, is also contained in $\hat{\Theta}_n$. For example, the sample extreme values (2.68) are, in the case of most distributions, obviously not sufficient, because they do not preserve the complete information that is contained in the sample elements $X_1, \ldots X_n$. For instance, the value of the sample minimum $X_{<1;n>}$ does not change if all components of the sample vector with exception of the sample minimum are changed. $X_{<1;n>}$ only contains the information that all these components are bigger than the statistic (2.68a).

A desirable property of a sample statistic $\hat{\Theta}_n = g(X_1, \ldots, X_n)$ is its linearity with respect to the sample variables. Linearity requires that $\hat{\Theta}_n$ is of form

Linearity: The statistic is a linear function of the sample elements.

$$\hat{\Theta}_n = a_0 + \sum_{i=1}^{n} a_i X_i$$

with suitable coefficients $a_0, a_1, \ldots, a_n$. Nonlinear sample statistics, for example (2.66) and (2.67) are more difficult to handle.

A sample statistic $\hat{\Theta}_n$ used to estimate the parameter Θ is called **unbiased** if

Unbiasedness: The expectation of the estimator aggrees with the parameter that is to be estimated.

$$E(\hat{\Theta}_n) = \Theta \quad \text{for all } n \in \mathbb{N}. \tag{2.71}$$

The difference $B(\hat{\Theta}_n) = E(\hat{\Theta}_n) - \Theta$ is called the **bias** of the estimator. Unbiasedness of an estimator $\hat{\Theta}_n$ implies that the expectation of $\hat{\Theta}_n$ agrees with the parameter that is to be estimated regardless of the sample size. In other words, the parameter is correctly estimated by the average. Statement (2.71) does not necessarily imply that $E[h(\hat{\Theta}_n)] = h(\Theta)$ holds for any function $h(.)$, , as we can see from (2.73) and (2.75).

Estimation of the expectation and variance

If the elements of a population are independently and identically distributed with expectation μ and variance σ^2, then μ is unbiasedly estimated by the sample average $\bar{X}_n$ of a random sample:

$$E(\bar{X}_n) = \frac{1}{n}\sum_{i=1}^{n} E(X_i) = \frac{1}{n} \cdot n \cdot \mu = \mu. \tag{2.72}$$

If the sample is drawn *with* replacement, i.e., if there is no possibility of stochastic dependence of the sample elements, then the sample variance S_n^2 is an unbiased estimator of σ^2

$$E(S_n^2) = \frac{1}{n-1}\sum_{i=1}^{n} E\left[(X_i - \bar{X}_n)^2\right] = \sigma^2. \tag{2.73}$$

In spite of this, the sample standard deviation S_n is a biased estimator of the standard deviation σ of the population, i.e., $E(S_n) \neq \sigma$. If the population is normally distributed then we have $E(S_n) = a_n\sigma$ (see GRAF/HENNING/STANGE/WILRICH 1987, p. 89). The factor

$$a_n := \sqrt{\frac{2}{n-1}} \cdot \frac{\Gamma\left(\frac{n}{2}\right)}{\Gamma\left(\frac{n-1}{2}\right)} \approx 1 - \frac{1}{4(n-1)} \cdot \quad ^{10} \tag{2.74}$$

is tabulated in table 5.3/1.

It follows from the above that in the case of sampling with replacement and a normally distributed population, an unbiased estimator of σ is given by S_n/a_n:

Estimation of the standard deviation of a normal distribution

$$E\left(\frac{S_n}{a_n}\right) = \sigma. \tag{2.75}$$

In the case of sampling *without* replacement and under the assumption of a finite population with size N, the following holds instead of (2.73):

$$E\left(S_n^2\right) = \frac{1}{n-1}\sum_{i=1}^{n} E\left[(X_i - \bar{X}_n)^2\right] = \frac{N}{N-1} \cdot \sigma^2. \tag{2.76}$$

Efficiency: unbiasedness and minimum variance

Within the class of unbiased estimators we can use their variances as a criterion for the comparison of their efficiency. Unbiased estimators with minimum variance are called **efficient**. If $\hat{\Theta}_{1;n}$ and $\hat{\Theta}_{2;n}$ are two unbiased estimators of the parameter Θ and if $V(\hat{\Theta}_{1;n}) < V(\hat{\Theta}_{2;n})$ then we say $\hat{\Theta}_{1;n}$ is **more efficient** than $\hat{\Theta}_{2;n}$. The ratio

$$w = \frac{V(\hat{\Theta}_{2;n})}{V(\hat{\Theta}_{1;n})}$$

[10] Γ(x) again denotes the gamma function introduced in (2.36a).

is a measure of the efficiency of $\hat{\Theta}_{1;n}$ compared to $\hat{\Theta}_{2;n}$. In practical applications we are always interested in estimators with smallest variance.

In some cases one can determine the minimum variance of an estimator of Θ and also the corresponding efficient estimator $\hat{\Theta}_n$. For example, $\bar{X}_n$ is an efficient estimator of the expectation μ of the units of a $no(\mu;\sigma^2)$-distributed population. The variance of $\bar{X}_n$ is given by

$$V(\bar{X}_n) = \frac{1}{n^2}\sum_{i=1}^{n} V(X_i) = \frac{\sigma^2}{n}, \qquad (2.77\text{ a})$$

when the sample is drawn *with* replacement. In the case of sampling *without* replacement from a finite population with N units, we get

$$V(\bar{X}_n) = \frac{\sigma^2}{n}\cdot\frac{N-n}{N-1}. \qquad (2.77\text{ b})$$

The application of formula (2.77) requires knowledge about the variance of the units in the population.

An estimator $\hat{\Theta}_n$ of the parameter Θ is called **asymptotically unbiased** if

Asymptotic unbiasedness: As $n \to \infty$, the bias tends to zero.

$$\lim_{n\to\infty} E(\hat{\Theta}_n) = \Theta.$$

The difference $\lim[E(\hat{\Theta}_n) - \Theta]$ is the **asymptotic bias**.

Another desirable asymptotic property of sample statistics is their consistency. An estimator $\hat{\Theta}_n$ is called **consistent** if, for any arbitrarily small $\epsilon > 0$, it holds that

Consistency: As $n \to \infty$, the sample statistic converges to the true parameter w.p.1.

$$\lim_{n\to\infty} Pr(|\hat{\Theta}_n - \Theta| < \epsilon) = 1.$$

Consistency of an estimator says that, provided the sample size n is large enough, the estimate almost certainly comes arbitrarily close to the true value of the parameter of interest. An estimator is always consistent if it is asymptotically unbiased and if its variance converges to zero as $n \to \infty$.

A further desirable property of a sample statistic $\hat{\Theta}_n$ is **asymptotic normality**. By this we mean that the distribution of $\hat{\Theta}_n$ converges to a normal distribution as $n \to \infty$.

Problem 2.2/5

The units of a population are independently and identically $no(\mu;\sigma^2)$-distributed.

a) Are the two estimators

$$\hat{\mu}_{1;n} := \frac{1}{n-1}\sum_{i=1}^{n} X_i, \quad \hat{\mu}_{2;n} := \frac{1}{n}\sum_{i=1}^{n}(X_i - 0.5)$$

unbiased, or at least asymptotically unbiased?

b) How big are the variances of $\hat{\mu}_{1;n}$ and $\hat{\mu}_{2;n}$ if the samples are drawn with replacement?

c) For which kind of function h does $E[h(\hat{\Theta}_n)] = h(\Theta)$ hold, when $\hat{\Theta}_n$ is an unbiased estimator of Θ ?

d) A sample statistic $\tilde{X}_n$ with $E(\tilde{X}_n) = \mu$ and $V(\tilde{X}_n) = (\pi/2)\cdot\sigma^2/n$ is used in sampling with replacement from the above lot. Compare the efficiency of $\tilde{X}_n$ to that of $\bar{X}_n$.

2.2.3 Distributions of Sample Statistics

a) The Normal Distribution as an Asymptotic Distribution of Sample Statistics

Characterization of unbiased and asymptotically normal sample statistics

We already mentioned that asymptotic normality is a desirable property of sample statistics, because the normal distribution is much easier to work with than most other distributions. Suppose now that $\hat{\Theta}_n$ is an unbiased and asymptotically normally distributed estimator of Θ with variance $V(\hat{\Theta}_n)$ ($n \in \mathbb{N}$, arbitrary). Then, for a large sample size n, the estimator $\hat{\Theta}_n$ is approximately normally distributed with expectation Θ and variance $V(\hat{\Theta}_n)$. By (2.59c), this implies

$$Pr\left[\Theta - z_{1-\alpha/2}\sqrt{V(\hat{\Theta}_n)} \le \hat{\Theta}_n \le \Theta + z_{1-\alpha/2}\sqrt{V(\hat{\Theta}_n)}\right] \approx 1-\alpha. \quad (2.78)$$

The terms in the square brackets of the above equality define the two-sided variation interval for $\hat{\Theta}_n$ of level $1-\alpha$. In other words, statement (2.78) says that, for a given Θ, approximately $(1-\alpha)\cdot 100\%$ of the realizations of $\hat{\Theta}_n$ lie within this interval. An elementary transformation of (2.78) gives

$$Pr\left[\hat{\Theta}_n - z_{1-\alpha/2}\sqrt{V(\hat{\Theta}_n)} \le \Theta \le \hat{\Theta}_n + z_{1-\alpha/2}\sqrt{V(\hat{\Theta}_n)}\right] \approx 1-\alpha. \quad (2.79)$$

The interval in the square brackets of (2.79) is the **twosided confidence interval for Θ with confidence level $1-\alpha$.** We observe that this interval in (2.79) is stochastic, because its boundaries depend on the random realization of the variable $\hat{\Theta}_n$. Thus the interpretation is that the above confidence interval covers the unknown parameter Θ with a probability of approximately $1-\alpha$.

In the following, we will present several other applications of the normal distribution as a limiting distribution. One can say that the most important asymptotically normal sample statistic is the sample mean $\bar{X}_n$. Its variance is given by (2.77), but recall that the application of this formula requires knowledge of the value of the population variance σ^2.

The fact, that $\bar{X}_n$ is asymptotically normally distributed, means, that for a sufficiently large sample size n, the statistic $\bar{X}_n$ can be considered to be approximately normally distributed. If the population units are independently and identically $no(\mu;\sigma^2)$-distributed, then $\bar{X}_n$ is **exactly normally distributed**, i.e., not only as $n \to \infty$ but for any finite n, it has a normal distribution.

Exact distributions: distributions for finite sample size

Unfortunately, not all sample statistics are at least asymptotically normal. Even in the case of asymptotic normality the sample size is often not large enough to justify the use of the normal approximation. Because of this, we also need to investigate exact distributions of sample statistics in addition to the approximation with the normal distribution.

Example 2.2/7

Let the characteristic X of a population be $re(5;9)$-distributed. Then, the expectation and variance of this rectangular distribution are, according to (2.27), given by $\mu = 7$ and $\sigma^2 = 4/3$. Suppose now that a sample of size $n = 48$ is drawn with replacement. Then according to (2.77a) the variance of the sample average $\bar{X}_{48}$ is found to be

$$V(\bar{X}_{48}) = \frac{\sigma^2}{n} = \frac{4}{3\cdot 48} = \frac{1}{36}.$$

The sample size $n = 48$ is large enough to justify the application of the normal approximation. Hence, the twosided variation interval of $\bar{X}_{48}$ of level 0.95 is, because of (2.78) and since $z_{0.975} = 1.96$, given by $[7 - 0.32\bar{6}, 7 + 0.32\bar{6}]$, i.e., it holds that

$$Pr(6.67\bar{3} \le \bar{X}_{48} \le 7.32\bar{6}) \approx 0.95.$$

If we observe the realization $\bar{x}_{48} = 6.6$, then the twosided confidence interval of μ with level 0.95 is given by $[6.6 - 0.32\bar{6}, 6.6 + 0.32\bar{6}]$. Note that, with the interval $[6.27\bar{3}, 6.92\bar{6}]$, we observed a realization of one of those 5% confidence intervals that do not cover the true parameter value $\mu = 7$.

Problem 2.2/6

A quality characteristic X in a population is $ex(0.01)$-distributed. A sample of size $n = 100$ is drawn with replacement.

a) Find the twosided variation interval with level 0.99 for $\bar{X}_{100}$.

b) For the realization $\bar{x}_{100} = 109$ calculate the twosided confidence interval of level 0.99 for the expectation $\mu = E(X)$.

b) The Hypergeometric and Negative Hypergeometric Distribution

Construction of a random variable with hypergeometric distribution

A sample of size n is drawn from an urn containing N balls, among which M are black and the remaining $N-M$ are white, i.e., we are sampling from a finite Bernoulli distributed population. Suppose that drawing a black ball means "success". Then the total number X_n^T of successes in the sample has a hypergeometric distribution.

The **hypergeometric distribution** is typical for attribute acceptance control. The population is, in this case, a lot with N units, of which M are nonconforming units (M unknown). The discovery of a nonconforming unit is considered to be a "success". The ratio $P := M/N$, already introduced in (2.10a) and also called the **fraction nonconforming** or **quality level** in acceptance sampling, characterises the quality standard of a lot.

Massfunction of the hypergeometric distribution

The massfunction $hy(k|N; M; n) := Pr(X_n^T = k)$ of the hypergeometric distribution is

$$hy(k|N;M;n) = \begin{cases} \dfrac{\dbinom{M}{k}\dbinom{N-M}{n-k}}{\dbinom{N}{n}} & \text{for } c_1 \le k \le c_2 \\ 0 & \text{elsewhere} \end{cases} \tag{2.80}$$

$$c_1 := \max(0; n + M - N); \quad c_2 := \min(n; M).$$

In the denominator of (2.80) we find $\binom{N}{n}$, the total number of all possible samples of size n from a population with N units (samples without replacement and without consideration in which order the elements were drawn). In the numerator stands the number of all those samples that draw exactly k successes out of the possible M successes and $n-k$ non-successes out of the possible $N-M$ non-successes, i.e., the product $\binom{M}{k}\binom{N-M}{n-k}$ (samples without replacement and without consideration of the order). This makes (2.80) a classical LAPLACE definition of a probability (PIERRE SIMON DE LAPLACE, 1749-1827): The number of outcomes in favour of an event divided by the total number of possible outcomes.

For the distribution function $Hy(k|N;M;n) := Pr(X_n^T \leq k)$ it follows from (2.80) that

Distribution function of the hypergeometric distribution

$$Hy(k|N;M;n) = \begin{cases} 0 & \text{for } k < c_1 \\ \sum_{i=c_1}^{k} hy(i|N;M;n) & \text{for } c_1 \leq k < c_2 \\ 1 & \text{for } k \geq c_2. \end{cases} \tag{2.81}$$

For a random variable X whose distribution is specified by (2.80) or (2.81), we will use the notation $X \sim hy(N;M;n)$. Similar to most other discrete distributions the distribution function (2.81) cannot be simplified or written in closed form. However, (2.81) can be evaluated numerically and tabulated as is partially presented in table 5.1/2.

We note – again without proof – the following functional parameters of the hypergeometric distribution. In acceptance sampling by attributes $Q := 1 - P$ is interpreted to be the proportion of conforming units in the lot:

Expectation and variance of the hypergeometric distribution

$$\mu = E(X) = nP \tag{2.82 a}$$

$$\sigma^2 = V(X) = nPQ \cdot \frac{N-n}{N-1}. \tag{2.82 b}$$

In practical applications the following recursion formulae are of importance:

Increasing recursion

$$hy(k+1|N;M;n) = \frac{(M-k)(n-k)}{(k+1)(N-M-n+k+1)} \cdot hy(k|N;M;n) \tag{2.83 a}$$

Decreasing recursion

$$hy(k-1|N;M;n) = \frac{k \cdot (N-M-n+k)}{(M-k+1)(n-k+1)} \cdot hy(k|N;M;n). \tag{2.83 b}$$

The hypergeometric distribution is symmetric around the function parameters M and n (see problem 2.2/7a):

Symmetry of the hypergeometric distribution

$$hy(k|N;M;n) = hy(k|N;n;M) \tag{2.84 a}$$

$$Hy(k|N;M;n) = Hy(k|N;n;M). \tag{2.84 b}$$

If one partitions the sample, as well as the rest of the population, into "successes" (nonconforming units) and "failures" (conforming units), one gets the following table 2.2/3.

Each of the four entries in the inner cells of the table can be seen to be the realization of a hypergeometric random variable with different parameters in each case. The appropriate parameters are found in the corresponding row and column of the outer cells of the table. This gives the following result for the massfunction:

$$\begin{aligned} hy(k|N;M;n) &= hy(n-k|N;N-M;n) && (2.85\text{ a})\\ &= hy(M-k|N;M;N-n) && (2.85\text{ b})\\ &= hy(N-n-M+k|N;N-M;N-n). && (2.85\text{ c}) \end{aligned}$$

Population	Outcome		Size
	Success	Non-success	
Sample	k	$n-k$	n
Rest of the population	$M-k$	$N-n-M+k$	$N-n$
Entire population	M	$N-M$	N

Table 2.2/3: Bernoulli distributed population and its partition

We note that the boundaries c_1 and c_2 in (2.80) are implicitly contained in table 2.2/3, if one considers that each entry in the four inner cells has to be a non-negative integer.

Taking into account that with $X_n^T \leq k$ and consequently $n - X_n^T \geq n-k$, the following equivalent representations of the distribution function are found in analogy to (2.85):

$$\begin{aligned} Hy(k|N;M;n) &= 1-Hy(n-k-1|N;N-M;n) && (2.86\text{ a})\\ &= 1-Hy(M-k-1|N;M;N-n) && (2.86\text{ b})\\ &= Hy(N-n-M+k|N;N-M;N-n). && (2.86\text{ c}) \end{aligned}$$

The hypergeometric distribution is somewhat unhandy and difficult to tabulate, because of its three function parameters N, M and n. The equalities in (2.86) allow us to reduce the tabulation to the entries

$$0 \leq k \leq M \leq n \leq 0.5\,N.$$

In table 5.1/2 this range is tabulated for $N = 20$.

Example 2.2/8

We want to calculate $hy(20;13;9)$ and $Hy(20;13;9)$ by means of table 5.1/2. As a result of (2.85a) and (2.86a), and since $N = 20, M = 13$ and $n = 9$, we get

$$hy(6|20;13;9) = hy(3|20;7;9) \approx 0.357585$$
$$Hy(6|20;13;9) = 1 - Hy(2|20;7;9) \approx 1 - 0.272446 = 0.727554.$$

Approximation of the hypergeometric distribution by distributions easier to handle

Candidates for approximating the three-parameter hypergeometric distribution are, under certain conditions, the normal distribution, the Poisson distribution and the binomial distribution. The latter will be introduced in section 2.2.3c. If $P = M/N$ denotes again the unknown fraction nonconforming of the population, then the following holds:

- **Binomial approximation**

$$hy(k|N;M;n) \approx bi(k|P;n) \tag{2.87 a}$$

Condition: $0.1 < P < 0.9$ and $n > 10$ and $n/N < 0.1$

- **Poisson approximation**

$$hy(k|N;M;n) \approx po(k|nP) \tag{2.87 b}$$

Condition: $P \leq 0.1$ (or $P \geq 0.9$) and $n > 30$ and $n/N < 0.1$

- **Normal approximation with continuity correction**

$$hy(k|N;M;n) \approx \Phi\left(\frac{k+0.5-nP}{\sqrt{nPQ\frac{N-n}{N-1}}}\right) - \Phi\left(\frac{k-0.5-nP}{\sqrt{nPQ\frac{N-n}{N-1}}}\right) \tag{2.87 c}$$

$$Hy(k|N;M;n) \approx \Phi\left(\frac{k+0.5-nP}{\sqrt{nPQ\frac{N-n}{N-1}}}\right)$$

Condition same as for the binomial approximation, but $n > 30$.

In table 2.2/4 we will compare these approximations of the hypergeometric massfunction, as well as its distribution function, for selected values of the function parameters.

The model of the negative hypergeometric distribution

In the context of curtailed inspection (see section 3.2.2d), we need the so-called **negative hypergeometric distribution**. It has the following underlying model: Suppose, from an urn with N balls among which there are M black and $N-M$ white balls, one successively draws balls without replacement until the c-th black ball is observed ($c \geq 1$). As before, in the case of attribute sampling, the black balls represent the nonconforming units in the lot. The counting variable in this model is the total number of balls, X, that are drawn until the occurrence of the c-th black ball. In other words, X is the random sample size. The negative hypergeometric distribution is also called the **hypergeometric waiting time distribution**. Its massfunction $nh(k|N;M;c) := Pr(X = k)$ is defined by

Massfunction of the negative hypergeometric distribution:

- first representation

$$nh(k|N;M;c) = \begin{cases} \dfrac{\binom{M}{c-1}\binom{N-M}{k-c}}{\binom{N}{k-1}} \cdot \frac{M-c+1}{N-k+1} & \text{for } c \leq k \leq N-M+c \\ 0 & \text{elsewhere.} \end{cases} \tag{2.88 a}$$

The first factor in (2.88a) represents the probability $hy(c-1|N;M;k-1)$ of the event that, in the first $k-1$ draws, exactly $c-1$ black balls occurred.

- second representation

Hence (2.88a) can equivalently be written as

$$nh(k|N;M;c) = \begin{cases} hy(c-1|N;M;k-1) \cdot \frac{M-c+1}{N-k+1} & \text{for } c \leq k \leq N-M+c \\ 0 & \text{elsewhere.} \end{cases} \tag{2.88 b}$$

The second factor in (2.88) represents the conditional probability that, at the k-th draw, a black ball occurs given that $c-1$ black balls were observed in the previous $k-1$ draws.

Through writing out the binomial coefficients in (2.88a) and appropriately combining them with the second factor one obtains a third representation of the massfunction of the negative hypergeometric distribution:

- third representation

$$nh(k|N;M;c) = \begin{cases} \dfrac{\binom{k-1}{c-1}\binom{N-k}{M-c}}{\binom{N}{M}} & \text{for } c \leq k \leq N-M+c \\ 0 & \text{elsewhere.} \end{cases} \tag{2.88 c}$$

For the distribution function $Nh(k|N;M;c) = Pr(X \leq k)$, we first get

Distribution function of the negative hypergeometric distribution:

- first representation

$$Nh(k|N;M;c) = \begin{cases} 0 & \text{for } k < c \\ \sum_{i=c}^{k} nh(i|N;M;c) & \text{for } c \leq k < N-M+c \\ 1 & \text{for } k \geq N-M+c\,. \end{cases} \tag{2.89 a}$$

- second representation

After appropriate transformation, this function can be expressed in terms of the hypergeometric distribution function (2.81):

$$Nh(k|N;M;c) = 1 - Hy(c-1|N;k;M). \tag{2.89 b}$$

We will only state, but not prove, the following properties of a random variable X with negative hypergeometric distribution:

Expectation and variance of a negative hypergeometric distribution

$$\mu = E(X) = c \cdot \frac{N+1}{M+1} \qquad (2.90\text{ a})$$

$$\sigma^2 = V(X) = c \cdot \frac{(n+1)(N-M)(M+1-c)}{(M+1)^2(M+2)}. \qquad (2.90\text{ b})$$

In analogy to (2.83), the following recursive relationships hold:

Increasing recursion

$$nh(k+1|N;M;c) = \frac{k \cdot (N-M+c-k)}{(k-c+1)(N-k)} \cdot nh(k|N;M;c), \qquad (2.91\text{ a})$$

Decreasing recursion

$$nh(k-1|N;M;c) = \frac{(k-c)(N-k+1)}{(k-1)(N-M+c-k+1)} \cdot nh(k|N;M;c). \qquad (2.91\text{ b})$$

If we let $N \to \infty$ and $M \to \infty$ while the fraction nonconforming is kept constant, or at least converges to a fixed value P_a $(0 < P_a < 1)$, then the negative hypergeometric distribution converges to a negative binomial distribution (see section 2.2.3c).

Problem 2.2/7

a) Prove the validity of (2.84a).
b) Derive from table 2.2/3 that k satisfies the conditions of formula (2.80).
c) Determine $hy(6|20;7;16)$ and $Hy(6|20;7;16)$.

Problem 2.2/8

A company receives a shipment of $N = 50$ condensers, among which there are $M = 5$ defectives.

a) A sample of size $n = 10$ is drawn without replacement. Denote the number of defective condensers in the sample by X_n^T and calculate the probabilities $Pr(X_n^T = k)$ for the possible realizations k of this variable. Also, determine the mode, expectation and variance of X_n^T.
b) Units are successively sampled without replacement from the above lot until the third defective condenser is observed in the sample. Let X denote the random size of the sample (i.e., the number of units that need to be sampled until the third nonconforming unit occurs). Calculate the probability that a sample size of $X = 25$ occurs. Also, find the corresponding probabilities for $X = 23, X = 24, X = 26$ and $X = 27$. Determine the expectation and variance of X.

c) The Binomial and Negative Binomial Distribution

We introduced the hypergeometric distribution with the help of the urn model. From an urn with M black and $N - M$ white balls a sample of n balls was drawn without replacement. The probability that a black ball was observed in the first draw is M/N. At the second draw the probability that a black ball occurs was $(M-1)/(N-1)$, given the first ball was black, and $M/(N-1)$, given the first ball was white. This illustrates that the probability of drawing a black ball is conditional on the previous outcomes and changes in this model with each draw.

Construction of a binomially distributed random variable

However, if a sample is drawn *with* replacement from the above Bernoulli distributed lot, then the probability of observing a black ball is the same for each draw, i.e., $P = M/N$. In the case of attribute sampling, this value is the fraction nonconforming of the lot. If we, as before, interpret the occurrence of a black ball as a "success" (in quality control the discovery of a nonconforming unit), then the total number X_n^T of successes in the sample follows a **binomial distribution**.

Massfunction of the binomial distribution

The massfunction $bi(k|P;n) = Pr(X_n^T = k)$ of the binomial distribution with $Q = 1 - P$ is defined by

$$bi(k|P;n) = \begin{cases} \binom{n}{k} P^k Q^{n-k} & \text{for } k = 0, 1, \ldots, n \\ 0 & \text{elsewhere.} \end{cases} \tag{2.92}$$

Distribution function of the binomial distribution

The distribution function $Bi(k|P;n) = Pr(X_n^T \leq k)$ is given by

$$Bi(k|P;n) = \begin{cases} 0 & \text{for } k < 0 \\ \sum_{i=0}^{k} \binom{n}{i} P^i Q^{n-i} & \text{for } 0 \leq k < n \\ 1 & \text{for } k \geq n. \end{cases} \tag{2.93}$$

For a discrete random variable X which is distributed according to (2.92) or (2.93) we introduce the notation $X \sim bi(P;n)$. Important functional parameters of a $bi(P;n)$-distributed random variable are

Expectation and variance of the binomial distribution

$$\mu = E(X) = nP \tag{2.94 a}$$

$$\sigma^2 = V(X) = nPQ. \tag{2.94 b}$$

Also helpful for the application of the binomial distribution are the following recursion formulas

Increasing recursion

$$bi(k+1|P;n) = \frac{n-k}{k+1}\frac{P}{Q}\, bi(k|P;n) \tag{2.95 a}$$

Decreasing recursion

$$bi(k-1|P;n) = \frac{k}{n-k+1}\frac{Q}{P}\, bi(k|P;n) \tag{2.95 b}$$

and symmetry relationships

$$bi(k|P;n) = bi(n-k|1-P;n) \tag{2.95 c}$$

Symmetry properties

$$Bi(k|P;n) = 1 - Bi(n-k-1|1-P;n). \tag{2.95 d}$$

The latter allow us to reduce the tabulation of the binomial distribution (table 5.1/3) to the range $0 < P \leq 0.5$. The statement of the symmetry relationships is easy to understand. For example, (2.95c) states that the probability of observing exactly k "successes" among n draws, when successes occur with probability P, is equal to the probability of observing $n-k$ "failures", when failures occur with probability $1-P$. The statement (2.95d) expresses a probability relationship of complementary events. The probability of observing at most k "successes" in n trials is related to the probability of observing at least $n-k$ failures in n trials.

Between the binomial distribution and the beta distribution there is the exact relationship

Relationships between the binomial distribution and other distributions:

$$Bi(k|P;n) = 1 - Bt(P|k+1;n-k). \tag{2.96}$$

- Beta distribution

We also want to mention that there is an exact relationship between the binomial and the F distribution (see section 2.2.3f), but unfortunately it does not simplify the calculation of binomial probabilities, because the F distribution cannot be evaluated in a general way. However, the relationship with the F distribution is important for the construction of percentiles of the binomial distribution.

- F distribution

The behaviour of the binomial distribution as $n \to \infty$, or respectively as $n \to \infty$, and $P \to 0$ is characterized by the two following limit theorems (see, for example, HARTUNG 1987, p.122):

▷ **Poisson limit theorem**

Let $\{X_n\}$ denote a sequence of $bi(P;n)$-distributed random variables with $n = 1, 2, \ldots$ and $0 < P < 1$.

- Poisson distribution

Then, as $n \to \infty$ and $P \to 0$ (with $n \cdot P \to \lambda =$ const.), the sequence of the distribution functions of the variables X_n converges to the distribution function of a Poisson distributed random variable with parameter $\lambda := nP$. This means that under the above conditions, X_n is asymptotically $po(n \cdot P)$-distributed.

▷ **Limit theorem by MOIVRE-LAPLACE**

- Normal distribution

Let $\{X_n\}$ denote a sequence of $bi(P;n)$-distributed random variables with $n = 1, 2, \ldots$ and $0 < P < 1$.

Then, for $n \to \infty$, the distribution functions of the sequence elements X_n converge to the distribution function of a normally distributed random variable with expectation nP and variance nPQ. In other words, X_n is asymptotically $no(nP;nPQ)$-distributed.

Approximations of the binomial distribution

Based on these limit theorems the following approximations are commonly applied in practice (see again section 2.1.4d for a presentation of the normal approximation with continuity correction):

- **Poisson approximation**

$$bi(k|P;n) \approx po(k|nP) \tag{2.97 a}$$

Condition: $nP \leq 10$ and $n \geq 1500P$.

- **Normal approximation with continuity correction**

$$bi(k|P;n) \approx \int_{k-0.5}^{k+0.5} no(x|nP;nPQ) = \Phi\left(\frac{k+0.5-nP}{\sqrt{nPQ}}\right) - \Phi\left(\frac{k-0.5-nP}{\sqrt{nPQ}}\right)$$

$$Bi(k|P;n) \approx No(k+0.5|nP;nPQ) = \Phi\left(\frac{k+0.5-nP}{\sqrt{nPQ}}\right) \tag{2.97 b}$$

Condition: $nPQ \geq 9$.

Example 2.2/9

Suppose that in a delivery of $N = 1,000$ units $M = 100$ are nonconforming. A sample of $n = 100$ is drawn *without* replacement. Let X_n^T denote the total number of nonconforming units in the sample. In table 2.2/4 the exact individual and cumulative probabilities $Pr(X_n^T = k) = hy(k|N;M;n)$ and $Pr(X_n^T \leq k) = Hy(k|N;M;n)$ are given in columns 2 and 7, respectively. The binomial, Poisson and normal approximations, according to (2.87a-c), are found in columns 3, 4, and 5 for column 2, and in columns 8, 9, and 10 for column 7. Although the conditions (rules of thumb) of (2.87) are not always satisfied, we find that the approximations work surprisingly well.

Table 2.2/4 also shows the quality of the approximations (2.97a-b) for the binomial distribution in columns 3 and 8, respectively. The Poisson

k	$hy(k\|1000; 100; 100)$	$bi(k\|0.1; 100)$	$po(k\|100)$	$\Phi\left(\frac{k+0.5-10}{2.8475}\right) - \Phi\left(\frac{k-0.5-10}{2.8475}\right)$	$\Phi\left(\frac{k+0.5-10}{3}\right) - \Phi\left(\frac{k-0.5-10}{3}\right)$	$Hy(k\|1000; 100; 100)$	$Bi(k\|0.1; 100)$	$Po(k\|10)$	$\Phi\left(\frac{k+0.5-10}{2.8475}\right)$	$\Phi\left(\frac{k+0.5-10}{3}\right)$
(1)	(2)	(3)	(4)	(5)	(6)	(7)	(8)	(9)	(10)	(11)
0	0.0000	0.0000	0.0000	0.0004	0.0008	0.0000	0.0000	0.0000	0.0004	0.0008
1	0.0002	0.0003	0.0005	0.0010	0.0015	0.0002	0.0003	0.0005	0.0014	0.0023
2	0.0011	0.0016	0.0023	0.0028	0.0039	0.0013	0.0019	0.0028	0.0042	0.0062
3	0.0045	0.0059	0.0076	0.0070	0.0089	0.0058	0.0078	0.0103	0.0112	0.0151
4	0.0130	0.0159	0.0189	0.0155	0.0183	0.0188	0.0237	0.0293	0.0267	0.0334
5	0.0297	0.0329	0.0378	0.0303	0.0334	0.0485	0.0576	0.0671	0.0570	0.0668
6	0.0558	0.0596	0.0631	0.0525	0.0549	0.1043	0.1172	0.1301	0.1095	0.1217
7	0.0874	0.0889	0.0901	0.0805	0.0806	0.1917	0.2061	0.2202	0.1900	0.2023
8	0.1171	0.1148	0.1126	0.1092	0.1062	0.3088	0.3209	0.3328	0.2992	0.3085
9	0.1362	0.1304	0.1251	0.1311	0.1253	0.4450	0.4513	0.4579	0.4303	0.4338
10	0.1391	0.1319	0.1251	0.1394	0.1324	0.5841	0.5832	0.5830	0.5697	0.5662
11	0.1264	0.1197	0.1137	0.1311	0.1253	0.7105	0.7030	0.6980	0.7008	0.6915
12	0.1027	0.0988	0.0948	0.1092	0.1062	0.8132	0.8018	0.7916	0.8100	0.7977
13	0.0751	0.0743	0.0729	0.0805	0.0806	0.8883	0.8761	0.8645	0.8905	0.8783
14	0.0497	0.0513	0.0521	0.0525	0.0549	0.9380	0.9274	0.9165	0.9430	0.9332
15	0.0300	0.0327	0.0347	0.0303	0.0334	0.9680	0.9601	0.9513	0.9733	0.9666
16	0.0166	0.0193	0.0217	0.0155	0.0183	0.9846	0.9794	0.9730	0.9888	0.9849
17	0.0086	0.0106	0.0128	0.0070	0.0089	0.9932	0.9900	0.9857	0.9958	0.9938
18	0.0040	0.0054	0.0071	0.0028	0.0039	0.9972	0.9954	0.9928	0.9986	0.9977
19	0.0017	0.0026	0.0037	0.0010	0.0015	0.9989	0.9980	0.9965	0.9996	0.9992
20	0.0007	0.0012	0.0019	0.0003	0.0006	0.9996	0.9992	0.9984	0.9999	0.9998
21	0.0003	0.0005	0.0009	0.0001	0.0001	0.9999	0.9997	0.9993	1.0000	0.9999
22	0.0001	0.0002	0.0004	0.0000	0.0001	1.0000	0.9999	0.9997	1.0000	1.0000
23	0.0000	0.0001	0.0002	0.0000	0.0000	1.0000	1.0000	0.9999	1.0000	1.0000
24	0.0000	0.0000	0.0001	0.0000	0.0000	1.0000	1.0000	1.0000	1.0000	1.0000

Table 2.2/4: Comparison of the hypergeometric, binomial, Poisson and normal distribution

approximation of columns 3 and 8 is found in columns 4 and 9, and their normal approximation in columns 6 and 11.

Construction of a random variable with negative binomial distribution

The binomial analogue of the negative hypergeometric distribution is the **negative binomial distribution**, also called **binomial waiting time distribution**. The underlying model is an urn with N balls, among which M are black and $N - M$ are white and the balls are successively sampled *with* replacement until the c-th black ball is observed. Then, the sample size X, that is required to reach the c-th occurrence of a black ball has a negative binomial distribution. The negative binomial distribution is used for curtailed inspection in acceptance sampling by attributes, e.g., when a plan specifies rejection of a lot after discovery of the c-th nonconforming unit in a sample from a lot of size N (see section 3.2.2d).

Massfunction of the negative binomial distribution:

- first representation

The massfunction $Pr(X = k) =: nb(k|P;c)$ of the negative binomial distribution is given by

$$nb(k|P;c) = \begin{cases} \binom{k-1}{c-1} P^c Q^{k-c} & \text{for } k = c, c+1, \ldots \\ 0 & \text{elsewhere} \end{cases} \tag{2.98 a}$$

and has the function parameters $0 < P < 1$ and $c \in \mathbb{N}$. In the case of $c = 1$, it is also called the **geometric distribution**, because then the probabilities in (2.98a) form a (decreasing) geometric sequence.

The massfunction in (2.98a) also has a second representation. The latter is verified with the identity

$$\binom{k-1}{c-1} P^c Q^{k-c} = \left[\binom{k-1}{c-1} P^{c-1} Q^{(k-1)-(c-1)}\right] P.$$

- second representation

The term in the square brackets is the probability $bi(c-1|P;k-1)$ of observing $c-1$ successes in $k-1$ draws. Consequently it holds that

$$nb(k|P;c) = \begin{cases} bi(c-1|P;k-1) \cdot P & \text{for } k = c, c+1, \ldots \\ 0 & \text{elsewhere.} \end{cases} \tag{2.98 b}$$

Distribution function of the negative binomial distribution:

- first representation

From (2.98a) we get the distribution function $Nb(k|P;c) := Pr(X \le k)$ of the negative binomial dir·.ibution

$$Nb(k|P;c) = \begin{cases} 0 & \text{for } k < c \\ \sum_{i=c}^{k} nb(i|P;c) & \text{for } k \ge c\,. \end{cases} \tag{2.99 a}$$

Under consideration of the symmetry relationship (2.95d), it follows that

- second representation

$$Nb(k|P;c) = 1 - Bi(c-1|P;k). \tag{2.99 b}$$

We note the following properties of a random variable with negative binomial distribution:

Expectation and variance of the negative binomial distribution

$$\mu = E(X) = \frac{c}{P} \tag{2.100 a}$$

$$\sigma^2 = V(X) = \frac{c \cdot Q}{P^2}. \tag{2.100 b}$$

Finally, we want to mention the recursive relationships

Increasing recursion

$$nb(k+1|P;c) = \frac{k \cdot Q}{k-c+1} \cdot nb(k|P;c) \tag{2.101 a}$$

Decreasing recursion

$$nb(k-1|P;c) = \frac{k-c}{(k-1) \cdot Q} \cdot nb(k|P;c). \tag{2.101 b}$$

Problem 2.2/9

a) For constant N, M and n, compare the values of the expectations and variances of the binomial, hypergeometric and Poisson distribution.
b) For the hypergeometric distribution with $N = 100, M = 10$ and $n = 5$, find the exact values of $Pr(X_n^T = 2)$ and $Pr(X_n^T \leq 2)$ and their approximations according to (2.87a) and (2.87c). Comment on the results.
c) Determine $bi(6|0.7;10)$ and $Bi(6|0.7;10)$ with the help of (2.95c,d) and table 5.1/3.

Problem 2.2/10

Answer the questions of problem 2.2/8 under the assumption that the sample is taken *with* replacement.

d) The t Distribution

If a random sample is drawn *with* replacement from a $no(\mu;\sigma^2)$-distributed population, then the sample average $\bar{X}_n$ is normally distributed with expectation μ and variance (2.77a):

$$\bar{X}_n \sim no\left(\mu; \frac{\sigma^2}{n}\right).$$

Thus the transformed variable

$$Z := \frac{\bar{X}_n - \mu}{\sigma} \cdot \sqrt{n} \tag{2.102}$$

has, according to (2.47), a standard normal distribution (standardized sample average). In practice the variance σ^2 of the population is in general only known approximately through the estimate of the sample variance S_n^2 from (2.66). Instead of (2.102) one uses the sample statistic:

$$T_n := \frac{\bar{X}_n - \mu}{S_n} \cdot \sqrt{n}. \tag{2.103}$$

This variable is no longer normally distributed but has a **central t distribution** with $\nu := n - 1$ degrees of freedom. As a synonym for the term t distribution the name **Student's t distribution** is often used. The latter term relates to the statistician WILLIAM SEALY GOSSET (1876-1937), who published derivations of the t distribution under the pseudonym STUDENT.

Density of the t distribution

The density $f(x) := f_t(x|\nu)$ of a random variable X with a t distribution having ν **degrees of freedom** ($\nu \in \mathbb{N}$) is given by

$$f_t(x|\nu) = \frac{\Gamma\left(\frac{\nu+1}{2}\right)}{\Gamma\left(\frac{1}{2}\right)\Gamma\left(\frac{\nu}{2}\right)\sqrt{\nu}}\left(1 + \frac{x^2}{\nu}\right)^{-(\nu+1)/2}. \tag{2.104 a}$$

Distribution function of the t distribution

The distribution function

$$F_t(x|\nu) := \int_{-\infty}^{x} f_t(u|\nu)du \tag{2.104 b}$$

Expectation and variance of the t distribution

can, in general, not be evaluated analytically. We note the following functional parameters of the t distribution with ν degrees of freedom:

$$\mu = 0 \qquad \text{for } \nu > 1 \tag{2.105 a}$$

$$\sigma^2 = \frac{\nu}{\nu - 2} \qquad \text{for } \nu > 2. \tag{2.105 b}$$

For a continuous random variable X with a t distribution according to (2.104) we also write $X \sim t(\nu)$.

The graph of the density (2.104a) is a bell shaped curve which is symmetric around $x = 0$ and resembles the normal distribution. Compared to the density of the standard normal distribution, the density of the t distribution has heavier tails. This can also be seen by means of the variance (2.105b), which is always greater than one. Similar to (2.104b), the percentile function $t_\nu := F_t^{-1}(y|\nu)$ of the central t distribution with ν degrees of freedom cannot be written in closed form. The values

Percentiles of the t distribution

$$t_{\nu;\omega} := F_t^{-1}(\omega|\nu) \tag{2.106 a}$$

of this function, i.e., the t percentiles of order ω, are tabulated in table 5.2/2 for various values of ν and ω. Since the distribution function (2.104b) is point symmetric around (0;0.5), as figure 2.1/8b illustrates for the distribution function of a $no(\mu; \sigma^2)$-distributed variable, it is sufficient to tabulate the function for $\omega \leq 0.5$. In analogy to (2.55), it holds that

$$t_{\nu;1-\omega} = -t_{\nu;\omega}. \tag{2.106 b}$$

As $\nu \to \infty$, the t distribution converges to the standard normal distribution. For $\nu > 30$, one can approximate the t distribution fairly well by the standard normal distribution. The convergence of $F_t(x|\nu)$ to $\Phi(x)$, for $\nu \to \infty$, also implies that the percentiles (2.106b) converge to the percentiles (2.54) of the standard normal distribution:

$$\lim_{\nu \to \infty} t_{\nu;\omega} = z_\omega. \tag{2.106 c}$$

When we constructed the t distributed statistic (2.103), we assumed that the underlying population has a normal distribution. But as long as its elements have any symmetric and unimodal distribution, the variable (2.103) is in most cases well approximated by the t distribution. Because of this, we also say that the t distribution is **robust**.

Example 2.2/10

Suppose the four filling weights X_i $(i = 1, \ldots, 4)$ of example 2.2/6 that were sampled in 30 minute intervals are independently and identically normally distributed with $E(X_i) = \mu$. Then the sample statistic $\bar{X}_4$ has the same expectation μ and is, in addition, asymptotically normal. Based on this information and the data of the first sample of table 2.2/2, we now want to calculate a twosided confidence interval of level 0.95 for μ.

The desired interval is given in the square brackets of (2.79), provided we replace $\hat{\Theta}_n$ by $\bar{x}_4$, $z_{1-\alpha/2}$ by $t_{3;0.975}$ and $\sqrt{V(\hat{\Theta}_n)}$ by $s_4/2$. With the help of table 5.2/2 we get

$$\bar{x}_4 \approx 1000.055; \quad s_4 \approx 0.286; \quad t_{3;0975} \approx 3.182.$$

Thus the desired interval is given by [1000.055-0.455, 1000.055+0.455], i.e., by [999.60, 1000.51].

Problem 2.2/11

Based on the data of the first sample of table 2.2/2, calculate the twosided 99% variation interval for $\bar{X}_4$. Assume that the sample statistic $\bar{X}_4$ is at least approximately $no(1000; 0.286^2)$-distributed.

Remark

If μ in (2.103) is replaced by an arbitrary real constant c, then the resulting variable is non-centrally t-distributed with $\delta := \sqrt{n} \cdot (\mu - c)/\sigma$, the so-called non-centrality parameter. The density function and other properties of a non-central t distribution can, for example, be found in JOHNSON/KOTZ (1970). We will need the non-central t distribution in section 3.3.3 for the discussion of sampling plans for variables in the case of unknown process variance.

e) The χ^2 Distribution

Let X_i $(i = 1, \dots, n)$ be independently and identically $no(\mu; \sigma^2)$-distributed. Then, according to (2.47), the variables $(X_i - \mu)/\sigma$ are independently standard normally distributed:

$$\frac{X_i - \mu}{\sigma} \sim no(0;1), \; i = 1, 2, \dots, n.$$

The distribution of the sample statistic

$$\chi^2 := \sum_{i=1}^{n} \left(\frac{X_i - \mu}{\sigma} \right)^2 = \frac{1}{\sigma^2} \sum_{i=1}^{n} (X_i - \mu)^2 \tag{2.107}$$

is called the **central χ^2 distribution** (say Chi-squared distribution) with $\nu := n$ degrees of freedom. The asymmetric and skewed to the right density $f(x) := ch(x|\nu)$ of the χ^2 distributed variable (2.107) satisfies the equation

Density of the χ^2 distribution

$$ch(x|\nu) = \begin{cases} \dfrac{x^{(\nu-2)/2} e^{-x/2}}{2^{\nu/2}\Gamma\left(\frac{\nu}{2}\right)} & \text{for } x \geq 0 \\ 0 & \text{elsewhere.} \end{cases} \tag{2.108 a}$$

Distribution function of the χ^2 distribution

Its distribution function

$$Ch(x|\nu) := \int_0^x ch(u|\nu)du = \frac{1}{2^{\nu/2}\Gamma\left(\frac{\nu}{2}\right)} \int_0^x u^{(\nu-2)/2} e^{-u/2} du \tag{2.108 b}$$

cannot be written in closed form. If the expectation μ of the population is unknown we can replace μ in (2.107) by its estimator, the sample mean $\bar{X}_n$.

Then, provided that the sample was taken *with* replacement, the resulting variable has a χ^2 distribution with $\nu = n-1$ degrees of freedom:

$$\sum_{i=1}^{k} \left(\frac{X_i - \bar{X}_n}{\sigma} \right)^2 = (n-1) \cdot \frac{S_n^2}{\sigma^2} \sim \chi^2(n-1). \qquad (2.109)$$

We mention the following parameters of the χ^2 distribution with ν degrees of freedom:

Expectation and variance of the χ^2 distribution

$$\mu = \nu \qquad (2.110\text{ a})$$

$$\sigma^2 = 2\nu. \qquad (2.110\text{ b})$$

Table 5.2/4 lists selected values

Percentiles of the χ^2 distribution

$$\chi^2_{\nu;\omega} := Ch^{-1}(\omega|\nu) \qquad (2.111\text{ a})$$

of the percentile function $\chi^2_\nu := Ch^{-1}(y|\nu)$. As $\nu \to \infty$, the χ^2 distribution converges to a normal distribution with parameters $\mu = \nu$ and $\sigma^2 = 2\nu$. For $\nu > 100$ the approximation of $Ch(x|\nu)$ by $No(x|\nu; 2\nu)$ is sufficiently good to allow us to replace the percentiles (2.111a) by the percentiles (2.56) of a normal distribution with $\mu = \nu$ and $\sigma = \sqrt{2\nu}$:

Relationship of the χ^2 distribution to other distributions:

- Normal distribution

$$\chi^2_{\nu;\omega} \approx \nu + z_\omega \sqrt{2\nu} \quad (\nu > 100). \qquad (2.111\text{ b})$$

In the case of $\nu = 2$, the χ^2 distribution is identical with the exponential distribution with $\lambda = 0.5$. Finally we want to mention the relationship with the Poisson distribution. Through partial integration of (2.108a), one can show that

- Exponential distribution

$$\sum_{i=0}^{k} \frac{\lambda^i}{i!} e^{-\lambda} = \frac{1}{2^{k+1}\Gamma(k+1)} \int_{2\lambda}^{\infty} u^k e^{-u/2} du.$$

With the help of (2.17) one can then prove, that this equation is equivalent to the relationship

- Poisson distribution

$$Po(k|\lambda) = 1 - Ch[2\lambda | 2(k+1)] \qquad (2.112\text{ a})$$

between the distribution functions of the Poisson and χ^2 distribution. If we set $Po(k|\lambda) =: \omega$ $(0 < \omega < 1)$, then we get $Ch[2\lambda|2(k+1)] = 1 - \omega$ and hence

$$\chi^2_{2(k+1);1-\omega} = 2\lambda. \qquad (2.112\text{ b})$$

The χ^2 distribution has two important applications:

Applications of the χ^2 distribution

- With the help of the χ^2 distribution we can draw inference about the variance of a normally distributed population. Drawing inference means being able to make statements about the variance estimator and to perform statistical tests.

- Because of its exact relationship (2.112) with the Poisson distribution the χ^2 distribution is important for the construction of sampling plans in acceptance sampling by attributes (see section 3.2.3a, construction of sampling plans with given properties).

Example 2.2/11

We want to illustrate the first application with the help of (2.109). According to the definition of a percentile, $(1-\alpha)\cdot 100\%$ of the realizations of the sample statistic (2.109) lie within the interval $[\chi^2_{n-1;\alpha/2};\ \chi^2_{n-1;1-\alpha/2}]$, the twosided variation interval of level $1-\alpha$ for the random variable $(n-1)\cdot S_n^2/\sigma^2$. In analogy to (2.58), it holds that

$$Pr\left(\chi^2_{n-1;\alpha/2} \leq (n-1)\cdot\frac{S_n^2}{\sigma^2} \leq \chi^2_{n-1;1-\alpha/2}\right) = 1-\alpha.$$

Through elementary transformations we get

$$Pr\left(\frac{\sigma^2}{n-1}\chi^2_{n-1;\alpha/2} \leq S_n^2 \leq \frac{\sigma^2}{n-1}\chi^2_{n-1;1-\alpha/2}\right) = 1-\alpha$$

$$Pr\left(\frac{(n-1)\cdot S_n^2}{\chi^2_{n-1;1-\alpha/2}} \leq \sigma^2 \leq \frac{(n-1)\cdot S_n^2}{\chi^2_{n-1;\alpha/2}}\right) = 1-\alpha.$$

Within the brackets of the first line we find the twosided variation interval of level $1-\alpha$ for the sample variance S_n^2. The interval in the second expression is the twosided confidence interval for σ^2 with level $1-\alpha$.

Example 2.2/12

We want to calculate $Ch(18|32) =: 1-P$. According to (2.112b) and table 5.1/4, we have

$$Ch(18|32) = 1 - Po(15|9) \approx 1 - 0.97796 \approx 0.02204.$$

This implies that the number 18 is the percentile $\chi^2_{32;0.02204}$ of the χ^2 distribution with 32 degrees of freedom. This result is compatible with table 5.2/4. There, we find that the closest percentile of order $P = 0.025$ is given by $\chi^2_{32;0.025} \approx 18,291$.

Problem 2.2/12

a) Suppose that the units of a population are independently and identically $no(\mu; \sigma^2)$-distributed. A sample of size $n = 10$ is taken with replacement. According to (2.73), S_n^2 is an unbiased estimator of σ^2. Find a variation interval of level 0.95 for the standardized estimation error $Y_n := (S_n^2 - \sigma^2)/\sigma^2$.

b) We are given that $\chi^2_{16;0.99} = 32$. Which value of $Po(k|\lambda)$ can be calculated with this information?

c) In analogy to (2.112a), express $po(k|\lambda)$ in terms of $Ch(x|\nu)$.

f) The F Distribution

Let X_1 and X_2 be two stochastically independent random variables with χ^2 distributions on ν_1 and ν_2 degrees of freedom, respectively. Then the distribution of the ratio

$$F := \frac{X_1/\nu_1}{X_2/\nu_2} \tag{2.113}$$

is called the **central F distribution** on ν_1 and ν_2 degrees of freedom. The quantities ν_1 and ν_2 are also called the degrees of freedom of the numerator and the denominator, respectively. The F distribution was first derived by the statistician R. A. FISHER (1890 - 1962).

Density of the F distribution

The density $f(x) =: fi(x|\nu_1; \nu_2)$ of the F-distributed variable (2.113) is defined by

$$fi(x|\nu_1;\nu_2) := \begin{cases} \dfrac{\Gamma\left(\frac{\nu_1+\nu_2}{2}\right)\cdot\left(\frac{\nu_1}{\nu_2}\right)^{\nu_1/2}}{\Gamma\left(\frac{\nu_1}{2}\right)\cdot\Gamma\left(\frac{\nu_2}{2}\right)}\cdot\dfrac{x^{(\nu_1-2)/2}}{\left(1+\frac{\nu_1}{\nu_2}\cdot x\right)^{(\nu_1+\nu_2)/2}} & \text{for } x \geq 0 \\ 0 & \text{elsewhere.} \end{cases} \tag{2.114}$$

Distribution function of the F distribution

The distribution function

$$Fi(x|\nu_1;\nu_2) := \int_0^x fi(u|\nu_1;\nu_2)du \tag{2.115}$$

of a $fi(\nu_1; \nu_2)$-distributed random variable cannot be written in closed form. Important functional parameters of the F distribution are

Expectation and variance of the F distribution

$$\mu = \frac{\nu_2}{\nu_2 - 2} \qquad (\nu_2 > 2) \tag{2.116 a}$$

$$\sigma^2 = \frac{2\nu_2^2(\nu_1+\nu_2-2)}{\nu_1(\nu_2-2)^2(\nu_2-4)} \qquad (\nu_2 > 4). \tag{2.116 b}$$

Percentiles of the F distribution

In table 5.2/3 we find a tabulation of the values

$$F_{\nu_1;\nu_2;\omega} := Fi^{-1}(\omega|\nu_1;\nu_2) \tag{2.117 a}$$

of the percentile function $F_{\nu_1,\nu_2} := Fi^{-1}(\omega|\nu_1,\nu_2)$ for selected ω. Since the percentiles satisfy the symmetry relationship

$$F_{\nu_1;\nu_2;\omega} := \frac{1}{F_{\nu_2;\nu_1;1-\omega}} \tag{2.117 b}$$

it is sufficient to tabulate the percentiles for $\omega \geq 0.5$ The F distribution is related to the binomial distribution by

Relationship between the F distribution and the binomial distribution

$$Bi(k|P;n) = 1 - Fi\left[\frac{n-k}{k+1}\frac{P}{1-P}\middle|2(k+1);2(n-k)\right]. \tag{2.118 a}$$

Substituting $Bi(k|P;n) = \omega$ $(0 < \omega < 1)$ we get

$$Fi\left[\frac{n-k}{k+1}\cdot\frac{P}{1-P}\middle|2(k+1);2(n-k)\right] = 1-\omega.$$

This implies for the corresponding percentile of the F distribution that

$$F_{2(k+1);2(n-k);1-\omega} = \frac{n-k}{k+1}\cdot\frac{P}{1-P}. \tag{2.118 b}$$

Applications of the F distribution

We mention two applications of the F distribution:

- With the help of the F distribution one can draw inference about the ratio of the variances of two normal distributions.
- Because of its relationship to the binomial distribution the F distributions is important in acceptance sampling (determination of sampling plans with specified properties).

Example 2.2/13

We want to determine the value of the parameter P of a binomial distribution, with $n = 14$, so that $Bi(4|14;P) = 0.05$.

The solution is found with the help of (2.118a,b) via the 95% percentile of the F distribution with $\nu_1 = 2\cdot(4+1) = 10$ degrees of freedom in the numerator and $\nu_2 = 2\cdot(14-4) = 20$ degrees of freedom in the denominator. According to table 5.2/3 this percentile has the value

$$F_{10;20;0.95} = 2.35.$$

It follows by (2.118b) that

$$2.35 = \frac{14-4}{4+1} \cdot \frac{P}{1-P};$$

i.e., we have to choose $P \approx 0.5402$.

Problem 2.2/13

a) What statements about the F distribution can be derived according to (2.118a,b) from $Bi(4|0.25;10) \approx 0.9219$?

b) Determine the percentile $F_{5;7;0.05}$.

c) In analogy to (2.118a), express $bi(k|P;n)$ through $Fi(x|\nu_1;\nu_2)$.

The following figure 2.2/2 summarises the relationships between the most important distributions mentioned before. This overview shows at first sight how many function parameters exist for each distribution and how we want to notate it. Distributions with special importance in SQA have been emphasized by shading.

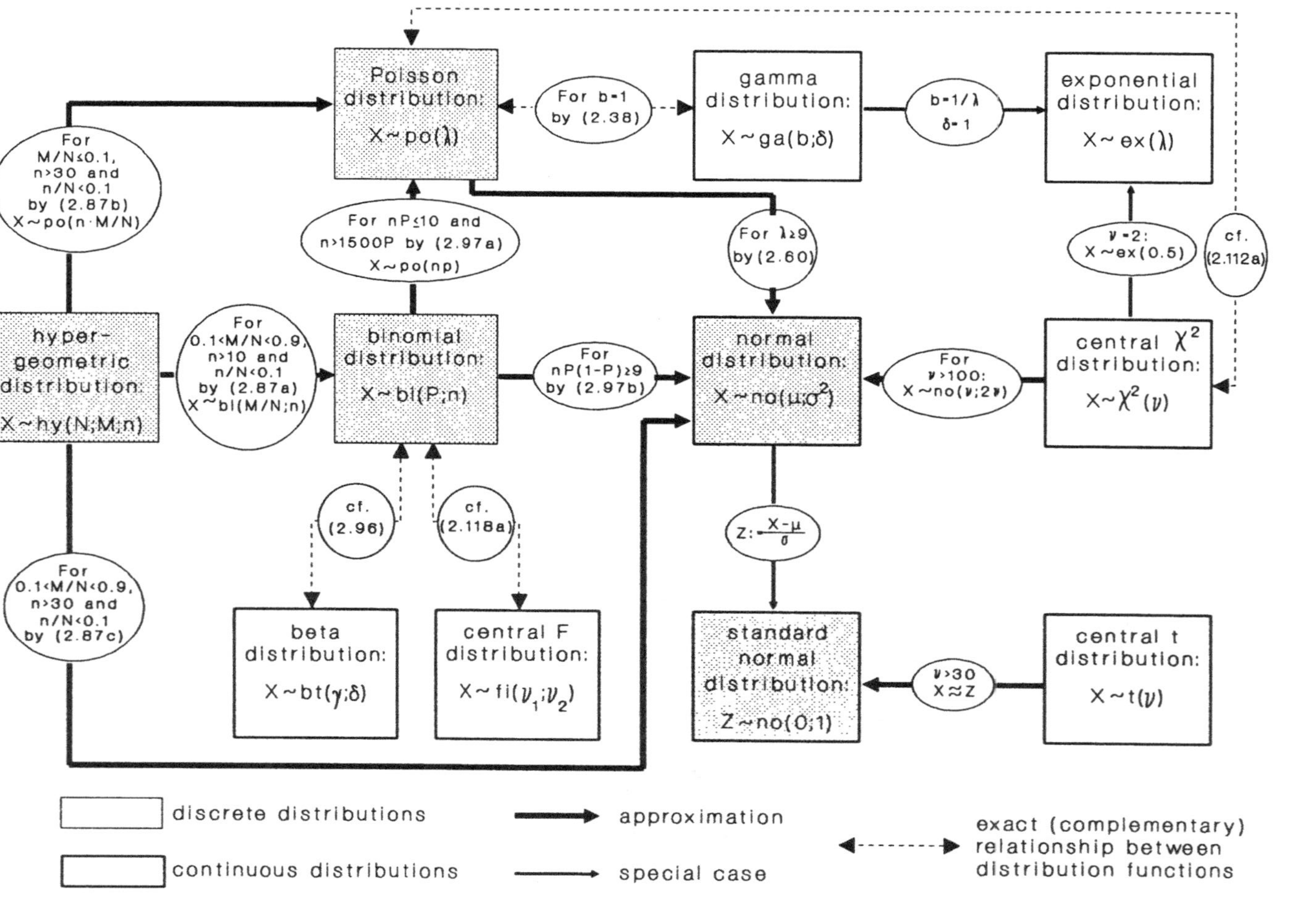

Figure 2.2/2: Relationships between several discrete and continuous distributions

2.3 Fundamentals of Hypothesis Testing

2.3.1 Basic Ideas of Hypothesis Testing

a) Errors in Hypothesis Tests

As already mentioned statistical quality control is basically an application of hypothesis testing, although the specific hypothesis is not always evident. A statistical **hypothesis** is a statement about the properties of a random variable. In SQA it is related to the quality characteristic of a population. A procedure to investigate a statistical hypothesis with the help of a sample from the relevant population is called **a statistical test**, or simply a **test**. According to the type of hypothesis, we distinguish between a parameter test and a goodness of fit test. In a **parameter test** the hypothesis H_0 specifies a value Θ_0 of a parameter Θ of a given distribution, i.e., $\Theta = \Theta_0$ (**point hypothesis** or **simple hypothesis**), or more than one value, for example $\Theta \geq \Theta_0$ (**composite hypothesis** or **range hypothesis**). In a **goodness of fit test** the hypothesis specifies a certain type of distribution. The goal is to test whether there is evidence that the sample values are realizations of a random variable distributed according to this distribution (for example, the normal distribution). In this book we will only deal with parameter tests.

Classification of statistical tests

In a statistical hypothesis test one determines whether an observed sample outcome supports the so-called **null hypothesis** H_0, and hence whether this hypothesis can be accepted, or whether the outcome of the sample is so unlikely under this hypothesis that one has good reason to reject the hypothesis H_0. Usually the outcome of the sample is expressed through the value of a sample statistic $g(\mathbf{X})$, usually called the **test statistic** or **test variable**. Since a statistical test is based on the outcome of a sample, which is a stochastically random result, it can never verify or falsify a hypothesis in the sense of proving or disproving it with certainty in a deterministic sense. The results of a statistical test are weaker. Acceptance does not mean the hypothesis is verified, only that the observed outcome gave evidence in favour of the hypothesis. Rejection does not imply that the hypothesis is proved wrong, only that the observed outcome gave evidence against the hypothesis. A wrong decision can occur in both cases.

Purpose and limitations of statistical tests

When performing a statistical hypothesis test there are two possibilities of making a wrong decision (see table 2.3/1). It can happen that the null hypothesis H_0 is rejected based on the sample, when in fact H_0 is true. This misjudgement of wrongly rejecting H_0 is called **a type I error**. Because its maximal probability of occurrence is usually denoted by α, it is sometimes called **α-error**. The probability α is the **significance level** of the

Types of errors in statistical tests

specific hypothesis test. In acceptance sampling, a type I error corresponds to rejecting a lot with tolerable quality level. The corresponding probability is also called the **producer's risk**. In process control a type I error corresponds to intervening in a production process that runs satisfactorily, a so-called **blind alarm**.

The other possibility for misjudgement is to accept the hypothesis H_0, when in fact it is false. This error of wrongly accepting a false hypothesis is called a **type II error** or **β-error**. The probability of committing a type II error is denoted by β. In acceptance sampling, a type II error corresponds to accepting a lot with an intolerable quality level. The corresponding probability is called the **consumer's risk**. In process control a type II error corresponds to not intervening in a production process that doesn't run satisfactorily, a **neglected alarm**.

Test decision	True state	
	H_0 true	H_0 false
H_0 is accepted	correct decision	type II error (β-error)
H_0 is rejected	type I error (α-error)	correct decision

Table 2.3/1: Types of errors in statistical tests

Descriptive and constructive aspects of test theory

It will be seen that the probabilities of committing type I and type II errors are conditional probabilities, each with a different condition. The *descriptive* aspect of the hypothesis testing theory is to determine these values for a given test. Conversely one can specify the maximal probabilities of occurrence of both types of errors and design a test, i.e., a decision rule, that at least approximately satisfies those error probabilities. This is the *constructive* aspect of testing theory.

In the discussion of acceptance sampling in chapter 3, the specification of both error probabilities is predominant. Since in this case α and β denote the producer's and consumer's risks, respectively, both the consumer's and producer's interests are taken into account by specifying these two values. In general only α is specified in process control (chapter 4). Since α represents the probability of a blind alarm, specification of α means that the risk of a blind alarm is kept under control.

b) Parameters Influencing the Error Probabilities

We begin with a simple example to demonstrate how the two error probabilities are related to each other and by which parameters they are influenced.

Consider a machine that can only produce in two different states. In the desirable state it produces output with a $no(10;4)$-distributed quality characteristic X, where X denotes, for example, the length of a work piece. In the undesirable state, we would have $X \sim no(11;4)$. In both cases the variance is $\sigma^2 = V(X) = 4$ and the only difference between the two states is the process level $\mu = E(X)$.

We want to test the null hypothesis that the process level is $\mu = 10$ against the only possible alternative $\mu = 11$. The alternative hypothesis is denoted by H_1:

$$\begin{aligned} H_0 &: \mu = 10 \\ H_1 &: \mu = 11. \end{aligned}$$

With this test we are trying to determine in which of the two states the machine is running. In this particular case, it does not make any difference which of the two hypotheses is chosen to be the null hypothesis H_0 (however see section 2.3.2d). In order to perform this described hypothesis test we will draw a sample of size n (without replacement) from the running production. The production can be ideally considered to be a population of infinite size.

The statistic of this test is the sample average $\bar{X}_n$. According to (2.72) it is an unbiased and efficient estimator of μ. If H_0 is true, it should hold that $\bar{X}_n \sim no(10;4/n)$, whereas if H_1 is true, then we would have $\bar{X}_n \sim no(11;4/n)$. Figure 2.3/1 shows the two density functions of $\bar{X}_n$ for $n = 4$ and $n = 25$, when H_0 and H_1 are true, respectively .

We can see that every possible realization of $\bar{X}_4$ and $\bar{X}_{25}$ can occur under both hypotheses, however with different probabilities of occurrence. We also observe that an increase in the sample size n leads to a reduction of the variance of the distribution of the test statistic and hence to a reduction in the error probabilities α and β (see also figure 2.3/2).

Acceptance and rejection region

Construction of a test requires the partitioning of the range of the test statistic into a critical region, the **rejection region** CR, and the corresponding complementary range, the **acceptance region** $\overline{CR}$. The decision rule of the test is to decide in favour of H_1 when $\bar{X}_n \in CR$ and in favour of H_0 when $\bar{X}_n \in \overline{CR}$. Based on figure 2.3/1 it seems that a sensible approach is to choose a number C with $10 < C < 11$, that determines the acceptance region $\overline{CR}$ to be the interval $(-\infty, C]$ and the rejection region CR to be the complementary interval (C, ∞). We can see from figure 2.3/1 that $\bar{X}_n \in CR$ can occur even when H_0 is true. In this case H_0 is mistakenly rejected, i.e., a type I error is committed. Vice versa, it can also happen that $\bar{X}_n \in \overline{CR}$, when actually H_1 holds. Then H_0 is wrongly accepted and a type II error is committed. The probability of committing a type I error is formally given by

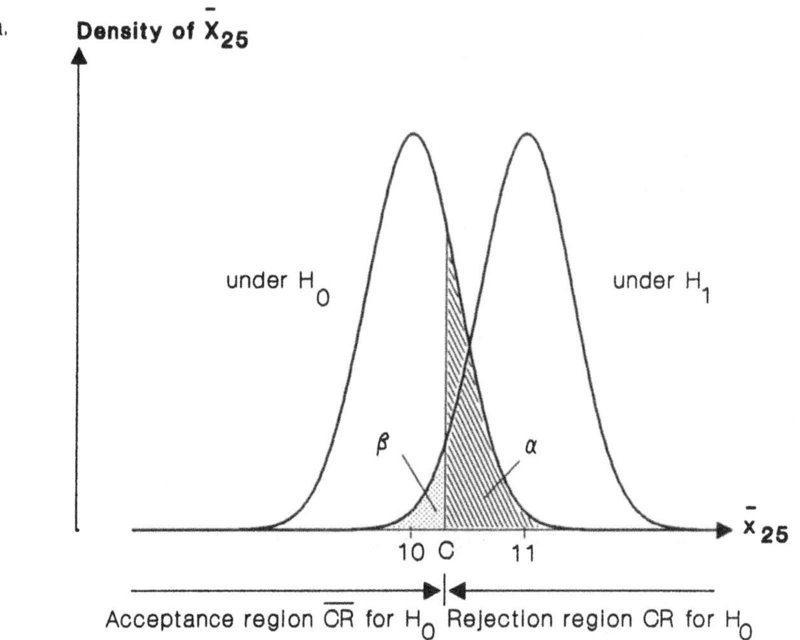

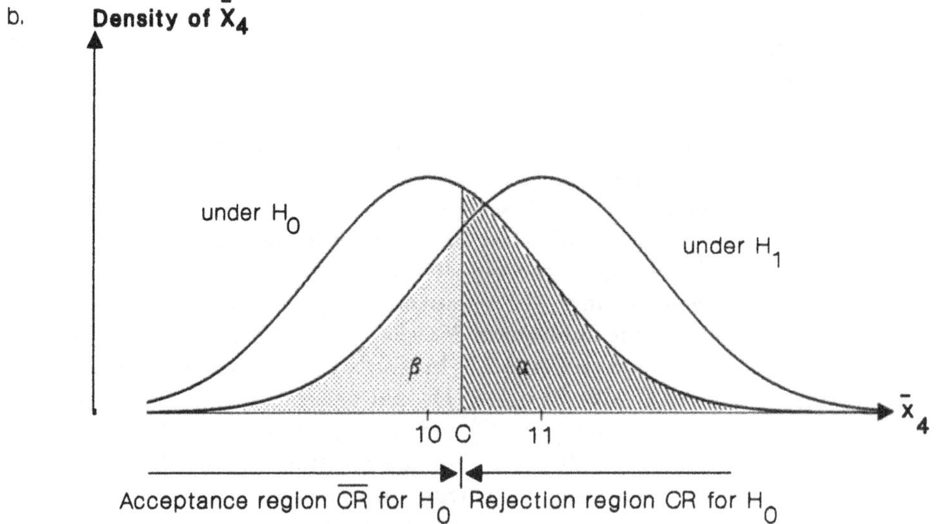

Figure 2.3/1: Distribution of the test statistic and critical region of a test for different sample sizes n

$$\begin{aligned}\alpha &:= Pr(\bar{X}_n \in CR|H_0) \\ &= Pr(\text{test rejects } H_0 \text{ given } H_0 \text{ is true})\end{aligned} \qquad (2.119 \text{ a})$$

and the probability that a type II error occurs is defined by

Formal definition of the two error probabilities

$$\begin{aligned}\beta &:= Pr(\bar{X}_n \in \overline{CR}|H_1) \\ &= Pr(\text{test accepts } H_0 \text{ given } H_1 \text{ is true}).\end{aligned} \qquad (2.119 \text{ b})$$

Because $\bar{X}_n \sim no(\mu; 4/n)$, with $H_0 : \mu = 10$ and $H_1 : \mu = 11$, we get for this example :

Calculation of the two error probabilities

$$\alpha = Pr(\bar{X}_n > C|\mu = 10) = 1 - \Phi\left(\frac{C-10}{2/\sqrt{n}}\right) \qquad (2.120 \text{ a})$$

$$\beta = Pr(\bar{X}_n \leq C|\mu = 11) = \Phi\left(\frac{C-11}{2/\sqrt{n}}\right). \qquad (2.120 \text{ b})$$

This gives us two equations for the four quantities α, β, C, and n. Hence, we can numerically specify two of these quantities and then solve (2.120a,b) for the remaining two. For example, if we fix $n = 25$ and $C = 10.4$ as in figure 2.3.1a, then this specifies a test. Its error probabilities can be determined to be:

$$\alpha = 1 - \Phi(1) \approx 0.151655; \quad \beta = \Phi(-1.5) \approx 0.066807.$$

With the specifications $n = 4$ and $C = 10.4$ of figure 2.3.1b we would get

$$\alpha = 1 - \Phi(0.4) \approx 0.344578; \quad \beta = \Phi(-0.6) \approx 0.274253.$$

We could also specify the error probabilities α and β in advance. Then they would determine n and C, in other words, the specific test.

The above hypothesis test illustrates two important issues. First, we can see from (2.120a,b) that the conditional probabilities α and β depend on different conditions. This explains why they do not add up to one. They each correspond to an area under a *different* density of figure 2.3/1. Thus the two error probabilities of the complementary actions "rejection" and "acceptance" of H_0 are related to different densities.

We also observe from figure 2.3/1 how a change in the rejection region would effect the two error probabilities. As the value of C increases, the probability of α becomes smaller and that of β becomes bigger. A smaller value of C increases α and reduces β. This shows that one cannot lower the probability of one type of error without automatically increasing the probability of the other type of error. This dilemma can only be solved by an increase in the sample size n.

The fact that the two quantities α and β counteract each other and that they do not add up to a constant is nicely illustrated in figure 2.3/2. The trade-off between the probabilities of committing a type I and type II error is graphically displayed for the simple hypothesis test $H_0 : \mu = 10$ versus $H_1 : \mu = 11$.

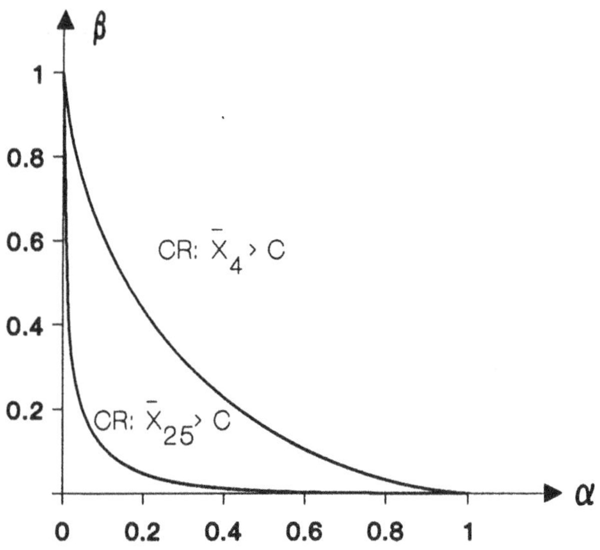

Figure 2.3/2: Trade-off between the error probabilities for different sample sizes

Points on the curve for $n = 25$ are determined according to (2.120a,b) as follows: For $\alpha = \alpha^*$, we get from (2.120a) that $z_{1-\alpha^*} = 5 \cdot (C - 10)/2$. Solving for C results in $C^* = 10 + 0.4z_{1-\alpha^*}$. Putting this C^* and $n = 25$ into (2.120b) yields the corresponding $\beta^* = \Phi(z_{1-\alpha^*} - 2.5)$. For $n = 4$, one obtains in a similar way that $\beta^* = \Phi(z_{1-\alpha^*} - 1)$. Note that each pair (α, β) has a different corresponding value of C. As figure 2.3/2 illustrates, the test with the larger sample size is better in regard to both error probabilities. This global superiority of the test with the larger sample is called **dominance**, i.e., the test with $n = 25$ dominates the test with $n = 4$.

Problem 2.3/1

Solve the equation system (2.120a,b) for all the six possible ways of specifying two of the four quantities α, β, C and n. Evaluate the solutions numerically for the specifications $\alpha = 0.10$, $\beta = 0.05$, $n = 16$ and $C = 10.7$. Don't forget to round the results for the sample size n to the next larger integer.

Problem 2.3/2

a) Determine the equations corresponding to (2.120a,b) for the test $H_0 : \mu = 10$ versus $H_1 : \mu = 11$ with CR: $\bar{X}_n < C$.

b) Sketch how to modify the curves in figure 2.3/2 for this test.

2.3.2 Design and Applications of Parameter Tests

a) Steps of a Parameter Test

We have already given an idea of the structure of a parameter test and also described how the error probabilities that are related to the various tests can be influenced. We will now give a more detailed and systematic description about how to approach the application of a hypothesis test and illustrate the procedure with the help of examples.

Application of a parameter test involves the following steps:

- **Step 1: Determination of the underlying population and its type of distribution**

One first needs to clarify the structure of the underlying population, where the units with the quality characteristic of interest come from (e.g., in acceptance sampling, a lot with finite size), and then determine the type of distribution of the quality characteristic.

- **Step 2: Statement of the hypothesis**

Let Θ be a parameter of the distribution of a quality characteristic X. Let Ω denote the **parameter space**, i.e., the set of all possible values of Θ and partition Ω into two mutually exclusive and exhaustive subsets Ω_0 and Ω_1. Then the null hypothesis H_0 and the alternative hypothesis H_1 are formally written as

$$\begin{aligned} H_0 &: \Theta \in \Omega_0 \\ H_1 &: \Theta \in \Omega_1. \end{aligned} \qquad (2.121)$$

The most common cases are that Ω_0 only consists of a single point (H_0: $\Theta = \Theta_0$) or of a half line (H_0: $\Theta \leq \Theta_0$ or, respectively, H_0: $\Theta \geq \Theta_0$). When constructing a hypothesis test of type (2.121) one should always choose H_0 in such a way that the most feared misjudgement becomes the type I error (see section 2.3.2d).

- **Step 3: Specification of the test statistic and determination of its distribution under H_0**

In order to investigate the stated hypothesis, or put differently, in order to make a statistical statement about the parameter value of a quality characteristic, we draw a sample of size n from the population. The sample values are given as the sample vector $\mathbf{X}$. In hypothesis testing one generally uses a scalar function $g(\mathbf{X})$ of the original vector $\mathbf{X}$ as a test statistic. This **test variable** needs to be chosen in a suitable way so that on the one hand it is able to give evidence in favour of H_0 or H_1. This requires that the distribution of the test statistic depends on whether H_0 or H_1 is true. On the other hand, one must be able to calculate the distribution of the scalar function $g(\mathbf{X})$ under H_0. Knowledge about the distribution of $g(\mathbf{X})$ under H_0 is necessary in order to determine whether the given significance level is exceeded or not (see step 4). In the case of composite hypotheses H_0: $\Theta \leq \Theta_0$, or respectively, H_0: $\Theta \geq \Theta_0$, the distribution of $g(\mathbf{X})$ is determined at the endpoint of the range of H_0, i.e., at $\Theta = \Theta_0$.

Hypothesis tests of the unknown expectation μ or variance σ^2 in a population commonly use the sample average $\bar{X}_n$ or the sample variance S_n^2, respectively, as their test statistics introduced in (2.65) and (2.66).

- **Step 4: Specification of the significance level and determination of the rejection region *CR***

Before a test can be performed, one has to specify the maximal admissible probability of a type I error. This upper bound

$$\alpha = \sup_{\Theta \in \Omega_0} Pr[g(\mathbf{X}) \in CR|\Theta] \quad ^{11} \tag{2.122 a}$$

for committing a type I error is called the **significance level** of the test. For a given value of α, formula (2.122a) can be seen as the determining equation of the rejection region CR. In other words, specification of α usually determines the rejection region CR. However, in the case of a discrete test statistic it is not always possible to satisfy (2.122a) exactly. If this is the case, one tries to comply with

$$\alpha \geq \sup_{\Theta \in \Omega_0} Pr[g(\mathbf{X}) \in CR|\Theta] \tag{2.122 b}$$

in such a way that, for a given α, the supremum is as close as possible to the value of α. Then, the rejection region CR is usually also determined by α.

The significance level of a test limits the probability of undesirably committing a type I error. One should however not choose its value to be arbitrarily small, because a reduction in α results in an increase in the probability of a type II error (see figure 2.3/2). Common values of α are 0.1, 0.05, 0.01, and occasionally 0.001.

[11] The smallest upper bound of a set that is bounded from above is in mathematical literature called the **supremum** and abbreviated by "sup".

- **Step 5: Test decision and interpretation**

After calculation of the test statistic for an observed sample, the null hypothesis H_0 is rejected when the value of the test statistic lies within the rejection region CR. Rejection of H_0 does not disprove the hypothesis in the formal sense of a proof, but the probability of a misjudgement (producer's risk, blind alarm) is at least below the given significance level. One can say that the null hypothesis H_0 is then "statistically disproved" or that there is significant statistical evidence against H_0, and that the alternative hypothesis H_1 is "statistically verified" or that there is significant statistical evidence in favour of H_1.

In the same way, non-rejection of H_0 – generally called acceptance of H_0 – should not be interpreted as a verification of H_0. Acceptance simply means that the result of the sample, i.e., the test statistic $g(\mathbf{X})$, did not give evidence against H_0 and that nothing speaks against working under the assumption that H_0 is true. However, this interpretation of the acceptance of H_0 as a decision to work with this hypothesis, is not statistically controlled. The probability of wrongly accepting H_0, i.e., of committing a type II error, is not kept below a specified small value and thus not under control, as in the case of wrongly rejecting H_0. In the worst case the probability of this β-error can be as large as $1 - \alpha$ (see section 2.3.2d).

Remarks

1. In classical hypothesis testing the error probability α is related to the procedure in general and not to a particular test result. The latter means that one interprets the significance level in the following way: If a test procedure with given significance level, say $\alpha = 0.05$, is repeated again and again, then in the long run we expect it to reject H_0 in 5% of the cases where H_0 is actually true. A statement like "when the hypothesis H_0 is rejected it is false with probability $1 - \alpha = 0.95$" does not have any statistical meaning.

   Some statistical software packages do not require the user to specify α in advance. Instead, these programs calculate the **critical significance level**. This value is related to the observed outcome of the test statistic $g(\mathbf{X})$ and gives the following probability of a specific significance level α^*: "If the observed sample data were tested with this significance level α^*, then $g(\mathbf{x})$ would be exactly the end point of the rejection region CR." This implies that the test would reject H_0 for any significance level α with $\alpha > \alpha^*$. Thus the final decision is left to the user and depends on his/her choice of α (which should be chosen before and not after obtaining α^*).

2. In classical hypothesis testing, contrary to the **Bayesian testing theory**, the null and alternative hypotheses are treated in an asymmetric way. The main interest of these procedures, also called **significance tests**, is the null hypothesis and, in particular, that it should be wrongly rejected as seldom as possible and only with controlled probability. In classical theory, rejection and non-rejection are statements of a different kind. This is caused by the different treatment of type I and type II errors, and consequently of null and alternative hypothesis, in the context of constructing the rejection region. In practical application, one

thus chooses H_0 and H_1 in a way that the least desirable misjudgement becomes the type I error, because its risk is controlled by the significance level. We will illustrate this procedure in detail in section 2.3.2d.

b) Two Examples from Practice

We now illustrate the procedure of hypothesis testing by means of two examples.

Example 2.3/1: Test on the filling volume of beer bottles

The first example from BAMBERG/BAUR (1989, p.176) concerns the filling of 0.5 l beer bottles in a brewery, and the quality characteristic of interest, X, is the actual filling volume of the individual bottles. Since X can theoretically take any value in the range between the smallest and largest possible volume, it is a continuous quality characteristic.

The population on which the test is applied can be seen to be the set of all bottles that have been filled in a certain period (e.g., a day's production). The kind of distribution of X must be determined through preliminary investigations. Suppose it was concluded that the filling volume is normally distributed with unknown expectation μ and known variance $\sigma^2 = 2.25$. We want to investigate the null hypothesis H_0: $\mu = \mu_0$ with the nominal value $\mu_0 = 500\ cm^3$. In this example of statistical process control the null hypothesis is related to the average level of the production process, the expectation of the filling volume. The statement of the alternative hypothesis depends on whether one is only interested in deviations in one direction (i.e., below or above the desired value) or in both possible directions. Let us assume that the brewery is interested in the latter statement of the problem. Then the hypotheses are written

$$\begin{aligned} H_0 &: \mu = \mu_0 \\ H_1 &: \mu \neq \mu_0. \end{aligned} \tag{2.123}$$

This is called a **twosided test** (see however problem 2.3/3b).

As a test statistic (step 3) we could choose the sample average $\bar{X}_n$, which, according to (2.72), is an unbiased estimator of μ. Under the null hypothesis H_0 we know that

$$\bar{X}_n \sim no\left(\mu_0; \frac{\sigma^2}{n}\right) \tag{2.124}$$

with $\mu_0 = 500$ and $\sigma^2 = 2.25$. Let the sample size be given by $n = 25$. Since we would prefer to directly work with the tables of the standard normal distribution, it is of advantage to choose instead of $\bar{X}_n$ the standardized test statistic $Z = \sqrt{n}(\bar{X}_n - \mu)/\sigma$ introduced in (2.102) instead of $\bar{X}_n$. Under H_0 this test statistic has a standard normal distribution. This is, strictly speaking, only true as long as the sample is taken with replacement. However, if the population size is sufficiently large one can assume in good approximation, even in the case of sampling without replacement, that the test statistic Z has a standard normal distribution under H_0.

In the next step (step 4) we are choosing the significance level α of the test. This means that we are limiting the probability of wrongly rejecting H_0 (producer's risk). We know that the test statistic Z has a standard normal distribution under H_0, and this tells us that, in the case that H_0 is true, its realizations lie with probability $1 - \alpha$ in the interval $[-z_{1-\alpha/2}; z_{1-\alpha/2}]$, according to (2.59c). This determines the rejection region of the test to be the union of the two open intervals:

$$CR = (-\infty; -z_{1-\alpha/2}) \cup (z_{1-\alpha/2}; \infty). \qquad (2.125)$$

If we specify $\alpha = 0.01$, for example, then we get from table 5.2/1 that

$$CR \approx (-\infty; -2.576) \cup (2.576; \infty).$$

The decision rule thus determines to reject H_0 if the realization of Z lies in the set CR. Suppose that the observed sample had a sample average of $\bar{x}_n = 499.28$. Then the test statistic takes the value

$$z = \frac{499.28 - 500}{1.5} \cdot \sqrt{25} = -2.4.$$

The result tells us that there is not sufficient evidence against H_0 and that rejection of H_0 is therefore not justified. With acceptance of H_0, the probability of a type II error cannot be determined directly. If the true value of μ were known, then we would be able to calculate this probability.

Example 2.3/2: Test on the fraction of nonconforming work pieces

A machine M_1 has so far produced work pieces with a fraction nonconforming $P_0 = 0.2$. It is planned to replace this machine by a new machine M_2. Of the latter it is assumed that it produces output of better quality. In a test run at the site of the manufacturer of the machine M_2, a random sample of $n = 30$ work pieces is taken. With this sample, one intends to test whether the unknown fraction nonconforming P of the Bernoulli distributed population (i.e., work pieces produced by M_2 within a certain time interval) is less than 0.2. In order to statistically ascertain the conjecture $P < 0.2$ one consequently chooses $P < 0.2$ to be the alternative hypothesis. The two hypotheses of the test are thus given by

$$\begin{aligned} H_0 &: P \geq P_0 \\ H_1 &: P < P_0 \end{aligned} \tag{2.126}$$

with $P_0 = 0.2$. The test statistic is chosen to be the discrete variable

$$X_n^T := \sum_{i=1}^{n} X_i; \; X_i := \begin{cases} 0, \text{ if } i\text{-th work piece is conforming} \\ 1, \text{ if } i\text{-th work piece is nonconforming} \end{cases} \tag{2.127}$$

which counts the number of nonconforming elements in a sample of size $n = 30$. If the sample is taken *without* replacement, then the test statistic (2.127) has a hypergeometric distribution, and in the case of sampling *with* replacement, it has a binomial distribution. However, because the above hypothesis concerns the parameter P of a population with unknown, but large, size, we can assume that the conditions for a binomial approximation of the hypergeometric distribution are satisfied. Consequently we can consider the variable X_n^T to be approximately $bi(P;n)$-distributed. In the case of $P = 0.2$ and $n = 30$, we have, in particular, that $X_n^T \sim bi(0.2;30)$.

The smaller the value of the test statistic, the more evidence it gives against H_0 and for H_1. Because of this we will choose the rejection region to be of the form

$$CR = \{0, 1, 2, \ldots, c\} \tag{2.128}$$

and require that

$$\begin{aligned} &\sup_{P \geq P_0} Pr(X_n^T \leq c|P) \leq \alpha \\ &\sup_{P \geq P_0} Pr(X_n^T \leq c+1|P) > \alpha \end{aligned} \tag{2.129}$$

with $P_0 = 0.2$ and the given significance level $\alpha = 0.05$. As we can see from table 5.1/3, the distribution function $Bi(c|P;n) = Pr(X_n^T \leq c|P)$ for $n = 30$ and fixed c is a monotone decreasing function of P. This implies that the supremum over P will be attained at the left side of the interval [0.2,1]. Consequently, one will specify the parameters of the binomial distribution to be $n = 30$ and $P = 0.2$ and determine the value of the realization c such that

$$\sum_{k=0}^{c} bi(k|0.2;30) = Bi(c|0.2;30) \leq \alpha = 0.05$$

and

$$\sum_{k=0}^{c+1} bi(k|0.2;30) = Bi(c+1|0.2;30) > \alpha = 0.05.$$

The result is obtained from table 5.1/3, with $n = 30$ and $P = 0.2$:

$$Bi(2|0.2; 30) \approx 0.0442 < 0.05$$

$$Bi(3|0.2; 30) \approx 0.1277 > 0.05.$$

This determines that $c = 2$ and hence that the rejection region is $CR = \{0, 1, 2\}$. The null hypothesis is thereby rejected if two or less nonconforming units are observed in the sample. In this case, one has strong statistical evidence in favour of the hypothesis H_1, i.e., that machine M_2 has a lower fraction nonconforming than M_1 and one will go ahead and replace M_1 by M_2.

If more than two nonconforming units are observed ($X_n^T > 2$), then one will decide to keep the old machine M_1. How the probability of a type II error can be calculated in this case will be discussed in the next section.

Problem 2.3/3

a) We assumed in example 2.3/1 that the filling volume X satisfies $X \sim no(\mu; \sigma^2)$, with known variance σ^2. Which test statistic has to be used instead of $Z = \sqrt{n}\,(\bar{X}_n - \mu)/\sigma$, when σ is unknown? What is the rejection region CR of H_0 in this case?

b) In example 2.3/1 we further assumed that the brewery is interested in deviations below as well as above the nominal value $\mu_0 = 500$. A consumer protection organization or a federal inspector would, however, only be interested in testing whether the expectation $\mu = E(X)$ lies significantly below the nominal value. How would the alternative hypothesis H_1 be formulated in this case? What would the form of the CR now be? Would a test in the case of $\bar{x}_{25} = 499.28$ and $\alpha = 0.01$ still result in acceptance of H_0?

c) How do we need to write (2.125), if, instead of standardizing, we would directly take $\bar{X}_n$ to be the test statistic?

Problem 2.3/4

On a certain plant site, the number of breakdowns of a machine per month is, based on past experience, known to be Poisson distributed with parameter $\lambda = 12$. Last month 20 stand stills were recorded. Perform a hypothesis test with $\alpha = 0.05$ to investigate whether the empirical value $\lambda = 12$ is reasonable for this last month.

c) Power Function, Operating Characteristic Function and OC Percentiles

When we are determining the rejection region CR of a parameter test, we need to take two things into account. First, the maximal probability of the type I error (wrongly rejecting H_0) should not be above the specified significance level α. The second point is that the probability of a type II error (wrongly accepting H_0) should be as small as possible. The probabilities of these two errors can be read of the graphs of either the power function or the operating characteristic function of the test. We will illustrate this with the fairly general hypothesis (2.121) of a parameter test.

The **power function** of the parameter test with hypotheses (2.121) is defined to be the function

$$\begin{aligned} G(\Theta) &:= Pr[g(\mathbf{X}) \in CR|\Theta] \\ &= Pr[\text{test statistic } g(\mathbf{X}) \text{ falls into the rejection} \\ &\quad \text{region } CR \text{ given that the parameter value is } \Theta]. \end{aligned} \tag{2.130}$$

The power function describes the relationship between the probability of rejecting H_0 and the unknown parameter Θ of this hypothesis. In order to calculate $G(\Theta)$ we need to know the distribution of $g(\mathbf{X})$ for every element Θ of Ω_0 and Ω_1 (the range of validity of Ω_0 and Ω_1 respectively), in other words over the whole parameter space Ω.

Interpretation of the graph of the power function

It follows that the parameter test (2.121) is a hypothesis test with significance level α, if and only if its power function satisfies

$$\sup_{\Theta\in\Omega_0} G(\Theta) = \alpha$$

i.e., if the smallest upper bound of the values of the power function over the range Ω_0 is α. In the special case when Ω_0 only contains a single point Θ_0 (point hypothesis $H_0 : \Theta = \Theta_0$) a continuous test statistic must satisfy $G(\Theta_0) = \alpha$. The graph of the power function, the power curve, not only gives us the maximal probability of committing a type I error (the significance level), but also all the other probabilities of committing a type I error for each value $\Theta \in \Omega_0$ as well. In the case of $\Theta \in \Omega_0$ the rejection of H_0 is a type I error and consequently its probability is directly given by $G(\Theta)$:

$$\Theta \in \Omega_0 \Rightarrow \begin{cases} G(\Theta) \text{ is the probability of the type I error} \\ \text{related to } \Theta. \end{cases} \tag{2.131 a}$$

In a similar way we can obtain the corresponding β-probabilities from the values of the power function over the range Ω_1. In the case of $\Theta \in \Omega_1$ the acceptance of H_0 is a type II error and it occurs with probability $1 - G(\Theta)$:

$$\Theta \in \Omega_1 \Rightarrow \begin{cases} 1-G(\Theta) \text{ is the probability of the type II error} \\ \text{related to } \Theta. \end{cases} \quad (2.131\text{ b})$$

If one knows the power function of a test, one knows the probability of rejecting H_0 for all values of the parameter space Ω. In statistical process control the power curve is called the **intervention line**. For evaluating the parameter test (2.121) one can instead of (2.130) also use the function, that describes the relationship between the **acceptance probability** of H_0 and the unknown parameter Θ. This function $L(\Theta)$ is called the **operating characteristic function** or simply **OC function**:

$$\begin{aligned} L(\Theta) &:= Pr[g(\mathbf{X}) \in \overline{CR}|\Theta] \\ &= Pr[\text{test statistic } g(\mathbf{X}) \text{ falls into the acceptance region } \overline{CR} \text{ given that the parameter value is } \Theta]. \end{aligned} \quad (2.132)$$

Since H_0 is either accepted or rejected, the probabilities of acceptance and rejection add up to one, and we get

$$L(\Theta) = 1 - G(\Theta). \quad (2.133)$$

Interpreting the OC curve

The graph of the OC function, the so-called **OC curve**, can be equally used to obtain the probabilities of wrongly rejecting or accepting H_0. It follows directly from (2.131a,b) and (2.132) that

$$\Theta \in \Omega_0 \Rightarrow \begin{cases} 1-L(\Theta) \text{ is the probability of the type I error} \\ \text{related to } \Theta. \end{cases} \quad (2.134\text{ a})$$

$$\Theta \in \Omega_1 \Rightarrow \begin{cases} L(\Theta) \text{ is the probability of the type II error} \\ \text{related to } \Theta. \end{cases} \quad (2.134\text{ b})$$

The power function and the OC function are equivalent in the sense that each of them completely describes the acceptance and rejection behaviour of a test procedure. One is free to choose whichever function one prefers. Traditionally one works with $L(\Theta)$ in acceptance control and with $G(\Theta)$ in process control.

Definition and characterisation of an ideal test

What are the general characteristics that we would like to see in a power function or an OC function? For $\Theta \in \Omega_0$, i.e. over Ω_0 where H_0 is true, we would like the power function $G(\Theta)$ to have small values or respectively the OC function $L(\Theta)$ to take on large values. Whereas for $\Theta \in \Omega_1$, i.e. over Ω_1 which is the range of validity of H_1, the power function $G(\Theta)$ should be high or respectively the OC curve $L(\Theta)$ should be low. In between we would like both curves to be as steep as possible. The ideal OC curve would be the graph of the function

$$L(\Theta) = \begin{cases} 1 & \text{for } \Theta \in H_0 \\ 0 & \text{for } \Theta \in H_1 \end{cases} \quad (2.135\text{ a})$$

which is called the **ideal OC function**. We can see that the ideal OC function is a step function with a jump at the endpoint of the range of validity of H_0. In the same way the **ideal power function** is given by

$$G(\Theta) = \begin{cases} 0 & \text{for } \Theta \in H_0 \\ 1 & \text{for } \Theta \in H_1. \end{cases} \qquad (2.135\text{ b})$$

A parameter test is called an **ideal test** if its OC function is given by (2.135a) or respectively its power function by (2.135b). Thus an ideal test is a test for which the probabilities of committing either a type I or a type II error are both zero.

If we know the OC function $y = L(\Theta)$ of a parameter test, then we can calculate the probability of accepting H_0 for each Θ. In SQA one is, however, frequently interested in the reverse question: How can one determine the value of the parameter Θ_ω for a given acceptance probability $y = \omega$? This question can be answered with the help of the inverse

$$\Theta = L^{-1}(y)$$

of the OC function. It is called the **percentile function of the OC function** $L(\Theta)$. For a given ω it gives the corresponding OC percentile Θ_ω of order ω. In analogy to (2.6) it holds that

Percentile function and percentiles of an OC function

$$\left.\begin{array}{l}\Theta_\omega \text{ is the } 100 \cdot \omega\% \text{ percentile of} \\ \text{the operating characteristic } L(\Theta)\end{array}\right\} \Leftrightarrow L(\Theta_\omega) = \omega. \qquad (2.136)$$

Determination of OC percentiles

An OC percentile Θ_ω is either determined numerically through substitution of $y = \omega$ into the OC percentile function $\Theta = L^{-1}(y)$ or graphically by reading Θ_ω from the OC curve. In the graphical method the percentile Θ_ω is the value on the abscissa that corresponds to the value of ω on the ordinate axis (see figure 5.2/1).

Special OC percentiles

If Θ denotes a quality parameter (i.e. the fraction nonconforming P), then in acceptance control there are special notations for selected OC percentiles. The particular (bad) level of quality Θ_ω of a lot for which a relatively low acceptance probability ω (usually $\omega = 0.1$) for protection of the consumer was agreed upon between the two parties, is called the **rejectable quality level** or **lot tolerance per cent defective** and abbreviated by **RQL** or **LTPD**. The particular (good) level of quality Θ_ω of a lot for which a relatively high acceptance probability of ω (usually $\omega = 0.99$) was aggreed upon between consumer and producer for the protection of the producer, is called the **acceptable quality level** and abbreviated by **AQL**. Finally, one calls the value $\Theta_{0.5}$ in acceptance sampling the **indifferent quality level** or **IQL**. The IQL value is the median of the OC function. We will discuss these terms in more detail in sec. 3.2.2.a.

Problem 2.3/5

The run length of a yarn is assumed to approximately have a normal distribution with average run length $\mu = E(X)$ and standard deviation $\sigma = 120\ m$. In a sample of $n = 25$ randomly selected rolls of yarn a sample average of 1560 m was observed.

a) Test $H_0 : \mu = 1600$ against $H_1 : \mu \neq 1600$ at a level of $\alpha = 0.05$.

b) What is the probability of a type II error, given that $\mu = 1620$ or $\mu = 1570$, respectively.

d) Derivation of the Power Function for two Tests

We want to determine the power function $G(P)$ for the test (2.126) of example 2.3/2 (inspection of the fraction of nonconforming work pieces) with $P_0 = 0.2$ and sketch its curve. After this we will interchange the hypotheses H_0 and H_1 in (2.126) and derive the power function of this new test.

Test 1 and its power function

First, we will consider the hypothesis test (2.126). The test statistic of example 2.3/2 was at least approximately binomially distributed with unknown parameter P and $n = 30$. Recall that the rejection region was found to be of form $CR = \{0, 1, 2\}$. With help of (2.93) we can represent the power function by

$$G(P) = \sum_{k=0}^{2} bi(k|P;30) = Bi(2|P;30). \tag{2.137}$$

Figure 2.3/3 shows the curve of $G(P)$. The values tabulated to the right of the graph can be found in table 5.1/3 under $n = 30$ with rounding to four decimal points.

For any fraction nonconforming $P \in \Omega$ we can, by (2.131a,b), read the values of the type I and II errors from the graph. We can also determine the maximal values of the two error probabilities. Let us first derive the type I error. It can only happen over the interval $\Omega_0 = [0.2, 1]$. For each $P \in \Omega_0$ the corresponding probability of a type I error is given by $G(P)$. Since $G(P)$ is strictly monotone decreasing over the interval Ω_0, its supremum is attained at the endpoint $P = 0.2$ and has the value $G(0.2) = 0.0442$. Thus $\alpha = 0.05$ determines (2.122b) to be

$$\alpha = 0.05 > G(0.2) = 0.0442.$$

Interpretation of the result

In this particular application, where the question is whether machine M_1 should be replaced by a new machine M_2, this implies the following: If

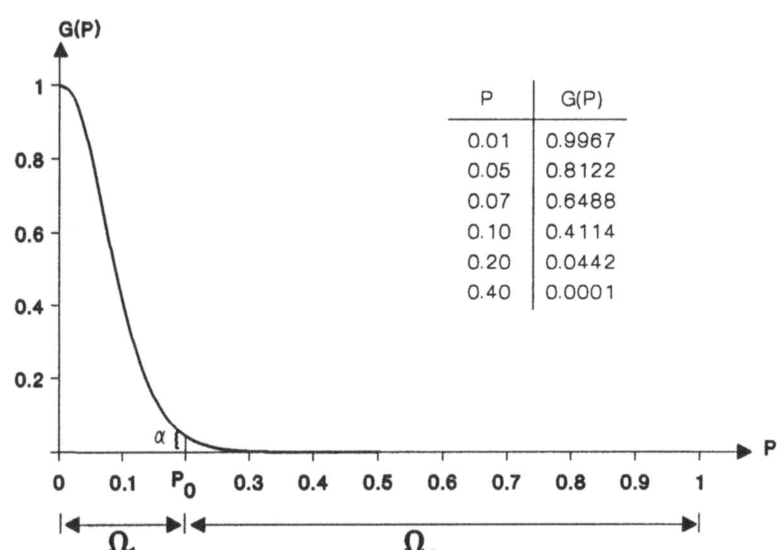

P	G(P)
0.01	0.9967
0.05	0.8122
0.07	0.6488
0.10	0.4114
0.20	0.0442
0.40	0.0001

Figure 2.3/3: Power curve of a test of $H_0 : P \geq P_0$ versus $H_1 : P < P_0$

machine M_2 produces an unknown fraction nonconforming P, that is at least as big as that of machine M_1, then the above test will decide to introduce this worse machine only with a probability of 0.0442.

The probability of committing a type II error is given for every $P \in \Omega_1$ by $L(P) = 1 - G(P)$. This value is largest as P approaches the endpoint $P = 0.2$, which is however not included in the half open interval $\Omega_1 = [0, 0.2)$. But we can argue that the probability of a type II error (wrongly rejecting H_0) can still be as much as $L(0.2) = 0.9558$, because for sufficiently small $\epsilon > 0$ it holds that $G(0.2 - \epsilon) \approx G(0.2) = 0.0442$ and consequently $L(0.2 - \epsilon) \approx L(0.2) = 0.9558$. This is a relatively high chance of keeping the old machine, even though the new machine M_2 is better in the sense of having a lower fraction nonconforming.

The above discussion illustrated that the chosen test procedure is only recommendable if the company primarily wants to control the risk of introducing a new, often more expensive machine M_2 with a higher fraction nonconforming than the old one. Then this risk of the test (2.126) is at most $G(0.2) = 0.0442$. The approach of (2.126) can however not be justified, if the company is primarily concerned about controlling the risk of keeping an old worse machine M_1. In this case we should test the hypotheses

Test 2 and its power function

$$\begin{aligned} H_0 &: P \leq P_0 \\ H_1 &: P > P_0 \end{aligned} \tag{2.138}$$

with $P_0 = 0.2$ and $\alpha = 0.05$. In this new test of the hypotheses (2.138) one will keep the old machine if the test rejects the null hypothesis H_0. The larger the value of X_n^T, the more evidence it gives in favour of H_1 and against H_0. Hence the rejection region is of form

$$CR = \{d, d+1, \ldots, n\} \tag{2.139}$$

with $n = 30$. Instead of (2.129) we now need to require

$$\begin{aligned} \sup_{P \leq P_0} P(X_n^T \geq d|P) &\leq \alpha \\ \sup_{P \leq P_0} P(X_n^T \geq d-1|P) &> \alpha \end{aligned} \tag{2.140}$$

with $P_0 = 0.2$ and $\alpha = 0.05$. The statistic X_n^T has a binomial distribution with the parameters P and n and the probability $Pr(X_n^T \geq d|P)$ is, for constant d, a monotone increasing function of P. From this it follows that the supremum is obtained at $P = 0.2$. The desired value is required to satisfy simultaneously the two equations

$$\begin{aligned} \sum_{k=d}^{n} bi(k|0.2;30) &= 1 - Bi(d-1|0.2;30) \leq 0.05 \\ \sum_{k=d-1}^{n} bi(k|0.2;30) &= 1 - Bi(d-2|0.2;30) > 0.05. \end{aligned} \tag{2.141}$$

From table 5.1/3 we get, for $n = 30$ and $P = 0.2$:

$$\begin{aligned} \sum_{k=11}^{30} bi(k|0.2;30) &\approx 1 - 0.9744 = 0.0256 < 0.05 \\ \sum_{k=10}^{30} bi(k|0.2;30) &\approx 1 - 0.9389 = 0.0611 > 0.05. \end{aligned}$$

This determines the rejection region to be $CR = \{11, 12, \ldots, 30\}$. If among the $n = 30$ inspected work pieces 11 or more are found to be nonconforming to specifications, then H_0 will be rejected and the old machine M_1 will be kept.

The power function of this test is given by

$$G(P) = \sum_{k=11}^{30} bi(k|P;30) = 1 - Bi(10|P;30). \tag{2.142}$$

The following figure shows the curve of $G(P)$. The tabulated values on the right can again be verified with table 5.1/3.

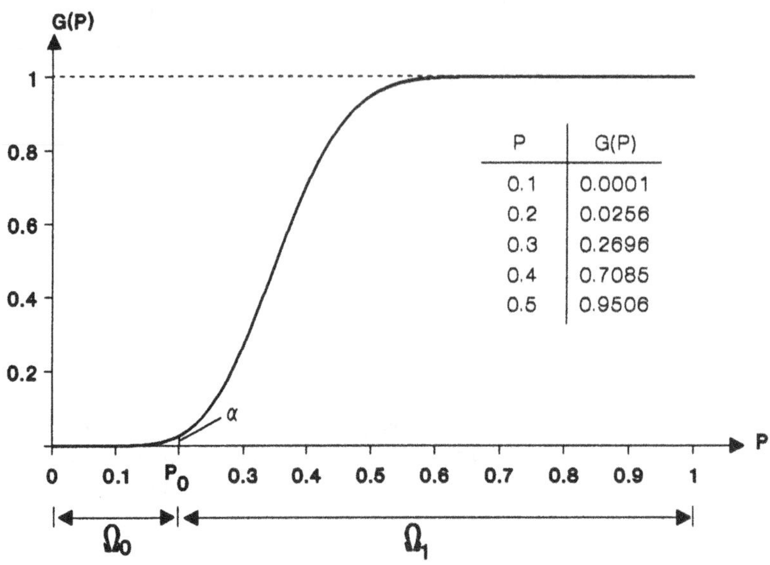

Figure 2.3/4: Power curve of a test of $H_0 : P \leq P_0$ against $H_1 : P > P_0$

Interpretation of the result

The type I error now corresponds to the decision to keep the old machine M_1 in the case that the fraction nonconforming of the new machine M_2 is at least as low as the fraction nonconforming $P_0 = 0.2$ of M_1. This error is committed with a probability of at most $G(0.2) = 0.0256$. The probability of introducing the new machine M_2 in the case of $P > P_0$ (type II error), which was kept under control as the type I error in the test of (2.126), can now be as high as $L(0.2) = 0.9744$. We see that the approach of the hypotheses (2.138) is apparently not recommendable, if the primary concern is to control the risk of a misinvestment (purchase of a new, but worse machine).

Problem 2.3/6

Test $H_0 : P \leq 0.5$ against $H_1 : P > 0.5$ with a sample of size $n = 3$ (sampling *with* replacement from a Bernoulli distributed population). Let X_n^T of (2.127) be the test statistic and reject H_0 for $X_n^T \geq 2$.

a) Determine the power function and the OC function of the test.

b) What are the maximal probabilities of a type I and type II error?

c) Find the power function of the test for the more realistic case of sampling *without* replacement. Assume that $N = 10$.

Problem 2.3/7

Design a significance test for $H_0 : P \geq 0.6$ with the approximately normally distributed test statistic $\Pi := X_n^T/n$ (proportion of "successes" in the sample) in such a way that $G(0.5) = 0.9$ and $G(0.64) = 0.001$.

a) Determine the sample size n and the rejection region CR of the test.

b) What is the significance level of the test?

e) Slope and Elasticity

We already mentioned that it is desirable to have the power curve or OC curve as steep as possible. The larger the slope of the OC curve the smaller are the probabilities of the type I and type II error. We say the test gains more **discriminatory power**. The more discriminatory power a test has, the smaller is the range of values in the parameter space, where the probabilities of type I and II errors cannot be neglected. It is only in an ideal test that these error probabilities are always zero. In a non-ideal test the range of values with high probabilities for the type I or type II errors becomes smaller as the steepness of the slope of the power or OC function increases. We can see from figure 2.3/4 and its table that for the test (2.138) with $P_0 = 0.2$ the probability of committing a type II error in the case of $P = 0.4$ is given by $1 - 0.7085$. If the curve $y = G(P)$ in figure 2.3/4 were steeper, then that would reduce this error probability. Of two curves of the type given by the figures 2.3/3 and 2.3/4 (strictly monotone increasing or decreasing curve with turning point), we find that the one with the larger slope (in terms of absolute values) at the turning point is the steeper curve.

The above discussion described how we can use the absolute value of the slope at the turning point as a **measure for the discriminatory power** of a test, provided that its power and OC function have a turning point. It is easily seen that the absolute value of the slope of the OC function and power function are the same, but that their signs are different.

Measuring the discriminatory power of a test

The slope at the turning point is also called **steepness**. In general, the IQL value is a good approximation of the turning point of the OC function. Thus we can approximate the steepness of a test by calculating the slope of its OC function at the indifference point. Instead of the absolute value of the steepness we then use the slope at the indifference point as an **approximate measure for the discriminatory power** of a test.

But how can we determine the slope and steepness of the OC function of a non-ideal test? If the OC function is defined over a real interval and if it is differentiable, then the slope is obtained by differentiation. The steepness, in this case, is given by the value of the first derivative at the turning point.

Slope and steepness of the OC function (discrete and continuous case)

For a differentiable OC function $y = L(P)$ with turning point $P = P_T$ and slope given by

$$m(P) := \frac{dL(P)}{dP} \tag{2.143}$$

the steepness is defined by

$$h := m(P_T). \tag{2.144}$$

For an OC function with a discrete argument variable a slope is strictly speaking not defined. However we can help ourselves by defining an auxiliary slope through joining the discrete points of the graph of the OC function by straight lines and interpreting the slopes of these pieces to be the slope at the individual points of the range (see figure 3.2/9). The point with the largest absolute slope is then considered to be the turning point.

We can illustrate this approach using the test (2.138) with $P_0 = 0.2$ and significance level $\alpha = 0.05$. We will first choose the sample size to be $n_1 = 30$ (test 1) and in the second case to be $n_2 = 100$ (test 2). The power function of test 1 is already determined by (2.142). Thus the OC function of test 1 is of form

$$L_1(P) = Bi(10|P; 30).$$

If we replace n in equation (2.141) by $n_2 = 100$ instead of $n_1 = 30$, then the rejection region is given by $CR = \{28, 29, \ldots, 100\}$. This implies that the OC function of test 2 results to be

$$L_2(P) = Bi(27|P; 100).$$

Figure 2.3/5 shows both OC curves. The OC curves were again constructed with the help of table 5.1/3.

Interpreting the OC curve

By just looking at the graphs we can immediately draw conclusions about the occurrence of type I and type II errors:

- If $P \leq P_0$ holds, i.e., if H_0 is true, then we would like to decide in favour of H_1, that is, to reject H_0. For both tests, the probability of wrongly rejecting H_0 (type I error) is, according to the design of the test, smaller than $\alpha = 0.05$ for all $P \in \Omega_0$. Because the quantity d in (2.139) is integer valued, the given significance level can only be satisfied approximately. The effective significance level of test 1 is $\alpha_1 = G_1(0.2) \approx 0.0256$ and $\alpha_2 = G_2(0.2) \approx 0.0341$ for test 2.

- If $P > P_0$ holds, i.e., if H_0 is not true, then we would prefer to decide against acceptance of H_0. We can see from the graphs that the probability of wrongly accepting H_0 (type II error) of test 2 is smaller than that of test 1 for all $P \in \Omega_1$, because the OC curve of test 2 lies below that of test 1 over the whole range of Ω_1.

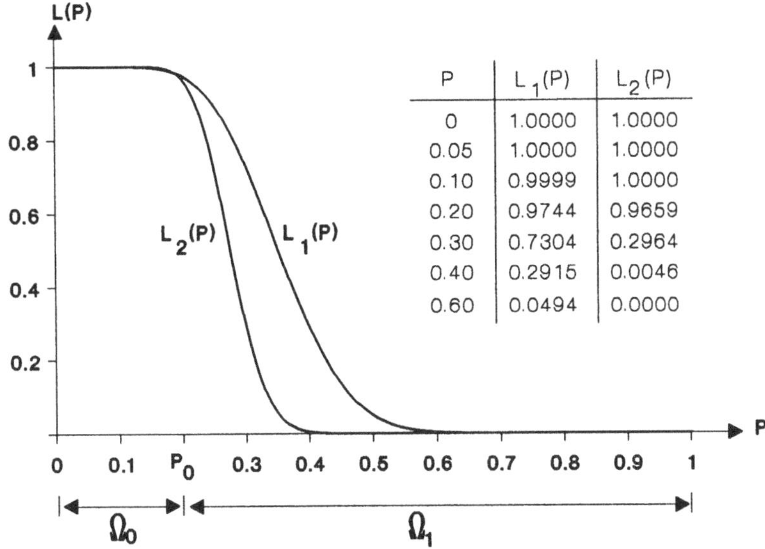

P	$L_1(P)$	$L_2(P)$
0	1.0000	1.0000
0.05	1.0000	1.0000
0.10	0.9999	1.0000
0.20	0.9744	0.9659
0.30	0.7304	0.2964
0.40	0.2915	0.0046
0.60	0.0494	0.0000

Figure 2.3/5: OC curves of two tests of $H_0 : P \leq P_0$ against $H_1 : P > P_0$ (test 1: $n_1 = 30$ and test 2: $n_2 = 100$)

We can conclude from the steeper course of $L_2(P)$ that test 2 has a greater discriminatory power. In general, it holds that the discriminatory power of a test can be improved by increasing the sample size n. If we increase n up to the size N of the finite lot (100% control) then we will get an ideal OC curve.

For both OC curves of figure 2.3/5 we can calculate the turning points P_{T_1} and P_{T_2} and the IQL values $P_{0.5_1}$ and $P_{0.5_2}$ and also the four corresponding slopes h_1, h_2, k_1 and k_2 respectively. We will omit the calculations (see (3/29a), (3/30a) and (3/40)) and only present the results:

$$P_{T_1} = \frac{10}{29} \approx 0.3448; \qquad P_{T_2} = \frac{27}{99} \approx 0.2727$$

$$P_{0.5_1} \approx \frac{10 + \frac{2}{3}}{30 + \frac{1}{3}} \approx 0.3516; \qquad P_{0.5_2} \approx \frac{27 + \frac{2}{3}}{100 + \frac{1}{3}} \approx 0.2757$$

$$\begin{aligned} h_1 &:= m_1(P_{T_1}) \approx -4.6300 & h_2 &:= m_2(P_{T_2}) \approx -8.9723 \\ k_1 &:= m_1(P_{0.5_1}) \approx -4.6165 & k_2 &:= m_2(P_{0.5_2}) \approx -8.9726. \end{aligned}$$

On the one hand these results verify analytically that, since $|h_2| > |h_1|$, test 2 has a larger steepness and hence greater discriminatory power. On the other hand, the results show that the turning points are approximated relatively well by the IQL values. As a consequence of this a comparison of the discriminatory power via the IQL values leads to the same conclusion, since $|k_2| > |k_1|$.

If the slope $m(P)$ of the OC function $y = L(P)$ is known, then we can determine at least approximately what size of change in the *absolute* value of $L(P)$ to expect when P is varied by a small amount ΔP. Provided the change in ΔP is small, the change

$$\Delta L(P) := L(P + \Delta P) - L(P)$$

that is effected by ΔP is approximately given by

$$\frac{\Delta L(P)}{\Delta P} \approx \frac{dL(P)}{dP} = m(P). \tag{2.145}$$

Definiton and explanation of the elasticity concept

Conclusions about these *relative* changes can be drawn with the help of the **elasticity** of the OC function $y = L(P)$. It is defined by

$$\varepsilon(P) := \frac{P}{L(P)} \cdot \frac{dL(P)}{dP} = \frac{P}{L(P)} \cdot m(P). \tag{2.146}$$

If we substitute the approximation (2.145) into (2.146) we get

$$\varepsilon(P) \approx \frac{P}{L(P)} \cdot \frac{\Delta L(P)}{\Delta P} = \frac{\Delta L(P)/L(P)}{\Delta P/P}. \tag{2.147}$$

Expression (2.147) illustrates that with the elasticity we are able to give an approximate value for the percent of change in $L(P)$, that occurs when P is increased by a small percentage. For example if $\varepsilon(P) = -3$, then this implies that, under an 1% increase in P, the original acceptance probability $L(P)$ is decreased by about 3%:

$$-3 \approx \frac{\Delta L(P)/L(P)}{0.01P/P} \Rightarrow \Delta L(P) \approx -0.03 \cdot L(P).$$

Problem 2.3/8

a) For the OC function $L_1(P)$ of figure 2.3/5 determine the OC percentiles P_ω for $\omega = 0.1, 0.5$ and 0.975 through reading them from the OC curve (graphical method; see figure 5.2/1).

b) Find the determining equation of the above OC percentiles.

2.3.3 Sequential Tests

We already described the different steps of testing the hypothesis $H_0 : \Theta \in \Omega_0$ against $H_1 : \Theta \in \Omega_1$. In this test the probability of committing a type I error was controlled by the significance level α. As we showed in sec. 2.3.2d the probability of the occurrence of a type II error can then be determined for every $\Theta \in \Omega_1$ given the sample size n.

An alternative approach would be to fix the upper limits α and β of *both* error probabilities and to work with a variable sample size. In practice this is done by successively increasing the sample size by one unit and at each step determining if the observed information is sufficient for a decision or whether one needs to continue sampling. Such tests, where the sample size and the number of steps until a final decision is reached are not known *a priori*, are called **sequential tests**. When administering a sequential test a significantly smaller sample size is usually needed than in the case of a comparable non-sequential test. In order to sketch an outline of the theory of sequential tests we will discuss a special case of (2.121), i.e., the test of the hypotheses $H_0 : \Theta = \Theta_0$ against $H_1 : \Theta = \Theta_1$. After this we will apply this theory first to a binomially and then to a normally distributed population. In the presentation of **sequential plans** in section 3.2.6 we will return to the application that was mentioned first and in section 4.6.2 about **cusum charts** we will come back to the latter.

a) The Likelihood Ratio Test (LR Test)

Let X be a stochastic variable and let its distribution within a population depend on the parameter Θ. Further, let the distribution of X be given by the massfunction $f(x|\Theta) = Pr(X = x)$ in the discrete case or by the density $f(x|\Theta) = dF(x|\Theta)/dx$ in the continuous case. For didactical reasons, we will assume that Θ can only have the values Θ_0 and Θ_1. We want to test the hypotheses:

$$\begin{aligned} H_0 &: \Theta = \Theta_0 \\ H_1 &: \Theta = \Theta_1. \end{aligned} \tag{2.148}$$

If a sample $\mathbf{x} = (x_1, \ldots, x_n)$ is taken from the population with replacement, then

$$L_n(\mathbf{x}|\Theta) := f(x_1|\Theta) \cdot f(x_2|\Theta) \ldots f(x_n|\Theta) \tag{2.149}$$

is called the **likelihood function** of the sample. The term likelihood function comes from the fact, that in the case of a discrete X, (2.149) is just the probability or likelihood $Pr(\mathbf{X} = \mathbf{x})$ of observing the realization $\mathbf{x} = (x_1, \ldots, x_n)$ of the vector $\mathbf{X}$ of sample elements (2.63a).

NEYMAN/PEARSON (1928) have chosen the **likelihood ratio**

$$LR_n := \frac{L_n(\mathbf{x}|\Theta_1)}{L_n(\mathbf{x}|\Theta_0)} = \frac{f(x_1|\Theta_1)\cdot f(x_2|\Theta_1)\ldots f(x_n|\Theta_1)}{f(x_1|\Theta_0)\cdot f(x_2|\Theta_0)\ldots f(x_n|\Theta_0)} \tag{2.150}$$

Interpretation of the likelihood ratio and definition of the *LR* test

to be the test statistic of the test (2.148). This ratio **LR** is a measure, which compares the evidence in favour of both hypotheses. A value much bigger than one speaks in favour of H_1 and a very small value below one in favour of H_0. A test using this test statistic is called the **likelihood ratio test** or simply the **LR test**. The classical *LR* test by NEYMAN and PEARSON works in the same way as described in sec. 2.3.1b. It specifies a sample size n and a critical value C before applying the test. In analogy to the discussion in sec. 2.3.2a one could equivalently specify n and α and determine the rejection boundary C for this specification. In both approaches one can then also calculate the probability of committing a type II error.

LR tests according to NEYMAN/PEARSON and WALD

The **sequential LR test** proposed by WALD (1947) works with two critical values A and B with $A < 1 < B$ and a variable sample size. The basic idea behind the test is immediately obvious: One keeps on testing as long as $LR_n \in (A, B)$, i.e., as long as the plausibility measure LR is not too far away from 1. In the case of the event $LR_n \leq A$ one decides in favour of H_0 and in the case of $LR_n \geq B$ in favour of H_1. In practice, it is common to specify the upper limits α and β for the error probabilities of the test and then to determine the critical values A and B based on these specifications. It can be shown that a choice of A and B with $A \geq \beta/(1-\alpha)$ and $B \leq (1-\beta)/\alpha$ ensures that the probabilities of type I and type II errors do not exceed the specified limits α and β. In practice one chooses

Determining the critical values of a sequential test

$$A := \frac{\beta}{1-\alpha}; \qquad B := \frac{1-\beta}{\alpha} \tag{2.151 a,b}$$

b) Sequential LR Test for a Bernoulli Distributed Population

We will first apply the *LR* test to the case of a dichotomous quality characteristic with the realizations "conforming" and "nonconforming" in a finite-sized population. This is a Bernoulli distributed population and we are considering the case of an unknown fraction nonconforming P. In order to keep things simple, we will first assume that P can only take the values P_0 and P_1. We are testing

$$\begin{aligned} H_0 &: P = P_0 \\ H_1 &: P = P_1 \end{aligned} \tag{2.152}$$

with $P_1 > P_0$ and given error probabilities α and β. If a sample of size n is taken *with* replacement from the population (for sufficiently large lot size, this also holds approximately in the case of sampling *without* replacement), then the probability $Pr(\mathbf{X} = \mathbf{x})$, that a particular realization $\mathbf{x} = (x_1, \ldots, x_n)$ of the sample vector $\mathbf{X}$ occurs is

$$L_n(\mathbf{x}|P) = P^k \cdot (1-P)^{n-k}.$$

The quantity k denotes the number of nonconforming units in the sample. The LR ratio (2.150) results as

$$LR_n = \frac{P_1^k(1-P_1)^{n-k}}{P_0^k(1-P_0)^{n-k}}. \tag{2.153}$$

Test procedure with LR as a test statistic

We are now able to calculate A and B according to (2.151) and accept H_0 when $LR_n \leq A$, or respectively H_1 when $LR_n \geq B$. If $LR_n \in (A, B)$ then no final decision is made, but another sample unit is drawn and LR_{n+1} is calculated. In practical applications of a LR test it is more convenient to work with the equivalent condition $\ln LR_n \in (\ln A, \ln B)$ instead of $LR_n \in (A, B)$. It is easily verified that

Calculation of the logarithmic test statistic

$$\begin{aligned}
\ln LR_n &= \ln\left[\left(\frac{P_1(1-P_0)}{P_0(1-P_1)}\right)^k \cdot \left(\frac{1-P_1}{1-P_0}\right)^n\right] \\
&= k \cdot \ln\left[\frac{P_1(1-P_0)}{P_0(1-P_1)}\right] - n \cdot \ln\left(\frac{1-P_0}{1-P_1}\right).
\end{aligned}$$

The numbers a, b and c are defined to be

$$a := \frac{\ln A}{\ln\left[\dfrac{P_1(1-P_0)}{P_0(1-P_1)}\right]} = \frac{\ln[\beta/(1-\alpha)]}{\ln\left[\dfrac{P_1(1-P_0)}{P_0(1-P_1)}\right]} \tag{2.154 a}$$

$$b := \frac{\ln B}{\ln\left[\dfrac{P_1(1-P_0)}{P_0(1-P_1)}\right]} = \frac{\ln[(1-\beta)/\alpha]}{\ln\left[\dfrac{P_1(1-P_0)}{P_0(1-P_1)}\right]} \tag{2.154 b}$$

$$c := \frac{\ln\left(\dfrac{1-P_0}{1-P_1}\right)}{\ln\left[\dfrac{P_1(1-P_0)}{P_0(1-P_1)}\right]}. \tag{2.154 c}$$

For a given sample size n we can now use the parameters in (2.154) to define the interval

$$I_n := (a + cn; b + cn). \tag{2.155}$$

Then the following statements are equivalent:

$$LR_n \in (A, B) \;\Leftrightarrow\; \ln LR_n \in (\ln A, \ln B) \;\Leftrightarrow\; k \in I_n.$$

Procedure using the test statistic $\ln LR$

When applying a sequential LR test we can thus proceed as follows: Start with a sample of size $n = 1$ and the specifications P_0, P_1, α and β. Next, determine the values of the parameters in (2.154) and the resulting indifference range I_n. Accept H_0, if the realization of k, the observed number of nonconforming units, satisfies $k \leq a + cn$ and in the case of $k \geq b + cn$ decide in favour of the alternative hypothesis H_1. For $k \in I_n$ increase the sample size by one unit and repeat the procedure for this new n. The upper and lower endpoints of the indifference intervals I_n for the increasing values of n can be graphically displayed. One finds that each of the two point sequences lie on a line with the same slope c. The upper line is called the **rejection boundary**, the lower line the **acceptance boundary** and the area in between the **continuation region** (see figure 3.2/23).

The above instructions can be easily transferred to the case where, instead of the hypotheses (2.152), one considers the more relevant hypotheses

$$\begin{aligned} H_0 &: P \leq P_0 \\ H_1 &: P \geq P_1 \end{aligned} \tag{2.156}$$

with $P_1 > P_0$. However, the probabilities of committing a type I or type II error are then no longer uniquely determined. In analogy to (2.122a), the specified α now represents the supremum of the type I error probabilities over the interval $[0,P_0]$ and β the supremum of the type II error probabilities over the range $[P_1,1]$.

Remark

The preceeding discussion can, after minor modifications, also be applied to the situation when the test statistic represents the *number of nonconformities* instead of the number of nonconforming units. If this new statistic can assumed to be $po(\lambda)$-distributed, then similar to (2.156), one can test the hypotheses $H_0 : \lambda \leq \lambda_0$ against $H_1 : \lambda \geq \lambda_0$ with $\lambda_1 > \lambda_0$ for the nonconformity rate λ. The indifference interval is then determined by

$$I_n^* := (a^* + c^*n; b^* + c^*n)$$

with the parameters

$$a^* := \frac{\ln A}{\ln(\lambda_1/\lambda_0)}; \qquad b^* := \frac{\ln B}{\ln(\lambda_1/\lambda_0)}; \qquad c^* := \frac{\lambda_1 - \lambda_0}{\ln(\lambda_1/\lambda_0)},$$

where A and B are as before given by (2.151).

Problem 2.3/9

Suppose that the parameters in (2.153) are given by $P_0 = AQL = 0.02$, $P_1 = RQL = 0.06, n = 20$ and $k = 4$. For these specifications calculate the values of the likelihood ratio and interprete the result.

c) Sequential LR Test for a Normally Distributed Population

We now want to apply the sequential LR test to a population of units with an identically and independently $no(\mu;\sigma^2)$-distributed quality characteristic X. The expectation μ is unknown, while the variance σ^2 is assumed to be known. We will again simplify the situation by allowing only two possible realizations for the parameter of interest, i.e., a nominal or desired level μ_0 and an undesirable level μ_1. We are now testing the hypotheses

$$\begin{aligned} H_0 &: \mu = \mu_0 \\ H_1 &: \mu = \mu_1 := \mu_0 + \delta\sigma \end{aligned} \tag{2.157}$$

with shift parameter $\delta > 0$ and specified error probabilities α and β. Because of (2.39) the likelihood function (2.149) takes the form

$$L_n(\mathbf{x}|\mu) = \left(\frac{1}{\sigma\cdot\sqrt{2\pi}}\right)^n \cdot \exp\left[-\frac{1}{2\sigma^2}\sum_{j=1}^{n}(x_j-\mu)^2\right].$$

The likelihood ratio (2.150) results as

$$LR_n = \exp\left[\frac{1}{2\sigma^2}\left\{\sum_{j=1}^{n}(x_j-\mu_0)^2 - \sum_{j=1}^{n}(x_j-\mu_0-\delta\sigma)^2\right\}\right]. \tag{2.158}$$

Procedure in the case of applying the test statistic LR

The first step of the test is to calculate the test statistic for the initial sample size of $n = 1$ and to check whether $LR_n \leq A$, $LR_n \geq B$ or $LR_n \in (A, B)$ (with A and B from (2.151)). If the first case occurs H_0 is accepted, in the second case H_1 is accepted, and in the latter case n is increased to $n+1$ and the procedure continues.

As above, the procedure can be simplified by taking logarithms. Then the test statistic LR is transformed to

Calculation of the logarithmic test statistic

$$\begin{aligned} \ln LR_n &= \frac{1}{2\sigma^2}\left[\sum_{j=1}^{n}(x_j-\mu_0)^2 - \sum_{j=1}^{n}(x_j-\mu_0-\delta\sigma)^2\right] \\ &= \frac{1}{2\sigma^2}\left[2\delta\sigma\cdot\sum_{j=1}^{n}(x_j-\mu_0) - n\cdot(\delta\sigma)^2\right] \\ &= \delta\cdot z_n - n\cdot\frac{\delta^2}{2}. \end{aligned}$$

The variable z_n here denotes the realization of Z_n, the sum of the standardized deviations of the sample variables X_j from the expectation μ_0:

$$Z_n := \frac{1}{\sigma}\sum_{j=1}^{n}(X_j - \mu_0). \tag{2.159}$$

If we put

$$a := \frac{\ln A}{\delta} = \frac{1}{\delta}\ln\frac{\beta}{1-\alpha} \tag{2.160 a}$$

$$b := \frac{\ln B}{\delta} = \frac{1}{\delta}\ln\frac{1-\beta}{\alpha} \tag{2.160 b}$$

$$c := \frac{\delta}{2} \tag{2.160 c}$$

and calculate the interval (in analogy to (2.154))

$$I_n^+ := (a + cn; b + cn), \tag{2.161}$$

then, in the same way as before, we get the following equivalent statements:

$$LR_n \in (A; B) \;\Leftrightarrow\; \ln LR_n \in (\ln A; \ln B) \;\Leftrightarrow\; z_n \in I_n^+.$$

Sequential test procedure using the test statistic $\ln LR$

In order to administer the sequential LR test we can thus proceed as follows: We start with the initial value of $n = 1$ and the specifications $\mu_0, \mu_1, \alpha, \beta$ and determine the parameters a, b and c and as a result the indifference interval I_n^+. If the realization z_n of the test statistic Z_n satisfies $z_n \leq a + cn$ or $z_n \geq b + cn$, then H_0 or respectively H_1 is accepted and otherwise the inspection continues. If the upper and lower endpoints of the indifference interval I_n^+ are plotted in a coordinate system against $n = 1, 2, \ldots,$ then we again get two point sequences, each on a line with slope c. As before, these lines are called the **rejection boundary** or the **acceptance boundary**, respectively and the area within the **continuation region**.

The test (2.157) was only concerned with a possible positive deviation from the expected value μ_0. However, in the same way we could equally test

$$\begin{aligned} H_0 &: \mu = \mu_0 \\ H_1 &: \mu = \mu_1 := \mu_0 - \delta\sigma \end{aligned} \tag{2.162}$$

with $\delta > 0$ (test for negative shift). The indifference interval is then no longer given by $I_n^+ = (a + cn, b + cn)$, but by

$$I_n^- := (-b - cn; -a - cn) \tag{2.163}$$

with a, b and c from (2.160). The two preceeding tests can be combined to a test of the hypotheses

$$\begin{aligned} H_0 &: \mu = \mu_0 \\ H_1 &: \mu = \mu_1 = \mu_0 \pm \delta\sigma \end{aligned} \tag{2.164}$$

where H_0 is tested against a twosided point alternative. If we divide the probability of committing a type I error equally between the two possible alternatives of H_1, then the **continuation region** results as

$$I_n := (a + cn; b + cn) \cup (-b - cn; -a - cn). \tag{2.165}$$

Because α is now divided between the two alternatives of H_1 we need to replace α in (2.151) by $\alpha/2$. This implies that the parameters a and b of the indifference interval I_n are no longer given by (2.160a,b), but instead by

$$a := \frac{\ln A}{\delta} = \frac{1}{\delta}\ln\frac{\beta}{1-\alpha/2} \tag{2.166 a}$$

$$b := \frac{\ln B}{\delta} = \frac{1}{\delta}\ln\frac{1-\beta}{\alpha/2}. \tag{2.166 b}$$

The continuation region of this test is made up of two bars, which look like the continuation regions of the first two tests with the onesided alternative hypotheses. Its shape thus looks like a transverse V, i.e., like $<$. The outer as well as the inner boundary each consist of one line with positive slope and one line with negative slope. The lines in the inside of the V are called the **acceptance boundary** and the lines at the outer edge the **rejection boundary** (see figure 4.6/6).

In analogy to (2.156), the above discussion can also be applied to composite hypotheses, where the parameter sets Ω_0 and Ω_1 that correspond to the two hypotheses contain a range of values. Then the specifications α and β give, as before, lower and upper limits for the probabilities of committing a type I and type II error.

2.3.4 Testing for Equality of Parameters for Normally Distributed Populations

In process control by variables one usually assumes that the quality characteristic of interest is $no(\mu;\sigma^2)$-distributed. In order to be able to estimate the parameters it is necessary that they are constant over time. There is a variety of tests which may be used to verify the hypothesis of a time constant process mean μ and process variance σ (i.e. see HARTUNG 1987,

p. 609 ff). In sec. 4.4.1 we will discuss two such tests, the so-called **F test** and the **Bartlett test**. The first is used to test the hypotheses

$$\begin{aligned} H_0 &: \mu_1 = \mu_2 = \ldots = \mu_m \\ H_1 &: \mu_{i_1} \neq \mu_{i_2} \text{ for at least one pair of indices } (i_1, i_2) \end{aligned} \tag{2.167}$$

under the assumption of a constant variance. The latter tests for equality of variances according to

$$\begin{aligned} H_0 &: \sigma_1^2 = \sigma_2^2 = \ldots = \sigma_m^2 \\ H_1 &: \sigma_{i_1}^2 \neq \sigma_{i_2}^2 \text{ for at least one pair of indices } (i_1, i_2). \end{aligned} \tag{2.168}$$

In the above μ_i and σ_i^2 denote distribution parameters of the quality characteristic in the i-th sample from the process.

3 Acceptance Sampling

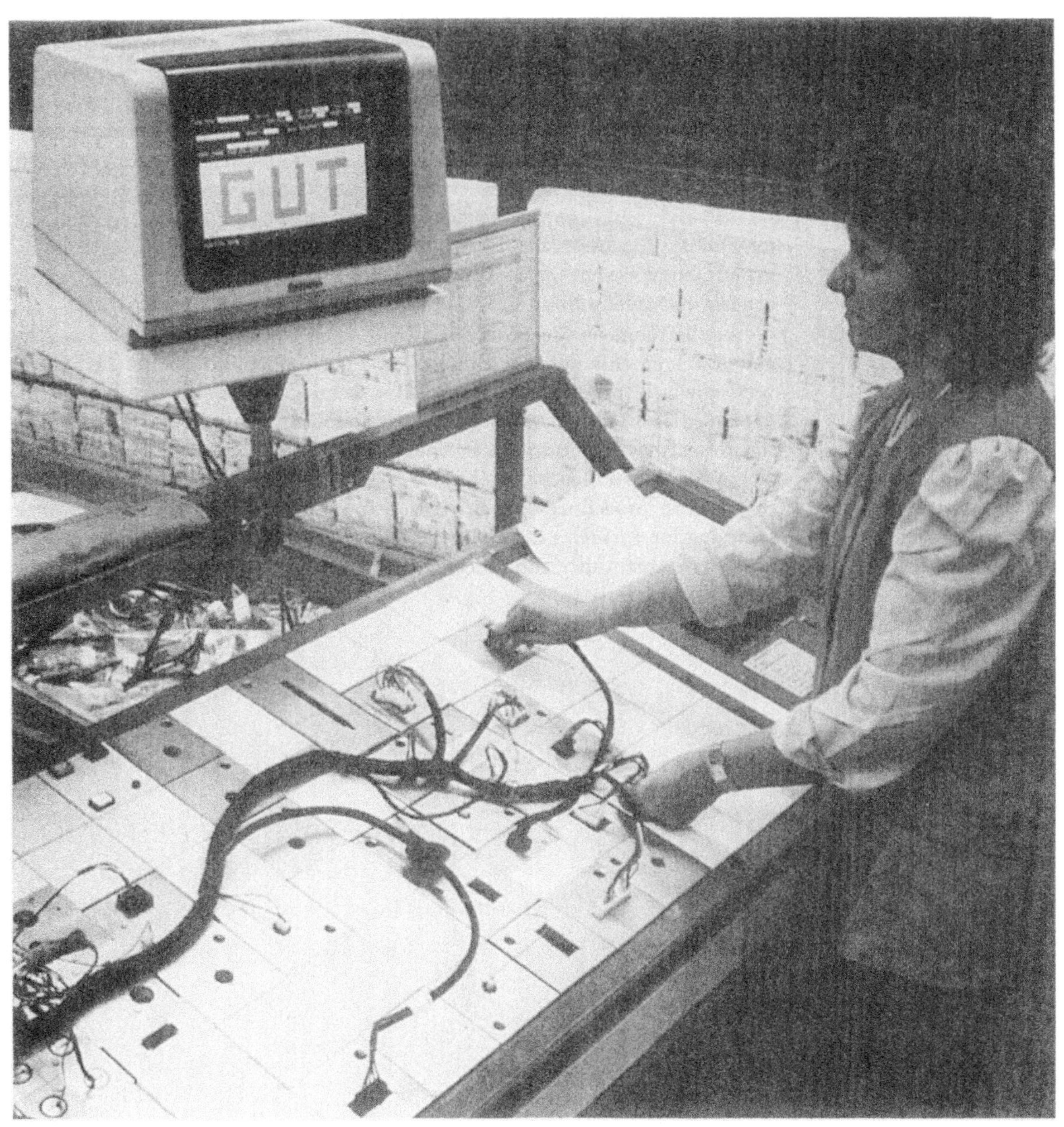

When we classified the different procedures of SQA in section 1.2.3 we distinguished between process control and acceptance control procedures. Through **process control** or process inspection we are trying to detect quality deficiencies during the production process in order to intervene immediately. In section 1.3.2 we used the term **online quality control** because of its integration into the manufacturing process. **Acceptance sampling** or **acceptance control** can only detect quality deficiency without being able to have a counteractive influence (**postline quality control**). Its underlying philosophy is defensive, i.e., it serves for quality control, not for quality improvement. In future preline and online techniques (mainly experimental design methods and control charting) will reduce and finally at least partly eliminate the need for postline control procedures.

Overview of Chapter 3

At the moment acceptance sampling is still quite popular because the new developments described in section 1.3.2 unfortunately are introduced very slowly in practice. Since acceptance sampling is still playing an important role in industrial practice the following chapter will describe its theoretical background very thoroughly. Section 3.1 will give an overview of the different kinds of acceptance sampling. In section 3.2 we will concentrate on procedures for *attributes* and, in section 3.3, on acceptance sampling for *variables*. In all of the above, we will only present the case of *univariate* acceptance sampling; in other words, only the case of one single quality characteristic.

Figure on title page of this chapter:
Electric wiring for automobiles is tested through attribute sampling (The photo is reproduced with the kind permission of AUDI, Ingolstadt, Germany.)

3.1 Overview

3.1.1 Basic Concepts

Acceptance sampling uses a random sample as a basis for assessing the quality of a finite population of units. The latter is also called **a lot**. The supplier of the lot is generally called the producer, the buyer is called the consumer. Quality control assesses whether and to what extent goods – or services (not covered in this book) – are fulfilling certain requirements that relate to their fitness of use. The test is performed on a selected number of quality characteristics. The observed realizations of these test characteristics are compared to a given required standard. In this book we will restrict ourselves to procedures that only test one single quality characteristic.

Definition of a lot and of acceptance sampling

A test lot is not required to be identical to the entire quantity which was produced over a specific time period nor with the whole order or shipment. The only requirement is the homogeneity of the lot in the sense that all units were produced under similar circumstances. The lot also has to consist of natural units and, consequently, its size is integer valued. These units are either pieces (screws, tablets, electronic parts) or packed quantities (1 *lb* bags of sugar, 0.7 *l* bottles of wine, 100 *m* rolls of yarn, steel tanks filled with 10 *l* of gas). This assumption excludes bulk goods like wire, paper, sand or fluids which are not divided into separate subunits.

Lot requirements

Depending on whether the test characteristic is a discrete or a continuous variable we distinguish between attributive and variable acceptance sampling. In **attributive acceptance sampling** or **acceptance control for attributes** (section 3.2) the number of nonconforming units or nonconformities in the sample is determined. In the first case, the test characteristic of every unit in the sample is recorded as either good/bad or nondefective/defective respectively (a dichotomous population). In this case, the acceptance control is a lot-sentencing procedure, i.e., either good or bad. The dichotomous test characteristic "quality of unit" has a Bernoulli distribution, and the total number of defective units in the sample has a hypergeometric distribution if the units are randomly sampled without replacement, or a binomial distribution if the units are sampled with replacement. We also talk of attributive acceptance control if a unit can have multiple defects (e.g., imperfections in a paint finish) and the total number of defects in the sample is determined. The total number of defects often has a Poisson distribution.

Classification of acceptance sampling procedures according to the type of Q-characteristic

Section 3.3 will describe **acceptance sampling for variables** or **acceptance control for measurements**. Here the characteristic of interest is a continuous variable, i.e., it is measured on a continuous scale. We almost always assume that the quality characteristic has a normal distribution. Assessment of the sample is made by means of various functions of the observed data. A frequently used sample statistic is the sample mean.

The statistical tool of acceptance control is the **sampling plan**, in the following, simply called a **plan**. Application of a plan is equivalent to performing the following hypothesis test:

$$\begin{aligned} H_0 &: \text{The test lot satisfies certain quality requirements.} \\ H_1 &: \text{The test lot does not satisfy these requirements.} \end{aligned} \tag{3.1}$$

Applying a sampling plan means performing a hypothesis test.

The above requirements are quality standards for the whole lot. The plan gives precise instructions about which hypothesis to accept after particular realizations have been observed. Regardless of whether we are sampling by attributes or by variables, the plan always specifies the size of the sample (or, in the case of multiple sampling, the sample sizes) as well as exact numerical conditions for acceptance or rejection of the lot. In an attribute procedure, plans would typically give this condition in the form of a maximum number of defective units or observed faults (**acceptance number**) and, in the case of a variable procedure, in the form of a critical value for the sample mean or some other statistic (**acceptance limit**). It is always possible to replace a variable procedure by an attribute procedure, but this also means not taking advantage of some information.

Types of plans

Depending on the way in which the quality characteristic is recorded, we distinguish between **sampling plans for attributes** (plans for count data) and **sampling plans for variables** (plans for measurements). Both types can be divided into single, double, multiple and sequential procedures depending on the maximum number of samples specified in the plan. A **single-sampling plan** requires only one sample of specified size n per lot. **Double-sampling plans** leave the possibility of a second sample, usually of smaller size. In the case of particulary "good" or "bad" lots, a decision is already reached after the first sample of given size n_1. The second sample of size n_2 is only drawn if the test lot was found to be of "medium" quality. The idea of double plans is to reduce the average testing costs by reaching a quick decision in the event of clear evidence in favour of one decision. This idea is further developed in multiple and sequential plans. A multiple (k sample) plan for a lot of size N will take a maximum number of k samples with given sizes $n_1, n_2, \ldots, n_k$ $(2 \leq k \leq N)$. The procedure of a **sequential plan** for a lot of total size N has at most N steps. In every step one unit is sampled and after every draw it is decided if the lot can be accepted or rejected. If not, the plan continues and another unit is drawn. A special characteristic of double, multiple and sequential plans is that the total number of units from the test lot that are sampled and tested (i.e., the sum of all sample sizes) is a random variable which depends on the quality of the lot. In particular the distribution of this random variable depends on the composition of the test lot.

3.1.2 Application of Sampling Plans in Practice

Acceptance control takes place in different departments of a company (see figure 1.2/1), for example

- when receiving goods (**inspection of incoming parts or raw materials**),
- when transferring goods from one manufacturing stage to the next (**intermediate inspection of semifinished products**),
- before shipping goods (**final inspection of finished products**).

All the sampling plans for acceptance control have one thing in common: at the end, one of two mutually exclusive decisions is made, acceptance or rejection of the lot. The rejection of a lot should have economic consequences for its producer, so that there is motivation to improve the quality of shipments. The next figure (3.1/1) shows what we can do with rejected lots.

Screening of a rejected lot can only be done if the testing does not destroy the units. Because of the high costs of testing, it may be advisable even in this case, to scrap the lot, to sell it at a special price, or - in the case of received parts - to return it to the producer. This also applies to defective units from an accepted lot.

Conditions for the application of sampling plans

The sampling plan only determines the sample size and the criteria for rejection and acceptance. Before it can be applied, one has to decide on the sampling procedure and to specify what one considers a defect or nonconformity. A unit is called **defective** or **nonconforming** if the realization of its quality characteristic does not fulfill given requirements. This conforms with the definition of quality from section 1.1.2, which defines quality as a measure of how well the product conforms with its design. Defects in a product can be classified, according to their practical relevance, into critical defects, major defects and minor defects. **Critical defects** may have hazardous consequences, for example, personal injury or material damage. **Major defects** significantly effect the fitness for use of the product, whereas **minor defects** do not significantly effect its fitness for use. For every acceptance control application it has to be specifically determined which kind of defects are to be recorded.

Classification of defects

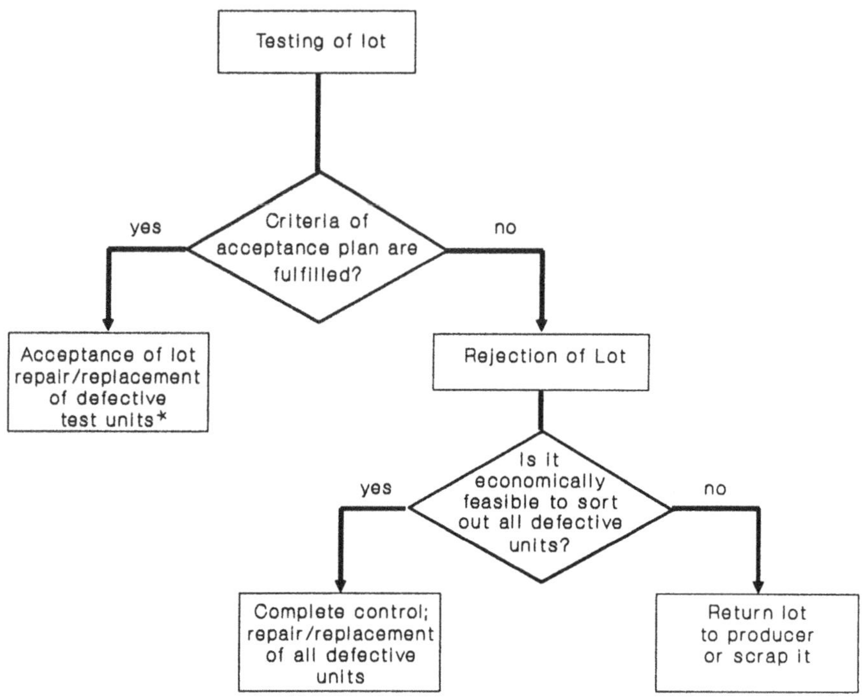

* Depending on the applicable law, the receiver of the lot may have the right to claim replacement or refund for defective units that still were discovered after acceptance.

Figure 3.1/1: Handling of test lots and defective units

Design and evaluation of plans

In order to evaluate a particular plan, and to compare different plans we use the **operating characteristic (OC function)** of the corresponding test. It is determined by the given parameters of the plan. However, it is often difficult to calculate – especially in the case of multiple plans. Conversely one can construct a plan by specifying the operating characteristic in a suitable way, e.g., by two points on the OC curve.

Combinations of plans: plan systems

When testing whole series' of lots, different plans are usually combined in practice to form a test system. The instructions for which plan to use and when to switch between plans are called switching rules. The most important **sampling schemes** or **sampling systems** of this kind are the so-called military standards MIL-STD 105 D (ISO 2859, DIN 40080) for sampling by attributes, and the MIL-STD 414 (ISO 3951) for variable sampling. These systems will be discussed in sections 3.2.7 and 3.3.6.

Figure 3.1/2 gives an overview on sampling plans and sampling systems covered by this book. The also quoted **continuous sampling plans** hold a special position because they are the only plans used for online control.

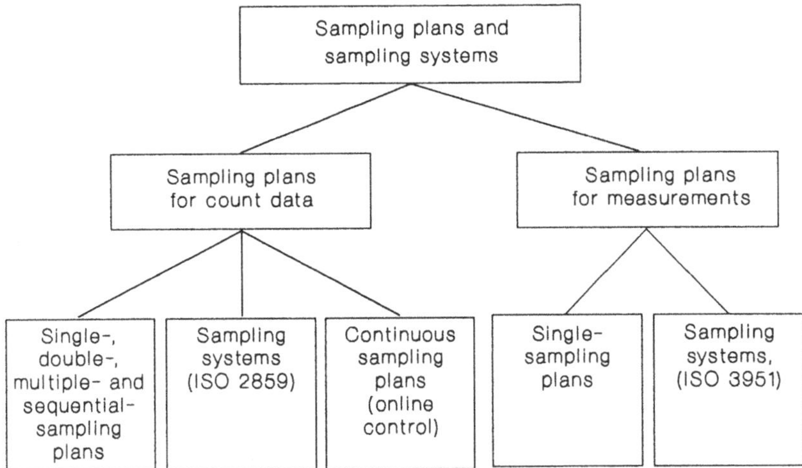

Figure 3.1/2: Sampling plans and sampling systems covered in this book

3.2 Acceptance Sampling for Attributes

In the following, we will assume that we have a lot of total size N. Unless stated otherwise, we will further assume that the quality characteristic of interest of each unit can be assigned into exactly one of the two possible categories "good" and "bad" and that each unit can be categorized accordingly into "non-defective/conforming" or "defective/nonconforming". Let M denote the unknown number of "bad" units in the lot. The quality of a lot of fixed size N can then be described by the number of defective units M. In practice, it is more appropriate to use a measure that allows a direct comparison of lots of different size. The **fraction defective** $P = M/N$ or the **percent defective** $100 \cdot P$ are examples of such measures.

3.2.1 Single-Sampling Plans

a) Single-Sampling Plan Procedure and MOOD's Theorem

Sampling plans for count data that work with one single sample per lot are called **single-sampling plans for attributes**. These procedures take a sample of n units from the lot and determine the total number of of defective units, X_n^T (T stands for total), and accept the lot if X_n^T does not exceed an integer valued critical number, c, called the **acceptance number**. Figure 3.2/1 describes the procedure.[1]

In figure 3.2/1, the variable Z denotes a register that contains the count of defective sample units. It is set to zero at the beginning and its value is increased by one for every defective unit that is found. After testing all n sample units the register Z contains the observed realization of X_n^T. Note that the index i in the structural chart goes from 1 to n, different from section 3.2.2d.

Notation for single attribute plans

A single-sampling plan for attributes is determined through three non-negative integer-valued parameters, N, n, and c, that satisfy $0 \leq c < n \leq N$. A sampling plan with given values N, n, and c will, in the following be called a plan $(N; n; c)$. How the parameters n and c are determined for a given N will be discussed in section 3.2.3. Instead of the acceptance number c, some sampling schemes give the **rejection number** $d := c + 1$. The latter is the smallest number of defective units for which the lot is rejected. Before administering a plan which is different from the plans given in this text it is important to find out which of these two numbers is being used.

[1] The procedure could also be described by a flowchart, but this technique is no longer commonly used since its design does not support structural programming. The structural chart design has the advantage of being easily modifiable (see problem 3.2/16).

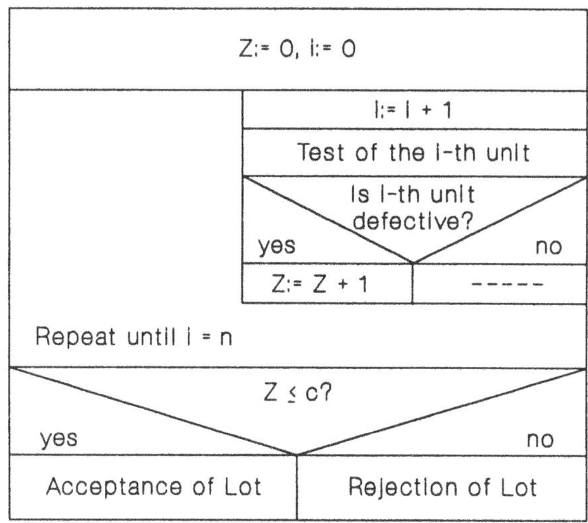

Figure 3.2/1: Structural chart of a single-sampling attribute plan

The procedure of a single-sampling plan for attributes, as described in the figure 3.2/1, is equivalent to a hypothesis test for the critical quality level P_0. We have already introduced this specific type of test in (2.138):

$$\begin{aligned} H_0 &: P \leq P_0 \\ H_1 &: P > P_0. \end{aligned} \tag{3.2}$$

The sample size and the statistic of the test are given by n and X_n^T, respectively, and the rejection and acceptance regions by $CR = \{d, d+1, \ldots, n\}$ and $\overline{CR} = \{0, 1, \ldots, c\}$. The hypothesis test (3.2) is characterized by its **OC function**, which was introduced in (2.132) and is written

$$L(P) = Pr(X_n^T \in \overline{CR}|P) = Pr(X_n^T \leq c|P). \tag{3.3}$$

The operating characteristic function (3.3) is strictly monotone decreasing in P. This means that with an increasing proportion of defectives P the probability that the lot is accepted decreases. We will analyze the OC curve under different assumptions for the distribution of X_n^T in the following sections.

The procedure described in figure 3.2/1 seems to be reasonable from a common sense point of view. If we observed a large number of defective units $m := X_n^T$ in the sample, it makes sense to suspect that in the remaining lot of size $N - n$ the remaining number of defectives $M - m$ will also be large and that the lot should consequently be rejected. In order to answer the question whether the above procedure is always valid, we will first discuss an important result by MOOD (1943, p. 415-425) and then present the well established theory and practice of acceptance sampling.

Introductory thoughts to MOOD's theorem

We need to assume that the lot is itself a sample of size N from the population of all units that are manfactured by the producer, which is considered to be of infinite size. The varying level of quality in the production process and the construction of the lot allow us to see M, the number of defective units in the test lot, as the realization of a random variable X_N^T. We do not know the particular realization M, but we can make probability statements about X_N^T, the number of defective units, called the **prior distribution**

$$\pi(M) := Pr(X_N^T = M), \tag{3.4}$$

This notion is taken from the Bayesian theory of statistics. We denote

$$\mu_N := E\left(X_N^T\right)$$

$$\sigma_N^2 := V\left(X_N^T\right)$$

to be the prior expectation and prior variance of the number of defective units in the test lot and

$$X_{N-n}^T := X_N^T - X_n^T \tag{3.5}$$

to be the number of defective units in the *remainder lot*. Using this notation the following statement can be proven:

▷ **MOOD's theorem**

A random sample of size n is taken without replacement from a lot of size N. Define

$$\mu_N^* := \mu_N\left(1 - \frac{\mu_N}{N}\right). \tag{3.6}$$

Then the correlation between the number of defective units X_n^T in the sample and the number of defective units X_{N-n}^T in the remainder lot is

- positive if $\sigma_N^2 > \mu_N^*$
- zero if $\sigma_N^2 = \mu_N^*$
- negative if $\sigma_N^2 < \mu_N^*$.

Note that MOOD's theorem contains a statement about the correlation between the number of defective units in the sample and in the remaining lot, and not in the whole lot. MOOD also showed that the correlation between the number of observed defective units X_n^T and the total number of defective units X_N^T is always non-negative. This is plausible, because the difference (3.5) is always positive and thus X_N^T has to be big if X_n^T is big.

At this point there are two questions of interest: What is the significance of MOOD's theorem for acceptance control? When is the procedure presented in figure 3.2/1 justifiable from a statistical point of view?

Significance of MOOD's theorem

Let us first consider the case when the variables X_n^T and X_{N-n}^T are *positively* correlated. Positive correlation means that on the average X_{N-n}^T is small (big) when X_n^T is small (big). Therefore, the rule of figure 3.2/1, to accept the lot as long as X_n^T does not exceed a critical number c, is an adequate strategy.

In the case when the variables X_n^T and X_{N-n}^T are *negatively* correlated the above does not apply. Negative correlation implies that on the average X_{N-n}^T is small (big) when X_n^T is big (small). Consequently we should reverse the decision rule from the first case; i.e., reject the lot if X_n^T is small ($X_N^T \leq c$) and accept the lot if X_n^T is big ($X_N^T > c$). It would however be hard to explain this procedure to the producer of the lot.

In the case when the variables X_n^T and X_{N-n}^T are *not correlated* it is not possible to use the quality in the sample, which is measured by X_n^T, to make conclusions about the quality in the remaining lot, which is represented by X_{N-n}^T. In this situation it would be appropriate to decide about the lot without inspection, or to inspect the entire lot.

In the following we will assume that the number of defective units in the sample X_n^T and the total number of defective units in the uninspected remainder lot X_{N-n}^T are positively correlated (see problem 3.2/1). This assumption assures that the procedure given in figure 3.2/1 is adequate.

Example 3.2/1

Suppose we have a series of lots with size N. These lots contain no defective units with probability ω and consist of only defective units with probability $1-\omega$ Then the prior distribution is of the form

$$\pi(M) = \begin{cases} \omega & \text{if } M = 0 \\ 1-\omega & \text{if } M = N \\ 0 & \text{if } M = 1, 2, ..., N-1. \end{cases}$$

This is a two point distribution with

$$\mu_N = N \cdot (1-\omega); \quad \sigma_N^2 = N^2 \cdot (1-\omega) \cdot \omega.$$

Here, equation (3.6) takes the form

$$\mu_N^* = N \cdot (1-\omega) \cdot [1-(1-\omega)] = N \cdot (1-\omega) \cdot \omega < \sigma_N^2.$$

This satisfies the condition of the first case of MOOD's theorem, where we have a positive correlation between the number of defective units X_n^T in the sample and the number of defective units X_{N-n}^T in the remainder lot, and consequently the decision rule in figure 3.2/1 is adequate.

Example 3.2/2

A production process is under "statistical control" if each unit has the same probability P $(0 < P < 1)$ of being defective, and if defective and non-defective units form a series of independent random variables which are identically Bernoulli distributed. If we take a lot of size N from this production, then the number of defective units X_N^T has a binomial distribution $bi(P;N)$. The prior distribution is

$$\pi(M) = bi(M|P;N).$$

The $bi(P;N)$-distributed variable X_N^T has, according to (2.94a,b), the moments

$$\mu_N = N \cdot P; \quad \sigma_N^2 = N \cdot P \cdot Q$$

where $Q := 1 - P$. Also it is easily verified that (3.6) results in

$$\mu_N^* = N \cdot P \cdot Q = \sigma_N^2.$$

This is the case of MOOD's theorem where X_n^T and X_{N-n}^T are uncorrelated. (It can even be shown that X_n^T and X_{N-n}^T are stochastically independent.) Therefore if one is given this a-priori information that the number of defective units in the lot has a binomial distribution, one would do without a test sample and accept the lot without inspection as long as there is past information about the producer's proportion of defective units and as long as this proportion is acceptable to the consumer. If the proportion of defective units is above an acceptable value, one can either make the producer sort out the defective units or try to find a producer with a lower proportion of defective units.

Example 3.2/3

Suppose again that we have a series of lots which have the same given size N and the same number of defective units $X_N^T = M$, with $0 < M < N$. The prior distribution (3.4) is

$$\pi(M) = \begin{cases} 1 & \text{for} \quad X_N^T = M \\ 0 & \text{for} \quad X_N^T \neq M. \end{cases}$$

This is a single point distribution with the moments

$$\mu_N = M; \quad \sigma_N^2 = 0$$

and equation (3.6) is of the form

$$\mu_N^* = M\left(1 - \frac{M}{N}\right) > \sigma_N^2 = 0.$$

We now have the situation of a negative correlation between X_n^T and X_{N-n}^T and, in this case, an unfavourable result from the test sample would result in accepting the lot, reversing the procedure in figure 3.2/1. However, it is not realistic to assume a constant proportion of defectives in practice.

Problem 3.2/1

In the case of a missing record about a producer's past quality one commonly assumes that all realizations $0, 1, \ldots, N$ of X_N^T, the number of defective units in the lot, have the same probability of occurrence, $1/(N+1)$.

a) What is the prior distribution under this assumption?

b) Is the procedure from figure 3.2/1 adequate in this case?

Remark

To determine which of the three cases in MOOD's theorem is given in a particular situation one needs the prior distribution $\pi(M)$. Then one can find the moments and the quantity (3.6). In practice, $\pi(M)$ is rarely known. One can then either subjectively determine $\pi(M)$ (subjectivist Bayesian approach, see also problem 3.2/1) or empirically estimate $\pi(M)$ from previous lots (empirical Bayesian approach). If one knows the distribution of the quality characteristic in the production process and the way the lot was obtained as a sample of size N from this process, then it is possible to deduce the distribution $\pi(M)$.

b) The Hypergeometric OC Function

We already pointed out that the application of a single plan for attributes is equivalent to performing a hypothesis test with the hypothesis described in (3.2). The OC function of the test can be calculated for a given distribution of the test statistic X_n^T. We want to first consider the case when X_n^T has a hypergeometric distribution. This happens when one takes a sample of size n from a lot *without* replacement. Suppose the lot contains N units $(N \geq n)$ of which M units are defective. Then under these conditions the variable X_n^T, which counts the number of "successes" detected by the inspection personnel (i.e., the number of defective units in the test sample)

When is the distribution of the test statistic hypergeometric?

is $hy(N;M;n)$-distributed. In this case, the OC function is called the **hypergeometric OC function** and is denoted by $L(P|N;n;c)$. Since $X_n^T \sim hy(N;M;n)$ we have $Pr(X_n^T \leq c|P) = Hy(c|N;M;n)$ and thus

$$L(P|N;n;c) = Hy(c|N;M;n) \tag{3.7 a}$$

holds with $M = N \cdot P$. By (2.80, 2.81), we can also write

$$L(P|N;n;c) = \sum_{i=0}^{c} \frac{\binom{M}{i}\binom{N-M}{n-i}}{\binom{N}{n}}. \tag{3.7 b}$$

Example of a hypergeometric OC function

Figure 3.2/2 gives the hypergeometric OC curve for a plan with $N = 3000, n = 89$ and $c = 2$. For reasons of better readability, the curves in this and the following figures are drawn continuously although the function (3.7) is only defined for $P \in \{0, 1/N, 2/N, \ldots, 1\}$ since $P = M/N$ and $M \in \{0, 1, \ldots, N\}$.

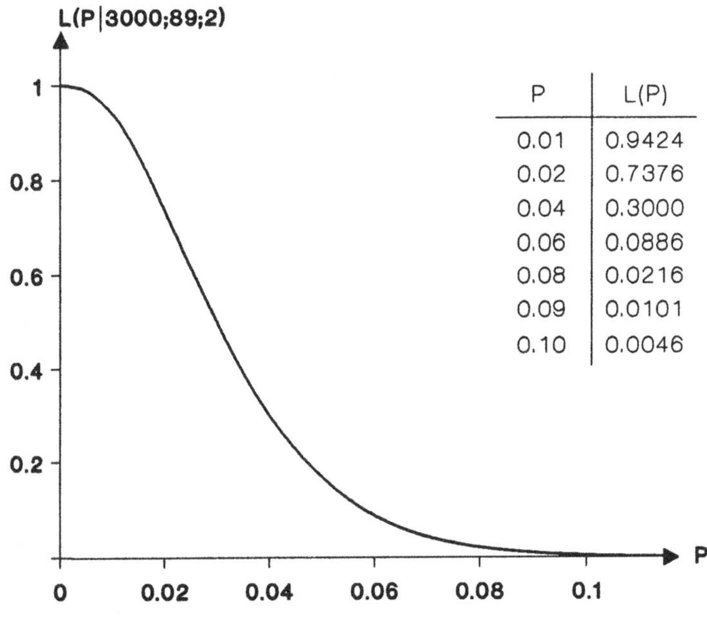

P	L(P)
0.01	0.9424
0.02	0.7376
0.04	0.3000
0.06	0.0886
0.08	0.0216
0.09	0.0101
0.10	0.0046

Figure 3.2/2: Hypergeometric OC curve for the plan (3000;89;2)

Interpretation of the OC curve

Using the above figure we can immediately see how, in this attribute plan (3000;89;2), the probability of accepting the lot changes with varying proportion P of defective units. We can see from the figure that the probability of acceptance in the case of $P = 0.06$ (6% defective units) is about

0.09, and in the case of $P = 0.01$ (1% defective units), about 0.94. For these two quality levels we will reject the lot with probabilities of about 0.91 and 0.06, respectively. For small values P the OC function should generally have a large value (protection of the producer from the return of "good" lots), and for large values P we require the OC function to take a small value (protection of the consumer from accepting "bad" lots). Whether this plan (3000;89;2) provides sufficient protection in both directions cannot be said in general, but has to be decided according to the desired protection of both consumer and producer.

Effect of variation of plan parameters onto the shape of the OC curve

The following figures will show in different examples how the shape of the hypergeometric OC curve changes when the plan parameters are changed. Figure 3.2/3 will demonstrate the effect of changes in the *lot size* N and the *sample size* n, while the acceptance number c and the sample proportion n/N are kept fixed.

- Variation of N and n for fixed n/N

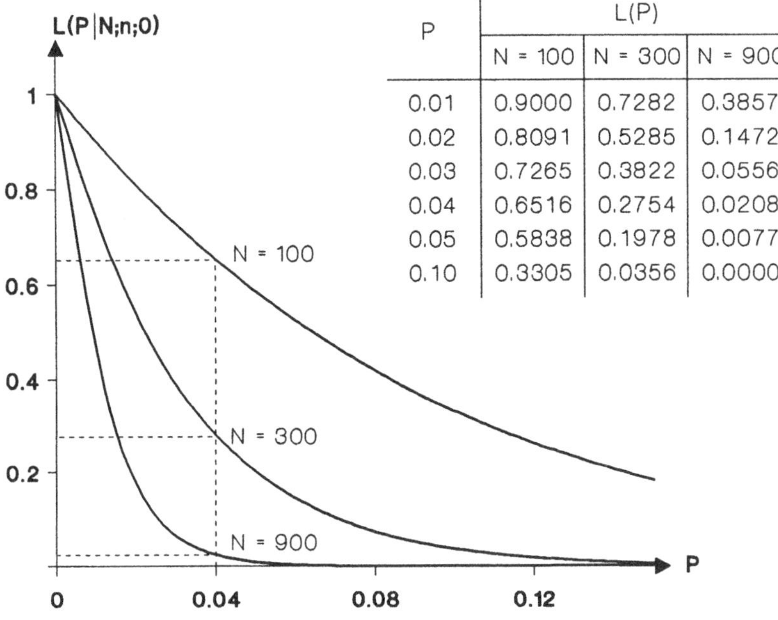

P	L(P)		
	N = 100	N = 300	N = 900
0.01	0.9000	0.7282	0.3857
0.02	0.8091	0.5285	0.1472
0.03	0.7265	0.3822	0.0556
0.04	0.6516	0.2754	0.0208
0.05	0.5838	0.1978	0.0077
0.10	0.3305	0.0356	0.0000

Figure 3.2/3: Hypergeometric OC curves for three plans $(N; n; 0)$ with fixed sampling proportion $n/N = 0.1$

We can see that the slope of the curve, and thus the discriminatory power of the underlying hypothesis test (3.2) increases when, for a fixed ratio n/N, N and, correspondingly, n are increased. The three plans presented above offer different protection. Let us, e.g., examine the protection of the consumer, in the case when he wants to reject the lot if the proportion of nonconforming units is 4% or above. For $P = 0.04$ the plan (900;90;0) undesireably accepts the lot with probability 0.02; this means that the consumer is 98% protected. For the plans (300,30,0) and (100,10,0) the corresponding probabilities are about 0.28 and 0.65. In these cases the consumer has less protection, only 72% and 35%, respectively.

- Variation of N

Let us now consider the case where the lot size N is varied while n and c remain fixed. It can be seen from figure 3.2/4 that the discriminatory power of the hypothesis test (3.2) only slowly increases as N increases.

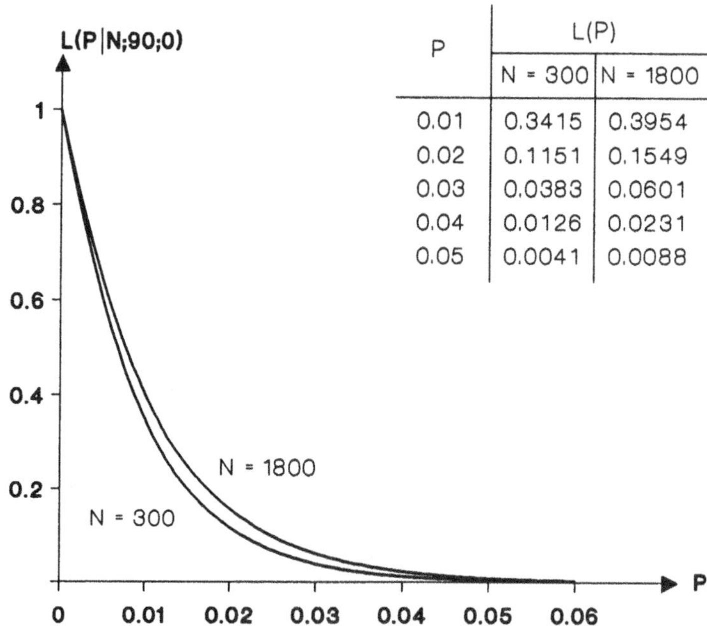

P	L(P)	
	N = 300	N = 1800
0.01	0.3415	0.3954
0.02	0.1151	0.1549
0.03	0.0383	0.0601
0.04	0.0126	0.0231
0.05	0.0041	0.0088

Figure 3.2/4: Hypergeometric OC curves for two plans $(N; 90; 0)$

- Variation of n

Variation of the *sample size* n has a strong effect on the slope of the OC function. Figure 3.2/5 shows that plans with a larger sample size have a higher discriminatory power between "good" and "bad" lots. In particular, as n increases the producer's as well as the consumer's risks decrease (simultaneous increase in the protection of the consumer and the producer). As $n \to N$ (total control), the OC curve approaches the **ideal OC curve**, which is, for example, in the case of $N = 5000$ and $c = 1$, a step function:

$$L(P|5000;5000;1) = \begin{cases} 1 & \text{if } P \in \left\{0, \frac{1}{5000}\right\} \\ 0 & \text{if } P \in \left\{\frac{M}{5000}\middle| M = 2, 3, ..., 5000\right\}. \end{cases}$$

This shows that total control corresponds to the application of an **ideal test**.

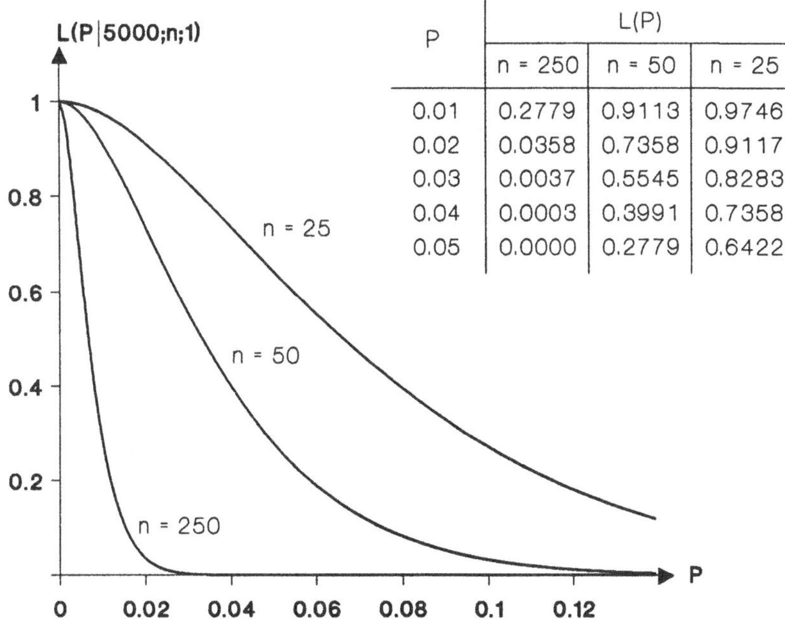

P	L(P)		
	n = 250	n = 50	n = 25
0.01	0.2779	0.9113	0.9746
0.02	0.0358	0.7358	0.9117
0.03	0.0037	0.5545	0.8283
0.04	0.0003	0.3991	0.7358
0.05	0.0000	0.2779	0.6422

Figure 3.2/5: Hypergeometric OC curves for three plans $(5000; n; 1)$

- Variation of c

Another way of controlling the discriminatory power of the test (3.2) is to vary the *acceptance number c*. We can see in figure 3.2/6 that decreasing c causes the curve to become steeper.

Are plans with $c = 0$ especially rigorous?

This fact is often used to justify the application of plans with $c = 0$. However, there are psychological reasons against this argument: Consumers as well as producers have an intuitive reluctance against the seemingly rigorous procedure of rejecting a lot in the case of one single defective sample unit. There is also a widespread misconception that "rigorous control", i.e., sampling with $c = 0$, is protecting the consumer from accepting lots with a high proportion of defective units. In reality even a plan $(N; n; 0)$ accepts lots with a considerable proportion of defective units with significant probability, unless the sampling proportion n/N is large.

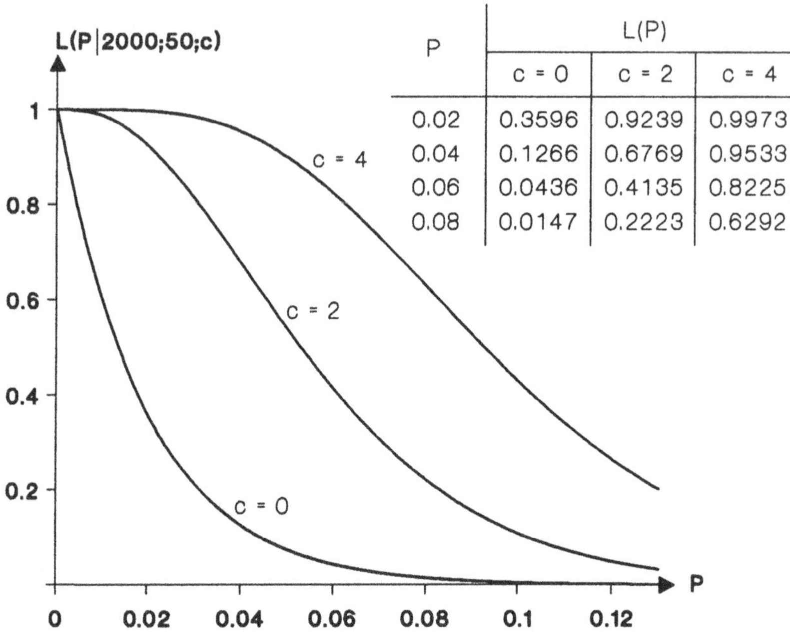

P	L(P)		
	c = 0	c = 2	c = 4
0.02	0.3596	0.9239	0.9973
0.04	0.1266	0.6769	0.9533
0.06	0.0436	0.4135	0.8225
0.08	0.0147	0.2223	0.6292

Figure 3.2/6: Hypergeometric OC curves for three plans (2000; 50; c)

This can be illustrated with an example of seven plans $(1000; n; 0)$. The following table lists the upper bounds of the 95% confidence interval for the unknown number M of defective units in the lot (recall M denotes the realization of X_N^T).

Sample Size	Upper Bound
8	312
13	205
20	138
32	88
50	57
80	36
125	21

Table 3.2/1: Upper bounds of a onesided 95% confidence interval for the number of defectives in the lot for several plans $(1000; n; 0)$

Table 3.2/1 shows with 95% level of confidence, that a lot of size $N = 1000$ that has been accepted by a plan with acceptance number $c = 0$ contains at most 168 defective units for a sample size of $n = 20$ and at most 71 defective units for $n = 50$. On the basis of this 95% level of confidence, the unknown proportion of defective units $100 \cdot M/N$ could be as high as 16.8% for $n = 20$ and 7.1% for $n = 50$.

Summary

We summarize that the steepness of the hypergeometric OC function (3.7), and consequently the discriminatory power of the corresponding test of type (3.2), increases when

- the size N of the lot increases as n/N remains constant (see figure 3.2/3)
- the size N of the lot decreases (see figure 3.2/4)
- the sample size n increases (see figure 3.2/5)
- the acceptance number c decreases (see figure 3.2/6).

Variation of several parameters

When several of the parameters are varied simultaneously the individual increasing or decreasing effects superimpose on each other. For example, if the acceptance number c increases while the remaining parameters remain fixed, then the plan with the smaller c has a steeper OC curve, as can be seen in figure 3.2/6. However, if we increase the sample size n sufficiently for the plan with the larger acceptance number c, its OC curve can be made steeper than the first, cf. figure 3.2/7.

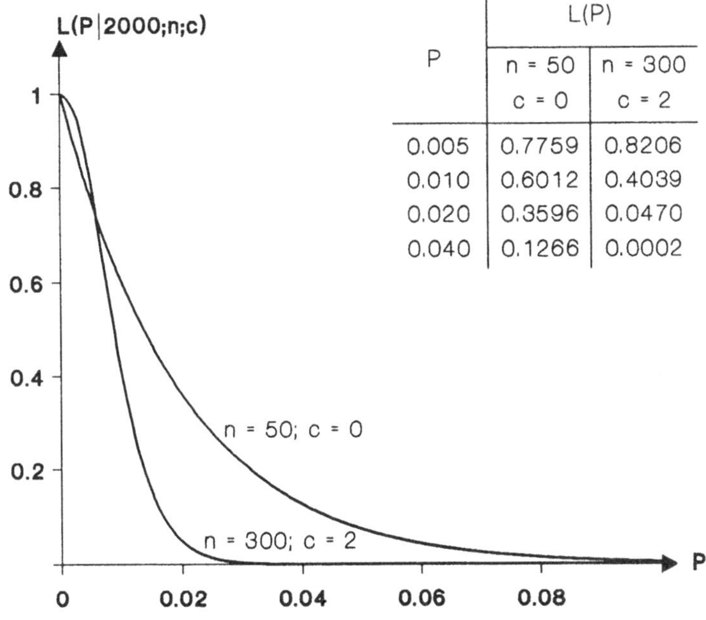

P	L(P) n = 50, c = 0	L(P) n = 300, c = 2
0.005	0.7759	0.8206
0.010	0.6012	0.4039
0.020	0.3596	0.0470
0.040	0.1266	0.0002

Figure 3.2/7: Hypergeometric OC curves for two plans $(2000; n; c)$

Problem 3.2/2

Calculate the values of the hypergeometric OC function $L(P|25;2;0)$ for all possible quality levels $P = M/25; M = 0, 1, \ldots, 25$.

Problem 3.2/3

Determine and sketch using table 5.1/2:

a) $L(0.45|20;n;2)$ for $n = 2, 3, \ldots, 12$

b) $L(0.4|20;5;c)$ for $c = 0, 1, \ldots, 5$.

Check whether your results are consistent with the results expressed by figures 3.2/5-6.

c) The Binomial OC Function

When is the distribution of the test statistic binomial?

Up to now we have considered the case where a sample of size n was taken without replacement from a lot with a total number of N units among which M units are defective. In this scenario X_n^T, the total number of defective units in the sample, had a hypergeometric distribution. We now want to consider the case when the sample is taken *with* replacement. Then the variable X_n^T has a binomial distribution: $X_n^T \sim bi(P;n)$. The probability, $Pr(X_N^T \leq c|P)$, for a given fraction defective P, that the hypothesis test (3.2) leads to acceptance of the null hypothesis H_0 takes the value $Bi(c|P;n)$ of the distribution function (2.93) for every $P \in [0;1]$. Denoting the OC function (3.3) of the binomial distributed statistic X_n^T by $L(P|n;c;)$ we get

$$L(P|n;c) = Bi(c|P;n). \qquad (3.8\text{ a})$$

We speak of (3.8a) as the **binomial OC function**. By (2.93) we have the equivalent representation

$$L(P|n;c) = \sum_{i=0}^{c} \binom{n}{i} P^i(1-P)^{n-i}. \qquad (3.8\text{ b})$$

The binomial OC function is used to approximate the hypergeometric OC function.

Sampling with replacement is not very common in practical statistical quality control applications. Nevertheless, the binomial OC function is frequently used as an approximation to the hypergeometric OC function because it is easier to handle. By (2.87a), we know that

$$Hy(c|N;M;n) \approx Bi(c|P;n) \qquad (3.9\text{ a})$$

provided that the conditions $0.1 < P < 0.9$ and $n > 10$, $n/N < 0.1$, are all satisfied. Hence by (3.7a) and (3.8a) it follows that under these conditions

$$L(P|N;n;c) \approx L(P|n;c). \qquad (3.9\text{ b})$$

Calculation of the binomial OC function:

- through the beta distribution

Alternative to (3.8), we can use the exact relationship between the binomial distribution and the beta distribution to calculate values of the binomial OC function. Through (2.96) and (3.8a) we get

$$L(P|n;c) = 1 - Bt(P|c+1;n-c). \tag{3.10}$$

The representation (3.10) has advantages over (3.8a) for the purpose of calculation, because computer based numerical evaluation of the integrals (2.29a,b) needed for $Bt(P|c+1;n-c)$ involve less rounding errors than the summation of binomial terms (2.93).

- through the F distribution

A third representation of the binomial OC function can be immediately obtained from (3.8a) and (2.118a):

$$L(P|n;c) = 1 - Fi\left[\frac{n-c}{c+1} \cdot \frac{P}{1-P}\middle|2(c+1);2(n-c)\right]. \tag{3.11}$$

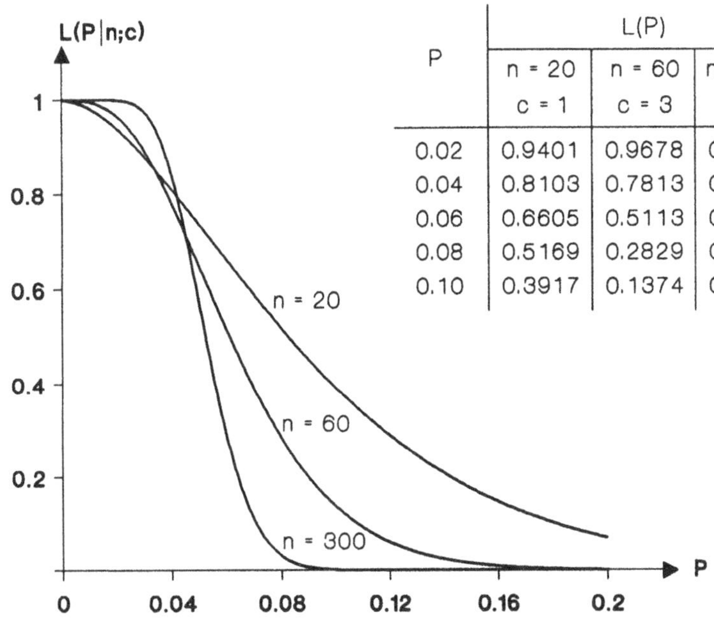

P	L(P)		
	n = 20, c = 1	n = 60, c = 3	n = 300, c = 15
0.02	0.9401	0.9678	0.9996
0.04	0.8103	0.7813	0.8489
0.06	0.6605	0.5113	0.2793
0.08	0.5169	0.2829	0.0292
0.10	0.3917	0.1374	0.0013

Figure 3.2/8: Binomial OC curves for a constant ratio $c/n = 0.05$

Effect of varying parameters

The binomial OC function (3.8) reacts to variation of n and c in the same way as the hypergeometric OC function. An increase in the sample size n or a decrease in the acceptance number c results in a steeper OC curve and thus in a better discriminatory power of the hypothesis test (3.2). Simultaneous variation of the parameters superimposes the individual effects. Figure 3.2/8 gives the curves of three binomial OC functions $L(P|n;c)$ for a fixed ratio c/n. The graphs demonstrate that the effect of an increase in c (less steep OC curve) is compensated by the effect of the increase in the sample size (steeper OC curve).

While the ratio c/n remains fixed, the OC curves from figure 3.2/8 converge, for $n \longrightarrow \infty$, to the ideal OC curve, which is a step function that jumps at $P = c/n$ from $L(P) = 1$ to $L(P) = 0$.

Problem 3.2/4

Use (3.9) to calculate approximations to the hypergeometric OC function $L(P|25;2;0)$ at the points $P = M/25$ with $M = 0, 1, \ldots, 25$ and compare the results to those of problem 3.2/2.

d) The Poisson OC Function

In the following, we will assume that the count variable is not counting the number of defective or nonconforming units but the number of *defects* or *nonconformities* in the sample. In order to distinguish this case from the previous we will denote this counting statistic by X_n^{*T}. The n units of the test sample are no longer either "bad" (defective/nonconforming) or "good" (nondefective/conforming), but each unit has more or less defects. Before, we described the unknown quality of the lot by its number of defective units M (absolute measure) or by its fraction defective $P = M/N$ (relative measure). In the same way, we can now use the total number of defects M^* or the *average number of defects per unit* $\lambda = M^*/N$. The test hypothesis is still (3.2), but P and P_0 are replaced by λ and λ_0 respectively.

When is the test statistic Poisson distributed?

The number of defects in the i-th unit of the lot is a random variable X_i for $i = 1, \ldots, N$. We are assuming that the random variables X_i are independent and identically po(λ)-distributed with $\lambda > 0$. We know from (2.18a) that a unit has on the average λ defects. Since by (2.22) the Poisson distribution is reproductive under summation, the total number of defects in the sample X_n^{*T} is po($n\lambda$)-distributed. Table 3.2/2 will clarify the present assumptions on the lot and the sample, and compare them to the previous situation of section 3.2.1b-c.

Since $X_n^{*T} \sim po(n\lambda)$, its expectation is $E(X_n^{*T}) = n\lambda$ (i.e., λ defects per element). Analogous to formula (3.3) the probability

$$L^*(\lambda|n;c) := Pr\left(X_n^{*T} \in \overline{CR}|n\lambda\right) = Pr\left(X_n^{*T} \leq c|n\lambda\right) \tag{3.12}$$

that the test statistic X_n^{*T} falls into the acceptance region $\overline{CR} = \{0, 1, \ldots, c\}$

Quality of a lot with N units	Relative measure of lot quality	Test statistic and its distribution	Expectation of the test statistic
The lot contains M *defective units.*	Fraction defective $P = M/N$	Number of defective units in the sample X_n^T Distribution: $X_n^T \sim hy(N;M;n)$ $X_n^T \sim bi(P;n)$ (drawn with or without replacement)	$E\left(X_n^T\right) = nP$
The lot has $M^* = N\lambda$ *defects.*	Average number of defects per unit $\lambda = M^*/N$	Number of defects in the sample X_n^{*T} Distribution: $X_n^{*T} \sim po(n\lambda)$	$E\left(X_n^{*T}\right) = n \cdot \lambda$

Table 3.2/2: Two standard scenarios for sampling by attributes

is exactly $Po(c|n\lambda)$. Hence, by (2.17), the probability that a lot with λ average defects per unit is accepted is found to be

$$L^*(\lambda|n;c) = Po(c|n\lambda) = \sum_{i=0}^{c} \frac{(n\lambda)^i}{i!} e^{-n\lambda}. \tag{3.13}$$

This operating characteristic function of a Poisson distributed test statistic X_n^{*T} is called the **Poisson OC function.**

Similar to the binomial OC function, the Poisson OC function is used in SQA to approximate the hypergeometric OC function. From (2.87b), it follows that

Poisson OC function is used for approximation

- of the hypergeometric OC function

$$Hy(c|N;M;n) \approx Po(c|nP) \tag{3.14 a}$$

with $P = M/N$. Further, we get by (3.7a) and (3.13)

$$L(P|N;n;c) \approx L^*(P|n;c), \tag{3.14 b}$$

provided that the conditions of (2.87b) are all satisfied, i.e., that $P \leq 0.1$ (or $P \geq 0.9$) for the fraction defective and $n > 30$ and $n/N < 0.1$ for the sample size and the sampled proportion.

The Poisson OC function can also be used to approximate the binomial OC function. By (2.97a), we have

- of the binomial OC function

$$Bi(c|P;n) \approx Po(c|nP), \tag{3.15 a}$$

if the sample size n and the fraction defective P satisfy the conditions of (2.97a), that is $nP \leq 10$ and $n \geq 1500P$. Using (3.8a) and (3.13) we can rewrite (3.15a) as

$$L(P|n;c) \approx L^*(P|n;c). \tag{3.15 b}$$

Note that, when used to approximate the hypergeometric and binomial OC function, the average number of defects λ in equation (3.13) is replaced by the fraction defective P:

$$L^*(P|n;c) = Po(c|nP) = \sum_{i=0}^{c} \frac{(nP)^i}{i!} e^{-nP}. \tag{3.16}$$

We also call the OC function (3.16) Poisson OC function, because it is formally the same function $L^*(x|n;c) = Po(c|nx)$. In practice, the Poisson OC function $L^*(P|n;c)$ is often used instead of $L(P|n;c)$ and of $L(P|N;n;c)$, since it is computationally easier to evaluate.

Calculating values of the Poisson OC function

Using (2.112a), the formulas (3.13) and (3.16) can be rewritten as

- by means of the χ^2 distribution

$$L^*(\lambda|n;c) = 1 - Ch[2n\lambda|2(c+1)], \tag{3.17 a}$$

$$L^*(P|n;c) = 1 - Ch[2nP|2(c+1)]. \tag{3.17 b}$$

- by means of the gamma distribution

We can also set $\delta := c+1$ in (2.38b) and get:

$$L^*(\lambda|n;c) = 1 - Ga(n\lambda|1, c+1), \tag{3.18 a}$$

$$L^*(P|n;c) = 1 - Ga(nP|1;c+1). \tag{3.18 b}$$

Example 3.2/4

A camera manufacturer has an intermediate screening stage before the camera bodies are transferred from the paint shop to the final assembly. The number X of imperfections in the paint finish per body can be seen as a po(λ)-distributed variable. In this situation, the Poisson rate λ has the meaning of an average number of imperfections in the paint finish of each body. The manufacturer wants to apply a plan that accepts lots when $\lambda \leq 0.1$ with at least 95% probability and, when $\lambda \geq 0.3$ with at most 10% probability. The following plan has been proposed: Take a random sample of size $n = 50$ from a series (lot) of $N = 500$ camera bodies, and let the lot go on to the final assembly if the inspection finds not more than 10 imperfections. In the case of more than 10 imperfections return the whole series to the paint shop for 100% reinspection and refinishing. Does this plan meet the given requirements?

The underlying hypothesis test of this plan tests $H_0 : \lambda \leq \lambda_0$ versus $H_1 : \lambda > \lambda_0$. The test statistic is X_{50}^{*T}, the number of impurities in the sample, and it is po(50λ)-distributed. The null hypothesis H_0 is accepted (and the lot) when $X_{50}^{*T} \leq 10$. For any value of λ, the probability of accepting the lot when $E(X_{50}^{*T}) = 50\lambda$ is given by formula (3.13) with $n = 50$ and $c = 10$:

$$L^*(\lambda|50; 10) = Pr(X_{50}^{*T} \leq 10|50\lambda) = Po(10|50\lambda).$$

Using table 5.1/4 for $\lambda = 0.1$ and $\lambda = 0.3$, we obtain

$$L^*(0.1|50; 10) = Po(10|5) \approx 0.98630$$

$$L^*(0.3|50; 10) = Po(10|15) \approx 0.11846.$$

Since $L^*(\lambda|50; 10)$ is strictly monotone decreasing in λ we know that $L^*(\lambda|50; 10) \geq L^*(0.1|50; 10)$ for $\lambda \leq 0.1$ and $L^*(\lambda|50; 10) \leq L^*(0.3|50; 10)$ for $\lambda \geq 0.3$. Hence, a series of bodies is accepted with at least 98.6% probability if $\lambda \leq 0.1$. However, only the first requirement is fulfilled. One can obtain a plan that conforms with both requirements by setting the acceptance number to $c = 9$, i.e., by accepting a series if $X_{50}^{*T} \leq 9$. After this modification we have

$$L^*(0.1|50; 9) = Po(9|5) \approx 0.96817$$

$$L^*(0.3|50; 9) = Po(9|15) \approx 0.06985.$$

The probabilities of acceptance for this plan are at least 96.8% for $\lambda \leq 0.1$ and at most 7.0% for $\lambda \geq 0.3$.

Example 3.2/5

Let us now modify example 3.2/4 by replacing the test statistic X_{50}^{*T}, the number of imperfections, by X_{50}^{T}, the number of imperfect bodies. We will classify a body imperfect if it has one or more imperfections. The new plan reads as follows: If, in a sample of size $n = 43$ from a series of $N = 500$ camera bodies, at most seven bodies are imperfect, then the series is accepted. Otherwise, the series is returned to the paint shop. What are the probabilities of accepting a series for $\lambda = 0.1$ and $\lambda = 0.3$, respectively?

The test statistic X_n^T has a hypergeometric distribution, and consequently we need to determine the acceptance probabilities by formula (3.7a). In order to apply (3.7a) we have to find the fraction defective P of the lot. The number of impurities is assumed to be $po(\lambda)$-distributed and thus $Pr(X = 0) = e^{-\lambda}$ is the probability that a body is perfect, implying that the probability of a body to be imperfect is $1-e^{-\lambda}$. This leads us to expect $500 \cdot e^{-\lambda}$ "bad" camera bodies among the $N = 500$ units. The quantity $500 \cdot e^{-\lambda}$, rounded to the next biggest integer (to be safe), corresponds to the value of the parameter

$$M = [500 \cdot (1 - e^{-\lambda})] + 1$$

of the hypergeometric distribution[2]. With $\lambda = 0.1$ and $\lambda = 0.3$, respectively, we get

$$M = [500 \cdot 0.09516] + 1 = [47.58] + 1 = 48$$

$$M = [500 \cdot 0.25918] + 1 = [129.59] + 1 = 130.$$

Since $P = M/500$ we need to take $P = 0.096$ for $\lambda = 0.1$ and $P = 0.26$ for $\lambda = 0.3$. Table 5.1/1 in this book does not cover the case $N = 500$, but we can use appropriate tables of the hypergeometric distribution to calculate the probabilities $L(P|500;43;7)$ given by formula (3.7a)

$$L(0.096|500;43;7) \approx 0.9580$$

$$L(0.26|500;43;7) \approx 0.0865.$$

We can see that the described plan (500;43;7) satisfies the requirements of example 3.2/4: When $\lambda \leq 0.1$ (equivalent to $P \leq 0.096$) a test lot is accepted with at least 95.8% probability and in the case of $\lambda \geq 0.3$ (equivalent to $P \geq 0.26$) with a probability of at most 8.65%.

Problem 3.2/5

Use the formulas (3.14b) and (3.15b) to calculate approximations to $L(P|25;2;0)$ and $L(P|2;0)$ at $P = M/25$, for $M = 0, 1, \ldots, 25$, and compare the results to those of the problems 3.2/4 and 3.2/2.

Problem 3.2/6

a) Calculate the OC functions $L(P|50;8;0)$, $L(P|8;0)$ and $L^*(P|8;0)$ at $P = M/50$, for $M = 0, 1, \ldots, 15$.

b) Plot the results.

[2] $[\cdot]$ denotes as before the Gauss bracket function.

Problem 3.2/7

a) What is the value of the Poisson OC function $L^*(P|100;3)$ at $P = 0.01, 0.05, 0.1$ and 0.15 ?

b) Calculate $L^*(0.01|n;2)$ for $n = 50, 100, 150$ and 200.

c) Calculate $L^*(0.01|100;c)$ for $c = 0, 1, 2$ and 3.

e) Comparison of the three OC Functions

We now want to further characterize the hypergeometric OC function $L(P|N;n;c)$, the binomial OC function $L(P|n;c)$ and the Poisson OC function $L^*(P|n;c)$, and make a comparison of them. For proofs of the properties that are listed below we refer to UHLMANN (1982, p. 106 ff).

First note that all three functions agree at $P = 0$ and are strictly monotone decreasing in P: Monotonicity property

$$L(0|N;n;c) = L(0|n;c) = L^*(0|n;c) = 1. \tag{3.19 a}$$

This monotonicity property implies that, among several lots of different quality, the one with the lowest fraction defective has the highest probability of acceptance.

For $P = 1$ the hypergeometric and binomial OC functions are zero, whereas the Poisson OC function is positive (see also problem 3.2/5):

$$L(1|N;n;c) = L(1|n;c) = 0;\ L^*(1|n;c) > 0. \tag{3.19 b}$$

All three OC functions are defined only on the interval $[0,1]$ for discrete values $P = M/N, M = 0, 1, \ldots, N$. The domains of the functions

$$L(P|n;c) = \sum_{i=0}^{c} \binom{n}{i} P^i (1-P)^{n-i} \tag{3.20}$$

$$L^*(P|n;c) = \sum_{i=0}^{c} \frac{(nP)^i}{i!} e^{-nP} \tag{3.21}$$

can be easily extended to the entire interval $[0, 1]$, since all terms of the sums in (3.20) and (3.21) can be calculated for any $P \in [0,1]$. On this interval the functions (3.20) and (3.21) are continuous and even differentiable in P. The corresponding derivatives are: Slope of the binomial and the Poisson OC function

$$m_B(P) := \frac{d}{dP} L(P|n;c) = -\frac{n!}{c!(n-c-1)!} P^c (1-P)^{n-c-1} \tag{3.22}$$

$$m_P(P) := \frac{d}{dP} L^*(P|n;c) = -\frac{n(nP)^c}{c!} e^{-nP}. \tag{3.23}$$

The hypergeometric OC function in its representation as a sum

$$L(P|N;n;c) = \sum_{i=0}^{c} = \frac{\binom{NP}{i}\binom{N-NP}{n-i}}{\binom{N}{n}} \tag{3.24}$$

can be continuously extended to the interval [0,1] by using the fact that the binomial coefficient may be expressed as

$$\binom{m}{k} = \frac{\Gamma(m+1)}{\Gamma(k+1) \cdot \Gamma(m-k+1)}.$$

This follows from (2.36b). Derivation of (3.24) in its gamma function representation with respect to P results in a complicated and not easy to handle expression. That is why another approach has been chosen.

In this situation it can help to connect, with a straight line, each point $(M/N; L(M/N|N;n;c))$ of the graph of the hypergeometric OC function to its right neighbour $((M+1)/N; L((M+1)/N|N;n;c))$, and to define the slope of this line to be the slope of $L(P|N;n;c)$ at $P = M/N$. The slope of the straight line, $\hat{m}_H(P)$, is given by

Slope of the hypergeometric OC function

$$\hat{m}_H(P) = \frac{\Delta L(P|N;n;c)}{1/N} = N \cdot \Delta L(P|N;n;c) \tag{3.25}$$

with

$$\Delta L(P|N;n;c) := L\left(\tfrac{M+1}{N}|N;n;c\right) - L\left(\tfrac{M}{N}|N;n;c\right). \tag{3.26 a}$$

The relationship (3.25) can be illustrated by figure 3.2/9. It can be shown that (3.26a) can be written as

$$\Delta L(P|N;n;c) = -\frac{\binom{M}{c}\binom{N-M-1}{n-c-1}}{\binom{N}{n}} \quad \text{for} \quad c \le M \le N-n-c. \tag{3.26 b}$$

If there is a fraction defective P_T for which the first derivatives (3.22) and (3.23) or the slope (3.25) have a maximum, we will call that P_T the **turning point** of that particular OC function. OC functions without a turning point are either **convex** or **concave** over their entire range. The graph of a convex function is "dome shaped" and a concave function is "cup shaped". If one of the three OC functions considered above has a turning point, then the graph will not be globally convex or concave, but it will be concave between the origin and the turning point and convex afterwards.

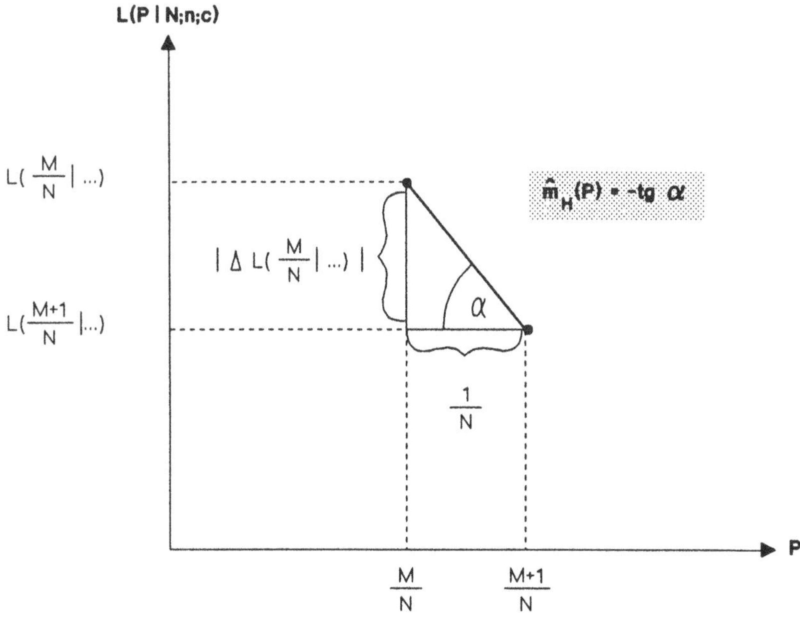

Figure 3.2/9: Slope $\hat{m}_H(P)$ of the hypergeometric OC function at $P = M/N$

For example the function $L(P|2000;50;0)$ in figure 3.2/6 is globally convex, but $L(P|2000;50;2)$ is partly convex and partly concave. We can see from this figure that the existence of a turning point depends on the value of the acceptance number c which obviously needs to satisfy $0 \leq c \leq n-1$. We will discuss the three cases $c = 0$, $0 < c < n-1$ and $c = n-1$ separately.

Properties of the OC functions:

When $c = 0$, all three OC functions are globally convex and hence do not have a turning point. It further holds (see problem 3.2/5) that

- globally convex for $c = 0$

$$L(P|N;n;c) < L(P|n;c) < L^*(P|n;c) \quad \text{for } P \in (0;1). \tag{3.27}$$

The three OC curves do not intersect each other on the open interval (0,1).

When $c = n-1$, which is only relevant if the sample size is extremely small, $L^*(P|n;c)$ has exactly one turning point $P_T^P = (n-1)/n$, and is partly concave and partly convex. The functions $L(P|N;n;c)$ and $L(P|n;c)$ are globally concave and it holds that

- globally or partly concave for $c = n-1$

$$L(P|N;n;c) > L(P|n;c) \quad \text{for } P \in (0;1). \tag{3.28}$$

The curve of $L^*(P|n;c)$ intersects each of the curves $L(P|N;n;c)$ and $L(P|n;c)$ exactly once.

When $0 < c < n-1$, all three OC functions have a turning point and thus are partly concave and partly convex. The turning points are

- partly concave / convex for $0 < c < n-1$

$$P_T^B = \frac{c}{n-1} \qquad \text{for } L(P|n;c), \tag{3.29 a}$$
$$P_T^P = \frac{c}{n} \qquad \text{for } L^*(P|n;c), \tag{3.29 b}$$
$$P_T^H = \frac{1}{N} \cdot \left[\frac{Nc}{n-1}\right] \qquad \text{for } L(P|N;n;c).\ ^3 \tag{3.29 c}$$

The OC functions intersect each other exactly once in the interval (0,1).

As we have already explained, the slope of the OC function at the turning point is a measure of the discriminating power of the single attributive plan (N;n;c) or, respectively, of the underlying hypothesis test (3.2). Before, we called this slope the **steepness** of the OC function. The steepness $h = m(P_T)$ can be obtained by applying (3.29a)–(3.29c) to (3.22), (3.23) or (3.25), respectively:

Steepness of the OC function

$$h^B = -\frac{n!}{c!(n-c-1)!} \cdot \frac{c^c(n-c-1)^{n-c-1}}{(n-1)^{n-1}} \quad \text{for } L(P|N;c) \tag{3.30 a}$$
$$h^P = -\frac{nc^c}{c!}e^{-c} \qquad \text{for } L^*(P|n;c) \tag{3.30 b}$$
$$h^H = -\frac{\binom{M_T}{c}\binom{N-M_T-1}{n-c-1}}{\binom{N}{n}} \cdot N \qquad \text{for } L(P|N;n;c). \tag{3.30 c}$$

In (3.30c) we used the notation $M_T := N \cdot P_T^H$. The slopes $k = m(P_{0.5})$ at the indifference points of the OC curve can be used as approximations of (3.30a)–(3.30c).

According to (2.146) the formulae (3.22), (3.23) and (3.25) which give the slopes $m(P)$ of the three OC functions can be used to calculate the elasticity $\varepsilon(P)$ of these functions. We only give the formula for the Poisson elasticity, because it is the only case where the elasticity $\varepsilon(P)$ can be written in a reasonably nice form:

Elasticity of the Poisson OC function

- at any point P

$$\varepsilon(P) = -\frac{P}{Po(c|nP)} \cdot \frac{n(nP)^c}{c!} \cdot e^{-nP}. \tag{3.31}$$

Since $L^*(P|n;c) = Po(c|nP)$ takes the value 0.5 at the indifference point, function (3.31) evaluated at $P = P_{0.5}^P$ is of the form

- at the indifference point

$$\varepsilon(P_{0.5}^P) = -2 \cdot \frac{\left(n\,P_{0.5}^P\right)^{c+1}}{c!} \cdot e^{-nP_{0.5}^P}. \tag{3.32 a}$$

HAMAKER (1950) gives the approximation

[3] $[\cdot]$ denotes again the Gauss bracket function.

$$\varepsilon(P^P_{0.5}) \approx -\sqrt{\frac{2}{\pi}(c+0.73)}. \qquad (3.32\text{ b})$$

If the Poisson OC function has a turning point P_T^P, i.e., in the case of $1 \leq c \leq n-2$, this point agrees approximately with $P^P_{0.5}$. In other words, the formulae (3.32a-b) also approximate the elasiticity $\varepsilon(P_T^P)$ at the turning point.

Example 3.2/6

Let $N = 50, n = 8, c = 2$. In practice the case $0 < c < n-1$ is most common. For this plan we will compare the hypergeometric OC function

$$L(P|50;8;2) = Hy(2|50;50P;8)$$

with its approximations (3.9b) and (3.14b)

$$L(P|8;2) := Bi(2|P;8)$$

$$L^*(P|8;2) := Po(2|8P).$$

The calculations result in the following table 3.2/3. The corresponding figure is omitted because the three OC curves are virtually identical for $P \leq 0.3$. It can be seen from table 3.2/3 that the three curves intersect each other once: $L(P|50;8;2)$ and $L(P|8;2)$ at about $P \approx 0.28$; $L(P|50;8;2)$ and $L^*(P|8;2)$ as well as $L(P|8;2)$ and $L^*(P|8;2)$ at $P \approx 0.26$.

We know from our previous discussion that, for $0 < c < n-1$, the turning points of the three OC functions are calculated by (3.29):

$$P_T^B = 2/7 \approx 0.2857$$

$$P_T^P = 2/8 = 0.25$$

$$P_T^H = \frac{1}{50} \cdot \left\lceil 50 \cdot \frac{2}{7} \right\rceil = \frac{2}{7} = 0.28.$$

The steepness at the turning point, i.e., the slope $h = m(P_T)$, is obtained from (3.30):

$$h^B = -\frac{8!}{2!\,5!} \cdot \frac{2^2 5^5}{7^7} \approx -2.5500$$

$$h^P = -\frac{8 \cdot 2^2}{2!} e^{-2} \approx -2.1654$$

$$h^H = -50 \cdot \frac{\binom{14}{2}\binom{35}{5}}{\binom{50}{8}} = -\frac{50 \cdot 91 \cdot 324632}{536878650} \approx -2.7512.$$

P	$L(P\|50;8;2)$	$L(P\|8;2)$	$L^*(P\|8;2)$
0	1	1	1
0.02	1	0.9996	0.9994
0.04	1	0.9969	0.9957
0.06	0.9971	0.9904	0.9871
0.08	0.9895	0.9789	0.9727
0.10	0.9758	0.9619	0.9526
0.12	0.9556	0.9392	0.9269
0.14	0.9287	0.9109	0.8964
0.16	0.8954	0.8774	0.8617
0.18	0.8563	0.8392	0.8238
0.20	0.8122	0.7969	0.7834
0.22	0.7640	0.7514	0.7413
0.24	0.7125	0.7033	0.6983
0.26	0.6590	0.6535	0.6550
0.28	0.6042	0.6027	0.6120
0.30	0.5492	0.5518	0.5697
0.32	0.4947	0.5013	0.5285
0.34	0.4417	0.4519	0.4887
0.36	0.3907	0.4042	0.4506
0.38	0.3423	0.3585	0.4143
0.40	0.2969	0.3154	0.3799

Table 3.2/3: Values of the three OC functions for the plan (50;8;2)

We further see that

$$|h^H| > |h^B| > |h^P|.$$

This means that the plan (50;8;2), and the underlying hypothesis test (3.2), has the best discriminating power when the statistic X_8^T (the number of nonconforming sample units) has a hypergeometric distribution.

The steepness h can also be expressed in terms of an angle α. For example, the result $h^B \approx -2.55$ implies that, at the turning point P_T^B, the angle α between the tangent on $L(P|n;c)$ and the negative direction of the P-axis is given by $-\tan(\alpha) = m_B(P_T) = h^B$, i.e., $\tan\alpha \approx 2.55$. From this we can calculate that the tangent at P_T^B has an angle of $\alpha \approx 68.59°$. In the same manner we derive from $h^P \approx -2.1654$, that the tangent of $L^*(P|n;c)$ at P_T^P has an angle $\alpha \approx 65.21°$. From the result $h^H \approx -2.7512$ it follows that the straight line that joins the values of the function $L(P|N;n;c)$ at $P_T^H = M_T/N$ and $P = (M_T + 1)/\text{N}$ has an angle of $\alpha \approx 70.02°$.

3.2.2 Measuring the Performance of Single-Sampling Plans

From a statistical point of view the performance of a sampling-plan is completely described by its OC function $L(P)$. The calculation of the entire OC curve requires a lot of work, unless one has access to a computer and the necessary software. In most applications, however, one does not use the complete OC function. Usually one works with only a few points of the OC curve. Section 3.2.2a will explain how to characterize the performance of a plan by percentiles, for example. In this approach one determines specific quality levels P_ω for which the acceptance probability of the test lot has value ω. Further, the user of a plan wants to know what proportion of nonconforming units slips through the inspection and, also, about the average costs involved with the special treatment that will be applied to "bad" lots. In sections 3.2.2b-c we will first answer these questions and then in section 3.2.2d we will talk about curtailed inspection using the average sample size as an additional performance measure.

Preview of section 3.2.2

a) OC Percentiles

In section 2.3.2c the inverse, $P = L^{-1}(y)$, of an OC function, $y = L(P)$, was denoted as the **percentile function of the OC function** $L(P)$. The percentile function gives the fraction defective, P_ω, of a lot for which the lot is accepted with a given probability ω. This value, P_ω, is named the **100·ω percentile of the OC function** or **percentile of order** ω. For the OC function $y = L(\lambda)$ we can replace the argument P, the average number of defectives, by the average number of defects λ, according to (2.136), and thus define a percentile function $\lambda = L^{-1}(y)$, the percentile λ_ω:

$$P_\omega \text{ is percentile of order } \omega \text{ of the OC function } L(P) \Leftrightarrow L(P_\omega) = \omega. \tag{3.33 a}$$

$$\lambda_\omega \text{ is percentile of order } \omega \text{ of the OC function } L(\lambda) \Leftrightarrow L(\lambda_\omega) = \omega. \tag{3.33 b}$$

For some special percentiles we introduced particular notations in section 2.3.2c. We now will recall this terminology in the context of percentiles of an OC function of type $y = L(P)$. The following also applies to percentiles of OC functions of type $y = L(\lambda)$.

An OC percentile, P_ω, of order ω with a rather small value of ω (usually $\omega = 0.1$), that the consumer and producer agreed upon, is called the **rejectable quality level**, and is abbreviated by **RQL**.[4] Since the OC

Special OC percentiles

[4] Other terms like **LQ** (limiting quality) and **LTPD** (lot tolerance per cent defective) are used in some literature.

function, $y = L(P)$, for the underlying test (3.2) is strictly monotone decreasing, it follows that the probability of accepting a lot with fraction defective $P \geq RQL$ is at most ω. In the case $\omega = 0.1$ we get

$$P \geq P_{0.1} = RQL \Rightarrow L(P) \leq 0.1 \tag{3.34 a}$$

(see figure 3.2/10). The agreement upon a RQL value aims at protecting the consumer from accepting lots with an untolerable fraction defective. Lots with fraction defective $P \geq RQL$ should usually be rejected. Consequently the smaller the RQL value is the more favourable the plan is for the consumer. The probability ω for the acceptance of "bad" lots, i.e., lots with $P \geq P_\omega = RQL$, is the **consumer's risk**. It is at most ω and represents the type II error probability of the underlying hypothesis test.

The OC percentile P_ω of order ω with a rather large value of ω (usually $\omega = 0.99$), that has been agreed upon between the consumer and producer, is called the **acceptable quality level**, abbreviated by **AQL**. Due to the strict monotonicity of $L(P)$, the probability of accepting lots with $P \leq AQL$ is at least ω. In other words the rejection probability $G(P) = 1 - L(P)$ is at most $1 - \omega$. For example, for $\omega = 0.99$ we get

$$P \leq P_{0.99} = AQL \Rightarrow L(P) \geq 0.99 \Rightarrow G(P) \leq 0.01. \tag{3.34 b}$$

Fixing the AQL value is in the interest of the producer. He wants to assure that lots which are conforming to the quality requirements are mostly accepted. It is clear that for larger AQL a plan is more favourable for the producer. The probability $1 - \omega$ of rejecting "good" lots, i.e., lots with $P \leq P_\omega = AQL$ is called the **producer's risk**. It is at most $1 - \omega$ and represents the type I error probability of the underlying hypothesis test.

The term **indifferent quality level**, abbreviated by **IQL**, denotes the quality level $P_{0.5}$ with lot acceptance probability $\omega = 0.5$:

$$P = P_{0.5} =: IQL \Rightarrow L(P) = 0.5. \tag{3.34 c}$$

We already illustrated the above concepts in section 2.3.2e with the example of a hypothesis test (3.2) with $P_0 = 0.2, c = 10$ and $n = 30$. Let $RQL = P_{0.05}$ and $AQL = P_{0.975}$, and assume the binomial case, i.e., the OC function is $L(P|30; 10) = Bi(10|P; 30)$. The graph of this function is given in figure 2.3/5 (see also solution of problem 2.3/8a). A type I error can only occur if the fraction defective P lies within the range Ω_0 of the null hypothesis $H_0 : P \leq P_0$; a type II error can only occur for a fraction defective P within Ω_1, the range of the alternative hypothesis $H_1 : P > P_0$. We know from (2.134) that, for any $P \in \Omega_0$, the probability of committing a type I error (rejecting H_0 when in fact H_0 is true) is given by $1 - L(P)$

and, for any $P \in \Omega_1$, the probability of committing a type II error is given by $L(P)$. We will introduce formula (3.38) to calculate the percentiles at a later point. Here the percentiles were found to be $AQL \approx 0.1993$, $IQL \approx 0.3526$ and $RQL \approx 0.4996$.

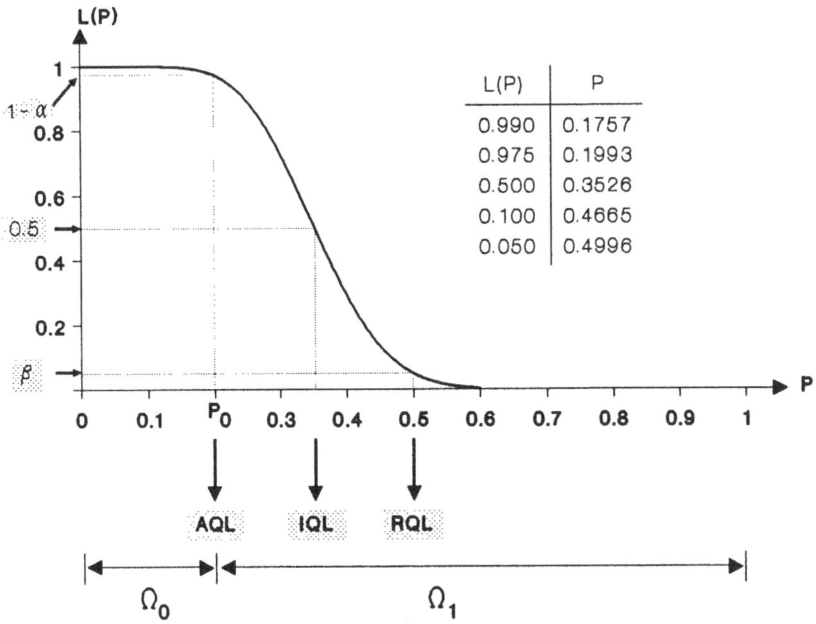

Figure 3.2/10: AQL, IQL and RQL of an OC function

It follows that $1 - L(AQL)$ is the probability of a type I error, because $AQL \in \Omega_0$, whereas $L(IQL)$ and $L(RQL)$ are probabilities of type II errors.

Depending on the underlying OC function, we speak of hypergeometric OC percentiles, binomial OC percentiles and Poisson OC percentiles, and we denote them as follows:

- P_ω^H hypergeometric OC percentile; percentile of $L(P|N;n;c)$
- P_ω^B binomial OC percentile; percentile of $L(P|n;c)$
- $P_\omega^P, \lambda_\omega$ Poisson OC percentile; percentile of $L^*(P|n;c)$ resp. $L^*(\lambda|n;c)$.

Calculation of Poisson percentiles:

Of the three different percentiles, Poisson OC percentiles are the easiest to calculate. They can be determined through the equations in (3.17), which are by (3.13) and (3.16) equivalent to (2.112a) when we set $k = c$

and replace λ by $n\lambda$ or nP, respectively. Since (2.112a) is equivalent to (2.112b), we can deduce the following equation for P_ω^P:

$$2nP_\omega^P = \chi^2_{2(c+1);1-\omega} = Ch^{-1}[1-\omega|2(c+1)].$$

- using percentiles of the χ^2 distribution

The same also holds for λ_ω. Thus we get

$$P_\omega^P = \lambda_\omega = \frac{1}{2n}\chi^2_{2(c+1);1-\omega}. \tag{3.35 a}$$

Table 5.2/4 gives selected percentiles $\chi^2_{\nu,\omega}$ of the χ^2 distribution. With this table, Poisson percentiles can be calculated for given values of n, c, and ω.

Alternatively, as a result of (3.18), we can determine P_ω and λ_ω by

$$P_\omega^P = \lambda_\omega = \frac{g_{c+1;1-\omega}}{n}, \tag{3.35 b}$$

- using percentiles of the gamma distribution

where

$$g_{c+1;1-\omega} := Ga^{-1}(1-\omega|1;c+1). \tag{3.36 a}$$

The term (3.36a) is a percentile of the gamma distribution (2.35) with $b = 1$. These percentiles are tabulated in table 5.2/5. They are defined not only for integer valued c, but for any real c with $c+1 > 0$. For integer valued c the percentiles in (3.35b) agree with those in (3.35a):

$$g_{c+1;1-\omega} = \frac{1}{2}\chi^2_{2(c+1);1-\omega}\,; \qquad c = 0, 1, 2, \ldots \tag{3.36 b}$$

Equation (3.35b) is especially useful for determining the IQL value $P_{0.5}^P$ of the Poisson OC function. An approximation is given by HALD (1981, p.39):

$$P_{0.5}^P \approx \frac{c+\frac{2}{3}}{n}. \tag{3.37}$$

This approximation is very useful in practical applications because it does not require the use of a table. By looking through the percentiles in table 5.2/5 for the column $\omega = 0.5$, one can verify that setting $g_{c+1;0.5}$ to $c+2/3$ yields a good approximation (see also problem 3.2/9a).

For the calculation of binomial OC percentiles we will give two exact and two approximate formulas. The first exact formula is derived from (3.11) and the fact that, by (3.8a), it agrees with (2.118a) when setting $k = c$. Since (2.118a) and (2.118b) are equivalent, it follows that P_ω^B is a binomial OC percentile of order ω if and only if

Calculation of binomial percentiles:

- using percentiles of the F distribution

$$\frac{n-c}{c+1}\cdot\frac{P_\omega^B}{1-P_\omega^B} = F_{2(c+1);2(n-c);1-\omega} := Fi^{-1}[1-\omega|2(c+1);2(n-c)].$$

Solving for P_ω^B yields

$$P_\omega^B = \frac{(c+1)\cdot F_{2(c+1);2(n-c);1-\omega}}{n-c+(c+1)\cdot F_{2(c+1);2(n-c);1-\omega}}. \tag{3.38 a}$$

Result (2.117b) allows us to substitute $F_{2(c+1);2(n-c);1-\omega}$ in (3.38a) by the reciprocal of $F_{2(n-c);2(c+1);\omega}$. This way we get

$$P_\omega^B = \frac{c+1}{c+1+(n-c)\cdot F_{2(n-c);2(c+1);\omega}}. \tag{3.38 b}$$

The percentiles $F_{\nu_1;\nu_2;\omega}$ of the F distribution are given in table 5.2/3. Since they are only given for $\alpha \geq 0.5$ we need to use formula (3.38a) if $\alpha < 0.5$ and (3.38b) if $\alpha \geq 0.5$.

If one has access to tables of percentiles $Bt^{-1}(\omega|\gamma;\delta)$ of the beta distribution function, one can use formula (3.10) to calculate binomial percentiles. Similar to (3.35b), we get for P_ω^B

- using percentiles of the beta distribution

$$P_\omega^B = Bt^{-1}(1-\omega|c+1;n-c). \tag{3.38 c}$$

Approximations for P_ω^B are based on the Poisson approximation of the binomial OC function $L(P|n;c)$. By (3.15b) and (3.35b) it follows that

- Poisson approximation

$$P_\omega^B \approx P_\omega^P = \frac{g_{c+1;1-\omega}}{n}. \tag{3.39 a}$$

An even better approximation is given by HALD (1981, p.40)

- modified Poisson approximation

$$P_\omega^B \approx \frac{g_{c+1;1-\omega}}{n+0.5\cdot(g_{c+1;1-\omega}-c)}. \tag{3.39 b}$$

The IQL value $P_{0.5}^B$ can be calculated exactly by (3.38) and appoximately by (3.39). HALD (1981, p. 39) also gives a simple formula for this special case of the IQL that is almost as exact as the approximation (3.39b) (see also problem 3.2/9b):

$$P_{0.5}^B \approx \frac{c+\frac{2}{3}}{n+\frac{1}{3}}. \tag{3.40}$$

Hypergeometric OC percentiles can only be determined approximately. For the binomial approximation (3.9a) of the hypergeometric OC function $L(P|N;n;c)$ we have the result

Calculation of hypergeometric OC percentiles

- binomial approximation

$$P_\omega^H \approx P_\omega^B \tag{3.41 a}$$

and for the Poisson approximation we have

- Poisson approximation

$$P_\omega^H \approx P_\omega^P \approx \frac{g_{c+1;1-\omega}}{n}. \tag{3.41 b}$$

- modified Poisson approximation

HALD (1981, p. 44) suggests replacing (3.41b) by the more exact approximation

$$P_\omega^H \approx \frac{g_{c+1;1-\omega} \cdot (2N - n + 1) + c \cdot (n - 0.5c)}{N \cdot (2n + g_{c+1;1-\omega} - c)}. \tag{3.41 c}$$

HALD (1981, p. 44) also gives a simplified approximation for the special case $IQL = P_{0.5}^H$ of the hypergeometric OC function, which is almost as good as the approximation formula (3.41c):

$$P_{0.5}^H \approx \frac{\left(c + \frac{2}{3}\right) - \frac{n}{3N}}{\left(n + \frac{1}{3}\right) - \frac{2n}{3N}}. \tag{3.42}$$

The most important results of sections 3.2.1c - 3.2.2a, which are the representations of the hypergeometric, binomial and Poisson OC functions and the calculation of the corresponding percentiles, are summarized in table 3.2/4.

Example 3.2/7

We are asked to determine the OC percentile $P_{0.95}^B$ for a plan $(N; n; c)$ with $n = 25$ and $c = 5$.
Using table 5.2/8 and (3.38b) gives

$$P_{0.95}^B = \frac{6}{6 + 20 \cdot F_{40;12;0.95}} \approx \frac{6}{6 + 20 \cdot 2.43} \approx 0.1099.$$

The approximation (3.39a) gives, together with (3.36b) and table 5.2/4,

$$P_{0.95}^B \approx P_{0.95}^P = \frac{1}{50} \cdot \chi_{12;0.05}^2 \approx \frac{5.226}{50} \approx 0.1045,$$

or equivalently, using (3.36a) instead of (3.36b), and table 5.2/5,

$$P_{0.95}^B \approx P_{0.95}^P = \frac{1}{25} \cdot g_{6;0.05} \approx \frac{2.613}{25} \approx 0.1045.$$

The more exact approximation (3.39b) yields

$$P_{0.95}^B \approx \frac{2.613}{25 + 0.5 \cdot (2.613 - 5)} \approx 0.1098.$$

OC function $L(P)$	Approximations of the OC function	OC percentile P_ω	HALD's approximations of the $IQL := P_{0.5}$
Hypergeometric OC function: $L(P\|N;n;c) = Hy(c\|N;NP;n) = \sum_{i=0}^{c} \frac{\binom{NP}{i}\binom{N-NP}{n-i}}{\binom{N}{n}}$ with $NP = 0, 1, 2, \ldots$	Binomial approximation: $L(P\|N;n;c) \approx L(P\|n;c)$ if $0.1 < P < 0.9$; $n > 10; n/N < 0.1$ Poisson approximation: $L(P\|N;n;c) \approx L^*(P\|n;c)$ if $P \leq 0.1$ (or $P \geq 0.9$); $n \geq 30;\ n/N < 0.1$	$P_\omega^H \approx \frac{g_{c+1;1-\omega}(2N - n + 1) + c(n - 0.5c)}{N\,(2n + g_{c+1;1-\omega} - c)}$ with $g_{c+1;1-\omega} = Ga^{-1}(1-\omega\|1;c+1)$	$P_{0.5}^H \approx \frac{\left(c+\frac{2}{3}\right) - \frac{n}{3N}}{\left(n+\frac{1}{3}\right) - \frac{2n}{3N}}$
Binomial OC function: $L(P\|n;c) = Bi(c\|P;n) = \sum_{i=0}^{c}\binom{n}{i}P^i(1-P)^{n-i} = 1 - Fi\left[\frac{n-c}{c+1}\frac{P}{1-P}\right\| 2(c+1); 2(n-c)\right] = 1 - Bt(P\|c+1;n-c)$	Poisson approximation: $L(P\|n;c) \approx L^*(P\|n;c)$ if $nP < 10$ and $n > 1500P$	$P_\omega^B = \frac{c+1}{c+1+(n-c)F_{2(n-c);2(c+1);\omega}} = \frac{(c+1)F_{2(c+1);2(n-c);1-\omega}}{n-c+(c-+1)F_{2(c+1);2(n-c);1-\omega}} = Bt^{-1}(1-\omega\|c+1;n-c)$ $P_\omega^B \approx \frac{g_{c+1;1-\omega}}{n+0.5\,(g_{c+1;1-\omega-c})}$	$P_\omega^B \approx \frac{c+\frac{2}{3}}{n+\frac{}{3}}$
Poisson OC function: $L^*(P\|n;c) = Po(c\|nP) = \sum_{i=0}^{c}\frac{(NP)^i}{i!}e^{-nP} = 1 - Ch[2nP\|2(c+1)] = 1 - Ga(nP\|1;c+1)$		$P_\omega^P = \frac{1}{2n}\chi^2_{2(c+1);1-\omega} = \frac{g_{c+1;1-\omega}}{n}$	$P_{0.5}^P \approx \frac{c+\frac{2}{3}}{n}$

Table 3.2/4: OC functions and OC percentiles for single-sampling plans by attributes

Problem 3.2/8

a) For $n = 100$ and $c = 3$ calculate the Poisson OC percentiles P_ω^P of order ω= 0.999, 0.99, 0.50, 0.1 and 0.01.

b) Determine the OC percentiles $P_{0.95}^B$ for the three OC functions in figure 3.2/8 using formula (3.38b).

c) Calculate the approximations (3.39a) and (3.39b) for the three binomial OC percentiles in part b) and compare them to the exact results.

Problem 3.2/9

a) Find the percentiles $P_{0.1}^P =: RQL$, $P_{0.5}^P =: IQL$ and $P_{0.95}^P =: AQL$ for the Poisson OC function in example 3.2/6 using (3.35b). What IQL value does the approximation (3.37) give?

b) Use (3.39b) to calculate the same percentiles for the binomial OC function $L(P|8;2)$. Obtain the exact IQL with (3.38b) and its alternative approximation (3.40).

c) Apply approximation (3.41c) to determine the above percentiles for the hypergeometric OC function $L(P|50;8;2)$ of example 3.2/6. What are the IQL values obtained by (3.41b) and (3.42)?

Problem 3.2/10

a) For the Poisson OC function $L(P|8;2)$ of example 3.2/6 obtain the elasticity $\varepsilon(P_{0.5}^P)$ at the indifference point $P_{0.5}^P$, where by (3.37) $P_{0.5}^P \approx \frac{1}{3}$. First use the exact formula (3.31) with $P = P_{0.5}^P$, then try the approximation (3.32) and interpret the second result.

b) Adapt (3.31) for the binomial case and use the result to determine the elasticity of $L(P|8;2)$ at the indifference point $P_{0.5}^B$. You can use the fact that $P_{0.5}^B \approx 0.32$, by (3.40).

Problem 3.2/11

a) Suppose it is required that the AQL and RQL values of the plan $(N;n;c)$ lie close together. Give a general description of such a plan.

b) Let P_ω^H $(0 < \omega < 1)$ be a given percentile of the OC function $L(P|N;n;c)$. Describe the relationship between this hypergeometric percentile and the corresponding OC percentiles P_ω^B and P_ω^P .

b) Average Outgoing Quality (AOQ and AOQL)

When administering a particular plan $(N; n; c)$, the consumer is not only interested in the probability $L(P)$ of accepting lots with quality level P, but also wants to know the proportion of defective units that slip through the inspection procedure. The application of the discussed plans $(N; n; c)$, even of those with $c = 0$, does not protect against accepting "bad" units. It only ensures that " good " lots are accepted with high probability and that "bad" lots are rejected with high probability.

In the following discussion, we will assume that the manufacturer delivers lots with constant quality level P. Thus a lot of N units contains exactly $M := N \cdot P$ defective units. A measure of the proportion of defective units that slip through inspection is the **average outgoing quality**, denoted **AOQ**.[5] Denote the number of defective units that slipped through inspection by Y_1 and the total number of accepted units by Y_2. It will be illustrated later that the variables Y_1 and Y_2 are to be seen as conditional expectations. We will define the AOQ by

Definition of AOQ

$$AOQ := \frac{E(Y_1)}{E(Y_2)}. \tag{3.43}$$

The average outgoing quality AOQ is a function of the quality level P in the incoming lots. This is expressed by the notation $AOQ = AOQ(P)$. This function attains a maximum for a particular $P = P_M$ The corresponding value $AOQ(P_M)$ is called the **average outgoing quality limit**, abbreviated by **AOQL**

Definition of $AOQL$

$$AOQL := \max_P AOQ(P) = AOQ(P_M). \tag{3.44}$$

We will first discuss the issue of finding the AOQ for a given quality level P. The number Y_2 in the numerator of (3.43) depends on the disposition of the n sample units after the inspection. There are three possible cases S_i, $(i = 1, 2, 3)$:

Disposition of the sample

- S_1: Neither the conforming nor the defective units of the test sample are put back into the lot after the inspection and no replacement is made.
- S_2: All defective units in the sample are sorted out and not replaced.
- S_3: All defect units in the sample are taken aside and replaced by "good" units (sample size n is preserved).

[5] See remark 1 at the end of this section for a comment on this definition.

Disposition of the remaining lot in the case of rejection

The variable Y_2 further depends on the disposition of the $N-n$ units in the remaining lot in the case of rejection of the original lot. We will again discuss three possibilities, denoted L_j, $(j = 1, 2, 3)$:

- L_1: All $N-n$ units in the remaining lot are discarded.
- L_2: The remaining lot is submitted to screening and all defective units are discarded without replacement.
- L_3: The remaining lot is submitted to screening and defective units are replaced by good units (the size $N-n$ of the remaining lot is preserved).

In general each type of sample disposition can be combined with each type of remaining lot disposition. If a rejected lot is 100% inspected and if defective units are replaced by good units, we speak of a **rectifying inspection**. The possible combinations for rectifying inspection are S_i/L_3.

Since we distinguished between nine disposition combinations S_i/L_j we need to consider the same cases for $AOQ(P)$. The results are summarized in table 3.2/5 (see also WORTHAM/MOGG 1970 and BEAINY/CASE 1981):

	L_1 remaining lot is not used	L_2 remaining lot is used after defectives are sorted out	L_3 remaining lot is used after replacement of defectives
S_1 sample is not used	$AOQ(P) = P$	$AOQ(P) = \frac{P \cdot L(P)}{1-P \cdot [1-L(P)]}$	$AOQ(P) = P \cdot L(P)$
S_2 conforming units in the sample are used, defectives are sorted out	$AOQ(P) = \frac{(N-n) \cdot P \cdot L(P)}{(N-n) \cdot L(P)+n \cdot (1-P)}$	$AOQ(P) = \frac{(N-n) \cdot P \cdot L(P)}{N-nP-(N-n) \cdot [1-L(P)]}$	$AOQ(P) = \frac{(N-n) \cdot P \cdot L(P)}{(N-n \cdot P}$
S_3 defective units are replaced and sample is used	$AOQ(P) = \frac{(N-n) \cdot P \cdot L(P)}{(N-n) \cdot L(P)+n}$	$AOQ(P) = \frac{(N-n) \cdot P \cdot L(P)}{N-(N-n) \cdot P \cdot [1-L(P)]}$	$AOQ(P) = \frac{(N-n)}{N} \cdot P \cdot L(P)$

Table 3.2/5: *AOQ* functions for different combinations of sample and remaining lot disposition for a single-sampling plan

In order to clarify the understanding of the *AOQ* formulas in table 3.2/5 we want to demonstrate that the expected value $E(Y_1)$ in the numerator of (3.43) is the same for all nine cases. First we notice that units that slip through the inspection can only come from the remaining lot and never from the sample, because either the whole sample is discarded (S_1) or the defective units are discarded (S_2) or replaced (S_3). The number of defective units in the remaining lot is the random variable X_{N-n}^T, which was introduced in (3.5). Its expectation is different for accepted and rejected lots. In the case of rejected lots, $X_n^T > c$, we respond with 100% control and either discarding (L_2) or replacement (L_3) of defective units, or by discarding the entire remaining lot without inspection. This ensures that in the case of a rejected lot no defective units can get to the consumer through the remaining lot:

Considerations with respect to AOQ calculations

$$Y_1 = E\left(X_{N-n}^T | X_n^T > c\right) = 0.$$

If $X_n^T \leq c$ the lot is accepted and the remaining $N - n$ units are not inspected. Hence

$$Y_1 = E\left(X_{N-n}^T | X_n^T \leq c\right) = (N - n) \cdot P.$$

Put together, the number of defectives Y_1 that slip through the inspection is given by

$$Y_1 = \begin{cases} (N-n) \cdot P & \text{if } X_n^T \leq c \\ 0 & \text{if } X_n^T > c. \end{cases} \tag{3.45}$$

The probabilities that the conditions $X_n^T > c$ and $X_n^T \leq c$ occur are the rejection probability $1 - L(P)$ and the acceptance probability $L(P)$, respectively. Consequently, the expectation $E(Y_1)$ is determined by

$$E(Y_1) = E\left(X_{N-n}^T | X_n^T > c\right) \cdot [1 - L(P)] + E\left(X_{N-n}^T | X_n^T \leq c\right) \cdot L(P).$$

Applying (3.45) yields

$$E(Y_1) = (N - n) \cdot P \cdot L(P). \tag{3.46}$$

In each of the nine cases of table 3.2/5, the AOQ is of the form

$$AOQ(P) = \frac{(N - n) \cdot P \cdot L(P)}{E(Y_2)}. \tag{3.47}$$

The expected value of Y_2, the number of accepted units in a lot, depends on the particular chosen combination of sample and remaining lot disposition. As an example we will discuss the combination S_2/L_2. Similar to Y_1, the variable Y_2 can be expressed in terms of a conditional expectation. When $X_n^T \leq c$, i.e., acceptance of the lot, the size of the accepted lot is $Y_2 = N - nP$, because, by disposition rule S_2, the lot size is reduced by the mean number of defectives in the sample (no replacement in the case of S_2). For $X_n^T > c$, when the lot is rejected, on the average nP units are sorted out from the sample by S_2 and $(N-n)P$ units are sorted out from the rest lot. This yields $Y_2 = N - nP - (N-n)P$. Put together, we finally have

$$Y_2 = \begin{cases} N - nP & \text{if } X_n^T \leq c \\ N - NP & \text{if } X_n^T > c. \end{cases} \tag{3.48}$$

The probabilities that the conditions $X_n^T \leq c$ and $X_n^T > c$ occur are again $L(P)$ and $1 - L(P)$, respectively, and this determines $\mathrm{E}(Y_2)$ to be

$$\begin{aligned} E(Y_2) &= (N - nP) \cdot L(P) + (N - NP) \cdot [1 - L(P)] \\ &= (N - nP) - (N - n) \cdot P \cdot [1 - L(P)]. \end{aligned} \tag{3.49}$$

Combining (3.47) and (3.49) confirms the AOQ formula for S_2/L_2 in table 3.2/5. In the same way, the AOQ formulas for the remaining cases can be verified.

Which disposition combinations are relevant in practice?

Among the nine possible combinations in table 3.2/5, the ones that are most commonly used in practice treat the sample and remaining lot in the same way. These combinations S_i/L_j with $i = j$ are on the principal diagonal of the table. **Destructive inspection** works with combination S_1/L_1. The result $AOQ(P) = P$ tells us that the output quality is the same as the input quality P, provided that the quality level P of the received lots does not change over time. If we rate a control procedure by how much the average outgoing quality falls below the input quality P, then the destructive inspection gives the worst result. The destructive inspection is only meaningful if lots of varying quality levels P are delivered. Then this procedure protects the consumer from accepting lots of extremely bad quality.

The combination S_2/L_2 is typically applied for **inspection of incoming products**, because the consumer is typically not able to replace the defectives in the sample and - in the case of rejection - in the remaining lot by good units. Consequently, nonconforming units can only be sorted out. The combination S_3/L_3 is most relevant for the case of **internal final inspection**, for example, by a manufacturer (finished or semifinished products). Then, new and conforming units are readily available and defectives can be replaced easily.

We will now determine the average outgoing quality limit $AOQL$. In the case of S_1/L_1 we have $AOQ(P) = P$ on the interval [0,1]. In other words, the average outgoing quality will have a maximum at P_M=1, the right boundary of the domain, and $AOQL = AOQ(1) = 1$. In the other cases of table 3.2/5 we need to solve the equation

Derivation of the $AOQL$

$$\frac{d[AOQ(P)]}{dP} = 0, \tag{3.50}$$

in order to obtain the value P_M which maximizes $AOQ(P)$. To solve the equation we need to require that $AOQ(P)$ is differentiable. We will use formula (3.50) to determine P_M and $AOQL = AOQ(P_M)$ for the cases S_1/L_3 and S_3/L_3. For these combinations the $AOQL$ determination is especially simple, because the AOQ functions have a simple form (for the other cases, see example 3.2/8).

Let us consider the application of a plan $(N; n; c)$ with disposition S_1/L_3 or S_3/L_3. According to table 3.2/5 the equations $AOQ(P) = P \cdot L(P)$ or $AOQ(P) = (N - n) \cdot P \cdot L(P)/N$ hold and we find in both cases P_M to be the solution of the equation

$$L(P) + P \cdot \frac{dL(P)}{dP} = 0. \tag{3.51}$$

The result for P_M from the non-linear equation (3.51) can be approximated only by numerical methods. The result obviously depends on whether the underlying OC function $L(P)$ is hypergeometric (3.7), binomial (3.8) or Poisson (3.16). For the case of a Poisson OC function, DODGE/ROMIG (1959, p. 37) give a table of auxiliary variables x and y for given acceptance numbers $0, 1, \ldots, 40$. With these auxiliary variables we can approximate the measures of interest P_M and $AOQL = AOQ(P_M)$ for given N and n in the following way:

$$P_M \approx \frac{x}{n} \tag{3.52 a}$$

$$AOQL \approx y \cdot \left(\frac{1}{n} - \frac{1}{N}\right). \tag{3.52 b}$$

The table below was developed by DODGE/ROMIG:

c	x	y	c	x	y
0	1.00	0.368	20	15.92	13.89
1	1.62	0.840	21	16.73	14.66
2	2.27	1.371	22	17.54	15.43
3	2.95	1.942	23	18.35	16.20
4	3.64	2.544	24	19.17	16.98
5	4.35	3.168	25	19.99	17.76
6	5.07	3.812	26	20.81	18.54
7	5.80	4.472	27	21.63	19.33
8	6.55	5.146	28	22.46	20.12
9	7.30	5.831	29	23.29	20.91
10	8.05	6.528	30	24.11	21.70
11	8.82	7.233	31	24.95	22.50
12	9.59	7.948	32	25.78	23.30
13	10.37	8.670	33	26.62	24.10
14	11.15	9.398	34	27.45	24.90
15	11.93	10.13	35	28.29	25.71
16	12.72	10.88	36	29.13	26.52
17	13.52	11.62	37	29.97	27.33
18	14.31	12.37	38	30.82	28.14
19	15.12	13.13	39	31.66	28.96
			40	32.51	29.77

Table 3.2/6: Auxiliary variables for the determination of the $AOQL$ and the corresponding quality level P_M for single-sampling plans

---

Example 3.2/8

The following table 3.2/7 lists values of the nine AOQ functions of table 3.2/5 for the plan (50;8;2). The OC function $L(P)$ was taken to be the hypergeometric OC function $L(P|50;8;2) = Hy(2|50;50P;8)$, that was discussed in example 3.2/6. The maximal value $AOQL$ of $AOQ(P)$ is marked in each case with *.

Analysis of table 3.2/7 shows:

- For lots of good quality (small P), the average outgoing quality is almost as high as the input quality P, because good lots are practically always accepted. The acceptance probabilities $L(P)$, which are listed in column 2, verify this.

- In the case of lots of bad quality (large P), we find for all combinations except S_1/L_1 that the $AOQ(P)$ is fairly small, at least well below the input quality P. The acceptance control procedure filters to a larger extent. Except for the case S_1/L_1, the $AOQ(P)$ goes to zero when

P	$L(P\|50;8;2)$	AOQ values for the combinations:								
		S_1/L_1	S_1/L_2	S_1/L_3	S_2/L_1	S_2/L_2	S_2/L_3	S_3/L_1	S_3/L_2	S_3/L_3
(1)	(2)	(3)	(4)	(5)	(6)	(7)	(8)	(9)	(10)	(11)
0	1.0000	0	0	0	0	0	0	0	0	0
0.02	1.0000	0.0200	0.0200	0.0200	0.0169	0.0169	0.0169	0.0168	0.0168	0.0168
0.04	1.0000	0.0400	0.0400	0.0400	0.0338	0.0338	0.0338	0.0336	0.0336	0.0336
0.06	0.9971	0.0600	0.0598	0.0598	0.0509	0.0508	0.0507	0.0504	0.0503	0.0503
0.08	0.9895	0.0800	0.0792	0.0792	0.0680	0.0674	0.0674	0.0671	0.0665	0.0665
0.10	0.9758	0.1000	0.0978	0.0976	0.0851	0.0835	0.0833	0.0837	0.0821	0.0820
0.12	0.9556	0.1200	0.1153	0.1147	0.1021	0.0987	0.0982	0.1001	0.0968	0.0963
0.14	0.9287	0.1400	0.1313	0.1300	0.1190	0.1127	0.1117	0.1162	0.1101	0.1092
0.16	0.8954	0.1600	0.1457	0.1433	0.1357	0.1253	0.1235	0.1319	0.1221	0.1203
0.18	0.8563	0.1800	0.1582	0.1541	0.1522	0.1364	0.1333	0.1472	0.1324	0.1295
0.20	0.8122	0.2000	0.1688	0.1624	0.1684	0.1457	0.1410	0.1620	0.1409	0.1364
0.22	0.7640	0.2200	0.1773	0.1681	0.1842	0.1533	0.1463	0.1761	0.1476	0.1412
0.24	0.7125	0.2400	0.1837	0.1710	0.1995	0.1590	0.1494	0.1894	0.1525	0.1436
0.26	0.6590	0.2600	0.1880	0.1713*	0.2142	0.1628	0.1502*	0.2017	0.1555	0.1439*
0.28	0.6040	0.2800	0.1902	0.1692	0.2282	0.1648	0.1488	0.2129	0.1567*	0.1421
0.30	0.5492	0.3000	0.1905*	0.1647	0.2414	0.1651*	0.1454	0.2227	0.1561	0.1384
0.32	0.4947	0.3200	0.1889	0.1583	0.2536	0.1636	0.1402	0.2310	0.1539	0.1330
0.34	0.4417	0.3400	0.1854	0.1502	0.2647	0.1605	0.1334	0.2376	0.1501	0.1261
0.36	0.3907	0.3600	0.1802	0.1406	0.2744	0.1558	0.1254	0.2420	0.1448	0.1181
0.38	0.3423	0.3800	0.1734	0.1301	0.2825	0.1498	0.1163	0.2441*	0.1383	0.1093
0.40	0.2969	0.4000	0.1652	0.1188	0.2888	0.1426	0.1066	0.2437	0.1306	0.0998
0.42	0.2548	0.4200	0.1558	0.1070	0.2930	0.1342	0.0964	0.2404	0.1220	0.0899
0.44	0.2164	0.4400	0.1453	0.0952	0.2947*	0.1250	0.0860	0.2340	0.1126	0.0800
0.46	0.1817	0.4600	0.1340	0.0836	0.2937	0.1151	0.0758	0.2246	0.1027	0.0702
0.48	0.1507	0.4800	0.1221	0.0723	0.2896	0.1046	0.0658	0.2120	0.0924	0.0608

Table 3.2/7: *AOQ* values of the plan (50;8;2) for the different combinations of sample and remaining lot disposition

$P \to 1$. It looks as though almost no lots are excepted without inspection if the fraction defective P is high.

- The $AOQ(P)$ in the case of sample disposition S_1 is, for any quality level P and any remaining lot disposition L_j, bigger than in the case of sample disposition S_2 which is bigger than in the case of disposition S_3. The same also holds for the $AOQL$ values for the different S-dispositions.

- Regardless of the kind of sample disposition S_i and the quality level P, L_1-disposition of the remaining lot (remaining lot is discarded if lot is rejected) has the highest $AOQ(P)$ and L_3-disposition (100% inspection of the remaining lot and replacement of defective units if the lot is rejected) has the smallest $AOQ(P)$. The equivalent result holds for the $AOQL$. For L_1-disposition of the remaining lot the $AOQL$ is reached for higher values of P than L_2-disposition, and, similarily, L_3-disposition reaches the $AOQL$ for smaller values of P than L_2-disposition. Figure 3.2/11 illustrates these results for the three cases S_3/L_j through plots of the AOQ functions (see columns $9-11$ in table 3.2/7).

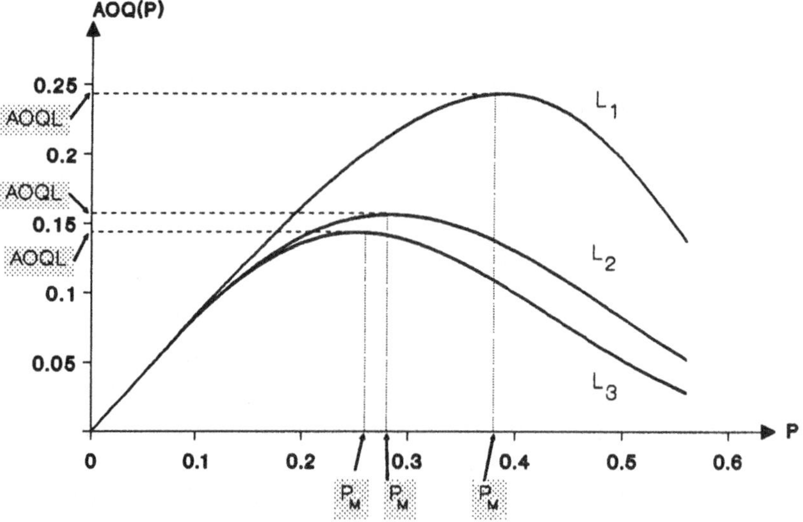

Figure 3.2/11: AOQ curves for the plan (50;8;2) for different types of remaining lot disposition

Table 3.2/7 also allows us to evaluate the quality of the approximation formulas (3.52). One can see from the table that for the case S_3/L_3 the $AOQL$ is attained at $P_M = 0.26$ and has the value

$$AOQL = AOQ(0.26) = 0.1439.$$

If we use the approximation equation (3.52) given by DODGE/ROMIG (1959), we can get from table 3.2/6 that $P_M = 2.27/8 \approx 0.2838$ and

$$AOQL = 1.371 \cdot \left(\frac{1}{8} - \frac{1}{50}\right) \approx 0.1440.$$

It is surprising that the approximation is so close to the actual value, since formula (3.52) is based on the Poisson approximation (3.14) and does not really apply to the plan (50;8;2).

Remarks

1. From an intuitive point of view it would be more appropriate to define the term "average outgoing quality" to be the expectation of the random quotient of undetected defectives and accepted units in the inspected lots. However, the determination of this measure often requires extensive statistical analysis, whereas definition (3.43) has the advantage of easy evaluation.
2. In SQA literature usually only the AOQ formulas $AOQ = P \cdot L(P)$ and $AOQ = (N-n) \cdot P \cdot L(P)/N$ are used. They are only adequate in the case of the disposition combinations S_1/L_3 and S_3/L_3, respectively. In all other cases they only give approximations. In particular, it holds that the smaller P and/or the sample proportion n/N, the better the approximation.

Problem 3.2/12

a) Calculate a table corresponding to table 3.2/7 for the plan (50;8;0). Use the 16 values of $L(P|50;8;0)$ obtained in problem 3.2/6a.

b) Use the table from a) to determine the $AOQL$ for the disposition combination S_3/L_3 and compare it to the approximation obtained by (3.52).

Problem 3.2/13

Compare the graphs of the AOQ functions for the plans (50;8;2) and (50;8;0) with disposition combination S_3/L_3. Comment on the difference.

c) Average Total Inspection and Average Fraction Inspected (ATI and AFI)

The preceding section described how to determine the average outgoing quality $AOQ(P)$ for the different combinations of sample and remaining lot disposition for a given quality level P. Depending on the particular combination of sample and remaining lot disposition, we get different numbers of items to inspect. The total number of inspected units Y_3 is only a random variable if defective units are sorted out and replaced by good units. Similar to Y_1 and Y_2 in (3.43), this variable can be expressed as a conditional expectation that takes a different value in the case of a rejected or an accepted lot. The expectation of Y_3 is called **average total inspection**, written **ATI**:

Definition of ATI and AFI

$$ATI := E(Y_3). \tag{3.53}$$

In some literature the abbreviation **AOI** (average amount of inspection) is used. Sometimes one is interested in the ratio of the average total inspection and the lot size N. One calls this measure **average fraction inspected** or **AFI**:

$$AFI := \frac{ATI}{N}. \tag{3.54}$$

Similar to the AOQ, ATI and AFI are again functions of the fraction defective P, and to illustrate this we write $ATI(P)$ and $AFI(P)$, respectively. Different from the AOQ, the functions $ATI(P)$ and $AFI(P)$ are only weakly monotone increasing, i.e., for $P_1 > P_2$ it follows that $ATI(P_1) \geq ATI(P_2)$ and $AFI(P_1) \geq AFI(P_2)$. As before in the case of the AOQ function, the graphs of the ATI and AFI functions depend on the choice of sample and remaining lot disposition.

Table 3.2/8 gives the ATI functions for the nine combinations of sample and remaining lot disposition S_i/L_j $(i, j = 1, 2, 3)$ that were introduced for the $AOQ(P)$. The disposition procedures S_1 and S_2 have the same amount of inspection, because in both cases only the n units in the sample are inspected.[6] Hence, the nine combinations S_i/L_j only have six different formulas for the ATI or AFI, respectively. The formulas for the AFI are not given below, since they can be directly obtained from the ATI formula through definition (3.54).

	L_1 remaining lot is not used	L_2 remaining lot is used after defectives are sorted out	L_3 remaining lot is used after replacement of defectives
S_1 sample is not used S_2 conforming units in the sample are used, defectives are sorted out	$ATI(P) = n$	$ATI(P) = N-(N-n)\cdot L(P)$	$ATI(P) = \frac{n\cdot(1-P)+(N-n)\cdot[1-L(P)]}{1-P}$
S_3 defective units are replaced and sample is used	$ATI(P) = \frac{n}{1-P}$	$ATI(P) = \frac{N-(N-n)\cdot[L(P)+P-P\cdot L(P)]}{1-P}$	$ATI(P) = \frac{n+(N-n)\cdot[1-L(P)]}{1-P}$

Table 3.2/8: ATI functions for different combinations of sample and remaining lot disposition for a single-sampling plan

[6] In the case of the curtailed inspection, which will be discussed later, the sample size needs to be replaced by the average sample number (ASN).

Derivation of the *ATI*

Instead of deriving all the *ATI* formulas, we will only give the derivation for the combination S_3/L_3. Suppose we accepted a lot with quality level P. The average amount of inspection Y_3 is identical to the number of all inspected units in the sampling stage. Since we are working with sample disposition S_3 we will first draw a sample of size n and inspect those units. On average, we will get nP defectives and we now need to inspect additionally as many units as it takes to obtain the nP non-defective units which are needed to replace the defective units in the sample. The variable X_n^{*T}, that denotes this number of additional inspected units, has a negative binomial distribution (see section 2.2.3c) with parameters $(1-P)$ and nP. In other words, we have $X_n^{*T} \sim nb(1-P; nP)$ and $E(X_n^{*T}) = nP/(1-P)$. Hence, it follows from (2.100a) that the total number Y_3 of inspected units is given by $n + nP/(1-P)$.

Now suppose that the lot was rejected. For the combination S_3/L_3 the average amount of inspection consists of the average number of units for the sample inspection $n+nP/(1-P)$ and the amount of inspection needed for the remaining lot. To obtain the latter we can use the formula of the sample case and replace the sample size n by the remaining lot size $N-n$. As the final result for the average total inspection in the case of a rejected lot, we get the sum of $n + nP/(1-P)$ and $(N-n) + (N-n) \cdot P/(1-P)$, i.e., $N + NP/(1-P)$.

We can simplify both results by using the identities

$$n + \frac{nP}{1-P} = \frac{n}{1-P}, \qquad N + \frac{NP}{1-P} = \frac{N}{1-P}.$$

By this way we finally get for the average number Y_3 of inspected units per lot

$$Y_3 := \begin{cases} \dfrac{n}{1-P} & \text{if } X_n^T \leq c \\ \dfrac{N}{1-P} & \text{if } X_n^T > c. \end{cases} \tag{3.55}$$

Hence, by (3.53) the average total inspection is obtained to be

$$\begin{aligned} ATI(P) &= \frac{n}{1-P} \cdot L(P) + \frac{N}{1-P} \cdot [1 - L(P)] \\ &= \frac{n}{1-P} - \frac{n}{1-P} \cdot [1 - L(P)] + \frac{N}{1-P} \cdot [1 - L(P)] \quad (3.56) \\ &= \frac{n + (N-n) \cdot [1 - L(P)]}{1-P}. \end{aligned}$$

The other *ATI* formulas of table 3.2/8 can be verified in the same way.

Interpreting the result

We can see from formula (3.56) that, if the lot is of bad quality, the amount of inspecton for the combination S_3/L_3 can theoretically exceed the lot size. This is generally true for all situations where nonconforming units are replaced by good ones (any disposition combination involving S_3 and/or L_3). For large values of P it can happen that $ATI(P) > N$ or $AFI > 1$, because, in addition to the N units required by 100% inspection, extra units need to be inspected from the ongoing production to replace the nonconforming units in the sample or remaining lot by good ones.

Example 3.2/9

In table 3.2/7 we tabulated the $AOQ(P)$ values of the AOQ functions corresponding to the different disposition combinations S_i/L_j for the plan (50;8;2). The following table 3.2/9 contains the $ATI(P)$ values of the corresponding ATI functions. As before, we took $L(P)$ to be the hypergeometric OC function $L(P|50;8;2)$.

Dividing the values in the table by the lot size $N = 50$ gives the AFI values. Analysis of the table 3.2/9 shows us that:

- The $ATI(P)$ grows very fast for combinations involving L_3 (columns 5 and 8).
- For combinations involving S_3 and L_3 (columns 5 to 8) the ATI value increases more and more as P increases. It can be shown analytically that the $ATI(P)$ converges to ∞ for $P \rightarrow 1$.
- For combinations S_1/L_2 and S_2/L_2 in column 4 the $ATI(P)$ seems to converge to $N = 50$ as $P \rightarrow 1$. This can also be shown analytically taking the limit of ATI(P)= $N - (N - n) \cdot L(P)$ as $P \rightarrow 1$. As a result of (3.19b), it follows that ATI(1)= $N - (N - n) \cdot 0 = N$.

P	$L(P\|50;8;2)$	$ATI(P)$ for the combinations:					
		$S_1/L_1, S_2/L_1$	$S_1/L_2, S_2/L_2$	$S_1/L_3, S_2/L_3$	S_3/L_1	S_3/L_2	S_3/L_3
(1)	(2)	(3)	(4)	(5)	(6)	(7)	(8)
0.00	1.0000	8	8	8	8	8	8
0.02	1.0000	8	8	8	8.1633	8.1633	8.1633
0.04	1.0000	8	8	8	8.3333	8.3333	8.3333
0.06	0.9971	8	8.1218	8.1296	8.5106	8.6324	8.6402
0.08	0.9895	8	8.4410	8.4793	8.6956	9.1367	9.1750
0.10	0.9758	8	9.0164	9.1293	8.8889	9.9053	10.0182
0.12	0.9556	8	9.8648	10.1191	9.0909	10.9557	11.2100
0.14	0.9287	8	10.9946	11.4821	9.3023	12.2969	12.7844
0.16	0.8954	8	12.3932	13.2300	9.5238	13.9170	14.7538
0.18	0.8563	8	14.0354	15.3603	9.7561	15.7915	17.1163
0.20	0.8122	8	15.8876	17.8595	10.0000	17.8876	19.8595
0.22	0.7640	8	17.9120	20.7077	10.2564	20.1684	22.9641
0.24	0.7125	8	20.0750	23.8882	10.5263	22.6013	26.4145
0.26	0.6590	8	22.3220	27.3541	10.8108	25.1328	30.1649
0.28	0.6040	8	24.6320	31.1000	11.1111	27.7431	34.2111
0.30	0.5492	8	26.9336	35.0480	11.4286	30.3622	38.4766
0.32	0.4947	8	29.2226	39.2097	11.7647	32.9873	42.9744
0.34	0.4417	8	31.4486	43.5282	12.1212	35.5698	47.6494
0.36	0.3907	8	33.5906	47.9853	12.5000	38.0906	52.4853
0.38	0.3423	8	35.6234	52.5539	12.9032	40.5266	57.4571
0.40	0.2969	8	37.5302	57.2170	13.3333	42.8635	62.5503
0.42	0.2548	8	39.2984	61.9628	13.7931	45.0915	67.7559
0.44	0.2164	8	40.9112	66.7700	14.2857	47.1969	73.0557
0.46	0.1817	8	42.3686	71.6456	14.8148	49.1834	78.4604
0.48	0.1507	8	43.6706	76.5973	15.3846	51.0552	83.9819

Table 3.2/9: *ATI* values of the plan (50;8;2) for different combinations of sample and remaining lot disposition

---

Remark

In practice, one often uses the formula $ATI(P) = N-(N-n)\cdot L(P)$ (see GRAF/HENNING/STANGE/WILRICH, 1987, for example). Strictly speaking, this formula is only valid for combinations S_1/L_2 and S_2/L_2. However, it is also valid for combinations S_1/L_3 and S_2/L_3 as well as S_3/L_2 and S_3/L_3, provided that the defectives found during the procedure are replaced from a stock of inspected good units instead of having to inspect them, since the output contains a proportion P of defectives.

Problem 3.2/14

Calculate the $ATI(P)$ and $AFI(P)$ values of the single-sampling plan (50;8;0) with $P = 0.1$ for the six cases of table 3.2/8. Assume that the OC function is hypergeometric.

d) Curtailed Inspection and Average Sample Number (ASN)

In the last section we determined the average amount of inspection that is needed for the different sample and remaining lot dispositions. One of the factors that is most influential on the ATI is the sample size of the plan. We will show that it is often possible to replace the parameter n by a smaller number without changing the OC function of the underlying hypothesis test (3.2).

So far, the procedure of the single-sampling attribute plan is to take a sample of size n from the lot and to decide on acceptance or rejection after inspecting all sample units. The lot is rejected if X_n^T, the number of nonconforming units in the sample, exceeds the given acceptance number c. In practice, however, one would not be able to simultaneously test all sample units, but would inspect them one by one. Thus, it is possible that the decision is already determined before all n units are inspected. This will especially happen in the case of very good or very bad lots. Now, in order to reduce the average amount of inspection ATI one can modify the procedure of figure 3.2/1 by terminating the inspection once the decision is determined. There are two different situations where this case applies and a **curtailed inspection** is reasonable:

Situations when curtailed inspection reduces the amount of inspection

- After inspection of less than n sample units the $(c+1)$-th defective unit is found. In this case the lot can be rejected.
- After inspection of less than n units the $(n-c)$-th non-defective unit is detected. This situation would allow us to accept the lot.

The first situation is more important, because it may terminate inspection at a very early stage, and, hence, significantly reduce the amount of inspection. For example, for a plan with $c = 0$ this could happen after inspection of the first sample unit. An inspection procedure that only stops in the case of an early rejection, but not in the case of an early decision to accept, is called **semicurtailed inspection**. The amount of inspection can be reduced further by stopping the procedure whenever the decision is determined regardless of whether the outcome is acceptance or rejection. This is called **fully curtailed inspection**. The following table illustrates the differences between curtailed and uncurtailed single-sampling procedures for attributes:

Variants of curtailed inspection

<table>
<tr><th rowspan="2">Single-sampling inspection procedure</th><th rowspan="2">Criterion for stopping inspection</th><th colspan="2">Number of sampled units</th></tr>
<tr><th>for rejected lots</th><th>for accepted lots</th></tr>
<tr><td>Inspection without curtailment</td><td>–</td><td colspan="2">n</td></tr>
<tr><td>Semicurtailed inspection</td><td>Discovery of the $(c+1)$-th defective unit</td><td>n</td><td rowspan="2">Random variable with realizations in $[c+1; n]$</td></tr>
<tr><td>Fully curtailed inspection</td><td>Discovery of the $(c+1)$-th defective or the $(n-c)$-th non-defective sample unit</td><td>Random variable with realizations in $[n-c; n]$</td></tr>
</table>

Table 3.2/10: Single-sampling attribute plan with or without curtailment

Advantages and disadvantages of curtailed inspection

A curtailed inspection is advantageous if the cost of testing sample units is high, or when the inspection is very difficult or time consuming (for example in life testing). One disadvantage is that one has to keep a log of the inspection in order to know when a stopping event occurs - i.e., the $(c+1)$-th defective or the $(n-c)$-th good unit. Another disadvantage is the difficulty in properly estimating the quality parameter P from such a procedure.

Graphical display of fully curtailed inspection

The **inspection diagram** describes the control procedure graphically. It is obtained by plotting the path of the observed number of defective units against the number n^* of inspected units. The **rejection boundary** $z = c+1$ is drawn parallel to the n^*-axis. It is sufficient to draw the line from $n^* = c+1$ to $n^* = n$, because, if the sample contains more than c defectives, this can only be detected after inspection of at least $c+1$ units and the maximum number of sample units is fixed by the plan to be $n^* = n$. For a fully curtailed inspection it is also necessary to mark the **acceptance boundary** in the figure. Its equation is $z = n^* - (n-c)$ and it is clear that the line only needs to be drawn for n^* between $n-c$ and n.

If the path of the observed number of defective units reaches the rejection boundary the lot is rejected. In the case of semicurtailed inspection the lot is accepted if the rejection boundary is not reached at $n^* = n$, and in the case of fully curtailed inspection possibly before, i.e., if the acceptance boundary is reached. The following figure shows an inspection diagram with acceptance and rejection boundaries and three different paths for a single-sampling plan with $n = 8$ and $c = 2$.

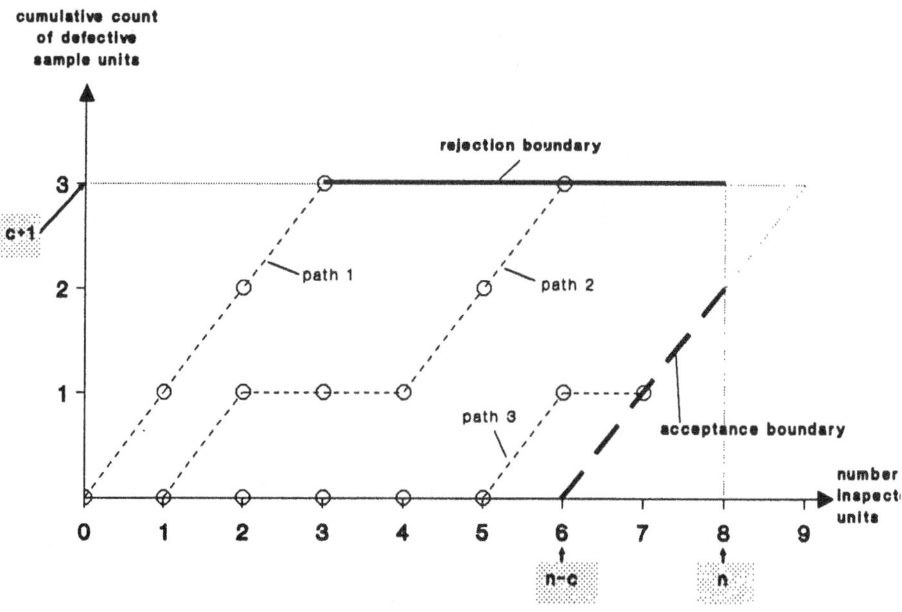

Figure 3.2/12: Inspection diagram for a single-sampling plan $(N; 8; 2)$ in the case of fully curtailed inspection

In all three cases, we see that the fully curtailed inspection leads to a decision before all n sample units are tested (early rejection for path 1 and path 2, and early acceptance for path 3). For path 3, note that semicurtailed inspection would have tested all n sample units before accepting the lot.

Definition of the *ASN*

The sample size that a curtailed inspection needs to reach a decision is a random variable, which we denote by Y^*. The possible realizations of the variable Y^* are $c+1, c+2, \ldots, n$ and their probabilities of occurrence can be calculated from the negative hypergeometric distribution or approximated by the negative binomial distribution (see sections 2.2.3b and 2.2.3c).[7] The distributions above also need to be cut off at $y^* = n$, because Y^* cannot take values above n. However, the main interest is not the complete distribution of Y^*, but its expectation, the **average sample number**, which is abbreviated by **ASN**:

$$ASN := E(Y^*). \tag{3.57}$$

Calculating the *ASN*:

The *ASN* is a function of the quality parameter P of the lot: $ASN = ASN(P)$. It further depends on the type of curtailed inspection that is applied (i.e., fully or semicurtailed). We will give the following formulas

[7] We are assuming that $c \leq n - c$, i.e., $n \geq 2c$. For $c > n - c$, the possible realizations of Y^* would be $n - c, n - c + 1, \ldots, n$.

without proof (see HALD 1981, p. 273 ff and SCHILLING 1982, p.91):

- for semicurtailing

$$ASN_1(P) = n \cdot F(c|n) + \frac{c+1}{P}[1 - F(c+1|n+1)], \qquad (3.58\text{ a})$$

for semicurtailed inspection and

$$ASN_2(P) = \frac{n-c}{1-P} \cdot F(c|n+1) + \frac{c+1}{P}[1 - F(c+1|n+1)] \qquad (3.58\text{ b})$$

- for fully curtailing

for fully curtailed inspection. The term $F(c|n)$ above denotes the probability of obtaining at most c defectives in a sample of size n, and refers to a quality characteristic X with distribution function $F(x) = Pr(X \leq x)$. For the special cases of discrete distributions that are discussed in this chapter we get

$$F(c|n) = \begin{cases} L(P|N;n;c) & \text{if } X \sim hy(N;NP;c) \\ L(P|n;c) & \text{if } X \sim bi(P;n) \\ L^*(P|n;c) & \text{if } X \sim po(nP). \end{cases} \qquad (3.58\text{ c})$$

One can also use approximations in place of the exact equations in the above formulas.

The function ASN_1 is monotone decreasing with respect to P and satisfies $ASN_1(0) = n$ and $ASN_1(1) = c+1$. The function ASN_2 is also monotone decreasing for $c = 0$ with $ASN_2(0) = n - c$ and $ASN_2(1) = c + 1$. For $c > 0$, it holds that $ASN_2(P)$ increases from $ASN_2(0) = n - c$ at $P = 0$ until it reaches at $P_M \in (0,1)$ a maximum $ASN_2(P_M)$, the **maximum ASN** or **ASNL** (average sample number limit), and then decreases to $ASN_2(1) = c + 1$ at $P = 1$. If the distribution of the quality characteristic is assumed to be hypergeometric or binomial we have the property that $ASN_1(P) > ASN_2(P)$ for all $P \in (0,1)$. The following example will demonstrate that there can be a significant reduction in the average sample number for small values of P if fully curtailed inspection is applied instead of semicurtailed.

Properties of the *ASN* function and definition of the *ASNL*

Example 3.2/10

In example 3.2/6 we calculated values of the OC function for the plan (50;8;2) under the assumption of the hypergeometric, binomial and Poisson distributions. For each of these three distributions one can calculate values of the *ASN* function for fully and semicurtailed inspection, using (3.58a-c). The results are given in table 3.2/11.

P	Hypergeometric case		Binomial case		Poisson case	
	$ASN_1(P)$	$ASN_2(P)$	$ASN_1(P)$	$ASN_2(P)$	$ASN_1(P)$	$ASN_2(P)$
(1)	(2)	(3)	(4)	(5)	(6)	(7)
0.00	8	6	8	6	8	6
0.04	8.0000	6.2500	7.9959	6.2426	8.0050	6.2522
0.08	7.9364	6.4412	7.9705	6.4667	8.0197	6.5207
0.12	7.8156	6.5582	7.9099	6.6468	8.0225	6.7737
0.16	7.6585	6.6118	7.8071	6.7672	7.9874	6.9778
0.20	7.4760	6.6103	7.6600	6.8211	7.8975	7.1103
0.24	7.2734	6.5605	7.4705	6.8076	7.7471	7.1615
0.30	6.9365	6.4081	7.1176	6.6705	7.4167	7.0901
0.40	6.2976	5.9907	6.4036	6.1983	6.6751	6.6633
0.50	5.5964	5.4395	5.6328	5.5547	5.8511	6.0292
0.60	4.8985	4.8363	4.9017	4.8788	5.0739	5.3549
0.70	4.2706	4.2551	4.2676	4.2631	4.4032	4.7410
0.80	3.7493	3.7479	3.7483	3.7479	3.8509	4.2445
0.90	3.3333	3.3333	3.3333	3.3333	3.4051	3.9645
1.00	3	3	3	3	3	3

Table 3.2/11: ASN values for the plan (50;8;2) for fully and semicurtailed inspection

Looking closer at the values in the table shows that:

- The Poisson approximation of the hypergeometric distribution is not as good as the binomial approximation and, in the case of semicurtailed inspection and if P is small, it can yield ASN values slightly above n.

- Comparison of the exact values in columns $2 - 3$ shows that the application of a fully curtailed inspection instead of the semicurtailed procedure results in a reduced sample size, and also that this reduction goes to zero as the quality parameter P approaches 1 ($P \to 1$). The graphs of the two ASN functions for the hypergeometric case, and also their difference (the reduction in sample size), are given in figure 3.2/13.

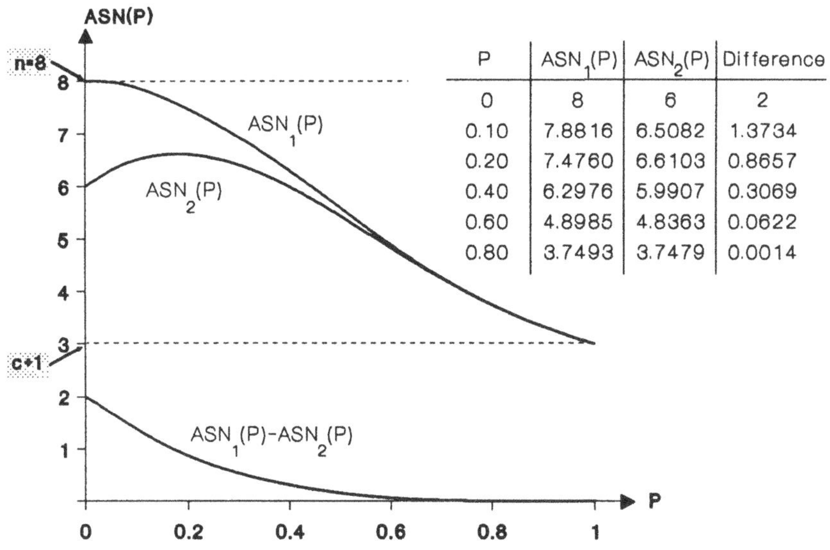

P	ASN1(P)	ASN2(P)	Difference
0	8	6	2
0.10	7.8816	6.5082	1.3734
0.20	7.4760	6.6103	0.8657
0.40	6.2976	5.9907	0.3069
0.60	4.8985	4.8363	0.0622
0.80	3.7493	3.7479	0.0014

Figure 3.2/13: *ASN* functions for the plan (50;8;2) for fully and semicurtailed inspection

---

Problem 3.2/15

a) Determine $ASN_1(P)$ and $ASN_2(P)$ for the plan $N = 50, n = 8, c = 0$ at $P = 0.1$.

b) Show that $ASN_1(P) = ASN_2(P)$ for the binomial distribution with $c = 0$.

Problem 3.2/16

The procedure of an uncurtailed single-sampling plan $(N; n; c)$ is described in figure 3.2/1. How do we have to modify this figure in order to apply it to curtailed inspection?

3.2.3 Designing Single-Sampling Plans with Specified Properties

We already mentioned that the application of a single-sampling attribute plan $(N; n; c)$ is equivalent to performing a hypothesis test of type (3.2). The test statistic of this test was X_n^T, the number of nonconforming units in the sample and the rejection region was given by $CR = \{c + 1, c + 2, \ldots, n\}$. For example, the test (3.2) can be completely charcterized by the OC function $L(P) = P(X_n^T \leq c|P)$, or equivalently by appropriate performance measures. In this section we want to reverse the approach. Instead of finding properties of given plans, we will discuss how to construct plans with an OC function that satisfies given properties. An attribute plan is characterized by its lot size N, which is still given and by the parameters n and c. This implies that we will need two different characteristics of the plan in order to be able to uniquely determine equations for n and c. The following list gives different characteristics that can be used for the determination of these parameters:

Options for constructing single-sampling plans

- given two points (P_1, L_1) and (P_2, L_2) of the OC curve;
- requiring the OC curve to go through one given point (P, L) and to have a given elasticity or slope at this point;
- given one point (P, L) on the OC curve or the $AOQL$ value. Among the class of plans that satisfy this requirement we will choose the one with the minimal amount of inspection ATI.

Due to lack of space, we will only elaborate on the first possibility for constructing single-sampling plans.

a) Specification of Consumer's and Producer's Risk

A common way to determine a single-sampling plan is to specify the quality levels AQL and RQL, with corresponding producer's risk α and consumer's risk β. The OC function is then required to pass through the two points $(AQL, 1-\alpha)$ and (RQL, β). In other words we specify $L(AQL) = 1 - \alpha$ and $L(RQL) = \beta$. Since the parameters n and c are integer valued we can usually only satisfy these requirements approximately. We write

$$L(AQL) = 1 - \alpha^* \tag{3.59 a}$$

$$L(RQL) = \beta^* \tag{3.59 b}$$

where $\alpha^* \approx \alpha$ and $\beta^* \approx \beta$. In order to avoid exceeding the given risks α and β we will require that $\alpha^* \leq \alpha$ and $\beta^* \leq \beta$, or equivalently

Specification of risk bounds at selected quality levels

$$L(AQL) \geq 1 - \alpha \tag{3.60 a}$$

$$L(RQL) \leq \beta. \tag{3.60 b}$$

Compliance with (3.60) means that the parameters n and c are determined so that the **effective consumer's risk** α^* and the **effective producer's risk** β^* are below the **specified consumer's risk** α and the **specified producer's risk** β.

Equation (3.59) implies that the OC percentiles AQL and RQL are percentiles of order $1 - \alpha^*$ and β^*:

$$AQL = P_{1-\alpha^*} \tag{3.61 a}$$

$$RQL = P_{\beta^*}. \tag{3.61 b}$$

We call these values of P the **specified OC percentiles**. The percentiles

$$AQL^* = P_{1-\alpha} \tag{3.62 a}$$

$$RQL^* = P_{\beta} \tag{3.62 b}$$

corresponding to the specified risks are called the **effective percentiles**. Because of (3.60), percentiles are related according to

$$AQL \leq AQL^* \tag{3.63 a}$$

$$RQL \geq RQL^*. \tag{3.63 b}$$

The above results are illustrated by figure 3.2/14.

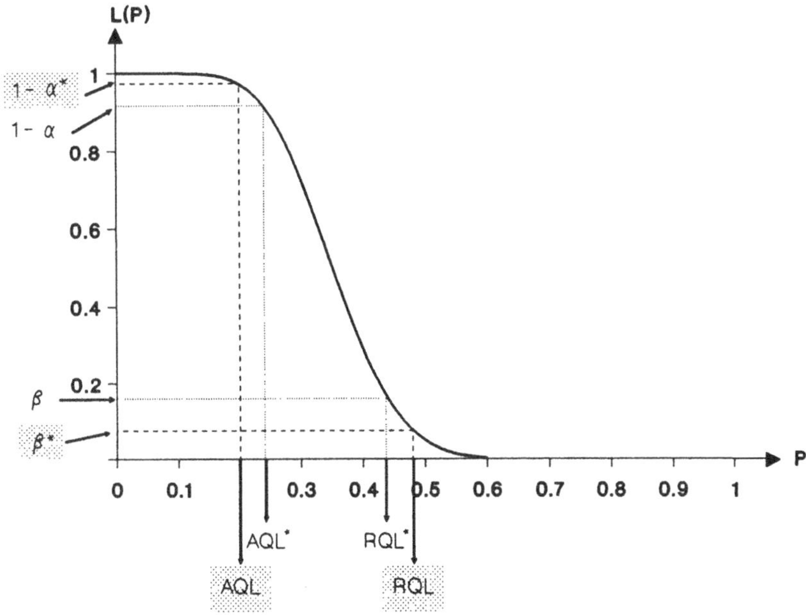

Figure 3.2/14: Effective and specified OC percentiles and risks of an attribute plan

A plan satisfying the inequalities in (3.60), or, equivalently in (3.63) is called an **admissible plan**. Admissible plans always exist. In figure 3.2/5 we can see that, through the choice of a sufficiently large n for fixed c we

Definition and existence of admissible plans

can always achieve that the OC function of a single-sampling plan $(N; n; c)$ at the point $P = RQL$ satisfies the condition $L(RQL) \leq \beta$. Figure 3.2/6 illustrates that one can get $L(P)$ to exceed $1-\alpha$ at $P = AQL$ by increasing c for fixed n.

Choosing an admissible plan

Which of the many admissible plans should we choose? From a cost point of view one is obviously interested in choosing the plan which satisfies the inequalities (3.60) and has the smallest sample size n. Hence, we will choose among all the pairs (n, c) of integers $n \geq 1$ and $c \geq 0$ the pair with minimal n. For the hypergeometric, binomial and Poisson distribution the determination of n and c cannot be done analytically but has to be solved through an iterative numerical procedure. GUENTHER (1969) found a suitable search algorithm and HAILEY (1980) came up with a programmable form. The structural chart of the algorithm is given below.

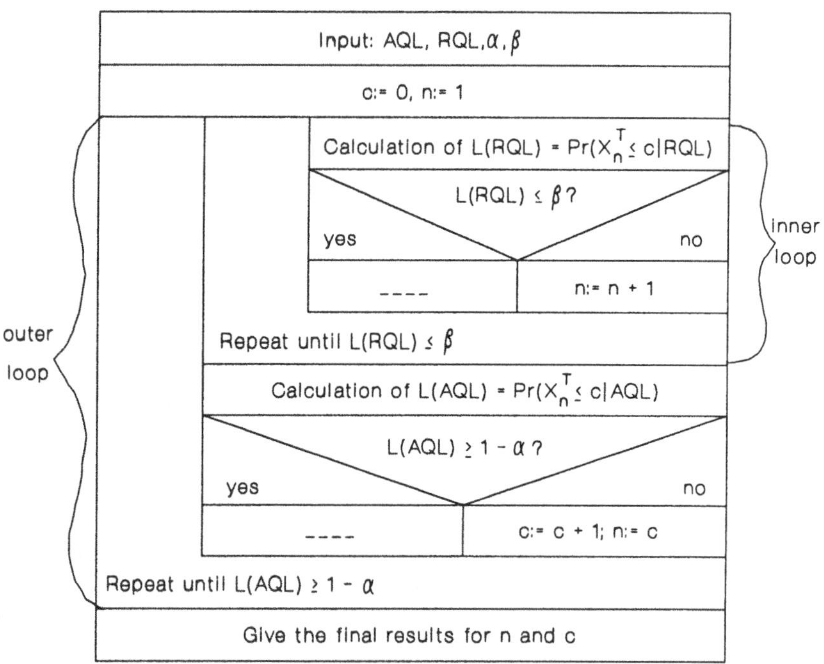

Figure 3.2/15: Structural chart of GUENTHER's search algorithm

Description of GUENTHER's algorithm

The basic idea behind the algorithm is the following: One starts with the acceptance number $c = 0$ and the sample size $n = 1$, and calculates for the particular discrete distribution (hypergeometric, binomial or Poisson) the OC function at $P = RQL$ by equation (3.7), (3.8) or (3.16), respectively. Then, while $c = 0$ remains fixed, one checks if the condition $L(RQL) \leq \beta$

is satisfied and, if not, one increases n stepwise by one until the condition is satisfied. After this, one verifies whether the condition $L(AQL) \geq 1-\alpha$ is satisfied for the given α with $c=0$. If it is, we have found the plan with minimal sample size. If the condition is not satisfied, we increase c in the outer loop by one and start with $n=c$ again in the inner loop until we find the minimal sample size for this new value of c. The plan with minimal sample size that results from this iterative procedure has the property that, among all admissible plans, it has the minimum difference between effective and specified producer's risk $|\alpha-\alpha^*|$ and the maximum difference between the effective and specified consumer's risk $|\beta-\beta^*|$.

Determination of the parameters of a plan

The application of the algorithm in figure 3.2/15 is not dependent on a particular distribution of the statistic X_n^T. In practice, one can use either sufficiently detailed tables of the particular distribution function or suitable software, if a personal computer is available. If one makes the assumption that the statistic X_n^T has a hypergeometric distribution, the previously mentioned requirements for the calculation of $L(AQL)$ and $L(RQL)$ are not always available. The situation looks a lot better in the case X_n^T is assumed to be binomial or Poisson distributed. In the binomial case we can use (3.11) to bring the inequalities (3.60) to the form

- in the binomial case

$$L(AQL|n;c)=1-Fi\left[\frac{n-c}{c+1}\cdot\frac{AQL}{1-AQL}\Big|2(c+1);2(n-c)\right]\geq 1-\alpha \tag{3.64 a}$$

$$L(RQL|n;c)=1-Fi\left[\frac{n-c}{c+1}\cdot\frac{RQL}{1-RQL}\Big|2(c+1);2(n-c)\right]\leq \beta \tag{3.64 b}$$

and in the Poisson case we get, by result (3.17b), that

- in the Poisson case

$$L^*(AQL|n;c)=1-Ch[2n\cdot AQL|2(c+1)]\ \geq\ 1-\alpha \tag{3.65 a}$$

$$L^*(RQL|n;c)=1-Ch[2n\cdot RQL|2(c+1)]\ \leq\ \beta. \tag{3.65 b}$$

Thus, in order to apply GUENTHER's search algorithm we only need to have access to tables of the F and χ^2 distribution functions.[8]

Since (3.60) is equivalent to (3.63) it is possible to transform equations (3.64) and (3.65) into inequalities for percentiles. As a result of (3.38), for the binomial case, we get

$$AQL\leq\frac{c+1}{c+1+(n-c)F_{2(n-c);2(c+1);1-\alpha}} \tag{3.66 a}$$

[8] If one uses a computer to calculate the required values of the OC function it is often better to use equations (3.10) and (3.18b) instead of (3.11) and (3.17b).

$$RQL \geq \frac{(c+1)F_{2(c+1);2(n-c);1-\beta}}{n-c+(c+1)F_{2(c+1);2(n-c);1-\beta}} \tag{3.66 b}$$

and, by (3.35a) in the Poisson case, we get

$$AQL \leq \frac{1}{2n}\chi^2_{2(c+1);\alpha} \tag{3.67 a}$$

$$RQL \geq \frac{1}{2n}\chi^2_{2(c+1);1-\beta}. \tag{3.67 b}$$

The two inequalities in (3.67) can be combined to

$$q_1(c) := \frac{\chi^2_{2(c+1);1-\beta}}{2 \cdot RQL} \leq n \leq \frac{\chi^2_{2(c+1);\alpha}}{2 \cdot AQL} =: q_2(c). \tag{3.68}$$

An alternative procedure to choose an admissible plan in the Poisson case

PEACH/LITTAUER (1946) proposed a procedure for determining n and c in the case of the Poisson distribution relying on (3.68).[9] This procedure iteratively compares the ratios $q_1(c)$ and $q_2(c)$ for $c = 0, 1, \ldots$ (using the χ^2 tables) and stops as soon as $q_1(c) \leq q_2(c)$. The acceptance number c of the plan is the smallest value of c for which this requirement is met. Every integer n that satisfies inequality (3.68) with this particular c is a sample size of an admissible plan. One will choose the smallest value of n. We again illustrate PEACH's and LITTAUER's procedure by means of a structural chart (figure 3.2/16).

In the Poisson case, GUENTHER's procedure is based on equation (3.65). Since (3.68) is eqivalent to (3.65), it is not surprising that GUENTHER's algorithm and the one proposed by PEACH/LITTAUER lead to the same result.

Testing the validity of the Poisson approximation

After construction of an admissible plan with minimal sample size, using the Poisson approximation one may ask whether the appropriate hypergeometric OC function satisfies the requirements for the consumer's and producer's risk for the particular n and c that emerged from the algorithm. In other words: We know that for the calculated values n and c $L^*(AQL|n;c) \geq 1-\alpha$ and $L^*(RQL|n;c) \leq \beta$, but is it also true that $L(AQL|N;n;c) \geq 1-\alpha$ and $L(RQL|N;n;c) \leq \beta$? Since a hypergeometric OC function is usually very hard to handle and since the binomial OC function approximates the hypergeometric OC function better than the Poisson OC function, one usually only checks whether the obtained

[9] HALD (1981, p. 50-51) describes a more complicated version of this procedure. It also requires the use of two different tables, whereas the original procedure proposed by PEACH/LITTAUER only requires the χ^2 percentiles.

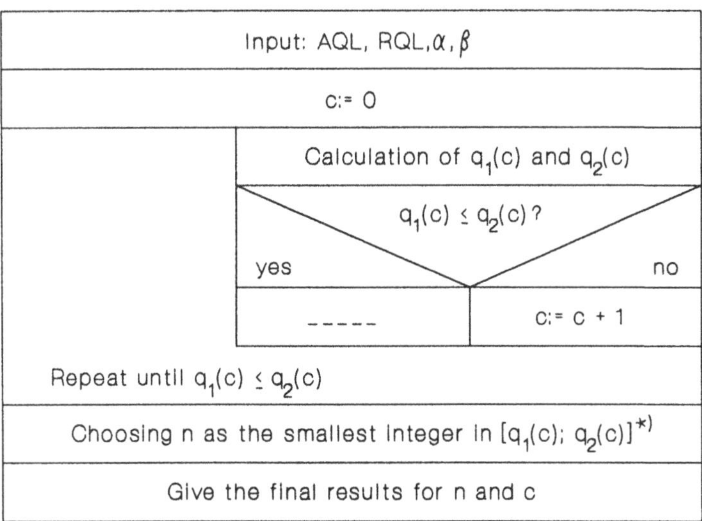

* If the interval $[q_1, q_2]$ does not contain an integer, the procedure needs to be repeated until a solution is found (see problem 3.2/33b).

Figure 3.2/16: Structural chart of PEACH/LITTAUER's search algorithm

Poisson OC function agrees with the binomial OC function reasonably well (see problem 3.2/17). This is considered to be true if the pair $(n; c)$ also satisfies the conditions (3.64), or, equivalently (3.66).

Note that the attribute plan determined by AQL, α, RQL and β can depend significantly on the underlying distribution of the statistic X_n^T. Under the assumption of a hypergeometric distribution the required sample size is usually smaller than in the case of the Poisson distribution (see also example 3.2/12). In general, a plan that is determined for an underlying Poisson distribution is also admissible, but not necessarily best (in the sense of minimal sample size), for the case of binomial or hypergeometric distribution.

Example 3.2/11

We want to construct a plan for lots of size $N = 100$ and we wish to have at least $AQL = 0.05$ with $\alpha = 0.05$, and $RQL = 0.20$ with $\beta = 0.10$. In other words, we want to construct a plan that on the one hand satisfies the inequalities $L(0.05) \geq 0.95$ and $L(0.2) \leq 0.1$ and on the other hand minimizes the sample size.

The following partial listing in table 3.2/12 describes the iterative procedure by GUENTHER (see figure 3.2/15) that determines the parameters n and c.[10] The OC function was assumed to be hypergeometric. We can see from the length of the sequences in the second column that the process had to go through the inner loop repeatedly. The table shows that the procedure had to repeat the outer loop four times before the algorithm stopped when the requirements (3.60) were fulfilled for $c = 3$ and $n = 29$. The plan (100;29;3) is found to be the sampling plan with the minimum amount of inspection.

We can see in table 3.2/12 that the resulting plan (100;29;3) attains an effective producer's risk of $\alpha^* = 0.024$ at $AQL = 0.05$ instead of the specified $\alpha = 0.05$, and an effective consumer's risk $\beta^* = 0.0993$ at $RQL = 0.2$ compared to the specified $\beta = 0.1$. Since the variable in the hypergeometric case is not continuous, but has stride length $1/N$, there is no difference between the effective percentiles AQL^* and RQL^* and the specified percentiles AQL and RQL.

An interesting question is how sensitive the constructed plan is to small increases in the specified risks α and β, i.e., how much does the sample size decrease if we do not require the effective parameters α^* and β^* to be strictly below the specified values (in other words we do not insist on being on the "safe" side). For example, if we were prepared to take a 10% increase in the stipulated producer's and consumer's risks α and β then the plan would not change at all. For a 20% increase in risks the acceptance number would remain at $c = 3$, but the sample size would drop to $n = 28$. The resulting effective risks would be $\alpha^* = 0.0209$ and $\beta^* = 0.1188$. A 50% increase in the specified risks would still leave $c = 3$ unchanged and would reduce the sample size to $n = 27$, resulting in a plan with effective risks $\alpha^* = 0.0189$ and $\beta^* = 0.1413$. We conclude that for the original specifications ($AQL = 0.05, \alpha = 0.05, RQL = 0.2, \beta = 0.1$ and $N = 100$), the plan is very robust under variations of the specified risks. In general, this need not be the case. For example, if one tries to construct a plan

[10]Note that the values of the operating characteristic in columns 3-4 of the following table were not obtained from table 5.1/2, since this table only lists the values for the special case of $N = 20$ for an underlying hypergeometric distribution.

c	n	$L(RQL\|100;n;c) = Hy(c\|100;20;n)$	$L(AQL\|100;n;c) = Hy(c\|100;5;n)$
(1)	(2)	(3)	(4)
0	1	0.8	
	2	0.6384	
	⋮	⋮	
	9	0.1219	
	10	$0.0951 < \beta = 0.10$	$0.5837 < 1 - \alpha = 0.95$
1	1	1	
	2	0.9616	
	⋮	⋮	
	16	0.1186	
	17	$0.0963 < \beta = 0,10$	$0.8006 < 1 - \alpha = 0.95$
2	2	1	
	3	0.9929	
	⋮	⋮	
	23	0.1017	
	24	$0.0837 < \beta = 0.10$	$0.9121 < 1 - \alpha = 0,95$
3	3	1	
	4	0.9988	
	⋮	⋮	
	28	0.1188	
	29	$0.0993 < \beta = 0.10$	$0.9760 > 1 - \alpha = 0.95$

Table 3.2/12: Log of the process of determing a plan by GUENTHER's procedure

with minimal sample size for $N = 2000, AQL = 0.02$ with $\alpha = 0.05$, and $RQL = 0.05$ with $\beta = 0.1$, the resulting parameters are $n = 301$ and $c = 10$. If one admits a 20% higher consumer's risk the parameters reduce to $n = 270$ and $c = 9$, which is more than a 10% reduction in the sample size. The corresponding effective risks are $\alpha^* = 0.035$ and $\beta^* = 0.1187$, i.e., the producer's risk α is still on the "safe" side.

Example 3.2/12

As in the previous example we want to construct a single-sampling attribute plan that lies below the specifications $AQL = 0.05$ with $\alpha = 0.05$ and $RQL = 0.2$ with $\beta = 0.01$. Different from example 3.2/11 where we assumed the distribution of X_n^T to be hypergeometric, we will now discuss the binomial and Poisson cases.

Assuming a *binomially* distributed X_n^T, the OC function is given by $L(P|n;c) = Bi(c|P;n)$. If one applies GUENTHER's search algorithm, the plan with minimal sample size that satisfies the conditions (3.64) is found to have parameters $n = 38$ and $c = 4$. Its corresponding effective risks are $\alpha^* = 0.0397$ and $\beta^* = 0.0986$. The effective percentiles for the specified risks $\alpha = 0.05$ and $\beta = 0.1$ are $AQL^* = 0.05331$ and $RQL^* = 0.19944$. This plan is also admissible for the case of $N = 100$ and a hypergeometric OC function (as in example 3.2/11), since it holds that $L(AQL|100; 38; 4) = 0.9933 > 1-\alpha = 0.95$ and $L(RQL|100; 38; 4) = 0.0520 < \beta = 0.1$. However, it does not have minimal sample size, since the resulting plan in example 3.2/11 is (100;29;3).

When the statistic X_n^T is *Poisson* distributed, the OC function takes the form $L^*(P|n;c) = Po(c|nP)$. If either the search algorithm by GUENTHER or the one proposed by PEACH/LITTAUER is applied one finds that the plan with minimal sample size that fulfills the requirements in (3.65) has the same parameters n and c in both cases. We will demonstrate how these values can be obtained by using the PEACH/LITTAUER algorithm. The procedure is given by figure 3.2/16. The χ^2 percentiles necessary for the calculation of the ratios $q_1(c)$ and $q_2(c)$ are obtained from table 5.2/4.

$$\left.\begin{aligned} c=0:\quad q_1(0) &= \frac{\chi^2_{2;0.90}}{2\cdot RQL} \approx \frac{4.605}{0.4} = 11.5125 \\ q_2(0) &= \frac{\chi^2_{2;0.05}}{2\cdot AQL} \approx \frac{0.103}{0.1} = 1.03 \end{aligned}\right\} \Rightarrow q_1(0) > q_2(0)$$

$$\vdots \qquad \vdots \qquad \vdots$$

$$\left.\begin{aligned} c=4:\quad q_1(4) &= \frac{\chi^2_{10;0.90}}{2\cdot RQL} \approx \frac{15.987}{0.4} = 39.9675 \\ q_2(4) &= \frac{\chi^2_{10;0.05}}{2\cdot AQL} \approx \frac{3.940}{0.1} = 39.40 \end{aligned}\right\} \Rightarrow q_1(4) > q_2(4)$$

$$\left.\begin{aligned} c=5:\quad q_1(5) &= \frac{\chi^2_{12;0.90}}{2\cdot RQL} \approx \frac{18.549}{0.4} = 46.3725 \\ q_2(5) &= \frac{\chi^2_{12;0.05}}{2\cdot AQL} \approx \frac{5.226}{0.1} = 52.26 \end{aligned}\right\} \Rightarrow q_1(5) < q_2(5)$$

The acceptance number of the plan is found to be $c = 5$. As a result of (3.68), any integer n in the interval $[q_1, q_2]$ is a sample size of an admissible plan. Here the set of these numbers is $n = 47, \ldots, 52$. Consequently the smallest sample size $n = 47$.

Thus we determined, for the Poisson case, that the parameters of the plan are $n = 47$ and $c = 5$. Note that the sample size increases from $n = 29$ to $n = 38$ and $n = 47$ as one goes from the hypergeometric to the binomial and Poisson cases, respectively. If one applies the plan that was found under the Poisson approximation to the hypergeometric case, because of $L(AQL|100; 47; 5) \approx 1 > 1 - \alpha = 0.95$ and $L(RQL|100; 47; 5) \approx 0.0239 < \beta = 0.1$, one would still have an admissible plan but not one with minimal sample size. The same holds if the Poisson based plan is applied to the binomial case (see problem 3.2/17).

For the assumption of an underlying Poisson distribution, the effective risks of the plan are found to be $\alpha^* = 0.0327$ and $\beta^* = 0.0935$ and the effective percentiles corresponding to the specified risks $\alpha = 0.05$ and $\beta = 0.1$ are given by $AQL^* = 0.0556$ and $RQL^* = 0.19733$, respectively. It is also of interest to investigate how the risks and percentiles are influenced if a sample size other than the minimal one is chosen. The following table gives the effective risks

$$\begin{aligned} \alpha^* &= 1 - Po(c|n \cdot AQL) = 1 - Po(5|n \cdot 0.05) \\ \beta^* &= Po(c|n \cdot RQL) = Po(5|n \cdot 0.20) \end{aligned}$$

and effective percentiles AQL^* and RQL^* for different choices of sample size n from the interval [47,52] for fixed acceptance number $c = 5$:

n	α^*	β^*	AQL^*	RQL^*
47	0.0327	0.0935	0.05560	0.19733
48	0.0367	0.0838	0.05444	0.19322
49	0.0388	0.0750	0.05345	0.18928
50	0.0420	0.0671	0.05225	0.18549
51	0.0454	0.0599	0.05121	0.18186
52	0.0490	0.0534	0.05025	0.17836

Table 3.2/13: Effect of choosing different admissible sample sizes on the effective percentiles and risks of a single-sampling plan

---

Problem 3.2/17

Example 3.2/12 determined a plan for the Poisson case with $AQL = 0.05, \alpha = 0.05, RQL = 0.2$ and $\beta = 0.1$. The search algorithm by PEACH/LITTAUER found the appropriate parameter values to be $n = 47$ and $c = 5$. Show that this plan is also admissible in the case of a binomially distributed test statistic. Does it also have minimal sample size under this distribution?

Problem 3.2/18

Let $N = 1000, AQL = 0.02$ with $\alpha = 0.05$, and $RQL = 0.1$ with $\beta = 0.05$.

a) Determine the parameters n and c of the corresponding plan in the in the Poisson case, using the inequalities (3.68).

b) Determine the range of n for which the requirements (3.65) and (3.68) are fulfilled, and calculate the effective producer's risk α^* and the effective consumer's risk β^* for each admissible n.

Problem 3.2/19

Assume that the statistic X_n^T has a binomial distribution. For a specified consumer's and producer's risk the parameters of the plan can be determined iteratively with the algorithm of GUENTHER using inequalities (3.64). GRAF/HENNING/STANGE/WILRICH (1987) proposed a way to directly determine n and c (in one step). This proposal, which involves an arcsin transformation of the binomial distribution and a subsequent normal approximation, determines the sample size to be

$$n \approx \frac{1}{4}\left(\frac{z_{1-\alpha} + z_{1-\beta}}{\phi_2 - \phi_1}\right)^2 - \frac{1}{4\phi_1\phi_2} \quad {}^{11}$$

where ϕ_1 and ϕ_2 are defined as

$$\phi_1 := \arcsin(\sqrt{AQL}), \qquad \phi_2 := \arcsin(\sqrt{RQL})$$

and z_ω is defined to be the percentile of order ω of the standard normal distribution (see table 5.2/1). Using this n, one obtains the acceptance number c according to

$$c \approx n \cdot \sin^2 \phi^* - 0.5 \quad {}^{11}$$

with

$$\phi^* := \frac{1}{2}(\phi_1 + \phi_2)\left(1 - \frac{1}{8n\phi_1\phi_2}\right) + \frac{z_{1-\alpha} + z_{1-\beta}}{4\sqrt{n}}.$$

a) Calculate the parameters n and c that result from using this formula for the specifications of example 3.2/12 ($AQL = 0.05$ with $\alpha = 0.05$ and $RQL = 0.2$ with $\beta = 0.1$).

b) Is the resulting plan admissible?

[11] If the terms on the left are not integers they need all to be rounded to the next largest integer.

b) Other Specifications

The Dutch electro corporation PHILIPS takes a different approach for constructing plans $(N; n; c)$ with given lot size N. Their procedure specifies the indifference point $P_{0.5} = IQL$ (see figure 3.2/10) and the elasticity $\varepsilon(P_{0.5})$. This technique can be best illustrated in the case of a Poisson distributed count statistic X_n^T. Assume now that $X_n^T \sim po(nP)$ is at least approximately true. Then the elasticity at the indifference point is estimated by (3.32). Solving (3.32) for c yields

PHILIPS' approach to specifying single-sampling plans

$$c \approx \frac{\pi}{2} \cdot \left[\varepsilon(P_{0.5}^P)\right]^2 - 0.73. \quad ^{12} \tag{3.69 a}$$

This c and the IQL approximation (3.37) is now used to calculate the sample size:

$$n \approx \frac{c + \frac{2}{3}}{P_{0.5}^P}. \quad ^{12} \tag{3.69 b}$$

DODGE and ROMIG developed plans with the main goal of minimizing the average amount of inspection ATI. The construction procedure assumes that the producer delivers lots with an average quality level $\overline{P}$. In their plans, DODGE/ROMIG (1929) specify the point (RQL, β) of the OC curve and require additionally that $ATI(\overline{P})$ is minimized with respect to n and c. In a different procedure by DODGE/ROMIG (1941) the $AOQL$ value is specified and again $ATI(\overline{P})$ is minimized with respect to n and c. Both plans are given in DODGE/ROMIG (1959).

Plans by DODGE and ROMIG

Problem 3.2/20

For the specifications $P_{0.5}^P = 0.05$ and $\varepsilon(P_{0.5}^P) = 1$, find the appropriate parameters n and c.

3.2.4 Double-Sampling Plans

So far the decision on accepting or rejecting a lot was based on a single sample. For the procedure of an uncurtailed single attribute plan (see figure 3.2/1) the size of this sample was independent of the quality P of the lot and fixed at n. Section 3.2.2d discussed curtailed versions of the single plan which allows the inspection to stop in the case of particularly bad lots (semicurtailed plan) and in the case of very good quality (fully curtailed plan). In these procedures the fixed sample size n was replaced by an average sample size ASN, with $ASN \leq n$. Consequently the average amount of inspection ATI was reduced.

Options to fall short of the ATI of an uncurtailed single-sampling plan

- through application of curtailed inspection

[12] The terms on the left have to be rounded to the next largest integer.

We can also reduce the ATI in a different way. This alternative procedure takes a first sample of size $n_1 < n$ to decide on acceptance or rejection of the lot in the more extreme situations of either especially good or bad quality. In doubtful situations a second sample of size n_2 is taken in order to guard against a wrong decision. Such plans, which perform acceptance control with at most two test samples, are called **double-sampling plans for attributes**. A double plan has the advantage of a decreased amount of total inspection over a single plan with an equivalent OC function. However, we will also see that the procedure of a double plan is somewhat more complicated.

- through application of a double plan

Advantages and disadvantages of a double plan

a) Double-Sampling Procedure

For the application of a double plan one first takes a sample of size n_1 from the given lot of size N. If either up to c_1 or d_1 and more units are found to be defective the lot is accepted or rejected, respectively. In other words, the decision is only based on the first sample if $X^T_{n_1}$, the number of defective units in this sample, satisfies $X^T_{n_1} \leq c_1$ or $X^T_{n_1} \geq d_1$. If $X^T_{n_1} \in (c_1, d_1)$ we will take a second sample of size n_2 and it is then decided to accept the lot if $X^T_{n_1+n_2}$, the total number of defectives in the two samples, does not exceed the critical value c_2. As before, the procedure can be described by a structural chart, e.g. figure 3.2/17. The register Z in this figure counts the number of defective units, and i is used as an index for the sample units.

A double-sampling plan is completely described by the lot size and five additional nonnegative integer valued parameters, n_1, c_1, d_1, n_2, and c_2. We will use the notation $(N; n_1; c_1; d_1; n_2; c_2)$ to specify double-sampling plans. The parameters n_1, c_1, d_1, n_2 and c_2 obviously cannot be chosen independently. We can deduce from the procedure that $c_1 < d_1 \leq n_1, c_2 < n_1 + n_2$ and $c_1 < c_2$. In order to allow the possibility of a second sample, the open interval (c_1, d_1) needs to contain at least one integer. Since this is not the case if $c_1 = d_1 - 1$ we need to tighten the condition $c_1 < d_1$ to $c_1 < d_1 - 1$. In order to insure that a decision made after taking a second sample could not already have been made after the first, we require that $d_1 - 1 \leq c_2$. The requirements for the parameters of a double-sampling plan can be summarized as follows:

Notation for double-sampling attribute plans

Requirements on the parameters of a double-sampling plan

$$0 \leq c_1 < d_1 - 1 \leq c_2 < n_1 < n_1 + n_2. \tag{3.70 a}$$

The basic idea that one wishes to make a decision after the first sample in the case of especially good or bad lots, suggests that the critical proportion c_1/n_1 of defectives in the first sample, that will lead to early acceptance,should be smaller than the critical proportion $c_2/(n_1 + n_2)$ of

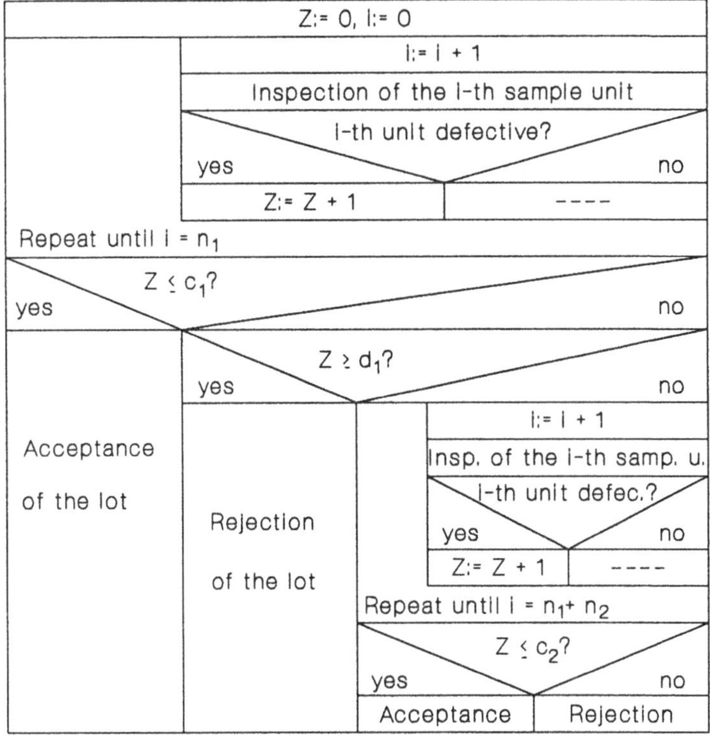

Figure 3.2/17: Structural chart of a double-sampling plan for attributes

defectives for acceptance for both samples. In the same way, the critical proportion d_1/n_1 for rejection after the first sample should be bigger than the critical proportion $(c_2 + 1)/(n_1 + n_2)$ for rejection after both samples have been taken. To take this into account we add to the requirement in (3.70a):

$$\frac{c_1}{n_1} < \frac{c_2}{n_1 + n_2} \tag{3.70 b}$$

$$\frac{d_1}{n_1} > \frac{c_2 + 1}{n_1 + n_2}. \tag{3.70 c}$$

The parameters c_1 and c_2 are called **acceptance numbers** and the parameters d_1 and $d_2 := c_2 + 1$ are the so-called **rejection numbers**.

Conventions in practice

The following conventions are used for sampling systems:

$$c_2 = d_1 - 1$$
$$d_1 - 1 = 3c_1 \quad \text{or} \quad d_1 - 1 = 5c_1$$
$$n_2 = n_1 \text{ for ISO 2859} \quad \text{or} \quad n_2 = 2n_1 \text{ for PHILIPS}$$

Following these conventions has the advantage that for a given lot size N only the two parameters n_1 and c_1 need to be specified. Thus, sampling schemes become clearer.

Graphical display of curtailed inspection

Figure 3.2/18 shows an **inspection diagram** that illustrates the filter effect of a double-sampling plan. The process of the inspection is drawn into the figure as a path by plotting the number of defectives that are found during inspection against the number of units that have been tested up to that point. For each of the four different outcomes of a double-sampling procedure (decision to accept/reject after first sample, decision to accept/reject after second sample) a path is given as an example.

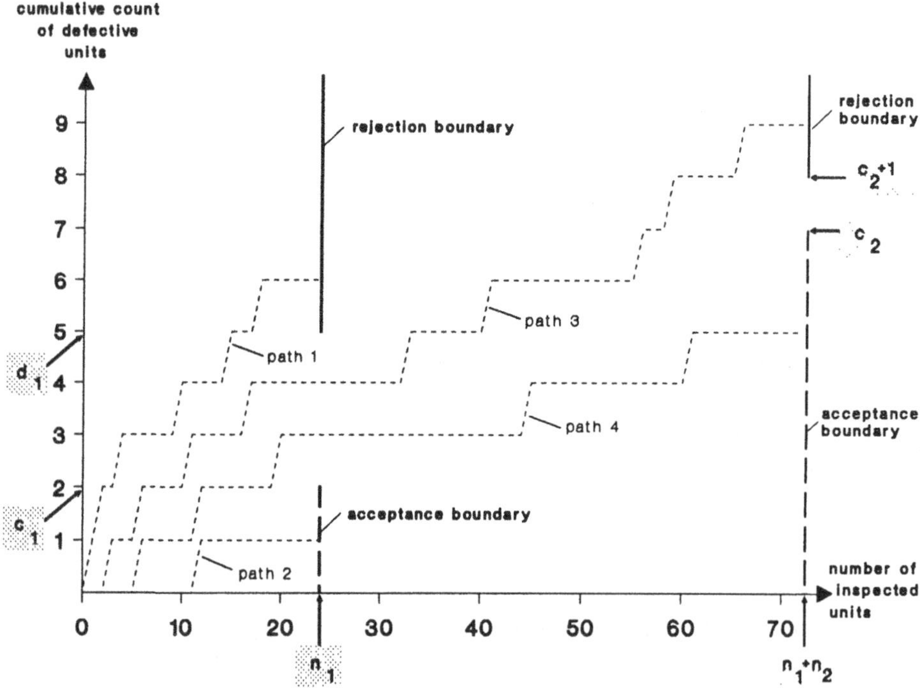

Figure 3.2/18: Inspection diagram for a double-sampling plan $(N; 24; 2; 5; 48; 7)$

Similar to the case of single-sampling plans, double-sampling plans can be modified so that the procedure stops once a definite decision is reached. This is again called **curtailed inspection**. There are four different situations in which the sampling of more units will not any longer effect the final decision:

Situations in which a curtailed sampling procedure reduces the amount of inspection

- Before all n_1 units of the first sample are inspected the d_1-th defective is found.
- Before inspection of all the $n_1 + n_2$ units in both samples the count of defectives reaches $c_2 + 1$. Since drawing of the second sample implies that at most $d_1 - 1$ defective units were found in the first sample, at least $(c_2 + 1) - (d_1 - 1) = c_2 - d_1 + 2$ units of the second sample have to be inspected before the $(c_2 + 1)$-th defective can occur.
- Before inspection of all n_1 units of the first sample the $(n_1 - c_1)$-th conforming unit is observed.
- Before the $n_1 + n_2$ units of both samples are all tested the count of conforming units reaches $n_1 + n_2 - c_2$. Since the number of conforming units had to be below $n_1 - (c_1 + 1)$ at the end of the inspection of the first sample it follows that at least $(n_2 - c_2) + (c_1 + 1)$ units need to be inspected before the above event can take place.

The first two situations allow an early rejection, and the last two an early acceptance of the lot. A procedure that only allows to stop the process in the first two cases, i.e., excludes the possibility of early acceptance, is called **semicurtailed inspection**. A procedure that allows acceptance as well as rejection before completion of the inspection is called **fully curtailed inspection**.

Variations of curtailed inspection

Figure 3.2/19 shows again the inspection diagram of the double-sampling plan with $n_1 = 24$, $c_1 = 2$, $d_1 = 5$, $n_2 = 48$ and $c_2 = 7$ for fully curtailed inspection. As in figure 3.2/18, four different paths are drawn in the diagram.

For all four paths, the fully curtailed inspection reaches a final decision before inspection of all units of the first sample (path $1 - 2$) or all units of the second sample (path $3 - 4$). In paths 2 and 4 the semicurtailed procedure would not reduce the amount of inspection.

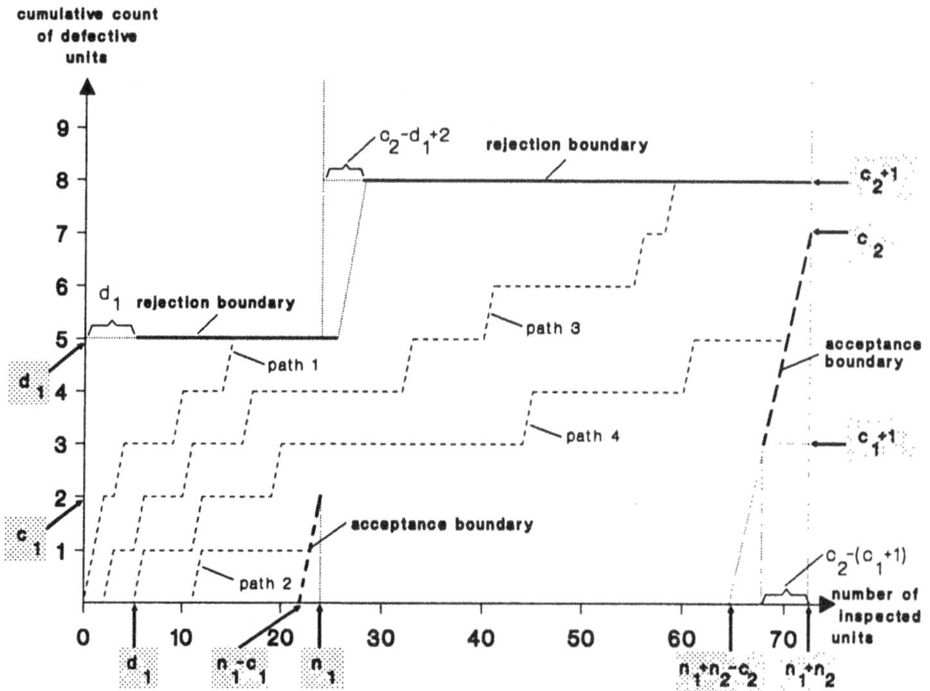

Figure 3.2/19: Inspection diagram of a double-sampling plan $(N; 24; 2; 5; 48; 7)$ for fully curtailed inspection

Problem 3.2/21

a) How do we need to modify the structural chart of the uncurtailed procedure in figure 3.2/17 for curtailed inspection?

b) Illustrate the differences between double-sampling plans with and without curtailed inspection by a table analogous to table 3.2/10.

b) OC Function

We will now derive the OC function of a double-sampling plan. We can assume without loss of generality the case of an uncurtailed double-sampling plan since curtailed inspection does not change the OC function. In the inspection diagram of figure 3.2/18 we illustrated the four different possible outcomes of this double-sampling. The probability of occurrence of these outcomes depends on the process quality P:

- Acceptance of lot based on first sample with probability $Pr_a^1(P)$ (see path 2 in figure 3.2/18);

- Rejection of lot based on first sample with probability $Pr_r^1(P)$ (see path 1);
- Acceptance of lot based on both samples with probability $Pr_a^2(P)$ (see path 4);
- Rejection of lot based on both samples with probability $Pr_r^2(P)$ (see path 3).

The four probabilities above are defined by the procedure in the following way:

Probabilities for the outcomes of double-sampling

$$P_a^1(P) := Pr(X_{n_1}^T \leq c_1|P) \tag{3.71 a}$$

$$Pr_r^1(P) := Pr(X_{n_1}^T \geq d_1|P) \tag{3.71 b}$$

$$Pr_a^2(P) := Pr(c_1 < X_{n_1}^T < d_1 \text{ and } X_{n_1+n_2}^T \leq c_2|P) \tag{3.71 c}$$

$$Pr_r^2(P) := Pr(c_1 < X_{n_1}^T < d_1 \text{ and } X_{n_1+n_2}^T > c_2|P). \tag{3.71 d}$$

Since the outcomes are mutually exclusive, we have

$$Pr_a^1(P) + Pr_r^1(P) + Pr_a^2(P) + Pr_r^2(P) = 1. \tag{3.72}$$

Hence, once the probabilities (3.71a-c) are obtained, $Pr_r^2(P)$ can easily be determined. In order to determine $Pr_a^2(P)$, it is best to condition on the outcome of the first sample. Suppose that the number of defectives $X_{n_1}^T$ has a realization j that leads to drawing of a second sample, i.e., $c_1 + 1 \leq j \leq d_1 - 1$. In order to be able to accept the lot we can have at most $c_2 - j$ defective units in the second sample. The probability of the composite event "$X_{n_1}^T = j$ and $X_{n_1+n_2}^T - X_{n_1}^T \leq c_2 - j$" is given as the product of the two individual probabilities. $Pr_a^2(P)$ is the sum of these products over all possible j:

$$Pr_a^2(P) = \sum_{j=c_1+1}^{d_1-1} Pr\left(X_{n_1}^T = j|P\right) \cdot Pr\left(X_{n_1+n_2}^T - X_{n_1}^T \leq c_2 - j|P\right). \tag{3.73}$$

The probability that a double-sampling procedure leads to drawing a second sample is called **sequel probability** $Pr_s(P)$. It is found to be

$$Pr_s(P) = 1 - \left[Pr_a^1(P) + Pr_r^1(P)\right] = Pr_a^2(P) + Pr_r^2(P). \tag{3.74}$$

The probability that the lot is accepted, regardless of the number of samples taken, is called the **total probability of acceptance** $L_{do}(P)$. It is seen as the **OC function** of the particular double-sampling plan, since $L_{do}(P)$ gives the probability that the lot is accepted as a function of P:

General formula for the OC function of a double-sampling plan

$$L_{do}(P) = Pr_a^1(P) + Pr_a^2(P). \tag{3.75}$$

Substituting (3.71a) and (3.73) into this formula gives

$$\begin{aligned} L_{do}(P) &= Pr\left(X_{n_1}^T \leq c_1 | P\right) + \\ & \textstyle\sum_{j=c_1+1}^{d_1-1} Pr\left(X_{n_1}^T = j | P\right) \cdot Pr\left(X_{n_1+n_2}^T - X_{n_1}^T \leq c_2 - j | P\right). \end{aligned} \tag{3.76}$$

In the case of sampling without replacement the number of defectives in the sample has a hypergeometric distribution. Then (3.76) becomes

OC formulas for different distributions:
- hypergeometric case

$$\begin{aligned} & L_{do}(P|N; n_1; c_1; d_1; n_2; c_2) = Hy(c_1|N; NP; n_1) + \\ & + \textstyle\sum_{j=c_1+1}^{d_1-1} hy(j|N; NP; n_1) \cdot Hy(c_2 - j|N - n_1; NP - j; n_2). \end{aligned} \tag{3.77 a}$$

This function is called the **hypergeometric OC function** of the double-sampling plan $(N; n_1; c_1; d_1; n_2; c_2)$. The **binomial OC function** corresponds to sampling with replacement:

- binomial case

$$L_{do}(P|n_1; c_1; d_1; n_2; c_2) = Bi(c_1|P; n_1) + \sum_{j=c_1+1}^{d_1-1} bi(j|P; n_1) \cdot Bi(c_2 - j|P; n_2). \tag{3.77 b}$$

- Poisson case

This function and the **Poisson OC function**

$$L_{do}^*(P|n_1; c_1; d_1; n_2; c_2) = Po(c_1|n_1P) + \sum_{j=c_1+1}^{d_1-1} po(j|n_1P) \cdot Po(c_2 - j|n_2P) \tag{3.77 c}$$

are commonly used to approximate formula (3.77a).

Example 3.2/13

Table 3.2/14 gives the probabilities (3.71), (3.74) and (3.75) for a double-sampling plan with $n_1 = 50$, $c_1 = 1$, $d_1 = 5$, $n_2 = 100$ and $c_2 = 7$ for different values of the quality level P. The values were calculated under the assumption of the binomial case.

We will discuss the calculation of these values for the example of $P = 0.06$. The probabilities $Pr_a^1(0.06)$ and $Pr_r^1(0.06)$ were obtained from table 5.1/3 and rounded to three decimal points:

$$\begin{aligned} Pr_a^1(0.06) &= Bi(1|0.06; 50) \approx 0.190 \\ Pr_r^1(0.06) &= 1 - Bi(4|0.06; 50) \approx 1 - 0.821 = 0.179. \end{aligned}$$

P	$Pr_a^1(P)$	$Pr_r^1(P)$	$Pr_a^2(P)$	$Pr_r^2(P)$	$Pr_s(P)$	$L_{do}(P)$
(1)	(2)	(3)	(4)	(5)	(6)	(7)
0.020	0.736	0.003	0.253	0.008	0.261	0.989
0.027	0.608	0.011	0.344	0.037	0.381	0.952
0.040	0.400	0.049	0.372	0.179	0.551	0.772
0.060	0.190	0.179	0.188	0.443	0.631	0.378
0.080	0.083	0.371	0.051	0.495	0.546	0.134
0.085	0.067	0.422	0.034	0.477	0.511	0.101
0.100	0.034	0.569	0.009	0.388	0.397	0.043
0.120	0.013	0.732	0.001	0.254	0.255	0.014

Table 3.2/14: Acceptance and rejection probabilities for the double-sampling plan $(N; 50; 1; 5; 100; 7)$

$Pr_a^2(0.06)$ is calculated by (3.73):

$$\begin{aligned} Pr_a^2(0.06) &= \sum_{j=2}^{4} bi(j|0.06;50)\cdot Bi(7-j|0.06;100) \\ &= bi(2|0.06;50)\cdot Bi(5|0.06;100)+bi(3|0.06;50)\cdot Bi(4|0.06;100) \\ &\quad +bi(4|0.06;50)\cdot Bi(3|0.06;100) \\ &\approx 0.226\cdot 0.440+0.231\cdot 0.277+0.173\cdot 0.143 \\ &= 0.188. \end{aligned}$$

The probability $Pr_r^2(0.06)$ is then determined by (3.72):

$$\begin{aligned} Pr_r^2(0.06) &= 1-Pr_a^1(0.06)-Pr_r^1(0.06)-Pr_a^2(0.06) \\ &\approx 1-0.190-0.179-0.188 \\ &= 0.443. \end{aligned}$$

The sequel probability (3.74) and acceptance probability (3.75) are found to be

$$\begin{aligned} Pr_s(0.06) &= Pr_a^2(0.06)+Pr_r^2(0.06)\approx 0.188+0.443=0.631 \\ L_{do}(0.06) &= Pr_a^1(P)+Pr_a^2(P)\approx 0.190+0.188=0.378. \end{aligned}$$

Figure 3.2/20 contains the curves of the OC function and probabilities $Pr_a^1(P)$ and $Pr_s(P)$. We can see that the sequel probability $Pr_s(P)$ is small for extremely good and bad quality levels and big for quality levels in the middle range.

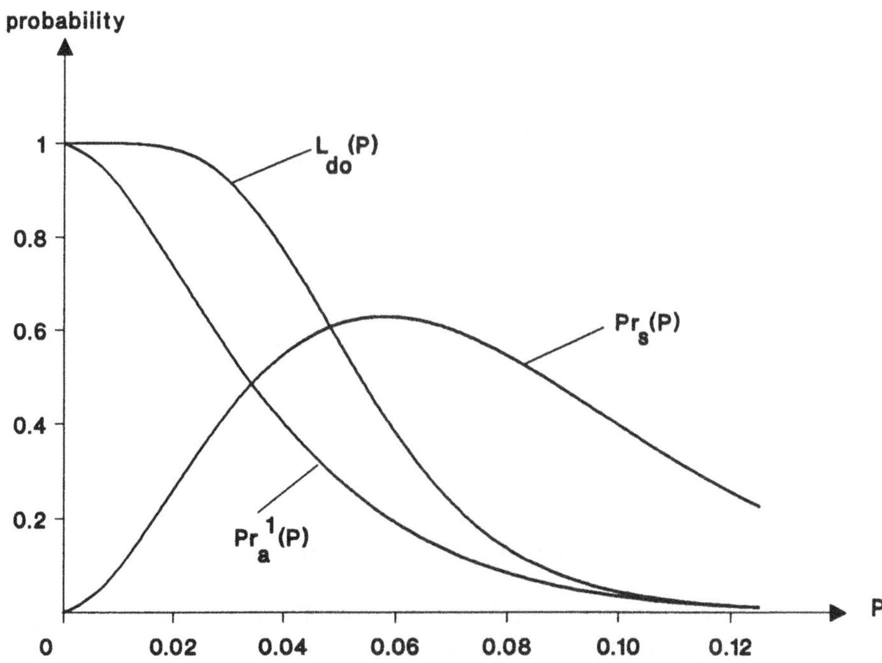

Figure 3.2/20: OC function and other probability curves for the double-sampling plan $(N; 50; 1; 5; 100; 7)$

Problem 3.2/22

Calculate for the plan in example 3.2/13 the probabilities (3.71), (3.74) and (3.75) by using the Poisson approximation. Suppose that the fraction nonconforming is $P = 0.06$.

Problem 3.2/23

Determine the probabilities mentioned above for a double-sampling plan with $N = 20, n_1 = 5, c_1 = 0, d_1 = 2, n_2 = 5, c_2 = 2$ by assuming the hypergeometric case and $P = 0.15$.

c) Average Sample Number (ASN)

In the case of single-sampling plans for attributes the total number of sample units necessary to decide about acceptance of the lot is a random variable only under curtailed inspection (see table 3.2/10). In double-sampling plans the effective sample size is always a random variable. Let us first consider uncurtailed inspection. Then Y^*, the number of sample units that is drawn, is a two-valued random variable:

$$Y^* = \begin{cases} n_1 & \text{if decision can be made after the first sample} \\ n_1 + n_2 & \text{if it is necessary to draw a second sample.} \end{cases} \tag{3.78}$$

The expectation of this random variable is again called the **average sample number** or **ASN** of the double-sampling plan:

Definiton of ASN and $ASNL$

$$ASN_{do} = E(Y^*). \tag{3.79}$$

The two values of Y^* occur with probabilities given by (3.71) and (3.74):

$$\begin{aligned} Pr(Y^* = n_1) &= Pr_a^1(P) + Pr_r^1(P) = 1 - Pr_s(P) \\ Pr(Y^* = n_1 + n_2) &= Pr_a^2(P) + Pr_r^2(P) = Pr_s(P) \end{aligned}$$

This determines the expectation (3.79) to be of the form

$$ASN_{do}(P) = n_1 \cdot [1 - Pr_s(P)] + (n_1 + n_2) \cdot Pr_s(P) = n_1 + n_2 \cdot Pr_s(P). \tag{3.80}$$

The function $ASN_{do} = ASN_{do}(P)$ attains its minimal value n_1 at $P = 0$ and $P = 1$, since $Pr_s(0) = Pr_s(1) = 0$. The maximum is attained at $P_M \approx (c_1 + d_1)/(2n_1)$. The corresponding value $ASNL_{do} := ASN(P_M)$ is denoted the **maximal ASN** or **ASNL** (average sample number limit) of the uncurtailed double-sampling plan.

For curtailed inspection, the realization n^* of the required sample size Y^* is at most as big as for uncurtailed inspection. This means that the ASN curve tends to be more flat. For semicurtailed inspection the following formula is obtained:

ASN curves in the case of semicurtailed and fully curtailed inspection

$$\begin{aligned} ASN_{do}^{(1)}(P) &= n_1 + \sum_{j=c_1+1}^{d_1-1} f(j|n_1) \cdot \left[\frac{c_2+1-j}{P} + n_2 \cdot F(c_2 - j|n_2) \right. \\ &\quad \left. - \frac{c_2+1-j}{P} \cdot F(c_2+1-j|n_2+1) \right] \end{aligned} \tag{3.81}$$

(see also SCHILLING 1982, p. 138). The terms $f(j|m)$ and $F(j|m)$ denote the probabilities that exactly or at least j defectives are found in a sample of size m, respectively.

Example 3.2/14

We want to calculate the ASN functions (3.80) and (3.81) for the double-sampling plan of example 3.2/13 that assumed an underlying binomial distribution. Its ASN function (3.80) has the following form

$$ASN_{do}(P) = 50 + 100 \cdot Pr_s(P) = 50 + 100 \cdot [1 - Pr_a^1(P) - Pr_r^1(P)].$$

Several values of this function can be easily calculated using column 6 of table 3.2/14. For calculation of additional values the formulas in (3.71) have to be used. Doing this we get $Pr_a^1(P) = Bi(1|P;50)$ and $Pr_r^1(P) = 1 - Bi(4|P;50)$ and the result is

$$ASN_{do}(P) = 50 + 100 \cdot [Bi(4|P;50) - Bi(1|P;50)].$$

The ASN function (3.81) is obtained through (3.58c) and (3.8a) to be

$$\begin{aligned} ASN_{do}^{(1)}(P) &= 50 + \sum_{j=2}^{4} bi(j|P;50) \\ &\quad \cdot \left[\frac{8-j}{P} + 100 \cdot Bi(7-j|P;100) - \frac{8-j}{P} \cdot Bi(8-j|P;101)\right] \end{aligned}$$

The following figure shows both ASN functions.

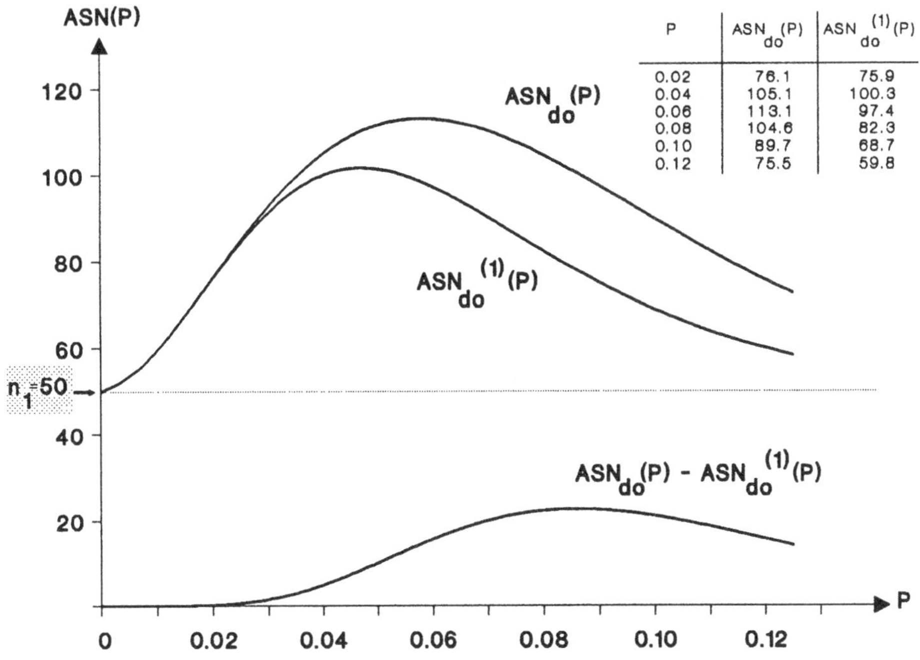

P	$ASN_{do}(P)$	$ASN_{do}^{(1)}(P)$
0.02	76.1	75.9
0.04	105.1	100.3
0.06	113.1	97.4
0.08	104.6	82.3
0.10	89.7	68.7
0.12	75.5	59.8

Figure 3.2/21: *ASN* functions of a double-sampling plan $(N; 50; 1; 5; 100; 7)$ for the cases of semicurtailed and uncurtailed inspection

---

Problem 3.2/24

a) Determine the value of the *ASN* function at $P = 0.15$ for the double-sampling plan of problem 3.2/23. Use formula (3.80) and assume the hypergeometric case.

b) Use (3.80) and (3.81) to calculate the values of the *ASN* function at $P = 0.06$ for the double-sampling plan in example 3.2/13. Use the Poisson approximation.

d) Other Measures of Performance (AOQ, AOQL, ATI and AFI)

As in single-sampling plans, defective units can slip undetected through the inspection in double-sampling plans. Analogous to (3.43) we define the **average outgoing quality (AOQ)** by

Definition of AOQ

$$AOQ_{do} := \frac{E(Y_1)}{E(Y_2)}. \tag{3.82}$$

The variable Y_1 again denotes the average number of defective units in the lot that pass the inspection undetected. The inspection procedure now consists of two stages and consequently Y_2 is the average number of units in the lot that are accepted at either stage of the process.

For the calculation of the average outgoing quality $AOQ_{do} = AOQ_{do}(P)$ we again distinguish between nine different combinations S_i/L_j of sample and remaining lot disposition, and the same assumptions and ideas of section 3.2.2b apply. Note that the value of the expectation $E(Y_1)$ in a double-sampling plan does as before not depend on a particular combination. Analogous to (3.45), it holds that

Considerations with respect to AOQ calculation

$$Y_1 = \begin{cases} (N-n_1)\cdot P & \text{if } X_{n_1}^T \leq c_1 \\ (N-n_1-n_2)\cdot P & \text{if } X_{n_1}^T \in (c_1, d_1) \text{ and } X_{n_1+n_2}^T \leq c_2 \\ 0 & \text{else.} \end{cases} \tag{3.83}$$

Applying (3.71a,c) and (3.75) gives

$$\begin{aligned} E(Y_1) &= (N-n_1)\cdot P\cdot Pr_a^1(P) + (N-n_1-n_2)\cdot P\cdot Pr_a^2(P) \\ &= P\cdot[(N-n_1)\cdot L_{do}(P) - n_2\cdot Pr_a^2(P)] \\ &=: A(P). \end{aligned} \tag{3.84}$$

Hence we find the AOQ of a double-sampling plan to be of the form

$$AOQ_{do}(P) = \frac{P\cdot[(N-n_1)\cdot L_{do}(P) - n_2\cdot Pr_a^2(P)]}{E(Y_2)} = \frac{A(P)}{E(Y_2)}. \tag{3.85}$$

The expected value of Y_2 depends on the choice of sample and remaining lot disposition S_i/L_j (see problem 3.2/25). The following table 3.2/15 gives the resulting AOQ formulas for the nine cases S_i/L_j according to BEAINY/CASE (1981).

The AOQ function of a double-sampling plan also attains a maximum at $P = P_M$. The corresponding value $AOQ(P_M)$ is called the **average outgoing quality limit** and, similar to (3.44), it is abbreviated by $AOQL_{do}$:

Definition of the $AOQL$

$$AOQL_{do} := \max_P AOQ_{do}(P) = AOQ_{do}(P_M). \tag{3.86}$$

	L_1 remaining lot is not used	L_2 remaining lot is used after defectives are sorted out	L_3 remaining lot is used after replacement of defectives
S_1 sample is not used	$AOQ_{do}(P) = P$	$AOQ_{do}(P) = \frac{A(P)}{A(P)+(1-P)[N-ASN_{do}(P)]}$	$AOQ_{do}(P) = \frac{A(P)}{N-ASN_{do}(P)}$
S_2 conforming units in the sample are used, defectives are sorted out	$AOQ_{do}(P) = \frac{P \cdot A(P)}{A(P)+(1-P) \cdot P \cdot ASN_{do}(P)}$	$AOQ_{do}(P) = \frac{A(P)}{A(P)+(1-P) \cdot N}$	$AOQ_{do}(P) = \frac{A(P)}{N-P \cdot ASN_{do}(P)}$
S_3 defective units are replaced and sample is used	$AOQ_{do}(P) = \frac{P \cdot A(P)}{A(P)+P \cdot ASN_{do}(P)}$	$AOQ_{do}(P) = \frac{A(P)}{A(P)+P \cdot ASN_{do}(P)+(1-P) \cdot N}$	$AOQ_{do}(P) = \frac{A(P)}{N}$

Table 3.2/15: *AOQ* functions for different combinations of sample and remaining lot disposition for a double-sampling plan

The $AOQL_{do}$ can again be approximated by (3.52) if one replaces n by $(n_1 + n_2)/2$ (see SCHILLING 1982, p.138):

Approximation of the *AOQL*

$$P_M \approx \frac{2x}{n_1 + n_2} \tag{3.87 a}$$

$$AOQL_{do} \approx y \cdot \left(\frac{2}{n_1 + n_2} - \frac{1}{N}\right). \tag{3.87 b}$$

The auxiliary variables x and y are obtained from table 3.2/6, which was developed by DODGE/ROMIG. Values of x and y are found in the row of the table corresponding to

$$c \approx \frac{1}{4}(c_1 + d_1 + 2 \cdot c_2 + 1). \tag{3.87 c}$$

Example 3.2/15

We already calculated the OC function $L_{do}(P)$ and the *ASN* function $ASN_{do}(P)$ of the double-sampling plan $(N; 50; 1; 5; 100; 7)$ in the binomial case (see examples 3.2/13-14). We now want to approximate the $AOQL_{do}$ for $N = 2000$. By (3.87a,b), we first get

$$P_M \approx \frac{x}{75}; \quad AOQL_{do} \approx y\left(\frac{1}{75} - \frac{1}{2000}\right).$$

As a result of (3.87c) we find that $c \approx 5.25$, and by table 3.2/6 taking $c = 5$, this determines the auxiliary variables to be $x = 4.35$ and $y = 3.168$:

$$P_M \approx \frac{4.35}{75} = 0.058; \qquad AOQL_{do} \approx 3.168\left(\frac{1}{75} - \frac{1}{2000}\right) \approx 0.0407.$$

Definition of *ATI* and *AFI*

For reasons of completeness, we will also discuss the performance measures *ATI* and *AFI*. The **average total inspection** or **ATI** was defined for a single-sampling plan in section 3.2.2c. Analogous to (3.53), for the double-sampling plan we get:

$$ATI_{do} := E(Y_3) \tag{3.88}$$

where Y_3 denotes the average number of all inspected units. Accordingly, the **average fraction inspected** or **AFI** is given by

$$AFI_{do} := \frac{ATI_{do}}{N}. \tag{3.89}$$

The table below gives the *ATI* formulas of an uncurtailed double-sampling plan for the nine disposition combinations S_i/L_j (for derivation see BEAINY/CASE 1981). Note that for the *AFI* formulas (3.89), we need to divide by the lot size N.

	L_1 remaining lot is not used	L_2 remaining lot is used after defectives are sorted out	L_3 remaining lot is used after replacement of defectives
S_1 sample is not used S_2 conforming units in the sample are used, defectives are sorted out	$ATI_{do}(P) = ASN_{do}(P)$	$ATI_{do}(P) = N - \frac{A(P)}{P}$	$ATI_{do}(P) = \frac{N-P\cdot ASN_{do}(P)-A(P)/P}{1-P}$
S_3 defective units are replaced and sample is used	$ATI_{do}(P) = \frac{ASN_{do}(P)}{1-P}$	$ATI_{do}(P) = N - \frac{A(P)}{P} + \frac{P\cdot ASN_{do}(P)}{1-P}$	$ATI_{do}(P) = \frac{N-A(P)/P}{1-P}$

Table 3.2/16: *ATI* **functions for different combinations of sample and remaining lot disposition for a double-sampling plan**

Remarks

1. In SQA literature the most commonly used formula for the average outgoing quality of a double plan is $AOQ_{do}(P) = P \cdot L_{do}(P)$. This is different from any formula in table 3.2/15, but, since the term $A(P)$ in (3.85) can be approximated by $A(P) \approx P \cdot N \cdot L_{do}(P)$ (provided N is big compared to n_1 and n_2), we can consider the above AOQ formula to be an approximation of the AOQ formula $AOQ_{do}(P) = A(P) \cdot N$ of the case S_3/L_3.
2. The AOQ formulas of table 3.2/15 are valid regardless of whether the inspection is curtailed or uncurtailed. Recall that curtailed inspection only effects the amount of inspection but not any characteristics of the plan.

Problem 3.2/25

Give a proof of the AOQ formula for the combination S_2/L_2 in table 3.2/15.

Problem 3.2/26

Give a proof of the ATI formula for the case S_3/L_3 in table 3.2/16.

Problem 3.2/27

Calculate $AOQ_{do}(P)$ and $ATI_{do}(P)$ for the double-sampling plan (2000;50;1;5;100;7) at the points $P_1 = 0.027$ and $P_2 = 0.085$ for all nine possible disposition combinations S_i/L_j. You can use the following results without proof:

$$Pr_a^2(P_1) = 0.344; \quad Pr_s(P_1) = 0.381; \quad L_{do}(P_1) = 0.952$$
$$Pr_a^2(P_2) = 0.034; \quad Pr_s(P_2) = 0.511; \quad L_{do}(P_2) = 0.101.$$

e) Equivalent Single-Sampling and Double-Sampling Plans

We have already pointed out that a sampling plan, or its underlying hypothesis test, is completely characterized by its OC function. We will call plans with the same OC function **OC equivalent sampling plans**. In particular, these plans have the same discriminatory power. Since the shape of the OC curve also depends on the underlying distribution of the test statistic, it is recommendable to compare plans with the same assumption on the underlying distribution. Even in this case it won't be possible to construct a single-sampling plan with exactly the same OC curve for a given double-sampling plan. At most, one can find a plan with an OC function that agrees at specified points with the OC function of the double-sampling

Definition of OC equivalence

plan. Such plans with approximately equivalent OC curves are called **approximately OC equivalent sampling plans**. An example of two approximately equivalent plans are the plans (N;50;1) and (N;32;0;2;32;1). We can see from table 3.2/17 that their OC functions are about the same. The calculations below were made under the assumption of a binomially distributed test statistic.

P	$L(P)$	$L_{do}(P)$
0.001	0.9988	0.9985
0.002	0.9954	0.9944
0.004	0.9827	0.9791
0.006	0.9635	0.9562
0.008	0.9391	0.9277
0.010	0.9106	0.8949
0.020	0.7358	0.7031
0.040	0.4005	0.3686
0.060	0.1900	0.1770
0.080	0.0827	0.0828
0.100	0.0338	0.0385
0.120	0.0131	0.0179

Table 3.2/17: Values of the OC function for the plans ($N; 50; 1$) and ($N; 32; 0; 2; 32; 1$)

Definition and measurement of the efficiency of a double-sampling plan

Among two (approximately) OC equivalent sampling plans, the one with the smaller average amount of inspection is called **more efficient**. In order to compare an OC equivalent single-sampling plan and an uncurtailed double-sampling plan we define the **efficiency** to be the ratio of the maximum value $ASNL_{do}$ of the function $ASN_{do}(P)$ in [0,1] and the sample size n of the single-sampling plan:

$$w_{do} := \frac{ASNL_{do}}{n}. \tag{3.90}$$

Example 3.2/16

We will use the uncurtailed plan ($N; 50; 1; 5; 100; 7$) of example 3.2/13 to demonstrate the general approach to constructing an OC equivalent single-sampling plan for a given double-sampling plan. The AQL and RQL are given by $AQL = P_{1-\alpha}$ and $RQL = P_\beta$, with $\alpha = 0.05$ and $\beta = 0.1$ (see (3.34)). Using table 3.2/14, we find that $AQL \approx 0.027$ and $RQL \approx 0.085$.

An approximately OC equivalent single-sampling plan is a plan ($N; n; c$) with an OC function that roughly goes through ($AQL; 1-\alpha$) and ($RQL; \beta$). Such a plan can be found with the search algorithm by GUENTHER that is desribed in table 3.2/15. The resulting plan has the parameter values $n = 136$ and $c = 7$. Since the ASN function of the double plan attains its maximum value $ASNL_{do} = ASN_{do}(P_M) = 113.1$ at about $P_M \approx 0.06$, we find the efficiency to be

$$w_{do} = \frac{113.1}{136} \approx 0.832.$$

The result tells us that, even in the worst case (i.e., at $P_M = 0.06$), the sample size of the double plan is on the average 16.8 % smaller than that of the OC equivalent single-sampling plan. If we had used the algorithm by PEACH/LITTAUER (Poisson approximation) to determine the OC equivalent single-sampling plan the results would have been almost the same, $n = 139$ and $c = 7$, and hence

$$w_{do} = \frac{113.1}{139} \approx 0.814.$$

Problem 3.2/28

The double-sampling plan with $n_1 = 50, c_1 = 0, d_1 = 3, n_2 = 50$ and $c_2 = 2$ has $AQL = 0.0116$ with $1 - \alpha = 0.9$, and $RQL = 0.057$ with $\beta = 0.1$. Suppose the average sample number limit is $ASNL_{do} = 76.7$. Use the search algorithm by PEACH/LITTAUER to determine a single-sampling plan with approximately the same producer's and consumer's risk. What is the efficiency of the double-sampling plan?

3.2.5 Multiple-Sampling Plans

With the help of an example we have just illustrated that double-sampling plans require less inspection on average than equivalent single-sampling plans. We would expect that one could reduce the amount of inspection even further if one uses a procedure that allows for more than two samples.

The procedure of a **k-stage multiple sampling plan** ($k = 2, 3, \ldots$) for attributes takes, at the j-th stage, a sample of size n_j from a lot of given size N and accepts the lot at this stage if the cumulative count of defective units in the first j samples

Description of the multiple-sampling procedure

$$X^T_{(j)} := X^T_{n_1+n_2+\ldots+n_j}$$

does not exceed the acceptance number c_j. If $X^T_{(j)}$ reaches the rejection number d_j the lot is rejected. The next sample is drawn when $X^T_{(j)} \in (c_j; d_j)$

and, unless the procedure stopped at an earlier stage, the lot is accepted at the k-th stage if $X^T_{(k)} \leq c_k$ and it is rejected if $X^T_{(k)} \geq d_k := c_k + 1$. Therefore, a multiple-sampling plan with k stages is specified by $3k$ parameters: the lot size N, k sample sizes $(n_1, n_2, \ldots, n_k)$, k acceptance numbers $(c_1, c_2, \ldots, c_k)$ and $k-1$ rejection numbers $(d_1, d_2, \ldots, d_{k-1})$. Analogous to (3.70a), the acceptance and rejection numbers form nondecreasing sequences of integers that satisfy the conditions

$$0 \leq c_j < d_j - 1 \leq c_{j+1} < n_1 + n_2 + \ldots + n_j; \quad j = 1, \ldots, k-1.$$

Requirements on the parameters of a multiple-sampling plan with k stages

Obviously, the sum of all sample sizes also has to satisfy the condition $k \leq n_1 + n_2 + \ldots + n_k \leq N$. The commonly applied sampling schemes (see section 3.2.7) generally use a constant sample size ($n_1 = n_2 = \ldots = n_k$).

We will omit the relatively long derivation of the OC function, as well as that of the *ASN*, *AOQ* and *ATI* functions of k-stage multiple-sampling plans, and refer interested readers to SCHILLING (1982, p.141-150). We only want to mention that in comparisons of multiple-sampling plans with their OC equivalent single-sampling plans $(N; n; c)$, analogous to (3.90), one can define the **efficiency** by the ratio

Efficiency of a k-stage multiple-sampling plan

$$w_k := \frac{ASNL_{k-stage}}{n} \tag{3.91}$$

of the average sample size limit of the k-stage plan and the sample size of the single-sampling plan. When $w_k < 1$, the multiple-sampling plan is more efficient.

Example 3.2/17

In order to illustrate the efficiency of a k-stage multiple-sampling plan with respect to its OC equivalent single-sampling plan, we will consider a 7-stage plan with $n_1 = n_2 = \ldots = n_7 = 20$ and the acceptance and rejection numbers

$$c_1 = *^{13},\ c_2 = 1,\ c_3 = 2,\ c_4 = 3,\ c_5 = 5,\ c_6 = 7,\ c_7 = 9$$
$$d_1 = 4,\ d_2 = 5,\ d_3 = 6,\ d_4 = 7,\ d_5 = 8,\ d_6 = 9,\ d_7 = 10.$$

By the sampling scheme ISO 2859 (see section 3.2.7) this is a plan that at least satisfies the conditions $AQL = 0.03$ with $\alpha = 0.025$, and $RQL = 0.115$ with $\beta = 0.1$. The following table contains values of the OC and *ASN* functions at selected quality levels P. The calculation of these values is omitted.

[13] The * denotes that acceptance after the first sample is not admissible.

P	$L_{\text{seven}}(P)$	$ASN_{\text{seven}}(P)$
0.01	1.000	41.64
0.02	0.995	46.80
0.03	0.975	54.24
0.04	0.916	62.02
0.05	0.809	68.14
0.06	0.661	70.42
0.07	0.508	70.46
0.08	0.366	67.68
0.09	0.257	64.34
0.10	0.174	59.44

Table 3.2/18: Selected values of the OC function of a 7-stage sampling plan

An approximately OC equivalent single-sampling plan is a plan with an OC function that at least approximately agrees with the OC function of the 7-stage plan at the two specified points $AQL = 0.03$ and $RQL = 0.115$. In other words, the single-sampling plan has about the same producer's and consumer's risks at the points AQL and RQL. The parameters of such a plan, with $L(0.05) \geq 0.975$ and $L(0.115) \leq 0.1$, can be determined under the assumption of a Poisson distributed test statistic using the search algorithm by PEACH/LITTAUER presented in figure 3.2/16. Using table 3.2/12 gives the following result (see again example 3.2/12):

$$\left.\begin{aligned} c=0: \quad q_1(0) &= \frac{\chi^2_{2;0.90}}{2\cdot RQL} \approx \frac{4.605}{0.23} = 20.02 \\ q_2(0) &= \frac{\chi^2_{2;0.025}}{2\cdot AQL} \approx \frac{0.051}{0.06} = 0.85 \end{aligned}\right\} \Rightarrow q_1(0) > q_2(0)$$

$$\vdots \qquad \vdots \qquad \vdots$$

$$\left.\begin{aligned} c=5: \quad q_1(5) &= \frac{\chi^2_{12;0.90}}{2\cdot RQL} \approx \frac{18.549}{0.23} = 80.65 \\ q_2(5) &= \frac{\chi^2_{12;0.025}}{2\cdot AQL} \approx \frac{4.404}{0.06} = 73.4 \end{aligned}\right\} \Rightarrow q_1(5) > q_2(5)$$

$$\left.\begin{aligned} c=6: \quad q_1(6) &= \frac{\chi^2_{14;0.90}}{2\cdot RQL} \approx \frac{21.064}{0.23} = 91.58 \\ q_2(6) &= \frac{\chi^2_{14;0.025}}{2\cdot AQL} \approx \frac{5.629}{0.06} = 93.82 \end{aligned}\right\} \Rightarrow q_1(6) < q_2(6).$$

The acceptance number of the resulting single-sampling plan is $c = 6$ and the sample size is chosen to be the smallest integer satisfying the condition $q_1(6) \leq n \leq q_2(6)$, i.e., $n = 92$.

The efficiency (3.91) of the 7-stage plan with respect to this single-sampling plan is found to be

$$w_7 = \frac{70.46}{92} = 0.766.$$

We can conclude that the amount of inspection of the 7-stage sampling plan is at least 24.4% less than that of the approximately OC equivalent single-sampling plan.

We will not discuss the construction of equivalent 2 to 6-stage plans and the comparison of their efficiency to that of the 7-stage plan. Also, the question of determining from which number of stages onward there is no more significant improvement in the efficiency of this 7-stage plan will not be considered.

Problem 3.2/29

a) Calculate the values of the OC function at $P = 0.02$ for a triple plan with $n_1 = n_2 = n_3 = 20, c_1 = 0, d_1 = 3, c_2 = 2, d_2 = 4, c_3 = 3$ using the binomial approximation. Analoguous to example 3.2/13, first determine the acceptance probabilities $P_a^1(0.02), P_a^2(0.02)$ and $P_a^3(0.02)$ after inspection of the first, second and third samples, respectively.

b) Also, find the value of the *ASN* function for the same 3-stage plan at $P = 0.02$.

3.2.6 Sequential-Sampling Plans

The logical continuation of the double- and multiple-sampling procedures for attribute plans is to set the sample size to one, to determine at every step if the lot can be accepted or rejected, respectively, and to continue sampling until a final decision is reached. Note that setting the sample size to one optimizes the efficiency of the procedure and that the number of steps to a final decision can theoretically be any integer from one to the total number of units in the lot. Such plans are called **sequential-sampling plans** and the procedure is called **sequential sampling**. Sequential-sampling plans are applications of the LR tests that were introduced in section 2.3.3b.

a) Sequential-Sampling Procedure

The application of a sequential plan is equivalent to performing a parameter test of type (2.156) with $P_0 = AQL$ and $P_1 = RQL$:

$$\begin{aligned} H_0: \quad & P \leq P_0 \quad := AQL \\ H_1: \quad & P \geq P_1 \quad := RQL. \end{aligned} \tag{3.92}$$

The upper limits for the probability of committing type I and type II errors are given by α and β, respectively. The lot on which the test is performed has an unknown proportion P of defectives. We are sampling without replacement, but we are assuming that the size of the lot is sufficiently large so that the proportion of defectives remains approximately constant. The test is performed by successively drawing one unit from the lot. At every step we are checking whether X_n^T, the number of defective units after n draws, takes on a value of $x_n^T =: k$ which is inside the interval $I_n = (a + cn, b + cn)$. For given α, β, P_0 and P_1, the parameters a, b and c are calculated by the following formulas, previously introduced in (2.154):

$$a = \frac{\ln A}{\ln\left[\frac{P_1(1-P_0)}{P_0(1-P_1)}\right]} = \frac{\ln A}{\ln\left[\frac{RQL(1-AQL)}{AQL(1-RQL)}\right]} \tag{3.93 a}$$

Parameters of the indifference interval

$$b = \frac{\ln B}{\ln\left[\frac{P_1(1-P_0)}{P_0(1-P_1)}\right]} = \frac{\ln B}{\ln\left[\frac{RQL(1-AQL)}{AQL(1-RQL)}\right]} \tag{3.93 b}$$

$$c = \frac{\ln\left(\frac{1-P_0}{1-P_1}\right)}{\ln\left[\frac{P_1(1-P_0)}{P_0(1-P_1)}\right]} = \frac{\ln\left(\frac{1-AQL}{1-RQL}\right)}{\ln\left[\frac{RQL(1-AQL)}{AQL(1-RQL)}\right]} \tag{3.93 c}$$

where A and B are as in (2.151)

$$A = \frac{\beta}{1-\alpha} \tag{3.94 a}$$

$$B = \frac{1-\beta}{\alpha}. \tag{3.94 b}$$

If $k \leq a + cn$ we accept the lot, if $k \geq b + cn$ we reject the lot, and if k lies within the interval I_n we continue sampling. The procedure can be described by the structural chart given in figure 3.2/22. The register that contains the present value of X_n^T is denoted by Z.

If you plot the endpoints of the indifference interval I_n, for $n = 1, 2, \ldots$, into a coordinate system, you will find that the upper end points lie on a straight line with slope c and the lower endpoints lie on a straight line parallel to and below the first one. We already called these lines **acceptance**

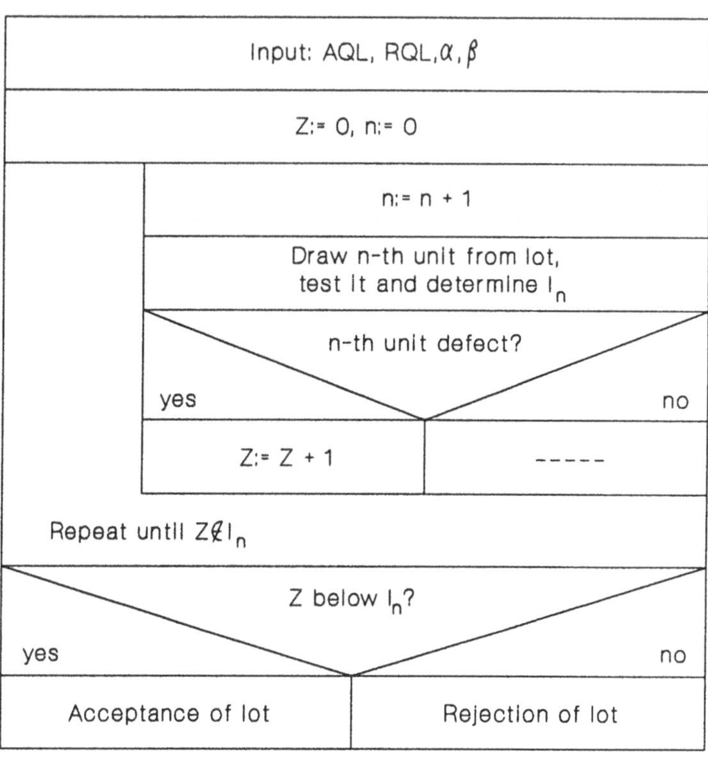

Figure 3.2/22: Structural chart of a sequential-sampling plan

Graphical display of the sequential inspection procedure

and **rejection boundaries**, and the area within, the **continuation region**. The whole process of performing a sequential test can be graphically displayed by an **inspection diagram**. This is obtained by plotting the path of the observed values of X_n^T against n. As soon as the path touches either the rejection or acceptance boundary the procedure is terminated with the respective decision to accept or reject the lot. The following inspection diagram for $a = -1.8, b = 2.4$ and $c = 0.05$ shows two possible paths.[14] In path 1 the decision to reject was reached after the 52nd drawing (five defective units) and in path 2 the procedure accepted the lot after 56 drawings (one defective unit).

[14] Strictly speaking the paths only consist of discrete points (see figure 3.2/12). Here, and also in figure 3.2/24, for the purpose of clearer presentation, we have drawn a line that results from connecting the individual points.

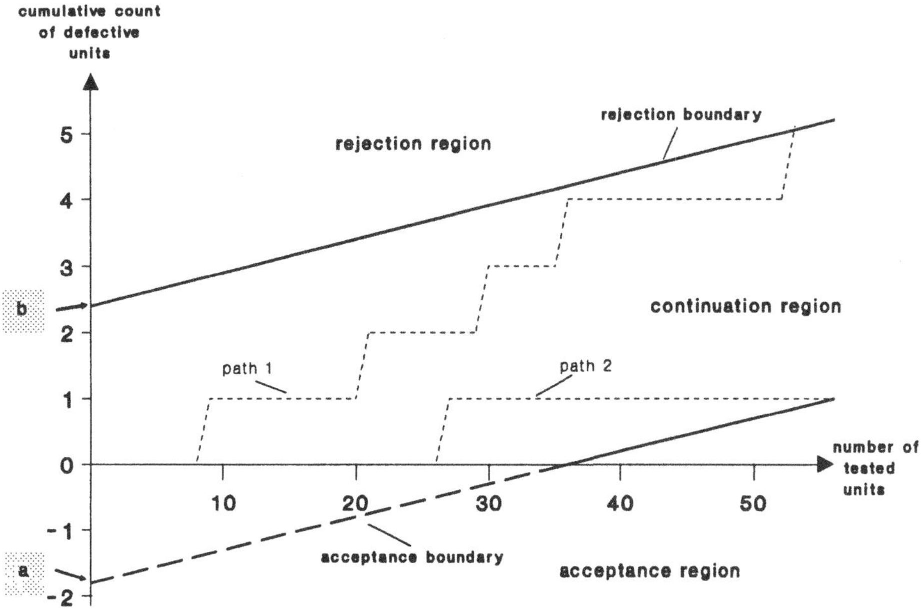

Figure 3.2/23: Inspection diagram of a sequential plan

It can be shown that the **final sample number**, which is the number of inspected units required to reach a decision, is finite with probability 1 as $N \to \infty$, provided the sample units are drawn independently (see UHLMANN 1982, p.161f). We are not going to give a rigorous proof of this result, but we will only illustrate the basic idea by means of a graph which is equivalent to figure 3.2/23. The inspection diagram in figure 3.2/23 gives the cumulative count of defective units as a function of the sample size n, whereas the **cone-shaped inspection diagram** in figure 3.2/24 gives the rejection and acceptance boundaries in terms of the proportion $p := k/n$ of the cumulated count of defective units. The continuation region is no longer defined by straight lines $k = a + cn$ and $k = b + cn$, but by the hyperbolas $p = a/n + c$ and $p = b/n + c$. The two curves form a cone and its peak converges to the abscissa $p = c$, for $n \to \infty$ and $N \to \infty$. The width of this continuation region is no longer constant, it actually converges to zero. The diagram in figure 3.2/24 was constructed for the same values of a, b, and c as figure 3.2/23. In order to keep the diagram easily understood, only one path is given.

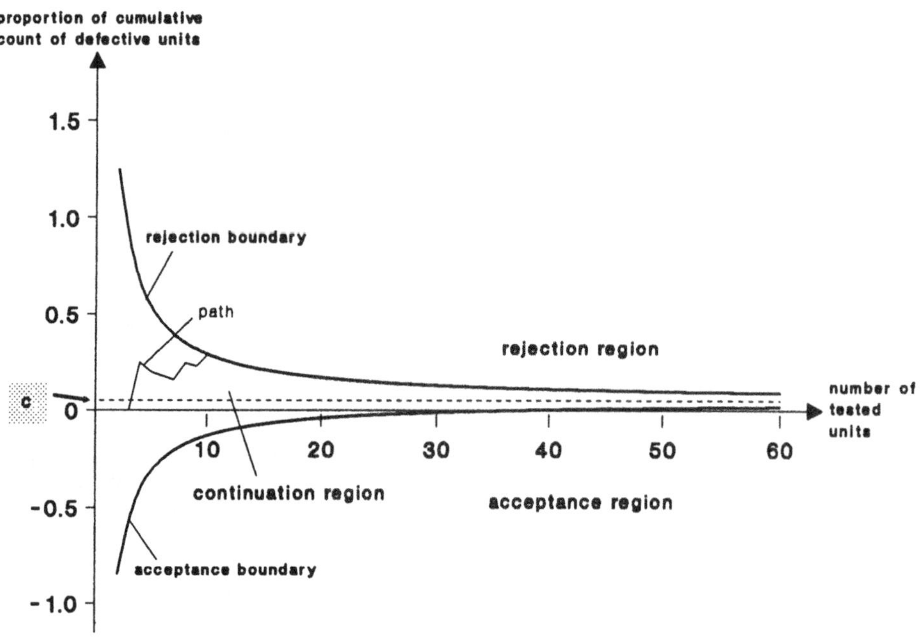

Figure 3.2/24: Cone representation of the inspection diagram of a sequential plan

In the cone representation the paths jump up after discovery of a defective unit and slowly decrease after this until the discovery of the next defective unit. The procedure continues as long as the path remains inside the cone. If the path touches or intersects either the lower or upper hyperbola the lot is accepted or rejected, respectively. In the path of figure 3.2/24 rejection occurs after ten units are drawn (three defectives). The diagram illustrates that, as the number of inspected units increases, it becomes more and more likely that the path leaves the narrowing cone and thus that a final decision is reached.

Transfer to the Poisson case

All the above concepts are easily transferred to the case when, instead of the number of defective units in the sample X_n^T, the number of defects in the sample X_n^{*T} is measured. If the assumption $X_n^{*T} \sim po(\lambda)$ is made we need to modify the test (3.92) to

$$\begin{aligned} H_0: &\quad \lambda \leq \lambda_0 \\ H_1: &\quad \lambda \geq \lambda_1, \end{aligned} \tag{3.95}$$

i.e., to a hypothesis test for the average number of defects per unit λ. The indifference interval is then given by $I_n^* = (a^* + c^*n, b^* + c^*n)$, where a^*, b^* and c^* are calculated with the following formulas (see the remark at the end of section 2.3.3b):

$$a^* = \frac{\ln A}{\ln(\lambda_1/\lambda_0)} \tag{3.96 a}$$

$$b^* = \frac{\ln B}{\ln(\lambda_1/\lambda_0)} \tag{3.96 b}$$

$$c^* = \frac{\lambda_1 - \lambda_0}{\ln(\lambda_1/\lambda_0)}. \tag{3.96 c}$$

Example 3.2/18

In example 3.2/16 we gave a single-sampling plan and its OC equivalent double-sampling plan, i.e., two plans with OC functions that approximately go through the same points $(AQL, 1-\alpha)$ and (RQL, β). We also found that $AQL \approx 0.027$ and $RQL \approx 0.085$ with $\alpha = 0.05$ and $\beta = 0.1$. We now want to add a sequential plan to the previous two equivalent plans.

The sequential plan is completely determined by specifying the indifference interval $I_n = (a + cn, b + cn)$ for every sample size n. This interval is determined by the parameters a, b and c of the acceptance and rejection boundaries and we can use (3.93) and (3.94) to find the appropriate values for the conditions $AQL = 0.027$ and $RQL = 0.085$, with $\alpha = 0.05$ and $\beta = 0.1$. Preliminary calculations yield

$$A := \frac{\beta}{1-\alpha} = \frac{0.10}{0.95} \approx 0.1053; \qquad B := \frac{1-\beta}{\alpha} = \frac{0.90}{0.05} = 18$$

$$\frac{1-AQL}{1-RQL} = \frac{0.973}{0.915} \approx 1.0634$$

$$\frac{RQL\,(1-AQL)}{AQL\,(1-RQL)} \approx \frac{0.085 \cdot 0.973}{0.027 \cdot 0.915} \approx 3.3477$$

and as a result we get the approximations:

$$\begin{aligned} a &\approx \frac{\ln 0.1053}{\ln 3.3477} \approx -1.8629 \\ b &\approx \frac{\ln 18}{\ln 3.3477} \approx 2.3922 \\ c &\approx \frac{\ln 1.0634}{\ln 3.3477} \approx 0.0509. \end{aligned}$$

There is very little difference between these acceptance and rejection boundaries and those of figure 3.2/23 which had a slope of $c = 0.05$ and intercepts $a = -1.8$ and $b = 2.4$, respectively.

Problem 3.2/30

a) At least how many units need to be inspected before the sequential-sampling plan in figure 3.2/23 can reach a decision about acceptance or rejection of the lot?

b) On what measures does the slope c of the acceptance and rejection boundaries in figure 3.2/23 depend?

c) Answer the last question for the vertical distance $b - a$ between the two lines.

Problem 3.2/31

a) Company R receives laminated tubes of 1 m length from company A in lots of $N = 1000$. At the acceptance control the defects in the lamination of the tubes is inspected and the number of defects per tube is recorded. Find a sequential-sampling plan with the number of defects per unit X_n^{*T} as its test statistic. Assume that this statistic is $po(n\lambda)$-distributed (this implies that the average number of defects per tube is λ). The underlying hypothesis test of the plan is given by $H_0 : \lambda \leq 2$ against $H_1 : \lambda \geq 5$, and the type I and type II errors are specified by $\alpha = 0.01$ and $\beta = 0.05$, respectively.

b) After inspection of five tubes a total number of ten defects were recorded. What is the decision of the plan (acceptance, rejection, continuation)?

b) OC Function and Average Sample Number (ASN)

The sequential-sampling plan of section 3.2.6a is designed to accept a lot with probabilities $1 - \alpha$ and β in the case of quality levels $P_0 = AQL$ and $P_1 = RQL$ respectively. This specifies two points $(AQL;\ 1 - \alpha)$ and $(RQL;\beta)$ on the OC curve. The derivation of the complete OC curve of a sequential-sampling plan is relatively complicated, so we will give the result without proof. A detailed treatment can be found in WALD (1947, p.51ff) or UHLMANN (1982, p.166ff).

For the description of the OC function it is helpful to define the continuous auxiliary function

$$P = \psi(h) := \begin{cases} \dfrac{\left(\frac{1-AQL}{1-RQL}\right)^h - 1}{\left[\frac{RQL(1-AQL)}{AQL(1-RQL)}\right]^h - 1} & \text{for } h \neq 0 \\ c & \text{for } h = 0. \end{cases} \tag{3.97}$$

Again, c denotes the slope (3.93c) of the acceptance and rejection boundaries. The function (3.97) is strictly increasing on its domain $(-\infty, \infty)$ and it takes on values in the interval (0,1). It further holds that

$$\lim_{h \to -\infty} \psi(h) = 1; \qquad \lim_{h \to \infty} \psi(h) = 0$$

(see UHLMANN 1982, p. 165f). Consequently, the inverse function h=$\psi^{-1}(h)$ of the function $P = \psi(h)$ exists. This implies that for every real number $P \in (0,1)$ there is a finite h with $\psi(h) = P$.

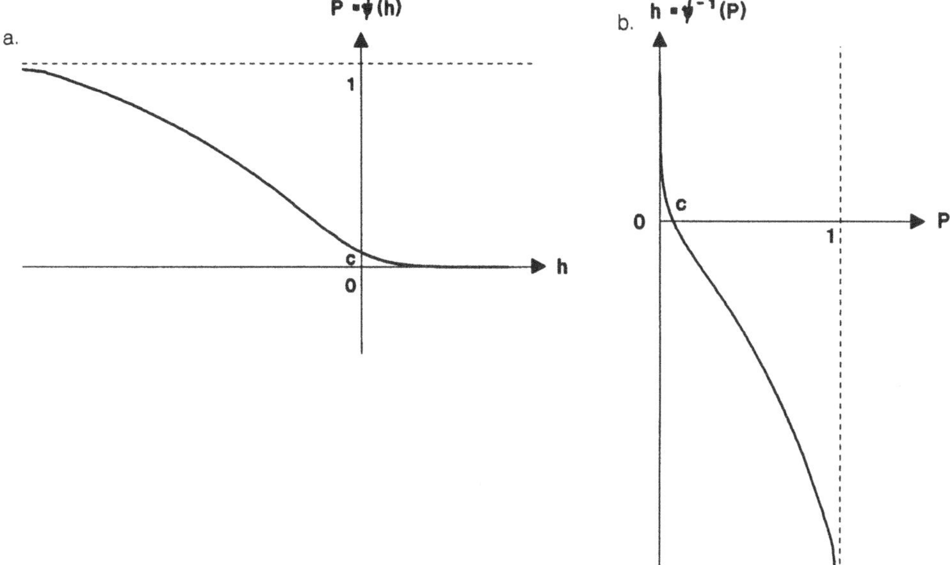

Figure 3.2/25: Graph of the auxiliary function $\psi(h)$ and its inverse

OC function of a sequential-sampling plan:

- 1st representation

It can be shown in the case of applying a sequential-sampling plan that $L_s(P)$, the probability of accepting a lot with quality parameter $P \in (0,1)$, can be written as

$$L_s(P) \approx \begin{cases} \dfrac{\left(\frac{\alpha}{1-\beta}\right)^{\psi^{-1}(P)} - 1}{\left[\frac{\alpha \cdot \beta}{(1-\alpha)(1-\beta)}\right]^{\psi^{-1}(P)} - 1} & \text{for } P \neq c \\[2ex] \dfrac{\ln\left(\frac{\alpha}{1-\beta}\right)}{\ln\left[\frac{\alpha \cdot \beta}{(1-\alpha)(1-\beta)}\right]} & \text{for } P = c. \end{cases} \tag{3.98}$$

One way of constructing the OC function $L_s(P)$ is to fix the fraction defective P and to determine $\psi^{-1}(P)$, the inverse of function (3.97), and then to put the result into formula (3.98). Since the determination of $h = \psi^{-1}(P)$ is computationally difficult, instead of (3.98), it is more practical to use the equivalent representation

- 2nd representation

$$L_s(P) = L_s[\psi(h)] \approx \begin{cases} \dfrac{\left(\frac{\alpha}{1-\beta}\right)^h - 1}{\left[\frac{\alpha \cdot \beta}{(1-\alpha)(1-\beta)}\right]^h - 1} & \text{for } P \neq c \\[2ex] \dfrac{\ln\left(\frac{\alpha}{1-\beta}\right)}{\ln\left[\frac{\alpha \cdot \beta}{(1-\alpha)(1-\beta)}\right]} & \text{for } P = c \end{cases} \tag{3.99}$$

Procedure for calculating OC function values

and to proceed as follows (also, see example 3.2/19):

- Fix a value of $h \in (-\infty, \infty)$ and determine the right side of (3.99).
- Then compute the corresponding quality level $P = \psi(h)$, i.e., the argument of the OC function, with formula (3.97).

Similar to double and multiple plans, in sequential sampling the number of units required to reach a final decision is a discrete random variable Y^* with a countable number of possible realizations. If one administers the procedure proposed in section 3.2.6a (successive sampling of one unit), then

$$Y^* = \begin{cases} 1 & \text{if a decision is reached after one sample is drawn} \\ 2 & \text{if a decision is reached after two samples are drawn} \\ \vdots & \quad \vdots \quad \vdots \\ k & \text{if decision is reached after k samples are drawn} \\ \vdots & \quad \vdots \quad \vdots \end{cases} \tag{3.100}$$

The expected value

$$ASN_s = E(Y^*) \tag{3.101}$$

is of interest for comparing the efficiency of different attribute plans. It is called the **average sample number (ASN)** of the sequential-sampling plan. The expectation (3.101) is a function of the process parameter P. It also depends on the parameters a, b, and c of the acceptance and rejection boundaries of the specific sequential-sampling plan (see again figure 3.2/23).

Of course, the plan parameters themselves depend on the specified values of AQL, RQL, α and β. UHLMANN (1982, p.170ff) derived the following form of the function $ASN_s = ASN_s(P)$:

$$ASN_s(P) \approx \begin{cases} \dfrac{b-(b-a)\cdot L_s(P)}{P-c} & \text{for } P \neq c \\ \dfrac{ba}{c(c-1)} & \text{for } P = c. \end{cases} \tag{3.102}$$

The graph of (3.102) is similar to the ASN curves in figure 3.2/21. The values of the curve increase from $ASN_s(0) = -a/c$ at $P = 0$ to a maximum at $P_M \approx c$, and then decrease to the value $ASN_s(1) = b/(1-c)$ at $P = 1$. Also note that the curve is relatively steep around the maximum.

The maximum $ASNL_s = ASN_s(P_M)$ of the ASN function can be used to compare the efficiency of a sequential-sampling plan to that of other OC equivalent single- or double-sampling plans. Analogous to (3.90) and (3.91) we define the **efficiency** for the comparison of a sequential-sampling plan to an OC equivalent single-sampling plan $(N; n; c)$ by

Efficiency of a sequential-sampling plan

$$w_s := \frac{ASNL_s}{n}. \tag{3.103}$$

Transfer to the Poisson case

Only minor modifications are necessary to apply these results for the OC and ASN functions to the case when the statistic used is the $po(\lambda)$-distributed count of defects variable X_n^{*T}. Instead of (3.97), we define an auxiliary function on $(0, \infty)$ through

$$\lambda = \psi^*(h) := \begin{cases} \dfrac{\lambda_1-\lambda_0}{\ln(\lambda_1/\lambda_0)}\cdot\dfrac{\ln h}{h-1} & \text{for } h \neq 1 \\ c^* & \text{for } h = 1, \end{cases} \tag{3.104}$$

and, analogous to (3.98), we find the representation

$$L_s(\lambda) = L_s[\psi^*(h)] = \begin{cases} \dfrac{1-h^{b^*}}{h^{a^*}-h^{b^*}} & \text{for } h \neq 1 \\ \dfrac{b^*}{b^*-a^*} & \text{for } h = 1 \end{cases} \tag{3.105}$$

for the **OC function**. The **ASN function** corresponding to (3.102) is

$$ASN_s(\lambda) \approx \begin{cases} \dfrac{b^*-(b^*-a^*)\cdot L_s(\lambda)}{\lambda-c^*} & \text{for } \lambda \neq c^* \\ \dfrac{b^*\cdot(-a^*)}{c^*} & \text{for } \lambda = c^*. \end{cases} \tag{3.106}$$

Example 3.2/19

We will use the sequential-sampling plan of example 3.2/18 with $AQL \approx 0.027$, $RQL \approx 0.085$, $\alpha = 0.05$ and $\beta = 0.1$, to calculate $L_s(P)$ and $ASN_s(P)$ values of the corresponding OC and ASN functions for several quality levels $P \in (0,1)$. As explained before, we will not specify P directly, but rather fix $h \in (-\infty, \infty)$ and use formula (3.97).

h	$P = \psi(h)$	$L_S(P)$	$ASN_S(P)$
(1)	(2)	(3)	(4)
$-\infty$	1	0	2.52
−10	0.4591	0.0000	5.86
−5	0.2652	0.0000	11.16
−2	0.1270	0.0110	30.81
−1	0.0850	0.1000	57.67
−0.5	0.0667	0.2685	79.09
−0.1	0.0538	0.4985	93.39
0	0.0509	0.5621	92.26
0.1	0.0480	0.6244	91.35
0.2	0.0452	0.6834	90.52
0.4	0.0401	0.7858	88.12
0.6	0.0353	0.8629	82.04
0.8	0.0309	0.9159	75.27
1	0.0270	0.9500	69.06
2	0.0128	0.9969	48.56
3	0.0055	0.9998	41.02
4	0.0022	1.0000	38.26
5	0.0009	1.0000	37.26
∞	0	1	36.61

Table 3.2/19: OC and ASN values for a sequential-sampling plan

We can see in columns 2 and 3 of the table that the OC curve actually passes through the points $(AQL, 1-\alpha)$ and (RQL, β). Column 4 shows that the average sample number limit is reached at about $P = 0.054$ and has the value $ASNL_s \approx 93.4$. In example 3.2/16 we presented two OC equivalent plans, one single and one double (uncurtailed), of which the first one had a sample size $n = 136$ and the second a sample size with a maximal value of $ASNL_{do} \approx 113.1$ at about $P_M = 0.06$. As a result, we can conclude that the sequential-sampling plan is the most efficient among the three. Comparison with the single-sampling plan gives an efficiency (3.103) of

$$w_s = \frac{93.4}{136} \approx 0.687.$$

This tells us that the average sample size of the sequential-sampling plan is at most 68.7% of that of the corresponding OC equivalent single-sampling plan. For the OC equivalent double-sampling plan we only get

$$w_{do} = \frac{113.1}{136} \approx 0.832,$$

in other words, its average sample size is at most 83.2% of that of the single-sampling plan.

Problem 3.2/32

Problem 3.2/28 introduced a double-sampling plan with $AQL = 0.0116, 1 - \alpha = 0.9, RQL = 0.057$ and $\beta = 0.1$, and an average sample number limit $ASNL_{do} = 76.7$. By applying the PEACH/LITTAUER search algorithm, we found the parameters $n = 94$ and $c = 2$ of the equivalent single-sampling plan.

a) Determine a sequential-sampling plan that is approximately OC equivalent to those two plans by specifying the parameters a, b and c of its acceptance and rejection boundaries (3.93).

b) Analogous to table 3.2/19, construct a table for the resulting sequential-sampling plan and set $h = \pm 1; \pm 0.5; \pm 0.3; \pm 0.1$; and 0 to obtain several values of the OC and ASN functions. At which point $P = P_M$ does the ASN function attain its maximal value and what is $ASNL_s$?

c) Compare the efficiency of the sequential-sampling plan with that of the single- and double-sampling plans.

Problem 3.2/33

a) For the sequential-sampling plan in problem 3.2/31a with $\lambda_0 = 2$, $1 - \alpha = 0.99$, $\lambda_1 = 5$ and $\beta = 0.05$, calculate the OC and ASN functions at the values of λ that result from setting $h = 0.2, 0.4, 0.6, 0.8, 1, 1.2, 2$, and 2.5. Again, construct a table analogous to table 3.2/19. Find $\lambda = \lambda_M$ that maximizes the ASN function and determine its value $ASNL_s = ASN_s(\lambda_M)$.

b) Specify the approximately OC equivalent plan, i.e., the plan with an OC function that approximately goes through the points (2, 0.99) and (5, 0.05). Use the search algorithm by PEACH/LITTAUER to specify this single-sampling plan (see figure 3.2/16).

c) What is the efficiency of the sequential-sampling plan compared to the single-sampling procedure?

3.2.7 Sampling Systems

a) Construction of Sampling Systems and New Developments

For inspecting *series'* of lots, in practice one administers a combination of several sampling plans with different discriminatory powers. The conditions for switching from one plan to another are laid out in the switching rules. Such sampling plan collections are called **sampling systems**, **sampling schemes** or **sampling tables**. Sampling schemes are categorized with respect to certain specifications or input criteria. One common input of every sampling system is the lot size N. Examples of other specifications are:

- OC percentiles, i.e., AQL, IQL and RQL;
- the average outgoing quality limit $AOQL$;
- prior information about the lot quality, e.g., in form of the average fraction defective $\overline{P}$ related to previous shipments or in form of a prior distribution $\pi(P)$; [15]
- cost parameters, for example, inspection cost (fixed cost and cost per unit) as well as the loss incurred by wrongly rejecting or accepting a lot.

With the help of a sampling system one tries to select from among all possible plans those suitable for ones needs. The guidelines for this selection are given in the form of input specifications. In general, one only uses one additional criterion besides the lot size, and in practice, these input criteria are specified according to the particular requirements. In order to reach a mutual agreement about the acceptance inspection procedure, both the consumer's and the producer's interests need to be taken into account.

Sampling schemes do not require the ad hoc calculation of OC functions or plan parameters since all the necessary information for the user is provided in the form of tables and curves. Recent new developments, made possible to a great extent by the advances in electronic data processing, have the goal of providing the user with more flexibility in selecting a particular sampling scheme. Instead of being limited by the strict procedures and few options of printed sampling scheme manuals that could only be used for specific applications, one now has a more or less user friendly data processing system with appropriate software and, without much effort, one can access sampling plans that are customized to one's specific needs.

[15] $\overline{P}$ can be interpreted to be an estimate of the expectation $E(P)$ of the prior distribution $\pi(P) := Pr(X_n^T/N = P)$.

In its most advanced form, the construction of sampling plans is per-rmed completely automatically by computer aided quality assurance or AQ **systems** (also see section 1.3.3). Figure 3.2/26 shows how accep-ance control is organized in **computer integrated manufacturing** or **IM**. We can see that the results of inspection effect the treatment of ture deliveries. Past quality determines the amount of inspection.

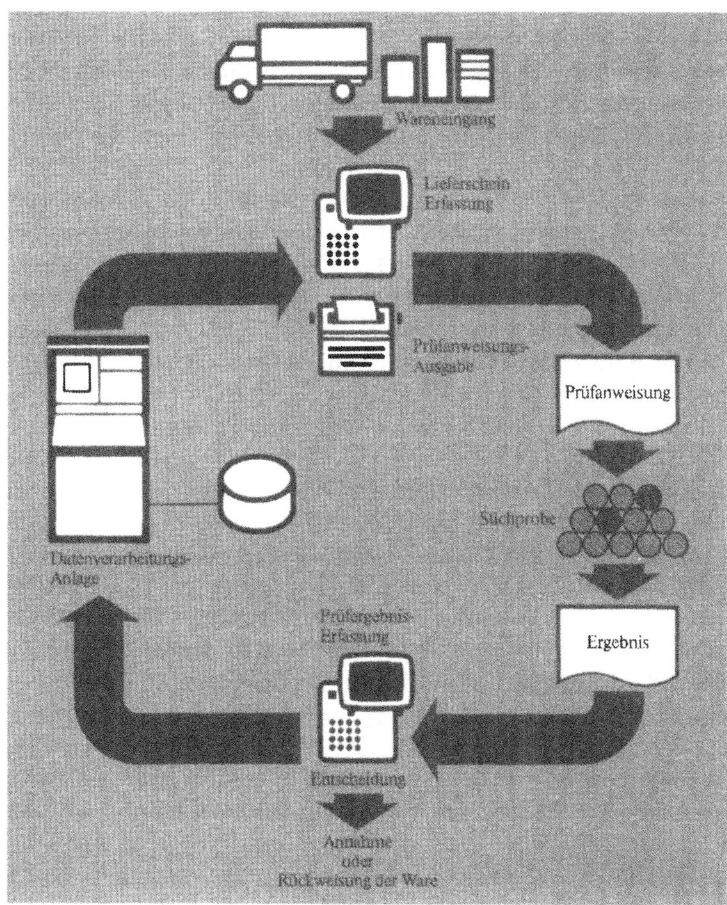

igure 3.2/26: **Scheme of automated acceptance sampling**
(Source: VOLKSWAGEN)

In the following discussion of sampling schemes for *attribute* acceptance ontrol we will introduce primarily the sampling system that is known in the SA as ANSI/ASQC Z 1.4 (MIL-STD 105; ISO 2859) and in Germany as

DIN 40080. Sampling systems for variables (ANSI/ASQC Z 1.9 MIL-STD 414; ISO 3951) will be treated in section 3.3.6.

b) The ANSI/ASQC Z 1.4 (ISO 2859)

Historical development of the ANSI/ASQC Z 1.4

The most widespread sampling scheme for attributes was first described in the MIL-STD 105D. The development of the standard of this sampling system started in the USA during World War II when a group of prominent statisticians working in the Statistical Research Group at the University of Columbia were commissioned by the Pentagon to develop quality control procedures for the inspection of incoming goods for the Army, Navy and Air Force. After many revisions and improvements, the sampling schemes for attributes were written down as the Military Standard 105D, abbreviated MIL-STD 105D. A detailed account of the development up to this point is given in DODGE (1973). The MIL-STD 105D has developed historically and is not based on an underlying mathematical model. Its first version was published in 1950 under the name MIL-STD 105A.

In 1974 the **American National Standard Institute (ANSI)** and the **American Society for Quality Control (ASQC)** designed an updated version of the MIL-STD 105D for civilian applications, called the ANSI/ASQC Z 1.4. In the same year this civilian standard was adopted by the **International Organization for Standardization (ISO)**, with only minor modifications, under the name of **ISO 2859**. The **DIN 40080** that was brought out by the German Institute for Standards (**Deutsches Institut für Normung, DIN**) is almost identical to the ISO 2859. One of the publications of the **German Society for Quality (DGQ)** contains an excerpt of the DIN 40080 and also instructions for its application.

The ISO 2859 is designed primarily for the inspection of series of lots. This implies that it is of interest to a buyer who receives regular shipments from a supplier. The ISO 2859 can be applied for assessing the quality in a given lot regardless of whether the measure of quality is the proportion of defective units - the fraction defective P - or the total number of defects in the lot.

Input criteria of the ISO 2859:

- lot size N and AQL value
- inspection levels

The application of the ISO 2859 requires some prior instruction. Besides the lot size N, an input parameter is usually the acceptable quality level AQL. This is why one sometimes speaks of an **AQL system**. Another input is the inspection level. In practice, one has three different inspection levels I, II and III. The default would be inspection level II. The discriminatory power of the plans increases from level I to III; in other words, the OC curve becomes steeper. There are also four special inspection levels S-1 to S-4 with less discriminatory power. These are employed when small sample sizes are necessary and when large sampling risks can or must be tolerated; for example, in the case of destructive inspection.

- number of sampling stages

At every inspection level the user of the scheme has the option between single, double or seven stage sampling plans. The decision of which of these plans to administer is usually based on what is more advantageous in the particular situation. While on the one hand the administration of plans becomes more difficult as the number of stages increases, on the other hand the average amount of inspection decreases. Within every inspection level there are three sublevels of inspection that are called **reduced, normal** and **tightened inspection**. If one is working with a particular inspection level and sublevel – usually one starts with normal inspection – the sublevel will be switched depending on the results of the current and previous inspection. Past quality regulates the discriminatory power of the test.

- sublevels

Procedure of selecting a sampling plan from ISO 2859

In practice, when selecting a plan from ISO 2859, the lot size N and one of the seven inspection levels (I to III; S-1 to S-4) are specified in advance. Each of these input pairs determines a **code letter** according to table 3.2/20.

Lot size N	Special inspection level				General inspection level		
	S-1	S-2	S-3	S-4	I	II	III
2 - 8	A	A	A	A	A	A	B
9 - 15	A	A	A	A	A	B	C
16 - 25	A	A	B	B	B	C	D
26 - 50	A	B	B	C	C	D	E
51 - 90	B	B	C	C	C	E	F
91 -150	B	B	C	D	D	F	G
151-280	B	C	D	E	E	G	H
281-500	B	C	D	E	F	H	J
501-1200	C	C	E	F	G	J	K
1201 - 3200	C	D	E	G	H	K	L
3201 - 10000	C	D	F	G	J	L	M
10001 - 35000	C	D	F	H	K	M	N
35001 - 150000	D	E	G	J	L	N	P
150001 - 500000	D	E	G	J	M	P	Q
$>$ 500000	D	E	H	K	N	Q	R

Table 3.2/20: Code letters according to ISO 2859

Each code letter denotes a specific inspection instruction and in addition one can also choose the most practical type of plan (single, double or seven stage). The following table 3.2/21 specifies the sample size for a given type of plan and code letter.[16]

Code letter	Sample size		
	single	double	seven
A	2	-	-
B	3	2	-
C	5	3	-
D	8	5	2
E	13	8	3
F	20	13	5
G	32	20	8
H	50	32	13
J	80	50	20
K	125	80	32
L	200	125	50
M	315	200	80
N	500	315	125
P	800	500	200
Q	1250	800	315
R	2000	1250	500

Table 3.2/21: Code letters and corresponding sample sizes for the ISO 2859 scheme

Interpreting the AQL specifications

The remaining parameters depend on the chosen discriminatory power (reduced, normal, tightened) and also the desired AQL value. We defined the acceptable quality limit AQL to be a quality level with the given high probability of acceptance ω. In the plans specified in the ISO 2859, the acceptance probability ω always lies between 0.8 and 0.99. The measure of lot quality is either percent defectives $100 \cdot P$ (for conforming/nonconforming classification) or the average number of defects per 100 units, $100 \cdot \lambda$ (if a unit can have more than one defect). In both situations one works with the same set of AQL values, that are called the **preferred AQL values**:

0.01	0.015	0.025	0.04	0.065
0.1	0.15	0.25	0.4	0.65
1	1.5	2.5	4	6.5
10	15	25	40	65
100	150	250	400	650
1000				

Table 3.2/22: Preferred AQL values (in percent) for ISO 2859

[16] In the case of double and seven stage sampling plans the sample size is kept constant and set to the value given in the table.

These AQL values form a geometric series in which the next value is obtained by multiplying the previous value by the factor $\sqrt[5]{10} \approx 1.585$. The scheme can only be applied for these 26 AQL values. Values below 10 can either be seen as the percentage of defectives or the count of defects per 100 units, but AQL values above 10 are used only for the number of defects per 100 units. For example, an AQL value of 0.4 in the terminology of the ISO 2859 could denote a fraction defective 0.004 (0.4%) or an average number of 0.4 defects per 100 units, but the value 25 can only denote an average number of 25 defects per 100 units.

The specification of a particular AQL value in the sampling scheme does not protect the buyer against accepting a *single* lot with nonconforming quality. The specification only gives the accuracy of the procedure for a *series* of lots (see DIN, 1979, p.3). A discussion and interpretation of the philosophy behind specifying an AQL value can be found in GEIGER (1973) and in DGQ (1984a).

An overview of the instructions for using the ISO 2859 sampling system can be graphically displayed as in figure 3.2/27.

Summary: How to handle the ISO 2859

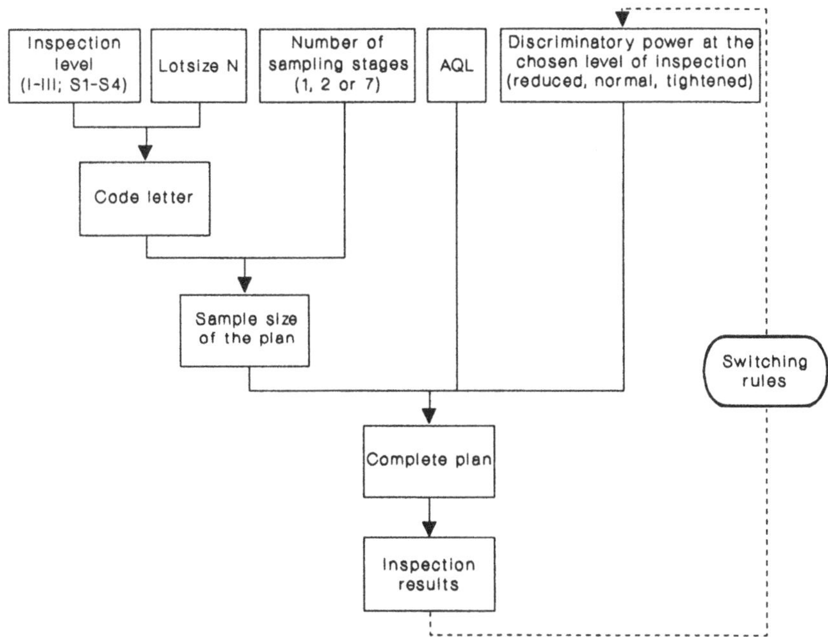

Figure 3.2/27: Determination of a sampling plan with the ISO 2859

The dotted line indicates the dynamic feature of the switching rules in the sampling scheme of the ISO 2859. The sampling system has a memory. For every code letter and every type of sampling plan (single, double, seven stages) the system will change between reduced, normal and tightened inspection according to the decisions of the recent inspections. Figure 3.2/28 shows the conditions under which transition between those three stages takes place. Unless there is a specific reason to do otherwise, the procedure will start with normal inspection. If condition ① is satisfied the procedure is ordered to switch to tightened inspection and it can only return to normal inspection after condition ② is satisfied (bold arrows). In the case of very negative inspection results, when condition ⑤ occurs, the process is stopped completely. Reduced inspection is optional and can be included if the supplier and buyer agree on it. Condition ③ determines when to switch from normal to reduced inspection and, if condition ④ occurs, the procedure is required to return to normal inspection.

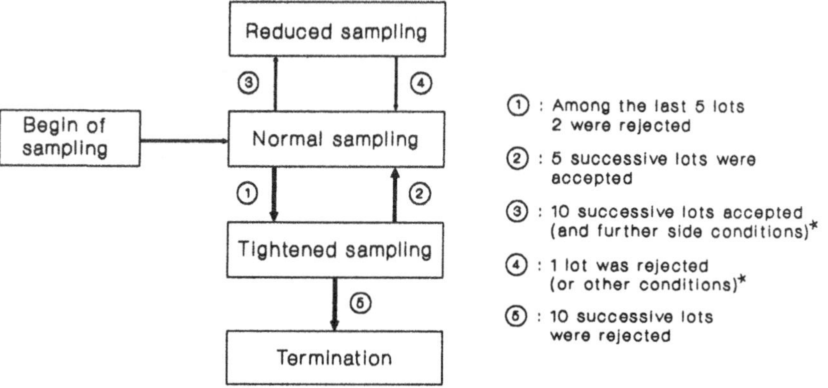

* Detailed instructions are given in DGQ (1986a, p.14).

Figure 3.2/28: Switching rules of the ISO 2859 (based on DGQ 1986a, p.14)

Special table for normal inspection at level II

Since inspection level II of the scheme is usually selected, it is helpful to use a subsystem of ISO 2859 sampling tables for level II. In this subsystem no code letters are needed and, as a result, the tables for reduced, normal and tightened inspection are much easier to use. Such a specialized AQL sampling scheme, that also omits the seven stage sampling option is described in DGQ (1986a). The following two tables for the case of normal inspection are taken from this source.

In the ISO 2859 scheme, table 3.2/23 is used to determine the sample size n and acceptance number c of a single-sampling plan $(N; n; c)$ for given AQL and lot size N. We see that for small lot sizes and small AQL values the plan requires 100% inspection (entry N). Otherwise the table gives pairs of numbers of which the left is the sample size n and the right one is the acceptance number c.

Table 3.2/24 specifies the parameters of an approximately OC equivalent double-sampling plan $(N; n_1; c_1; d_1; n_2; c_2)$ for the same AQL values. The ISO 2859 sets $n_1 = n_2$ and, hence – for a given lot size and resulting sample size – it is only necessary to specify three more AQL dependent parameters, i.e., the acceptance number c_1, the rejection number d_1 for the first sample and the acceptance number c_2 for both samples. In addition, the table also gives the rejection number $d_2 := c_2 + 1$. The four values $c_1; d_1; c_2; d_2$ are given in the cells of the inner table. The first row of the cell gives the acceptance number c_1 and the rejection number d_1 for the first sample and the row below contains the values of c_2 and d_2, provided that the cell is not empty.

Lot size N	*AQL* (in percent)												
	0.10	0.15	0.25	0.40	0.65	1.0	1.5	2.5	4.0	6.5	10	15	25
2 - 8	*N*	*N*	*N*	*N*	*N*	*N*	*N*	*N* resp. 5 - 0	*N* resp. 3 - 0	*N* resp. 2 - 0	*N* resp. 5 - 1	*N* resp. 3 - 1	*N* resp. 2 - 1
9 - 15	*N*	*N*	*N*	*N*	*N*	*N* resp. 13 - 0	8 - 0	5 - 0	3 - 0	2 - 0	5 - 1	3 - 1	3 - 2
16 - 25	*N*	*N*	*N*	*N*	*N* resp. 20 - 0	13 - 0	8 - 0	5 - 0	3 - 0	8 - 1	5 - 1	5 - 2	5 - 3
26 - 50	*N*	*N*	*N*	*N* resp. 32 - 0	20 - 0	13 - 0	8 - 0	5 - 0	13 - 1	8 - 1	8 - 2	8 - 3	8 - 5
51 - 90	*N*	*N* resp. 80 - 0	50 - 0	32 - 0	20 - 0	13 - 0	8 - 0	20 - 1	13 - 1	13 - 2	13 - 3	13 - 5	13 - 7
91 - 150	*N* resp. 125 - 0	80 - 0	50 - 0	32 - 0	20 - 0	13 - 0	32 - 1	20 - 1	20 - 2	20 - 3	20 - 5	20 - 7	20 - 10
151 - 280	125 - 0	80 - 0	50 - 0	32 - 0	20 - 0	50 - 1	32 - 1	32 - 2	32 - 3	32 - 5	32 - 7	32 - 10	32 - 14
281 - 500	125 - 0	80 - 0	50 - 0	32 - 0	80 - 1	50 - 1	50 - 2	50 - 3	50 - 5	50 - 7	50 - 10	50 - 14	50 - 21
501 - 1200	125 - 0	80 - 0	50 - 0	125 - 1	80 - 1	80 - 2	80 - 3	80 - 5	80 - 7	80 - 10	80 - 14	80 - 21	50 - 21
1201 - 3200	125 - 0	80 - 0	200 - 1	125 - 1	125 - 2	125 - 3	125 - 5	125 - 7	125 - 10	125 - 14	125 - 21	80 - 21	50 - 21
3201 - 10000	125 - 0	315 - 1	200 - 1	200 - 2	200 - 3	200 - 5	200 - 7	200 - 10	200 - 14	200 - 21	125 - 21	80 - 21	50 - 21
10001 - 35000	500 - 1	315 - 1	315 - 2	315 - 3	315 - 5	315 - 7	315 - 10	315 - 14	315 - 21	200 - 21	125 - 21	80 - 21	50 - 21
35001 - 150000	500 - 1	500 - 2	500 - 3	500 - 5	500 - 7	500- 10	500 - 14	500 - 21	315 - 21	200 - 21	125 - 21	80 - 21	50 - 21
150001 - 500000	800 - 2	800 - 3	800 - 5	800 - 7	800 - 10	800 - 14	800 - 21	500 - 21	315 - 21	200 - 21	125 - 21	80 - 21	50 - 21
> 500000	1250 - 3	1250 - 5	1250 - 7	1250 - 10	1250 - 14	1250 - 21	800 - 21	500 - 21	315 - 21	200 - 21	125 - 21	80 - 21	50 - 21

Table 3.2/23: Determination of the parameters n and c of a single-sampling plan according to the ISO 2859 sampling scheme for normal inspection at level II

Lot size N	n_1 $n_1 + n_2$	*AQL* (in percent)												
		0.1	0.15	0.25	0.4	0.65	1.0	1.5	2.5	4.0	6.5	10	15	25
2 - 8		•	•	•	•	•	•	•	•	•	•		↓	•
9 - 15	2 4	•	•	•	•	•	•	•	•	•	•	↓	0 - 2 1 - 2	0 - 3 3 - 4
16 - 25	3 6	•	•	•	•	•	•	•	•	•	↓	0 - 2 1 - 2	0 - 3 3 - 4	1 - 4 4 - 5
26 - 50	5 10	•	•	•	•	•	•	•	•	↓	0 - 2 1 - 2	0 - 3 3 - 4	1 - 4 4 - 5	2 - 5 6 - 7
51 - 90	8 16	•	•	•	•	•	•	•	↓	0 - 2 1 - 2	0 - 3 3 - 4	1 - 4 4 - 5	2 - 5 6 - 7	3 - 7 8 - 9
91 - 150	13 26	•	•	•	•	•	•	↓	0 - 2 1 - 2	0 - 3 3 - 4	1 - 4 4 - 5	2 - 5 6 - 7	3 - 7 8 - 9	5 - 9 12 - 13
151 - 280	20 40	•	•	•	•	•	↓	0 - 2 1 - 2	0 - 3 3 - 4	1 - 4 4 - 5	2 - 5 6 - 7	3 - 7 8 - 9	5 - 9 12 - 13	7 - 11 18 - 19
281 - 500	32 64	•	•	•	•	↓	0 - 2 1 - 2	0 - 3 3 - 4	1 - 4 4 - 5	2 - 5 6 - 7	3 - 7 8 - 9	5 - 9 12 - 13	7 - 11 18 - 19	11 - 16 26 - 27
501 - 1200	50 100	•	•	•	↓	0 - 2 1 - 2	0 - 3 3 - 4	1 - 4 4 - 5	2 - 5 6 - 7	3 - 7 8 - 9	5 - 9 12 - 13	7 - 11 18 - 19	11 - 16 26 - 27	↑
1201 - 3200	80 160	•	•	↓	0 - 2 1 - 2	0 - 3 3 - 4	1 - 4 4 - 5	2 - 5 6 - 7	3 - 7 8 - 9	5 - 9 12 - 13	7 - 11 18 - 19	11 - 16 26 - 27	↑	
3201 - 10000	125 250	•	↓	0 - 2 1 - 2	0 - 3 3 - 4	1 - 4 4 - 5	2 - 5 6 - 7	3 - 7 8 - 9	5 - 9 12 - 13	7 - 11 18 - 19	11 - 16 26 - 27	↑		
10001 - 35000	200 400	↓	0 - 2 1 - 2	0 - 3 3 - 4	1 - 4 4 - 5	2 - 5 6 - 7	3 - 7 8 - 9	5 - 9 12 - 13	7 - 11 18 - 19	11 - 16 26 - 27	↑			
35001 - 150000	315 630	0 - 2 1 - 2	0 - 3 3 - 4	1 - 4 4 - 5	2 - 5 6 - 7	3 - 7 8 - 9	5 - 9 12 - 13	7 - 11 18 - 19	11 - 16 26 - 27	↑				
150001 - 500000	500 1000	0 - 3 3 - 4	1 - 4 4 - 5	2 - 5 6 - 7	3 - 7 8 - 9	5 - 9 12 - 13	7 - 11 18 - 19	11 - 16 26 - 27	↑					
> 500000	800 1600	1 - 4 4 - 5	2 - 5 6 - 7	3 - 7 8 - 9	5 - 9 12 - 13	7 - 11 18 - 19	11 - 16 26 - 27	↑						

•: use single-sampling plan for same *AQL* value ↓, ↑: use parameters below/above of the arrow

Table 3.2/24: Determination of the parameters $n_1; n_2; c_1; d_1$ of a double-sampling plan according to ISO 2859 for normal inspection at level II

Remark

It often occurs that the units within a lot can have different types of defects. The ISO 2859 scheme distinguishes between critical, major and minor defects according to their potential consequences. The first kind could result in hazardous or unsafe conditions for individuals using or maintaining that product, whereas the latter two effect the fitness of use of the product to a greater or lesser extent, respectively.

In the case of critical defects with responsibility for the health and safety of other persons, it would be irresponsible to perform partial inspection. Therefore, every outgoing unit should be tested. In the case of the other two kinds of defects, if they can occur simultaneously, there are different possibilities. One option is to test separately for each kind of defect and to reject a lot if it does not satisfy the acceptance conditions for at least one kind of defect. Another possibility is to pool major and minor defects and to set the AQL value to be the sum of the two individual AQL values. This approach is only sensible if the two kind of defects occur independently.

Problem 3.2/34

For the specifications $N = 5000$ and $AQL = 0.01$ (1% defectives) the ISO 2859 determines the single-sampling plan (5000;200;5), according to table 3.2/23 for normal inspection at level II.

a) How big is the producer's risk for this AQL value, i.e., the maximal probability of rejecting lots with quality parameter $P \leq AQL$?

b) How big is the consumer's risk, i.e., the maximal probability of accepting lots with quality $P \geq RQL$ when $RQL = 0.02, 0.03, 0.04,$ and 0.05 respectively?

Use the Poisson approximation $L(P|5000; 200; 5) \approx L^*(P|200; 5)$.

Problem 3.2/35

What decision has to be made according to ISO 2859, if after the process switched to

a) normal,

b) tightened,

c) reduced

inspection six lots ago the current lot is the first one to be rejected after the switch?

Problem 3.2/36

a) One can see from table 3.2/24 that, according to the ISO 2859 scheme, the double-sampling plan $(N; n_1; c_1; d_1; n_2; c_2)$ for a lot size $N = 200$ and $AQL = 0.04$ (4% defectives) and normal inspection at level II is given by $n_1 = n_2 = 20$, $c_1 = 1$ and $d_1 = c_2 = 4$. What is the exact probability that this plan accepts a lot with quality level $P = AQL$ (at either stage 1 or stage 2)?

b) In the case of tightened inspection at level II, the parameters c_1, d_1 and c_2 of the double-sampling plan in a) with the same $N = 200$ and $AQL = 0.04$ would change to $c_1 = 0$ and $d_1 = c_2 = 3$. Find the above acceptance probability for this situation.

c) Evaluation of Plans in the ISO 2859

The International Standard ISO 2859 contains a number of figures and tables with information that can be used to evaluate a particular sampling plan. For example, for normal and tightened inspection the sampling tables display an OC function for every combination of code letter and AQL value. In addition, the OC percentiles of order 0.01, 0.05, 0.25, 0.5, 0.75, 0.9, 0.95 and 0.99 are given. For reduced inspection this information is not available. Even in the case of normal and tightened inspection, the OC curves and percentiles should be used with caution because they were determined without taking into account that the process can switch between the sublevels. The calculation of the **effective OC functions** - those that determine the acceptance probabilities under consideration of the switching rules - is not easy (refer to ROSSOW 1971 and SCHILLING/SHEESLEY 1978).

Usual basis for evaluating sampling plans: OC curves and OC percentiles

Shortcomings:
- Dynamic element is not considered

The OC curves and percentiles in the ISO 2859 have been partially calculated with the help of approximations, some of which are not always exact. For AQL values below 10, the approximations are based on the binomial distribution, provided the sample size does not exceed 80, and on the Poisson distribution otherwise. Values of the OC function with AQL above 10 were calculated with the Poisson OC function. This implies that, when the fraction defective is used in acceptance sampling (good/bad classification, $AQL < 10$), the appropriate hypergeometric distribution is either approximated by the binomial or the Poisson distribution. Especially for percentiles of lower order, this can result in significant approximation errors (see figure 6.2/3).

- Approximation errors

The ISO 2859 contains two tables (V/A and V/B) with factors that allow the calculation of the average outgoing quality limit $AOQL$ for normal and tightened inspection. Further, the ISO 2859 contains graphs (table IX) that can be used to determine the average sample number ASN for

Other measures for evaluating ISO 2859 sampling plans: $AOQL, ASN, RQL$

normal and tightened, double and multistage sampling. In addition, for single-sampling plans only, the rejectable quality limit RQL is given for the acceptance probabilities 0.1 and 0.05. In the case of inspection of single lots, the ISO 2859 scheme emphasizes that not only the AQL, but also the RQL value, is of significant importance.

With the specification $AQL = 0.04$ (in the notation of the ISO 2859: $AQL = 4$, i.e., 4% defectives), table 3.2/25 lists the resulting single-sampling plans for normal, reduced and tightened inspection for selected lot sizes N (columns 2, 3, 7, 8, 12, 13). The lot sizes were chosen to represent the midpoints of the ranges of N that are specified in table 3.2/23. The given measures of the plans are the OC function value $L(AQL)$ and the RQL value (columns 4, 5, 9, 10, 14, 15), where, analogous to (3.61b), the RQL is defined to be the percentile of order β^* with $\beta^* \leq 0.1$. The results for the $L(AQL)$ and RQL are – different from similar calculations – not based on approximations but were determined exactly via the hypergeometric distribution. Table 3.2/25 also contains the turning point P_T^H previously introduced in (3.29c).

At first glance, analysis of table 3.2/25 gives a seemingly paradoxical result: The acceptance probability $L(AQL)$ for the chosen $AQL = 0.04$ under normal inspection is higher than under tightened inspection, and hence, the producer's risk of normal inspection is lower than under tightened inspection (compare columns 4 and 9). The reduced inspection has a lower producer's risk compared to the other levels of inspection. We can conclude from this fact that, in spite of its focus on the AQL value, the ISO 2859 is not one sided in favour of the producer, since, for a given AQL, the producer's risk increases from reduced to normal to tightened inspection.

The greater discriminatory power of the tightened inspection causes the OC curve to be steeper, which can be seen by the fact that the value $AQL = 0.04$ is closer to the RQL value and, also, the AQL and P_T^H values are closer, than under reduced or normal inspection (compare the AQL value of 0.04 to columns 5, 10, 15 and to columns 6, 11, 16).

Lot size	Normal inspection					Tightened inspection					Reduced inspection				
	para.		$L(AQL)$	RQL	P_T^H	para.		$L(AQL)$	RQL	P_T^H	para.		$L(AQL)$	RQL	P_T^H
N	n	c				n	c				n	c			
(1)	(2)	(3)	(4)	(5)	(6)	(7)	(8)	(9)	(10)	(11)	(12)	(13)	(14)	(15)	(16)
5	3	0	1	0.4000	-	5	0	Total	Total	Total	2	0	1	0.6000	-
12	3	0	1	0.5000	-	5	0	1	0.3333	-	2	0	1	0.6667	-
20	3	0	1	0.5500	-	5	0	1	0.3500	-	2	0	1	0.7000	-
40	13	1	1	0.2500	0.0750	20	1	1	0.1500	0.0500	5	0	0.8750	0.3500	-
70	13	1	0.9677	0.2571	0.0714	20	1	0.9217	0.1714	0.0429	5	0	0.8613	0.3714	-
120	20	2	0.9855	0.2333	0.1000	20	1	0.8710	0.1750	0.0500	8	1	0.9780	0.4000	0.1417
220	32	3	0.9829	0.1909	0.0955	32	2	0.9060	0.1545	0.0636	13	1	0.9261	0.2636	0.0818
400	50	5	0.9915	0.1750	0.1000	50	3	0.8740	0.1250	0.0600	20	2	0.9605	0.2425	0.1050
850	80	7	0.9897	0.1412	0.0882	80	5	0.9092	0.1106	0.0624	32	3	0.9654	0.1953	0.0965
2200	125	10	0.9904	0.1195	0.0805	125	8	0.9415	0.1009	0.0641	50	5	0.9867	0.1768	0.1018
6600	200	14	0.9862	0.0988	0.0703	200	12	0.9430	0.0873	0.0602	80	7	0.9858	0.1424	0.0885
22500	315	21	0.9916	0.0883	0.0668	315	18	0.9498	0.0776	0.0573	125	10	0.9883	0.1205	0.0806
92500	315	21	0.9913	0.0884	0.0669	315	18	0.9488	0.0776	0.0573	125	10	0.9881	0.1206	0.0806
325000	315	21	0.9912	0.0884	0.0669	315	18	0.9486	0.0776	0.0573	125	10	0.9881	0.1206	0.0806

Table 3.2/25: Examination of ISO 2859 single-sampling plans (normal, tightened and reduced inspection at level II with $AQL = 0.04$)

Problem 3.2/37

A supplier delivers lots of size $N = 1000$. He is wondering if it would be advantageous for him to deliver two lots of $N = 500$, instead of one lot of $N = 1000$, when the buyer administers normal inspection at level II and uses single-sampling plans.

a) What is the probability of accepting a "large" lot ($N = 1000$)?

b) What is the probability of accepting two "smaller" lots ($N = 500$ each)? Which choice is better for the producer?

Assume that the unknown quality parameter of the lot is $P = AQL$ and use table 3.2/25 (column 4).

Problem 3.2/38

Lots of size $N = 400$ with fixed but unknown fraction defective P are inspected by administering a single-sampling plan for normal inspection at level II with $AQL = 0.04$ (i.e., 4% defectives). After initial normal inspection, it became necessary to switch to tightened inspection.

a) After the switch, what is the probability that the first five successive lots are accepted? (This would imply staying at the tightened inspection level for a minimal amount of time.) Answer this question for $P = AQL = 0.04, P = IQL = 0.0725$ and $P = RQL = 0.125$.

b) For these three quality levels find the probability that the first ten successive lots are rejected. (This would cause termination of inspection.)

Hint: $L(AQL)$ can be found in table 3.2/25, and use $L(RQL) \approx 0.0982$.

d) Dynamic Sampling Systems

The single, double, multiple and sequential procedures of attribute acceptance sampling, previously introduced in sections 3.2.1 - 3.2.6 are *static* and memoryless in the sense that the decision about a lot is based solely on the inspection result of that particular lot. With the switching rules of the ISO 2859, we introduced a method for determining the appropriate sampling plan and decision rule contingent upon the inspection results of preceding lots. Through advances in electronic data processing, one is able now to design flexible and *dynamic* sampling schemes that integrate the inspection history. In addition to the switching rules of the ISO 2859, we will now introduce other selected **dynamic sampling systems**.

DODGE (1955a) gives the following requirements for the application of a dynamic system:

Requirements for the application of dynamic systems

- The lots should form a continuous series of deliveries from the same supplier.
- The variation in the quality of the lots should be small, i.e., the production process that produces the lots should be under control.
- The buyer should not have the impression that the present lot is of lower quality than the preceding ones.
- The buyer should be certain that, after acceptance of preceding lots, the supplier is not deliberately delivering lots of lesser quality.

Contrary to the sampling scheme of the ISO 2859 that requires inspection of *every* lot and allows switching the inspection intensity between the three levels of normal, tightened and reduced, the **skip lot sampling plans** proposed by DODGE allow the acceptance of lots without inspection under certain conditions. There is a close connection between the skip lot scheme and the continuous sampling inspection that will be introduced in section 4.1. The basic assumption of the **continuous sampling plans (CSP)** is that one inspects a stream of *individual product units* by administering either 100% inspection or inspection of samples from the process, depending on the observed quality level. Because one repeatedly skips units, not every unit from the production line is tested. A skip lot system is applied to a series of *lots*. It also has two levels of inspection intensity, normal inspection (of every lot) and skipping inspection, i.e., for positive quality history the inspection procedure skips lots.

Skip lot systems: Transfering the CSP principle to inspection of lots

The first skip-lot procedure, called **SkSP-1**, was developed by DODGE (1955b). It concerns the bulk sampling of lots that consist of raw materials, such as rubble, fluids, gases or similar. When a lot has to be inspected it is classified as conforming or nonconforming depending on lab test results. Thus, each lot is seen as a unit and those units are treated by a CSP. The SkSP-1 plan inspects every incoming lot until a certain number i of successive lots are accepted ($i \geq 1$). Then it switches to skip mode in which only one out of k lots is randomly selected and inspected. If this lot is accepted the remaining $k-1$ are also accepted and out of the next k lots one is selected and inspected and so forth, otherwise the procedure switches back to normal inspection and again all incoming lots are inspected until i successive lots are accepted. Similar to a manufacturer's final inspection, every rejected lot is replaced by a good one.[17]

Procedure of a SkSP-1

[17] DODGE (1955b) also gives a second procedure for the case when replacement of nonconforming lots by good lots is technically not possible or not planned.

Thus, a SkSP-1 procedure is specified by two parameters, the **relaxation number** or clearing interval i and the **selection distance** k. The quotient $f := 1/k$ with $0 < f < 1$ is called the **sampling fraction**. The parameters i and k need to be chosen so that on the average the proportion of nonconforming lots that slip through inspection does not exceed a given value. This measure corresponds to the average outgoing quality limit $AOQL$. In section 4.1 we will show how i and k (or f respectively) can be chosen for a given $AOQL$. For example, we can choose $i = 14$ and $f = 0.5$, as well as $i = 76$ and $f = 0.05$, in order to satisfy the specification $AOQL = 0.02$.

Of course, the SkSP procedure presented above can also be applied to lots that consist of natural units (pieces). The decision of whether the lot is conforming or not is then not based on lab test, but determined with the help of a sampling plan, the so-called **reference plan**. Such a reference plan can be found in the ISO 2859 sampling tables, for example. A skip lot system that is specified by i and k of a SkSP-1 plan and a reference plan is called a **SkSP-2 procedure**. The first SkSP-2 plan was proposed by DODGE/PERRY (1971); further developments were made by PERRY (1970, 1973a, 1973b) and others.

Procedure of a SkSP-2

For examination of the SkSP-2 plan, we will state its **OC function** and two additional measures without proof. Let P be the quality level of the incoming lots and $L(P)$ their acceptance probability based on the reference plan. Then under the SkSP-2 plan the acceptance probability of lots is given by

OC, AFI and ASN function of a SkSP-2

$$L_{Sk}(P) = \frac{(1-f) \cdot L(P)^i + f \cdot L(P)}{(1-f) \cdot L(P)^i + f}. \tag{3.107}$$

Further, for the SkSP-2 plan the **average fraction inspected**, previously introduced in (3.54), is determined by

$$AFI_{Sk} = \frac{f}{(1-f) \cdot L(P)^i + f}. \tag{3.108}$$

If the reference plan is a single-sampling plan with sample size n, then the **average sample number** of the SkSP-2 results to be

$$ASN_{Sk}(P) = AFI_{Sk}(P) \cdot n. \tag{3.109}$$

Among skip-lot systems there are two kinds of outgoing quality. The first is the average proportion of outgoing nonconforming units (combined from skipped and inspected lots) and the second is the average proportion of outgoing nonconforming lots, (i.e., the nonconforming lots among those that were skipped by the procedure). For the calculation of the average outgoing quality limits of these measures (i.e.,the maximal values) see SCHILLING (1982, p.447ff).

Chain sampling plans are another kind of sampling with memory. The first system of this kind, chain-sampling-plan 1, abbreviated **ChSP-1**, was introduced by DODGE (1955a). He and other statisticians later modified this first version (refer to STEPHENS/DODGE 1974, 1976a, 1976b and SOUNDARARAJAN 1978). Originally, the ChSP-1 was designed to eliminate the lack of discriminatory power of plans with $c = 0$. The idea is to chain consecutive inspections in such a way that the resulting OC curve has a turning point which is missing in plans with $c = 0$. This is especially useful in situations when a small sample size is required because a large amount of inspection is technically or economically not feasible; for example, in the case of destructive inspection. In the ChSP-1 a sample of small size is drawn and the lot is accepted if there were either no defectives in the sample or, if the previous i samples did not contain any defectives, in the case of one defective. Otherwise, the lot is rejected.

Description of the ChSP-1

The ChSP-1 is specified by the parameters i and n. Let $P(X_n^T = k)$ denote again the probability – calculated with the hypergeometric, binomial or Poisson distribution according to the specific situation – that k defectives are found in a sample of size n. Then the probability that a lot of given quality P is accepted is given by

OC and AOQ function of a ChSP-1

$$L_{Ch}(P) = Pr(X_n^T = 0) + Pr(X_n^T = 1) \cdot [Pr(X_n^T = 0)]^i. \qquad (3.110)$$

With this OC function we can calculate the average outgoing quality through

$$AOQ_{Ch}(P) = P \cdot L_{Ch}(P). \qquad (3.111)$$

The maximum is the average outgoing quality limit $AOQL_{Ch}$.

With respect to statistical calculations, **serial sampling** is more complicated than skip-lot and chain-sampling. In this type of dynamic inspection the current and several previous inspection results can be integrated into the decision making in various ways. There are also versions that only decide on the current lot when the inspection result of the following lot is known. This case is called **deferred sampling**.

Serial sampling

The first known version of deferred sampling was applied during World War II by the British Ministry of Supply for acceptance control of amunition (see ANSCOMBE/GODWIN/PLACKETT 1947). The procedure which was discussed in depth by the three authors is the simplest case when the stream of products from a production line is grouped into small lots. One unit is randomly sampled from each of the lots. If this unit is found to be conforming to the requirements, the lot is accepted. If more than m defectives are found in the last d consecutive units, one rejects all the last

Description of a special deferred sampling procedure

d lots beginning with the lot where the first defective was found up to the lot with the m–th defective unit. The idea behind this procedure is that before accepting a lot with a defective sample unit one waits until it is clear that the the next $d-1$ consecutive lots contain less than $m-1$ defective units. If this is the case one accepts all lots up to the next defective unit and starts the queue again. For small lots, where a sample size of one is sufficient, this procedure is definitely appropriate. The same is true in the case of bulk sampling. Variations of this approach can be found by ANSCOMBE/GODWIN/PLACKETT (1947) and in later work by HILL/HORSNELL/WARNER (1959).

Further dynamic sampling schemes

To conclude we will also mention two more versions of dynamic sampling systems that are described by SCHILLING (1982, p.463). The first is the **demerit rating plan**, which assigns scores to the defects according to their gravity and uses a cumulative count of these scores as the test statistic. The second plan is the **cumulative results criterion plan** with a statistic that adds measures of the inspected units instead of counting punishment points as with the previous plan.

Problem 3.2/39

Let $(N; 20; 1)$ be the reference plan of a SkSP-2 procedure (N is assumed very large). For $i = 4$ and $f = 0.25$, determine the values of functions (3.107) - (3.109) at $P = 0.05$. The OC function of the plan is specified to be binomial.

Problem 3.2/40

We want to apply a ChSP-1 with $n = 10$ and $i = 2$. The lot size is assumed to be so large that X_n^T, the number of defectives in the sample, has approximately a binomial distribution. For these specifications, calculate the value of the OC function (3.110) and the average outgoing quality (3.111) at $P = 0.1$.

e) Further Sampling Systems

We will now also introduce several *static* sampling systems.

Sampling systems with fixed sample quota

In **percent sampling plans** one always inspects a fixed quota n/N of the lot. In practice, such plans are no longer commonly used. We also do not recommend them, because their discriminatory power depends on the lot size (see figure 3.2/3).

PHILIPS' IQL system

The **Philips standard sampling system** was developed at the end of the 1940's by HAMAKER for the Dutch electronic corporation PHILIPS (refer to HAMAKER/TAUDIN, CHABOT/WILLEMZE 1950, HAMAKER 1950 and

SCHAAFSMA/WILLEMZE 1973). The input parameters are the lot size N and the OC percentile $P_{0.5} = IQL$. The sampling tables consist of only one page and are very simple to administer. The plan is printed in SCHILLING (1982, p. 366), for example. The table specifies single- and double-sampling plans for $P_{0.5} = 0.0025, 0.005, 0.01, 0.02, 0.03, 0.05, 0.07, 0.1$ and 11 different classes of lot size. The construction of these plans is based on the elasticity $\epsilon(P)$ at the indifference point $P = P_{0.5}$. All the calculations are based on the Poisson approximation (3.32b). Nowadays, PHILIPS plans are hardly used any more because they are not flexible enough.

DODGE-ROMIG plans

In the **LTPD- or RQL-Sampling system** proposed by DODGE and ROMIG in the late 1920's the input parameter is the RQL. The latest version of this system came out in 1959 (DODGE/ROMIG 1959) and contains single- and double-sampling plans with minimal total inspection ATI. At the same time, the authors also developed $AOQL$ **sampling systems** for single and double sampling. Again the plans mimimize the average amount of inspection. The latest version can be found in DODGE/ROMIG (1959).

ANSCOMBE system

With the **Anscombe sampling plan** it is possible to construct plans for specified RQL and $AOQL$ values in a fairly simple way (see ANSCOMBE 1949 or SCHILLING 1982, p. 395ff). For a lot of given size N, the procedure first takes a sample of size $f_1 \cdot N$ with $0 < f_1 < 1$, then inspects the sample units, and, if need be, draws further samples of size $f_2 \cdot N (0 < f_2 < f_1 < 1)$. The inspection is terminated after the first sample if the latter does not contain any defectives, after the second sample if the first two samples contain only one defective together, or, in general, after the first $(r + 1)$ samples if they contain together not more than r defectives. Otherwise, the procedure goes on until the entire lot is inspected.

Systems for sequential sampling

A sampling system design for sequential inspection was presented by the International Standard Organization in the ISO 8422 standard. The instructions contained in this standard result in plans with OC functions that agree with those of the MIL-STD 105D at $L(P) = 0.9$ and $L(P) = 0.1$.

Sampling systems with prior information

The last systems that we want to mention are **Bayes sampling systems**. They are based on the knowledge of a prior distribution (3.4) and thus assume extensive prior knowledge about the quality parameter in the incoming lots. Frequently, inspection costs and resulting loss factors are integrated into the Bayes approach. The description and discussion of these plans will have to be omitted in this book and we refer interested readers to STANGE (1977), HALD (1981) and RENDTEL/LENZ (1990).

3.2.8 Special Topics

In the conclusion of this section, we intend to discuss two special issues of attribute acceptance sampling. The first topic is concerned with the effect of misclassification on the effectiveness and on measures of single-sampling plans. By misclassification we mean the false classification of "good" sample units as "bad" and vice versa. A large number of empirical studies has shown that these mistakes frequently occur in acceptance control by inspection personnel. The second issue is the search for sampling plans with minimal costs of inspection. So far we selected single, double, multiple and sequential plans solely based on statistical criteria; for example, when we constructed plans by specifying two points on the OC curve. We will discuss what we mean by minimal costs and show how to construct such plans.

a) Effects of Misclassification on the OC Function and other Performance Measures for Single-Sampling Plans

Errors occur not only in the production of goods, but also during their inspection. For example, in acceptance sampling by variables, which will be discussed in section 3.3, measurement errors can occur through improper use of the measuring instrument, false readings, transfer of results or insufficient calibration of an instrument. When sampling by attributes – which is discussed here – **errors of classification** caused by the inspector or by the counting device (see figure 1.3/11) may occur. In the following, we will call those errors **inspection errors**.

We can distinguish between two types of inspection errors. Analogous to the terminology of hypothesis testing (see table 2.3/1), we will denote them by **type I inspection error** if a good unit is classified as bad and **type II inspection error** if a bad unit is mistakenly classified as good. We introduce an unobservable stochastic variable

Types of data errors in acceptance sampling by attributes

$$T := \begin{cases} 0 & \text{if sample unit is “good”,} \\ 1 & \text{if sample unit is “bad”,} \end{cases} \tag{3.112}$$

that represents the *true* state of a sample unit and a random variable

$$K := \begin{cases} 0 & \text{if sample unit is classified “good”,} \\ 1 & \text{if sample unit is classified “bad”,} \end{cases} \tag{3.113}$$

that records the *observed* value of a sample unit. The following table gives all possible combinations of the realizations of the two random variables and the two types of errors:

Inspection result	True state	
	$T = 0$	$T = 1$
$K = 0$	no inspection error	type II inspection error
$K = 1$	type I inspection error	no inspection error

Table 3.2/26: Types of inspection errors

As long as the lot size is sufficiently large the probability $Pr(T = 1)$ that a particular unit is actually "defective" as defined by the process, is approximately the **true fraction defective** in the lot P (see also section 3.3.1). In a similar way, we define the **empirical fraction defective** π to be the probability $Pr(K = 1)$ that a randomly selected unit is classified "defective".

State variable	Realizations	Probability of occurrence	Interpretation of the probabilities
T	1	P	true fraction defective
	0	$1 - P$	true proportion of "good" units
K	1	Π	observed fraction defective
	0	$1 - \Pi$	observed proportion of "good" units

Table 3.2/27: Probabilities of the realizations of the two state variables

The probabilities of the inspection errors in table 3.2/26 are conditional probabilities. For a type I error we get the probability

Definition of the two inspection error probabilities

$$\varepsilon := Pr(K = 1|T = 0) = \frac{Pr(K = 1, T = 0)}{Pr(T = 0)}, \qquad (3.114\text{ a})$$

and for a type II inspection error it is given by

$$\phi := Pr(K = 0|T = 1) = \frac{Pr(K = 0, T = 1)}{Pr(T = 1)}. \qquad (3.114\text{ b})$$

We will not discuss why these inspection errors occur and how these probabilities can be estimated (note problem 3.2/41). In BAUER (1987,

p. 7) one can find reports on studies of these issues. According to these reports, ε and ϕ were found to be as high as $\varepsilon = 0.4$ and $\phi = 0.9$.

When inspection errors occur, one has to ask and investigate whether they effect the OC function and other performance measures of a given sampling plan. In the following, we will discuss this issue for a *single* uncurtailed plan with test statistic X_n^T (number of defectives in the sample). We will assume that the statistic has a binomial distribution, i.e., we assume sampling *with* replacement. Under the conditions given in (2.87a) the results are also good approximations for the more commonly used case of sampling *without* replacement.

Assumption of a single random sample with replacement

Let us first investigate the expected value of the observed fraction defective for a lot with true fraction defective P in the case of administering **100% inspection**. Inspection errors occur with probability ε for the type I error and with probability ϕ for the type II error. This determines the probability that a defective unit is actually classified defective to be $Pr(K = 1|T = 1) = 1 - \phi$. Type II inspection error has the effect that instead of observing the actual P we observe a lower fraction defective, namely $P \cdot (1 - \phi)$. Type I inspection error has the opposite effect, since among the proportion $1 - P$ of good units each is classified defective with probability ε. Combining these two types of errors results in an observed fraction defective of the form

$$\Pi = P \cdot (1 - \phi) + (1 - P) \cdot \varepsilon. \tag{3.115}$$

Effect of inspection errors on the OC function:

Apart from the rare case that the two inspection errors cancel each other out, the inspection errors distort the true fraction defective P. Through P they also change the OC function and, instead of the theoretical or **true OC function**

$$L(P|n;c) = \sum_{i=0}^{c} \binom{n}{i} P^i (1 - P)^{n-i}, \tag{3.116}$$

given by (3.8), the resulting **empirical OC function** is of the form [18]

$$L^e(P) := L(\Pi|n;c) = \sum_{i=0}^{c} \binom{n}{i} \Pi^i (1 - \Pi)^{n-i}. \tag{3.117}$$

- general case: both inspection errors occur

Using (3.115), we can rewrite the above formula to

$$L^e(P) = \sum_{i=0}^{c} \binom{n}{i} [P(1 - \phi) + (1 - P)\varepsilon]^i \cdot [P\phi + (1 - P)(1 - \varepsilon)]^{n-i}. \tag{3.118}$$

[18] Since Π depends on P, ε and ϕ, we could also use the more exact but tedious notation $L_{\varepsilon;\phi}(P)$ instead of $L^e(P)$ for the OC function.

If the inspection involves errors then the decision of acceptance or rejection of the lot is based on wrong information. Also, the protection of the plan $(N; n; c)$ against acceptance and rejection errors is determined by the empirical OC function. This can be read from the empirical OC function (3.118) in the same way as indicated in figure 3.2/10, and one finds that the results do not agree with the specifications for which the plan was constructed.

In order to better understand the effects of inspection errors on the effective OC function, we need to investigate separately how the type I and type II inspection errors effect the OC function *individually*. Suppose that only type I inspection errors can occur ($\varepsilon > 0, \phi = 0$). If 100% inspection is administered, the resulting empirical fraction defective for a lot with actual quality parameter $P \in [0,1)$ is $\Pi = P + (1-P)\varepsilon$. It follows that $\Pi > P$ always, so that the quality level of the lot is "underestimated". As a consequence, the acceptance probability of a lot decreases. By (3.117) and the property that the OC function $L(P)$ is strictly monotone decreasing, we find that

- **1st special case: only type I inspection errors**

$$L^e(P) = L[P + (1-P)\varepsilon] < L(P) \quad \text{for} \quad P \in [0;1). \qquad (3.119\text{ a})$$

For $P = 1$ the functions $L(P)$ and $L^e(P)$ are both zero.

Suppose now that only type II inspection errors can occur ($\varepsilon = 0, \phi > 0$). Then 100% inspection would determine a fraction defective of $\Pi = P(1-\phi)$ and, for any actual fraction defective $P \in (0,1]$, we have $\Pi < P$. Thus the quality of the lot is "overestimated" and the inequality corresponding to (3.119a) is

- **2nd special case: only type II inspection errors**

$$L^e(P) = L[P(1-\phi)] > L(P) \quad \text{for} \quad P \in (0;1]. \qquad (3.119\text{ b})$$

Under this assumption and for $P = 0$, both $L(P)$ and $L^e(P)$ take on the value 1.

In summary, we can see that type I error pushes the OC curve down, while type II error pushes it up. Figure 3.2/29 illustrates this result. It shows the true binomial OC curve $L(P) = L(P|30;10)$ of the single-sampling plan $(N;30;10)$, previously introduced in figure 2.3/5. Besides this reference curve, two empirical curves $L^e(P)$ that arise in the case of only one type of inspection error are also displayed. The lower curve $L_1^e(P)$ corresponds to the case of only type I inspection error with error probability $\varepsilon = 0.2$, and the upper curve $L_2^e(P)$ is based on only type II error with probability $\phi = 0.2$.

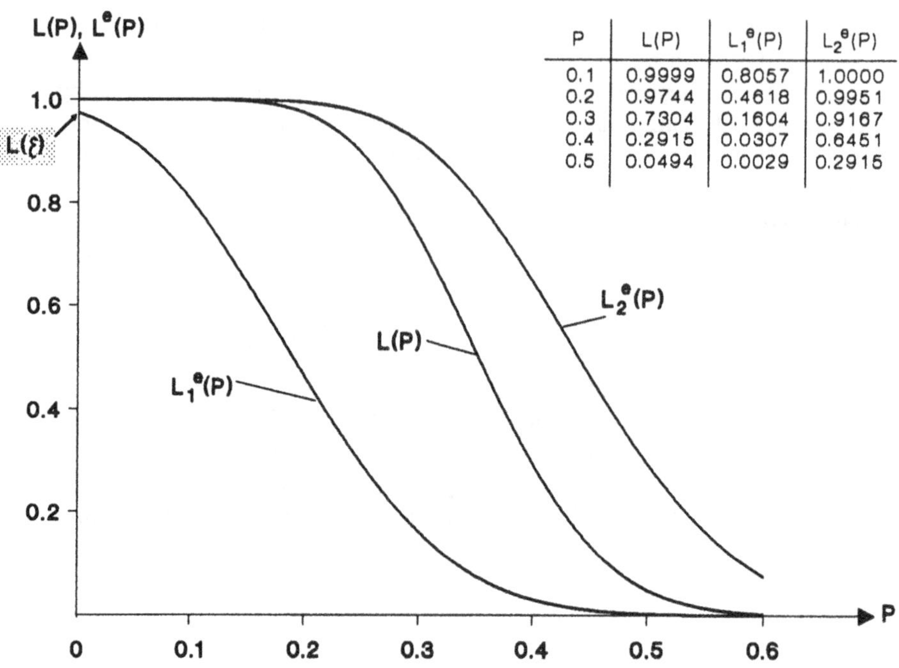

P	L(P)	$L_1^e(P)$	$L_2^e(P)$
0.1	0.9999	0.8057	1.0000
0.2	0.9744	0.4618	0.9951
0.3	0.7304	0.1604	0.9167
0.4	0.2915	0.0307	0.6451
0.5	0.0494	0.0029	0.2915

Figure 3.2/29: True OC curve of the single-sampling plan $(N; 30; 10)$ and two empirical OC curves for the cases that only one type of inspection error occurs $(L_1^e(P) : \varepsilon = 0.2,\ \phi = 0;\quad L_2^e(P) : \varepsilon = 0,\ \phi = 0.2)$

When type I and II inspection errors occur *simultaneously* they have, by (3.115), a counteractive effect on the empirical fraction defective II and hence, also on the OC function $L^e(P)$. Figure 3.2/30 shows again the actual OC reference curve $L(P)$ from above, and in addition, two empirical OC curves $L_3^e(P)$ and $L_4^e(P)$ that arise as a result of containing the error probabilities $\varepsilon = 0.1$, $\phi = 0.2$ and $\varepsilon = 0.2$, $\phi = 0.2$, respectively. The latter two both intersect the reference OC curve at a point $P_I \in (0, 1)$.

When inspection errors are possible they not only affect the OC function but also the other performance measures of a sampling plan. We will mention only the average outgoing quality AOQ and the average total inspection ATI. We will determine these functions for the case when all defectives in the sample are replaced by good units and when, in the case of rejection, 100% inspection with replacement of all defectives by good units is administered. This disposition combination was denoted in table 3.2/5 by S_3/L_3. There we also found that for the case of no inspection errors and disposition S_3/L_3 the average outgoing quality is given by

Effect of inspection errors on the AOQ function:

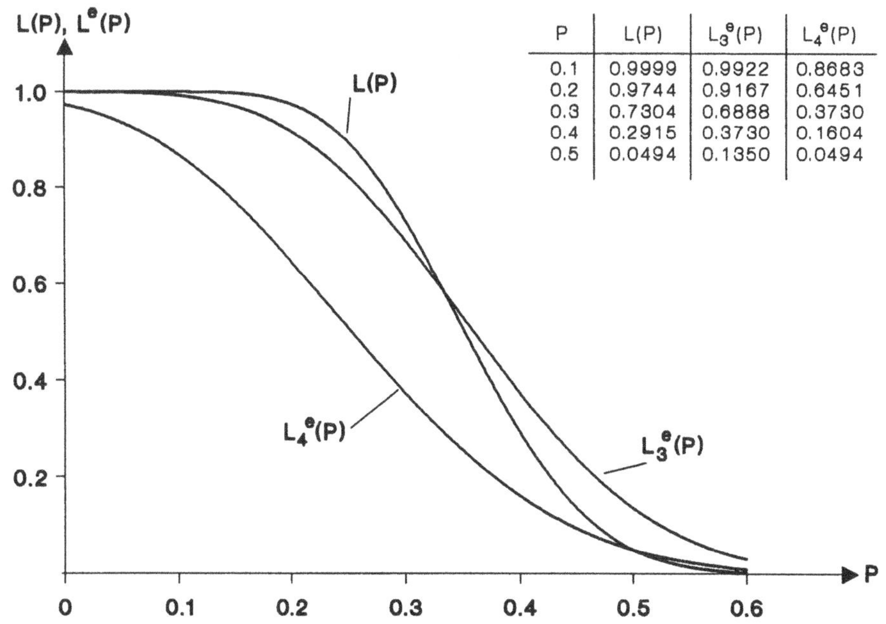

P	L(P)	$L_3^e(P)$	$L_4^e(P)$
0.1	0.9999	0.9922	0.8683
0.2	0.9744	0.9167	0.6451
0.3	0.7304	0.6888	0.3730
0.4	0.2915	0.3730	0.1604
0.5	0.0494	0.1350	0.0494

Figure 3.2/30: True OC curve of the plan $(N; 30; 10)$ and two empirical OC curves related to the simultaneous occurrence of both inspection error types
$(L_3^e(P) : \varepsilon = 0.1,\ \phi = 0.2;\quad L_4^e(P) : \varepsilon = 0.1,\ \phi = 0.2)$

$$AOQ(P) = \frac{N-n}{N} \cdot P \cdot L(P). \tag{3.120 a}$$

When inspection errors are involved, we have to replace the **true AOQ function** by the **empirical AOQ function** (see BAUER 1987, p. 37)

$$AOQ^e(P) = \frac{P}{N} \cdot \frac{n\phi + (N-n) \cdot [P\phi + (1-P)(1-\varepsilon)L^e(P) + \phi\{1 - L^e(P)\}]}{P\phi + (1-P)(1-\varepsilon)}. \tag{3.120 b}$$

As before, the effect of inspection errors on the AOQ function is better understood when the errors are first considered *individually*. We already discovered that, as a result of type I inspection error, the fraction defective of a lot is overestimated ($\Pi > P$). This causes more rejections and hence more inspection of remainder lots. Thus, the inspection is more strict. This explains why the graph of the empirical AOQ function (3.120b) lies below the actual reference curve (3.120a). Type II inspection error reduces the empirical fraction defective, i.e., the plan will reject lots less often and a

- special case: occurrence of only one inspection error type smaller number of remainder lots will need to be inspected. As a result, the *AOQ* value increases, i.e., more defectives slip through inspection undetected. As before, we will illustrate these findings for the plan $(N;30;10)$ with $N = 1000$. Figure 3.2/31 shows the true OC curve $AOQ(P)$ and the two empirical *AOQ* curves $AOQ_1^e(P)$ and $AOQ_2^e(P)$ that arise from the inspection error combinations $\varepsilon = 0.2, \phi = 0$ and $\varepsilon = 0, \phi = 0.2$, respectively. The values of the OC function that are needed in (3.120a,b) were calculated by (3.116) and (3.118).

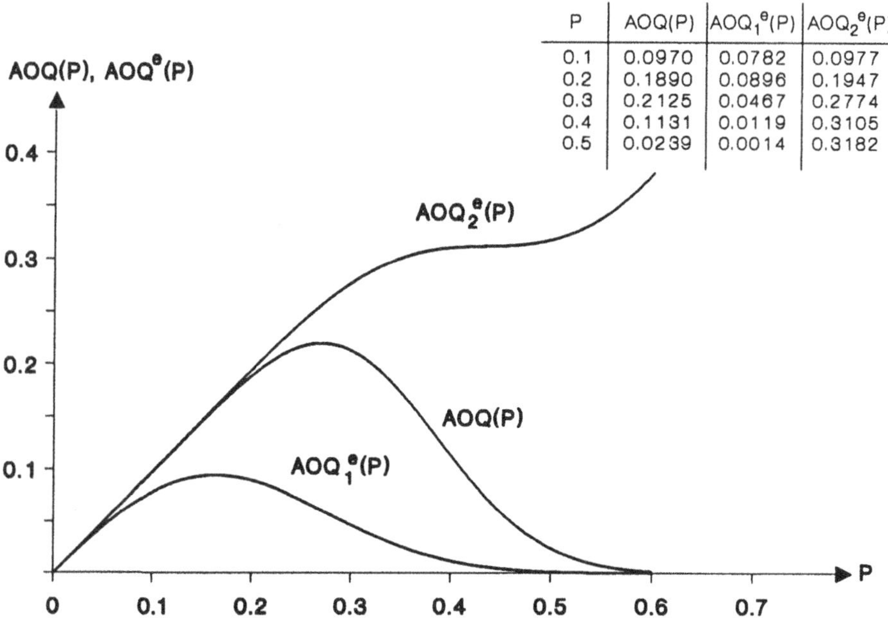

P	AOQ(P)	$AOQ_1^e(P)$	$AOQ_2^e(P)$
0.1	0.0970	0.0782	0.0977
0.2	0.1890	0.0896	0.1947
0.3	0.2125	0.0467	0.2774
0.4	0.1131	0.0119	0.3105
0.5	0.0239	0.0014	0.3182

Figure 3.2/31: True *AOQ* curve for the sampling plan (1000;30;10) and two empirical *AOQ* functions for only one type of inspection error ($AOQ_1^e : \varepsilon = 0.2, \phi = 0$; $AOQ_2^e : \varepsilon = 0, \phi = 0.2$)

- general case: both types of errors occur

Hence, the effect of inspection errors on the *AOQ* curve is the same as on the OC curve: type I inspection error causes the curve to be below the reference curve and type II inspection error causes it to be above. If type I and II inspection errors occur ***simultanously***, these effects superimpose each other. In this case, the *AOQ* curve lies below the actual *AOQ* curve up to the intersection point $P_I \in (0,1)$ and then above of it. This is illustrated in figure 3.2/32. This figure contains the true *AOQ* curve $AOQ(P)$ and two empirical AOQ^e curves $AOQ_3^e(P)$ and $AOQ_4^e(P)$ for the error specifications $(\varepsilon = 0.1, \phi = 0.2)$ and $(\varepsilon = 0.2, \phi = 0.2)$, respectively.

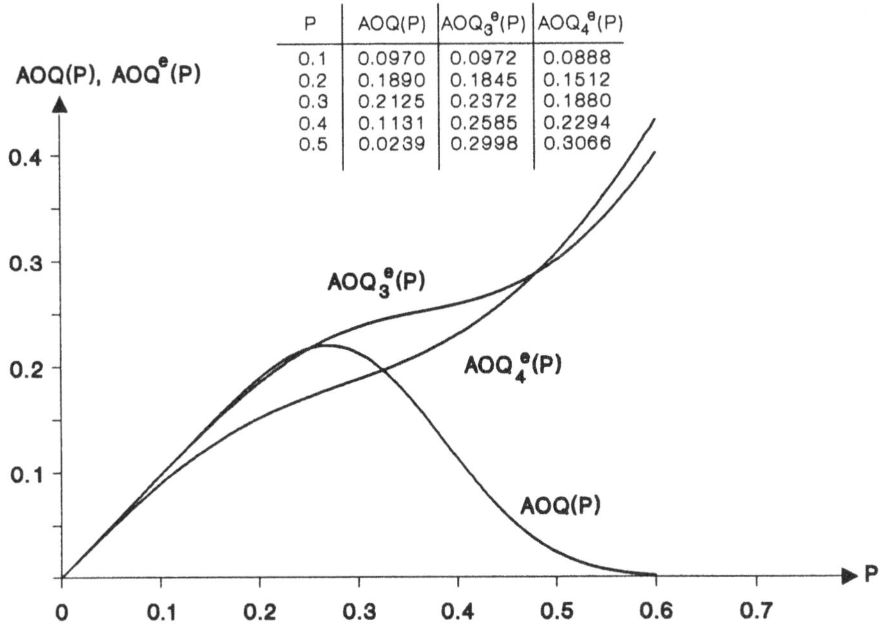

Figure 3.2/32: True AOQ curve for the sampling plan (1000;30;10) and two empirical AOQ curves related to the simultaneous occurrence of both inspection error types
($AOQ_3^e : \varepsilon = 0.1,\ \phi = 0.2;\quad AOQ_4^e : \varepsilon = 0.2,\ \phi = 0.2$)

The **true ATI function** (average amount of inspection without inspection errors) was presented in table 3.2/8. Recall that, in the case of disposition combination S_3/L_3, its formula is

$$ATI(P) = \frac{n + (N-n)\cdot[1 - L(P)]}{1-P}. \tag{3.121 a}$$

When we need to take into account inspection errors of type I and II, the true function (3.121a) has to be replaced by the **empirical ATI function** (see BAUER 1987, p. 52)

Effect of inspection errors on the ATI function

$$ATI^e(P) = \frac{n + (N-n)\cdot[1 - L^e(P)]}{P\phi + (1-P)(1-\varepsilon)}. \tag{3.121 b}$$

The two following figures 3.2/33-34 each show two empirical ATI curves for the sampling plan (1000;30;10). The first figure considers the inspection errors separately and the second their simultaneous occurrence. For comparison, the true ATI curve is given as reference. The inspection errors were specified in the same way as in the previous figures 3.2/29-32.

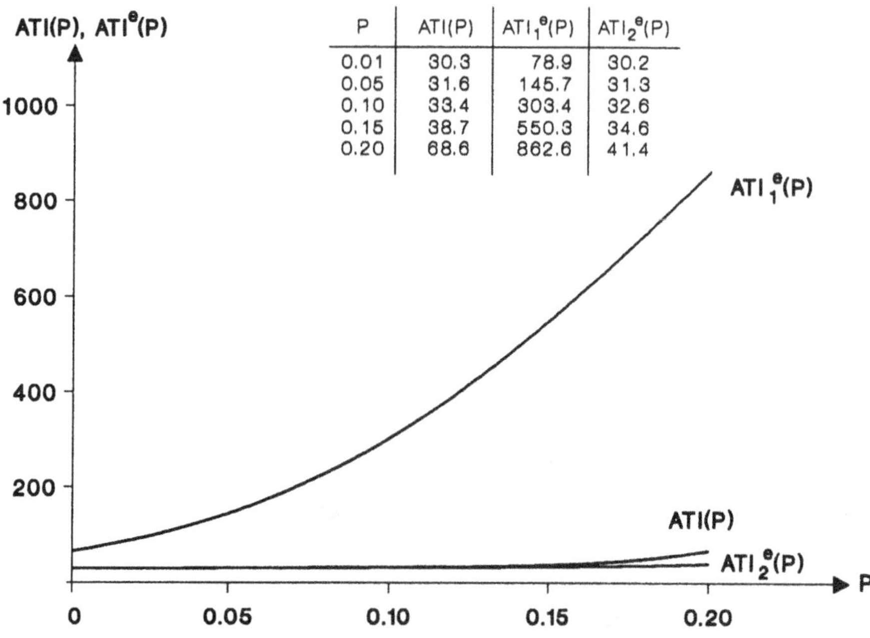

P	ATI(P)	$ATI_1^e(P)$	$ATI_2^e(P)$
0.01	30.3	78.9	30.2
0.05	31.6	145.7	31.3
0.10	33.4	303.4	32.6
0.15	38.7	550.3	34.6
0.20	68.6	862.6	41.4

Figure 3.2/33: True ATI curve for the sampling plan (1000;30;10) and two empirical ATI curves for only one type of inspection error ($ATI_1^e : \varepsilon = 0.2,\ \phi = 0;\quad ATI_2^e : \varepsilon = 0,\ \phi = 0.2$)

Designing sampling plans in the error free case meeting specified consumer's and producer's risk

In section 3.2.3a we constructed single-sampling plans by specifying the two quality levels AQL and RQL, along with their respective producer's risk α and consumer's risk β. These plans were determined by an iterative procedure and their OC functions satisfied according to (3.60) the condition

$$L(AQL) \geq 1 - \alpha \tag{3.122 a}$$

$$L(RQL) \leq \beta. \tag{3.122 b}$$

Design procedure for the case of inspection errors

Taking inspection errors into account, the acceptance probability $L(P)$ becomes $L^e(P) = L[P(1-\phi) + (1-P)\varepsilon]$. Suppose the effective acceptance probabilitiy $L^e(P)$ takes the values $1-\alpha$ and β at about $P = AQL$ and $P = RQL$, then the true OC function $L(P)$ attains these values at

$$AQL^* := AQL(1-\phi) + (1 - AQL)\varepsilon \tag{3.123 a}$$

$$RQL^* := RQL(1-\phi) + (1 - RQL)\varepsilon. \tag{3.123 b}$$

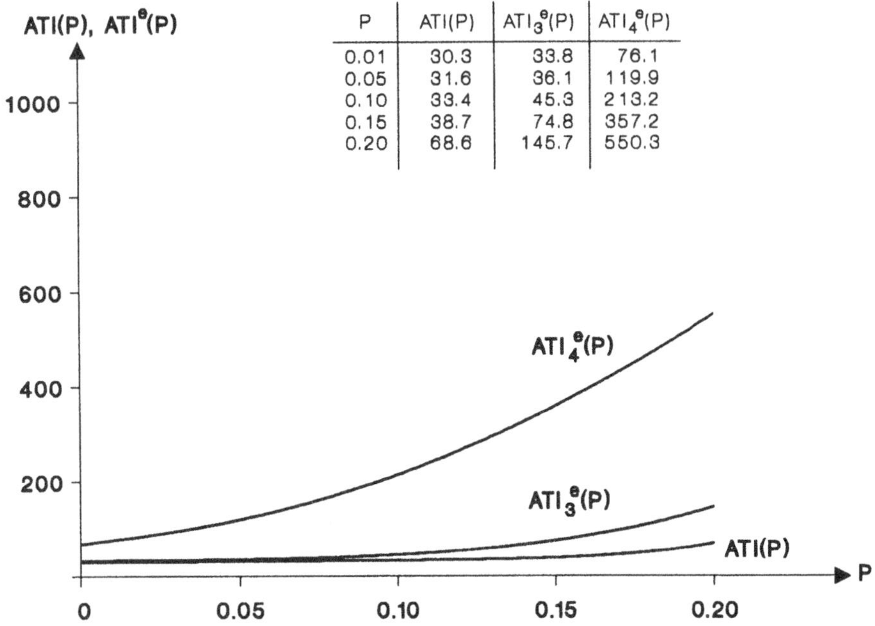

P	ATI(P)	$ATI_3^e(P)$	$ATI_4^e(P)$
0.01	30.3	33.8	76.1
0.05	31.6	36.1	119.9
0.10	33.4	45.3	213.2
0.15	38.7	74.8	357.2
0.20	68.6	145.7	550.3

Figure 3.2/34: True ATI curve for the sampling plan (1000;30;10) and two empirical ATI curves related to the simultaneous occurrence of both inspection error types ($ATI_3^e : \varepsilon = 0.1,\ \phi = 0.2;\quad ATI_4^e : \varepsilon = 0.2,\ \phi = 0.2$)

If the inspection error probabilities ε and ϕ are known, it is possible to apply a search algorithm to determine a sampling plan with an empirical OC curve that approximately agrees with the true OC curve that arose in the error free case (agreement at the points AQL and RQL). The resulting plan is called the **error adjusted plan**. The discussion above suggests that this plan can be obtained by applying a search algorithm like the one by GUENTHER with the specifications AQL^*, RQL^*, α and β, instead of AQL, RQL, α and β (see example 3.2/20).

This discussion has illustrated that inspection errors can have serious consequences. In practice, one needs to pay more attention to this problem.

Example 3.2/20

With the specifications $AQL = 0.2$, $\alpha = 0.025$ and $RQL = 0.47$, $\beta = 0.1$, the search algorithm by GUENTHER determines the parameters of the plan for error free inspection with a lot size of $N = 1000$ to be $n = 30$ and $c = 10$. The calculations were based on the assumption of a binomially specified OC function (see example 3.2/12 for the calculations). Suppose that type I and type II inspection errors occur with probability ε and ϕ, respectively. Then the specifications for the search algorithm by GUENTHER are

$$\begin{aligned} AQL^* &= AQL(1-\phi)+(1-AQL)\varepsilon &= 0.24 \\ RQL^* &= RQL(1-\phi)+(1-RQL)\varepsilon &= 0.43 \end{aligned}$$

and the above values of α and β. Under the assumption of a binomial OC function the algorithm determines the sample size to be $n^* = 67$ instead of $n = 30$, and the acceptance number $c^* = 23$ in place of $c = 10$. Figure 3.2/35 displays the true OC curve $L(P) := L(P|30;10)$ and the empirical OC curve $L_3^e(P) = L_3^e(P|30;10)$ for the case of inspection with type I and type II error probabilities of $\varepsilon = 0.1$ and $\phi = 0.2$, respectively. The figure also contains the empirical OC curve $L_*^e(P) := L^e(P|67;23)$ of the error adjusted plan and we observe that the adjustment was very successful since $L(P)$ and $L_*^e(P)$ approximately agree.

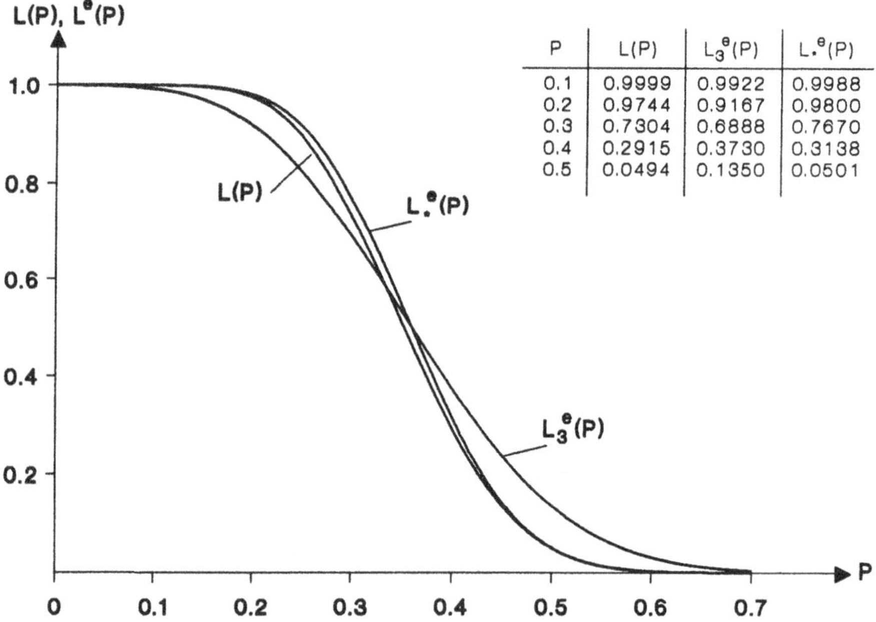

P	$L(P)$	$L_3^e(P)$	$L_*^e(P)$
0.1	0.9999	0.9922	0.9988
0.2	0.9744	0.9167	0.9800
0.3	0.7304	0.6888	0.7670
0.4	0.2915	0.3730	0.3138
0.5	0.0494	0.1350	0.0501

Figure 3.2/35: True OC curve for the sampling plan $(N;30;10)$, empirical OC curve related to the ocurrence of both inspection error types ($\varepsilon = 0.1, \phi = 0.2$) and OC curve of the error adjusted plan

However, we cannot assume that the adjustment with regard to the OC curve also automatically adjusts the measures of performance (AOQ, ATI). We will demonstrate for the average outgoing quality that this is not neccessarily the case. Figure 3.2/36 shows the AOQ functions $AOQ(P), AOQ_3^e(P)$ and $AOQ_*^e(P)$ corresponding to the three OC functions of the previous figure ($N = 1000$).

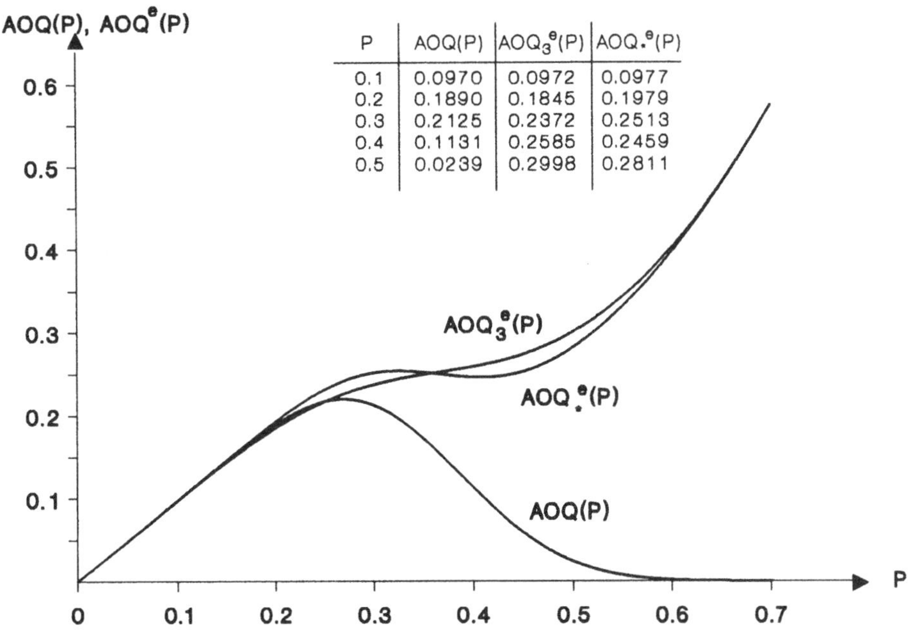

P	AOQ(P)	AOQ3e(P)	AOQ.e(P)
0.1	0.0970	0.0972	0.0977
0.2	0.1890	0.1845	0.1979
0.3	0.2125	0.2372	0.2513
0.4	0.1131	0.2585	0.2459
0.5	0.0239	0.2998	0.2811

Figure 3.2/36: True AOQ curve for the plan (1000; 30; 10), empirical AOQ curve related to the ocurrence of both inspection error types ($\varepsilon = 0.1, \phi = 0.2$) and AOQ curve of the error adjusted plan

---

Problem 3.2/41

a) Name the causes of inspection errors.

b) What problems arise in practice when estimating the error probabilities ε and ϕ?

c) In the case of simultaneous occurrence of type I and II inspection errors, the true and the empirical OC function intersect at one point $P_I \in (0, 1)$. Determine this point.

Problem 3.2/42

a) Determine the equations of the four empirical OC functions $L^e(P)$ in figures 3.2/29-30.

b) Calculate the values of these functions at $P = 0.15$ and compare them to the value $L(0.15)$ of the true OC function.

b) Economic Acceptance Sampling

Sampling plans can also be developed under economic considerations by using of the tools of decision theory and Bayesian statistics. The goal is to construct sampling plans that minimize the costs (inspection costs as well as misclassification costs). In the following we will briefly outline this approach. As in section 3.2.3, we will only consider the case of *single-sampling plans*.

Acceptance sampling is a typical application of decision theory (refer to textbooks, for example, by SCHNEEWEISS 1967 or BAMBERG/COENENBERG 1985). The **decision maker** – in this case the buyer of the lot – has to choose between the two possible **actions** "accept the lot" and "reject the lot". The **action space** consists of these two options. In acceptance sampling, the consequences of the decision depend on the fraction nonconforming P. In the terminology of decision theory every possible value of P is a **state of nature**. The collection of all possible states of nature - here the interval [0,1] - forms the **state space**. [19] The state space and the action space are connected through the **result function**. This function specifies the consequences or **results** for every possible combination of states and actions. The collection of all consequences is also called the **result space**. In order to make a rational decision one must be able to compare two elements of the result space in terms of "equally good", "better" and "worse". If this is the case, we say that a complete preference relation is defined on the result space. Often the preference relation is represented by a **utility function**. The utility function transforms the results to utility values. In other words, the consequence of an action is represented by the utility value. If the results can be transferred to a monetary scale, one usually defines a loss or **gain function** to be the utility function. The utility values are then given in terms of losses or gains:

Basic concepts of decision theory

$$\text{loss} := \text{costs - profits}$$

$$\text{gain} := \text{profits - costs}.$$

[19] Since $P = M/N$ with $M \in \{0, 1, \dots, N\}$, strictly speaking the state space consists only of rational numbers $P \in [0, 1]$.

In the literature of economic acceptance sampling (see, for example, UHLMANN 1969, HALD 1981, VON COLLANI 1984, VOGT 1988), a loss function is commonly used to compare results. Since gain can be seen as negative loss we can actually do without the term gain. The construction of plans has the goal of minimizing costs. For fixed returns, minimizing the loss is equivalent to minimizing the costs. Consequently the terms **minimal cost inspection** and **minimal loss inspection** can be seen as synonyms to economic acceptance sampling.

Classification of decision situations

Before we give a brief introduction to the theory of economic sampling we want to introduce three typical decision situations. If the state space consists of one single element we have a **decision under certainty**. In all other cases we have **decisions under doubt**. The latter type is divided into **decisions under risk** and **uncertain decisions** depending on whether the probability distribution of the elements in the state space is known or not. In the case of acceptance sampling, the second case is given, if the prior distribution of quality parameter P is known, i.e., in the form of a prior density $\Pi(P)$. The different decision situations are summarized below in table 3.2/28 and illustrated by examples from acceptance control.

Decision situation	General characteristics	Example from acceptance sampling
Decision under certainty	Selection of an optimal action in the case of only one possible state	Decision on a lot for given quality level P
Decision under risk	Selection of an optimal action in the case of more than one possible state and known distribution of the state space	Decision on the lot with unknown quality level P, but known prior distribution of P
Decision under uncertainty	Selection of an optimal action in the case of more than one possible state and unknown distribution of the state space	Decision on the lot with unknown quality level P and unknown prior distribution of P

Table 3.2/28: Decision situations

There are also intermediate categories between the decision under risk and decision under uncertainty, that arise for example, when the prior distribution of P is ***partially known***, e.g., in the form of percentiles, expectation or variance of P.

The above classification into three types of decision situations by the extent of information on P is neither in theory nor in practice sufficient. In the cases of decision under risk and under uncertainty, one has to further determine whether the information about the unknown fraction nonconforming P was or will be available in the form of a sample or whether one wants or has to decide without sample data.[20] The sample information for the decision on the lot with unknown quality parameter is the number of defective units in the sample. We can now distinguish between five different basic decision situations, as given in figure 3.2/37.

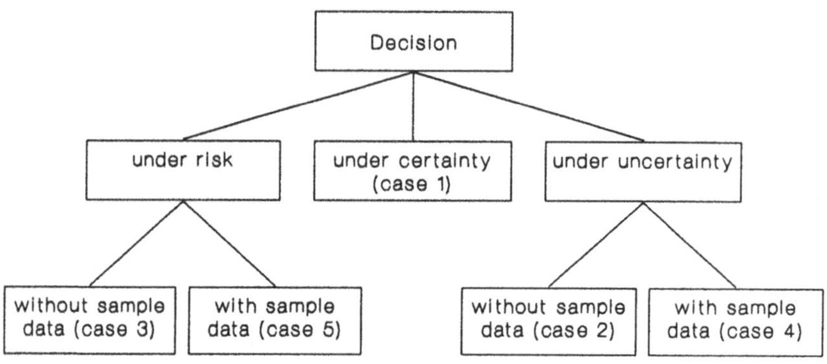

Figure 3.2/37: Basic decision situations

Before we can discuss these five situations, we need to first introduce their common loss function. For every possible action the loss is seen as a function of the state of nature (here the quality level P). In the following argument we will assume this function to be linear. Since in acceptance sampling we only have two choices of actions (acceptance or rejection), we only need to consider two different loss functions. By "loss" we mean the loss of the decision maker, which is the buyer in our case.

Acceptance loss function

If each ***accepted good*** unit results in a loss of size α (usually $\alpha < 0$) and every ***accepted bad*** unit results in a loss of size β, the **acceptance loss per lot** for a lot of size N and fraction nonconforming P is given by

$$V_a(P) = N(1-P)\alpha + N \cdot P \cdot \beta = N\alpha + (\beta - \alpha)NP, \qquad (3.124\text{ a})$$

and the **acceptance loss per unit** is given by

$$v_a(P) = \frac{V_a(P)}{N} = \alpha + (\beta - \alpha)P =: a_1 + a_2 P. \qquad (3.124\text{ b})$$

[20] In the case of decision under certainty a sample is not needed.

Rejection loss function

Analogous to (3.124), we get the loss function for rejection by specifying the loss of a *rejected good* unit by γ and that of a *rejected bad* unit by δ. The **rejection loss per lot** is then determined by

$$V_r(P) = N \cdot (1-P) \cdot \gamma + N \cdot P \cdot \delta = N \cdot \gamma + (\delta - \gamma) \cdot N \cdot P \qquad (3.125\text{ a})$$

and the **rejection loss per unit** by

$$v_r(P) = \frac{V_r(P)}{N} = \gamma + (\delta - \gamma)P =: r_1 + r_2 P. \qquad (3.125\text{ b})$$

In practice, it is often difficult to evaluate the four coefficients a_1, a_2, r_1 and r_2 from the accounting department or other sources.

Determining the break even point

Which action results in minimal loss? - It is reasonable to assume that the loss of accepting a lot with only good units is smaller than the loss of rejecting it, so that

$$v_a(0) = a_1 < r_1 = v_r(0) \qquad (3.126\text{ a})$$

has to hold. It is also reasonable to assume that the loss of rejecting a lot with only bad units is smaller than the loss of accepting it, and thus we get

$$v_r(1) = r_1 + r_2 < a_1 + a_2 = v_a(1). \qquad (3.126\text{ b})$$

It follows from the conditions (3.126) and the linearity of the loss functions, that the two loss functions intersect at exactly one point. This point $P = P_0$ at which the loss functions have the same value is called the **break even point**. Using

$$v_a(P_0) = a_1 + a_2 P_0 = r_1 + r_2 P_0 = v_r(P_0)$$

the point P_0 is determined by

$$P_0 = \frac{r_1 - a_1}{a_2 - r_2}. \qquad (3.127)$$

Using inequalities (3.126) it can be easily shown that $P_0 \in (0,1)$.

Figure 3.2/38a shows the graph of the loss functions

$$\begin{aligned} v_a(P) &= -10 + 50P \\ v_r(P) &= 30 - 20P. \end{aligned}$$

By (3.127), the break even point is found to be at $P_0 = 4/7 \approx 0.5714$. Under the reasonable assumptions stated for (3.126), the two loss functions always have the pattern of figure 3.2/38a, i.e., neither of the two loss functions can be above the other on the entire range [0,1]. Thus none of the two actions

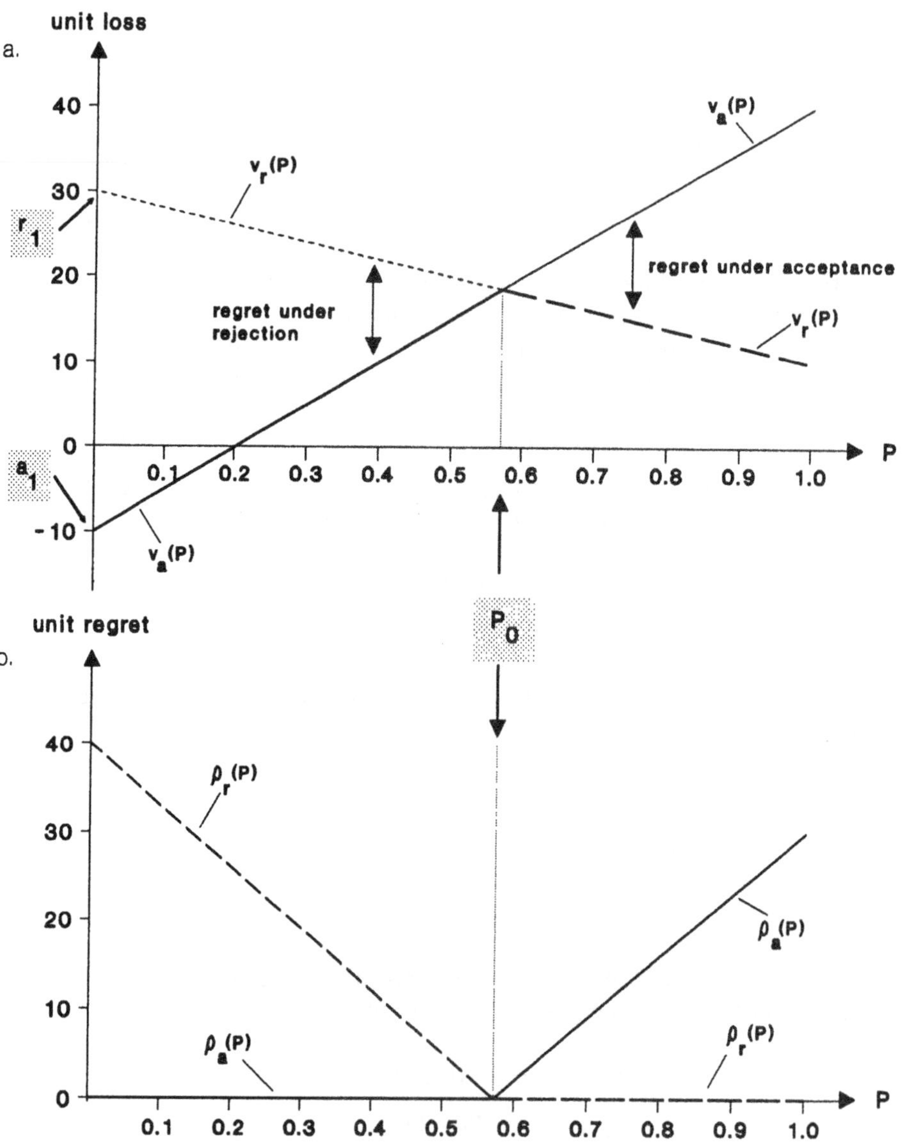

Figure 3.2/38: Loss and regret function for acceptance and rejection (a) loss function (b) regret function

"acceptance" and "rejection" dominates the other on the whole state space. We also say there is no **uniformly best action**. Which of these two actions is optimal, in the sense of resulting in smaller loss, depends on the quality level P. Hence, we have a non-trivial decision problem.

Case 1: Decision under certainty

In the case of decision under *certainty* the quality level of the lot is known and one can determine whether the given value P lies in the interval $[0, P_0]$, in which case the acceptance loss dominates or if P lies in the interval $(P_0, 1]$, where the rejection loss dominates.[21] Thus, in the case of decision under certainty we can present the following optimal, i.e., minimal loss **decision rule**:

- Accept lot if $0 \leq P \leq P_0$
- Reject lot if $P_0 < P \leq 1$.

The loss function for this decision rule is

$$v_u(P) = \begin{cases} a_1 + a_2 P & \text{for } 0 \leq P \leq P_0 \\ r_1 + r_2 P & \text{for } P_0 < P \leq 1. \end{cases} \tag{3.128}$$

The loss (3.128) is called the **unavoidable unit loss** and it denotes the loss that cannot be avoided even if one has complete information on the quality parameter P of the lot (as in the case of decision with certainty). In figure 3.2/38a, the graph of (3.128) is drawn bold. We see that it has a fold at P_0.

Derivation of the regret function

In the case of risk or uncertainty the quality level P of the lot is not known. If one accepts a lot and finds out later – for example, during the use of the units – that for this lot $P \in (P_0, 1]$, then one apparently committed a decision error. It would have been more advantageous to reject the lot, since for $P \in (P_0, 1]$ we have $v_r(P) < v_a(P)$. The portion of the loss that exceeds the unavoidable loss is called **regret**. It represents the costs of false decision.[22] If a lot with $P \in [0, P_0]$ is accepted the resulting regret is obviously zero. The **acceptance regret per unit** is defined by

$$\rho_a(P) = v_a(P) - v_u(P) = \begin{cases} 0 & \text{for } 0 \leq P \leq P_0 \\ (a_2 - r_2)(P - P_0) & \text{for } P_0 < P \leq 1. \end{cases} \tag{3.129 a}$$

[21] It is arbitrary to which interval the point P_0 is assigned.

[22] It should make sense that the costs of a sample that is drawn to obtain (incomplete) information about the quality level P should not be more than the regret.

In the same way the **rejection regret per unit** is found to be

$$\rho_r(P) = v_r(P) - v_a(P) = \begin{cases} (a_2 - r_2)(P_0 - P) & \text{for } 0 \leq P \leq P_0 \\ 0 & \text{for } P_0 < P \leq 1. \end{cases} \tag{3.129 b}$$

The two regret functions are displayed in figure 3.2/38b.

Case 2:
Decision in the case of uncertainty without sample data

In the case of ***decision under uncertainty and no sample data*** neither the quality level nor its prior distribution are known, and it was also not possible to obtain information through a sample. For this situation we need to find an optimal **blind strategy**. A popular strategy is the **minimax rule**. Every action is rated by the maximal loss that can result from choosing it, and in the end, one selects the action with the lowest maximal loss (**minimax loss action**). The minimax rule only looks at the worst possible consequences of each action. Hence, it represents the approach of a risk avoiding decision maker.

For linear loss functions the maximum can only be attained at the end points of the state space, i.e., at $P = 0$ or $P = 1$. Let

$$\begin{aligned} a^* &:= \max(a_1; a_1 + a_2) \\ r^* &:= \max(r_1; r_1 + r_2) \end{aligned}$$

be the maxima of the unit loss functions of acceptance or rejection, respectively. Then the optimal action is acceptance if $a^* < r^*$ and rejection if $r^* < a^*$. If $a^* = r^*$ the choice of action is arbitrary. For the situation in figure 3.2/38, we get

$$\begin{aligned} a^* &= \max(-10; 40) &= 40 \\ r^* &= \max(30; 10) &= 30, \end{aligned}$$

so that rejection of the uninspected lot is the optimal decision. This minimax action guarantees that the loss per lot is at most $30 \cdot N$.

The minimax rule can also be applied to the regret function. Similar to the loss function, it is linear and hence, obtains its maximum at an endpoint of its domain. The maximum of the unit regret function (3.129a) is attained at $P = 1$ and has the value

$$a^{**} = v_a(1) - v_r(1) = (a_1 + a_2) - (r_1 + r_2). \tag{3.130 a}$$

The unit regret function (3.129b) attains its maximal value

$$r^{**} = v_r(0) - v_a(0) = r_1 - a_1 \tag{3.130 b}$$

at $P = 0$. Through comparison of (3.130a) and (3.130b) one can obtain the minimax regret action. For the example in figure 3.2/38, it follows that

$$\begin{aligned} a^{**} &= 40 - 10 &= 30 \\ r^{**} &= 30 - (-10) &= 40 \end{aligned}$$

and thus that acceptance of the (uninspected) lot is optimal. The regret per lot is then at most $30 \cdot N$. This example illustrates that the resulting optimal action depends on whether one uses the regret or the loss function. Note that an action can only be "optimal" in the sense of "optimal with respect to a given goal". Since the goals of loss and regret are different, it makes sense that the resulting optimal actions are not the same.

Case 3: Decision under risk and no sample data

In the case of *decision under risk and no sample data* the buyer has prior information about the distribution of the quality level P, i.e., in the form of a prior density $\pi(P)$. Since no sample is drawn, we again want to find an optimal blind strategy. A commonly used decision rule for this situation is the so-called **μ rule**. We can think of μ as the expected value of the loss or regret with respect to the prior density $\pi(P)$. For the unit loss functions (3.124) for acceptance and rejection, respectively, the expected values are

$$E[v_a(P)] = \int_0^1 (a_1 + a_2 \cdot p) \cdot \pi(p) \cdot dp \qquad (3.131\text{ a})$$

$$E[v_r(P)] = \int_0^1 (r_1 + r_2 \cdot p) \cdot \pi(p) \cdot dp. \qquad (3.131\text{ b})$$

One can interprete (3.131a) to be the **average loss per unit** that is incurred if one accepts every lot and if the lot quality level P is distributed according to $\pi(P)$. In the same way, (3.131b) represents the average loss per unit for the rule of rejecting every lot. If one has to choose between these two procedures, one will decide in favour of acceptance if $E[v_a(P)] < E[v_r(P)]$.

Suppose we want to use the regret function instead of the loss function. Then the corresponding expectations are

$$E[\rho_a(P)] = \int_0^1 \rho_a(p) \cdot \pi(p) \cdot dp = \int_{P_0}^1 (a_2 - r_2) \cdot (p - P_0) \cdot \pi(p) \cdot dp \quad (3.132\text{ a})$$

$$E[\rho_r(P)] = \int_0^1 \rho_r(p) \cdot \pi(p) \cdot dp = \int_0^{P_0} (a_2 - r_2) \cdot (P_0 - p) \cdot \pi(p) \cdot dp. \quad (3.132\text{ b})$$

The interpretation of (3.132) and choice of action are analogous to the approach (3.131). Again it is possible that the loss and regret function approaches result in different optimal actions (see problem 3.2/43).

Case 4: Decision under uncertainty and with sample data

If one is not willing to use a blind strategy one can obtain at least partial information about the unknown quality of a lot by means of a sample. Contrary to the last two cases, in the situation of decision under uncertainty, one does not decide once and for all on an optimal action for all lots, but selects actions depending on the sample result. The **statistical decision function** assigns an action to every possible sample result. Here the statistical decision function is of the form:

- Accept lot if $X_n^T \leq c$.
- Reject lot if $X_n^T > c$.

We now need to specify the sample size n and the acceptance number c in an optimal way.

Suppose our goal is to minimize the loss. The loss incurred by applying the plan $(N; n; c)$ with OC function $L(P)$ is determined by

$$V(P|n;c) = V_a(P) \cdot L(P) + V_r(P) \cdot [1 - L(P)] + k_1 + k_2 \cdot n. \qquad (3.133)$$

Under the assumption that the incoming lots all have the same quality level P and that for inspection the plan $(N; n; c)$ is administered, we can interpret (3.133) to be the resulting **average loss per lot**. In the above k_1 denotes the fixed inspection cost and k_2 the extra inspection cost per unit. We can modify the formulas for the **average regret per unit**. It is given by

$$R(P|n;c) = V(P|n;c) - V_u(P) \qquad (3.134\text{ a})$$

where $V_u(P)$ is, by (3.124a) and (3.125a), defined to be

$$V_u(P) = \begin{cases} V_a(P) & \text{for } 0 \leq P \leq P_0 \\ V_r(P) & \text{for } P_0 < P \leq 1. \end{cases} \qquad (3.134\text{ b})$$

If no prior information about the lot is available, one can apply the minimax rule to (3.133) or (3.134a) respectively. In UHLMANN (1982, p. 1237ff) and VOGT (1988, p. 215ff) the decision rule for the regret function is presented under the assumption of a binomial OC function, whereas VON COLLANI (1984, p.99ff) presents it for the hypergeometric OC function.

Case 5: Decision under risk and with sample data

In the situation of *decision under risk and with sample data*, one has prior information on the distribution of P in the form of the density $\pi(P)$ and partial information, usually in the form of X_n^T, about the lot. For a description of how to find the **optimal Bayes decision function** for this case refer to HALD (1981).

Problem 3.2/43

We need to make a blind decision on a lot (i.e., without sample data). The unit loss functions for the two actions "acceptance" and "rejection" are given by (3.124b) and (3.125b).

a) Use the minimax rule to decide between these two actions for the two different utility functions of, first, the given loss function and, second, the regret function (3.129). Under which conditions do both cases give the same result?

b) Find the minimal cost decision of the minimax procedure under assumption of the loss functions (3.124b) and (3.125b), the parameters $a_1 = -10, a_2 = 50, r_1 = 30, r_2 = -20$, and a prior distribution of

$$\pi(P) = \begin{cases} 2(1-P) & \text{for } P \in [0;1] \\ 0 & \text{else} \end{cases}$$

for the quality level P.

c) Use the regret function (3.129) instead of the loss function and find the result of question (b).

d) Suppose that all we know is that the quality level lies between 0.5 and 0.7 and that it has a rectangular distribution. For the last two questions find the cost minimal actions in the case of applying the loss and regret functions, respectively.

3.3 Acceptance Sampling by Variables

Comparison of attribute and variable acceptance sampling

In the attribute procedures of acceptance sampling that were discussed in section 3.2, one records either the number of defectives or the total number of defects in the sample, and bases the decision to accept or reject the lot on this count. The quality characteristic of interest typically has a *discrete distribution* , e.g., a binomial or Poisson distribution. Occasionally it is of interest to use a *continuous* quality characteristic in acceptance sampling. In such cases, the attribute procedure would not take full advantage of the available information, i.e., the exact measurement, because it only records if the value is within certain bounds or not. In the following presentation of **acceptance sampling by variables** we will discuss sampling procedures for continuous quality characteristics and we will further assume that the characteristic of interest in the lot is at least approximately normally distributed. This assumption can be checked, for example, by a goodness of fit test, (e.g., the χ^2-test or the Kolmogorov-Smirnov-test) or graphically by a normal probability plot (see GRAF/HENNING/STANGE/WILRICH 1987, p. 130ff). It is theoretically possible to modify the following results for non-normally distributed continuous quality characteristics, but this is usually not considered in practice.

Sampling by variables under the assumption of a normally distributed test statistic

Different from the attribute case in section 3.2, we will only discuss single-sampling plans, i.e., plans that only draw *one* sample of size n from the lot.

3.3.1 Relationship between Fraction Defective and Process Mean

Let X be a quality characteristic of a product unit, e.g., weight, length, diameter, electric resistance or tensile strenght, etc., and assume that it is at least approximately normally distributed. A unit is called defective or nonconforming if the measurement x of the characteristic X lies below a certain lower specification limit (minimal value) G_l or above an upper specification limit (maximal value) G_u or if it lies outside of a closed specification interval $[G_l, G_u]$.

Three cases: specification G_l, G_u or $[G_l, G_u]$

Which of these cases is appropriate depends on the specific situation. The following example will illustrate this further.

Example 3.3/1

The requirement on the production of thread is that it at least has a minimal tensile strength G_l. Thread with a tensile strength $x < G_l$ needs to be sorted out of the lot. When inspecting automobile brakes we may want to require that the braking distance does not exceed a certain value G_u. Brakes with a too long braking distance ($x > G_u$) are classified defective. The diameter of the pistons of a motor is required to lie within a certain range $[G_l, G_u]$. Cylinders with diameter $x < G_l$ or $x > G_u$ are not fit for use.

The three cases are summarized below:

Case	Specification limit	A unit is	
		conforming if	nonconforming if
1	lower tolerance limit G_l	$x \geq G_l$	$x < G_l$
2	upper tolerance limit G_u	$x \leq G_u$	$x > G_u$
3	lower tolerance limit G_l and upper tolerance limit G_u with $G_l < G_u$	$x \in [G_l; G_u]$	$x \notin [G_l; G_u]$

Table 3.3/1: Conforming and nonconforming units

If X is no(μ, σ^2) then the probability P that a randomly drawn unit is classified "defective" can be easily determined for each of these three cases. By (2.47), one can reduce the problem to the standard normal case and use the standard normal distribution function $\Phi(z)$ defined by (2.50). The **defective probabilities** P for onesided specification limits are [23]

Calculating the probability of a unit to be defective for the three cases

$$P = Pr(X < G_l|\mu;\sigma) = \Phi\left(\frac{G_l - \mu}{\sigma}\right) = 1 - \Phi\left(\frac{\mu - G_l}{\sigma}\right) \qquad (3.135\text{ a})$$

$$P = P(X > G_u|\mu;\sigma) = 1 - \Phi\left(\frac{G_u - \mu}{\sigma}\right) = \Phi\left(\frac{\mu - G_u}{\sigma}\right). \qquad (3.135\text{ b})$$

In the case of a lower and upper specification limit we get

$$\begin{aligned} P &= Pr(X \notin [G_l, G_u]|\mu;\sigma) = 1 - \Phi\left(\frac{G_u - \mu}{\sigma}\right) + \Phi\left(\frac{G_l - \mu}{\sigma}\right) \\ &= \Phi\left(\frac{\mu - G_u}{\sigma}\right) + \Phi\left(\frac{G_l - \mu}{\sigma}\right). \end{aligned} \qquad (3.135\text{ c})$$

The equations in (3.135) are, strictly speaking, formulas for the defective probabilities of individual units but, especially for large lot sizes, they can also be seen as the previously introduced **fraction defective** of the lot. We will illustrate this with an example. Suppose that each unit of a production

[23] For the derivation of these formulas look back to the normal distribution introduced in section 2.1.4c and especially to problems 2.1/8 and 2.1/10b.

line is defective with probability 0.01 and that the units are grouped into large lots of size N. Then we expect that a lot contains on the average $M = 0.01 \cdot N$ defective units. As a result, the fraction defective of the lot is on the average $P = M/N = 0.01$.

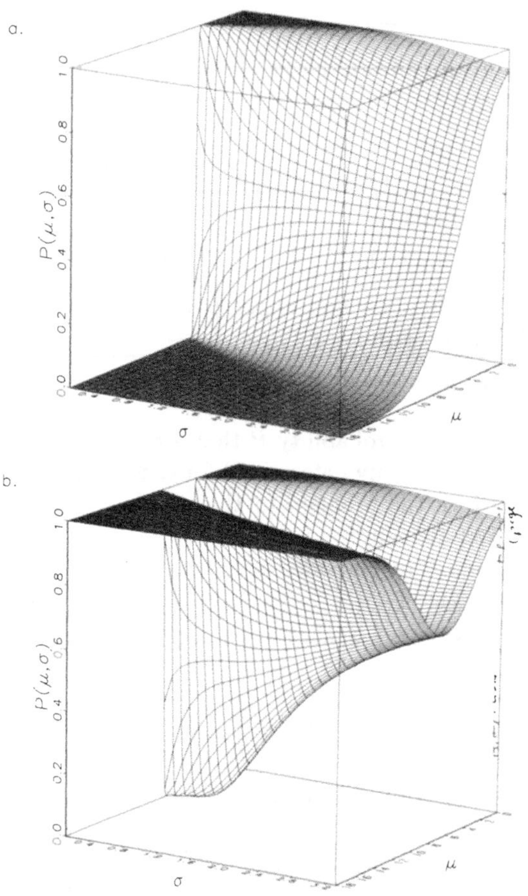

Figure 3.3/1: Fraction defective P as a function of μ and σ
(a) 3D-graph for $G_l = 5$ (b) 3D-Graph for $G_l = 5$ and $G_u = 8$

From now on we will consider the probability P to be the fraction defective of the lot. We can see immediately that the value of P depends, for given specification limits (G_l and/or G_u), on the parameters μ and σ^2. Figure 3.3/1 shows the 3D-graphs of P when either a single specification limit $G_l = 5$ or a specification interval $[G_l; G_u]$ with $G_l = 5$ and $G_u = 8$ are given.

In practice, one almost always assumes that the **process variance** σ^2 is constant. This means that there is constant variation in the production process. In this case the only variable is the expectation μ and we call it the **production** or **process mean**. The following discussion will be based on these assumptions. Note that the fraction defective P only depends on the expectation μ of the normal distribution. We will write $P = P(\mu)$ whenever we want to emphasize this relationship and thus (3.135) becomes

Notation when assuming a constant process variance σ^2

$$P(\mu) = \Phi\left(\frac{G_l - \mu}{\sigma}\right) = 1 - \Phi\left(\frac{\mu - G_l}{\sigma}\right) \qquad (3.136\text{ a})$$

$$P(\mu) = \Phi\left(\frac{\mu - G_u}{\sigma}\right) = 1 - \Phi\left(\frac{G_u - \mu}{\sigma}\right) \qquad (3.136\text{ b})$$

$$P(\mu) = \underbrace{\Phi\left(\frac{G_l - \mu}{\sigma}\right)}_{P_1(\mu)} + \underbrace{\Phi\left(\frac{\mu - G_u}{\sigma}\right)}_{P_2(\mu)}. \qquad (3.136\text{ c})$$

For a given lower specification limit G_l (i.e., case 1) we have the relationship $\Phi[(G_l - \mu)/\sigma] = P$. Figure 5.2/1 demonstrates that z_P, the standard normal percentile of order P, takes the value $(G_l - \mu)/\sigma$:

$$z_P = \frac{G_l - \mu}{\sigma}. \qquad (3.137\text{ a})$$

By the same argument, we get for the case 2

$$z_P = \frac{\mu - G_u}{\sigma}. \qquad (3.137\text{ b})$$

Solving (3.137) for μ and applying (2.55) yields the formula for $\mu = \mu(P)$:

Process mean μ as a function of the fraction defective P for given G_l or G_u

$$\mu(P) = G_l - z_P \cdot \sigma = G_l + z_{1-P} \cdot \sigma \qquad (3.138\text{ a})$$

$$\mu(P) = G_u + z_P \cdot \sigma = G_u - z_{1-P} \cdot \sigma. \qquad (3.138\text{ b})$$

We have seen that in the case of onesided specification limits, one cannot only calculate the fraction defective for given μ, but also determine the process mean for given fraction defective P.

Figure 3.3/2 illustrates the functional relationship (3.136a) between μ and P in two ways. In both parts of the figure we set $G_l = 5$ and $\sigma = 1$. This determines the formula for the fraction defective to be $P(\mu) = \Phi(5 - \mu)$. Figure 3.3/2a shows that, for varying μ, the corresponding values $P(\mu)$ can be represented by areas under the normal density function. For fixed lower specification limit G_l the fraction defective $P(\mu)$ is strictly monotone

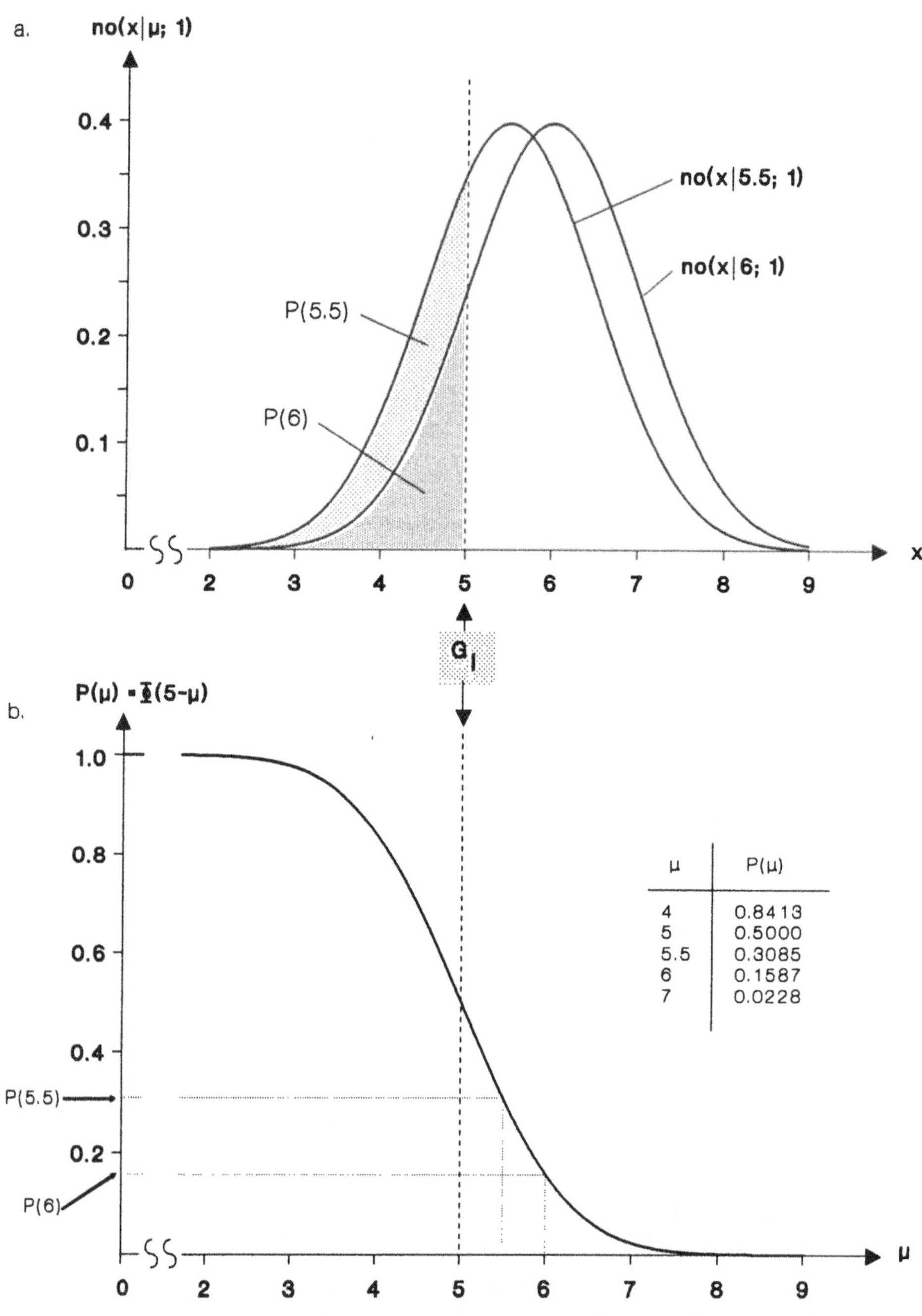

Figure 3.3/2: Fraction defective P as a function of μ in the case of given lower specification limit $G_l = 5$
(a) Values of the function $P(\mu)$ described by areas under the density
(b) Graph of the function $P(\mu)$

decreasing in μ. The latter property is illustrated by the curve of $P = P(\mu)$ in figure 3.3/2b. This curve results when cutting the 3D-graph in figure 3.3/1a by a plane erected in $\sigma = 1$. Accordingly the following figure 3.3/3b results from the graph in figure 3.3/1b by a cutting plane in $\sigma = 1$.

We can see that for given onesided lower specification limit the **minimal fraction defective** P^*

$$P^* := \min_{\mu} P(\mu) \tag{3.139}$$

is zero and is attained as $\mu \to \infty$:

Minimal fraction defective for given G_l

$$P^* = \lim_{\mu \to \infty} P(\mu) = \lim_{\mu \to \infty} \Phi\left(\frac{G_l - \mu}{\sigma}\right) = 0. \tag{3.140 a}$$

To derive this, take the derivative of $P(\mu)$ with respect to μ and evaluate it at zero (see problem 2.1/10c).

Analogous to figure 3.3/2a, one can illustrate the relationship (3.136b) by drawing the upper specification limit instead of the lower limit into the same figures and shading the respective areas under the densities to the right of G_u. For example, setting $G_u = 8$ results in $P(5.5) \approx 0.062$ and $P(6) \approx 0.0228$. For given upper specification limit the function $P(\mu)$ is strictly decreasing as μ decreases. The minimal value P^* is now attained as $\mu \to -\infty$ and is zero, as before:

Minimal fraction defective for given G_u

$$P^* = \lim_{\mu \to -\infty} P(\mu) = \lim_{\mu \to -\infty} \Phi\left(\frac{\mu - G_u}{\sigma}\right) = 0. \tag{3.140 b}$$

The relationship (3.136c) for given upper and lower limits can also be illustrated. Figure 3.3/3 gives the example of $G_l = 5$, $G_u = 8$ and $\sigma = 1$ (also see figure 6.1/3).

For a given interval $[G_l, G_u]$ the fraction defective function $P(\mu)$ consists of the two terms $P_1(\mu) := \Phi[(G_l - \mu)/\sigma]$ and $P_2(\mu) := \Phi[(\mu - G_u)/\sigma]$. The first term $P_1(\mu)$ contributes the proportion of units with quality characteristic below the lower specification limit G_l and $P_2(\mu)$ represents the proportion of units with characteristics exceeding the upper specification limit G_u. As $\mu \to \pm\infty$, the function $P(\mu)$ converges to 1, since in either case one of the components $P_1(\mu)$ and $P_2(\mu)$ converges to one and the other to zero. The minimal fraction defective is non-zero and is attained at the midpoint of the interval (the proof is the same as in problem 2.1/10c):

Minimal fraction defective for given $[G_l, G_u]$

$$P^* = P(\mu^*) = 2 \cdot \Phi\left(\frac{G_l - G_u}{2\sigma}\right) = 2 \cdot \left[1 - \Phi\left(\frac{G_u - G_l}{2\sigma}\right)\right] \tag{3.141 a}$$

$$\mu^* = \frac{G_u - G_l}{2} =: G_m. \tag{3.141 b}$$

The minimal fraction defective P^* only depends on the ratio of the length of the specification interval $[G_l, G_u]$ and the variance σ^2 of the manufacturing process. If this interval is larger than 8σ then, as a rule, the minimal fraction defective P^* is negligibly small; it is smaller than $\Phi(-4) \approx 0.00006$. Thus, in the case of $G_u - G_l > 8\sigma$ the calculation of $P(\mu)$ for $\mu \neq \mu^*$ also becomes simpler, since the smaller of the two terms $P_1(\mu)$ and $P_2(\mu)$ can be neglected.

Symmetry of $P(\mu)$ for given $[G_l, G_u]$

The second part of figure 3.3/3 shows that $P(\mu)$ is symmetric with respect to $\mu = \mu^*$. This symmetry implies that if two expected values μ_1 and μ_2 have the same distance $d = |\mu - \mu^*|$ to the point μ^*, the corresponding processes have the same fraction defective. Formally, this can be shown by (3.136c) and (3.141b):

$$\begin{aligned} P(\mu^* - d) &= \Phi\left(\frac{G_l - G_u - 2d}{2\sigma}\right) + \Phi\left(\frac{G_l - G_u + 2d}{2\sigma}\right) \\ &= \Phi\left(\frac{-\mu^* - d}{\sigma}\right) + \Phi\left(\frac{-\mu^* + d}{\sigma}\right) \qquad (3.142) \\ &= P(\mu^* + d). \end{aligned}$$

In the case of a given specification interval $[G_l, G_u]$, every fraction defective $P > P^*$ corresponds to an infinite number of expected values of μ and, consequently, the function $P(\mu)$ cannot have an inverse. The expectation μ is uniquely defined only if either $P_1(\mu)$ or $P_2(\mu)$ is specified (see problem 3.3/2).

Summary

The preceding discussion concluded that under the assumption that the quality characteristic X of a lot is approximately normally distributed with constant σ^2, the quality of the lot is described by the fraction defective as well as the manufacturing process mean. If a onesided specification limit is given the relationship between P and μ is invertible, i.e., P and μ are equivalent characterizations of the process. However, in the case of a specification interval with upper and lower limits the relationship between P and μ is no longer uniquely invertible. We want to note that, in practice, the quality of the lot is described by the fraction defective P rather than the process mean μ.

In the case of a tolerance interval with onesided specification limits the producer only has to comply with one limit G_l or G_u and, hence, he could achieve any fraction defective P by simply increasing or decreasing the process mean μ sufficiently (for given G_l see figure 3.3/2). In practice, this would usually involve unreasonably high production costs. If the producer has to comply with upper and lower specification limits, then he has far less control. For a given constant production variance σ^2 he cannot achieve a fraction defective below the minimal value $P^* = 2 \cdot \Phi[(G_l - G_u)/\sigma] > 0$,

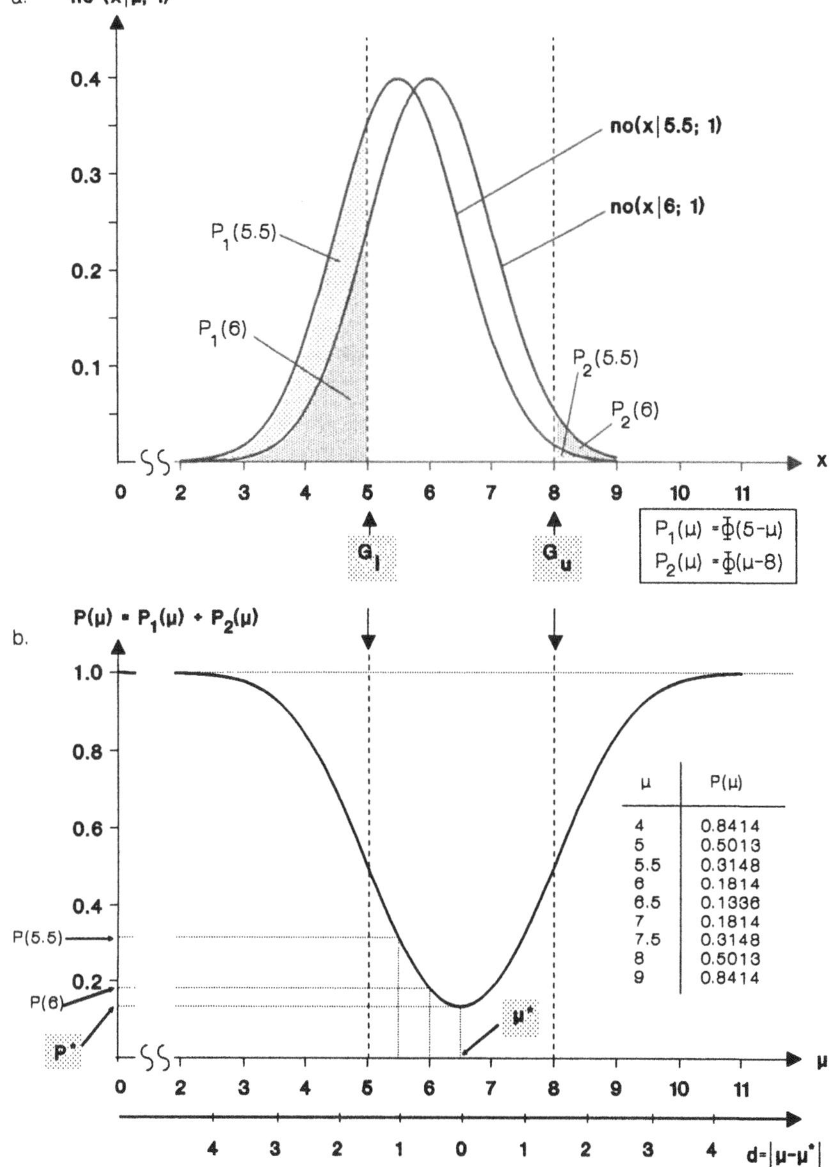

μ	P(μ)
4	0.8414
5	0.5013
5.5	0.3148
6	0.1814
6.5	0.1336
7	0.1814
7.5	0.3148
8	0.5013
9	0.8414

Figure 3.3/3: Fraction defective P as a function of μ in the case of given specification limits $G_l = 5$ and $G_u = 8$
(a) Fraction defective $P(\mu)$ described by areas under the density curve
(b) Graph of the function $P(\mu)$

given by (3.141a). If the acceptable quality limit AQL is below P^* the producer will not be able to produce lots with quality $P < AQL$. He is then uncapable to meet the quality specifications. **Process capability studies** have gained increasing importance in process control. For a "capable" production process, sampling plans are actually superfluous. At the other extreme, if one chooses $AQL = P^*$ then the producer is forced to keep the process mean μ exactly at the mid point $\mu^* = (G_l + G_u)/2$ of the tolerance region, unless he wants to risk many rejected lots. Since it is very difficult to fix the process mean at a single point in practice, one usually has to choose an acceptable quality limit well above the minimal fraction defective, e.g., $AQL = 2 \cdot P^*$.

Problem 3.3/1

A manufacturing process produces units with a $no(\mu, 1)$-distributed quality characteristic X. Suppose the upper specification limit is $G_u = 5$.

a) What is the relationship between μ and P? Sketch the graph of $P = P(\mu)$.

b) What are the resulting fractions defective $P(\mu)$ if the process mean μ takes the values 3, 4, 4.5, 5, 5.5, 6, 7 and 8?

Problem 3.3/2

The tolerance interval of a production process with $no(\mu, 4)$-distributed quality characteristic is given by [6,12].

a) Find the minimal fraction defective P^* and the corresponding process mean μ^*?

b) Suppose we require the fraction defective to be $P = 0.2$ and the side conditions that both components $P_1(\mu)$ and $P_2(\mu)$ of (3.136c) have the same value 0.1. What value of the process mean μ satisfies this condition?

c) What is the result of (b) if one requires $P_1(\mu) = 0.05$?

d) Answer the same question for $P_1(\mu) = 0.12$. Also find the solutions for μ without the side condition.

3.3.2 Sampling Plans for a Single Specification Limit and Known Variance

As explained before, a quality characteristic is either an attribute or a variable. In ***sampling by attributes*** of a measurable quality characteristic one only records whether the value of an inspected item is below or above a specification limit. One way of doing this is to compare it to a template. If the realization x of the characteristic is outside the tolerance range the unit is classified nonconforming or defective (see table 3.3/1). The exact value of x is not significant in this approach and does not necessarily have to be measured. In *sampling by variables* one takes a measurement of every unit and feeds this datum into the test statistic. Since variable sampling makes use of the exact measurement instead of a dichotomous characteristic, and in this way takes better advantage of the available information, one would expect that it will require smaller sample sizes than attribute sampling.

Differences between sampling by attributes and by variables

In the following, we will explain the concepts of sampling by variables, present methods to evaluate such plans and describe the construction of "optimal" procedures. We need to distinguish between the cases of known and unknown variance and also of one and two specification limits. If the variance σ^2 of the quality characteristic is unknown it has to be estimated from the sample. We will first present the simplest case of known variance and one specification limit. In all the situations presented the decision is either based on the sample mean $\bar{X}_n$ or – with no effect on the operating characteristic – on three other test statistics that depend on $\bar{X}_n$.

a) Procedure and Introduction of Appropriate Test Statistics

Suppose the quality characteristics $X_1, \ldots, X_N$ of the units in a lot are identically $no(\mu, \sigma^2)$-distributed. To administer a **single-sampling plan by variables** one draws a sample of size n and takes a measurement to determine the realization $\mathbf{x} = (x_1, \ldots, x_n)$ of the sample vector $\mathbf{X} = (X_1, \ldots, X_n)$ and also the realization $g(\mathbf{x})$ of the **test statistic** $g(\mathbf{X})$. If $g(\mathbf{x})$ falls in a specified acceptance region $\overline{CR}$ the lot is accepted, otherwise, it is rejected. Analogous to figure 3.2/1, the procedure can be described by the structural chart given in figure 3.3/4.

Procedure of a single-sampling plan by variables

The numerical register Z is set to zero at the beginning of the procedure and keeps track of the measurements that are obtained from the sample units. At the end, the value of the test statistic is obtained from these data. The variable i is the index of the sample units and takes the values 1 to n.

Applying a single-sampling plan by variables is equivalent to performing a hypothesis test of type (2.138). In the case of a given lower specification limit G_l the test (2.138) takes the form

$$\begin{aligned} H_0 &: \mu \geq \mu_0 \\ H_1 &: \mu < \mu_0 \end{aligned} \tag{3.143}$$

where the particular "critical" process parameter μ_0 is not explicitly specified. The sample size of the hypothesis test is n. The test statistic and its

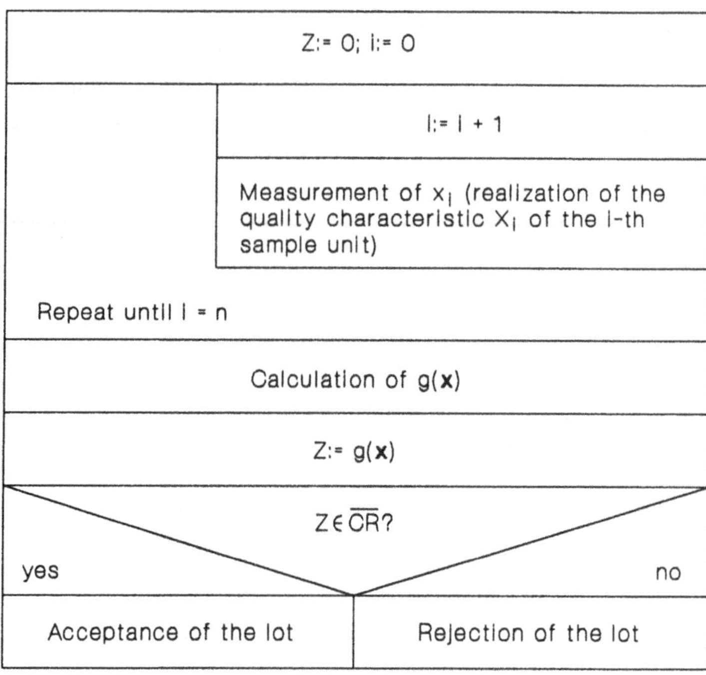

Figure 3.3/4: Structural chart of a single-sampling plan for variables

corresponding acceptance and rejection region can be specified in various ways. The most natural test statistic is the sample mean

$$\bar{X}_n := \frac{1}{n}\sum_{i=1}^{n} X_i .$$

Since $X_i \sim no(\mu, \sigma^2)$ the sample mean is normally distributed. In the typical case of sampling *without* replacement its variance is given by (2.77b). We will assume that the sample size is small compared to the lot size, say in the range $n \leq 0.1N$. Then the exact expression (2.77b) for the variance can be approximated by the variance (2.77a) of the case of sampling *with* replacement. The approximate distribution of the sample mean is found to be

Assumptions:

- sample size is small compared to the lot size

$$\bar{X}_n \sim no\left(\mu; \frac{\sigma^2}{n}\right).$$

By (2.47) the standardized variable

$$Z := \frac{\bar{X}_n - \mu}{\sigma} \cdot \sqrt{n} \tag{3.144}$$

has a standard normal distribution. Here the variance of the process is assumed to be known (for the case of unknown variance see section 3.3.3). The construction and evaluation of the sampling plan are very straightforward. We are assuming that only one specification limit is given and, without loss of generality, that it is the lower limit G_l. The change to the situation of specified upper limit G_u is no problem. At the end of this section we will give a summary of the results for the different cases.

- process variance known

- only one specification limit

By (2.72), the sample statistic $\bar{X}_n$ is an unbiased estimator of the unknown process mean μ. A large realization of $\bar{X}_n$ is seen as evidence of a large process mean μ and, consequently in the case of working with a lower specification limit G_l as evidence of a small fraction defective in the lot. Thus for sufficiently large $\bar{X}_n$, we will assume that the fraction defective in the lot is small and consequently accept the lot. If the process mean μ is equal to G_l the resulting fraction defective $P = P(G_l)$ is 0.5 (see figure 3.3/2b). In order to avoid such a large fraction defective one needs to require $\bar{X}_n > G_l$. The actual requirement is much stronger. One requires that $\bar{X}_n$ is not smaller than an **acceptance limit** $G_l + k\sigma$, i.e.,

Test statistic is the sample mean.

$$\bar{X}_n \geq G_l + k \cdot \sigma, \tag{3.145}$$

where $k > 0$ is a real-valued **acceptance factor**. From now on an acceptance sampling plan by variables with given parameters n and k will be denoted as a plan $(n; k)$. The rejection and acceptance region of the underlying hypothesis test (2.138) for this situation of specified lower specification limit and test statistic $\bar{X}_n$ are given by $CR = (-\infty, G_l + k\sigma)$ and $\overline{CR} = [G_l + k\sigma, \infty)$. In section 3.3.2b we will derive the OC function of a given plan $(n; k)$ (*descriptive* approach), while in section 3.3.2c we will discuss how to determine a plan for a given OC function (*constructive* approach).

Notation of single-sampling plans by variables

In (3.145) the sample mean is directly used as a decision variable. Through a suitable transformation of (3.145) one can obtain the lower specification limit G_l as the acceptance limit. By (3.145) we have

Alternative test statistics

$$\bar{X}_n - k\sigma \geq G_l, \tag{3.146}$$

and one can define

$$Z_n := \bar{X}_n - k\sigma. \tag{3.147}$$

The acceptance limit of this new test statistic is exactly G_l. Z_n is called the **type I test statistic**. Its acceptance region is $\overline{CR} = [G_l, \infty)$.

Another possibility is to use a test statistic with the acceptance factor k as its acceptance limit. By (3.145) it follows immediately that

$$\frac{\bar{X}_n - G_l}{\sigma} \geq k, \tag{3.148}$$

and we define

$$Q_n := \frac{\bar{X}_n - G_l}{\sigma} \tag{3.149}$$

to be the **type II test statistic** or **quality index**. The acceptance region of (3.149) is $\overline{CR} = [k, \infty)$. It has the name quality index because, by

$$\hat{P}_n := 1 - \Phi\left(Q_n \cdot \sqrt{\frac{n}{n-1}}\right) \tag{3.150}$$

the variable Q_n can be used directly to obtain an unbiased estimate of the unknown fraction defective in the lot (refer to LIEBERMANN/RESNIKOFF 1955). Since the relationship between $\hat{P}_n$ and Q_n is uniquely determined and invertible one can use equivalently the test statistic (3.150) instead of (3.149). $\hat{P}_n$ is called the **type III test statistic** and its acceptance region is $\overline{CR} = [0, M_n]$ with

$$M_n := 1 - \Phi\left(k \cdot \sqrt{\frac{n}{n-1}}\right). \tag{3.151}$$

The acceptance limit M_n can be interpreted as the upper acceptable limit for the fraction defective in the sample.

k-method: test statistic II is used

M-method: test statistic III is used

Besides the sample mean $\bar{X}_n$, we just introduced three alternative test statistics Z_n, Q_n and $\hat{P}_n$ with their different acceptance and rejection regions for the test (3.143). Since the critical value of the test statistic Q_n is k its application is also called the **k-method**. In the same way we use the term **M-method** for a plan $(n; k)$ with test statistic $\hat{P}_n$ (see MONTGOMERY 1991, p.631). Since the application of each of the four statistics yields the same decision, one can choose the one that is most convenient in a particular situation (see problem 3.3/3). For a given sample the decision to accept or reject the lot depends only on the plan parameters n and k. The OC function also depends only on these parameters and not on the choice of test statistic. The advantage of the M-method is that it transforms the statistic $\bar{X}_n$ into an estimate of the fraction defective in the lot.

The following table lists all four approaches of sampling plans for variables and also presents the results for the case of a single *upper* specification limit G_u.

		$\overline{X}_n$	Type I: Z_n	Type II: Q_n	Type III: $\widehat{P}_n$
G_l	Definition of test statistic	$\overline{X}_n = \frac{1}{n}\sum_{i=1}^{n} X_i$	$Z_n = \overline{X}_n - k \cdot \sigma$	$Q_n = \frac{\overline{X}_n - G_l}{\sigma}$	$\widehat{P}_n = 1 - \Phi\left(Q_n\sqrt{\frac{n}{n-1}}\right)$
	Acceptance of the lot if	$\overline{X}_n \geq G_l + k \cdot \sigma$	$Z_n \geq G_l$	$Q_n \geq k$	$\widehat{P}_n \leq M_n = 1 - \Phi\left(k\sqrt{\frac{n}{n-1}}\right)$
	Rejection of the lot if	$\overline{X}_n < G_l + k \cdot \sigma$	$Z_n < G_l$	$Q_n < k$	$\widehat{P}_n > M_n$
G_u	Definition of test statistic	$\overline{X}_n = \frac{1}{n}\sum_{i=1}^{n} X_i$	$Z_n = \overline{X}_n + k \cdot \sigma$	$Q_n = \frac{G_u - \overline{X}_n}{\sigma}$	$\widehat{P}_n = 1 - \Phi\left(Q_n\sqrt{\frac{n}{n-1}}\right)$
	Acceptance of the lot if	$\overline{X}_n \leq G_u - k \cdot \sigma$	$Z \leq G_u$	$Q_n \geq k$	$\widehat{P}_n \leq M_n = 1 - \Phi\left(k\sqrt{\frac{n}{n-1}}\right)$
	Rejection of the lot if	$\overline{X}_n > G_u - k \cdot \sigma$	$Z > G_u$	$Q_n < k$	$\widehat{P}_n > M_n$

Table 3.3/2: Alternative test statistics for acceptance sampling by variables in the case of a single specification limit and known variance

Problem 3.3/3

For the series production of a product with a $no(\mu, \sigma^2)$-distributed quality characteristic X the lower specification limit is $G_l = 10$ [mm]. Acceptance control monitors the compliance with this requirement through applying a single-sampling plan $(n; k)$ with $n = 10$ and $k = 2$. The drawing of a sample of size $n = 10$ produced the sample average $\bar{x}_{10} = 10.9$ [mm]. Show that the lot is rejected for all four approaches with the respective test statistics $\bar{X}_n, Z_n, Q_n$ and $\hat{P}_n$.

Problem 3.3/4

When applying the test statistic Q_n the lot is accepted if $Q_n \geq k$ and in the case of the test statistic $\hat{P}_n$ for $\hat{P}_n \leq M_n$, where M_n is given by (3.151). Prove that the two conditions $\hat{P}_n \leq M_n$ and $Q_n \geq k$ are equivalent.

b) OC Functions and Measures of Performance

We already stated that, in the case of a $no(\mu, \sigma^2)$-distributed quality characteristic X, the quality of the lot can be determined equivalently by the fraction defective P as well as by the process mean μ. If one wants to charactericterize a single-sampling plan for variables by the OC function of the underlying hypothesis test then one can choose the argument of the

OC function to be either P or μ. We will denote these two functions by $L_1(\mu)$ and $L_2(P)$:

$$\begin{aligned} L_1(\mu) &:= Pr(\text{ test statistic} \in \overline{CR}_1|\mu) \\ L_2(P) &:= Pr(\text{ test statistic} \in \overline{CR}_2|P). \end{aligned}$$

In practice one usually works with $L_2(P)$, i.e., in a plan $(n; k)$ one specifies the probability of acceptance for the lot depending on the fraction defective P.

Assumptions:

- known process variance

- single specification limit

We will now derive both versions of the operating characteristic for the plan $(n; k)$. Assume as before that the process variance σ^2 is known and that we have a single *lower* specification limit G_l. The analogous formulae for the case of a single upper specification limit will be given in table 3.3/3 at the end of this section.

Recall that the decision to reject or accept a lot and the OC function (3.143) are determined by the sample data and the parameters n and k, and are independent of the choice of one of the four previously discussed test statistics $\bar{X}_n, Z_n, Q_n$ and $\hat{P}_n$. Thus we can derive $L_1(\mu)$ and $L_2(P)$ for the case of the statistic $\bar{X}_n$ without loss of generality. By the acceptance condition (3.145) and by (3.144), the **OC function with argument** μ is found to be

$$\begin{aligned} L_1(\mu) &= Pr(\bar{X}_n \geq G_l + k\sigma|\mu) \\ &= Pr\left(Z \geq \frac{G_l + k\sigma - \mu}{\sigma}\sqrt{n} \mid \mu\right) \\ &= 1 - \Phi\left[\sqrt{n}\left(\frac{G_l - \mu}{\sigma} + k\right)\right], \end{aligned}$$

OC function with argument μ

and as a result of (2.51)

$$L_1(\mu) = \Phi\left[\sqrt{n}\left(\frac{\mu - G_l}{\sigma} - k\right)\right]. \tag{3.152}$$

Figure 3.3/5 shows two ways of illustrating the relationship (3.152) between the process mean μ and the acceptance probability $L_1(\mu)$. As in figure 3.3/2, we specified $G_l = 5$ and $\sigma = 1$ and the plan parameters are assumed to be $n = 25$ and $k = 0.2$. It follows that $\bar{X}_{25} \sim no(\mu; 0.04)$. Part (a) of the figure represents the acceptance probabilities $L_1(\mu)$ by areas under the density of $\bar{X}_{25}$. Obviously for a fixed lower specification limit the acceptance probability is strictly monotone increasing in μ. The OC curve $L_1(\mu)$ in part (b) of the figure also shows this very clearly. Here the formula of the OC function is $L_1(\mu) = \Phi[5(\mu - 5.2)]$.

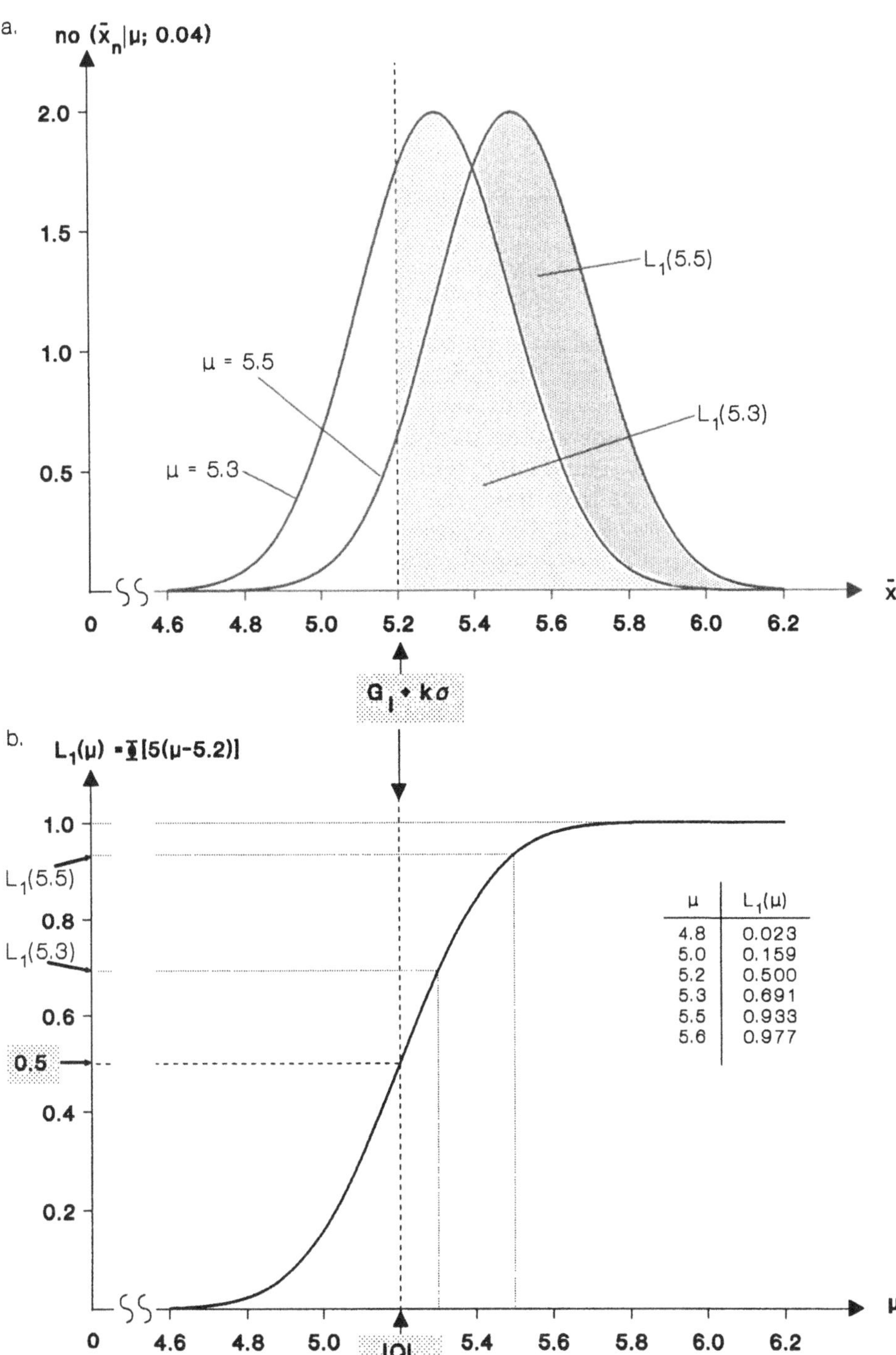

μ	$L_1(\mu)$
4.8	0.023
5.0	0.159
5.2	0.500
5.3	0.691
5.5	0.933
5.6	0.977

Figure 3.3/5: OC function $L_1(\mu)$ of the plan (25;0.2) in the case of a given lower specification limit $G_l = 5$
(a) OC function $L_1(\mu)$ described by areas under the density curve
(b) Graph of the OC function $L_1(\mu)$

The **OC function with argument** P is obtained directly from (3.152) if one defines

$$L_2(P) := L_1[\mu(P)]. \qquad (3.153\text{ a})$$

By (3.138a) we get

$$L_2(P) = L_1(G_l + z_{1-P} \cdot \sigma), \qquad (3.153\text{ b})$$

OC function with argument P

and, because of (3.152)

$$L_2(P) = \Phi\left[\sqrt{n}(z_{1-P} - k)\right]. \qquad (3.154)$$

For a plan $(n;k)$ and given process quality P the acceptance probability $L_2(P)$ is found by first determining the percentile z_{1-P} using table 5.2/1 and then the argument in the square brackets of $\Phi[..]$ in (3.154). For this argument $L_2(P)$ is finally obtained from table 5.1/1.

Figure 3.3/6 contains the graph of $L_2(P) = \Phi[5(z_{1-P} - 0.2)]$ that is derived by (3.153) from the previously introduced OC function $L_1(\mu) = \Phi[5(\mu - 5.2)]$. For a given lower specification limit the two parameters μ and P are related by a non-linear strictly monotone *decreasing* transformation. As μ increases P decreases and vice versa. Since $L_1(\mu) = \Phi[5(\mu - 5.2)]$ in figure 3.3/5b is strictly monotone increasing it follows that P is necessarily strictly monotone decreasing. In figure 3.3/6 below, $L_2(P)$ is plotted against the P-axis, but for comparison the corresponding scale of μ is also given. For given P the corresponding μ value is obtained by (3.138a) and in the case of $G_l = 5$ and $\sigma^2 = 1$, the equation is $\mu = 5 + z_{1-P}$.

Definition and calculation of OC percentiles

Analogous to (3.33) we call the quality level μ_ω, or the respective fraction defective P_ω, that correspond to an acceptance probability of exactly ω the **OC percentile** of order ω. We can verify through (3.152) and figure 5.2/1 that

$$L_1(\mu_\omega) = \omega \Leftrightarrow z_\omega = \sqrt{n} \cdot \left(\frac{\mu_\omega - G_l}{\sigma} - k\right).$$

Solving for μ_ω on the right side yields

$$\mu_\omega = G_l + \left(\frac{z_\omega}{\sqrt{n}} + k\right) \cdot \sigma. \qquad (3.155\text{ a})$$

The OC percentile P_ω defined by $L_2(P_\omega) = \omega$ is obtained by substituting μ_ω into (3.136a):

$$P_\omega = \Phi\left(\frac{G_l - \mu_\omega}{\sigma}\right) = \Phi\left(-\frac{z_\omega}{\sqrt{n}} - k\right) = \Phi\left(\frac{z_{1-\omega}}{\sqrt{n}} - k\right). \qquad (3.155\text{ b})$$

The average outgoing quality (AOQ) and average total inspection (ATI, AFI) of a single-sampling plan for variables will not be presented. These

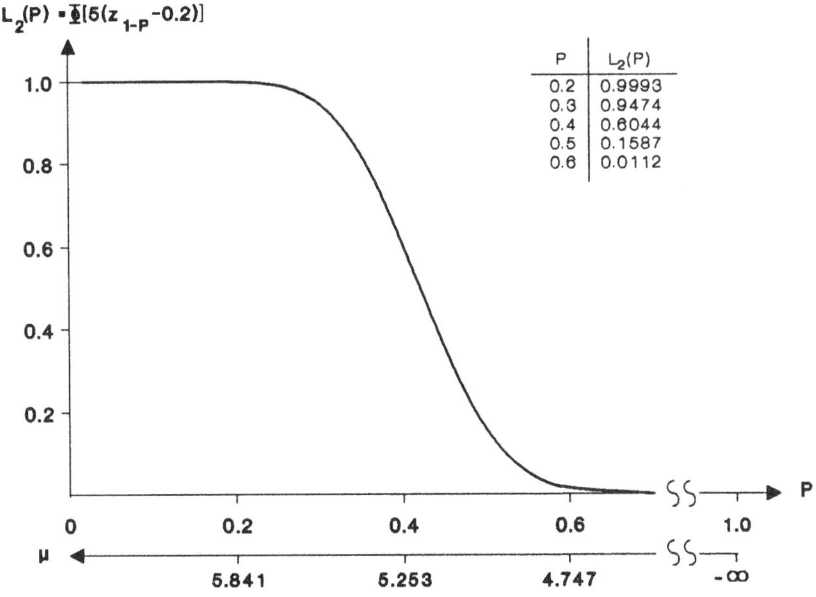

Figure 3.3/6: OC function $L_2(P)$ of the plan (25;0.2) in the case of a given lower specification limit $G_l = 5$

Measuring the performance of a single-sampling plan for variables

measures can also be given as functions of either P or μ. For example, the functions with argument P result from substituting the second form $L_2(P)$ of (3.154) for the OC function $L(P)$ in table 3.2/5 and table 3.2/8.

The following table 3.3/3 presents the OC functions $L_1(\mu)$ and $L_2(P)$ and their corresponding OC percentiles. The table also gives formulae for the case of a single *upper* specification limit G_u. Note that the OC function $L_2(P)$ and its percentiles are the same for a lower and an upper limit.

	Specification of a single lower limit G_l	Specification of a single upper limit G_u
OC function with argument μ and corresponding OC percentile	$L_1(\mu) = \Phi\left[\sqrt{n}\left(\frac{\mu - G_l}{\sigma} - k\right)\right]$ $\mu_\omega = G_l + \left(\frac{z_\omega}{\sqrt{n}} + k\right)\sigma$	$L_1(\mu) = \Phi\left[\sqrt{n}\left(\frac{G_u - \mu}{\sigma} - k\right)\right]$ $\mu_\omega = G_u - \left(\frac{z_\omega}{\sqrt{n}} + k\right)\sigma$
OC function with argument P and corresponding OC percentile	$L_2(P) = \Phi\left[\sqrt{n}\,(z_{1-P} - k)\right]$ $P_\omega = \Phi\left(\frac{z_{1-\omega}}{\sqrt{n}} - k\right)$	

Table 3.3/3: OC functions and OC percentiles for acceptance sampling by variables in the case of a given single specification limit and known variance

Problem 3.3/5

a) What is the effect of increasing the sample size n on the OC function of a sampling plan $(n; k)$? Use figure 3.3/5 to illustrate the effect and compare the result to that of sampling by attributes.

b) Answer the same question for the other sampling plan parameter k.

Problem 3.3/6

a) The underlying hypothesis test for a single sampling plan for variables with given lower specification limit is of type (3.143). Modify (3.143) for the case of an upper specification limit G_u.

b) A manufacturing process produces units with $no(\mu, 1)$-distributed quality characteristic X. We require the realizations x to lie below the upper specification limit $G_u = 5$. Sketch the graph of the OC function $L_1(\mu)$ for the plan (25, 0.2).

Problem 3.3/7

a) Calculate the IQL value of the OC function $L_1(\mu)$, i.e., the process mean $\mu = \mu_{0.5}$ with lot acceptance probability 0.5.

b) Also determine the IQL value of the OC function $L_2(P)$.

c) Designing Plans for a Specified Consumer's and Producer's Risk

We will now transfer the results about constructing single-sampling plans for attributes (section 3.2.3a) for two given points of the OC curve to the case of sampling by variables. As before, we will assume that the process variance σ^2 is known.

Suppose that, as in section 3.2.3a, we have specified the values AQL and RQL and the related producer's and consumer's risks α and β ($AQL < RQL; 1-\alpha > \beta$). We want to determine the parameters of a single-sampling plan for variables such that its OC function $L_2(P)$, introduced in (3.154), satisfies the conditions $L_2(AQL) = 1 - \alpha$ and $L_2(RQL) = \beta$. The following holds regardless of upper or lower specification limits, because the OC function $L_2(P)$ in table 3.3/3 turned out to be the same for both cases. Since the sample size is necessarily integer valued, the above conditions for $L_2(P)$ can only be approximately satisfied, i.e.,

$$L_2(AQL) = 1 - \alpha^* \tag{3.156 a}$$

$$L_2(RQL) = \beta^* \tag{3.156 b}$$

with $\alpha^* \approx \alpha$ and $\beta^* \approx \beta$. The risks α^* and β^* were called **effective producer's risk** and **effective consumer's risk** and the given probabilities α and β are denoted as **specified producer's risk** and **specified consumer's risk**. The requirements $\alpha^* \leq \alpha$ and $\beta^* \leq \beta$ will ensure that we are on the safe side:

$$L_2(AQL) \geq 1 - \alpha \tag{3.157 a}$$

$$L_2(RQL) \leq \beta. \tag{3.157 b}$$

As a result of (3.154), these inequalities are equivalent to

$$\Phi[\sqrt{n}(z_{1-AQL} - k)] \geq 1 - \alpha \tag{3.158 a}$$

$$\Phi[\sqrt{n}(z_{1-RQL} - k)] \leq \beta. \tag{3.158 b}$$

One can easily verify by means of figure 5.2/1 that the form

$$\sqrt{n}(z_{1-AQL} - k) \geq z_{1-\alpha} \tag{3.159 a}$$

$$\sqrt{n}(z_{1-RQL} - k) \leq z_\beta \tag{3.159 b}$$

is equivalent to (3.158). Solving for n and k and using the equality $z_\beta = -z_{1-\beta}$ yields the parameters of the desired plan:

Formulae for the calculation of the plan parameters in the case of known variance

$$n = \left(\frac{z_{1-\beta} + z_{1-\alpha}}{z_{1-AQL} - z_{1-RQL}}\right)^2 = \left(\frac{z_\beta + z_\alpha}{z_{AQL} - z_{RQL}}\right)^2, \tag{3.160 a}$$

$$k = \frac{z_{1-\beta}z_{1-AQL} + z_{1-\alpha}z_{1-RQL}}{z_{1-\alpha} + z_{1-\beta}} = -\frac{z_\beta z_{AQL} + z_\alpha z_{RQL}}{z_\alpha + z_\beta}. \tag{3.160 b}$$

The result (3.160a) for the sample size is always rounded to the next biggest integer. Note that the specified plan has minimum amount of inspection among all plans which fulfil the requirements (3.157).

Example 3.3/2

Suppose we want to construct a sampling plan $(n; k)$ for variables based on the requirements of $AQL = 0.05$ with $\alpha = 0.05$ and $RQL = 0.2$ with $\beta = 0.1$. In examples 3.2/11-12 we already determined such a plan for attribute acceptance sampling under various assumptions for the underlying distribution. In the case of a binomially distributed count variable the desired plan parameters were a sample size of $n = 38$ and an acceptance number of $c = 4$, and for the hypergeometric case we found $n = 29$ and $c = 3$.

The parameters n and k of the variable sampling plan are culculated by (3.160). Table 5.2/1 gives the required percentiles

$$z_{1-AQL} = z_{0.95} = 1.645 \qquad z_{1-\alpha} = z_{0.95} = 1.645$$
$$z_{1-RQL} = z_{0.80} = 0.841 \qquad z_{1-\beta} = z_{0.90} = 1.282.$$

Substituting into (3.160) gives

$$n = \left(\frac{1.282 + 1.645}{1.645 - 0.841}\right)^2 \approx 13.25, \qquad \text{that is } n = 14,$$

$$k = \frac{1.282 \cdot 1.645 + 1.645 \cdot 0.841}{1.645 + 1.282} \approx 1.1931.$$

According to (3.156) the effective producer's risk at $AQL = 0.05$ is

$$\alpha^* = 1 - L_2(0.05) = 1 - \Phi[\sqrt{14}(1.645 - 1.1931)] \approx 1 - \Phi(1.69)$$

and the effective consumer's risk at $RQL = 0.2$ is found to be

$$\beta^* = L_2(0.2) = \Phi[\sqrt{14}(0.841 - 1.1931)] \approx \Phi(-1.32).$$

Using table 5.2/1 we get the final result

$$\alpha^* \approx 1 - 0.9545 = 0.0455 < \alpha = 0.05$$
$$\beta^* \approx 0.0934 < \beta = 0.10.$$

Note that the effective risks of both the consumer and the producer for this resulting plan are below the specified limits α and β.

Comparison of the sample sizes of the approximately OC equivalent sampling plan for variables and attributes shows that the variable sampling plan significantly reduces the sample size and, as a result, the amount of inspection. In this example, the reduction is about 63.1% compared to the binomial case and about 51.7% for the hypergeometric case.

The OC function $L_2(P) = \Phi[\sqrt{14}(z_{1-P} - 1.1931)]$ of the plan (14;1.1931) is given in figure 3.3/7. In order to draw an additional scale for the process parameter μ we need to specify suitable values of σ and G_l or G_u. We have chosen $\sigma = 10$ and $G_u = 100$. According to (3.138b) for given P, the process mean μ is determined by $\mu = 100 + 10z_P$. Since μ and P are related in this case through a non-linear strictly monotone *increasing* transformation, μ and P change in the same way. The IQL value is given by $P_{0.5} = \Phi(-1.1931) \approx 0.1164$ on the P-axis and by $\mu_{0.5} = 88.069$ on the μ-axis (see problem 3.3/7).

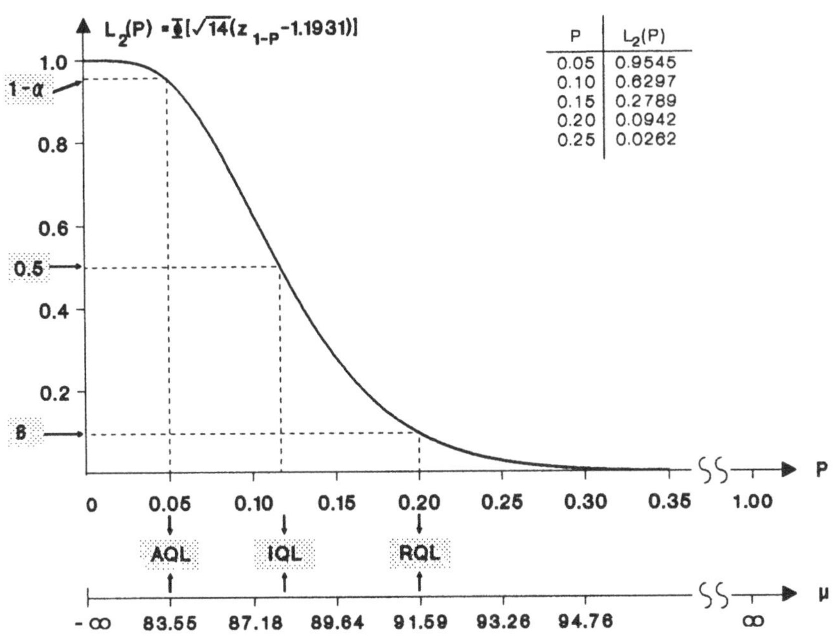

P	$L_2(P)$
0.05	0.9545
0.10	0.6297
0.15	0.2789
0.20	0.0942
0.25	0.0262

Figure 3.3/7: OC curve $L_2(P)$ for the plan (14;1.1931) for given upper specification limit $G_u = 100$

Problem 3.3/8

In the production of units with a $no(\mu, 0.25)$-distributed quality characteristic X a lower specification limit $G_l = 10$ is given. As before, the fulfillment of this requirement is monitored with a single-sampling plan for variables (10;2).

a) Determine the operating characteristic function with argument μ for this plan. What are the values of the OC function at $\mu = 10.8, 11$ and 11.2?

b) Calculate the OC percentiles $\mu_{0.05}, \mu_{0.5}$, and $\mu_{0.95}$.

c) Also find the OC function $L_2(P)$. What are its values at $P = 0.05, 0.1$ and 0.15?

d) Calculate the OC percentiles $P_{0.05}, P_{0.5}$, and $P_{0.95}$.

3.3.3 Sampling Plans for a Single Specification Limit and Unknown Variance

We will continue to assume that our quality characteristic of interest is $no(\mu, \sigma^2)$-distributed, but now we consider the case of unknown variance σ^2. Since the test statistics (3.147), (3.149) and (3.150), previously introduced, require the knowledge of the process standard variation $\sigma = \sqrt{\sigma^2}$ they can no longer be evaluated. We need to introduce new test statistics that only require an estimate $\hat{\sigma}$ of the unknown standard deviation σ. The following derivations are based mainly on a single *lower* specification limit G_l.

a) Introduction of Appropriate Test Statistics

The sample mean $\bar{X}_n$ gave an unbiased estimate of the process mean μ. In the case of unknown standard deviation σ one uses the sample data to obtain an estimate of the the standard deviation σ. We will use the previously introduced sample standard deviation (2.66-67) as an estimator of the standard deviation σ

$$\hat{\sigma} := S_n = \sqrt{\frac{1}{n-1}\sum_{i=1}^{n}(X_i - \bar{X}_n)^2}. \tag{3.161}$$

Analogous to (3.145), the acceptance condition in the case of a given lower specification limit is of form

$$\bar{X}_n \geq G_l + k \cdot S_n \tag{3.162}$$

with $k > 0$. Again the sample size n and the acceptance number k are the parameters of the sampling plan. Similar to section 3.3.2a, we can introduce alternative test statistics besides of $\bar{X}_n$. The **type I test statistic** with acceptance region $\overline{CR} = [G_l, \infty)$ previously introduced in (3.147) is now modified to

$$Z_n^* := \bar{X}_n - k \cdot S_n. \tag{3.163}$$

Analogous to (3.149), the **type II test statistic** with acceptance region $\overline{CR} = [k, \infty)$ is given by

$$Q_n^* := \frac{\bar{X}_n - G_l}{S_n}. \tag{3.164}$$

However, the formulae (3.150) and (3.151) of the **type III test statistic** cannot be transferred without major modifications. In the case of estimated process standard deviation, an unbiased estimator of the unknown lot quality P is found to be

$$\hat{P}_n^* := 1 - \Phi\left(Q_n^* \sqrt{\frac{2n-1}{2n - Q_n^{*2}}}\right). \tag{3.165}$$

The acceptance region of this test statistic is determined by $[0; M_n^*]$ with

$$M_n^* := 1 - \Phi\left(k \cdot \sqrt{\frac{2n-1}{2n - z_{1-\alpha}^2}}\right), \tag{3.166}$$

where $1-\alpha$ denotes the acceptance probability for a lot with quality level $P = AQL$ and $z_{1-\alpha}$ is defined to be the corresponding percentile of the standard normal distribution.

Similar to table 3.3/2, the following table 3.3/4 summarizes the formulae for the four equivalent approaches to variable sampling in the case of unknown variance. It also gives the results for the case of a single *upper* specification limit:

		$\overline{X}_n$	Type I: Z_n^*	Type II: Q_n^*	Type III: $\widehat{P}_n^*$
G_l	Definition of test statistic	$\overline{X}_n = \frac{1}{n}\sum_{i=1}^{n} X_i$	$Z_n^* = \overline{X}_n - kS_n$	$Q_n^* = \frac{\overline{X}_n - G_l}{S_n}$	$\widehat{P}_n^* = 1 - \Phi\left(Q_n^* \sqrt{\frac{2n-1}{2n-(Q_n^*)^2}}\right)$
	Acceptance of the lot if	$\overline{X}_n \geq G_l + kS_n$	$Z_n^* \geq G_l$	$Q_n^* \geq k$	$\widehat{P}_n^* \leq M_n^* = 1 - \Phi\left(k \cdot \sqrt{\frac{2n-1}{2n-z_{1-\alpha}^2}}\right)$
	Rejection of the lot if	$\overline{X}_n < G_l + kS_n$	$Z_n^* < G_l$	$Q_n^* < k$	$\widehat{P}_n^* > M_n^*$
G_u	Definition of test statistic	$\overline{X}_n = \frac{1}{n}\sum_{i=1}^{n} X_i$	$Z_n^* = \overline{X}_n + kS_n$	$Q_n^* = \frac{G_u - \overline{X}_n}{S_n}$	$\widehat{P}_n^* = 1 - \Phi\left(Q_n^* \sqrt{\frac{2n-1}{2n-(Q_n^*)^2}}\right)$
	Acceptance of the lot if	$\overline{X}_n \leq G_u - kS_n$	$Z \leq G_u$	$Q_n^* \geq k$	$\widehat{P}_n^* \leq M_n^* = 1 - \Phi\left(k \cdot \sqrt{\frac{2n-1}{2n-z_{1-\alpha}^2}}\right)$
	Rejection of the lot if	$\overline{X}_n > G_u - kS_n$	$Z > G_u$	$Q_n^* < k$	$\widehat{P}_n^* > M_n^*$

Table 3.3/4: Alternative test statistics and alternative approaches to acceptance sampling by variables in the case of single specification limit and unknown variance

Remark

In some sampling systems for variables, i.e., the MIL-STD 414 and the ISO 3951, the process variation is not estimated by (3.161) but by the less accurate but easily calculated sample range R_n.

b) OC Functions and Designing Plans with Specified Consumer's and Producer's Risk

Assumptions:

- unknown process variance
- lower specification limit given

We want to derive the two OC functions, previously denoted by $L_1(\mu)$ and $L_2(P)$, for the case where the unknown process variance is estimated by the sample variance $\hat{\sigma}^2 = S_n^2$. As before, we will base the derivation on a single lower specification limit G_l.

The decision to accept or reject a lot depends only on the sampling plan parameters n and k and not on the choice of the test statistics of table 3.3/4. Consequently, we can derive the **OC function with argument** μ for the case of applying the test statistic $\bar{X}_n$ without loss of generality. We write

$$L_1(\mu) = Pr(\bar{X}_n \geq G_l + k\, S_n | \mu).$$

- sample size much smaller than lot size

We will also assume that the sample size is much smaller than the lot size, i.e., $n \leq 0.1N$. Then the test statistic $\bar{X}_n$ is approximately $no(\mu, \sigma^2/n)$-distributed. After elementary standardizing transformations we get

$$L_1(\mu) = Pr(Y_{n-1;\delta} \geq k\,\sqrt{n}|\mu) \tag{3.167 a}$$

Exact OC function with argument μ

with the random variable

$$Y_{n-1;\delta} := \frac{\dfrac{\sqrt{n}\,(\bar{X}_n - \mu)}{\sigma} + \dfrac{\sqrt{n}\,(\mu - G_l)}{\sigma}}{\dfrac{S_n}{\sigma}} = \frac{\sqrt{n}\,(\bar{X}_n - G_l)}{S_n}. \tag{3.167 b}$$

This variable has a non-central t distribution with non-centrality parameter

$$\delta = \frac{\sqrt{n}\,(\mu - G_l)}{\sigma}. \tag{3.167 c}$$

As a result of (3.137a), the parameter δ and the probability of the event $Y_{n-1;\delta} \geq k \cdot \sqrt{n}$ can also be expressed as functions of P. The **OC function with argument P** is determined by

Exact OC function with argument P

$$L_2(P) = Pr(Y_{n-1;\delta} \geq k \cdot \sqrt{n}|P). \tag{3.168 a}$$

For the non-centrality parameter with argument P we get the form

$$\delta = -z_P \cdot \sqrt{n}. \tag{3.168 b}$$

The exact evaluation of (3.168) involves using tables of the non-central t distribution and is fairly complicated. We will omit the description of this approach (see SCHILLING 1982, p. 244ff) and present instead a normal approximation for the OC function that gives good results for $n > 5$.

We will start to derive the normal approximation of the OC function (3.167a) from the equivalent form

Derivation of approximate OC functions

$$L_1(\mu) = Pr(\bar{X}_n - k \cdot S_n \geq G_l|\mu) = Pr(Z_n^* \geq G_l|\mu).$$

The test statistic Z_n^*, introduced in (3.163) is approximately normally distributed and it holds that

$$E(Z_n^*) \approx \mu - k\sigma$$

$$V(Z_n^*) \approx \frac{\sigma^2}{n}\left(1 + \frac{k^2}{2}\right).$$

Standardizing Z_n^* to Z according to (2.47) yields the approximation

$$\begin{aligned} L_1(\mu) &\approx Pr\left(Z \geq \frac{G_l - \mu + k\sigma}{\sigma\sqrt{1+k^2/2}} \cdot \sqrt{n}|\mu\right) \\ &= 1 - \Phi\left(\sqrt{n} \cdot \frac{G_l - \mu + k\sigma}{\sigma\sqrt{1+k^2/2}}\right) \\ &= \Phi\left(\sqrt{n} \cdot \frac{\mu - G_l - k\sigma}{\sigma\sqrt{1+k^2/2}}\right) \end{aligned}$$

for $L_1(\mu)$. We will denote the resulting **approximate OC function with argument** μ by

$$L_1^*(\mu) := \Phi\left(\sqrt{n} \cdot \frac{\mu - G_l - k\sigma}{\sigma\sqrt{1+k^2/2}}\right). \tag{3.169}$$

Observe its similarity to formula (3.152). However, we cannot apply this formula in practice since in this case the variance σ^2 is not known. Fortunately, the standard deviation in (3.169) can be easily eliminated. By (3.137a) and the fact that $z_P = -z_{1-P}$, we know that $\mu - G_l = z_{1-P} \cdot \sigma$. Solving for σ and substituting yields the normal approximation

$$L_2^*(P) := \Phi\left(\sqrt{n} \cdot \frac{z_{1-P} - k}{\sqrt{1+k^2/2}}\right) \tag{3.170}$$

of the OC function (3.168a), which we will call the **approximate OC function with argument P**. It is easily seen that, in the case of a single *upper* specification limit G_u, the OC function with argument P is also approximated by (3.170). Comparison of (3.170) and (3.154) shows that the formulae for the cases of known and unknown variances only differ by the factor $\sqrt{1+k^2/2}$ of the denominator.

In SQA literature (i.e., SCHILLING 1982, p. 243) the more exact approximation

$$L_2(P) \approx \Phi\left[(z_{1-P} - k)\sqrt{\frac{n}{1 + 0.5k^2 n/(n-1)}}\right] \tag{3.171}$$

is proposed instead of (3.170). Table 3.3/5 compares the exact values of the OC function $L_2(P)$ in column 2 to the approximate values according to (3.170) in column 3. We can see that, even for this small sample size of $n = 5$, the approximation (3.170) gives satisfactory results as long as the quality level is good. For $P > 0.05$ the approximations are less exact because of the effect of the asymmetry of the non-central t distribution.

P	$L_2(P)$	
	exact	approximate
(1)	(2)	(3)
0.001	0.995	0.996
0.0025	0.985	0.987
0.004	0.975	0.977
0.010	0.934	0.930
0.025	0.837	0.813
0.040	0.751	0.712
0.065	0.628	0.572
0.100	0.490	0.425
0.150	0.343	0.282
0.250	0.164	0.124

Table 3.3/5: Exact and approximate values of the OC function $L_2(P)$ for the plan (5;1.4)

Formula (3.170) can be used to construct a plan with an OC function $L_2(P)$ that approximately goes through the points $(AQL; 1-\alpha)$ and $(RQL; \beta)$. The parameters n and k of the desired plan are then determined by

$$k = \frac{z_{1-\beta} z_{1-AQL} + z_{1-\alpha} z_{1-RQL}}{z_{1-\alpha} + z_{1-\beta}} \tag{3.172 a}$$

$$n = \left(1 + \frac{k^2}{2}\right)\left(\frac{z_{1-\beta} + z_{1-\alpha}}{z_{1-AQL} - z_{1-RQL}}\right)^2. \tag{3.172 b}$$

The result of (3.172b) needs to be rounded to the next largest integer.

In order to compare the plan parameters (3.160) and (3.172) that arise in the case of known variance and unknown variance, we will denote the pair of parameters in the first case by $n = n_\sigma$ and $k = k_\sigma$, and in the second case, by $n = n_s$ and $k = k_s$. Analysis of the formulae shows that k_σ and k_s are equal and that the sample size n_s is larger than n_σ by a factor of $(1 + k_s^2/2)$.

Example 3.3/3

In this example we will consider a sampling plan for variables based on the requirements of $AQL = 0.05$ at $\alpha = 0.05$ and $RQL = 0.2$ at $\beta = 0.1$. The process variance is now assumed to be unknown.

The percentiles for (3.172a) were already given in example 3.3/2 and we get

$$k_s = \frac{1.282 \cdot 1.645 + 1.645 \cdot 0.841}{1.645 + 1.282} \approx 1.1931.$$

By (3.172b) we find that

$$n_s = \left(1 + \frac{1.1931^2}{2}\right)\left(\frac{1.282 + 1.645}{1.645 - 0.841}\right)^2 \approx 22.69,$$

i.e., the sample size is $n_s = 23$, compared to $n_\sigma = 14$ in example 3.3/2. Thus the sample size of this OC equivalent plan is about 64% higher.

Problem 3.3/9

Analogous to (3.155b), find formulae for calculating the OC percentiles μ_ω and P_ω of the approximate OC functions (3.169) and (3.170).

Problem 3.3/10

Suppose the plan in problem 3.3/8 is one for the case of unknown variance. The parameters are now $n_s = 10$ and $k_s = 2$.

a) What are the values of the approximate OC function (3.170) at the points $P = 0.05, 0.1$ and 0.15?
b) Find the values of the approximate OC percentiles $P_{0.05}, P_{0.1}$, and $P_{0.15}$.
c) Compare the graphs of the OC function $L_2(P)$ for the cases of known and unknown variance and state a general conclusion.

3.3.4 Sampling Plans with Double Specification Limits

Until now the presentation has dealt only with the case of variable sampling plans for $no(\mu, \sigma^2)$-distributed quality characteristics with a single lower or upper specification limit G_l or G_u. If the quality characteristic is required to be within two specification limits G_l and G_u, the formula (3.136c) for the fraction defective $P = P(\mu)$ was shown to be the sum of the two terms $P_1(\mu) = \Phi[(G_l - \mu)/\sigma]$ and $P_2(\mu) = \Phi[(\mu - G_u)/\sigma]$. $P_1(\mu)$ represents the contribution of units with characteristic values below the lower specification limit to the fraction defective $P(\mu)$ and $P_2(\mu)$ represents the contribution of units with values above the upper specification limit.

Case 1: $G_u - G_l > 6\sigma$

Let us first consider the case when the length of the tolerance interval $[G_l, G_u]$ exceeds 6σ. Then the smaller of the two components $P_1(\mu)$ and $P_2(\mu)$ can be neglected. If the fraction defective is too high, then this either means that the process mean μ is shifted too far to the right or too far to the left of the midpoint $\mu^* = (G_l + G_u)/2$ of the tolerance interval. Consequently, we can go back to the sampling plans for a single specification limit. Thus, for the test statistic $\bar{X}_n$, the lot is rejected if either $\bar{X}_n < G_l + k\sigma$ or $\bar{X}_n > G_u - k\sigma$. For test statistics other than $\bar{X}_n$, equivalent conditions can be easily formulated (see again tables 3.3/2 and 3.3/4). The construction of plans for given two-sided specifications is approached in the same way as for plans with single specification limits, i.e., in the case of known variance as described in section 3.3.2 and, in the case of unknown process variance, as in section 3.3.3.

Case 2: $G_u - G_l \leq 6\sigma$

In the case of $G_u - G_l \leq 6\sigma$ one applies the M-method and a test statistic analogous to (3.150). We will omit the presentation of this statistic and its corresponding OC function. The description of the procedure and the necessary tables can be found in the sampling systems MIL-STD 414 or ISO 3951, and also in textbooks like SCHILLING (1982) or SCHINDOWSKI/SCHÜTZ (1965).

Remark

In the context of sampling by variables there are many possibilities for extensions and special problems similar to those discussed for attribute sampling plans. A presentation of **double-sampling plans for variables** can be found in SCHILLING (1982, p. 260ff), for example. GRAF/HENNIG/STANGE/WILRICH (1987, sec. 11.6) present the subject of **sequential sampling for variables**. In German SQA literature, **minimal cost plans** for variables are discussed by MÄDER (1986), SCHRÖDER (1985), STANGE (1964) and UHLMANN (1982, p. 196ff).

3.3.5 Comparison of Acceptance Sampling by Variables and by Attributes

In general, it is possible to apply attribute sampling procedures to variable quality characteristics. For example, a series of measurements can be reduced to an attribute data set by only recording if the values are within specified limits or not, but clearly one is not taking advantage of the full amount of available information. Thus, if the quality characeristic is a variable, one can apply both attribute and variable procedures. The best choice will depend on the particular situation, since both approaches have their advantages and disadvantages.

Acceptance sampling by variables has the following advantages over attribute procedures:

Advantages of sampling by variables

- For an equivalent OC function, i.e., with the same discriminatory power, variable plans have a significantly lower sample size. This is an important economic advantage, especially in the case of expensive or destructive inspection.
- With measurement data it is much easier to draw inference on the stability of the production process, and to detect trends and disturbances, than with count data.
- In sampling by variables one gets a much clearer picture of the exact location of individual measurements within the tolerance interval. One also has a much better chance of detecting outliers among the data.

Compared to attribute plans acceptance sampling by variables has the following disadvantages:

Disadvantages of sampling by variables

- The validity of the decisions based on measurements depends on the validity of the assumption that the quality characteristic is at least approximately normally distributed. The type III test statistic (M-method) is most sensitive to deviations from this assumption. This is especially true if the quality of the lot is close to the specification limits G_l or G_u.
- In the case of acceptance control for several quality characteristics, univariate variable sampling requires a separate plan for each characteristic. One may have to take a separate sample for each characteristic, while an attribute approach would only require one sample.
- Since the measurement instruments may be very expensive the fixed inspection costs for sampling by variables can be much higher than

those of attribute sampling. However, in many cases this is compensated by lower variable inspection costs as a result of the reduction in the amount of inspection.

- It is possible that a sampling plan for variables will reject a lot although no measurement is found outside the specification limits.

Example 3.3/4

We have already seen in example 3.3/2 that sampling by variables can significantly reduce the amount of inspection. SCHILLING (1982, p. 224ff) gives another numerical example of this result. He found the following sample sizes n and corresponding ASN values of several approximately OC equivalent attribute and variable sampling plans.

Acceptance sampling for ***attributes***:

- single-sampling plan: $n = 50$
- double-sampling plan: $ASN = 43$
- seven-stage-sampling plan: $ASN = 37$
- sequential-sampling plan: $ASN = 33.5$

Acceptance sampling for ***variables***:

- in the case of unknown process variance: $n = 27$
- in the case of known process variance: $n = 12$

The calculation of the plan parameters for the attribute plans in this example was based on a binomially distributed test statistic. The conclusion is that, for attribute procedures, the amount of inspection goes down as the number of inspection stages goes up, and in the case of sampling by variables, that improved prior information reduces the sample size.

3.3.6 Sampling Systems by Variables

For acceptance sampling by attributes we introduced a series of sampling systems in section 3.2/7 of which only the **Military Standard 105D (MIL-STD 105D)** and its modern civilian versions ISO 2859 and ANSI/ ASQC Z 1.4 have gained world wide importance. For variable acceptance control there is also a sampling system with international significance.

It was first presented in 1957 under the name **Military Standard 414 (MIL-STD 414)** and is based on the MIL-STD 105A, a previous version of the MIL-STD 105D proposed in 1950. The plan assumes that the quality characteristic has a normal distribution. Similar to the MIL-STD 105, it is AQL oriented and has different levels of inspection as well as switching rules between reduced, normal and tightened inspection, but different from the attribute system it does not have double and multiple stage sampling plans. The standard is divided into four sections A, B, C and D. Section A contains the general description, while sections B and C cover the case of unknown variance. In part B the variance is estimated by the sample variance and, in part C, by the more simple sample range. Section D presents the procedure for known process variance. The flow chart in figure 3.3/8 describes the structure of the sampling scheme.

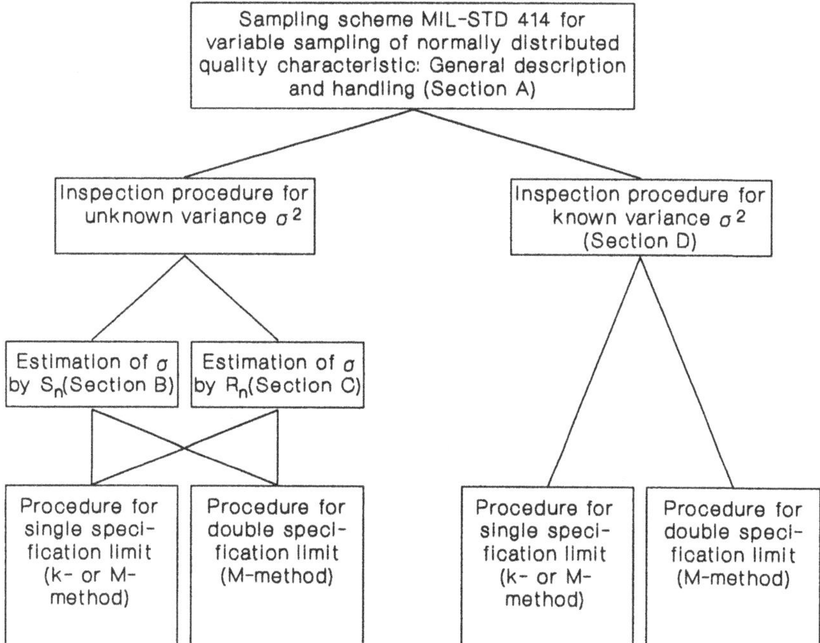

Figure 3.3/8: Outline of the MIL-STD 414 sampling scheme

Similar to the MIL-STD 105D, the user of the MIL-STD 414 first has to determine a code letter from a table analogous to tables 3.2/20-21. This code letter depends on the lot size and the chosen inspection level. In addition the AQL value needs to be specified.

Further development of the MIL-STD 414

In the beginning the MIL-STD 105A proposed in 1950 and the MIL-STD 414, which was published seven years later, were very much in accordance with each other. Once the former became updated to MIL-STD 105D there began to be major differences between the two systems that make it difficult to compare them directly. From this point on the two schemes had not only different switching rules, but also the assignment of the code letters and the possible *AQL* values were different. In 1980 the **American National Standards Institute (ANSI)** and the **American Society for Statistical Quality Control (ASQC)** developed an updated civilian version **ANSI/ASQC Z 1.9** of the MIL-STD 414. This sampling system has the same structure as indicated in figure 3.3/8, but is now comparable to the updated military standard MIL-STD 105D. The norm ANSI/ASQC Z 1.9 scheme for sampling by variables was actually designed analogous to the norm ANSI/ASQC Z 1.4 scheme for attribute sampling from 1974. Both systems have the same set of possible *AQL* values, the same levels of inspection and the same grouping of lot sizes. The **International Institute for Standardization** presented an adaption of the ANSI/ASQC Z 1.9 called **ISO 3951**. This version works with nomograms. The **Deutsche Gesellschaft für Qualität** presented a standard for a variable sampling system similar to the ISO 3951 (DGQ 1980). Different from the ISO 3951 it does not cover the variable sampling procedure for double specification limits. Also, the *M*-method that is presented in the MIL-STD 105D and also in the ISO 3951, in the case of a single specification limit as an alternative to the *k*-method, is not mentioned in the DGQ paper.

Remarks

1. A detailed description of the MIL-STD 414 procedure can be found in BANKS (1989, p. 413ff), WADSWORTH/STEPHENS/GODFREY (1986, p. 552ff), GRANT/LEAVENWORTH (1988, p. 554ff) and MONTGOMERY (1991, p. 630ff), for example.
2. The fact that the MIL-STD 414 and even the newer ISO 3951 discuss in detail how to estimate σ by the sample range R_n (see section C in table 3.3/7) is due to historical reasons. When σ had to be estimated by very primitive means there were good reasons in favour of the sample range. In the age of computer aided quality assurance these reasons have lost their validity.

4 Statistical Process Control

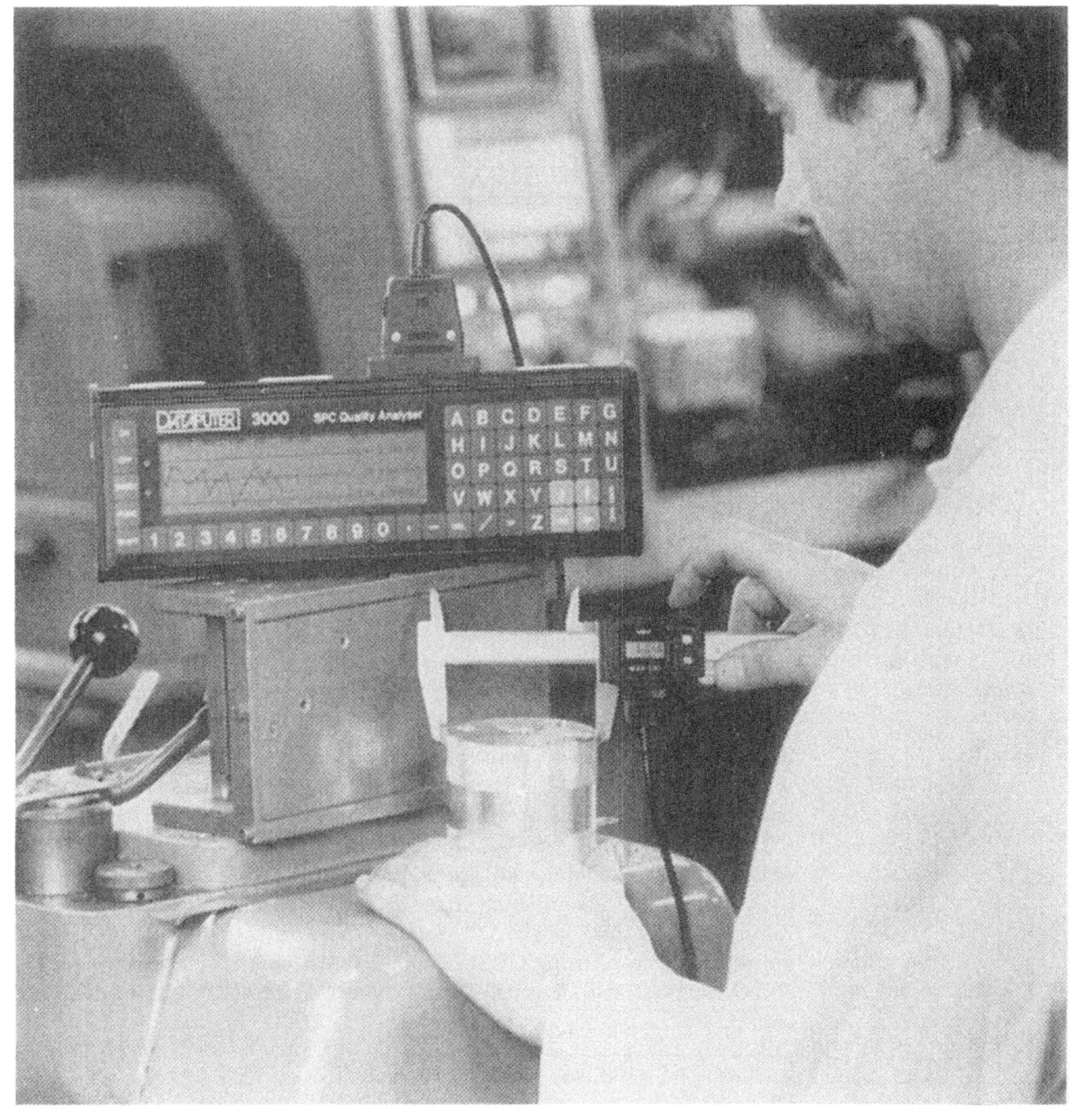

The theory of acceptance sampling in chapter 3 dealt with the question of rating the quality of a finite population of product units (lot) after completion of the manufacturing process (**offline inspection**). The following chapter presents the basic ideas of **statistical process control**, which tries to detect quality deficiencies during the manufacturing process (**online inspection**). A characteristic of process control is that a *stream* of individual product units continually arrives at the inspection station. We consider this population of units to be potentially of infinite size. A typical example of process control is the control of a manufacturing process that involves a conveyor or a moving assembly-line. In practice, the term statistical process control is often abbreviated by **SPC**.

Goals of statistical process control

In statistical process control, sampling has the following two non-exclusive goals:

- **control of the outgoing quality**, i.e., the proportion of nonconforming units passing inspection without being detected;
- **production control** through intervention in the process as a result of unsatisfactory sample results.

Preview of chapter 4

In section 4.1 we will first introduce **continuous sampling plans** which primarily serve the first of the two purposes mentioned above. Through continuous inspection with varying intensity these plans intend to ensure that the average outgoing quality stays below a specified upper limit. After discussion of this method we will present the subject of monitoring a process by means of **quality control charts**. Here, the second goal is primarily addressed. We will first present the general purpose and structure of control charts in section 4.2, and also give an overview of the different types and the underlying statistical background. Sections 4.3 - 4.4 will then be devoted to the **classical control chart**, which goes back to W. A. SHEWHART (1891-1967). After these so-called classical SHEWHART charts and one of its modifications presented in 4.5 we will discuss the lesser known CUSUM and EWMA charts. In chapter 4, as before, we will exclusively consider the case of *univariate* process control, i.e., control of only one quality characteristic of a product. Readers interested in multivariate process control will find this topic in ALT/SMITH (1988) or RYAN (1989). Multivariate process control using CUSUM and EWMA charts is treated, e.g., by PIGNATIELLO/RUNGER (1990) and LOWRY/WOODALL/CHAMP/RIGDON (1992).

Figure on the title page of this chapter:
Inspection of the diameter of cylindrical work pieces with the help of a SHEWHART type control chart. We are grateful to the Co. Elcometer (Eßlingen, Germany) for their kind permission to print this photo.

4.1 Continuous Sampling Plans

So far we have introduced inspection procedures based on the assumption that the production flow naturally divides into finite subsets and that a decision has to be made about each one of these. The subsets were called lots. We took samples from them and, based on the sample outcome, we drew conclusions about the quality of the lot. This assumption is frequently not satisfied in industrial practice. In the following we will assume that there is a *continuous* stream of product units. For example, manufacturing of high-tech products is usually performed on a conveyor assembly line. Our goal will be to monitor the realizations of a dichotomous quality characteristic (good-bad-inspection, Bernoulli distributed quality characteristic).

Defining the term "fraction nonconforming" in the context of a continuous production

We first need to clarify what is meant by the term *fraction nonconforming* or *fraction defective* in the context of a population with potentially infinite size. Let P denote the probability that a randomly chosen product unit from the manufacturing process is found to be defective. If the occurrence of nonconforming units in a process is stochastically independent (i.e., nonconforming units neither occur in groups nor at constant intervals), then the proportion nonconforming in any sufficiently large subset of the population agrees approximately with the individual probability P of being defective. Under this assumption of independence, we can thus define P as the **fraction nonconforming of the production process**, also called the **process fraction nonconforming**.

Goal of continuous sampling

If the fraction nonconforming is constant over time, then we also say that the process is *under statistical control.* The average outgoing quality of such a process, i.e., the expected value of the fraction nonconforming after inspection, can be reduced through more or less intensive screening. To be exact, the average outgoing quality can theoretically range from $AOQ(P) = P$, in the case of no inspection, to $AOQ(P) = 0$, in the case of screening every unit, provided the latter is performed without inspection errors. The goal of all **continuous sampling plans (CSP)** is to control the intensity of inspection depending on the inspection results in such a way so that the maximum of the average outgoing quality does not exceed a specified upper limit $AOQL$.

To a large extent, the development of continuous sampling plans is due to DODGE (1893-1976). His first continuous sampling plan, CSP-1, dates back to 1943 (DODGE 1943). Later, CSP-1 was modified several times by DODGE as well as by others. In section 4.1.1, we will introduce CSP-1 and discuss its characteristics in detail. In section 4.1.2 we will present various modifications and extensions of sampling for continuous production.

4.1.1 The CSP-1

a) Description of a CSP-1

As described above, we are dealing with a continuous production stream of good (conforming, non-defective) and bad (nonconforming, defective) units. Unless stated otherwise, we will assume that the following assumptions are satisfied:

Assumptions for application of a CSP

- The production process is under statistical control.
- Every detected bad unit is replaced by a good one or is repaired immediately.

In addition, we are assuming that the inspection does not require more time than the manufacturing process, so that there is no danger of congestion at the inspection station. The question is how to ensure that not too many nonconforming units remain undetected. For this scenario, DODGE (1943) presented an inspection procedure commonly referred to as CSP-1, which always starts with 100% inspection (screening). This screening is performed until i successive non-defective units are observed. Then the procedure samples only one of the following k units (sampling inspection or partial inspection). If the sampled unit is found to be good, then the procedure continues to sample one unit from the next k, etc. As soon as a defective sample unit is observed, the procedure switches back to screening every unit and continues until again i consecutive good units are observed. Thus, the inspection procedure consists of alternating periods of 100% inspection and periods with $f \cdot 100\%$ inspection, where $f := 1/k$.

Procedure of a CSP-1

Figure 4.1/1 illustrates the approach of a CSP-1 for the case of $i = 8$ and $k = 4$. The horizontal axis (time axis) represents the production stream beginning with the start of inspection. On this axis "good" units are denoted by white points and "bad" units by black points. Units sampled during a partial inspection stage are marked with an arrow. The inspection intensity is given on the vertical axis.

Thus a CSP-1 is determined by two integer-valued parameters, i.e., the **clearance number** i and the **sampling interval** k. Instead of k, we could use the equivalent proportion $f = 1/k$ of sampled units of the sampling period as the second parameter. This quantity is called **sampling fraction**.

Parameters of a CSP-1

The previous description of the CSP-1 procedure is that given by DODGE (1943). However, in this text DODGE does not uniquely specify how the sampling during the partial inspection periods should be done. DODGE only recommends that biased samples be avoided. When applying a CSP-1 plan there is a choice between three different ways of sampling,

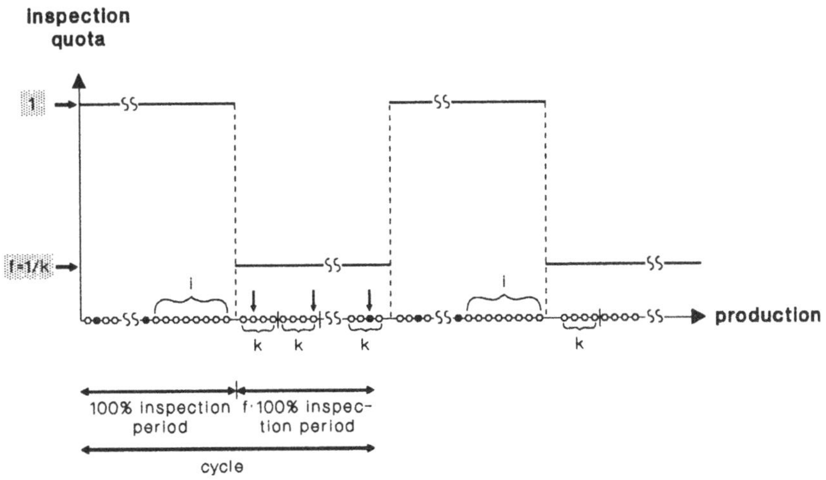

Figure 4.1/1: Inspection intensities and inspection cycles of a CSP-1

all of which satisfy DODGE's requirement and all lead to the same OC function, as shown by DERMAN/JOHNS/LIEBERMAN (1959):

Three possible approaches to sampling during the partial inspection period of a CSP-1

- systematic sampling;
- block or random sampling;
- probability sampling.

When performing **systematic sampling**, after the i-th consecutive conforming unit is observed, one simply draws every k-th unit for inspection and leaves out the $k-1$ units in between. If the sampled unit is found to be nonconforming, the procedure begins 100% inspection with the next unit.

In **block** or **random sampling**, after the i-th consecutive good unit is observed, one looks at every sequence of k units as a block and randomly draws one unit from each block. This unit is inspected, whereas the remaining $k-1$ pass without being inspected. If the inspected unit is good, one goes to the next block, but if it is bad, one starts 100% inspection with the first unit of the next block. This approach is presented in figure 4.1/1. Note that it is more appropriate here to call k the *average* sampling interval, because the interval between sampled units is a random variable with expectation k.

In the case of **probability sampling** one decides for every unit, beginning after the i-th consecutive good unit, whether to sample or not. Here, the probability of being selected for inspection has to have the constant value $f = 1/k$ (constant selection probability f). The best way to select sample units during the partial inspection periods according to this approach is to use random numbers which are uniformly distributed on [0,1]. For each arrival of a new unit such a random number U is either generated by a computer or obtained from a table.[1] If $U \leq f = 1/k$ then the corresponding unit is inspected. If the unit is determined to be good, one continues this random selection with the next unit, else one switches back to 100% inspection beginning with the next unit. In this approach, the parameter k again denotes the average sampling interval.

This description of the different approaches to sampling completes the presentation of the CSP-1. We will now illustrate the CSP-1 procedure using a structural chart. For convenience, we assume systematic sampling during the partial inspection sequences.

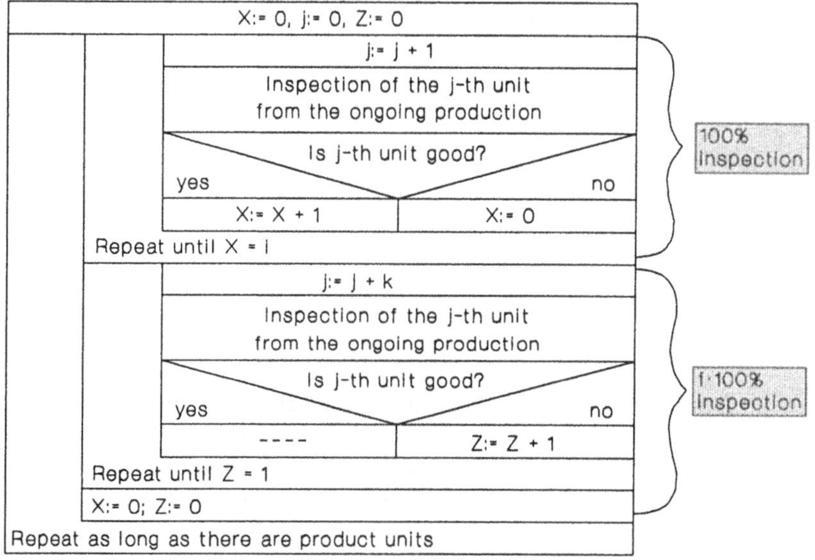

Figure 4.1/2: Structural chart of a CSP-1

In figure 4.1/2 the quantities X, j and Z denote registers with the initial value zero. The register X counts the number of consecutive good units during the 100% inspection period. Each time a nonconforming unit is observed, X is reset to zero. The number of nonconforming units during

[1] Random numbers with a uniform distribution on [0,1] can be obtained from table 2.2/1, for example, or from any other digital random number table, by taking a certain number of consecutive random digits – say, four or five – and setting a "0." in front of them.

the $f \cdot 100\%$ inspection period is contained in the register Z. As soon as it reaches the value 1 the partial inspection period is terminated, the procedure returns to 100% inspection and Z is reset to zero. During each period the register j keeps track of the total number of inspected units.

b) Measuring the CSP-1 Performance

We now want to investigate how the specification of the parameters i and k (or $f = 1/k$) effects the various performance measures of a CSP-1. As mentioned before, we will assume that the production process is under statistical control. In other words, the occurrence of nonconforming units is stochastically independent and has constant probability P. Thus the product units, or more exactly, their quality characteristics, form a sequence of Bernoulli distributed random variables. We further assume that every detected nonconforming unit is either mended or replaced by a good one.

The operation mode of a CSP-1 with parameters i and k is described by six performance measures:

Six measures for the perfomance of a CSP-1

▷ Characteristic 1: *Average length of a 100% inspection period*

By **length of an inspection period** we mean the number of product units that are processed during this particular sequence. In a screening period every manufactured unit is also an inspected unit automatically. The length of such a 100% inspection period is a random variable the distribution of which cannot be easily written down in an explicit form. Thus, the minimal duration of a screening period is i units which occurs if, immediately after the start of the period, the first i consecutive units are all found to be non-defective. This case occurs with a probability of $(1-P)^i$. In theory, it is also possible that the 100% inspection period never ends, but the corresponding probability is zero. In order to prevent the procedure from remaining too long in 100% inspection, for a given i, one sometimes introduces so-called **stopping rules** (see remark 2 at the end of section 4.1.2b). In practice, the **average length of a 100% inspection period**, i.e., the value of the expected number of processed product units per screening period, is of particular importance. Since it only depends on i and P, this measure is denoted by $u(P|i)$ and is given by

$$u(P|i) = \frac{1-(1-P)^i}{P(1-P)^i}. \tag{4.1}$$

An analysis of (4.1) shows that the average length $u(P|i)$ of a 100% inspection period increases as the clearance number i or the fraction defective P of the process increase.

▷ Characteristic 2: *Average length of a* $f \cdot 100\%$ *inspection period*

During the sampling stage of a CSP-1 we have *exactly* one inspected unit per k processed product units ($k-1$ uninspected and 1 inspected unit) when the sampling is performed in blocks or systematically, or *on average* one inspected unit per k processed units for probability sampling. The length of a $f \cdot 100\%$ inspection period is a random variable of the form $Y = X \cdot k$. The variable X in this expression has a negative binomial distribution with parameters P and $c = 1$ (i.e., a geometric distribution, see (2.98a)). The smallest possible realization of X is one which occurs if the first inspected unit of the $f \cdot 100\%$ inspection period is found to be defective. The expectation $E(Y)$ of the **average length of a** $f \cdot$ **100% inspection period** is denoted by $v(P|k)$ and is determined by

$$v(P|k) = \frac{k}{P} = \frac{1}{fP}. \tag{4.2}$$

We can see from (4.2) that the the length $v(P|k)$ of a sampling inspection period increases as either the sampling interval k increases or the process fraction defective P decreases.

▷ Characteristic 3: *Average cycle length*

We define a **cycle** to be the portion of the production stream which includes all units between the start of a screening period and the end of the following partial inspection sequence. A cycle consists of exactly one 100% inspection period and one $f \cdot 100\%$ inspection period. The length of a cycle is thus the number of product units, which are processed during this cycle (see figure 4.1/1). Since the length of a screening period and the length of a sampling period are both random variables, it follows that this also has to be the case with the cycle length. The **average cycle length**, denoted by $z(P|i;k)$, is the sum of the two previously introduced quantities $u(P|i)$ and $v(P|k)$:

$$z(P|i;k) = u(P|i) + v(P|k). \tag{4.3 a}$$

With (4.1) and (4.2) we get

$$z(P|i;k) = \frac{1 + (k-1)(1-P)^i}{P(1-P)^i}. \tag{4.3 b}$$

The average cycle length is a strictly monotone increasing function of the parameters i and k. With respect to the parameter P, however, it is neither monotone increasing nor decreasing. As P increases the two components of $z(P|i;k)$ do not change in the same way: $u(P|i)$ increases and $v(P|k)$ decreases. For $P \to 0$ and $P \to 1$, it holds that $z(P|i;k) \to \infty$, because in both cases one of its components goes to infinity while the other converges to a finite value (see figure 4.1/4). In the open interval (0,1), the function $z(P|i;k)$ has a unique minimum at the point P_M. This minimum can be determined from (4.3b) by differentiating with respect to P and setting the whole term to zero. This results in the nonlinear determining equation

$$(1+i)P - 1 = (k-1)(1-P)^{i+1}. \tag{4.4}$$

Although P_M cannot be solved analytically from this equation, it is possible to determine its solution by iterative numerical methods. Substituting the obtained value P_M into (4.3b) gives the minimal average cycle length.

$$z(P_M|i;k) = \frac{i}{(1-P_M)^{i+1}}. \tag{4.5}$$

▷ Characteristic 4: *Average fraction of units inspected*

In acceptance sampling, we introduced two measures for the amount of inspection. One was the absolute measure **ATI**, the average total inspection, and the other **AFI**, the average fraction inspected. Both quantities were related to the inspection of lots, i.e., populations of finite size. In continuous sampling inspection we are dealing with a potentially infinite number of units. Instead of the lot size N, we can work here with the average cycle length (4.3). The average total inspection per cycle is then denoted by $ATI(P|i;k)$ and defined to be the sum of the average total inspection of a 100% inspection period and the average total inspection of a $f \cdot 100\%$ inspection period. The first term of the sum is equivalent to the average length of a screening period, because every unit is inspected. The second term is the k-th fraction of the average length of a $f \cdot 100\%$ inspection period, since during this period only one out of every k units is inspected. Thus, we get

$$ATI(P|i;k) = u(P|i) + \frac{v(P|k)}{k} = u(P|i) + f \cdot v(P|k). \tag{4.6 a}$$

With (4.1) and (4.2) it follows that

$$ATI(P|i;k) = \frac{1}{P(1-P)^i}. \tag{4.6 b}$$

This shows that the average number of inspected units of a cycle is independent of the sampling interval k. It is a monotone increasing function of the clearance number i and the fraction defective P.

A relative measure of the amount of inspection is the **average fraction inspected**, denoted by $AFI(P|i;k)$. It is defined to be the ratio of the $ATI(P|i;k)$ and the average cycle length $z(P|i;k)$:

$$AFI(P|i;k) = \frac{ATI(P|i;k)}{z(P|i;k)} = \frac{u(P|i) + f \cdot v(P|k)}{u(P|i) + v(P|k)}. \tag{4.7 a}$$

Using (4.3b) and (4.6b) it follows that

$$AFI(P|i;k) = \frac{1}{1 + (k-1)(1-P)^i}. \tag{4.7 b}$$

The function $AFI(P|i;k)$ tells us what proportion of the total produced units is inspected on average. It is monotone decreasing in k, but monotone increasing in i and P. We observe that

$$AFI(0|i;k) = \frac{1}{k} = f; \qquad AFI(1|i,k) = 1. \tag{4.7 c}$$

▷ Characteristic 5: *Average outgoing quality*

What is the average outgoing quality of a CSP-1? Analogous to acceptance sampling, we can define the **average outgoing quality of a continuous sampling plan** as the ratio of the number of nonconforming units which slip undetected through inspection, and the number of all processed units using the average cycle length as a reference population. Under the assumption that all detected nonconforming units are replaced by good ones, no defective units can pass inspection during a screening period. During the $f \cdot 100\%$ inspection period, on the average $v(P|k) \cdot P - 1$ nonconforming units slip undetected through the inspection. Thus the average outgoing quality of a CSP-1, denoted by $AOQ(P|i;k)$, is defined by

$$AOQ(P|i;k) = \frac{v(P|k)P - 1}{z(P|i;k)}. \tag{4.8 a}$$

Substituting (4.2) and (4.3b) results in

$$AOQ(P|i;k) = \frac{k-1}{z(P|i;k)} = \frac{(k-1)P(1-P)^i}{1 + (k-1)(1-P)^i}. \tag{4.8 b}$$

As k increases, the average outgoing quality converges to P, and as i increases it goes to zero:

$$\lim_{k \to \infty} AOQ(P|i;k) = P; \qquad \lim_{i \to \infty} AOQ(P|i;k) = 0. \tag{4.8 c}$$

With respect to P, the behaviour of $AOQ(P|i;k)$ is not monotone. At the edges of the interval [0,1], the range of the process level P, the average outgoing quality is zero:

$$AOQ(0|i;k) = AOQ(1|i;k) = 0. \tag{4.8 d}$$

On the interval (0,1) the function $AOQ(P|i;k)$ has a unique maximum at the point $P = P_M$. The value of P_M can be calculated by differentiating (4.8b) with respect to P and setting the derivation to zero. The resulting determining equation is identical to (4.4). This tells us that the value P_M, which minimizes the cycle length, maximizes the average outgoing quality. Similar to (3.44), we call this value the **average outgoing quality limit** and denote it by **AOQL**:

$$AOQL := \max_P AOQ(P|i;k) = AOQ(P_M|i;k). \tag{4.9 a}$$

Substituting the iteratively obtained value P_M into (4.8b) yields

$$AOQL = \frac{(i+1)P_M - 1}{i}. \tag{4.9 b}$$

▷ Characteristic 6: *The OC function*

In acceptance sampling, the OC function gives the probability that a lot with a fraction defective P is accepted. Since we do not have lots in continuous sampling, we have to find a concept – similiar to the ATI and AFI – which comes as close as possible to the concept of the OC function in acceptance control. Let us again first look back to the situation of acceptance sampling. There we applied an attribute plan $(N;n;c)$ to lots with a quality level P and rejected lots were submitted to 100% inspection. For a given P the value $L(P)$ of the OC function of the plan could be interpreted as the proportion of lots with this process level P which were accepted under sampling in the long run. When administering a CSP-1 we can make a similar statement. Here $v(P|k)/z(P|i;k)$ is the proportion of accepted units among those processed during the partial inspection periods. Because of this analogy, it seems appropriate to define the **OC function of a continuous sampling plan** to be the function which relates the parameter P to the proportion of units accepted during the $f \cdot 100\%$ inspection periods, i.e., during sampling inspection. For this function we will use the notation $L(P|i;k)$:[2]

$$L(P|i;k) := \frac{v(P|k)}{z(P|i;k)}. \tag{4.10 a}$$

[2]The OC function (4.10a) of a CSP-1 should not be confused with the binomial OC function $L(P|n;c)$ of a single sampling plan. In order to avoid an excessively complicated notation, we are not differentiating the notation of these terms.

Using (4.2), (4.3), (4.8b) and $f = 1/k$ it follows that

$$L(P|i;k) = \frac{k(1-P)^i}{1+(k-1)(1-P)^i} = \frac{AOQ(P|i;k)}{P(1-f)}. \tag{4.10 b}$$

The OC function (4.10) behaves in the same way as the one from acceptance control, i.e., it is monotone decreasing with respect to P and it holds that

$$L(0|i;k) = 1; \qquad L(1|i;k) = 0. \tag{4.10 c}$$

Under variation of the parameters i and k, the graph of (4.10), the so-called **OC curve of the continuous sampling plan**, behaves in the same way as the OC curves of single attribute plans $(N; n; c)$ under variation of n and c. The OC curve becomes steeper (increasing discriminatory power) as the clearance number i increases and/or the (average) sampling interval k decreases. Similar to figure 3.2/7, this is illustrated by figure 4.1/3.

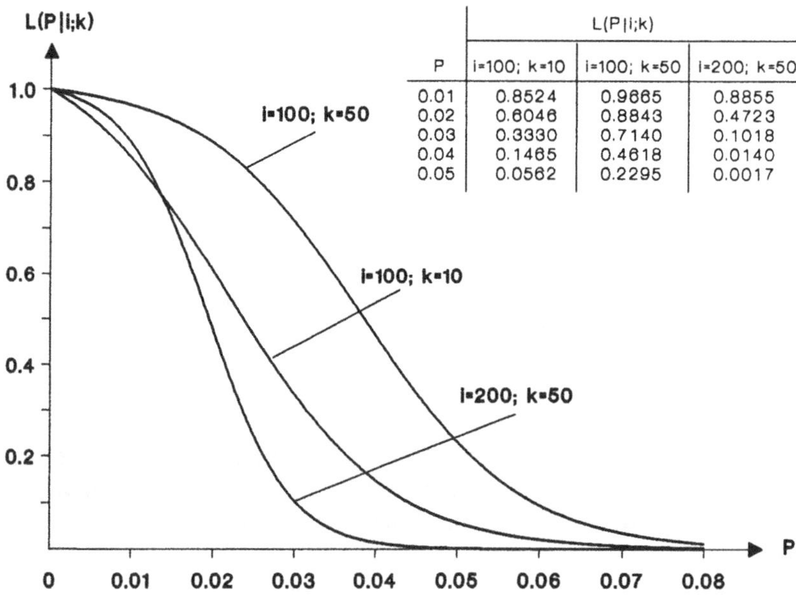

P	L(P|i;k) i=100; k=10	i=100; k=50	i=200; k=50
0.01	0.8524	0.9665	0.8855
0.02	0.6046	0.8843	0.4723
0.03	0.3330	0.7140	0.1018
0.04	0.1465	0.4618	0.0140
0.05	0.0562	0.2295	0.0017

Figure 4.1/3: OC curves of three CSP-1 plans

Comparison with acceptance sampling

In order to illustrate the similarities and differences between acceptance control with a single-sampling plan $(N; n; c)$ and continuous sampling inspection with a CSP-1, we are concluding our discussion with the summary table 4.1/1.

	Acceptance control with a single-sampling plan (I)	Continuous process control with a CSP-1 (II)
Population	lots with N product units	production stream with a potentially infinite number of units
Parameters of the sampling plan	lot size N sample size n acceptance number c	clearance number i (average) sampling interval k
ATI function	average number of inspected units per lot (I) or per cycle (II) [1]	
AFI function	average proportion of inspected units per lot (I) or per cycle (II) [1]	
AOQ function	average proportion of undetected nonconforming units after inspection per lot (I) or per cycle (II) [1]	
OC function	probability of accepting the lot[1]	average proportion of processed units per sampling period [1]

[1] "depending on the quality level P" is to be added.

Table 4.1/1: Similarities and differences between single sampling for attributes in acceptance control and continuous sampling with a CSP-1

Example 4.1/1

We are now going to present a CSP-1 with parameters $i = 50$ and $k = 25$, then determine the six performance measures previously introduced and illustrate how they change for varying P.

We can see from figure 4.1/4 how the average cycle length $z(P|50;25)$ and its components, $u(P|50)$ and $v(P|25)$, behave under variation of the process fraction defective P. Since $z(P|50;25)$ takes on very large values for small as well as for large values of $P \in (0,1)$ we are presenting all three characteristics on a logarithmic scale (base 10 logarithm).

We can observe from the graph that the minimal average cycle length $z(P_M|50;25)$ is attained at $P_M \approx 0.05$. Substituting the parameter values $i = 50$ and $k = 25$ into (4.5) and solving the equation determines the exact result to be $P_M \approx 0.05144$. With this exact value, according to (4.4), the minimal average cycle length of this CSP-1 is found to be

$$z(0,05144|50;25) = \frac{50}{0.94856^{51}} \approx 739.$$

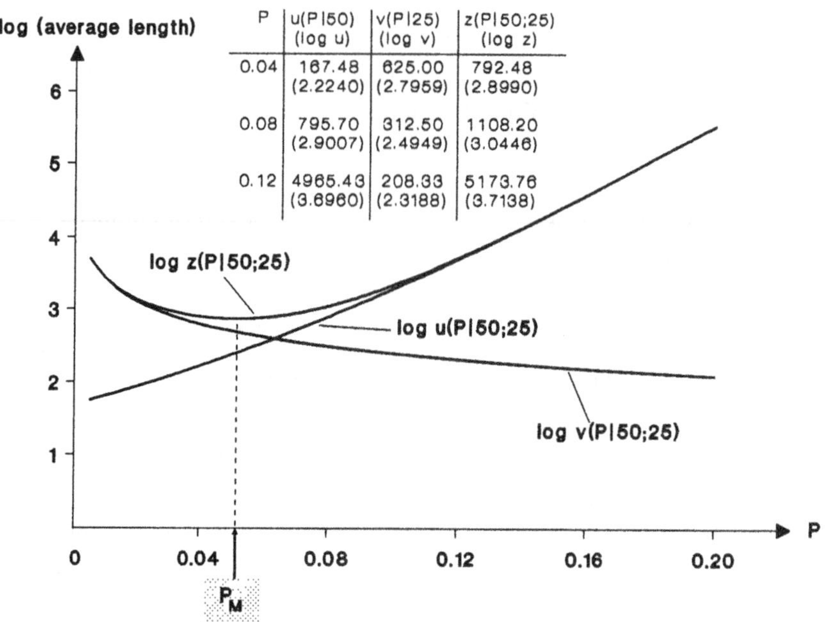

P	u(P|50) (log u)	v(P|25) (log v)	z(P|50;25) (log z)
0.04	167.48 (2.2240)	625.00 (2.7959)	792.48 (2.8990)
0.08	795.70 (2.9007)	312.50 (2.4949)	1108.20 (3.0446)
0.12	4965.43 (3.6960)	208.33 (2.3188)	5173.76 (3.7138)

Figure 4.1/4: Average cycle length of a CSP-1 and its two components

This determines the average number of processed units during the 100% inspection periods to be

$$u(0.05144|50) = \frac{1 - 0.94856^{50}}{0.054144 \cdot 0.94586^{50}} \approx 253$$

and

$$v(0.05144|25) = \frac{25}{0.05144} \approx 486$$

during the 4% inspection periods. The maximal average outgoing quality is also attained at $P_M \approx 0.05144$ and by (4.9) has the value

$$AOQL \approx AOQ(0.05144|50;25) = \frac{1}{50} \cdot (51 \cdot 0.05144 - 1) \approx 0.0325.$$

Figure 4.1/5 presents the complete graph of the function $AOQ(P|50;25)$.

The strictly monotone increasing function $AFI(P|50;25)$ according to (4.7c) takes the value $f = 0.04$ at $P = 0$. At $P = 1$, it has the value one. Its graph and the graph of the OC function $L(P|50;25)$ are presented in figure 4.1/6.

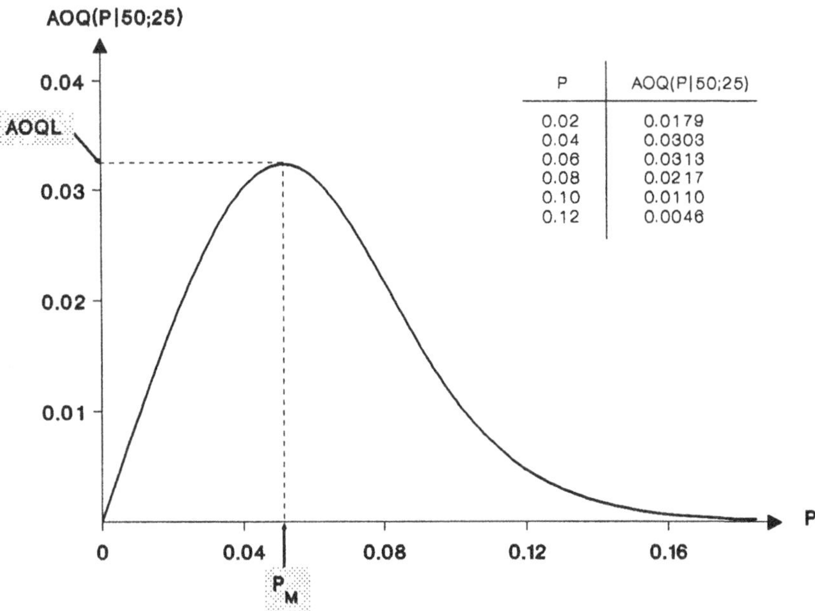

Figure 4.1/5: *AOQ* curve of a CSP-1

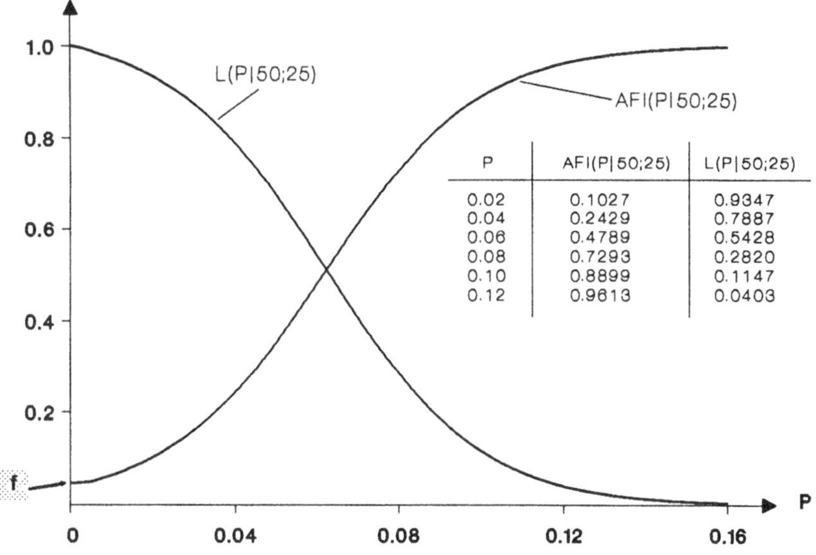

Figure 4.1/6: *AFI* and OC curve of a CSP-1

For $P_M \approx 0.05144$, by (4.7b), the average fraction inspected is determined to be

$$AFI(0.05144|50;25) = \frac{1}{1 + 24 \cdot 0.94856^{50}} \approx 0.3688.$$

At $P_M \approx 0.05144$ the OC function attains the value

$$L(0.05144|50;25) = \frac{AOQ(0.05144|50;25)}{0.05144 \cdot 0.96} \approx 0.6581.$$

Problem 4.1/1

For a CSP-1 with parameter $i \geq 2$ and given process level P find the probabilities that

a) $i+1$ or $i+2$ units are processed during a 100% inspection period,

b) k, $2k$ or $3k$ units are processed during a $f \cdot 100\%$-inspection period.

c) Designing a CSP-1 with Specified Properties

Options for constructing a CSP-1:

We have already described how to determine the six characteristics of a CSP-1 for given plan parameters i and k. Alternatively, we can obtain determining equations for i and k for two given specifications. We will now present three possible ways of giving such specifications:

- Specification of the average lengths of the 100% inspection period and the $f \cdot 100\%$ inspection period for a given quality level P^*.
- Specification of two points on the OC curve.
- Specification of the $AOQL$ and one additional condition.

- specifying the two components of the average cycle length

The first case is the most simple. With the specifications $u(P^*|k) = u^*$ and $v(P^*|k) = v^*$, we get from (4.1) and (4.2) that

$$i = -\frac{\ln(u^* \cdot P^* + 1)}{\ln(1 - P^*)} \tag{4.11 a}$$

$$k = P^* \cdot v^*. \tag{4.11 b}$$

Since i and k are integer valued, the solutions of (4.11a,b) have to be rounded to integers. In order to prevent the average cycle length from becoming too large, one always rounds to the next smallest integer. In practice, it is not common to specificy parameters i and k via (4.11a,b).

- specifying two points on the OC curve

Another approach to specifying i and k – similar to that which is discussed in section 3.2.3a for single sampling plans for attributes – is to give two points $(P_{1-\alpha}, 1-\alpha)$ and (P_β, β) of the OC function (4.10) so that the inequalities $P_{1-\alpha} < P_\beta$ and $1-\alpha < \beta$ are satisfied. Because the parameters i and k are integer-valued this requirement can only be approximately satisfied. To ensure that one stays on the "safe side" one requires, analogous to (3.60), that

$$L(P_{1-\alpha}|i;k) \geq 1-\alpha \tag{4.12 a}$$

$$L(P_\beta|i;k) \leq \beta. \tag{4.12 b}$$

From (4.12) and the result in (4.10) we get two interdependent nonlinear equations which can be solved numerically only by iterative procedures. This approach of determining the parameters is also seldom applied in practice.

- $AOQL$ specification and protection against not detecting short sequences of nonconforming units

A commonly used way to specify the parameters i and k of a CSP-1 is related to the goal of continuous sampling, which is to reduce the process fraction defective P into a lower average outgoing quality level AOQ. If one specifies a maximal value $AOQL$, then the first determining equation follows from (4.9b):

$$AOQL = \frac{(i+1)\cdot P_M - 1}{i}. \tag{4.13}$$

However, from this equation one cannot determine the parameter i, since, according to (4.4), the value of P_M, belonging to the maximum average outgoing quality, depends on i and k. In any case, there are several combinations of i and k with the same value of the average outgoing quality limit $AOQL$. If one disregards that the parameters have to be integer-valued then, for any given $AOQL$, there is an infinite number of solutions. If one specifies one of the two plan parameters besides the $AOQL$, then the other can be calculated. The relationship between i and k for a given $AOQL$ is described by the so-called **iso-AOQL function**. In order to obtain this function, one first solves (4.13) for P_M and then solves (4.4) with $P = P_M$ for k. From the resulting equations

$$P_M = \frac{1+i\cdot AOQL}{i+1} \tag{4.14 a}$$

$$k = 1 + \frac{(i+1)P_M - 1}{(1-P_M)^{i+1}} \tag{4.14 b}$$

one finally gets the iso-$AOQL$ function by substituting (4.14a) into (4.14b):

$$k = 1 + \left[\frac{i+1}{i(1-AOQL)}\right]^{i+1} \cdot i \cdot AOQL = 1 + \left(1 + \frac{1}{i}\right)^{i+1} \cdot \frac{i \cdot AOQL}{(1-AOQL)^{i+1}}. \tag{4.15 a}$$

Under the assumption that $i \geq 10$ and $AOQL \leq 0.1$, we get

$$k \approx 1 + (i+1) \cdot AOQL \cdot \exp[1 + (i+1) \cdot AOQL]. \tag{4.15 b}$$

A graph of (4.15a) or (4.15b), is called an **iso-AOQL curve**. This curve contains all points (i, k) with the same $AOQL$. If one varies the $AOQL$ value the result is a system of iso-$AOQL$ curves. Figure 4.1/7 shows such a system. For practical reasons, we plotted the values $f = 1/k$ instead of k as a function of i.

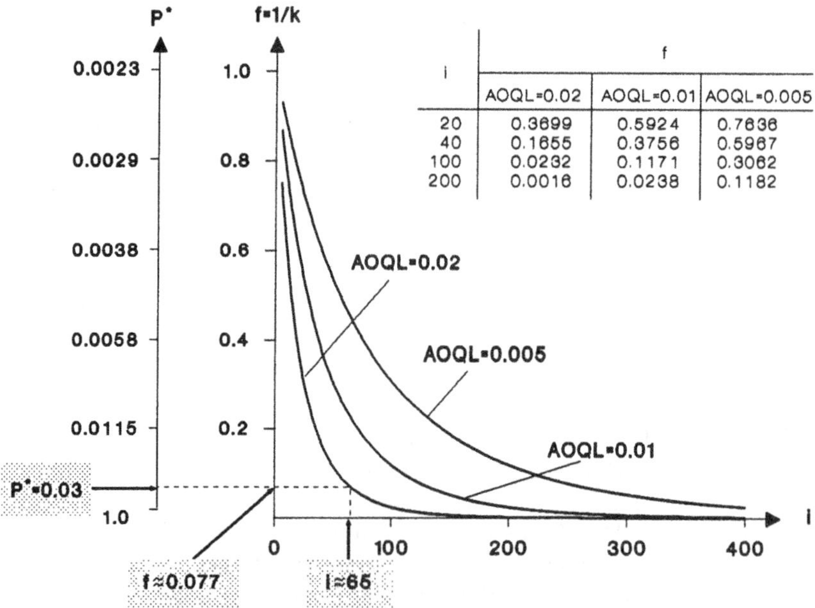

i	f		
	AOQL=0.02	AOQL=0.01	AOQL=0.005
20	0.3699	0.5924	0.7636
40	0.1655	0.3756	0.5967
100	0.0232	0.1171	0.3062
200	0.0016	0.0238	0.1182

Figure 4.1/7: Iso-$AOQL$ curves for determining the parameters i and k of a CSP-1

The question is how to choose a point (i, f) on a certain $AOQL$ curve. How can we best use the remaining degree of freedom in choosing a particular plan? If the sampling interval k is chosen to be small, i.e., f is large, then this protects against not detecting short sequences of nonconforming units. Hence, one should choose a combination of a small i and a large f. DODGE/TORREY (1951) introduced a special functional parameter, a certain quality level P^*, for this purpose. Since nonconforming units can only slip through the inspection during the partial inspection periods, DODGE/TORREY wanted to control the probability that a sequence of units with a critical quality level P^* passes the inspection undetected. They specified the length of the sequence to be 1000 units and the probability of accepting such a sequence during the $f \cdot 100\%$ inspection period to be at most 0.1. We now want to show how the critical quality level P^* can be determined for these two specifications and a given $f = 1/k$.

Let us first determine the probability of accepting one unit from an output stream with quality level P^*. The unit is accepted without inspection with probability $1 - f$. With probability f it is inspected, in which case it is only accepted if not defective. Hence, the probability of accepting a unit under inspection is $f \cdot (1 - P^*)$ and the acceptance probability comes out to be $f \cdot (1 - P^*) + (1 - f)$, i.e., $1 - f \cdot P^*$. As a result, the probability of accepting a sequence of *1000 units* with quality level P^* is $(1 - f \cdot P^*)^{1000}$. For a given acceptance probability of 0.1, we get the following representation for P^*:

$$P^* = \left(1 - \frac{1}{10^{0.001}}\right) \cdot \frac{1}{f} \approx \frac{0.0023}{f} = 0.0023k. \tag{4.16}$$

Constructing a CSP-1 according to DODGE/TORREY

In the approach of constructing a CSP-1 proposed by DODGE/TORREY one can proceed in the following way:

- Specification of the $AOQL$ value and the critical quality level P^*.
- Determination of the sampling interval k and the sampling fraction $f \approx 0.0023k$.
- Reading the clearance number i corresponding to the determined value f from the iso-$AOQL$ curve corresponding to the specified $AOQL$ value.

Since P^* and f are uniquely related to each other, figure 4.1/7 displays the P^*-axis next to the f-axis. This way the four quantities P^*, $AOQL$, i and f can be found in one glance.

Example 4.1/2

We are looking for a CSP-1 with an average outgoing quality limit of 0.02. First we will randomly pick two such representatives from the group of plans with this property. Then we will give an additional condition in order to have a unique solution of the problem.

To obtain two admissible combinations (i, k) we only need to pick two values for i, substitute them into (4.15) and with these results, and the specified $AOQL$, determine the plan parameter k. For example, for $i = 100$

it follows by (4.15b) that $k \approx 43.03$. In order to be on the "safe side", i.e., if we want to ensure that the average outgoing quality limit is really at most 2% we need to round k to the next smallest integer ($k = 43$). In the same way, for $i = 50$ we would i get $k \approx 8.69$, i.e., $k = 8$.

Should one specify $P^* = 0.03$ as well as $AOQL = 0.02$, then it follows from (4.16) that $f \approx 0.077$ or $k \approx 13.04$, i.e., $k = 13$. In figure 4.1/7, one can read from the correponding iso-$AOQL$ curve that $i \approx 65$ roughly corresponds to $f \approx 0.077$.

---

d) Average Outgoing Quality Limit under Altered Model Assumptions

Hitherto we have assumed that the monitored manufacturing process is under statistical control and, in particular, that it has a constant fraction defective P. We have further assumed that all units found to be defective during inspection are either repaired or replaced by conforming units. The formulae which were derived for the six performance measures of a CSP-1 depend significantly on these assumptions. We will now alternatively drop each one of these assumptions and discuss the effects on the $AOQL$ value.

Dropping the assumption that the process is under statistical control

Let us first drop the assumption that the manufacturing process is under statistical control. In this situation, we can no longer be sure that a plan which is constructed for a given $AOQL$ with the help of (4.15) and (4.16) actually has an average outgoing quality limit below the specified $AOQL$. There are various papers which derive the $AOQL$ in the case of a production process with unknown stochastical properties (see LIEBERMANN 1953, WHITE 1965, ENDRES 1969, BANZHOF/BRUGGER 1970 and SACKROWITZ 1975). Such an $AOQL$ is called an **unrestricted AOQL** and abbreviated by **UAOQL**.

We will first consider the CSP-1 under the assumption that sampling during the $f\cdot 100\%$ inspection period is administered using *random sampling* or *probability sampling*. In order to determine the $UAOQL$ of a CSP-1 with parameters i and k, we only need to analyze the situation which is least favourable with respect to the average outgoing quality. This is obviously the case when the first i units arriving at inspection are all conforming, the following k all defective and the next i again all conforming etc. In this special case of feedback between the quality level and the inspection procedure the performance measures of a CSP-1 all have constant values. Since during each screening period i units are processed, and during every sampling inspection period k units are processed it follows that the average cycle length (4.3a) has the constant value $z(P|i;k) = i + k$. Because $k - 1$ defectives per cycle remain undetected the AOQ function is given by

$$AOQ(P|i;k) = \frac{k-1}{i+k}.$$

As a result of the AOQ constancy, the unrestricted average outgoing quality limit is found to be

$$UAOQL_1 = \frac{k-1}{i+k}. \tag{4.17}$$

This value lies significantly above the $AOQL$ (4.9) which was calculated for the case of a production process with a Bernoulli distributed quality characteristic. For the CSP-1 of example 4.1/1, with $i = 50$ and $k = 25$ instead of $AOQL \approx 0.0325$ we would get the almost ten times larger value $UAOQL_1 = 0.32$. We want to note, however, that this extreme state of the manufacturing process, which leads to the outgoing quality (4.17), is very unlikely to occur in practice provided there is no deliberate sabotage.

One could actually think of an even worse situation, which can happen when a CSP-1 with parameters i and k is administered through *systematic sampling*. The worst-case scenario here would be that the first i units and thereafter only every k-th unit – i.e., every inspected unit – are non-defective. Under this behaviour of the process we would have no more screening periods after the first 100%-inspection period, although the fraction defective of the process is very high. If we denote the number of sample inspections by m, we can describe the unrestricted $AOQL$ of this case to be

$$UAOQL_2 = \lim_{m\to\infty} \frac{m(k-1)}{i+mk} = \frac{k-1}{k}. \tag{4.18}$$

Finally, we want to introduce a third unrestricted $AOQL$ which occurs when a CSP-1 with parameters i and k (assuming probability sampling during the partial inspection periods) is applied to a production process which is not under statistical control, but is assumed to not have a feedback to the inspection procedure. SACKROWITZ (1975) showed that for this case the unrestricted average outgoing quality limit is given by

$$UAOQL_3 = \frac{(k-1)\left[1-\left(1-\frac{1}{k}\right)^{\lambda_M}\right]}{i+\lambda_M}. \tag{4.19}$$

The parameter λ_M denotes the integer which maximizes the expression $[1-(1-\frac{1}{k})\lambda]/(i+\lambda)$.

Table 4.1/2 contains the maximum average outgoing quality for four CSP-1 plans which are obtained through formulae (4.9), (4.17), (4.18) and (4.19) and are valid under the respective assumptions made for the derivation of these formulae. In order to facilitate the verification of $UAOQL_3$ results we have also tabulated the values of λ_M from (4.19).

i	k	$AOQL$	$UAOQL_1$	$UAOQL_2$	$UAOQL_3$	λ_M
5	2	0.048	0.143	0.500	0.109	3
5	5	0.103	0.400	0.800	0.269	5
2	2	0.106	0.250	0.500	0.188	2
2	5	0.250	0.571	0.800	0.394	4

Table 4.1/2: *AOQL* and *UAOQL* of several CSP-1 plans

Dropping the assumption that nonconforming units are replaced

We will now discuss how the average outgoing quality limit changes when the detected defective units are not replaced but only sorted out. The manufacturing process is now assumed to be under statistical control.

The average outgoing quality of a CSP was defined to be the ratio of the number of undetected nonconforming units and the number of all processed units where these numbers were related to a cycle. The sorting out of defective units effects this characteristic. What is left of the average cycle length after the sorting is

$$z^*(P|i;k) = u(P|i)\cdot(1-P) + [v(P|k)-1] \tag{4.20}$$

because $u(P|i)$ reduces to $u(P|i)\cdot(1-P)$ and $v(P|k)$ to $v(P|k)-1$. Instead of (4.8a), we get

$$AOQ^*(P|i;k) = \frac{v(P|k)\cdot P - 1}{z^*(P|i;k)}. \tag{4.21 a}$$

As a consequence of (4.1), (4.2) and (4.20), it follows that

$$AOQ^*(P|i;k) = \frac{k-1}{z^*(P|i;k)} = \frac{(k-1)P(1-P)^{i-1}}{1+(k-1)(1-P)^{i-1}}. \tag{4.21 b}$$

Compared to (4.8b) the only difference is that the exponent i is replaced by $i-1$. The unrestricted $AOQL$ for the assumptions in (4.17) now becomes

$$UAOQL_1^* = \frac{k-1}{(i-1)+k}. \tag{4.22}$$

The remaining performance measures, i.e., $u(P|i)$, $v(P|k)$, $ATI(P|i;k)$, $AFI(P|i;k)$ and $L(P|i;k)$, will not change when the detected nonconforming units are not replaced.

Problem 4.1/2

a) Determine a CSP-1 with $AOQL = 0.01$ and specifications $i = 100$ and $i = 200$, respectively.

b) Determine a CSP-1 with $AOQL = 0.01$ and the side condition $P^* = 0.05$ referring to the quality level (4.16).

c) For each of the three plans determined above, calculate the values of all performance measures at $P = 0.01, 0.02, 0.03, 0.04$ and 0.05. Also calculate the average outgoing quality for the case when detected defectives are not replaced by good units.

d) Determine the unrestricted $AOQL$ values for all three plans according to (4.17) – (4.19). Analogous to table 4.1/2, summarize your results in a table. Include the $AOQL$ from (4.13) and $UAOQL$ from (4.22).

Remark

The effect of **inspection errors** (misclassification of inspected units) on the performance measures of a CSP-1 is investigated by CASE/BENNETT/SCHMIDT (1973). LUDWIG (1974), UHLMANN (1982) and VOGT (1986, 1988) discuss **economic continuous sampling plans.** RESNIKOFF (1960) describes how one can minimize the average fraction inspected $AFI(P)$ of a CSP-1 and thus talks only implicitly about the economical aspect. The **consumer protection** that a CSP-1 provides and which is expressed by the OC percentile RQL, is explored by STEPHENS (1979, 1981).

4.1.2 Modifications and Extensions of the CSP-1

a) The CSP-2 and CSP-3

In a CSP-1 the *first* detected nonconforming unit results in switching to the work intensive 100% inspection. Relatively soon after the development of the CSP-1, this was found to be a disadvantage. As a result, DODGE and TORREY developed two variations of their first plan, CSP-2 and CSP-3 (see DODGE/TORREY 1951). In a CSP-2, switching from partial to complete inspection is delayed through changes to the switching rule (protection from "premature" switching), whereas a CSP-3 also protects from not detecting short sequences of nonconforming units.

Procedure of a CSP-2

A **CSP-2** differs from a CSP-1 in the sense that during the sampling inspection period the first observed defective unit does not immediately require the procedure to change to 100% inspection. Switching only takes place if another defective is found in the following m sampled units. Frequently, one chooses $m = i$. This choice of m implies that, after discovery of the first nonconforming unit during the $f \cdot 100\%$ inspection period, the inspection needs to draw only good units in the next i sampled units, i.e., among $i \cdot k$ processed units, before the register Z in figure 4.1/2 is reset from $Z = 1$ to $Z = 0$. If $Z = 2$ is reached before this happens, then the procedure switches to screening at this point.

Besides the parameters i and k of a CSP-1, a CSP-2 thus has a third parameter m. We will only determine one of the characteristic measures of a CSP-2, the **average outgoing quality**. Analogous to (4.8b) and (4.22) one gets different formulae depending on whether the inspection procedure works *with* or *without* replacing detected nonconforming units. In the case of replacement of nonconforming units, the average outgoing quality of a CSP-2 with parameters i, k and m is given by

AOQ function of a CSP-2 under different model assumptions

$$AOQ(P|i;k;m) = \frac{(k-1)PQ^i(2-Q^m)}{(1-Q^i)(1-Q^m)+kQ^i(2-Q^m)}, \tag{4.23 a}$$

where $Q := 1 - P$. If defective units are sorted out without replacement, then we get

$$AOQ^*(P|i;k;m) = \frac{AOQ(P|i;k;m)}{Q + AOQ(P|i;k;m)} \tag{4.23 b}$$

and $AOQ(P|i;k;m)$ according to (4.23a).

Procedure of a CSP-3

The difference between a **CSP-3** and a CSP-2 is that, after discovery of the first defective unit during a sampling inspection period, the next four consecutive units are inspected (insertion of a short screening period of four units in length). If a second nonconforming unit is found during this time, then one switches to screening (100% inspection with random length). However, if all four units are found to be good, then one continues with the CSP-2. In other words, one then "forgets" this first observed nonconforming unit (Z is reset to zero) after m additional samples, provided there were no more nonconforming units. If there are, one appropriately switches back to 100% inspection.

The formula for the average outgoing quality of a CSP-3 with replacement of detected nonconforming units is

AOQ function of a CSP-3 under different model assumptions

$$AOQ(P|i;k;m) = \frac{(k-1)PQ^i(1+Q^4-Q^{m+4})}{(1-Q^i)(1-Q^{m+4})+4PQ^i+kQ^i(1+Q^4-Q^{m+4})}. \tag{4.24 a}$$

When nonconforming units are not replaced, the formula is

$$AOQ^*(P|i;k;m) = \frac{AOQ(P|i;k;m)}{Q + AOQ(P|i;k;m)}. \tag{4.24 b}$$

and $AOQ(P|i;k;m)$ according to (4.24a).

Example 4.1/3

We will continue with the CSP-1 of example 4.1/1 with $i = 50$ and $k = 25$. This plan attained the average outgoing quality limit $AOQL = AOQ(P_M) \approx 0.0325$ at $P_M \approx 0.0514$. For this quality level, we will now calculate the average outgoing quality for the plans introduced above using formulae (4.23) and (4.24):

Type of CSP	$AOQ(0.0514)$	$AOQ^*(0.0514)$
CSP-1 with $i = 50; k = 25$	0.0325	0.0331
CSP-2 with $i = m = 50; k = 25$	0.0395	0.0399
CSP-3 with $i = m = 50; k = 25$	0.0384	0.0389

Table 4.1/3: Average outgoing quality limits of a CSP-1, CSP-2 and CSP-3 for $P = 0.0514$

We can see that the average outgoing quality of all three plans without replacement is slighty larger than that of a CSP with replacement. It is the most difficult to return to 100% inspection for the CSP-2. Consequently, its average outgoing quality has a higher value than that of the CSP-1 and the CSP-3.

Problem 4.1/3

a) A stream of manufactured units is to be inspected by a CSP-2 with parameters $i = 8$, $k = 4$ and $m = 8$. Suppose that the output stream is as described by figure 4.1/1. Assuming systematic sampling during the sampling inspection periods (sampling every fourth unit), determine the number of samples needed to complete the first partial inspection period.

b) What would be the course of the inspection procedure, if one administers a CSP-3 with $i = 8, k = 4$ and $m = 4$ under the same assumptions?

Problem 4.1/4

Simplify the formulae in (4.23) for the special case of $m = i$.

Problem 4.1/5

a) For the quality level $P = 0.02$, calculate the average outgoing quality of a CSP-2 and a CSP-3 with $i = 100$ and $k = 20$ (AOQ in the case of replacement of detected nonconforming units by good units). Successively choose the values 20, 50, 100 and 150 for m and describe how the average outgoing quality changes for increasing m.

b) Determine the limit of the average outgoing quality in (4.23a) and (4.24a) of a CSP-2 and CSP-3 for $m \to \infty$. What effect does $m \to \infty$ have on the two plans?

b) Multilevel Continuous Sampling Plans

So far all the introduced continuous plans had in common that they possessed, besides the screening mode, exactly *one* additional inspection intensity, i.e., inspection with the sampling fraction f during the sampling period ($0 < f < 1$; see figure 4.1/1). The various inspection intensities of a CSP are called **inspection levels** or **inspection stages**. When specifying the number of inspection levels it is not usual to count the starting level (screening mode). Counting in this way the CSP-1, CSP-2 and CSP-3 are all considered to be **single-level continuous plans**. It is also possible to design CSP with additional inspection levels where the inspection intensity decreases as the number of the corresponding level increases. After observing a sufficient number of good samples one will switch from one level to the next higher level with a smaller sampling fraction. In case of finding a nonconforming unit one will go one level or even two or more levels down to a larger sampling fraction. Such an approach of flexibly adapting the inspection intensity according to the recent inspection history usually reduces the amount of inspection compared to a single-level CSP.

Procedure of a multilevel CSP

In a **multilevel continuous sampling plan** or **multilevel CSP** the abrupt switching from a sampling inspection mode with a low inspection intensity to 100% inspection is diminished by inserting intermediary stages. In a CSP-2 this is achieved through a modification of the switching rules. A s-level CSP is specified by the sampling fraction $f_0 := 1$ (screening mode) and s different sampling fractions $f_1, f_2, \ldots, f_s$ with

$$1 > f_1 > f_2 \ldots > f_s$$

and s positive integer-valued clearance numbers $i_0, i_1, \ldots, i_{s-1}$. When operating with the sampling fraction f_j the plan is said to be on level j. In analogy to the CSP-1 the transition from level j ($j = 0, 1, \ldots, s-1$) to level $j+1$ with the lower sampling fraction f_{j+1} is controlled by the clearance number i_j. If a nonconforming unit is observed while the procedure operates on level j ($f_j \cdot 100\%$ inspection period; $j \geq 1$), then the inspection is switched back to a level with higher inspection intensity. There are several possible options for switching back. For example one could require that the procedure always switches back to level 0 (100% inspection). Another possibility would be to always go back exactly one level or exactly r levels ($r > 1$).

History of the multilevel CSP

Multilevel CSP were first proposed by LIEBERMAN and SOLOMON (1955). They discussed a s-level CSP with

$$f_j := f^j; \qquad (0 < f < 1; \;\; j = 0, 1, \ldots, s) \qquad (4.25\text{ a})$$

$$i_0 = i_1 = \ldots = i_{s-1} =: i; \qquad (4.25\text{ b})$$

i.e., a plan with a constant clearance number i and sampling fractions, which form a decreasing geometric series. The procedure always switches back to the next lower level, i.e., from j to $j-1$ ($j \geq 1$).

We will not go into further details about the different variations of this plan or the calculation of the performance measures of a multilevel CSP and refer the reader to the literature on the subject by DERMAN/LITTAUER/SOLOMON (1957), IRESON/BIEDENBENDER (1958), DERMAN/JOHNS/LIEBERMAN (1959), ELFVING (1962/63) and VON COLLANI (1974).

Remarks

1. In practice, the selection of a specific single-level or multilevel CSP is supported by **sampling tables for continuous sampling inspection**. The four different presently available tables have all been published by the US military administration (U.S.-Government Printing Office, Washington 1958, 1959, 1975 and 1982). The latter two sampling systems are known under the names MIL-STD 1235A and MIL-STD 1235B. The structure and procedure of the Military Standard 1235B is for example described by SCHILLING (1982) or BANKS (1989).
2. All the CSP-systems mentioned above work with a **stopping rule** during the 100% inspection periods. If it turns out that during the screening an unreasonable number of units has to be processed before switching occurs, then this is a sign that the defective fraction of the process has increased. The stopping rule gives the condition for terminating the screening period. In this case one has the option of either stopping the manufacturing process or to take other measures for correcting the process level. Stopping rules are discussed in detail by MURPHY (1959).
3. So far all the discussed continuous sampling plans have assumed that the manufacturing process will continue for an infinite time. Modifications for processes with a finite time span can be found in BLACKWELL (1977).

c) Block Continuous Plans

So far all the considered continuous sampling plans have assumed that there is a continuous stream of output, in other words that the production stream is not split up into lots or segments. There are, however, manufacturing processes with a naturally segmented or blocked output stream. Such blocks can for example be a charge, an edition, the output of a particular shift or hour or similar. For these situations there are special continuous sampling plans called **continuous sampling plans with subgrouping** or **block continuous plans**. When administering such a plan one successively takes samples from each block of the production output. In the case that a critical number of observed nonconforming units is exceeded, the rest of the block is submitted to 100% inspection. Different to the CSP-1, CSP- 2 and CSP-3, which specify the clearance number i as well as the sampling fraction $f = 1/k$, and the multilevel continuous plans, which specify i and leave the sampling fraction flexible, this type of continuous sampling plan has a specified parameter f and the clearance number varies randomly from block to block.

Procedure of continuous sampling plans with subgrouping

Continuous sampling plans with subgrouping were introduced by WALD and WOLFOWITZ (1945) (see also GIRSHICK 1954 and ALBRECHT/GULDE/ MCLEAN/THOMPSON 1955). We will introduce one of the plans proposed by them as an example. In this CSP with subgrouping, denoted plan C by WALD/WOLFOWITZ, the output stream is divided into *blocks* of fixed size N and within the blocks the units are divided into *groups* of size k. The blocks are successively inspected and one proceeds with the inspection as follows:

Procedure of the plan C proposed by WALD and WOLFOWITZ

- One first successively samples one unit from each of the groups of the block (beginning with the first group in the block), inspects the units and adds up the number of nonconforming units from all these random samples of size one.
- In case the observed number of nonconforming units reaches a critical value M^* before the last group is inspected, one submits all remaining groups to 100% inspection. Otherwise one continues with sampling inspection until the last group.

Thus the plan C of WALD/WOLFOWITZ is specified by the block size N, the group size k and the critical value M^*. The number of groups is obviously given by $g = N/k$. Instead of k one can also use the sampling fraction $f = 1/k$ as an alternative parameter. Figure 4.1/8 clearly illustrates the procedure of such a plan, every block is divided into $g = 10$ groups and the critical number was choosen to be $M^* = 2$. Groups where a nonconforming unit was observed are marked with a black dot and groups which are submitted to screening are shaded.

Performance measures for the plan C

If a plan C is specified by N, k and M^* then the fraction of inspected units per block, the so-called **average fraction inspected** or **AFI(P)**

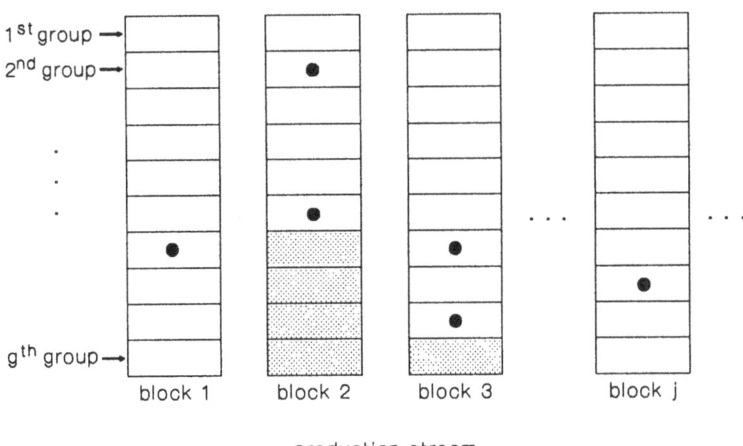

Figure 4.1/8: Procedure of a block continuous sampling plan by WALD/WOLFOWITZ (1945)

is, for a given process level P and under the assumption that detected nonconforming units are replaced, determined by

$$AFI(P) = 1 - \frac{M^*(1-f)}{P \cdot f \cdot N} + \frac{1-f}{P \cdot f \cdot N} \sum_{i=0}^{M^*-1} (M^* - 1) \binom{fN}{i} P^i (1-P)^{fN-i}. \tag{4.26}$$

The corresponding formula for the average fraction of undetected nonconforming units per block, the **average outgoing quality** $AOQ(P)$ is

$$AOQ(P) = \frac{M^*(1-f)}{f \cdot N} \cdot \left[1 - \frac{1}{M^*} \sum_{i=0}^{M^*-1} (M^* - i) \binom{fN}{i} P^i (1-P)^{fN-i} \right]. \tag{4.27}$$

Maximising (4.27) with respect to P results in

$$AOQL := \max_P AOQ(P) = \frac{M^*(1-f)}{f \cdot N}. \tag{4.28}$$

Remarks

1. The principle of *block continuous* inspection can, besides process control, also be applied to attribute acceptance sampling. In this case a lot would be considered to be a block. The skip-lot-inspection described in section 3.2.7d can be seen as a version of *continuous* inspection for acceptance sampling, but the difference is that in continuous inspection with subgrouping no lot passes without inspection.
2. At present continuous sampling plans are not widely used. This can be seen from the fact that they do not appear on the training syllabus of the American and most

European quality assurance organisations. However, there are publications on this subject, for example in Germany by the DGQ (DGQ 1988). The development of continuous sampling plans in the USA until about 1955 is presented by BOWKER (1956). A very comprehensive presentation of results in continuous sampling theory is also contained in the monograph by STEPHENS (1979).

Problem 4.1/6

The continuous sampling plan with subgrouping discussed by WALD/ WOLFOWITZ is supposed to be applied to the assembly line manufacturing of a product (inspection with replacement of detected nonconforming units). The block size is given to be $N = 1000$, the sampling fraction to be $f = 0.1$ and the average outgoing quality limit to be $AOQL = 0.018$.

a) Determine the third plan parameter M^*.
b) Calculate the average fraction inspected and average outgoing quality for a process level of $P = 0.02$.

Problem 4.1/7

Describe the parallels between attribute acceptance sampling with the ISO 2859 (see figure 3.2/27) and process control with a s-level CSP.

4.2 Control Charts

The manufacturing of a product always involves a certain amount of variation in the production conditions. This natural fluctuation has the effect, that the realizations of each product quality characteristic X are also subject to a certain variability. In a carefully designed and implemented manufacturing process these inherent variations are small and cannot be attributed to controllable single factors. Under these conditions we say that the manufacturing process is *under statistical control* or that it runs *undisturbed*. During the ongoing production it can happen that these variations increase and exceed a reasonable amount, due to significant changes in the controllable factors of the process. For example, wear and tear of a tool or fatigue of the personnel could lead to a systematic change in the process level or to an increase of the process variance. Then we would say that the process is *out of statistical control* or that it is *disturbed*.

Control charts serve the primary purpose of continuously monitoring whether the manufacturing process is under statistical control. As we will elaborate later one can also use control charts for other purposes besides this. However, we want to first illustrate the procedure of quality control charts with the example of the SHEWHART chart. After this we will give an overview of the different kinds of quality control charts and present their test theoretical background. A detailed discussion of special quality control charts will then be given in the following sections.

Basic assumption: uncorrelated quality data

When dealing with control charts we always assume that the state of statistical control is characterized by a process generating *independent* and *identically distributed* random variables. In particular this assumption implies *lack of autocorrelation*. Approaches for control charting in the case of autocorrelated quality data are described by ALWAN/ROBERTS (1988) and MONTGOMERY/MASTRANGELO (1991).

4.2.1 Control Chart Principles

a) Basic Idea of a Control Chart

When applying a control chart one draws samples of fixed size n from the manufacturing process at specified time points. The intervals between these timepoints are in general constant. The observable values $X_1, X_2, \ldots, X_n$ of the monitored quality characteristic are summarized in the sample vector $\mathbf{X}$ and are either used in their original form or are condensed to a sample statistic, for example the sample sum, sample average, sample median, sample standard deviation or sample range. A control chart is the graphical display of these sample results, in either a manual way or through electronic

Definition of a control chart

data processing. The results are plotted on the vertical axis against the specific time points of their observation or respectively the sample index numbers on the horizontal axis. In addition to these two axes the coordinate system contains several fixed lines. We will here only describe the lines that are found in the **classical control chart**, which goes back to SHEWHART. **Modified SHEWHART control charts** will be presented in section 4.5. Non-SHEWHART control charts, also called **control charts with memory**, will be discussed in sec. 4.6.

Lines of a classical control chart

As an aid for orientation the coordinate system of a SHEWHART type control chart usually contains a straight **centre line** parallel to the abscissa. The height of this center line **CL** is given by the target value of the manufacturing process. This value can for example be a **nominal value** required by a law, a standard or the manufacturing specifications. It can also be a **value based on past experience** from the process or an **estimated value** taken from a prerun of the manufacturing process under undisturbed conditions.

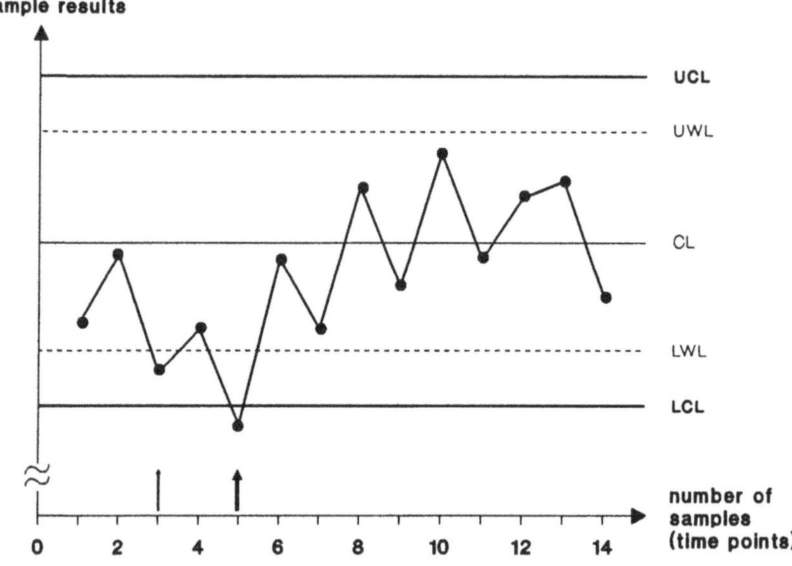

Figure 4.2/1: SHEWHART control chart with twosided warning and control lines

Whereas one can generally do without the centre line in a control chart, it is absolutely necessary to have *one* or *two* **control lines**. Depending on whether one will either monitor deviations of the quality characteristic above *and* below the target value or only onesided deviations one works with two control lines or with one control line. In accordance with this one distinguishes between **twosided control charts** and **onesided control charts**. The control lines are called **upper control limit** and **lower control limit**, abbreviated by **UCL** and **LCL**, respectively. These lines have to be calculated and drawn into the chart before the start of the sampling inspection. They serve the purpose of deciding whether the process is under statistical control or whether disturbances might have occurred. Besides these control lines SHEWHART control charts sometimes contain one or two additional **warning lines**. The levels corresponding to these lines are called the **upper warning limit UWL** and **lower warning limit LWL** and the distance between them and, if applicable, the centre line is shorter than those between the control lines UCL and LCL.

Figure 4.2/1 shows a SHEWART control chart with twosided warning and control lines. Several sample results are drawn into the chart. In order to facilitate orientation the sample points are connected by straight lines.

Different actions depending on the sample outcomes

During the application of a control chart there are three different possible outcomes for each sample: The observed value lies within the warning limits, between the warning and control limits or outside the control limits. In the process described by figure 4.2/1 each of these three events occur. The third sample observation (thin arrow) lies within the lower warning and control boundaries, the fifth sample result (thick arrow) even outside the control limit. Beginning with the sixth sample all values lie within the warning lines. Before using a control chart one has to clearly determine the consequences of these three different events. In practice, one often uses the following **decision rules**:

- Case 1: *The sample result lies within the warning limits*

  Here one assumes that the manufacturing process runs under statistical control. Hence it is not necessary to take any particular action and the process is allowed to continue as before.

- Case 2: *The sample result lies between the warning and control limits*

  In this case there is the suspicion of a disturbance. Usually one will draw a second sample immediately. If the new result lies within the warning limits, then this suspicion is considered to be disproved. Should the new observation again lie outside the warning limits one will regard the suspicion to be justified and take a corrective action in order to bring the manufacturing process under statistical control.

- Case 3: *The sample result lies on or outside the control limits*

  If this occurs we are forced to assume that the manufacturing process is no longer under statistical control. One will immediately intervene in the process. What this means in a concrete situation depends on the particular process, one's knowledge about it and on the kind of disturbance indicated by the inspection result. Under certain circumstances one may even be forced to screen all units, which were produced after the last sample.

In a control chart without warning limits the first decision rule refers to the control limits and the second decision rule is omitted.

Critical remark concerning the use of warning limits or run rules

Please note, that the use of warning limits considerably changes the statistical properties of a control chart. In particular it changes its power curve in an uncontrolled manner. The same holds in the case of taking account for seemingly nonrandom sample data patterns (application of so-called **run rules**).

b) Designing a Control Chart

Phase 1: Design of the chart

When working with control charts one has to distinguish between two different phases. In the first phase the control chart is designed and implemented. The design of a control chart mainly involves

- a suitable choice of the sample size and the time interval between consecutive samples;
- the specification of the control limits and, if appropriate, the warning limits.

During the design period test theoretical and economic considerations are of great importance. This phase also includes the evaluation of a control chart with the help of its power function.

Phase 2: Ongoing application of the chart

The second phase contains the continuous application of the control chart on site. It includes drawing the samples at the specified times, the determination of the observed values or counts for the inspected sample units, the evaluation of the sample statistic, entering of the results into the control chart as well as making the decision according to the given decision rule. We want to note that there is a tremendous potential for rationalization during this phase. Measuring machines, for example, directly convert their observations into digital data and transfer them to a computer. A suitable computer program could then evaluate these data using specified sample statistics and display the control chart with the plotted values on a monitor.

Economic considerations for specifying sample size and sampling interval

In the following we want to describe in detail how to design a classical SHEWHART chart. When determining the sample size and the sampling interval one can use economic criteria. The relevant costs are:

- the **inspection costs**, which are an increasing function of the sample size and a decreasing function of the sampling interval;
- the **costs of production standstill** due to interrupting the process for making the adjustments required by the control chart (decreasing function of the sampling interval);
- the **costs of an undetected disturbance**, which are an increasing function of the sampling interval.

In practice the sample size n and the sampling frequency are arbitrarily chosen, usually based on past experience. The sample size n is rarely bigger than 15 and – because of numerical reasons – an odd number.

Specifying the control limits of a classical SHEWHART chart:

The specification of the control limits and possibly the warning limits is a central issue in the design of a control chart. The control limits are specified in a way that the test statistic g(**X**) reaches or exceeds these values only with a given small probability α, when the process runs without disturbance. For a quality control chart with *twosided* control limits UCL and LCL this means

$$Pr[g(\mathbf{X}) \notin (LCL, UCL)|\text{process is under statistical control}] = \alpha. \quad (4.29)$$

In practice one uses test statistics with symmetric distributions and consequently one will always proceed as described in figure 4.2/1 and specify the limits LCL and UCL at the same distance from the centre line CL. The probability (4.29) then consists of two equal probabilities $Pr[g(\mathbf{X}) \geq UCL|\cdots]$ and $Pr[g(\mathbf{X}) \leq LCL|\cdots]$. As a result two separate determining equations for UCL and LCL are obtained from (4.29):

- in the case of a two-sided control chart

$$Pr[g(\mathbf{X}) \geq UCL|\text{ process is under statistical control}] = \alpha/2 \quad (4.30)$$

$$Pr[g(\mathbf{X}) \leq LCL|\text{ process is under statistical control}] = \alpha/2. \quad (4.31)$$

When designing a *onesided* control chart one proceeds in an analogous way. One only does not split the probability α into two probabilities and determines UCL or respectively LCL from one of the following two equations:

- in the case of a one-sided control chart

$$Pr[g(\mathbf{X}) \geq UCL|\text{ process is under statistical control}] = \alpha \quad (4.32)$$

$$Pr[g(\mathbf{X}) \leq LCL|\text{ process is under statistical control}] = \alpha. \quad (4.33)$$

It is important not to specify the control limits too close to the centre line, because otherwise the unavoidable natural "background noise" at times when the process is in state of statistical control, can induce an intervention. The probability α of interfering in an undisturbed process (**false alarm**) increases as the distance between the control limits decreases. However, if the control lines are too far away from the centre line then one runs the risk of responding too late to an actual systematic disturbance of the process. The probability of (unwantingly) not intervening into a disturbed process (**neglected alarm**) increases as the distance between the control lines and the centre line increases. In general one thus has to make a compromise that takes into account the risks of both kinds of decision errors. In practice certain conventions for the specification of the control and warning limits have evolved. In Europe, for example, these critical boundaries are usually calculated in a way that the sample statistic g($\mathbf{X}$) of an undisturbed process lies within the control lines with a probability of 99% and, if applicable, between the warning lines with 95% probability. Consequently, for the determination of the control lines one generally sets $\alpha = 0.01$ in (4.29) respectively in (4.32) or (4.33). Similarily the specification conditions for the warning lines are obtained from these equations by substituting UCL and LCL by UWL and LWL and setting $\alpha = 0.05$.

European convention for specifying the control and warning limits

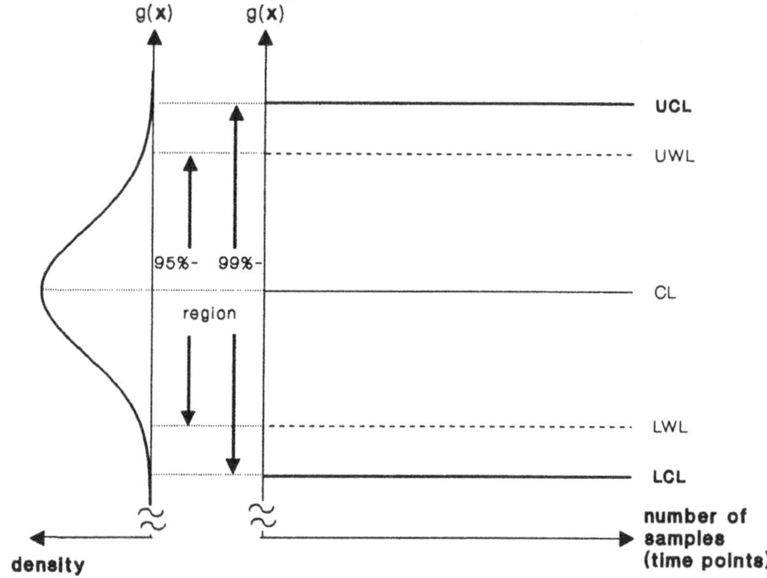

Figure 4.2/2: Specification of control and warning limits of a classical SHEWHART control chart

Figure 4.2/2 illustrates the approach of specifying the limits according to (4.29). The sample statistic $g(\mathbf{X})$ is assumed to have a continuous and symmetric distribution, e.g. the normal distribution. We further assume that its density exists. In the figure above the density of $g(\mathbf{X})$ in the case of an undisturbed process is plotted beside the vertical axis of the chart. The centre line CL thus represents the expectation of the test statistic.

In the anglosaxon literature the limiting boundaries are usually calculated in a different way. If the scalar test statistic $Y = g(\mathbf{X})$ has, under in-control conditions, a distribution with expectation μ_Y (level of the centre line CL) and standard deviation σ_Y, then the control limits UCL and LCL are placed at the $\mu_Y \pm 3\sigma_Y$ level and the warning lines at $\mu_Y \pm 2\sigma_Y$. In the case of a normally distributed test statistic these **2-Sigma** and respectively **3-Sigma** lines are a little further apart than the 95% and 99%-lines, which we use. In practice one often uses **nomograms** from which one can easily read the location of these lines.

Anglosaxon convention for specifying the control and warning limits

Remark

When administering process control by means of control charts, three parameters need to be specified: the sample size, the control limits and the time interval between consecutive samples. The control limits are generally determined solely based on statistical criteria, i.e., as described above one computes the limits for the given probability α of a false alarm. When specifying the other two parameters one usually resorts to values based on experience or rules of thumb. Approaches to specify the three decision parameters according to economic criteria will be presented in section 4.4.5 b.

c) Benefits from Using Control Charts

The implementation and application of a control chart serves several goals at the same time. In general these are:

▷ *Increase in quality and productivity*

A quality control chart monitors the conformity between the actual and the desired state of a process with respect to a certain quality characteristic. The application of a control chart is supposed to have the effect that undesired changes in the behaviour of the quality characteristic – i.e., a change in the mean, an increase in the spread or an increasing number of nonconforming units or nonconformities – are discovered and corrected as soon as possible. As a result the fraction defective of the process or respectively the amount of mending of nonconformities is reduced and consequently the productivity is increased.

▷ *Documentation of the in-house quality assurance*

Completed control charts, i.e., charts, which already fulfilled their purpose as an instrument of process control, serve a company as proof and documentation in several ways:

- They document the quality assurance efforts of a producer for the consumer. The control charts can be handed over to the buyer with the corresponding production output. Then the buyer can reduce the amount of his inspection or possibly completely stop to administer it.

In the automotive industry documentation on the side of the supplier is for example legally required for certain safety related parts.

- They document the quality assurance before the trade inspection and technical inspection. In some trades it is legally required to keep the process data about quality assurance, i.e., through laws concerning measures and gauges and their directives (e.g., about fill weights) or environmental laws and decrees (e.g., about emission of pollutants).
- Finally quality control charts can also be used for internal evaluation of the precision of machinery and tools. In this respect they can also serve as an aid in decisions about additional investments or the scheduling of general overhauls.

▷ *Conducting process capability studies*

Before producing in large quantities it is important to ensure that the implemented process and its supervision via control charts is actually capable of fulfilling the required specifications with respect to the expectation and variance of the monitored quality characteristic X. Otherwise the process would be continually interrupted whenever the control chart limits are exceeded. The control chart is a useful tool for conducting **process capability studies** (see sec. 4.5.1) before the actual start of production.

4.2.2 Types of Control Charts

Criteria for the classification of control charts

There are several criteria according to which control charts can be classified. One criterion has already been mentioned: with respect to the number of control limits one distinguishes between **onesided control charts** and **twosided control charts**. We will now introduce further criteria for classification.

First, SHEWHART control charts can be classified according to whether the calculation of the control limits involves technical specifications (tolerance limits) or not. With respect to this point we distinguish between **classical** and **modified** SHEWHART **control charts**. We will discuss classical SHEWHART control charts for attributes in section 4.3 and for variables in section 4.4. Modified SHEWHART control charts will be presented in section 4.5.2.

We speak of a **single-tracked control chart** when the control chart only contains one coordinate sytem in which the inspection results for monitoring *one* aspect of the manufacturing process (location *or* spread) are entered. A **double-tracked control chart** contains two coordinate systems for *two* different sample statistics from each sample in order to simultaneously monitor location *and* spread. Thus double-tracked control charts are nothing but two simultaneously applied single-tracked control charts, both related to the same quality characteristic. Different to these, **multivariate control charts** are control charts for simultaneously monitoring several different quality characteristics. In the following we will always restrict ourselves to **univariate control charts**.

According to how the quality characteristic is measured one distinguishes between **control charts for attributes** and **control charts for variables**. Synonym terms are **control charts for count data** and **control charts for measurements** Charts for attributes always use a test statistic with *discrete* distribution whereas the sample statistic of a chart for variables has a *continuous* distribution.

Finally we can differentiate control charts according to whether the decision on interfering with the process is solely based on the present sample outcome or also on the preceeding samples. SHEWHART type control charts only use the current sample result. This is why they are called **control charts without memory**. **Control charts with memory**, for example CUSUM charts and EWMA charts, in addition use the results of preceeding samples.

The above description can be summarized in table 4.2/1. Summary

Classification	Differentiation criterion
one-/ twosided control chart	number of control lines
classical SHEWHART control chart / modified SHEWHART chart	mode of calculating the control limits
single-/ double-tracked control chart	number of sample statistics for one quality characteristic
univariate / multivariate control chart	number of quality characteristics monitored by one chart
control chart for attributes / for variables	distribution type of the sample statistic
control chart with / without memory	consideration of previous sample results

Table 4.2/1: Classifications of control charts

For the notation of control charts we are frequently using one or two letters (for single-tracked or double-tracked control charts, respectively), which refer to the applied sample statistic. In practice the following notations have established themselves:

Notations for control charts operating with different sampling statistics

- **x chart**

  Single-tracked control chart for attributes where the test statistic is the *cumulative count of nonconformities per product unit* or the *number of nonconforming units* in the sample. These charts are also called **c chart** or **np chart**, respectively.

- **p chart**

  Control chart for attributes, which uses the *proportion of nonconforming units* in the sample as its test statistic.

- **u chart**

  Control chart for attributes. Its test statistic is the *cumulative count of nonconformities per physical unit.*

- **$\bar{x}$ chart and $\tilde{x}$ chart**

  Control chart for variables with the *sample mean* or respectively the *sample median* as its test statistic. Accordingly, these control charts are also called **mean chart** and **median chart**. Both serve the purpose of monitoring the process level.

- **r chart and s chart**

  Control chart for variables where the test statistic is the *sample range* or respectively the *sample standard deviation.* Accordingly these charts are also called **range chart** and **standard deviation chart**. They both monitor the spread of the production process.

- **Extreme value chart**

  Control chart for variables where all the individual observations (elements of the sample vector) are directly drawn into the chart. This type of chart can be used for monitoring the location as well as the spread of a quality characteristic. Hence, it can be universally applied. However, its performance compared to a specialized control chart has to be questioned. Since, when working with this kind of chart, the only vector elements of importance are the smallest and/or largest value it is called **extreme value chart**.

- **$\bar{x}$-s chart, $\bar{x}$-r chart, $\tilde{x}$-s chart and $\tilde{x}$-r chart**

  Double-tracked control charts for variables which use the *sample average* or the *sample median* for monitoring the process level and the *sample standard deviation* or the *sample range* for controlling the process spread. These charts are appropriately named as above, for example **mean range chart** in the case of the $\bar{x}$-r chart.

Figure 4.2/3 shows the SHEWHART control charts, which will be presented in sections 4.3 - 4.5. For the control charts with memory, treated in section 4.6, there is a similar, but more simple scheme. There are also CUSUM charts for attribute and variable inspection, but there is no chart corresponding to the modified SHEWHART chart. In practice double-tracked control charts with memory are not used either.

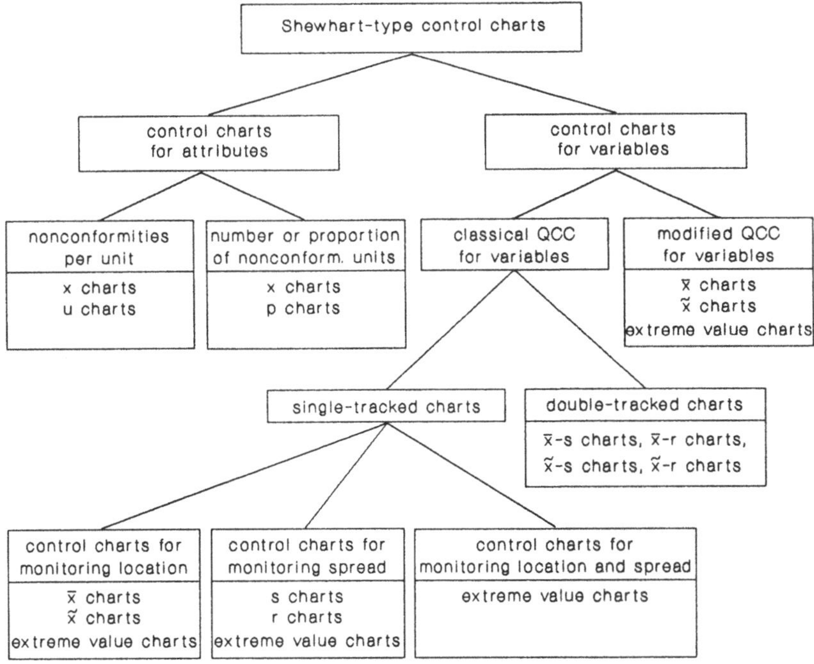

Figure 4.2/3: SHEWHART-type control charts covered in this manuscript

4.2.3 Hypothesis Testing and Control Charts

When comparing control charts one can, besides differences, also look for their common properties. As mentioned above, control charts are mainly a graphical display of a sample statistic $g(\mathbf{X})$ as a function of time. All control charts have in common that their application is equivalent to repeatedly performing a test of the hypotheses

Applying a control chart is equivalent to hypothesis testing

$$
\begin{aligned}
H_0 &: \text{ The manufacturing process is under statistical control.} \\
H_1 &: \text{ The manufacturing process is out of statistical control.}
\end{aligned}
\tag{4.34}
$$

If the realization of the sample function reaches or exceeds the control limits UCL and LCL (twosided control chart) or one of these limits (in the case of a onesided control chart), then the hypothesis H_0 is rejected and adjustment of the process is undertaken. The acceptance region $\overline{CR}$ for H_0 is thus given by the set of all those realizations of the test statistic, which lie within the control limit(s). Accordingly the rejection region CR for H_0 is defined to be the complement of $\overline{CR}$. Consequently the decision rule of the test reads as follows:

- If the test statistic $g(\mathbf{X})$ lies on or outside the control line(s), then intervene in the process.
- If the test statistic $g(\mathbf{X})$ lies within the control lines, then do not take any action.

In a given situation the hypothesis H_0 says that a location parameter (μ, λ, P) or a spread parameter (σ) of the monitored quality characteristic agrees with a desired value. This target value can either be an actual nominal value or an estimate obtained from a prerun of the process. The choice of a test statistic depends on the monitored aspect of the manufacturing process (spread or location of a quality characteristic). A further criterion can be the time and complexity involved in calculating the test statistic and the qualifications required by the inspection personnel. However, with the advance of the computerization in statistical quality control these criteria are loosing their significance. Simple and unassuming handling of a test statistic and its efficiency sometimes are, as the reader will see, antagonistic features. For example, extreme value charts are easier to apply than mean charts, but the latter ones are more powerful.

Test theoretical background of the control lines

The control lines of a control chart – compare figure 4.2/2 – are the boundaries of the variation interval of the test statistic, when the process runs in state of control. The 99% control lines represent the boundaries between the acceptance and rejection region of the hypothesis test (4.34) in case of assuming a significance level of $\alpha = 0.01$. The optional 95% warning lines do not have an analogous test theoretical background.

Evaluating the performance of a control chart:

Behind every control chart stands a hypothesis test of type (4.34). Since every hypothesis test can be completely characterized by the power function (2.130) or alternatively the OC function (2.132) one can generally use either of those functions to describe the performance of a control chart. Recall that behind all sampling plans presented in chapter 3, there also were underlying hypothesis tests. In their case we worked with the OC function, because in acceptance sampling one is primarily interested in calculating the probability of accepting a lot under a given decision rule (probability of not rejecting H_0). For the evaluation of control charts we want to use the

power function, because in process control the probability of intervening in the process (probability of rejecting H_0) is of particular importance; there are however textbooks that work with the OC function, for example MONTGOMERY (1991) and WADSWORTH/STEPHENS/GODFREY (1986). With the help of the power function one can study how the probability of intervening in the manufacturing process changes for varying process states. The graph of the power function is called the **power curve** or **power characteristic**. In order not to mix up the application and evaluation of a control chart the power curve is not displayed on a chart.

- by means of the OC or the power curve

Along with the power and the OC functions there exists another instrument describing the performance of control charts, the **ARL function** (**a**verage **r**un **l**ength). To explain this new function one first has to explain the meaning of the **run length**. The run length of a control chart is the number of samples to be drawn from one intervention in the process to the next intervention. The *ARL* value is the expectation of the discrete random variable "run length". The *ARL* function of a control chart shows how the *ARL* value depends on the state of the process. When the process is undisturbed this function should have a high value, whereas it should have a rather low value for a process being disturbed.

- by means of the *ARL* curve

Problem 4.2/1

a) Explain why, when working with control charts, one speaks of a "false alarm" and a "neglected alarm". Relate these two terms to the type I and type II error in the theory of hypothesis testing.

b) Obviously, there also is a "false warning" and a "neglected warning". What is understood by these terms?

c) What is the probability of a "false alarm" and of a "false warning" for a control chart of the type displayed in figure 4.2/2?

4.3 SHEWHART Control Charts for Attributes

Different sample statistics in process control for count data:

The result in process control for count data based on a sample is either the number of nonconforming units or the number of nonconformities in the sample. Different control charts are used in these two situations. In the following we will introduce these **control charts for attributes**, but restrict ourselves to SHEWHART-type charts.

- number of nonconformities in the sample

If one counts the *number of nonconformities in the sample*, then the reference unit can be either a *product unit* (i.e. weaving flaws per bale of cloth, impurities per piece of glass, nonconformities in the varnish per roll of varnished wire) or a *physical unit* or quantity (i.e. flaws in the weaving of 100 m^2 cloth, impurities per dm^2, nonconformities in the varnish per m). For a physical unit one usually chooses a round and common number. A product unit may comprise a multiple of physical units. A sampled roll of 990 m of varnished wire (product unit) would, for example, consist of 9.9 physical units, given that 100 m is the physical unit. One uses **x charts** (sometimes referred to as **c charts**) for the number of nonconformities per product unit and **u charts** for the number of nonconformities per physical unit. In both cases the Poisson distribution is the underlying distribution, provided it is reasonable to assume that the nonconformities per unit occur according to a Poisson process. The Poisson distribution can be approximated by a normal distribution according to (2.60).

- number or proportion of nonconforming sample units

If one records the number of *nonconforming sample units* one can either use this number directly or divide it by the sample size and use the resulting *proportion of nonconforming units in the sample* as a test statistic. In the first case one works with **x charts**, in this context also called **np charts**, and in the second case with **p charts**. The underlying distribution in both cases is the binomial distribution, since the sample is drawn from a process, which is assumed to be of potentially infinite size. Thus the hypergeometric distribution, frequently used in section 3.2, is no longer of importance. The binomial distribution can again be approximated by the normal distribution with the help of (2.97b).

4.3.1 Control Charts for the Number of Nonconformities

Test theoretical background

For every product unit or physical unit the number of nonconformities referring to a certain quality characteristic[3] can be determined through

[3] If one intends to control several quality characteristics one either has to implement a separate control chart for each characteristic or a chart for the number or proportion of nonconforming units. Charts for multiple nonconformities would also be an option (see sec. 4.3.3).

appropriate rules. The numbers of nonconformities are assumed to be independently $po(\lambda_t)$-distributed, i.e., a unit manufactured at time t has λ_t nonconformities on average. Provided the process is considered to be undisturbed for $\lambda_t \leq \lambda_0$ and disturbed for $\lambda_t > \lambda_0$, i.e., if one is only interested in deviations from above, then the hypotheses of type (4.34) take on the special form

- of onesided x and u charts

$$\begin{aligned} H_0 &: \lambda_t \leq \lambda_0 \\ H_1 &: \lambda_t > \lambda_0 \end{aligned} \tag{4.35}$$

If, however, the process is considered to be undisturbed for $\lambda_t = \lambda_0$ and disturbed in the case of $\lambda_t \neq \lambda_0$, then (4.34) takes the form

- of twosided x and u charts

$$\begin{aligned} H_0 &: \lambda_t = \lambda_0 \\ H_1 &: \lambda_t \neq \lambda_0 \end{aligned} \tag{4.36}$$

An *onesided* control chart with test statistic λ_t always corresponds to a hypothesis test of type (4.35), whereas (4.36) is tested in the case of a *twosided* control chart. The information about λ_0 is either given by

- a specified **nominal value** $\lambda_0 = \lambda_N$ or
- an **empirical value** $\lambda_0 = \lambda_E$ from **past process experience** or
- an **estimate** $\hat{\lambda}_0$ of λ_0 obtained from a prerun.

In order to reach a decision a sample of constant size n ($n \geq 1$) is taken in fixed time intervals from the manufacturing process. The test statistic is the cumulative number X_n^{*T} of observed nonconformities in the sample. The cumulation process refers either to a product unit (x chart) or to a physical unit (u chart).

a) Onesided x Charts for Nonconformities per Product Unit

Without loss of generality we will assume that the target value λ_0 is given as a nominal or empirical value. In practice, however, one will generally use an estimate $\hat{\lambda}_0$ instead of λ_0. In this case, the parameter is estimated from the process during a prerun. One randomly samples m ($m \geq 25$) inspection units from the undisturbed process at arbitrary intervals. Let X_i denote the number of nonconformities in the i-th sample unit and X_m^{*T} be the cumulative number of nonconformities over all sample units. Then

Estimating the target value

$$\hat{\lambda}_0 := \frac{1}{m}\sum_{i=1}^{m} X_i = \frac{1}{m} X_m^{*T} \tag{4.37}$$

is an unbiased minimum variance estimator of λ_0.

As already mentioned we will in the following assume that λ_0 is directly given and prepare a control chart which works with samples of size n and centre line $CL = n\lambda_0$ and uses the cumulative count of nonconformities X_n^{*T} as its test statistic. The purpose of this chart is to monitor the Poisson rate λ_t of the process. Using the hypothesis test (4.35), we will draw inference about the unknown present intensity λ_t, in other words, the present state of the process. Under the null hypothesis H_0 we are claiming that the manufacturing process has a sufficiently low intensity of nonconformities compared to the desired target value λ_0. A large total number of nonconformities would give evidence against H_0. Consequently, all we need to do is to specify an onesided upper control line UCL and possibly an upper warning line UWL for the x chart. Since the test statistic X_n^{*T} is integer valued the parameters UCL and UWL are chosen to be integers.

According to (4.32) the control line UCL of an **onesided chart** has to be specified such that the probability of the test statistic X_n^{*T} reaching or exceeding the limit UCL in the case of an undisturbed manufacturing process – i.e., under H_0 – satisfies the specified small value of α. Thus, we keep the probability

$$Pr(X_n^{*T} \geq UCL|\lambda_t = \lambda_0) = \alpha \tag{4.38}$$

for the occurrence of a type I error (false alarm probability) under control. If the test statistic has a discrete distribution, this given probability α can usually be satisfied only approximately, for example, by

$$Pr(X_n^{*T} \geq UCL|\lambda_t = \lambda_0) = \alpha^* \tag{4.39}$$

with $\alpha^* \approx \alpha$. One then stays on the "safe side" by requiring that the effective intervention probability α^* satisfies the condition $\alpha^* \leq \alpha$, i.e., that the condition

$$Pr(X_n^{*T} \geq UCL|\lambda_t = \lambda_0) \leq \alpha \tag{4.40}$$

is satisfied. In other words, one is looking for the largest integer UCL that satisfies (4.40). This value UCL has the property that

$$Pr(X_n^{*T} \geq UCL|\lambda_t = \lambda_0) \leq \alpha < Pr(X_n^{*T} \geq UCL - 1|\lambda_t = \lambda_0). \tag{4.41}$$

As a result of the reproductivity property (2.22) of the Poisson distribution, it follows that $X_n^{*T} \sim po(n\lambda_t)$, i.e., in the case of an undisturbed process, $X_n^{*T} \sim po(n\lambda_0)$. This implies that

$$Pr(X_n^{*T} \geq UCL|\lambda_t = \lambda_0) = \sum_{j=UCL}^{\infty} po(j|n\lambda_0) = 1 - Po(UCL - 1|n\lambda_0) \tag{4.42 a}$$

$$Pr(X_n^{*T} \geq UCL-1|\lambda_t = \lambda_0) = \sum_{j=UCL-1}^{\infty} po(j|n\lambda_0) = 1-Po(UCL-2|n\lambda_0). \tag{4.42 b}$$

Instead of (4.41), one can also write

$$1 - Po(UCL - 1|n\lambda_0) \leq \alpha < 1 - Po(UCL - 2|n\lambda_0) \tag{4.43}$$

or, eqivalently,

Determining the control limits in the Poisson case

$$Po(UCL - 2|n\lambda_0) < 1 - \alpha \leq Po(UCL - 1|n\lambda_0). \tag{4.44}$$

For given values of n and α – usually $\alpha = 0.01$ for the determination of the control lines according to (4.32) – the value of UCL is determined using table 5.1/4. For $n\lambda_0 \geq 9$, the Poisson distribution can be approximated by the normal distribution (normal approximation with continuity correction) and, by (2.60b), it holds that

$$Po(UCL - 1|n\lambda_0) \approx \Phi\left(\frac{UCL - 0.5 - n\lambda_0}{\sqrt{n\lambda_0}}\right). \tag{4.45}$$

Since in the case of a *continuous* distribution it is possible to satisfy condition (4.38) exactly, one does not have to work with its weakened version (4.40). Hence, using (4.42a) and (4.45) and for given n, λ_0 and $\alpha = 0.01$, the upper control limit UCL is found via the approach

$$Pr(X_n^{*T} \geq UCL|\lambda_t = \lambda_0) = \alpha \approx 1 - \Phi\left(\frac{UCL - 0.5 - n\lambda_0}{\sqrt{n\lambda_0}}\right).$$

This implies

$$\Phi\left(\frac{UCL - 0.5 - n\lambda_0}{\sqrt{n\lambda_0}}\right) \approx 1 - \alpha. \tag{4.46}$$

The argument of the function in (4.46) approximately agrees with the percentile $z_{1-\alpha}$ of the standard normal distribution (see figure 5.2/1). Solving for UCL yields

Approximate control limits under the normal approximation with continuity correction

$$UCL \approx n\lambda_0 + z_{1-\alpha} \cdot \sqrt{n\lambda_0} + 0.5. \tag{4.47}$$

Because the control limits of a control chart for count data are chosen to be integer-valued, one rounds the result to the next largest integer.

Determination of warning limits

The warning lines are determined according to (4.32) in the same manner. In (4.44) and (4.47) respectively, one has to replace UCL by UWL, choose $\alpha = 0.05$ and round the result of (4.47) to the next largest integer.

Power function of a onesided x chart:

- in the Poisson case

For the **power function** $G(\lambda_t) = P(X_n^{*T} \geq UCL|\lambda_t)$, which specifies the intervention probability depending on the process state, we get, because of $X_n^{*T} \sim po(n\lambda_t)$, the result

$$G(\lambda_t) = \sum_{j=UCL}^{\infty} po(j|n\lambda_t) = 1 - Po(UCL - 1|n\lambda_t). \qquad (4.48)$$

- under the normal approximation with continuity correction

Again, one can use the normal approximation with continuity correction given by (4.45), provided that $n\lambda_t \geq 9$. The result is

$$G(\lambda_t) \approx 1 - \Phi\left(\frac{UCL - 0.5 - n\lambda_t}{\sqrt{n\lambda_t}}\right). \qquad (4.49)$$

Example 4.3/1

In a textile mill, the quality inspection of bales of cloth with equal length found the following intensities of flaws in the weaving during $m = 30$ days of a production prerun:[4]

Day	Flaws per bale					
1 - 6	8	12	5	11	12	8
7 - 12	10	7	10	5	6	14
13 - 18	2	5	8	3	8	7
19 - 24	6	10	6	9	7	11
25 - 30	9	4	11	13	9	4

Table 4.3/1: Prerun data of weaving flaws

We need to determine an x chart with an upper warning limit ($\alpha = 0.05$) and an upper control limit ($\alpha = 0.01$) for samples of size $n = 1$. From the prerun, we get according to (4.37) that

$$\hat{\lambda}_0 = \frac{1}{30}\sum_{i=1}^{30} x_i = \frac{240}{30} = 8.$$

Hence, the test statistic $X := X_1^{*T}$ is considered to be $po(8)$-distributed under undisturbed process conditions. For the determination of UCL we have to set $n = 1, \lambda_0 = 8$ and $\alpha = 0.01$ in formula (4.44):

$$Po(UCL - 2|8) < 0.99 \leq Po(UCL - 1|8).$$

[4] A similar example can be found in MASING (1988, p. 174ff).

Using table 5.1/4 it can be verified that these inequalities are satisfied for $UCL = 16$:

$$Po(14|8) = 0.9827 < 0.99 \leq 0.9918 = Po(15|8).$$

According to (4.39) and (4.42a), the effective probability of intervention results to be

$$\alpha^* = Pr(X \geq UCL|\lambda_0 = 8) = 1 - Po(15|8) \approx 1 - 0.9918 = 0.0082.$$

Substituting UWL for UCL in (4.44) and using $n = 1, \lambda = 8$ and $\alpha = 0.05$ we get

$$Po(UWL - 2|8) < 0.95 \leq Po(UWL - 1|8).$$

These inequalities are satisfied for $UWL = 14$:

$$Po(12|8) = 0.9362 < 0.95 \leq 0.9658 = Po(13|8).$$

Note that, although the normal approximation is only recommended for $\lambda \geq 9$, we would get the same results for the control and warning lines if we used it here. For UCL we would get by (4.47) that

$$UCL \approx 8 + z_{0.99} \cdot \sqrt{8} + 0.5 \approx 8 + 2.326 \cdot 2.828 + 0.5 \approx 15.079$$

which after rounding gives $UCL = 16$. Similarly, UWL would be found to be

$$UWL \approx 8 + z_{0.95} \cdot \sqrt{8} + 0.5 \approx 8 + 1.645 \cdot 2.828 + 0.5 \approx 13.153,$$

i.e., $UWL = 14$. The procedure for the determination of the UCL and UWL described above is illustrated by the following figure. The figure also shows the graph of the massfunction $po(j|8)$ of the test statistic X. Beside this graph the values of the massfunction $po(j|8)$ as well as that of the distribution function $Po(j|8)$ are tabulated. The values of $Po(j|8)$ which are closest to $1 - \alpha = 0.99$ and $1 - \alpha = 0.95$, respectively, are shaded. Between the graph and the table there are arrows which assign values to the covered areas. These values represent the probabilities that the $po(8)$-distributed test statistic has a realization in the specific interval. The ranges which result in a warning or a corrective action are emphasized through bold arrows. We can see from this figure that the effective warning probability results to be 0.0260.

Figure 4.3/2 shows the x chart calculated above with $UCL = 16$ and $UWL = 14$. The observed realizations of the prerun from table 4.3/1 are plotted into the chart, although this is generally not done in practice. We can see that the process was under statistical control during the prerun.

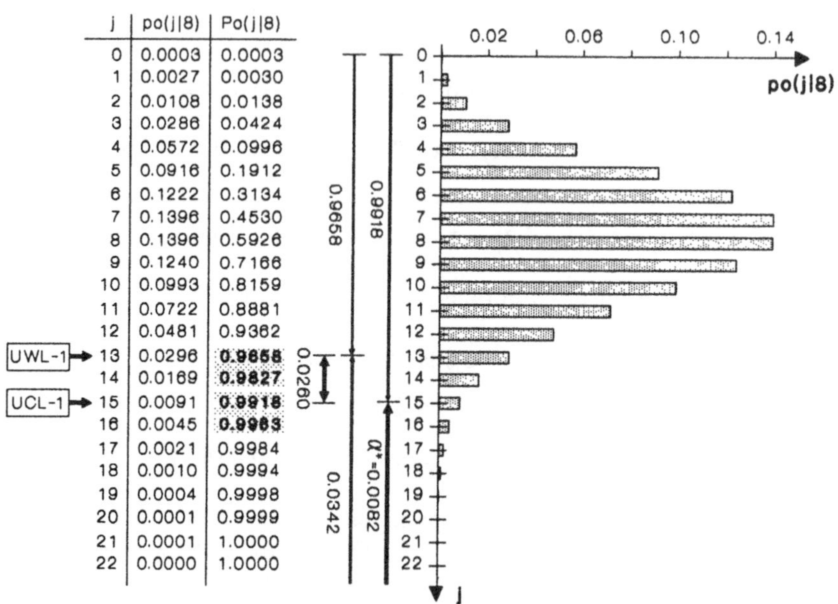

j	po(j|8)	Po(j|8)
0	0.0003	0.0003
1	0.0027	0.0030
2	0.0108	0.0138
3	0.0286	0.0424
4	0.0572	0.0996
5	0.0916	0.1912
6	0.1222	0.3134
7	0.1396	0.4530
8	0.1396	0.5926
9	0.1240	0.7166
10	0.0993	0.8159
11	0.0722	0.8881
12	0.0481	0.9362
13	0.0296	**0.9658**
14	0.0169	**0.9827**
15	0.0091	**0.9918**
16	0.0045	**0.9963**
17	0.0021	0.9984
18	0.0010	0.9994
19	0.0004	0.9998
20	0.0001	0.9999
21	0.0001	1.0000
22	0.0000	1.0000

Figure 4.3/1: Determination of the control and warning lines in a onesided control chart for nonconformities

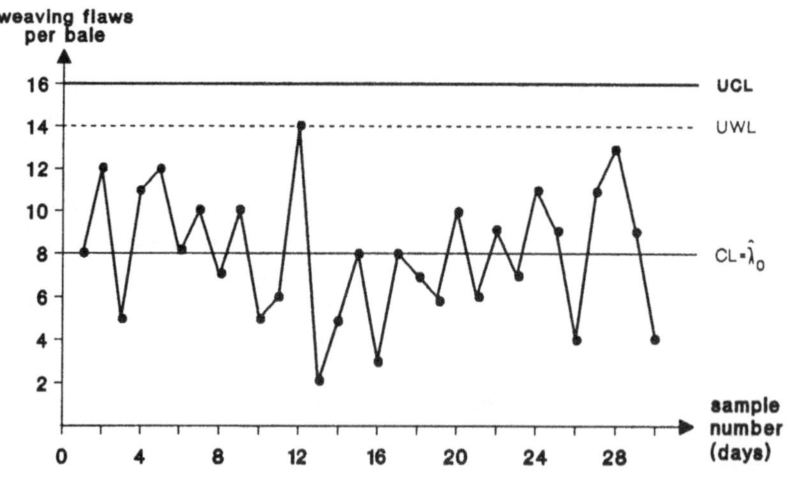

Figure 4.3/2: Onesided control chart for nonconformities

Finally figure 4.3/3 displays the graph of the power function corresponding to this x chart. According to (4.48) it is given by

$$G(\lambda_t) = 1 - Po(15|\lambda_t).$$

When calculating the values of this function one can also work with the normal approximation (4.49) for $\lambda_t \geq 9$:

$$G(\lambda_t) \approx 1 - \Phi\left(\frac{15.5 - \lambda_t}{\sqrt{\lambda_t}}\right).$$

For $\lambda_t \leq \lambda_0$, i.e., within the range $\Omega_0 = [0; \lambda_0]$ of the null hypothesis H_0, the term $G(\lambda_t)$ represents the probability of a false alarm. For $\lambda_t > \lambda_0$, i.e., within the range $\Omega_1 = (\lambda_0, \infty)$ of the alternative hypothesis H_1, the probability of a neglected alarm is given by $1 - G(\lambda_t)$ (see also figure 2.3/4).

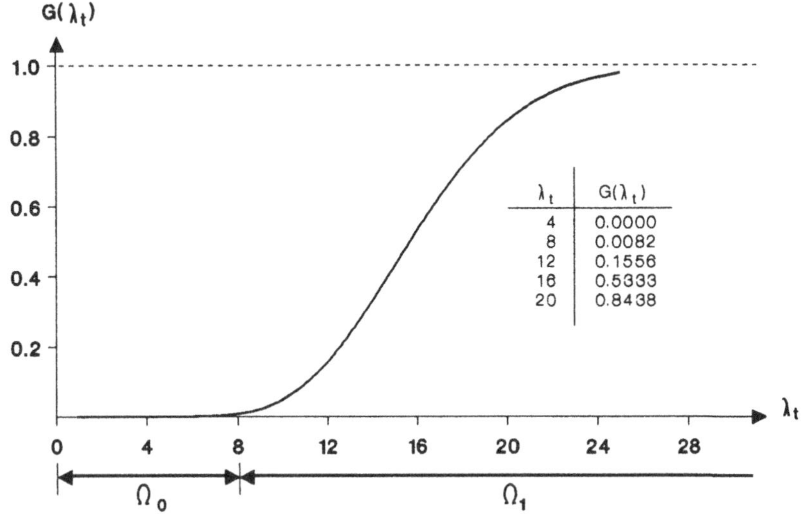

Figure 4.3/3: Power curve of a onesided control chart for nonconformities

Problem 4.3/1

a) In the context of the control chart for count data of example 4.3/1, the power function $G(\lambda_t)$ specified the effective intervention probability depending on the process state. Now find the corresponding function $H(\lambda_t)$ for the probability of giving a warning.

b) Under the assumption that $\lambda_t \geq 9$, find the appropriate normal approximation of $H(\lambda_t)$.

c) Calculate the probability $H(\lambda_t)$ for $\lambda_t = 2, 4, \ldots, 18$. For $\lambda_t \geq 9$, use the approximation of part b).

Problem 4.3/2

Recalculate the control chart lines UCL and UWL in example 4.3/1 for the case when the sample size is set to $n = 3$.

b) Twosided x Charts for Nonconformities per Product Unit

In practice, one also works with **twosided x charts for nonconformities.** Analogous to (4.38) the determining equations for the control lines are based on

$$Pr(X_n^{*T} \geq UCL|\lambda_t = \lambda_0) = \alpha/2 \quad (4.50\text{ a})$$

$$Pr(X_n^{*T} \leq LCL|\lambda_t = \lambda_0) = \alpha/2. \quad (4.50\text{ b})$$

The chain of inequalities in (4.41) for a onesided x chart now becomes

$$Pr(X_n^{*T} \geq UCL|\lambda_t = \lambda_0) \leq \alpha/2 < Pr(X_n^{*T} \geq UCL-1|\lambda_t = \lambda_0) \quad (4.51\text{ a})$$

$$Pr(X_n^{*T} \leq LCL|\lambda_t = \lambda_0) \leq \alpha/2 < Pr(X_n^{*T} \leq LCL+1|\lambda_t = \lambda_0) \quad (4.51\text{ b})$$

Determining the control lines in the Poisson case

and (4.44) takes the form

$$Po(UCL-2|n\lambda_0) < 1-\alpha/2 \leq Po(UCL-1|n\lambda_0) \quad (4.52\text{ a})$$

$$Po(LCL|n\lambda_0) \leq \alpha/2 < Po(LCL+1|n\lambda_0). \quad (4.52\text{ b})$$

For determining UCL and LCL, one again specifies n, λ_0 and $\alpha = 0.01$. Provided that $n\lambda_0 \geq 9$, one can apply the normal approximation with continuity correction as before and thus gets, analogous to (4.46), that

$$\Phi\left(\frac{UCL-0.5-n\lambda_0}{\sqrt{n\lambda_0}}\right) \approx 1-\frac{\alpha}{2} \quad (4.53\text{ a})$$

$$\Phi\left(\frac{LCL+0.5-n\lambda_0}{\sqrt{n\lambda_0}}\right) \approx \frac{\alpha}{2}. \quad (4.53\text{ b})$$

Solving for UCL and LCL yields

Approximate control lines under the normal approximation with continuity correction

$$UCL \approx n\lambda_0 + z_{1-\alpha/2} \cdot \sqrt{n\lambda_0} + 0.5 \quad (4.54\text{ a})$$

$$LCL \approx n\lambda_0 - z_{1-\alpha/2} \cdot \sqrt{n\lambda_0} - 0.5. \quad (4.54\text{ b})$$

The result for UCL is rounded to the next largest integer and that for LCL to the next smallest.

Determination of the warning lines

For determining the warning lines one only has to substitute UWL and LWL for UCL and LCL respectively and to choose $\alpha = 0.05$.

Power function of the twosided x chart:

The **power function** of the twosided x chart is given by

$$G(\lambda_t) = Pr(X_n^{*T} \geq UCL|\lambda_t) + Pr(X_n^{*T} \leq LCL|\lambda_t). \quad (4.55\text{ a})$$

- in the Poisson case

With $X_n^{*T} \sim po(n\lambda_t)$ it follows that

$$\begin{aligned} G(\lambda_t) &= \sum_{j=UCL}^{\infty} po(j|n\lambda_t) + \sum_{j=0}^{LCL} po(j|n\lambda_t) \\ &= 1 - Po(UCL - 1|n\lambda_t) + Po(LCL|n\lambda_t). \quad (4.55\text{ b}) \end{aligned}$$

- under the normal approximation with continuity correction

For $n\lambda_t \geq 9$, the normal approximation (2.60b) yields

$$G(\lambda_t) \approx 1 - \Phi\left(\frac{UCL - 0.5 - n\lambda_t}{\sqrt{n\lambda_t}}\right) + \Phi\left(\frac{LCL + 0.5 - n\lambda_t}{\sqrt{n\lambda_t}}\right). \quad (4.56)$$

In practice, twosided x charts are handled in two ways. In the first approach both limits are strictly observed in the sense that reaching or exceeding them results in taking actions to correct the process. In the second approach the lower limit LCL is ignored. One only intervenes with the process when $X_n^{*T} \geq UCL$. Should samples with $X_n^{*T} \leq LCL$ occur at an increasing rate, one concludes that the process level is improving. Then one would estimate this new process level, declare a new target value and apply a new control chart with a smaller UCL. In the second approach the values of the power function are calculated according to (4.48) and (4.49), respectively.

Remark

In practice, the control and warning lines are often determined by graphical methods. For the one- and twosided x chart with a $po(n\lambda_t)$-distributed test statistic, one can use the so-called THORNDIKE nomograms, for example. From these one can read the levels of the control lines for different Poisson intensities. Nomograms of this kind are found in GRAF/HENNING/STANGE/WILRICH (1987, p.494), for example.

Problem 4.3/3

a) Using the data of example 4.3/1 and specifying $\lambda_0 = 8$, determine the limiting lines of a twosided control chart with sample size $n = 1$.

b) Determine the power function for the case when this chart is actually used as a twosided chart (first approach) as well as for the case when an intervention with the process only takes place when the upper limit UCL is reached or exceeded (second approach).

c) For both cases mentioned above calculate the values of $G(\lambda_t)$ assuming $\lambda_t = 2, 4, \ldots,$ and 18.

c) u Charts for Nonconformities per Physical Unit

In practice it is often the case that one counts *the number of nonconformities per* suitably chosen *physical unit* instead of the number of nonconformities per product unit. The **u chart**, which is appropriate in this case, can be derived from the x chart described in the previous section. We will assume that every product unit consists of d physical units. Further, let U_j denote the number of nonconformities in the j-th physical unit. Under the assumption that the number of nonconformities per product unit are again independently $po(\lambda_t)$-distributed, it holds that $U_j \sim po(\lambda_t^r)$ with

$$\lambda_t^r := \frac{\lambda_t}{d}. \tag{4.57}$$

Thus, the number of nonconformities per physical unit, also called the **relative number of nonconformities**, and the number of nonconformities per product unit are both Poisson distributed, where the Poisson intensities only differ by the factor $1/d$. The u chart uses the cumulative count of nonconformities per physical unit as its test statistic, whereas the x chart uses the cumulative count of nonconformities per product unit in the entire sample. Consequently the centre line CL^r and the limiting lines UCL^r, LCL^r, UWL^r and LWL^r of the u chart can be obtained by dividing the corresponding levels of the x chart by d:

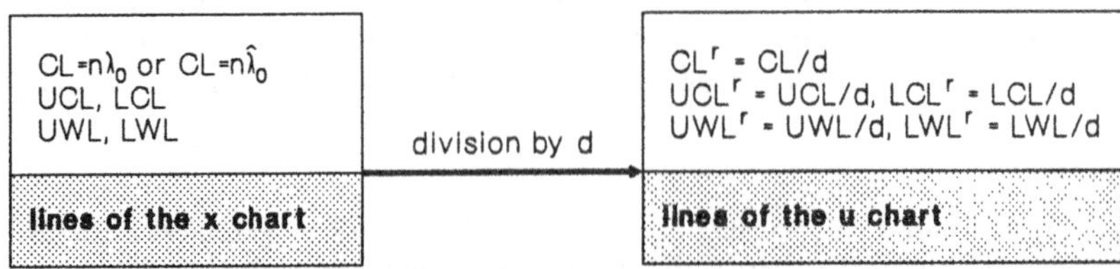

Figure 4.3/4: Relationship between the x chart and u chart for nonconformities

The **power function** of the u chart agrees with the power function $G(\lambda_t)$ of the x chart. We will proof this for the case when only the upper limit UCL, or UCL^r, is given. Using the notation $G^r(\lambda_t^r)$ for the power function of the u chart, we get the following chain of equalities:

$$G^r(\lambda_t^r) = Pr(X_n^{*T}/d \leq UCL^r|\lambda_t^r) = Pr(X_n^{*T} \leq UCL|\lambda_t) = G(\lambda_t). \quad (4.58)$$

Example 4.3/2

In example 4.3/1 we determined a onesided x chart for individual observations with the cumulative number of weaving flaws per bale of cloth as the test statistic. The x chart had its centre line at $CL = 8$ and its limiting lines at $UCL = 16$ and $UWL = 14$. We will now assume that a bale consists of 200 m of cloth and determine a u chart with the cumulative number of nonconformities per 100 m cloth as its test statistic. Then $d = 2$ and, hence, $CL^r = 4$, $UCL^r = 8$ and $UWL^r = 7$. The power function for both charts is

$$G(\lambda_t) = 1 - Po(15|\lambda_t).$$

---

d) Randomized Tests

When the test statistic is *discrete*, conditions (4.29) or (4.32) and (4.33), respectively, which are used for determining the control lines of a control chart, can be satisfied only approximately. We already presented this issue in detail for the case of a onesided x chart. However, we can alter the test (4.34) behind the control chart in a way that the test decision is randomized for certain sample outcomes. Through this approach the condition $\alpha = 0.01$ for the probability of a false alarm can be exactly satisfied even in the case of a discrete test statistic. Using this trick, the critical region of the test is extended so that the desired parameter value α is achieved. In order to achieve this, one has to modify the decision rule of section 4.2.3 as follows:

- If the test statistic $g(\mathbf{X})$ – i.e., X_n^{*T} in this case – satisfies the conditions $g(\mathbf{X}) \geq UCL$ or $g(\mathbf{X}) \leq LCL$, then intervene in the process.
- If $g(\mathbf{X}) < UCL - 1$ or $g(\mathbf{X}) > LCL + 1$, do not take any action.
- If $g(\mathbf{X}) = UCL - 1$ or $g(\mathbf{X}) = LCL + 1$, readjust the process with probability α' or α'', respectively. The value of α' and α'' are determined so that the total probability of interfering with the undisturbed process has the desired value α.

Example 4.3/3

We will now describe the procedure of control charting based on randomized testing for the x chart with $n = 1$ from example 4.3/1. There the specification of $UCL = 16$ resulted in a critical region of $CR = \{16, 17, \ldots\}$. The probability that a realization of the test statistic $X := X_1^{*T}$ falls into this range during an undisturbed process state was found to be $\alpha^* = 0.0082$. Since the effective probability α^* of a false alarm lies 0.0018 below the specified value $\alpha = 0.01$, we must extend the critical region. In order to raise the effective probability of a false alarm to the desired value 0.01, we can change the decision rule so that we will always intervene in the process for $X \geq 16$ and, in addition, intervene with probability α' for $X = 15$. The value of α' is given by the equation

$$\alpha' \cdot Pr(X = UCL - 1 | \lambda_t = \lambda_0) = \alpha' \cdot po(15|8) = 0.0018.$$

From this equation and by reading that $po(15|8) \approx 0.0091$ from figure 4.3/1, we get the result that $\alpha' \approx 0.2$.

Thus, one has to perform a second random experiment, the randomization, if the inspected unit (first random experiment) is found to have 15 nonconformities. Consequently, for $x = 15$ it depends on the outcome of the second experiment whether or not one will interfere with the process. Through this randomization the critical region is extended in the sense that one occasionally takes measures to readjust the process as a result of observing $x = 15$, i.e., one will reject the null hypothesis $H_0 : \lambda_t \leq \lambda_0$ in 20% of the occurrences of this value. The second random experiment could be performed by generating a random number Z which is uniformly distributed on [0,1], for example, or by reading it from a table. $Z \leq 0.2$ means intervention whereas $Z > 0.2$ is interpreted as a warning.

Problem 4.3/4

What are the conditions for intervening in the process for the twosided x chart introduced in problem 4.3/3? Assume that both control limits are strictly observed and a randomization is chosen.

4.3.2 Control Charts for the Number or the Fraction of Nonconforming Units

The control charts introduced so far had the number of nonconformities in the sample as their test statistic. We will now consider the case when the *number of nonconforming sample units* is measured. At any time t, the process level is now described by the fraction nonconforming P_t. The quantity P_t denotes the fraction nonconforming of the process at time t. Under the assumption that the manufacturing process is considered to be undisturbed for $P_t \leq P_0$ and disturbed for $P_t > P_0$, hypotheses (4.34) take the form

Test theoretical background

- in the case of onesided x or p charts

$$H_0 \; : \; P_t \leq P_0$$
$$H_1 \; : \; P_t > P_0. \qquad (4.59\text{ a})$$

If the process is considered to be undisturbed for $P_t = P_0$ and disturbed for $P_t \neq P_0$, then (4.34) takes the form

- in the case of twosided x or p charts

$$H_0 \; : \; P_t = P_0$$
$$H_1 \; : \; P_t \neq P_0. \qquad (4.59\text{ b})$$

The underlying hypothesis test of a *onesided* control chart for the number or proportion of nonconforming units in the sample is always of type (4.59a), while that of the corresponding twosided control chart is of type (4.59b).

In practice, the parameter P_0 is taken to be one of the following:

- a given **nominal value** $P_0 = P_N$ or
- an **empirical value** $P_0 = P_E$ or
- an **estimate** $\hat{P}_0$ of P_0.

In order to decide which of the two hypotheses H_0 and H_1 holds, samples of constant size $n > 1$ are drawn from the process at equidistant time points. The test statistic can either be the $bi(P_t; n)$-distributed number of nonconforming units in the sample X_n^T (x chart) or the proportion of nonconforming sample units X_n^T/n (p chart).

a) x Charts for the Number of Nonconforming Units

We will assume without loss of generality that P_0 is given as a nominal or empirical value. In practice, one will generally use an estimate $\hat{P}_0$ instead of P_0. This estimate is obtained during a prerun of the process, when there are no apparent disturbances, by taking m samples of constant size n ($m \geq 25$). Let X_{in}^T be the observed number of nonconforming units in the i-th sample from the process prerun ($i = 1, \ldots, m$). Then

Estimating the target value

$$\hat{P}_0 := \frac{1}{m \cdot n} \sum_{i=1}^{m} X_{in}^T \qquad (4.60)$$

is a minimum variance unbiased estimator of P_0.

In the following, we will sketch how to construct a control chart with centre line $CL = nP_0$ for a sample of size n and with the number X_n^T of nonconforming sample units as its test statistic. Provided that the process fraction defective is P_0, it holds that $X_n^T \sim bi(P_0; n)$. The control lines of the x chart for the number of nonconforming units are found in the same manner as those of the x chart for the number of nonconformities. Let us first consider a **onesided x chart for the number of nonconforming units** with upper control limit UCL. The chain of inequalities in (4.41) now becomes

$$Pr(X_n^T \geq UCL|P_t = P_0) \leq \alpha < Pr(X_n^T \geq UCL - 1|P_t = P_0). \quad (4.61)$$

Determining the control limits in the binomial case (onesided x chart)

For $X_n^T \sim bi(P_0; n)$, after elementary transformations it results that

$$Bi(UCL - 2|P_0; n) < 1 - \alpha \leq Bi(UCL - 1|P_0; n). \quad (4.62)$$

Hence, for given values of n and P_0 and specified $\alpha = 0.01$, one can determine UCL from table 5.1/3. For $nP_0(1 - P_0) \geq 9$, one can use the normal approximation according to (2.97b)

$$Bi(UCL - 1|P_0; n) \approx \Phi\left(\frac{UCL - 0.5 - nP_0}{\sqrt{nP_0(1 - P_0)}}\right). \quad (4.63)$$

Using this approximation, one can find the following condition for UCL, analogous to (4.46):

$$\Phi\left(\frac{UCL - 0.5 - nP_0}{\sqrt{nP_0(1 - P_0)}}\right) \approx 1 - \alpha. \quad (4.64)$$

Approximate control limits under the normal approximation with continuity correction (onesided x chart)

Solving for UCL yields

$$UCL \approx nP_0 + z_{1-\alpha} \cdot \sqrt{nP_0(1 - P_0)} + 0.5. \quad (4.65)$$

The above result should be rounded to the next biggest integer. The determination of the upper warning limit UWL is done in the same way. One only has to substitute UWL for UCL in (4.62) and (4.65) and choose the value $\alpha = 0.05$ instead of $\alpha = 0.01$.

Power function of the onesided x chart:

- in the binomial case

For the **power function** $G(P_t) = P(X_n^T \geq OEG|P_t)$ of the onesided x chart it follows with $X_n^T \sim bi(P_t; n)$ that

$$G(P_t) = \sum_{j=UCL}^{n} bi(j|P_t; n) = 1 - Bi(UCL - 1|P_t; n). \quad (4.66)$$

Provided that $nP_t(1-P_t) \geq 9$, one can again use the normal approximation (2.97b) and get

- under the normal approximation with continuity correction

$$G(P_t) = 1 - \Phi\left(\frac{UCL - 0.5 - nP_t}{\sqrt{nP_t(1 - P_t}}\right). \quad (4.67)$$

In order to determine the control limits for a **twosided x chart** for the number of nonconforming units one starts from the following chain of inequalities which corresponds to (4.51):

$$Pr(X_n^T \geq UCL|P_t = P_0) \leq \alpha/2 < Pr(X_n^T \geq UCL - 1|P_t = P_0) \quad (4.68\text{ a})$$

$$Pr(X_n^T \leq LCL|P_t = P_0) \leq \alpha/2 < Pr(X_n^T \leq LCL + 1|P_t = P_0). \quad (4.68\text{ b})$$

By using these relationships and $X_n^T \sim bi(P_0; n)$ one gets

Determining the control limits in the binomial case (twosided x chart)

$$Bi(UCL - 2|P_0; n) < 1 - \alpha/2 \leq Bi(UCL - 1|P_0; n) \quad (4.69\text{ a})$$

$$Bi(LCL|P_0; n) \leq \alpha/2 < Bi(LCL + 1|P_0; n). \quad (4.69\text{ b})$$

For given n, P_0 and $\alpha = 0.01$ the values of UCL and LCL can now be calculated. Analogous to (4.54) the normal approximation with continuity correction gives

Approximate control lines under the normal approximation with continuity correction (twosided x chart)

$$UCL \approx nP_0 + z_{1-\alpha/2} \cdot \sqrt{nP_0(1 - P_0)} + 0.5 \quad (4.70\text{ a})$$

$$LCL \approx nP_0 - z_{1-\alpha/2} \cdot \sqrt{nP_0(1 - P_0)} - 0.5. \quad (4.70\text{ b})$$

As before, the result for UCL has to be rounded to the next largest integer and that for LCL to the next smallest integer.

For the determination of the warning limits one again proceeds in the same manner, i.e., by replacing UCL and LCL with UWL and LWL, respectively, and choosing $\alpha = 0.05$.

The **power function** of the twosided x chart is given by

Power function of the twosided x chart:

$$G(P_t) = Pr(X_n^T \geq UCL|P_t) + Pr(X_n^T \leq LCL|P_t). \quad (4.71\text{ a})$$

Since $X_n^T \sim bi(P_t; n)$, this becomes

- in the binomial case

$$\begin{aligned} G(P_t) &= \sum_{j=0}^{LCL} bi(j|P_t; n) + \sum_{j=UCL}^{n} bi(j|P_t; n) \\ &= 1 - Bi(UCL - 1|P_t; n) + Bi(LCL|P_t; n). \end{aligned} \quad (4.71\text{ b})$$

- under the normal approximation

For $nP_t(1-P_t) \geq 9$, the normal approximation (2.97b) yields

$$G(P_t) \approx 1 - \Phi\left(\frac{UCL - 0.5 - nP_t}{\sqrt{nP_t(1-P_t)}}\right) + \Phi\left(\frac{LCL + 0.5 - nP_t}{\sqrt{nP_t(1-P_t)}}\right). \quad (4.72)$$

The two previously described approaches to operating a twosided x chart for the number of nonconformities can also be applied to this x chart for the number of nonconforming units. If one intervenes in the process only when UCL is reached or exceeded and ignores the LCL, then the power function is no longer given by (4.71), but by (4.66).

Randomized test

Finally we want to mention that the specified value α for the probability of a false alarm can be satisfied exactly by again using a randomized test.

Remark

The control and warning lines of a one- or twosided x chart with a $bi(P_t; n)$-distributed test statistic can also be determined by graphical methods. For this, one uses the so-called LARSON nomograms, which can be found in GRAF/HENNING/STANGE/WILRICH (1987, p.435), for example.

b) p Charts for the Fraction of Nonconforming Units

Instead of the number X_n^T of nonconforming units in a sample of size n, we can also use the **sample fraction nonconforming**

$$\hat{P}^r := \frac{X_n^T}{n} \quad (4.73)$$

as a test statistic in the hypothesis test of type (4.59). The p chart, which is used in this situation, is analogous to the u chart, because both (4.73) and (4.57) are relative measures. Since the test statistic of the p chart is obtained from the above x chart through division by n, one can obtain the centre line CL^r and the lines UCL^r, LCL^r, UWL^r and LWL^r of the p chart by dividing the corresponding levels of the x chart by n.

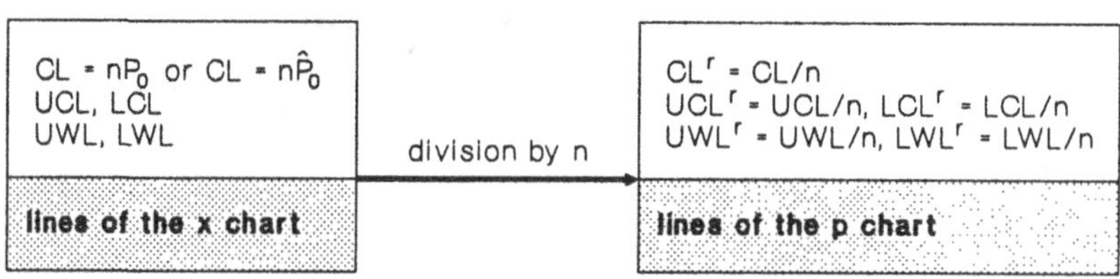

Figure 4.3/5: Relationship between the x chart for the number and the p chart for the proportion of nonconforming sample units

The power function of the p chart agrees with the power function $G(P_t)$ of the x chart.

Problem 4.3/5

a) Let $n = 100$ and $P_0 = 0.07$. With $\alpha = 0.01$ and $\alpha = 0.05$ calculate the control and warning lines, respectively, of a twosided x chart for the number of nonconforming units and the corresponding p chart without using the normal approximation.
b) Determine the power functions of the charts constructed above and also find the relationship between the quality level P_t and the effective intervention probability $G(P_t)$. Also determine the functional relationship between P_t and the effective warning probability $H(P_t)$.
c) How big are the effective intervention and effective warning probabilities for $P_t = P_0$? Compare the results to the desired nominal values 0.01 and 0.04.
d) Also calculate $G(P_t)$ for $P_t = 0.01, 0.02, \ldots, 0.09, 0.1, 0.2$.

4.3.3 Charts for Multiple Nonconformities and the PARETO Diagram

If a unit has to be inspected for several different types of nonconformities one can work with a **chart for multiple nonconformities**. Figure 4.3/6 shows the structure of such a chart.

Upper part of the chart: analysis of the individual effects

The *upper* part of the chart contains r rows for the "types of nonconformities" for which one wants to control and k consecutively numbered columns for the samples. For each sample, the observed number of each type of nonconformity is entered. The second to the last column list the absolute frequency of the nonconformities over all k samples, while the last column contains the observed relative frequencies of the different types of errors in the samples.

Lower part of the chart: evaluation of cumulative effects

In the *lower* part of the chart for multiple nonconformities a cross is entered to indicate the total number of observed nonconformities in each sample. Because of the differences in the kind of nonconformities, control lines would not be meaningful in this chart. By making crosses in this part of the chart, it becomes apparent that the total number of nonconformities changes with the sample number and, consequently, with time, as in the x chart for the number of nonconformities. Thus this chart provides data for quality analysis in a simple way. We want to note that this kind of chart can also be used for acceptance control and for quality audits.

		Sample number							Frequency	
		1	2	3	4	. . .	k-1	k	$\sum_1^k$	%
Type of nonconformity	F_1									
	F_2									
	F_3									
	. . .									
	F_r									
Number of nonconformities per sample	≥ 10									
	9									
	. . .									
	2									
	1									
	0									

Figure 4.3/6: Structure of a chart for multiple nonconformities

Interpreting the results of a PARETO chart

From the frequencies of the individual nonconformity types, which are indicated in the upper part of the chart, one can recognize the location of the weak points in the manufacturing process. Thus, one determines the types of nonconformities which need to be given special attention. If we put the relative frequencies in decreasing order and display them in a coordinate system, then we get a very illustrative graphical representation, called the PARETO **diagram**. In the following PARETO diagram we can see that the nonconformity types F_2, F_5 and F_3 account for about 90% of all observed nonconformities.

The diagram is named after the economist VILFREDO PARETO (1848-1923) who suggested a certain function for the description of the distribution of income. This function has a density extremely skewed to the right, as is generally the case for the distribution of types of nonconformities according to their frequencies. There are several versions of PARETO diagrams. These as well as other graphical methods in quality assurance can be found in WADSWORTH/STEPHENS/GODFREY (1986, p.241ff),BANKS (1989, p.459ff) or MONTGOMERY (1991, p.118ff).

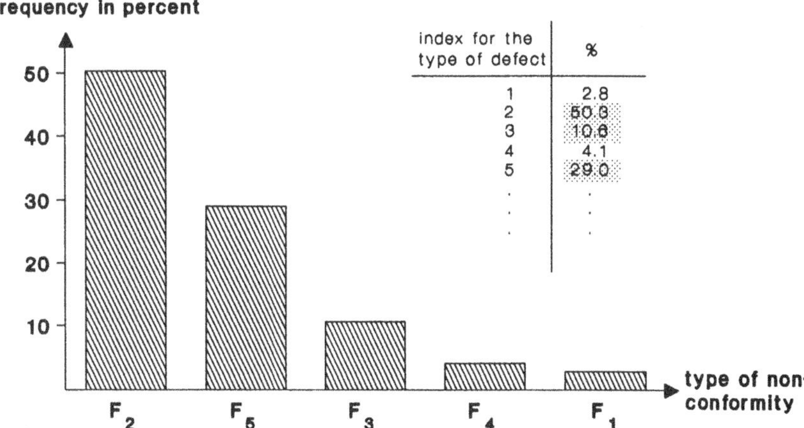

Figure 4.3/7: PARETO Diagram

4.4 SHEWHART Control Charts for Variables

Characterization of process control for count data and for measurements

In control charting for attributes introduced in section 4.3 the monitored quality characteristic and the test statistic had a *discrete* distribution. Of course, control charts for attributes can also be applied to *continuous* quality characteristics, but this implies a waste of information contained in the observed data. In the following, we will assume that the quality characteristic of interest has a *continuous* distribution and apply a SHEWHART **control chart for variables**. We will further assume that the quality characteristic is normally distributed. This is actually true for a wide range of quality characteristics. If it is doubtful whether this assumption is fulfilled, then one should perform either a **goodness of fit test** (χ^2**-test** or **Kolmogorov-Smirnov test**) or verify the assumption graphically with a **normal probability plot**.

Assumption of a normally distributed quality characteristic in control charting for variables

Let us now assume that, at time t, the monitored quality characteristic X is exactly or at least approximately $no(\mu_t; \sigma_t^2)$-distributed. If the process is not disturbed then μ_t and σ_t are constant over time. A disturbance results in a shift of the process location parameter μ_t or/and a change (usually an increase) in the process standard deviation σ_t. Such disturbances can lead to an increasing proportion P_t of nonconforming product units (see again figures 1.1/2 and 1.1/3). For given specification limits for X, one can also determine the fraction nonconforming P_t which corresponds to the process parameters μ_t and σ_t. We can further distinguish between three different cases, depending on whether we have an upper specification limit G_u (maximal value), a lower specification limit G_l (minimal value) or a specification range $[G_l, G_u]$. In any of these three situations the process fraction nonconforming is determined according to (3.136).[5]

In variables process control with given specification limits one can try to control the parameters μ_t and/or σ_t in such a way that the fraction nonconforming does not become too high. This issue will not be discussed until section 4.5. Here, in section 4.4, we will only consider situations where the specification limits are either not known or, when they are known, are not explicitly taken into account. The goal is to control the process so that its expectation and/or standard deviation are in accordance with the target values μ_0 and σ_0. These target values can be:

- **nominal values** μ_N, σ_N specified by a law, a standard or by product design;
- **empirical values** μ_E, σ_E from past process experience;
- **estimates** $\hat{\mu}_0$, $\hat{\sigma}_0$ from an undisturbed prerun.

[5] In equations (3.136) the time index t was omitted.

In section 4.4.1 we will show how to process data from a prerun, how to test for disturbances during the prerun and, in the case of no statistical evidence for disturbances, how to estimate the two process parameters from the prerun data. In section 4.4.2 we will introduce control charts for monitoring the process level and, in section 4.4.3, control charts for the process spread. In section 4.4.4 we will briefly talk about control charts for the simultaneous control of both process parameters.

4.4.1 Evaluation of a Prerun

a) Aggregating the Prerun Data

In the context of a prerun, m samples $X_{i1}, \ldots, X_{in}$ of size n are taken from the process ($i = 1, \ldots, m; m \geq 25$).[6] In a prerun, the time interval between consecutive samples can be shorter than in the actual control chart. The extensive data collected during the prerun, i.e., the realizations of the $m \cdot n$ sample variables X_{ij}, can be suitably condensed with the help of the sample statistics introduced in (2.65-70). Since we are dealing here with m samples instead of one, it is necessary to introduce the additional sample index i in the formulae (2.65-70). In this manner, the **mean**, **median**, **variance**, **standard deviation** and **range of the i-th sample** are denoted in the following way:

Statistics for describing individual samples

$$\bar{X}_{in} := \frac{1}{n} \sum_{j=1}^{n} X_{ij} \tag{4.74}$$

$$\tilde{X}_{in} := \begin{cases} X_{i;<k+1;n>} & \text{if } n = 2k+1 \\ \frac{1}{2}(X_{i;<k;n>} + X_{i;<k+1;n>}) & \text{if } n = 2k \end{cases} \tag{4.75}$$

$$S_{in}^2 := \frac{1}{n-1} \sum_{j=1}^{n} \left(X_{ij} - \bar{X}_{in}\right)^2 = \frac{1}{n-1} \left[\sum_{j=1}^{n} X_{ij}^2 - n\bar{X}_{in}^2\right] \tag{4.76 a}$$

$$S_{in} := +\sqrt{S_{in}^2} \tag{4.76 b}$$

$$R_{in} := X_{i;<n;n>} - X_{i;<1;n>}. \tag{4.77}$$

In the above, $X_{i;<k;n>}$ denotes the element of the i-th sample vector $\mathbf{X}_i = (X_{i1}, \ldots, X_{in})$ which takes the k-th place when the components of $\mathbf{X}_i$ are put in increasing order.

[6] For instructional reasons, in the following examples and problems we will disregard the assumptions on n and m.

Aggregating all prerun data:

The information in the prerun data can be further condensed by taking the means of $\bar{X}_{in}, \tilde{X}_{in}, S^2_{in}, S_{in}$ and R_{in}, respectively. We then speak of the **mean of the sample means**, the **mean of the sample medians**, the **mean of the sample variances**, the **mean of the sample standard deviations** and the **mean of the sample ranges**, respectively, and use the following notation:

$$\bar{\bar{X}}_m := \frac{1}{m}\sum_{i=1}^{m} \bar{X}_{in} \tag{4.78}$$

$$\bar{\tilde{X}}_m := \frac{1}{m}\sum_{i=1}^{m} \tilde{X}_{in} \tag{4.79}$$

- by taking the mean of the individual statistics

$$\overline{S^2_m} := \frac{1}{m}\sum_{i=1}^{m} S^2_{in} \quad ^7 \tag{4.80}$$

$$\bar{S}_m := \frac{1}{m}\sum_{i=1}^{m} S_{in} \quad ^7 \tag{4.81}$$

$$\bar{R}_m := \frac{1}{m}\sum_{i=1}^{m} R_{in}. \tag{4.82}$$

Instead of the mean, one can also take the median of the m individual statistics (4.74)-(4.77). In the following we will only need the median of (4.74), (4.75) and (4.77), i.e., the **median of the sample means**, the **median of the sample medians** and the **median of the sample ranges**:

- by taking the median of the individual statistics

$$\tilde{\bar{X}}_m := \begin{cases} \bar{X}_{<k+1;m>} & \text{if } m = 2k+1 \\ \frac{1}{2}(\bar{X}_{<k;m>} + \bar{X}_{<k+1;m>}) & \text{if } m = 2k. \end{cases} \tag{4.83}$$

$$\tilde{\tilde{X}}_m := \begin{cases} \tilde{X}_{<k+1;m>} & \text{if } m = 2k+1 \\ \frac{1}{2}(\tilde{X}_{<k;m>} + \tilde{X}_{<k+1;m>}) & \text{if } m = 2k. \end{cases} \tag{4.84}$$

$$\tilde{R}_m := \begin{cases} R_{<k+1;m>} & \text{if } m = 2k+1 \\ \frac{1}{2}(R_{<k;m>} + R_{<k+1;m>}) & \text{if } m = 2k. \end{cases} \tag{4.85}$$

Here, $\bar{X}_{<k;m>}$ denotes the k-th element when the sequence of the m sample means $\bar{X}_{in}$ is arranged in increasing order. $\tilde{X}_{<k;m>}$ and $R_{<k;m>}$ are defined in the same way.

---

[7]Please note that $\bar{S}_m \neq \sqrt{\overline{S^2_m}}$.

The $m \cdot n$ prerun variables X_{ij} can also be transformed directly to a scalar quantity without determination of the individual sample statistics. One way to do this is to consider all $m \cdot n$ variables as elements of a single sample of size $m \cdot n$ and to calculate the sample mean $\bar{X}_{m \cdot n}$ and the sample variance $S^2_{m \cdot n}$ or the sample standard deviation $S_{m \cdot n}$, according to (2.65-67). These functions are also called the **total sample mean** , the **total sample variance** and the **total sample standard deviation**. The first function is identical to (4.78):

- by calculating total statistics

$$\bar{X}_{m \cdot n} := \frac{1}{m \cdot n} \sum_{i=1}^{m} \sum_{j=1}^{n} X_{ij} = \bar{\bar{X}}_m \tag{4.86}$$

$$S^2_{m \cdot n} := \frac{1}{m \cdot n - 1} \sum_{i=1}^{m} \sum_{j=1}^{n} \left(X_{ij} - \bar{X}_{m \cdot n}\right)^2 = \frac{1}{m \cdot n - 1} \left[\sum_{i=1}^{m} \sum_{j=1}^{n} X^2_{ij} - m \cdot n \cdot \bar{X}^2_{m \cdot n}\right] \tag{4.87 a}$$

$$S_{m \cdot n} := +\sqrt{S^2_{m \cdot n}} \tag{4.87 b}$$

The sum

$$Q_{m \cdot n} := \sum_{i=1}^{m} \sum_{j=1}^{n} \left(X_{ij} - \bar{X}_{m \cdot n}\right)^2 \tag{4.88}$$

of the squared deviations between the variables X_{ij} and $\bar{X}_{m \cdot n}$ is also called the **total sum of squares**. With the help of (4.88) we can write the total sample variance in the form

$$S^2_{m \cdot n} = \frac{Q_{m \cdot n}}{m \cdot n - 1}. \tag{4.89}$$

b) Testing for Disturbances in the Prerun Data

When the parameters μ_0 and σ_0 of the undisturbed process are unknown, they can be estimated with the sample statistics introduced in (4.74)-(4.87). Before estimating them, however, one should perform a test to ensure that the production was not disturbed during the prerun. One first tests whether the process variance had a constant value during the prerun. Provided there is no evidence against the hypothesis of a constant process variance, one proceeds with testing the hypothesis of a constant process.

The hypothesis of constant process variance can be tested using the **BARTLETT test** mentioned in section 2.3.4. One tests the hypotheses

Testing for constancy of the process variance

$$\begin{aligned} H_0 &: \sigma_1^2 = \sigma_2^2 = \ldots = \sigma_m^2 \\ H_1 &: \sigma_{i_1}^2 \neq \sigma_{i_2}^2 \text{ for at least one index pair } (i_1; i_2). \end{aligned} \tag{4.90}$$

Hypothesis H_1 says that the process variances were not equal at two or more sampling time points. The BARTLETT test assumes that the quality characteristic X is normally distributed and uses the test statistic

$$\chi^2 := \frac{3m \cdot (n-1)^2}{3mn - 2m + 1} \cdot \left(m \cdot \ln \overline{S^2_m} - \sum_{i=1}^{m} \ln S^2_{in} \right). \tag{4.91}$$

Under H_0 the test statistic (4.91) is $\chi^2(m-1)$-distributed. Too large values of this statistic give evidence against H_0. Thus, the rejection region CR of the test is given by the set

$$CR = \left\{ \chi^2 | \chi^2 > \chi^2_{m-1;1-\alpha} \right\}.$$

Percentiles of the central χ^2 distribution can be found in table 5.2/4.

If the hypothesis of a constant variance is not rejected, then one can proceed with testing the hypothesis of a time constant process level with an **F test**. This test requires X to be normally distributed with constant variance. The hypotheses are

Testing for constancy of the process level

$$\begin{aligned} H_0 &: \mu_1^2 = \mu_2^2 = \ldots = \mu_m^2 \\ H_1 &: \mu_{i_1}^2 \neq \mu_{i_2}^2 \text{ for at least one index pair } (i_1; i_2). \end{aligned} \tag{4.92}$$

The total sum of squares $Q_{m \cdot n}$ introduced in (4.88) can be decomposed into two additive components:

$$Q_{m \cdot n} = Q_1 + Q_2 \tag{4.93 a}$$

$$Q_1 := n \cdot \sum_{i=1}^{m} \left(\bar{X}_{in} - \bar{\bar{X}}_m \right)^2 = n \cdot \left(\sum_{i=1}^{m} \bar{X}^2_{in} - m \cdot \bar{\bar{X}}^2_m \right) \tag{4.93 b}$$

$$Q_2 := \sum_{i=1}^{m} \sum_{j=1}^{n} \left(X_{ij} - \bar{X}_{in} \right)^2 = (n-1) \cdot \sum_{i=1}^{m} S^2_{in}. \tag{4.93 c}$$

The partial sum Q_1 is a measure for the deviation in level *between* the m samples, while Q_2 measures the variations in level *within* each of the m samples. The test statistic of the hypothesis test (4.92) is given by

$$F = \frac{Q_1/(m-1)}{Q_2/[m(n-1)]}. \tag{4.94}$$

Under H_0, this variable has an F distribution with $\nu_1 = m - 1$ degrees of freedom in the numerator and $\nu_2 = m(n-1)$ degrees of freedom in the denominator. Large values of F give evidence against H_0. For a given significance level α the critical region is found to be:

$$CR = \left\{ F | F > F_{m-1;m(n-1);1-\alpha} \right\}.$$

Percentiles of the F distribution are given in table 5.2/3.

Example 4.4/1

A manufacturer of carbonated soft drinks wants to use control charts for monitoring the manufacturing process with respect to the CO_2-content of the beverage. In a prerun $m = 15$ samples of size $n = 5$ were taken. The monitored quality characteristic X was the CO_2 content measured in grams/litre. Table 4.4/1 contains the observed measurements x_{ij} in column 2 and results that we will need repeatedly in the following analysis in columns 3 to 9.

i	Prerun data x_{ij}					$\sum_{j=1}^{5} x_{ij}$	$\sum_{j=1}^{5} x_{ij}^2$	$\bar{x}_{i5}$	$\tilde{x}_{i5}$	s_{i5}^2	s_{i5}	r_{i5}
(1)	(2)					(3)	(4)	(5)	(6)	(7)	(8)	(9)
1	7.3	7.0	7.2	6.5	7.0	35.0	245.38	7.00	7.0	0.095	0.3082	0.8
2	6.4	6.8	6.8	6.6	6.9	33.5	224.61	6.70	6.8	0.040	0.2000	0.5
3	6.7	6.7	6.4	6.8	7.0	33.6	225.98	6.72	6.7	0.047	0.2168	0.6
4	6.9	7.1	7.4	7.0	7.2	35.6	253.62	7.12	7.1	0.037	0.1924	0.5
5	6.3	6.6	7.2	6.6	7.2	33.9	230.49	6.78	6.6	0.162	0.4025	0.9
6	6.5	7.0	6.8	7.0	7.0	34.3	235.49	6.86	7.0	0.048	0.2190	0.5
7	7.1	7.1	6.9	7.1	6.8	35.0	245.08	7.00	7.1	0.020	0.1414	0.3
8	7.4	7.0	6.8	6.6	6.8	34.6	239.80	6.92	6.8	0.092	0.3033	0.8
9	7.0	7.2	7.2	6.8	6.8	35.0	245.16	7.00	7.0	0.040	0.2000	0.4
10	7.2	6.6	7.3	7.0	6.8	34.9	243.93	6.98	7.0	0.082	0.2864	0.7
11	6.4	6.8	6.8	7.2	7.2	34.4	237.12	6.88	6.8	0.112	0.3347	0.8
12	6.8	7.0	7.4	6.6	7.0	34.8	242.56	6.96	7.0	0.088	0.2966	0.8
13	6.2	7.0	7.2	6.6	6.8	33.8	229.08	6.76	6.8	0.148	0.3847	1.0
14	6.4	7.2	7.4	7.1	7.0	35.1	246.97	7.02	7.1	0.142	0.3768	1.0
15	7.0	6.8	7.2	6.6	7.0	34.6	239.64	6.92	7.0	0.052	0.2280	0.6
	sum					518,1	3584.91	103.62	103.8	1.205	4.0908	10.2

Table 4.4/1: Measurements during a prerun and results of the analysis (CO_2-content of a soft drink)

We will first perform a BARTLETT test with $\alpha = 0.01$. Using column 9 we get:

$$\overline{s_{15}^2} = \frac{1}{15}\sum_{i=1}^{15} s_{i5}^2 = \frac{1}{15} \cdot 1.205 \approx 0.0803$$

$$\ln \overline{s_{15}^2} \approx -2.5220; \qquad \sum_{i=1}^{15} \ln s_{i5}^2 \approx -40.2405$$

As a result, the test statistic (4.91) is found to be

$$\chi^2 \approx \frac{45 \cdot 16}{225 - 30 + 1} \cdot (40.2405 - 15 \cdot 2.5220) \approx 8.8548.$$

Since $8.8548 < \chi^2_{14;0.99} = 29.141$, the hypothesis H_0 of a time constant variance cannot be rejected. Consequently, we can continue with the F test which assumes the variances to be constant. When performing an F test with $\alpha = 0.01$, we first get

$$Q_1 = 5 \cdot \left(\sum_{i=1}^{15} \bar{x}_{i5}^2 - 15 \cdot \bar{\bar{x}}_{15}^2 \right) = 5 \cdot (716.018 - 15 \cdot 6.908^2) \approx 1.0552$$

$$Q_2 = 4 \cdot \sum_{i=1}^{15} s_{i5}^2 = 4 \cdot 1.205 = 4.82.$$

Substituting into (4.94) yields

$$F = \frac{1.0552/14}{4.82/60} \approx 0.9382.$$

Since $0.9382 < F_{14;60;0.99} = 2.39$, the hypothesis of a time constant expectation cannot be rejected. Thus, we conclude that the prerun can be considered undisturbed and, consequently, that its results can be used for estimation of μ_0 and σ_0.

Problem 4.4/1

The following table contains prerun measurements from $m = 10$ samples of $n = 5$ units each (tensile strength of wire measured in Deca-Newton):

Sample number i	Measurements x_{ij}				
1	235	235	230	232	226
2	238	234	229	231	240
3	235	239	234	230	236
4	234	233	235	227	226
5	238	236	230	235	231
6	230	231	229	237	235
7	237	239	231	233	240
8	231	240	232	231	228
9	231	230	232	237	238
10	230	235	228	233	240.

Perform a BARTLETT test with $\alpha = 0.05$ and (in the case of non-rejecting the hypothesis of a constant variance) an F test.

c) Estimating the Process Level

If the target value μ_0 of the process level is not given in the form of a nominal or empirical value, it must be estimated from the prerun data. There are several possibilities for doing this. We will introduce four different methods for estimating μ_0. All the estimators are ***unbiased*** and at least asymptotically normally distributed. However, they have different variances, which means that they do not have the same efficiency.

▷ First estimator : **Total sample mean**

The total sample mean $\bar{X}_{m \cdot n} = \bar{\bar{X}}_m$ introduced in (4.86) has expectation μ_0 and variance

$$V(\bar{\bar{X}}_m) = \frac{\sigma_0^2}{m \cdot n}, \tag{4.95}$$

where σ_0^2 is the process variance. Provided that the X_{ij} are normally distributed, this estimator also has a normal distribution.

▷ Second estimator: **Median of the sample medians**

If the prerun variables X_{ij} are $no(\mu_0; \sigma_0^2)$-distributed, then the medians $\tilde{X}_{1n}, \ldots, \tilde{X}_{mn}$ of the individual samples have a normal distribution with expectation μ_0 and variance

$$V(\tilde{X}_{in}) = \frac{\sigma_0^2}{n} \cdot c_n^2. \tag{4.96}$$

The median $\tilde{\tilde{X}}_m$ of the sample medians is approximately normally distributed with expectation μ_0 and variance

$$V(\tilde{\tilde{X}}_m) = \frac{\sigma_0^2}{m \cdot n} \cdot c_m^2 \cdot c_n^2. \tag{4.97}$$

The values of the factors c_ν can be found in table 5.3/1 for $\nu = 2, 3, \ldots, 20$. For $\nu > 20$, there is an approximation

$$c_\nu \approx \sqrt{\frac{\pi}{2}} \approx 1.253.$$

▷ Third estimator: **Mean of the sample medians**

The mean $\bar{\tilde{X}}_m$ of the sample medians, previously introduced in (4.83), is approximately normally distributed with expectation μ_0 and variance

$$V(\bar{\tilde{X}}_m) = \frac{\sigma_0^2}{m \cdot n} \cdot c_n^2. \tag{4.98}$$

▷ Fourth estimator: **Median of the sample means**

The median $\tilde{\bar{X}}_m$ of the sample means is approximately normally distributed with expectation μ_0 and variance

$$V(\tilde{\bar{X}}_m) = \frac{\sigma_0^2}{m \cdot n} \cdot c_m^2. \tag{4.99}$$

Comparison of efficiency

Which of these four unbiased estimators should one choose? Since $c_\nu > 1$ for $\nu > 2$ and $c_{\nu+2} > c_\nu$, we get the following ranking of the variances for $m > n$:

$$V(\bar{\bar{X}}_m) < V(\bar{\tilde{X}}_m) < V(\tilde{\bar{X}}_m) < V(\tilde{\tilde{X}}_m). \tag{4.100}$$

Consequently one would choose the total sample mean when **efficiency** is the decision criterion. With respect to **robustness**, i.e., sensitivity towards outliers, the median of the sample medians would be preferred.

d) Estimating the Process Spread

If the target value σ_0 of the process spread is not given in the form of a nominal or empirical value, it can also be estimated from prerun data. In the following, we will present five possibilities for its estimation. The estimators $\hat{\sigma}_0$ are all *unbiased* but differ with respect to their variances (see STANGE 1975, p.54ff).

▷ First estimator : **Corrected total sample standard deviation**

The first candidate for an estimator is the total standard deviation $S_{m \cdot n} = \sqrt{S_{m \cdot n}^2}$ introduced in (4.87b). As shown in (4.93), the sum $Q_{m \cdot n}$ in $S_{m \cdot n}^2$ consists of the two terms Q_1 and Q_2. These two components reflect different sources of variation. The variation resulting from the spread of the means is contained in Q_1, whereas the variation of the individual values with respect to their corresponding sample mean is measured by Q_2. For the variation of the process spread one can use only the latter component. Since $Q_1 > 0$ usually, $S_{m \cdot n}^2$ is an unbiased estimate of the actual process variance only when the process level is constant. Thus, one will use the F test (4.92) in order to justify the assumption of a time constant process level. If this is the case, it follows that $\hat{\sigma}_0^2 = S_{m \cdot n}^2$ is an unbiased estimator for σ_0^2. However, it does not follow from this that $S_{m \cdot n}$ is also an unbiased estimator of σ_0. Analogous to (2.75), one has to divide $S_{m \cdot n}$ by a correction term $a_{m \cdot n}$ in order to achieve unbiasedness. Thus, the **corrected total sample standard deviation** $S_{m \cdot n}/a_{m \cdot n}$ results in an unbiased estimator of σ_0. The variance of this estimator is given by

$$V\left(\frac{S_{m\cdot n}}{a_{m\cdot n}}\right) = \left(1 - a_{m\cdot n}^2\right) \cdot \sigma_0^2 = b_{m\cdot n}^2 \cdot \sigma_0^2 \qquad (4.101)$$

with $b_\nu := \sqrt{1 - a_\nu^2}$. The values of the terms a_ν and b_ν are given in table 5.3/1 for $\nu = 2, 3, \ldots, 20$. For $\nu > 20$, one can use the approximations

$$a_\nu \approx 1 - \frac{1}{4(\nu - 1)}; \qquad b_\nu \approx \frac{1}{\sqrt{2(\nu - 1)}}.$$

▷ Second estimator: **Corrected mean of the sample standard deviations**

For normally distributed prerun variables X_{ij} the m standard deviations $S_{1n}, \ldots, S_{mn}$ of (4.76b) have the expectation $E(S_{in}) = a_n \cdot \sigma_0$ and the variance

$$V(S_{in}) = (1 - a_n^2) \cdot \sigma_0^2, \qquad i = 1, \ldots, m. \qquad (4.102)$$

Thus, the **corrected mean of the sample standard deviations** $\bar{S}_m/a_n$ is an unbiased estimator of σ_0. Its variance is

$$V\left(\frac{\bar{S}_m}{a_n}\right) = \frac{(1 - a_n^2)}{a_n^2} \cdot \frac{\sigma_0^2}{m} = \left(\frac{b_n}{a_n}\right)^2 \cdot \frac{\sigma_0^2}{m}. \qquad (4.103)$$

For $n = 2, \ldots, 20$ the ratios b_n/a_n are given in table 5.3/1.

▷ Third estimator: **Corrected square root of the average sample variance**

As an alternative to $\overline{S}_m/a_n$, we also present $\sqrt{\overline{S_m^2}}/a_{m\cdot(n-1)+1}$. This estimator, which is based on (4.80), is also unbiased and has variance

$$V\left(\frac{\sqrt{\overline{S_m^2}}}{a_{m\cdot(n-1)+1}}\right) = b_{m\cdot(n-1)+1}^2 \cdot \sigma_0^2. \qquad (4.104)$$

▷ Fourth estimator: **Corrected mean of the sample ranges**

If the prerun variables X_{ij} prerun are normally distributed, then the sample ranges $R_{1n}, \ldots, R_{mn}$ of the individual samples have a distribution with expectation $E(R_{in}) = d_n\sigma_0$ and variance

$$V(R_{in}) = e_n^2\sigma_0^2; \qquad i = 1, \ldots, m. \qquad (4.105)$$

The **corrected mean of the sample ranges** $\bar{R}_m/d_n$ is then unbiased and has variance

$$V\left(\frac{\bar{R}_m}{d_n}\right) = \left(\frac{e_n}{d_n}\right)^2 \cdot \frac{\sigma_0^2}{m}. \tag{4.106}$$

The values of the factors e_n and d_n as well as those of the ratios e_n/d_n can be found in table 5.3/1.

▷ Fifth estimator: **Corrected median of the sample ranges**

Instead of the corrected mean $\bar{R}_m/d_n$, one can also use the **corrected median of the sample ranges** $\tilde{R}_m/\tilde{d}_n$ for estimating σ_0. Its variance is

$$V\left(\frac{\tilde{R}_m}{\tilde{d}_n}\right) = \frac{\sigma_0^2}{4m \cdot \tilde{e}_n^2}. \tag{4.107}$$

The conversion factors $\tilde{d}_n$ and $\tilde{e}_n$ can also be found in table 5.3/1.

Comparison of efficiency

When comparing the variances of these five unbiased estimators, the following ranking can be verified for $n > 2$:

$$V\left(\frac{S_{m\cdot n}}{a_{m\cdot n}}\right) < V\left(\frac{\sqrt{\overline{S^2_m}}}{a_{m\cdot(n-1)+1}}\right) < V\left(\frac{\bar{S}_m}{a_n}\right) < V\left(\frac{\bar{R}_m}{d_n}\right) < V\left(\frac{\tilde{R}_m}{\tilde{d}_n}\right). \tag{4.108}$$

Thus, the corrected total sample standard deviation has the highest efficiency, but the differences from the other four estimators are small for $2 < n \leq 12$ (m arbitrary).

Table 4.4/2 summarizes the above presentation referring to the estimation of the target values μ_0 and σ_0.

Θ	Estimator for Θ	Variance of the estimator
μ_0	$\hat{\mu}_0 = \bar{\bar{X}}_m$	$V(\hat{\mu}_0) = \dfrac{\sigma_0^2}{m \cdot n}$
	$\hat{\mu}_0 = \tilde{\tilde{X}}_m$	$V(\hat{\mu}_0) = \dfrac{\sigma_0^2}{m \cdot n} \cdot c_m^2 \cdot c_n^2$
	$\hat{\mu}_0 = \bar{\tilde{X}}_m$	$V(\hat{\mu}_0) = \dfrac{\sigma_0^2}{m \cdot n} \cdot c_n^2$
	$\hat{\mu}_0 = \tilde{\bar{X}}_m$	$V(\hat{\mu}_0) = \dfrac{\sigma_0^2}{m \cdot n} \cdot c_m^2$
σ_0	$\hat{\sigma}_0 = \dfrac{S_{m \cdot n}}{a_{m \cdot n}}$	$V(\hat{\sigma}_0) = b_{m \cdot n}^2 \cdot \sigma_0^2$
	$\hat{\sigma}_0 = \dfrac{\bar{S}_m}{a_n}$	$V(\hat{\sigma}_0) = \left(\dfrac{b_n}{a_n}\right)^2 \cdot \dfrac{\sigma_0^2}{m}$
	$\hat{\sigma}_0 = \dfrac{\sqrt{\overline{S_m^2}}}{a_{m \cdot (n-1)+1}}$	$V(\hat{\sigma}_0) = b_{m \cdot (n-1)+1}^2 \cdot \sigma_0^2$
	$\hat{\sigma}_0 = \dfrac{\bar{R}_m}{d_n}$	$V(\hat{\sigma}_0) = \left(\dfrac{e_n}{d_n}\right)^2 \cdot \dfrac{\sigma_0^2}{m}$
	$\hat{\sigma}_0 = \dfrac{\tilde{R}_m}{\tilde{d}_n}$	$V(\hat{\sigma}_0) = \dfrac{\sigma_0^2}{4m \cdot \tilde{e}_n^2}$

Table 4.4/2: Estimation of the target values for the process level and process spread based on prerun data

---

Example 4.4/2

We will now apply the estimators for μ_0 and σ_0, which were introduced above, to the data of table 4.4/1. The quantity μ_0 is the target value for the expectation of the normally distributed CO_2-content X of a soft drink and σ_0 is the target value for its standard deviation. From columns 5 – 6 of table 4.4/1 we get the following estimates for μ_0:

$$\hat{\mu}_0 = \bar{\bar{x}}_{15} = \frac{1}{15} \sum_{i=1}^{15} \bar{x}_{i5} = \frac{1}{15} \cdot 103.62 \approx 6.908$$

$$\hat{\mu}_0 = \tilde{\tilde{x}}_{15} = \tilde{x}_{<8;15>} = 7.0$$

$$\hat{\mu}_0 = \bar{\tilde{x}}_{15} = \frac{1}{15} \sum_{i=1}^{15} \tilde{x}_{i5} = \frac{1}{15} \cdot 103.8 \approx 6.92.$$

$$\hat{\mu}_0 = \bar{\bar{x}}_{15} = \tilde{x}_{<8;15>} = 6.92$$

The five estimates $\hat{\sigma}_0$ are calculated using columns $7-9$ in table 4.4/1. By (4.89) and (4.93) and using $Q_1 \approx 1.0552$ and $Q_2 \approx 4.82$ in example 4.4/1, it follows that:

$$s_{75} = \sqrt{s_{75}^2} \approx \sqrt{\frac{1.0552 + 4.82}{74}} \approx 0.2817$$

$$\bar{s}_{15} = \frac{1}{15} \cdot 4.0908 \approx 0.2727$$

$$\sqrt{\overline{s_{15}^2}} = \sqrt{\frac{1}{15} \cdot 1.205} \approx \sqrt{0.0803} \approx 0.2834$$

$$\bar{r}_{15} = \frac{1}{15} \cdot 10.2 \approx 0.68$$

$$\tilde{r}_{15} = r_{<8;15>} = 0.7.$$

The corrected results are found using table 5.3/1 and the approximation formulas for a_ν ($\nu > 20$):

$$\hat{\sigma}_0 = \frac{s_{75}}{a_{75}} \approx \frac{0.2817}{0.9966} \approx 0.2827$$

$$\hat{\sigma}_0 = \frac{\bar{s}_{15}}{a_5} \approx \frac{0.2727}{0.940} \approx 0.2901$$

$$\hat{\sigma}_0 = \frac{\sqrt{\overline{s_{15}^2}}}{a_{61}} \approx \frac{0.2834}{0.9958} \approx 0.2846$$

$$\hat{\sigma}_0 = \frac{\bar{r}_{15}}{d_5} \approx \frac{0.68}{2.326} \approx 0.2923$$

$$\hat{\sigma}_0 = \frac{\tilde{r}_{15}}{\tilde{d}_5} \approx \frac{0.7}{2.257} \approx 0.3101.$$

Among these estimates, the last one differs significantly from the rest.

Remark

For $n = 1$ the presented approaches to estimate σ_0 fail. Since $m \cdot n = m$, one has only m prerun variables $X_1, \ldots, X_m$ in this case. An unbiased estimate is then given by

$$\hat{\sigma}_0 = \sqrt{\Delta/2}; \qquad \Delta := \frac{1}{m-1} \cdot \sum_{i=1}^{m-1} (X_{i+1} - X_i)^2.$$

(see GRAF/HENNING/STANGE/WILRICH 1987, p.397).

Problem 4.4/2
Apply the estimators of table 4.4/2 to the prerun data in problem 4.4/1.

4.4.2 Control Charts for Monitoring the Process Level

a) Introductory Remarks

Before installing a control chart for the process level μ_t, one has to decide whether one wants to detect increasing and decreasing shifts or a shift in only one direction. If one is interested in the latter case, one will use a **onesided control chart for the process level**. The underlying hypothesis test for this chart is of the type

Test theoretical background of control charts for the process level:

- in the case of one-sided monitoring

$$\begin{aligned} H_0 &: \mu_t \leq \mu_0 \\ H_1 &: \mu_t > \mu_0 \end{aligned} \tag{4.109}$$

or

$$\begin{aligned} H_0 &: \mu_t \geq \mu_0 \\ H_1 &: \mu_t < \mu_0, \end{aligned} \tag{4.110}$$

depending on whether one wants to detect an *increasing* or *decreasing* shift in the process (control charts with a single upper or respectively lower limit). However, if increasing and decreasing movements of the process level are relevant, then one will implement a **twosided control chart for the process level**. Its underlying hypothesis test is of the form

- in the case of two-sided monitoring

$$\begin{aligned} H_0 &: \mu_t = \mu_0 \\ H_1 &: \mu_t \neq \mu_0. \end{aligned} \tag{4.111}$$

Due to lack of space, we will discuss only control charts with *twosided* limits. After working through this section the reader will have no difficulties in applying the necessary modifications for the onesided cases.

Determining the lines of a twosided control chart for the process level

In all of the presented control charts for the process level the location CL of the **centre line** will be obtained from the available information about the target value μ_0. It is either given by $CL = \mu_0$ with $\mu_0 = \mu_N$ or $\mu_0 = \mu_E$ (nominal or empirical values) or by $CL = \hat{\mu}_0$ (estimate from the undisturbed process). How the levels UCL, LCL, UWL and LWL of the limiting lines are determined will depend on the information about the spread of the process which is assumed to be constant. If σ_0 is given in the form of a nominal or empirical value, i.e., if $\sigma_0 = \sigma_N$ or $\sigma_0 = \sigma_E$, then the levels of the limiting lines are

$$\left.\begin{matrix} UCL \\ LCL \end{matrix}\right\} = CL \pm c^C \cdot \sigma_0 \tag{4.112}$$

$$\left.\begin{array}{c} UWL \\ LWL \end{array}\right\} = CL \pm c^W \cdot \sigma_0. \tag{4.113}$$

The factors c^C and c^W are determined according to figure 4.2/2 so that the probability of observing a realization of the test statistic outside of the interval (LCL, UCL) or (LWL, UWL) is $\alpha = 0.01$ or $\alpha = 0.05$ when the process is undisturbed. If one has only an estimate $\hat{\sigma}_0$ of σ, then this estimate is used instead of σ_0. Thus, a control chart for the process level has the form given in figure 4.4/1.:

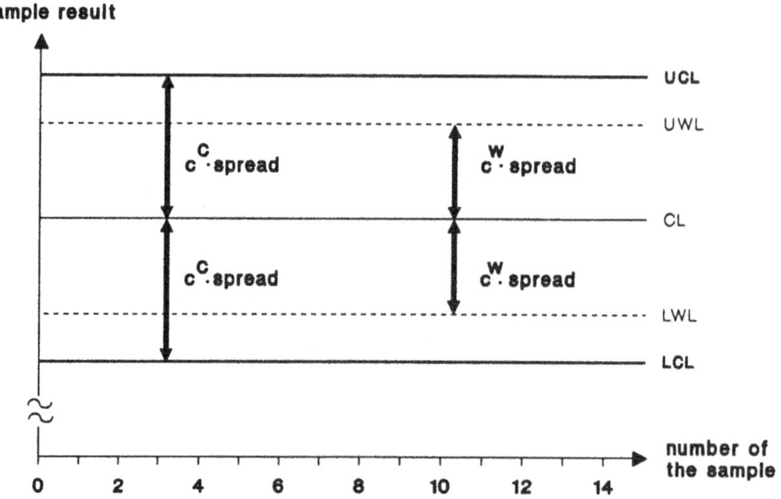

Figure 4.4/1: Structure of a twosided control chart for the process level

When σ_0 has to be estimated one can use one of the alternatives listed in table 4.4/2. Table 4.4/3 summarizes all the discussed possibilities for constructing a control chart for the process level.

The magnitude of the coefficients c^C and c^W not only depends on the sample size n, but also on the chosen test statistic of the chart. In order to emphasize the dependency on the sample size, we sometimes use the notation $c^C = c^C(n)$ and $c^W = c^W(n)$. One can also refer to the underlying test statistic by using a subscript, i.e., $c^C = c^C_{\bar{x}}(n)$.

Assuming a normally distributed test statistic with constant variance

In the following, we will introduce four different control charts for the process level. We will assume that the monitored quality characteristic X is $no(\mu_t; \sigma_0^2)$-distributed. In general one will take a sample of size $n > 1$ from the manufacturing process at constant time intervals. Depending on whether the sample mean $\bar{X}_n$, the sample median $\tilde{X}_n$, or the original sample

<table>
<tr><th rowspan="2">Level CL of the centre line</th><th rowspan="2">Information about σ_0</th><th colspan="2">Levels of the limiting lines</th></tr>
<tr><th>UCL, LCL</th><th>UWL, LWL</th></tr>
<tr><td rowspan="7">$CL = \mu_0$
or
$CL = \hat{\mu}_0$</td><td>$\sigma_0 = \sigma_N$</td><td rowspan="2">$CL \pm c^C \cdot \sigma_0$</td><td rowspan="2">$CL \pm c^C \cdot \sigma_0$</td></tr>
<tr><td>$\sigma_0 = \sigma_E$</td></tr>
<tr><td>$\hat{\sigma}_0 = \frac{s_{m \cdot n}}{a_{m \cdot n}}$</td><td rowspan="5">$CL \pm c^C \cdot \hat{\sigma}_0$</td><td rowspan="5">$CL \pm c^W \cdot \hat{\sigma}_0$</td></tr>
<tr><td>$\hat{\sigma}_0 = \frac{\sqrt{\overline{s^2_m}}}{a_{m \cdot (n-1)+1}}$</td></tr>
<tr><td>$\hat{\sigma}_0 = \frac{\bar{s}_m}{a_n}$</td></tr>
<tr><td>$\hat{\sigma}_0 = \frac{\bar{r}_m}{d_n}$</td></tr>
<tr><td>$\hat{\sigma}_0 = \frac{\bar{r}_m}{\tilde{d}_n}$</td></tr>
</table>

Table 4.4/3: Control lines and warning lines of a twosided control chart for the process level

vector $\mathbf{X} = (X_1, \ldots, X_n)$ is chosen to be the test statistic, one uses a mean chart ($\bar{x}$ chart), a median chart ($\tilde{x}$ chart) or an extreme value chart (**x** chart), respectively. These three charts agree in the special case of $n = 1$. The corresponding chart is then called an individual observation chart.

b) Mean Charts ($\bar{x}$ charts)

The test statistic of a **mean chart** is always the arithmetic mean

$$\bar{X}_n = \frac{1}{n} \sum_{i=1}^{n} X_i$$

of a sample of size n from the ongoing production. The assumption of a constant process variance σ_0^2 implies that this test statistic is $no(\mu_t; \sigma_0^2/n)$-distributed. Hence, by applying (2.59c) we get

$$Pr\left(\mu_0 - z_{1-\alpha/2}\frac{\sigma_0}{\sqrt{n}} \leq \bar{X}_n \leq \mu_0 + z_{1-\alpha/2}\frac{\sigma_0}{\sqrt{n}} | \mu_t = \mu_0\right) = 1 - \alpha. \quad (4.114)$$

The interval within the brackets, the so-called **twosided variation interval** of the test statistic $\bar{X}_n$ with level $1 - \alpha$, has the property that in the case of undisturbed production $(1 - \alpha) \cdot 100\%$ of all the realizations of $\bar{X}_n$

are expected to lie within this interval. The control lines and the warning lines are given by the endpoints of this interval with $\alpha = 0.01$ and with $\alpha = 0.05$, respectively. If μ_0 and σ_0 are given in the form of fixed values, then we get from (4.114) and (4.112) - (4.113) that

Limiting lines of a two-sided mean chart for known μ_0 and σ_0

$$\left.\begin{matrix} UCL \\ LCL \end{matrix}\right\} = CL \pm c_{\bar{x}}^{C} \cdot \sigma_0 = \mu_0 \pm \frac{z_{0.995}}{\sqrt{n}} \cdot \sigma_0 \tag{4.115}$$

$$\left.\begin{matrix} UWL \\ LWL \end{matrix}\right\} = CL \pm c_{\bar{x}}^{W} \cdot \sigma_0 = \mu_0 \pm \frac{z_{0.975}}{\sqrt{n}} \cdot \sigma_0. \tag{4.116}$$

Using table 5.2/1 it follows that

$$c_{\bar{x}}^{C} = c_{\bar{x}}^{C}(n) = \frac{z_{0.995}}{\sqrt{n}} \approx \frac{2.576}{\sqrt{n}} \tag{4.117}$$

$$c_{\bar{x}}^{W} = c_{\bar{x}}^{W}(n) = \frac{z_{0.975}}{\sqrt{n}} \approx \frac{1.960}{\sqrt{n}}. \tag{4.118}$$

If μ_0 and/or σ_0 in (4.114) are replaced by estimates then this probability statement holds only approximately. For an undisturbed process the limiting lines, which then result from the appropriately modified determining equations (4.115) - (4.116), are reached or exceeded only with probability $\alpha^* \approx \alpha$ in this case.

Analogous to (4.71a), the **power function** of the twosided mean chart is given by

$$G_{\bar{x}}(\mu_t) = Pr(\bar{X}_n \geq UCL|\mu_t) + Pr(\bar{X}_n \leq LCL|\mu_t). \tag{4.119 a}$$

For a control chart with centre line $CL = \mu_0$ and fixed process spread σ_0, the values of UCL and LCL are given by (4.115). We get

$$G_{\bar{x}}(\mu_t) = Pr(\bar{X}_n \geq CL + c_{\bar{x}}^{C} \cdot \sigma_0|\mu_t) + Pr(\bar{X}_n \leq CL - c_{\bar{x}}^{C} \cdot \sigma_0|\mu_t). \tag{4.119 b}$$

Taking into account that $\bar{X}_n \sim no(\mu_t; \sigma_0^2/n)$ and standardizing according to (2.52a) gives

$$\begin{aligned} G_{\bar{x}}(\mu_t) &= 1 - No(\mu_0 + c_{\bar{x}}^{C} \cdot \sigma_0|\mu_t) + No(\mu_0 - c_{\bar{x}}^{C} \cdot \sigma_0|\mu_t) \qquad (4.119\text{ c}) \\ &= \Phi\left(-\frac{\mu_0 + c_{\bar{x}}^{C} \cdot \sigma_0 - \mu_t}{\sigma_0} \cdot \sqrt{n}\right) + \Phi\left(\frac{\mu_0 - c_{\bar{x}}^{C} \cdot \sigma_0 - \mu_t}{\sigma_0} \cdot \sqrt{n}\right). \end{aligned}$$

Substituting (4.117) yields

$$G_{\bar{x}}(\mu_t) = \Phi\left(-z_{0.995} + \frac{\mu_t - \mu_0}{\sigma_0} \cdot \sqrt{n}\right) + \Phi\left(-z_{0.995} - \frac{\mu_t - \mu_0}{\sigma_0} \cdot \sqrt{n}\right). \tag{4.119 d}$$

In practice, it is more useful to express the intervention probability as a function $G^*_{\bar{x}}(\delta_t)$ of the dimensionless variable

$$\delta_t := \frac{\mu_t - \mu_0}{\sigma_0} \tag{4.120}$$

(standardized shift) instead of as a function $G_{\bar{x}}(\mu_t)$ of the process mean. The variable δ_t measures the deviation of the actual process mean μ_t from the target value μ_0 with respect to the standard deviation σ_0 of the undisturbed process as a basic unit. From (4.119d) we get

Power function of the twosided mean chart for known μ_0 and σ_0

$$G^*_{\bar{x}}(\delta_t) = \Phi\left(-z_{0.995} + \delta_t \cdot \sqrt{n}\right) + \Phi\left(-z_{0.995} - \delta_t \cdot \sqrt{n}\right) \tag{4.121}$$

with $z_{0.995} \approx 2.576$. If estimates $\hat{\mu}_0$ and/or $\hat{\sigma}_0$ are used for the construction of the control chart, then the power function no longer holds exactly. A demonstration of the evaluation of (4.121) can be found in section 4.4.2e.

With the power function (4.121), the **average run length** is almost instantly provided. The average run length is the expectation of the discrete random variable "run length" which denotes the number of samples drawn between one intervening action and the following one. This random variable – for a process shift δ_t and $P := G^*_{\bar{x}}(\delta_t)$ – takes the values $k = 1, 2, 3, \ldots$, with probabilities $(1 - P)^{k-1} \cdot P$. Hence, according to the definition of the expectation of a discrete random variable, the average run length is given by

$$\sum_{k=1}^{\infty} k \cdot (1-P)^{k-1} \cdot P = P \cdot \sum_{k=1}^{\infty} k \cdot (1-P)^{k-1} = \frac{1}{P}.$$

Abbreviating the average run length of a mean chart by $ARL_{\bar{x}}(\delta_t)$ one gets

ARL function of the mean chart

$$ARL_{\bar{x}}(\delta_t) = \sum_{k=1}^{\infty} k \cdot G^*_{\bar{x}}(\delta_t) \cdot [1 - G^*_{\bar{x}}(\delta_t)]^{k-1} = \frac{1}{G^*_{\bar{x}}(\delta_t)}. \tag{4.122}$$

Applying this formula, the average run length $ARL_{\bar{x}}(\delta_t)$ for any process shift δ_t is readily computed. It should be noted that the expression $1/G^*_{\bar{x}}(\delta_t)$ can be considered as the expectation (2.98a) of a negative binomial distribution with parameters $c = 1$ and $P = G^*_{\bar{x}}(\delta_t)$, i.e., as the expectation of a geometric distribution.

Example 4.4/3

With the prerun data of example 4.4/1 we will now construct a mean chart. Its limiting lines are determined by (4.115) - (4.116). Instead of μ_0 and σ_0 we need to use estimates:

$$\left.\begin{matrix} UCL \\ LCL \end{matrix}\right\} = CL \pm c_{\bar{x}}^{C}(5) \cdot \hat{\sigma}_0 = \hat{\mu}_0 \pm \frac{z_{0.995}}{\sqrt{5}} \cdot \hat{\sigma}_0 = \hat{\mu}_0 \pm 1.152 \cdot \hat{\sigma}_0$$

$$\left.\begin{matrix} UWL \\ LWL \end{matrix}\right\} = CL \pm c_{\bar{x}}^{W}(5) \cdot \hat{\sigma}_0 = \hat{\mu}_0 \pm \frac{z_{0.975}}{\sqrt{n}} \cdot \hat{\sigma}_0 = \hat{\mu}_0 \pm 0.877 \cdot \hat{\sigma}_0 .$$

Our estimates are

$$\hat{\mu}_0 = \bar{\bar{x}}_{15} \approx 6.908; \qquad \hat{\sigma}_0 = \frac{\bar{s}_{15}}{a_5} \approx 0.2901$$

of example 4.4/2. With these values we can now calculate:

$$\left.\begin{matrix} UCL \\ LCL \end{matrix}\right\} = 6.908 \pm 1.152 \cdot 0.2901 \approx 6.908 \pm 0.334 = \left\{\begin{matrix} 7.242 \\ 6.574 \end{matrix}\right.$$

$$\left.\begin{matrix} UWL \\ LWL \end{matrix}\right\} = 6.908 \pm 0.877 \cdot 0.2901 \approx 6.908 \pm 0.254 = \left\{\begin{matrix} 7.162 \\ 6.654. \end{matrix}\right.$$

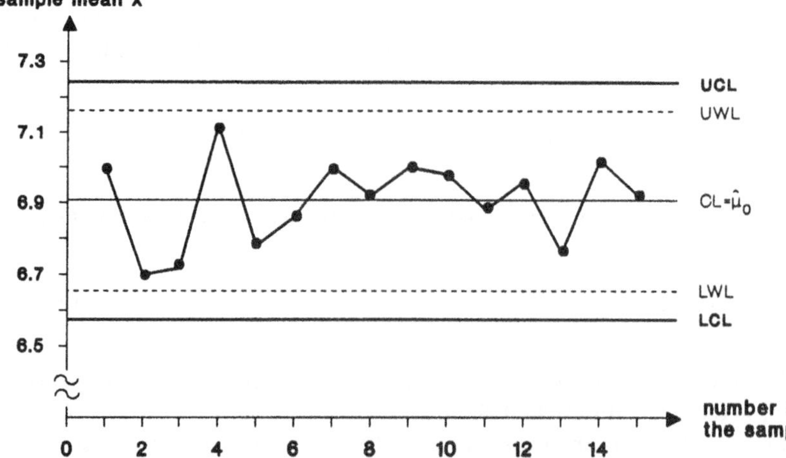

Figure 4.4/2: Mean chart with twosided limiting lines

Figure 4.4/2 shows the mean chart with these limiting lines and the centre line $CL = \hat{\mu}_0$. The control chart contains the 15 sample means of the prerun (column 5 of table 4.4/1).

With respect to the process level, we can see that the prerun was undisturbed, although we observe some instability at the beginning. The conclusion that the process is undisturbed agrees with the results of the F test performed in example 4.4/1.

---

c) Median Charts ($\tilde{x}$ charts)

The test statistic of a **median chart** is always the median

$$\tilde{X}_n := \begin{cases} X_{<k+1;n>} & \text{if } n = 2k+1 \\ \frac{1}{2}(X_{<k;n>} + X_{<k+1;n>}) & \text{if } n = 2k \end{cases}$$

based on a sample of size n from the ongoing production. If n is chosen to be odd, then the determination of $\tilde{X}_n$ does not require any calculation. One simply orders the observations by their magnitude in an increasing sequence and chooses the middle value. The test statistic $\tilde{X}_n$ is normally distributed with expectation $E(\tilde{X}_n) = \mu_t$ and variance $V(\tilde{X}_n) = \sigma_0^2 \cdot c_n^2/n$. Analogous to (4.114), we get

$$Pr\left(\mu_0 - z_{1-\alpha/2}\frac{\sigma_0 \cdot c_n}{\sqrt{n}} \leq \tilde{X}_n \leq \mu_0 + z_{1-\alpha/2}\frac{\sigma_0 \cdot c_n}{\sqrt{n}} \middle| \mu_t = \mu_0\right) = 1 - \alpha \tag{4.123}$$

with c_n from table 5.3/1. For given values μ_0 and σ_0 the limiting lines corresponding to (4.115) - (4.116) have the form:

Limiting lines of a twosided median chart for known μ_0 and σ_0

$$\left.\begin{matrix} UCL \\ LCL \end{matrix}\right\} = CL \pm c_{\tilde{x}}^C \cdot \sigma_0 = \mu_0 \pm \frac{z_{0.995} \cdot c_n}{\sqrt{n}} \cdot \sigma_0 \tag{4.124}$$

$$\left.\begin{matrix} UWL \\ LWL \end{matrix}\right\} = CL \pm c_{\tilde{x}}^W \cdot \sigma_0 = \mu_0 \pm \frac{z_{0.975} \cdot c_n}{\sqrt{n}} \cdot \sigma_0. \tag{4.125}$$

Thus, it holds that

$$c_{\tilde{x}}^C = c_{\tilde{x}}^C(n) = c_{\bar{x}}^C(n) \cdot c_n = \frac{z_{0.995}}{\sqrt{n}} \cdot c_n \approx \frac{2.576}{\sqrt{n}} \cdot c_n \tag{4.126}$$

$$c_{\tilde{x}}^W = c_{\tilde{x}}^W(n) = c_{\bar{x}}^W(n) \cdot c_n = \frac{z_{0.975}}{\sqrt{n}} \cdot c_n \approx \frac{1.960}{\sqrt{n}} \cdot c_n. \tag{4.127}$$

Power function of a twosided median chart for known μ_0 and σ_0

The **power function** with argument δ_t corresponding to (4.121) is defined by

$$G^*_{\tilde{x}}(\delta_t) = \Phi\left(-z_{0.995} + \frac{\delta_t \cdot \sqrt{n}}{c_n}\right) + \Phi\left(-z_{0.995} - \frac{\delta_t \cdot \sqrt{n}}{c_n}\right). \qquad (4.128)$$

If a median chart is constructed with estimates $\hat{\mu}_0$ and/or $\hat{\sigma}_0$ instead of μ_0 and σ_0, respectively, then formula (4.128) holds only approximately.

Example 4.4/4

We will again use the prerun data of example 4.4/1. Based on these data and the estimates $\hat{\mu}_0 = \bar{\bar{x}}_{15} \approx 6.908$ and $\hat{\sigma}_0 = \bar{s}_{15}/a_5 \approx 0.2901$, we determined a mean chart in example 4.4/3. We now want to determine a median chart with these estimates. According to (4.124) - (4.125), its limiting lines satisfy

$$\left.\begin{array}{l} UCL \\ LCL \end{array}\right\} = CL \pm c^C_{\tilde{x}}(5) \cdot \hat{\sigma}_0 = \hat{\mu}_0 \pm c^C_{\bar{x}}(5) \cdot c_5 \cdot \hat{\sigma}_0 \approx \hat{\mu}_0 \pm 1.152 \cdot c_5 \cdot \hat{\sigma}_0$$

$$\left.\begin{array}{l} UWL \\ LWL \end{array}\right\} = CL \pm c^W_{\tilde{x}}(5) \cdot \hat{\sigma}_0 = \hat{\mu}_0 \pm c^W_{\bar{x}}(5) \cdot c_5 \cdot \hat{\sigma}_0 \approx \hat{\mu}_0 \pm 0.877 \cdot c_5 \cdot \hat{\sigma}_0.$$

Substituting $\hat{\mu}_0$ and $\hat{\sigma}_0$, as well as $c_5 = 1.198$ from table 5.3/1, yields

$$\left.\begin{array}{l} UCL \\ LCL \end{array}\right\} \approx 6.908 \pm 1.380 \cdot 0.2901 \approx 6.908 \pm 0.400 = \left\{\begin{array}{l} 7.308 \\ 6.508 \end{array}\right.$$

$$\left.\begin{array}{l} UWL \\ LWL \end{array}\right\} = 6.908 \pm 1.051 \cdot 0.2901 \approx 6.908 \pm 0.305 = \left\{\begin{array}{l} 7.213 \\ 6.603. \end{array}\right.$$

A comparison of the 15 individual prerun medians in column 6 of table 4.4/1 with the control limits of the chart shows that all medians lie within the control lines.

---

d) Extreme Value Charts (x charts)

The test statistic of an **extreme value chart** is always the original sample vector

$$\mathbf{X} = (X_1, \ldots, X_n)$$

of a sample of size n from the ongoing production. All n realizations of the sample vector are individually plotted into the control chart. No intervention or warning occurs only if *all* n observations lie within the control lines or warning limits, respectively. A corrective action is taken after a sample depending solely on the extreme values $X_{<1;n>}$ (sample minimum) and $X_{<n;n>}$ (sample maximum) of the sample. Because of this, the chart is called extreme value chart. The n components $X_1, \ldots, X_n$ of the sample vector are again assumed to be independently and identically $no(\mu_t; \sigma_0^2)$-distributed. The limiting lines are determined according to figure 4.4/2 so that in the case of an undisturbed process, i.e., when $\mu_t = \mu_0$, all components lie within the limits with probability $1 - \alpha$. Since the individual variables X_i are independently and identically distributed, we can formulate the condition mentioned above as follows: The limiting lines are to be determined such that an arbitrarily chosen component X_i of $\mathbf{X} = (X_1, \ldots, X_n)$ lies with probability $\sqrt[n]{1-\alpha}$ within the limits. Because of $X_i \sim no(\mu_t; \sigma_0^2)$ this implies

$$Pr(\mu_0 - z_{P_n} \cdot \sigma_0 \leq X_i \leq \mu_0 + z_{P_n} \cdot \sigma_0) = \sqrt[n]{1-\alpha}, \tag{4.129}$$

where

$$P_n = P_n(\alpha) := \tfrac{1}{2}\left(1 + \sqrt[n]{1-\alpha}\right). \tag{4.130}$$

Consequently, for given values μ_0 and σ_0, the determining equations for the limiting lines of a twosided extreme value chart have the form

Limiting lines of a twosided extreme value chart for known μ_0 and σ_0

$$\left.\begin{matrix} UCL \\ LCL \end{matrix}\right\} = CL \pm c_{\mathbf{X}}^{C} \cdot \sigma_0 = \mu_0 \pm z_{P_n(0.01)} \cdot \sigma_0 \tag{4.131}$$

$$\left.\begin{matrix} UWL \\ LWL \end{matrix}\right\} = CL \pm c_{\mathbf{X}}^{W} \cdot \sigma_0 = \mu_0 \pm z_{P_n(0.05)} \cdot \sigma_0. \tag{4.132}$$

Analogous to (4.119b) and (4.119c), the **power function** of a twosided extreme value chart is given by [8]

$$G_{\mathbf{X}}(\mu_t) = 1 - \prod_{i=1}^{n} Pr(\mu_0 - c_{\mathbf{X}}^C \cdot \sigma_0 < X_i < \mu_0 + c_{\mathbf{X}}^C \cdot \sigma_0 | \mu_t) \tag{4.133 a}$$
$$= 1 - [No(\mu_0 + c_{\mathbf{X}}^C \cdot \sigma_0 | \mu_t; \sigma_0^2) - No(\mu_0 - c_{\mathbf{X}}^C \cdot \sigma_0 | \mu_t; \sigma_0^2)]^n.$$

Standardizing according to (2.52a) gives

$$G_{\mathbf{X}}(\mu_t) = 1 - \left[\Phi\left(\frac{\mu_0 + c_{\mathbf{X}}^C \cdot \sigma_0 - \mu_t}{\sigma_0}\right) - \Phi\left(\frac{\mu_0 - c_{\mathbf{X}}^C \cdot \sigma_0 - \mu_t}{\sigma_0}\right)\right]^n \tag{4.133 b}$$
$$= 1 - \left[\Phi\left(c_{\mathbf{X}}^C - \frac{\mu_t - \mu_0}{\sigma_0}\right) - \Phi\left(-c_{\mathbf{X}}^C - \frac{\mu_t - \mu_0}{\sigma_0}\right)\right]^n.$$

When using the dimensionless shift variable δ_t introduced in (4.120), the **power function** is given by

Power function of a twosided extreme value chart for known μ_0 and σ_0

$$G_{\mathbf{X}}^*(\delta_t) = 1 - [\Phi(c_{\mathbf{X}}^C - \delta_t) - \Phi(-c_{\mathbf{X}}^C - \delta_t)]^n. \tag{4.134}$$

Formula (4.134) holds only approximately if an extreme value chart is constructed with estimates $\hat{\mu}_0$ and/or $\hat{\sigma}_0$, instead of μ_0 and σ_0.

Example 4.4/5

As before, we will use the prerun data from example 4.4/1 for determining an extreme value control chart based on the estimates $\hat{\mu}_0 = \bar{\bar{x}}_{15} \approx 6.908$ and $\hat{\sigma}_0 = \bar{s}_{15}/a_5 \approx 0.2901$, which were obtained in example 4.4/3. According to (4.131) - (4.132), the limiting lines are defined by

$$\left.\begin{matrix} UCL \\ LCL \end{matrix}\right\} = CL \pm c_{\mathbf{X}}^C \cdot \hat{\sigma}_0 = \hat{\mu}_0 \pm z_{P_5(0.01)} \cdot \hat{\sigma}_0$$

$$\left.\begin{matrix} UWL \\ LWL \end{matrix}\right\} = CL \pm c_{\mathbf{X}}^W \cdot \hat{\sigma}_0 = \hat{\mu}_0 \pm z_{P_5(0.05)} \cdot \hat{\sigma}_0,$$

where

$$P_5(0.01) = \tfrac{1}{2}\left(1 + \sqrt[5]{0.99}\right) \approx 0.9990$$
$$P_5(0.05) = \tfrac{1}{2}\left(1 + \sqrt[5]{0.95}\right) \approx 0.9949.$$

[8] Π denotes the product operator.

After substituting the values of $\hat{\mu}_0$ and $\hat{\sigma}_0$ as well as $z_{0.999} \approx 3.09$ and $z_{0.9949} \approx 2.57$, we get

$$\left.\begin{array}{l} UCL \\ LCL \end{array}\right\} \approx 6.908 \pm 3.09 \cdot 0.2901 \approx 6.908 \pm 0.896 = \left\{\begin{array}{l} 7.804 \\ 6.012 \end{array}\right.$$

$$\left.\begin{array}{l} UWL \\ LWL \end{array}\right\} \approx 6.908 \pm 2.57 \cdot 0.2901 \approx 6.908 \pm 0.746 = \left\{\begin{array}{l} 7.654 \\ 6.162. \end{array}\right.$$

Figure 4.4/3 shows an extreme value chart with these limiting lines and the centre line $CL = \hat{\mu}_0$. The components of the observed 15 sample vectors are also plotted into this control chart (column 2 in table 4.4/1). The ranges of the individual observations in each sample are shaded. We can see that all 75 observations lie within the warning limits.

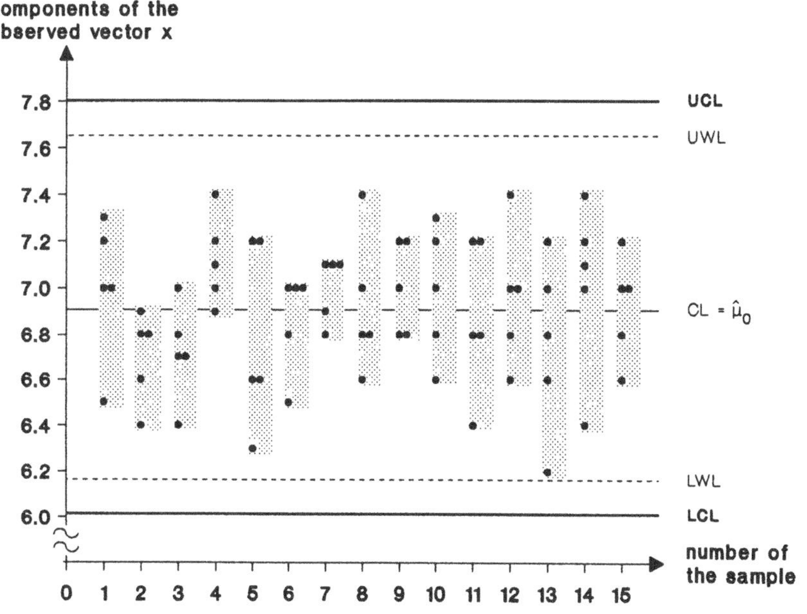

Figure 4.4/3: Extreme value chart with twosided limiting lines

e) Comparison of Mean, Median and Extreme Value Charts

Comparing the power functions of the three twosided control charts for the process level

The three control charts for the process level introduced above can be evaluated and compared using their power functions or, graphically, by the corresponding power curves. Recall that the formulas of the three power functions were:

$$G^*_{\bar{x}}(\delta_t) = \Phi\left(-z_{0.995} + \delta_t \cdot \sqrt{n}\right) + \Phi\left(-z_{0.995} - \delta_t \cdot \sqrt{n}\right) \qquad (4.135\text{ a})$$

$$G^*_{\tilde{x}}(\delta_t) = \Phi\left(-z_{0.995} + \frac{\delta_t \cdot \sqrt{n}}{c_n}\right) + \Phi\left(-z_{0.995} - \frac{\delta_t \cdot \sqrt{n}}{c_n}\right). \qquad (4.135\text{ b})$$

$$G^*_{\mathbf{x}}(\delta_t) = 1 - [\Phi(-z_{P_n(0.01)} - \delta_t) - \Phi(z_{P_n(0.01)} - \delta_t)]^n. \qquad (4.135\text{ c})$$

During an undisturbed process, i.e., for $\mu_t = \mu_0$, all three functions have the same value $\alpha = 0.01$, which was specified for the blind alarm probability:

$$G^*_{\bar{x}}(0) = G^*_{\tilde{x}}(0) = G^*_{\mathbf{x}}(0) = 0.01.$$

Since the coefficients of table 5.3/1 have the property that $c_n > 1$ for $n \geq 3$, it follows that the limiting lines of a median chart are for $n \geq 3$ farther apart than the corresponding lines of the mean chart. Thus, the median chart

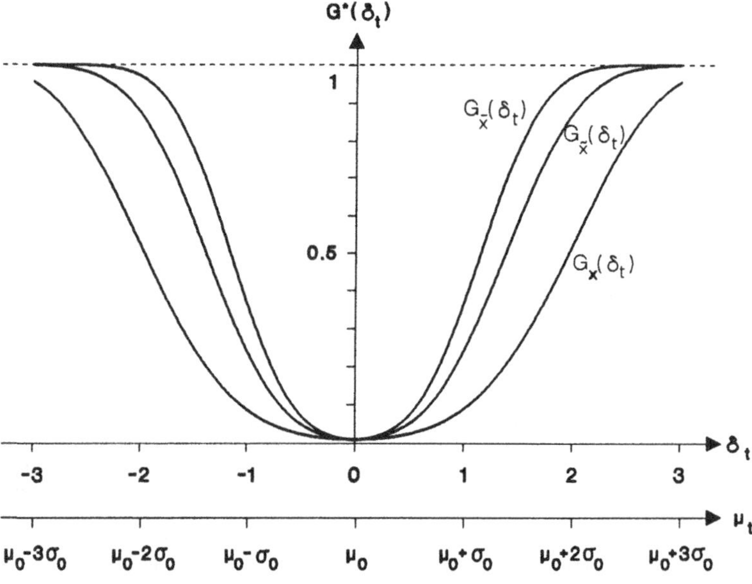

Figure 4.4/4: Power curves of a twosided mean chart, median chart and extreme value chart for $n = 5$

has a lower intervention probability when there is a shift $\delta_t \neq 0$. Hence its power curve is less steep. Figure 4.4/4 displays three power curves for $n = 5$.

One can see that the performance of the extreme value chart is even worse than that of the median chart, in the sense that it has a lower intervention probability when a shift $\delta_t \neq 0$ in the process actually occurs. However, the extreme value chart has the advantage that it can simultaneously control the process spread and location.

Remark

It occasionally happens that quality characteristics have unavoidable variations in their level, even when the process is undisturbed. In such cases, the F test for constant process level, which is performed during the process prerun, can lead to a rejection of the null hypothesis. If one ignores these variations and installs the $\bar{x}$, $\tilde{x}$ or x chart as described above, then the probability α^* of a false alarm can exceed the specified value $\alpha = 0.01$. In such a situation, one speaks of a false alarm when μ_t actually lies within an interval $[\mu^L, \mu^U]$, which one has accepted to be a satisfactory process level. In order to achieve $\alpha^* \leq \alpha$, one has to replace μ_0 by μ^L in the formulas for LCL and LWL, and by μ^U in the formulas for UCL and UWL. How the endpoints of the interval μ^L and μ^U can be estimated and how the power function of such a **control chart with extended limiting lines** can be obtained from (4.135) is described by GRAF/HENNING/STANGE/WILRICH (1987, p.320).

Problem 4.4/3

Calculate the limiting lines of twosided mean, median and extreme value charts from the prerun data of problem 4.4/1 ($n = 5$). Among the estimates obtained in problem 4.4/2, choose the alternatives $\hat{\mu}_0 = \tilde{\bar{x}}_{10}$ and $\hat{\sigma}_0 = \bar{r}_{10}/d_5$.

f) Single Observation Charts (x charts)

If the measurement of the quality characteristic is very expensive or takes a rather long time compared to the process speed, one has the option of applying a **single observation chart** which is also called **control chart for individuals**. Its test statistic is the observation X_t of a sample of size $n = 1$. Thus, the single observation chart is a special case of the mean value, median and extreme value charts (special case $n = 1$). Since the variables X_t are assumed to be $no(\mu_t; \sigma_0^2)$-distributed, it holds that

$$Pr(\mu_0 - z_{1-\alpha/2} \cdot \sigma_0 \leq X_t \leq \mu_0 + z_{1-\alpha/2} \cdot \sigma_0 | \mu_t = \mu_0) = 1 - \alpha. \quad (4.136)$$

This is the same as (4.114) with $n = 1$. The endpoints of the twosided variation interval of level $1 - \alpha$ in the brackets of expression (4.136) again give us the control lines for $\alpha = 0.01$ and the warning lines for $\alpha = 0.05$. Hence, for fixed μ_0 and σ_0, we get the formulas

Limiting lines of a two-sided single value chart for known μ_0 and σ_0

$$\left.\begin{matrix} UCL \\ LCL \end{matrix}\right\} = CL \pm c_x^C \cdot \sigma_0 = \mu_0 \pm z_{0.995} \cdot \sigma_0 \tag{4.137}$$

$$\left.\begin{matrix} UWL \\ LWL \end{matrix}\right\} = CL \pm c_x^W \cdot \sigma_0 = \mu_0 \pm z_{0.975} \cdot \sigma_0 . \tag{4.138}$$

From this we get

$$c_x^C = z_{0.995} \approx 2.576 \tag{4.139}$$

$$c_x^W = z_{0.975} \approx 1.960. \tag{4.140}$$

When using estimates $\hat{\mu}_0$ and $\hat{\sigma}_0$, these are substituted into (4.137) - (4.138). Note that the estimators for σ_0 in table 4.4/2 cannot be used for $n = 1$ (see the remark at the end of section 4.4.1d).

Because the single value chart can be seen as a special case of the $\bar{x}$, $\tilde{x}$ and **x** charts, its power function can be obtained by specializing the power functions of these charts. Setting $n = 1$ in (4.121) we get

Power function of a twosided single value chart for known μ_0 and σ_0

$$G_x^*(\delta_t) = \Phi\left(-z_{0.995} + \delta_t\right) + \Phi\left(-z_{0.995} - \delta_t\right). \tag{4.141}$$

The power curve is even shallower than that of the extreme value chart (see figure 4.4/4). Consequently one should only apply a chart for individual measurements when economic or technical considerations make it necessary and only when relatively large deviations $|\mu_t - \mu_0|$ need to be detected. By large we mean deviations in the range of $|\mu_t - \mu_0| > 3\sigma_0$, i.e. $|\delta_t| > 3$.

Example 4.4/6

With the prerun data of example 4.4/1 we now want to construct a single value chart based on a given target value $\mu_0 = \mu_N$=7.0 [g CO_2/litre] for the process location and an estimate $\hat{\sigma}_0$ for the process standard deviation. The single values are taken to be the first measurements of the 15 sample vectors in column 2 of table 4.4/1.

As an estimate of σ_0 we first get (see the remark at the end of 4.4.1d):

$$\Delta = \frac{1}{14}\sum_{i=1}^{14}(x_{i+1} - x_i)^2 = \frac{3.55}{14} \approx 0.2536,$$

$$\hat{\sigma}_0 = \sqrt{\Delta/2} \approx \sqrt{0.1268} \approx 0.3561.$$

Replacing σ_0 by $\hat{\sigma}_0$ in (4.137) - (4.138), we get:

$$\left.\begin{array}{l} UCL \\ LCL \end{array}\right\} = CL \pm c_x^C \cdot \hat{\sigma}_0 \approx 7.0 \pm 2.576 \cdot 0.356 \approx \left\{\begin{array}{l} 7.92 \\ 6.08 \end{array}\right.$$

$$\left.\begin{array}{l} UWL \\ LWL \end{array}\right\} = CL \pm c_x^W \cdot \hat{\sigma}_0 \approx 7.0 \pm 1.960 \cdot 0.356 \approx \left\{\begin{array}{l} 7.70 \\ 6.30. \end{array}\right.$$

We can see that all 15 observations of the prerun lie within these control limits.

4.4.3 Control Charts for Monitoring the Process Spread

a) Introductory Remarks

When constructing control charts for the process spread, one again has to first decide whether the chart is supposed to detect shifts in both directions or in only one direction. In the last case an **onesided control chart for the process spread** is used. Its underlying hypothesis test is of the form

$$\begin{array}{lcl} H_0 & : & \sigma_t \leq \sigma_0 \\ H_1 & : & \sigma_t > \sigma_0, \end{array} \tag{4.142}$$

if one is only interested in an *increasing* shift (control chart with onesided upper limits). Of course, one can also construct control charts which detect a shift of the process variance in either direction. The application of such a **twosided control chart for the process spread** corresponds to applying a hypothesis test of the type

$$\begin{array}{lcl} H_0 & : & \sigma_t = \sigma_0 \\ H_1 & : & \sigma_t \neq \sigma_0, \end{array} \tag{4.143}$$

Since the first type of control charts is much more relevant in practice, we will restrict ourselves to it. The modifications for the twosided case can be made appropriately.

Determining the centre line and the limiting lines of a onesided control chart for the process spread

In all the control charts for the process spread to be discussed, the level CL of the **centre line** is defined by the available information about the target value σ_0. In other words, it is given by $CL = \sigma_0$ with $\sigma_0 = \sigma_N$ or $\sigma_0 = \sigma_E$ or by $CL = \hat{\sigma}_0$ (estimate from an undisturbed prerun). The level of the limiting lines is obtained by multiplying the centre line level CL by a factor c^C or c^W, respectively:

$$UCL = c^C \cdot CL \tag{4.144}$$

$$UWL = c^W \cdot CL. \tag{4.145}$$

The factors c^C and c^W have to be determined so that, in an undisturbed process state, the test statistic exceeds the values UCL and UWL with a probability of $\alpha = 0.01$ and $\alpha = 0.05$, respectively.

The above discussion can be summarized as follows:

<table>
<tr><th rowspan="2">Level CL of the centre line</th><th rowspan="2">Information about σ_0</th><th colspan="2">Levels of the limiting lines</th></tr>
<tr><th>UCL</th><th>UWL</th></tr>
<tr><td rowspan="7">$CL = \sigma_0$
or
$CL = \hat{\sigma}_0$</td><td>$\sigma_0 = \sigma_N$</td><td rowspan="2">$c^C \cdot \sigma_0$</td><td rowspan="2">$c^W \cdot \sigma_0$</td></tr>
<tr><td>$\sigma_0 = \sigma_E$</td></tr>
<tr><td>$\hat{\sigma}_0 = \frac{s_{m \cdot n}}{a_{m \cdot n}}$</td><td rowspan="5">$c^C \cdot \hat{\sigma}_0$</td><td rowspan="5">$c^W \cdot \hat{\sigma}_0$</td></tr>
<tr><td>$\hat{\sigma}_0 = \frac{\sqrt{\overline{s_m^2}}}{a_{m \cdot (n-1)+1}}$</td></tr>
<tr><td>$\hat{\sigma}_0 = \frac{\bar{s}_m}{a_n}$</td></tr>
<tr><td>$\hat{\sigma}_0 = \frac{\bar{r}_m}{d_n}$</td></tr>
<tr><td>$\hat{\sigma}_0 = \frac{\tilde{r}_m}{\tilde{d}_n}$</td></tr>
</table>

Table 4.4/4: Control and warning limits of a onesided control chart for the process spread

The magnitude of the factors c^C and c^W depends again on the sample size n, in other words, $c^C = c^C(n)$ and $c^W = c^W(n)$. In addition, the magnitude also depends on the choice of test the statistic. The latter is again referred to by means of an index, e.g. $c^C = c^C_s(n)$.

Assuming a normally distributed quality characteristic with constant mean

We will discuss three different control charts for the process spread, the standard deviation chart (s chart), the sample range chart (r chart) and the extreme value chart (x chart). In all cases, the monitored quality characteristic is assumed to be $no(\mu_0; \sigma_t^2)$-distributed.

b) Standard Deviation Charts (*s* charts)

The test statistic of a **standard deviation chart** is always the sample standard deviation

$$S_n = \sqrt{S_n^2} = \sqrt{\frac{1}{n-1}\sum_{i=1}^{n}(X_i - \bar{X}_n)^2}$$

of a sample of size n from the ongoing production. Since $X_i \sim no(\mu_0; \sigma_t^2)$, it follows according to (2.109) that $(n-1) \cdot S_n^2/\sigma_t^2$ has a χ^2 distribution with $n-1$ degrees of freedom. For an undisturbed process, i.e., for $\sigma_t^2 = \sigma_0^2$, it then holds that

$$Pr\left(\frac{(n-1) \cdot S_n^2}{\sigma_0^2} \leq \chi^2_{n-1;1-\alpha}\right) = 1 - \alpha. \tag{4.146}$$

From this it follows that

$$Pr\left(S_n \leq \sqrt{\frac{\chi^2_{n-1;1-\alpha}}{n-1}} \cdot \sigma_0\right) = 1 - \alpha. \tag{4.147}$$

The term on the right side of the inequality within the brackets is the upper limit of the **onesided variation interval** with level $1-\alpha$ of the test statistic S_n. This means that $(1-\alpha) \cdot 100\%$ of all realizations s_n are expected to lie below this limit when the process is undisturbed. Thus, for a given centre line value CL, the limiting lines of an onesided s chart are obtained by setting $\alpha = 0.01$ and $\alpha = 0.05$, respectively.

Limiting lines of an onesided standard deviation chart for known σ_0

$$UCL = c_s^C \cdot CL = \sqrt{\frac{\chi^2_{n-1;0.99}}{n-1}} \cdot \sigma_0 \tag{4.148}$$

$$UWL = c_s^W \cdot CL = \sqrt{\frac{\chi^2_{n-1;0.95}}{n-1}} \cdot \sigma_0. \tag{4.149}$$

Thus, the factors c_s^C and c_s^W are given by

$$c_s^C = c_s^C(n) = \sqrt{\frac{\chi^2_{n-1;0.99}}{n-1}} \tag{4.150}$$

$$c_s^W = c_s^W(n) = \sqrt{\frac{\chi^2_{n-1;0.95}}{n-1}}. \tag{4.151}$$

The percentiles $\chi^2_{n-1;1-\alpha}$ can be found in table 5.2/4. When only an estimate $\hat{\sigma}_0$ of σ_0 is available for the construction of the control chart, it is substituted for σ_0 in (4.148) - (4.149).

For the **power function** of the onesided standard deviation chart, it holds that

$$G_s(\sigma_t) = Pr(S_n \geq UCL|\sigma_t) = 1 - Pr(S_n < UCL|\sigma_t). \qquad (4.152)$$

With (4.148) we get

$$G_s(\sigma_t) = 1 - Pr(S_n < c_s^C \cdot \sigma_0|\sigma_t) = 1 - Pr(S_n^2 < \frac{\chi^2_{n-1;0.99}}{n-1} \cdot \sigma_0^2|\sigma_t).$$

If σ_t denotes the momentary process standard deviation, then we get $(n-1) \cdot S_n^2/\sigma_t^2 \sim \chi^2(n-1)$. From this it follows that

$$G_s(\sigma_t) = 1 - Ch\left[\frac{\chi^2_{n-1;0.99}}{(\sigma_t/\sigma_0)^2}|n-1\right]. \qquad (4.153)$$

In the above, $Ch(.|n-1)$ denotes the cumulative distribution function of the χ^2 distribution with $n-1$ degrees of freedom. There are no tables available for this distribution, but it is possible to calculate some of its values via the percentile function $Ch^{-1}(.|n-1)$ using table 5.2/4 (see example 4.4/7).

Formula (4.153) can be simplified further by expressing the intervention probability not as a function $G_s(\sigma_t)$ of the absolute process spread σ_t, but as a function $G_s^*(\varepsilon_t)$ of the relative spread

$$\varepsilon_t := \frac{\sigma_t}{\sigma_0}. \qquad (4.154)$$

The variable ε_t measures the process spread as a multiple of the target value σ_0 (σ_0 is taken as the measuring unit). Thus, we get for (4.153) that

Power function of the onesided standard deviation chart for known σ_0

$$G_s^*(\varepsilon_t) = 1 - Ch\left(\frac{\chi^2_{n-1;0.99}}{\varepsilon_t^2}|n-1\right). \qquad (4.155)$$

When constructing an s chart with an estimate $\hat{\sigma}_0$ instead of a known value σ_0 the formulas for the power function hold only approximately.

Example 4.4/7

We now want to construct a standard deviation chart with the prerun data of example 4.4/1, where $\sigma_0 = 0.3$ [g CO_2/litre] is given as a target value.

We also want to find out the power function, to graphically display this function and to calculate some of its values.

With the help of table 5.2/4, the factors c_s^C and c_s^W from (4.150) - (4.151) are found to be

$$c_s^C = c_s^C(5) = \frac{1}{2}\sqrt{\chi^2_{4;0.99}} \approx \frac{1}{2}\sqrt{13.277} \approx 1.822$$

$$c_s^W = c_s^W(5) = \frac{1}{2}\sqrt{\chi^2_{4;0.95}} \approx \frac{1}{2}\sqrt{9.488} \approx 1.540.$$

Consequently, according to (4.148) - (4.149), the limiting lines of the s chart are given by

$$UCL = c_s^C \cdot CL \approx 1.822 \cdot 0.3 = 0.547$$

$$UWL = c_s^W \cdot CL \approx 1.540 \cdot 0.3 = 0.462.$$

Figure 4.4/5 displays the standard deviation chart with these limiting lines and the centre line $CL = \sigma_0$. The fifteen s values from the prerun are drawn into the control chart (column 8 of table 4.4/1). Since none of the values lies above the upper warning limit, we can conclude that during the prerun the process was under statistical control with respect to its spread.

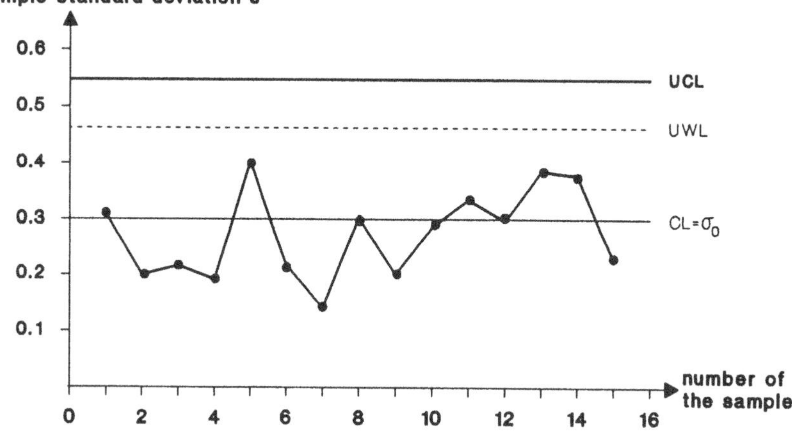

Figure 4.4/5: Standard deviation chart with onesided upper limit

If the index t is omitted, then according to (4.155) the power function of this s chart is given by:

$$G_s^*(\varepsilon) = 1 - Ch\left(\frac{\chi^2_{n-1;0.99}}{\varepsilon^2}|4\right).$$

We now want to calculate several points of the power curve. Since we have not tabulated the cumulative distribution function of the χ^2 distribution, we cannot take the straightforward approach of simply looking up the intervention probability

$$P := G_s^*(\varepsilon) = 1 - Ch\left(\frac{\chi^2_{4;0.99}}{\varepsilon^2}|4\right).$$

for given values of ε. Instead, we will need to specify the intervention probability P and then determine the corresponding value $\varepsilon = \varepsilon_P$ through table 5.2/4. This is the percentile of the power function $G_s^*(\varepsilon)$ of order P, which is defined by $G_s^*(\varepsilon_P) = P$.

By definition it holds that $Ch(\chi^2_{4;\omega}|4) = \omega$ for each percentile $\chi^2_{4;\omega}$ of the $\chi^2(4)$ distribution. Thus, it follows from $Ch(\chi^2_{4;0.99}/\varepsilon_P^2|4) = 1 - P$ that

$$\chi^2_{4;1-P} = \frac{\chi^2_{4;0.99}}{\varepsilon_P^2}.$$

Solving for ε_P yields

$$\varepsilon_p = \sqrt{\chi^2_{4;0.99}/\chi^2_{4;1-P}}.$$

Thus, for a given intervention probability P, the corresponding percentile of the power function can be calculated by the above formula. Table 4.4/5 displays the results ε_P and some intermediary results for several values of P.

$P = G_s^*(\varepsilon_P)$	$\chi^2_{4;1-P}$	$\chi^2_{4;0.99}/\chi^2_{4;1-P}$	ε_P
0.995	0.207	64.1401	8.0088
0.990	0.297	44.7037	6.6861
0.975	0.484	27.4318	5.2375
0.950	0.711	18.6737	4.3213
0.900	1.064	12.4784	3.5325
0.750	1.923	6.9043	2.6276
0.250	5.385	2.4656	1.5702
0.100	7.779	1.7068	1.3064
0.050	9.488	1.3993	1.1829
0.025	11.143	1.1915	1.0916
0.010	13.277	1	1
0.005	14.860	0.8935	0.9052

Table 4.4/5: Values of the power curve of a standard deviation chart

c) Range Charts (r charts)

The test statistic of a **range chart** is the sample range

$$R_n = X_{<n;n>} - X_{<1;n>}$$

previously introduced in (2.70). It is based on a sample of size n from the ongoing production, where the quality characteristic X is asssumed to be $no(\mu_0; \sigma_t^2)$-distributed. The sample range is the difference between the largest observation $X_{<n;n>}$ in the sample and the smallest observation $X_{<1;n>}$. If we denote the percentiles of R_n of order ω with $r_{n;\omega}$ and those of the **standardized sample range**

$$R_n^* := \frac{R_n}{\sigma_t} \tag{4.156}$$

by $r_{n;\omega}^*$, then by definition of the percentiles it holds that

$$Pr(R_n \le r_{n;1-\alpha}) = Pr(R_n^* \le r_{n;1-\alpha}^*) = 1 - \alpha.$$

For an undisturbed process we have $\sigma_t = \sigma_0$ and thus $R_n^* = R_n/\sigma_0$. Consequently, it follows that

$$Pr(R_n \le r_{n;1-\alpha}^* \cdot \sigma_0) = 1 - \alpha. \tag{4.157}$$

The term $r_{n;1-\alpha}^* \cdot \sigma_0$ is the upper limit of the onesided variation interval with level $1 - \alpha$ of the test statistic R_n. Thus, for a given value of σ_0 the limiting lines of the onesided r chart are determined by substituting $\alpha = 0.05$ and $\alpha = 0.01$, respectively:

Limiting lines of the onesided sample range chart for known σ_0

$$UCL = c_r^C \cdot CL = r_{n;0.99}^* \cdot \sigma_0 \tag{4.158}$$

$$UWL = c_r^W \cdot CL = r_{n;0.95}^* \cdot \sigma_0. \tag{4.159}$$

Hence, the factors c_r^C and c_r^W are given by

$$c_r^C = c_r^C(n) = r_{n;0.99}^* \tag{4.160}$$

$$c_r^W = c_r^W(n) = r_{n;0.95}^*. \tag{4.161}$$

The percentiles $r_{n;0.99}^*$ and $r_{n;0.95}^*$ for $n = 2, 3, \ldots, 20$ are tabulated in table 5.3/2.

For the **power function** of the onesided sample range chart, analogous to (4.152), it holds that

$$G_r(\sigma_t) = Pr(R_n \ge UCL|\sigma_t) = 1 - Pr(R_n < UCL|\sigma_t). \tag{4.162}$$

Substituting (4.157) yields

$$G_r(\sigma_t) = 1 - Pr(R_n < r^*_{n;0.99} \cdot \sigma_0 | \sigma_t) = 1 - Pr\left(R^*_n < \frac{r^*_{n;0.99}}{\sigma_t/\sigma_0}\right).$$

Power function of the onesided sample range chart for known σ_0

If the intervention probability is again expressed as a function $G^*_r(\varepsilon_t)$ of the relative spread $\varepsilon_t = \sigma_t/\sigma_0$, then we get

$$G^*_r(\varepsilon_t) = 1 - Pr\left(R^*_n < \frac{r^*_{n;0.99}}{\varepsilon_t}\right). \tag{4.163}$$

We note that this formula holds only approximately, if an estimate $\hat{\sigma}_0$ is used instead of σ_0 for constructing the control chart.

Example 4.4/8

We will continue with example 4.4/7 and construct a sample range chart and its corresponding power function for the target value $\sigma_0 = 0.3$ and $n = 5$.

The limiting lines of the r chart are determined by (4.158) - (4.159). Using table 5.3/2 we find that

$$UCL = c^C_r(5) \cdot CL \approx r^*_{5;0.99} \cdot 0.3 \approx 4.60 \cdot 0.3 = 1.38$$

$$UWL = c^W_r(5) \cdot CL \approx r^*_{5;0.95} \cdot 0.3 \approx 3.86 \cdot 0.3 = 1.16.$$

The 15 sample ranges of the prerun (column 9 of table 4.4/1) all lie below $UWL = 1.16$. Thus, the r chart indicates that during the prerun the production was under statistical control with respect to its spread. According to (4.163) and table 5.3/2, the power function of the above r chart is given by

$$G^*_r(\varepsilon) = 1 - Pr\left(R^*_5 < \frac{r^*_{5;0.99}}{\varepsilon}\right).$$

Similar to example 4.4/7, one can determine values of the power function by specifying intervention probabilities $P := G^*_r(\varepsilon)$ and determining the corresponding values $\varepsilon = \varepsilon_P$, i.e., the percentile of order P of $G^*_r(\varepsilon)$. From $Pr(R^*_5 < r^*_{5;0.99}/\varepsilon_P) = 1 - P$, we first get

$$r^*_{5;1-P} = \frac{r^*_{5;0.99}}{\varepsilon_p}.$$

From this it results by table 5.3/2 that

$$\varepsilon_P = \frac{r^*_{5;0.99}}{r^*_{5;1-P}} = \frac{4.60}{r^*_{5;1-P}}.$$

With this last formula it is possible to calculate, for a given intervention probability P, the corresponding percentile ε_P of the power function using table 5.3/2. Listed in table 4.4/6 are the values of ε_P, including intermediary results for several P.

$P = G_r^*(\varepsilon_P)$	$r^*_{5;1-P}$	ε_P
0.999	0.37	12.43
0.995	0.55	8.36
0.990	0.67	6.87
0.975	0.85	5.41
0.950	1.03	4.47
0.900	1.26	3.65
0.700	1.82	2.53
0.500	2.26	2.04
0.300	2.73	1.68
0.100	3.48	1.32
0.050	3.86	1.19
0.025	4.20	1.10
0.010	4.60	1.00
0.005	4.89	0.94
0.001	5.48	0.84

Table 4.4/6: Power curve of a sample range chart

Problem 4.4/4

With the prerun data of problem 4.4/1 calculate the limiting lines of a onesided sample standard deviation chart as well as a sample range chart. Use the estimate $\hat{\sigma}_0 = \bar{r}_{10}/d_5$ of problem 4.4/2 for constructing the charts.

d) Extreme Value Charts (x charts)

We already introduced the **extreme value chart** (**x** chart) as a chart for monitoring the process level, which works with the original sample vector $\mathbf{X} = (X_1, \ldots, X_n)$. The twosided extreme value chart, with the limiting lines (4.131) - (4.132), can also be used for monitoring the process variation. Hence, in the case of an intervention it is not clear whether the cause of the intervention was a shift in location, in spread or in both parameters. In practice, one generally works with the following interpretation:

Interpreting the results of an extreme value chart

- If only *one* of the control limits is reached in the sample, and if there is no obvious increase in the range, then one will conclude that there was an undesirable shift in the process level.

- If *both* control limits are reached or exceeded, then one will interpret this result as an indication of an undesired increase in the process spread.

We derived the **power function** of the twosided extreme value chart under the assumption that all n components $X_1, \ldots, X_n$ of the sample vector $\mathbf{X}$ were independently and identically $no(\mu_t; \sigma_0^2)$-distributed (assumption of constant process spread). We will now derive the power function of the $\mathbf{x}$ chart with limiting lines (4.131) - (4.132) under the assumption that the components X_i are independently and identically $no(\mu_0; \sigma_t^2)$-distributed (assumption of a constant process level). Then (4.133a) becomes

$$\begin{aligned} G_{\mathbf{X}}(\sigma_t) &= 1 - \prod_{i=1}^{n} Pr(\mu_0 - c_{\mathbf{X}}^C \cdot \sigma_0 < X_i < \mu_0 + c_{\mathbf{X}}^C \cdot \sigma_0 | \sigma_t) \\ &= 1 - [No(\mu_0 + c_{\mathbf{X}}^C \cdot \sigma_0 | \mu_0; \sigma_t^2) - No(\mu_0 - c_{\mathbf{X}}^C \cdot \sigma_0 | \mu_0; \sigma_t^2)]^n. \end{aligned} \tag{4.164 a}$$

Standardizing gives

$$G_{\mathbf{X}}(\sigma_t) = 1 - \left[\Phi\left(\frac{c_{\mathbf{X}}^C \cdot \sigma_0}{\sigma_t}\right) - \Phi\left(-\frac{c_{\mathbf{X}}^C \cdot \sigma_0}{\sigma_t}\right)\right]^n = 1 - \left[2\Phi\left(\frac{c_{\mathbf{X}}^C \cdot \sigma_0}{\sigma_t}\right) - 1\right]^n. \tag{4.164 b}$$

Power function of the twosided extreme value chart for known σ_0

If the intervention probabilities are again expressed as a function of the relative spread $\varepsilon_t = \sigma_t/\sigma_0$, then we get

$$G_{\mathbf{X}}^*(\varepsilon_t) = 1 - \left[2\Phi\left(\frac{c_{\mathbf{X}}^C}{\varepsilon_t}\right) - 1\right]^n, \tag{4.165}$$

where $c_{\mathbf{X}}^C$ is given by the percentile of order $\frac{1}{2}(1 + \sqrt[n]{0.99})$ of the standard normal distribution. It is comparatively simple to determine values of this power function; one only needs tables 5.1/1 and 5.2/1.

e) Comparison of Standard Deviation, Range and Extreme Value Charts

Control charts for monitoring the process spread are again evaluated and compared through their power functions or their corresponding power curves, respectively. We will not display the graphs resulting from tables 4.4/5-6 and (4.165) with $n = 5$, because the first two curves would be quite inaccurate due to too few points and insufficient accuracy of the calculations. If the formulas for the control lines (4.148) and (4.158) for the s and r chart are evaluated for different values of n, one finds that the distance between the control line and the centre line of the r chart is a little bigger ($n \geq 3$). Thus, the r chart has a smaller intervention probability compared to the s chart for every increase of the process spread. This implies that its power curve is less steep. However, for small sample sizes the difference is very small. This is why we have not drawn a graph for $n = 5$. For a sample size of $n = 5$ the power curve of the extreme value chart is above that of the s chart, indicating that this chart is even better than the s chart. As the sample size n increases the superiority of the extreme value chart over the s chart decreases.

For the case of $n = 5$ one can easily verify the superior performance of the s chart compared to the r chart by looking in the last column of tables 4.4/5-6. For example, in the s chart the process variance σ_t has to reach $\sigma_t \approx 8.01 \cdot \sigma_0$ ($\varepsilon_t \approx 8.01$) before its intervention probability reaches the value $P = 0.995$. In an r chart, the same probability of intervention is achieved for $\sigma_t \approx 8.36 \cdot \sigma_0$.

4.4.4 Control Charts for Simultaneously Monitoring Process Level and Process Spread

If one wants to ***simultaneously*** control the location and spread of a production process, there are two options:

▷ Option 1: **Application of a double-tracked control chart**

First there is the option of combining two single-tracked control charts either manually on graph paper or electronically on a monitor. A median or a mean chart can be used for the process level, and a standard deviation or sample range chart for the spread. With every sample the realization $\tilde{x}$ or $\bar{x}$ is entered into the location chart, and the observed value r or s into the spread chart. One intervenes in the process when the control limit is reached or exceeded in at least one of the two charts.

▷ Option 2: **Application of an extreme value chart**

One can also monitor both process parameters with the twosided extreme value chart, i.e. by applying only one single-tracked chart. Unless one has the support of electronic data processing, administering this chart is simpler than simultaneously administering a location and a spread chart. However, with the advance of automatized data collection and data analysis this argument is losing more and more weight.

Figure 4.4/6 gives an example of an electronically processed $\bar{x}$-s chart. The monitor displays 38 sample results for $\bar{x}$ and s. For both control charts the levels of the centre and limiting lines are displayed next to the graphs. In addition, specification limits and process capability indices are set out

(C_p value, C_{pk} value). We will discuss these indices in detail in section 4.5.1. The chart was implemented and applied through a CAQ system.

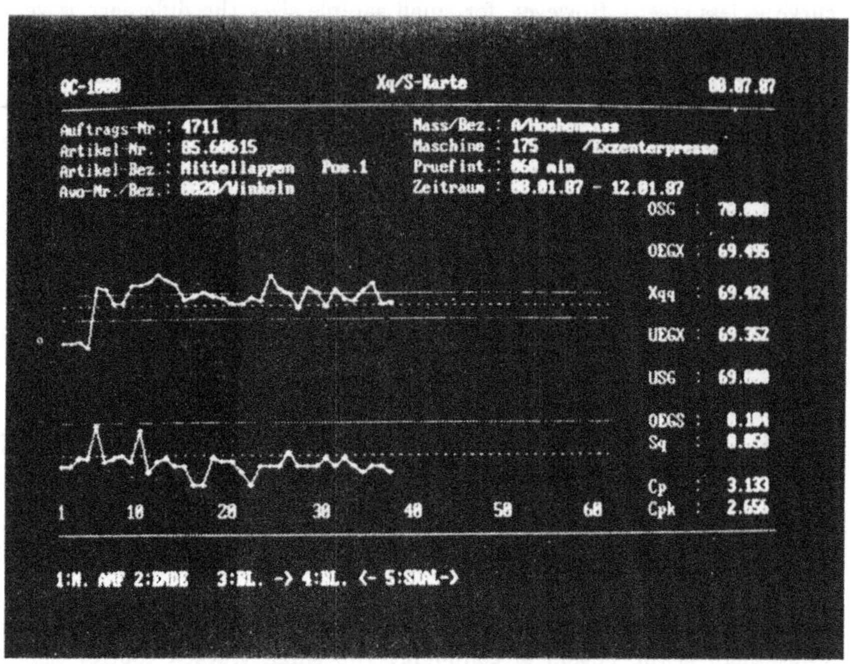

Figure 4.4/6: Example of an electronically administered $\bar{x}$-s chart (Source: Co. Dr. Brankamp, Erkrath, Germany)

Assumption: Normally distributed quality characteristic with two non-constant distribution parameters

Both control charts mentioned above can be evaluated again and compared via their power functions. When deriving these functions, the previous assumption that one of the two parameters is constant has to be dropped. The quality characteristic is then assumed to be $no(\mu_t; \sigma_t^2)$-distributed. In the following, we will show how to calculate the power function of a double-tracked control chart and a twosided extreme value chart under this more general assumption.

In order to illustrate the approach to deriving the power function of a double-tracked control chart, we will consider the example of a **mean-standard deviation chart** ($\bar{x}$-s chart; combination of a twosided $\bar{x}$ chart and an onesided s chart). The power function of the $\bar{x}$-s chart specifies the intervention probability $G_{\bar{x};s}(\mu_t; \sigma_t)$ depending on the process parameters μ_t and σ_t. The probability $1 - G_{\bar{x};s}(\mu_t; \sigma_t)$ of a non-intervention is obviously identical with the probability that $\bar{X}_n$ lies within the control limits (4.115) and *at the same time* S_n below the control limit (4.148). Since these two individual events occur with a probability of $1 - G_{\bar{x}}(\mu_t)$ and $1-G_s(\sigma_t)$, respectively, and since $\bar{X}_n$ and S_n are stochastically independent under the normality assumption, the probability of the event "The production is under statistical control with respect to *both* process parameters" (non-intervention probability) is obtained as the product of $1-G_{\bar{x}}(\mu_t)$ and $1-G_s(\sigma_t)$. For the power function, we thus get

$$G_{\bar{x};s}(\mu_t;\sigma_t) = 1 - [1 - G_{\bar{x}}(\mu_t)] \cdot [1 - G_s(\sigma_t)]. \tag{4.166}$$

If we are using the variables $\delta_t = (\mu_t - \mu_0)/\sigma_0$ and $\varepsilon_t = \sigma_t/\sigma_0$ instead of μ_t and σ_t, then the resulting power function is of the form

Power function of a $\bar{x}$-s chart for known μ_0 and σ_0

$$G^*_{\bar{x};s}(\delta_t;\varepsilon_t) = 1 - [1 - G^*_{\bar{x}}(\delta_t)] \cdot [1 - G^*_s(\varepsilon_t)]. \quad ^9 \tag{4.167 a}$$

Substituting (4.121) and (4.155) yields

$$G^*_{\bar{x};s}(\delta_t;\varepsilon_t) = 1-[1-\Phi(-z_{0.995}+\delta_t\cdot\sqrt{n})-\Phi(-z_{0.995}-\delta_t\cdot\sqrt{n})]\cdot Ch\left(\frac{\chi^2_{n-1;0.99}}{\varepsilon_t^2}\middle|n-1\right). \tag{4.167 b}$$

If the production process is in a desirable state with respect to its location and spread ($\mu_t = \mu_0, \sigma_t = \sigma_0$ or $\delta_t = 0, \varepsilon_t = 1$, respectively), then intervention would be the wrong decision. Since $\Phi(z_\omega) = 1 - \Phi(-z_\omega) = \omega$ and $Ch(\chi^2_{n-1;\omega}|n-1) = \omega$, the probability of a blind alarm is given by

Blind alarm probability

$$G^*_{\bar{x};s}(0;1) = 1 - [0.995 - 0.005] \cdot 0.99 = 1 - 0.99^2 = 0.0199. \tag{4.168}$$

The power function of a twosided extreme value chart for the simultaneous control of spread and location is denoted by $G_{\mathbf{X}}(\mu_t;\sigma_t)$. Analogous to (4.133a) and (4.164a) it is of the form

$$\begin{aligned} G^*_{\mathbf{X}}(\mu_t;\sigma_t) &= 1 - \prod_{i=1}^{n} Pr(\mu_0 - c^C_{\mathbf{X}} \cdot \sigma_0 < X_i < \mu_0 + c^C_{\mathbf{X}} \cdot \sigma_0 | \mu_t;\sigma_t) \qquad (4.169\text{ a}) \\ &= 1 - [No(\mu_0 + c^C_{\mathbf{X}} \cdot \sigma_0|\mu_t;\sigma_t^2) - No(\mu_0 - c^C_{\mathbf{X}} \cdot \sigma_0|\mu_t;\sigma_t^2)]^n. \end{aligned}$$

Standardizing gives

$$\begin{aligned} G_{\mathbf{X}}(\mu_t;\sigma_t) &= 1 - \left[\Phi\left(\frac{\mu_0 + c^C_{\mathbf{X}}\cdot\sigma_0 - \mu_t}{\sigma_t}\right) - \Phi\left(\frac{\mu_0 - c^C_{\mathbf{X}}\cdot\sigma_0 - \mu_t}{\sigma_t}\right)\right]^n \qquad (4.169\text{ b}) \\ &= 1 - \left[\Phi\left(c^C_{\mathbf{X}}\cdot\frac{\sigma_0}{\sigma_t} - \frac{\mu_t - \mu_0}{\sigma_t}\right) - \Phi\left(-c^C_{\mathbf{X}}\cdot\frac{\sigma_0}{\sigma_t} - \frac{\mu_t - \mu_0}{\sigma_t}\right)\right]^n. \end{aligned}$$

[9] The 3D graph on the book cover represents the power curve of a $\bar{x}$-s control chart (axes suppressed).

If one again introduces the standardized variables δ_t and ε_t and uses the relationship

$$\frac{\mu_t-\mu_0}{\sigma_t}=\frac{(\mu_t-\mu_0)/\sigma_0}{\sigma_t/\sigma_0}=\frac{\delta_t}{\varepsilon_t}$$

Power function of the extreme value chart for the simultaneous control of spread and location

then one gets the more simple representation

$$G^*_{\mathbf{x}}(\delta_t;\varepsilon_t)=1-\left[\Phi\left(\frac{c^C_{\mathbf{x}}-\delta_t}{\varepsilon_t}\right)-\Phi\left(\frac{-c^C_{\mathbf{x}}-\delta_t}{\varepsilon_t}\right)\right]^n. \qquad (4.170)$$

By using the fact that

$$\Phi(c^C_{\mathbf{x}})=\tfrac{1}{2}\cdot(1+\sqrt[n]{0.99})$$

Probability of a blind alarm

the probability of a blind alarm can be expressed as

$$G^*_{\mathbf{x}}(0;1)=1-\left[2\Phi\left(c^C_{\mathbf{x}}\right)-1\right]^n=1-\left[(1+\sqrt[n]{0.99})-1\right]^n=0.01. \qquad (4.171)$$

In order to make the $\bar{x}$-s and the extreme value chart comparable, we have to modify one of the charts so that the probability of a false alarm is the same for both charts. For this purpose we will leave the $\bar{x}$-s chart unchanged and replace the factor $c^C_{\mathbf{x}}$ in (4.170) by a new factor $C^C_{\mathbf{x}}$. For the power function $G^{**}_{\mathbf{x}}(\delta_t;\varepsilon_t)$ of the adapted extreme value chart with this new factor, it holds that

$$G^{**}_{\mathbf{x}}(0;1)=1-\left[2\Phi\left(C^C_{\mathbf{x}}\right)-1\right]^n\approx 0.0199.$$

The determining equation of $C^C_{\mathbf{x}}$ is thus found to be

$$C^C_{\mathbf{x}}=C^C_{\mathbf{x}}(n)=\Phi^{-1}\left[\frac{1}{2}\cdot(1+\sqrt[n]{0.9801})\right]. \qquad (4.172)$$

Analoguous to (4.170) the power function of the adapted extreme value chart now results to be

Power function of the adapted extreme value chart

$$G^{**}_{\mathbf{x}}(\delta_t;\varepsilon_t)=1-\left[\Phi\left(\frac{C^C_{\mathbf{x}}-\delta_t}{\varepsilon_t}\right)-\Phi\left(\frac{-C^C_{\mathbf{x}}-\delta_t}{\varepsilon_t}\right)\right]^n. \qquad (4.173)$$

Example 4.4/9

We will now determine the power functions of an $\bar{x}$-s chart and a twosided extreme value chart for $n=5$ and given target values μ_0 and σ_0. Both charts operate with $\alpha=0.0199$ and, in particular, we want to consider these functions for the special case of $\varepsilon=1$ (constant process spread).

The power function of the $\bar{x}$-s chart with the limiting lines (4.115) or (4.148) is given by (4.167b) with $n = 5$. In the special case of $\varepsilon = 1$, with $z_{0.995} \approx 2.576$ it follows that

$$G_{\bar{x};s}(\delta_t; 1) = 1 - [\Phi(2.576 - \delta_t \cdot \sqrt{5}) - \Phi(-2.576 - \delta_t \cdot \sqrt{5})] \cdot 0.99.$$

According to (4.172) the comparable extreme value chart has the control limits $CL \pm C_x^C \cdot \sigma_0$, where

$$C_{\mathbf{X}}^C = \Phi^{-1}\left[\tfrac{1}{2}(1 + \sqrt[5]{0.9801})\right] \approx \Phi(0.9980) \approx 2.8782.$$

The power function corresponding to this modified chart is given by (4.173) with $n = 5$. In the special case of $\varepsilon = 1$, we get

$$G_{\mathbf{X}}^{**}(\delta_t; 1) = 1 - [\Phi(2.8782 - \delta_t) - \Phi(-2.8782 - \delta_t)]^5 .$$

The following table lists, for several shifts δ, the corresponding intervention probabilities $G_{\bar{x};s}^{*}(\delta; 1)$ and $G_{\mathbf{X}}^{**}(\delta; 1)$:

δ	$G_{\bar{x};s}^{*}(\delta; 1)$	$G_{\mathbf{X}}^{**}(\delta; 1)$
0	0.0199	0.0199
±0.5	0.0817	0.0452
±1.0	0.3732	0.1422
±1.5	0.7822	0.3555
±2.0	0.9711	0.6513
±2.5	0.9987	0.8864
±3.0	1.0000	0.9812

Table 4.4/7: **Values of the power curve of an $\bar{x}$-s chart and an extreme value chart with $n = 5$ for varying process levels**

The fact that for $\delta \neq 0$ the intervention probability of the $\bar{x}$-s chart is consistently higher than that of the extreme value chart shows the superiority of the $\bar{x}$-s chart in the case where only the process level is shifting.

Problem 4.4/5

What values do the power functions $G_{\bar{x};s}^{*}(\delta; 1)$ and $G_{\mathbf{X}}^{**}(\delta; 1)$ of example 4.4/9 take at the point $(\delta; \varepsilon) = (1.5; 1.3064)$? Which of the two control charts is more sensitive in this case?

4.4.5 Special Topics

At the conclusion of this section on SHEWHART control charts we want to address the issues of economic process control and measurement error effects on control charting. These topics are often neglected in textbooks on quality assurance. The effects of error contaminated quality data are rarely covered, not even in the journals of statistical quality assurance. Nevertheless, the analysis of measurement error effects gains more and more importance because it provides the theoretical foundation and justification for gauge capability studies. The following presentation of this isssue is based mainly on the work by MITTAG (1991). Finally, we will briefly describe the most recent approaches to minimal cost process control. In order to point out the basic ideas we illustrate the design procedure for economic SHEWHART charts by means of a rather simple model. As before in section 4.4.2 we will restrict ourselves to *twosided* SHEWHART control charts.

a) Effects of Measurement Errors on the Performance of SHEWHART Control Charts

In the literature on control charting it is tacitly assumed that the quality data involved do not contain any measurement errors. However, this assumption is not always justified, for example in the case of insufficiently calibrated measuring instruments and machines where the measurements are influenced by exterior circumstances like temperature or humidity. With the occurrence of measurement errors one needs to distinguish between the **true** or **latent variables** X and the **empirical** or **observable variables** X^e. The latent variables are the quantities which one would observe in the case that no measurement errors occur. One typically distinguishes between systematic and random measurement errors. Synonyms are nonstochastic and stochastic measurement errors. In the following, the effects of these two types of measurement errors will be dealt with separately. If both error types occur simultaneously then their effects superimpose each other.

Systematic measurement errors are characterised by the fact that the variable X^e is a deterministic function of the variable X. The most simple and most important case for industrial practice is the special case of **a constant** or systematic additive **measurement error**. When analysing the effects of systematic measurement errors we will restrict ourselves to this case. Instead of the quality characteristic of interest X, here we are measuring

Example of a systematic measurement error

$$X^e := X + c \tag{4.174}$$

where c denotes a real valued constant which can be interpreted to be a measure of gauge miscalibration. A measurement error of this type does not have any effect on the performance of the SHEWHART chart (and other control charts), provided it not only occurs during the manufacturing process but also during the installation of the control chart, i.e., when calculating the control limits. Instead of the control limits UCL and LCL of the error free case we now have the **empirical control limits**

Effects of constant measurement errors

$$\left.\begin{matrix} UCL^e \\ LCL^e \end{matrix}\right\} := \left.\begin{matrix} UCL \\ LCL \end{matrix}\right\} + c \tag{4.175}$$

but because of the uniform shift in the observed data the effect of the shift of the control limits is exactly compensated. In particular, the power function and false alarm probability α remain unchanged. However, this does by no means imply that the constant measurement error is without significance. In this situation the control chart monitors the compliance with a false target value $CL^e = CL + c$ which can result in the production of a high quota of non-conforming units.

The situation is completely different if the constant measurement error only occurs after the installation of a control chart, for example through a change of the measuring instrument. In this case the error c leads to a horizontal shift of the power curve by c/σ_0 units, which means the location, but not the shape of the power curve has changed. The latter effect can be easily illustrated with the mean chart. In the beginning the control limits of this chart for the error free state are according to (4.115) given by UCL and LCL with the false alarm probability again specified to be $\alpha = 0.01$. If a constant measurement error of size c occurs the test statistic $\bar{X}_n$ in (4.119a) has to be replaced by $\bar{X}_n^e = \bar{X}_n + c$ with $\bar{X}_n^e \sim no(\mu_t + c; \sigma^2/n)$. If the standardization formulas connected with (4.119c/d) are applied in an analogous way and if one defines the **relative constant measurement error**

$$a := \frac{c}{\sigma_0} \tag{4.176}$$

as a measure for error contamination we get instead of the true power function $G_{\bar{x}}^*(\delta_t)$ presented in (4.121) the **empirical power function**

Power function of the twosided mean chart in case of constant measurement error (error occurs after installing the chart)

$$G_{\bar{x}}^{*e}(\delta_t) = \Phi\left[-z_{0.995} + (\delta_t + a)\cdot\sqrt{n}\right] + \Phi\left[-z_{0.995} - (\delta_t + a)\cdot\sqrt{n}\right]. \tag{4.177}$$

Obviously (4.121) and (4.177) are related by

$$G_{\bar{x}}^{*e}(\delta_t) = G_{\bar{x}}^*(\delta_t + a). \tag{4.178}$$

We can see from this relationship that a measurement error c seemingly changes the standardized measurement error by the amount of $a = c/\sigma_0$. Thus, if in a practical application a control chart indicates an intolerable shift in the production level one has to be aware that this indicated shift may in fact only be fictitious because the alarm may have been caused by a sudden occurrence of a constant measurement error.

If one sets $\delta_t = 0$ in (4.177) then one gets the false alarm probability. Due to the occurrence of a constant measurement error c, it takes instead of $\alpha = 0.01$ the value

$$\alpha^e = \Phi\left(-z_{0.995} + a \cdot \sqrt{n}\right) + \Phi\left(-z_{0.995} - a \cdot \sqrt{n}\right). \tag{4.179}$$

The size of α^e can be illustrated graphically. One can see in figure 4.4/7 that the sum of the two shaded areas has for $c = 0$ the value $\alpha^e = a$, but for any constant measurement error $c \neq 0$ a value $\alpha^e > \alpha$:

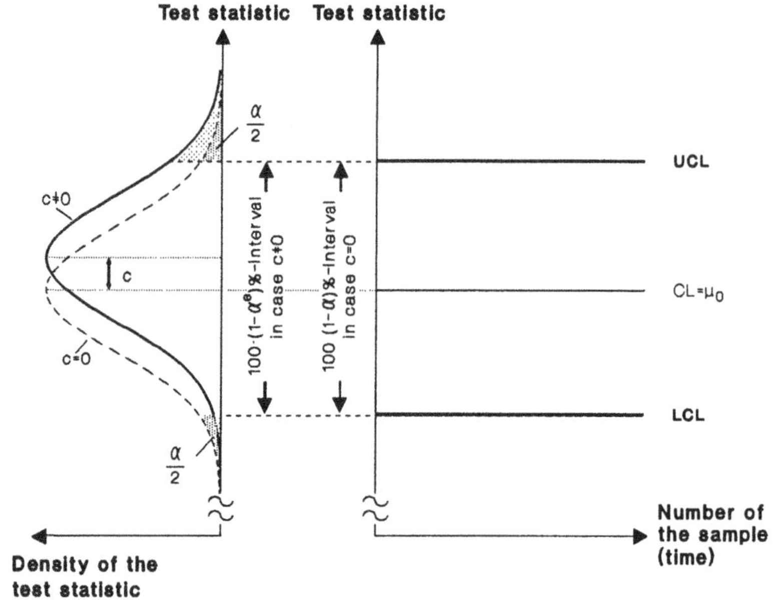

Figure 4.4/7: Increase in the false alarm probability for a twosided mean chart due to a constant measurement error (Source: MITTAG 1991)

Example of a stochastic measurement error

We speak of **random measurement errors** if the errors can be modeled by a stochastic variable V. The most important case is the one where, analogous to (4.174), X and V are additively related to the empirical variable X^e according to

$$X^e = X + V, \tag{4.180}$$

where X and V are assumed to be stochastically independent. Before, the variable X at time t was denoted X_t and we assumed the X_t are independently, identically $no(\mu_t; \sigma_0^2)$-distributed. The error variables V_t are regarded to be independently and identically $no(0, \sigma_v^2)$-distributed. Different to (4.174) we here have a situation where the measurement error V does on the average not have any influence on the process level $E(X^e) = \mu$. Contrary to systematic data errors the stochastic measurement error effects the performance of a control chart not only when it occurs during the manufacturing process but also if it occurs before or during the installation of the chart. Also, a random measurement error does not lead to a shift but to flattening of the power curve of a control chart.

Effects of additive stochastic measurement errors

We will again illustrate the effects of stochastic measurement errors with the example of the previously used mean chart. When random measurement errors V may occur the test statistic $\bar{X}^e = \bar{X} + \bar{V}$ is under the above assumptions $no[\mu_t; (\sigma_{\bar{x}}^e)^2]$-distributed. If we introduce the **relative measurement error variance**

$$r^2 = \frac{\sigma_v^2}{\sigma_0^2} \tag{4.181}$$

then the following relationship holds for the standard deviation $\sigma_{\bar{x}}^e$:

Seemingly increased spread through stochastic measurement error

$$\sigma_{\bar{x}}^e = \sqrt{\frac{\sigma_0^2 + \sigma_v^2}{n}} = \sigma_{\bar{x}} \cdot \sqrt{1 + r^2}.$$

The variance of the test statistic is increased due to the measurement error V by the factor $(1 + r^2)$. The effect on the power curve depends on whether the measurement error already occured before or during the installation of the $\bar{x}$ chart or after. If the error V is already present at the time of the installation then it is already taken into account when the control limits are determined. With the help of figure 4.4/8 it can be verified that in this case the increased spread of the test statistic $\bar{X}^e$ will lead to dislocating the control limits.

Case 1: Stochastic measurement error occuring before the installation of the control chart

The control limits are no longer given by (4.115) but are

$$\left.\begin{matrix} UCL^e \\ LCL^e \end{matrix}\right\} := \mu_0 \pm z_{0.995} \cdot \sigma_{\bar{x}}^e = \mu_0 \pm \frac{z_{0.995}}{\sqrt{n}} \cdot \sigma_0 \cdot \sqrt{1 + r^2}. \tag{4.182}$$

The **empirical power function** is found to be

Power function of a twosided mean chart in case of stochastic measurement error (error already present when designing the chart)

$$G_{\bar{x}}^{*e}(\delta_t) = \Phi\left(-z_{0.995} + \delta_t \frac{\sqrt{n}}{\sqrt{1 + r^2}}\right) + \Phi\left(-z_{0.995} - \delta_t \frac{\sqrt{n}}{\sqrt{1 + r^2}}\right). \tag{4.183}$$

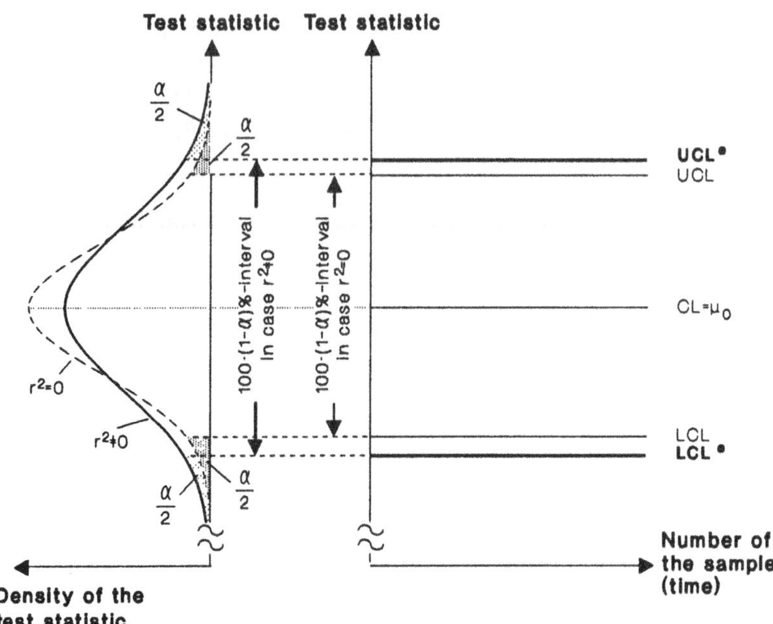

Figure 4.4/8: Effect of stochastic measurement errors on the control limits of a twosided mean chart (Source: MITTAG 1991)

In the case of $r^2 = 0$ (no measurement errors present) the function (4.183) becomes the true power function (4.121).

Case 2: Stochastic measurement error only occurs after designing the control chart

We will now consider the case when the random measurement error only occurs after the design of the $\bar{x}$ chart. Although in this situation the control chart works with the true control limits (4.115) because of the increased variance of the test statistic these limits are lying too close together. Since we are not taking into account the increased variance the false alarm probability of the test has instead of the desired value $\alpha = 0.01$ the larger value

$$\alpha^e = 2\Phi\left(-\frac{z_{0.995}}{\sqrt{1+r^2}}\right). \tag{4.184}$$

The relationship $\alpha^e > \alpha$ which is true for any $r^2 \neq 0$ can be easily verified by means of a figure analogous to figure 4.4/7 (see MITTAG 1991). For the **empirical power function** it now holds that

Power function of the twosided mean chart in the case of stochastic measurement error (error occurs after designing the control chart)

$$G_{\bar{x}}^{*e}(\delta_t) = \Phi\left[\frac{1}{\sqrt{1+r^2}}\left(-z_{0.995} + \delta_t\sqrt{n}\right)\right] + \Phi\left[\frac{1}{\sqrt{1+r^2}}\left(-z_{0.995} - \delta_t\sqrt{n}\right)\right]. \tag{4.185}$$

If we put $\delta_t = 0$ in (4.185) we get formula (4.184) for the false alarm probability α^e.

Example 4.4/10

In figure 4.4/4 the power function (4.121) of a twosided mean chart with specified blind alarm probability $\alpha = 0.01$ is given for the common sample size of $n = 5$. For this case we now want to demonstrate the effects of constant and stochastic measurement errors on the power curve.

Let us first consider the case that a *constant* measurement error occurs *after* the design of the control chart. The error c can be expressed in terms of multiples of the process standard deviation σ_0. Figure 4.4/9 shows the power curve of the $\bar{x}$ chart after occurrence of the error c. For c we have chosen the value $c = 0$ (reference curve) as well as $c = 0.5 \cdot \sigma_0$ and $c = -2\sigma_0$. This corresponds to a choice of $a = 0, a = 0.5$ and $a = -2$ in (4.176).

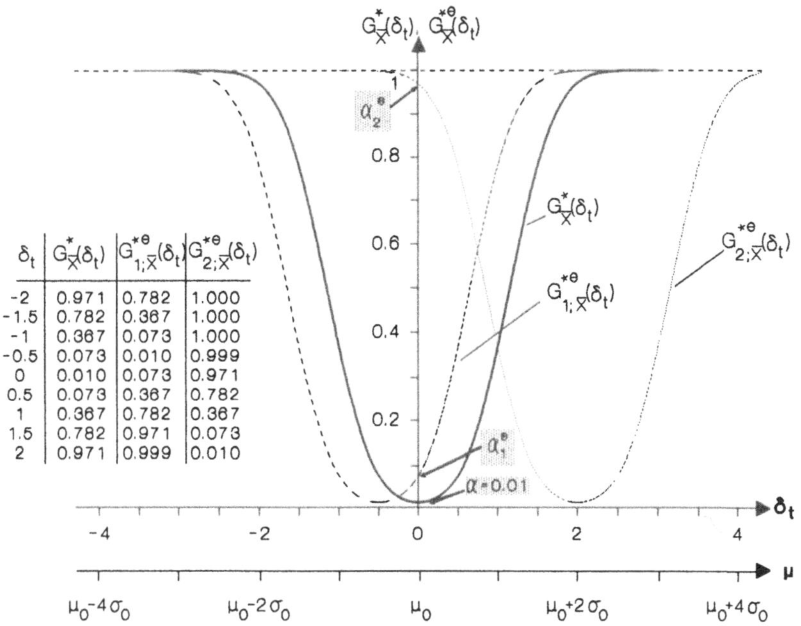

δ_t	$G^*_{\bar{X}}(\delta_t)$	$G^{*e}_{1;\bar{X}}(\delta_t)$	$G^{*e}_{2;\bar{X}}(\delta_t)$
-2	0.971	0.782	1.000
-1.5	0.782	0.367	1.000
-1	0.367	0.073	1.000
-0.5	0.073	0.010	0.999
0	0.010	0.073	0.971
0.5	0.073	0.367	0.782
1	0.367	0.782	0.367
1.5	0.782	0.971	0.073
2	0.971	0.999	0.010

Figure 4.4/9: True and empirical power curves of a twosided mean chart in the case of constant measurement errors and various error contamination degrees a ($G^{*e}_{1;\bar{x}} : a = 0.5$; $G^{*e}_{2;\bar{x}} : a = -2$; Source: MITTAG 1991)

We can see that the true power curve $G^{e*}_{\bar{x}}(\delta_t)$ in case of $c = 0.5 \cdot \sigma_0$ is shifted to the left by 0.5 units and in case of $c = -2\sigma_0$ to the right by 2 units. These shifts of the power curve lead to significant changes in the intervention probability for a given shift δ_t. If, for example, the process level drifts σ_0 units below the target value μ_0 ($\delta_t = -1$) then this leads in case of $c = 0$ with probability 0.367 to a process intervention. For $c = 0.5 \cdot \sigma_0$ and $c = -2\sigma_0$ the rounded probabilities are 0.072 or respectively 1.00. In case of $c = 0$ the false alarm probability results to be the desired value $\alpha = 0.01$ but for $c = 0.5 \cdot \sigma_0$ and $c = -2\sigma_0$ this probability changes to $\alpha_1^e \approx 0.072$ or respectively $\alpha_2^e \approx 0.971$. Thus, a shift of twice the process standard deviation in the measuring instrument origin has the effect that the probability of a false alarm is no longer 1% but 97%.

We will now assume that instead of a constant measurement error c a *stochastic* measurement error V with $V \sim no(0; \sigma_v^2)$ occurs independently of the quality characteristic X. We will restrict ourselves to the case that V is already present *during* the design phase of the control chart (also see problem 4.4/6b). The variance σ_v^2 of the measurement error will be expressed in multiples of σ_0. For σ_v^2 we have chosen the values $\sigma_v^2 = 0$ as well as $\sigma_v^2 = 0.25 \cdot \sigma_0^2$ and $\sigma_v^2 = \sigma_0^2$. This corresponds to a choice of $r^2 = 0$, $r^2 = 0.25$ and $r^2 = 1$ in (4.181). Figure 4.4/10 shows the power curves given by (4.183) for these three cases.

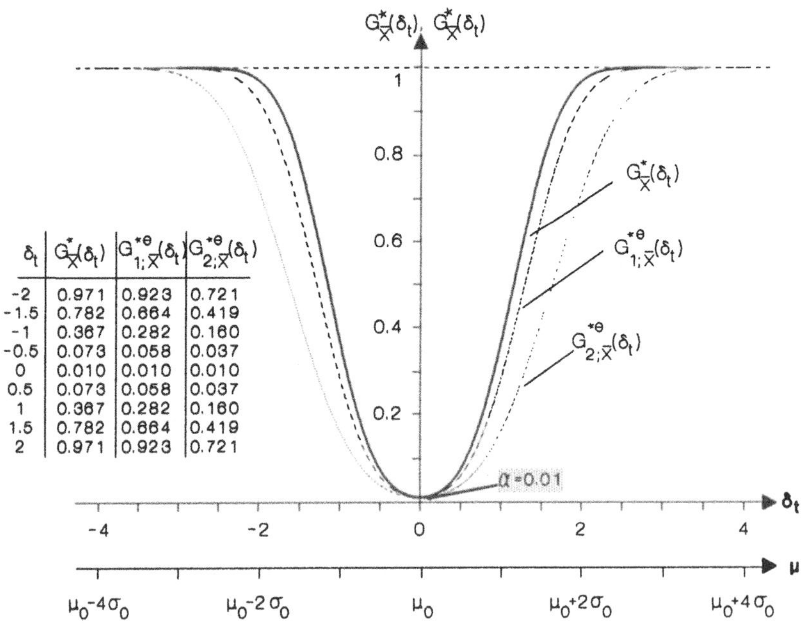

δ_t	$G^*_{\bar{X}}(\delta_t)$	$G^{*e}_{1;\bar{X}}(\delta_t)$	$G^{*e}_{2;\bar{X}}(\delta_t)$
-2	0.971	0.923	0.721
-1.5	0.782	0.664	0.419
-1	0.367	0.282	0.160
-0.5	0.073	0.058	0.037
0	0.010	0.010	0.010
0.5	0.073	0.058	0.037
1	0.367	0.282	0.160
1.5	0.782	0.664	0.419
2	0.971	0.923	0.721

Figure 4.4/10: True and empirical power curves of a twosided mean chart in the case of stochastic measurement errors and various error contamination degrees r^2 ($G^{*e}_{1;\bar{x}} : r^2 = 0.25$; $G^{*e}_{2;\bar{x}} : r^2 = 1$; Source: MITTAG 1991)

One can see that the alarm probability for a given shift $\delta_t \neq 0$ decreases as r^2 increases. If the process level is, for example, shifted by σ_0 below the target value μ_0 ($\delta_t = -1$) then the mean chart will detect this shift with probability 0.367 in the error free case, and only with probability 0.282 or respectively 0.160 in case of $r^2 = 0,25$ and $r^2 = 1$.

Remark

BENNETT (1954), MIZUNO (1961) and ABRAHAM (1977) also discuss the effects of error contaminated quality data on single-tracked control charting. The effects of stochastic measurement errors on the mean-range chart and the mean-standard deviation chart are treated by KANAZUKA (1986) and MITTAG/STEMANN (1993a) respectively. MITTAG (1991) outlines how to compensate the effects of measurement errors on the performance of SHEWHART charts. SCHNEEWEISS/MITTAG (1986) discuss the effects of measurement errors in the context of regression analysis.

Besides the issue of measurement errors there are other significant questions connected with the performance of SHEWHART charts which, so far, have not been sufficiently investigated. For example, this is the case with the consequences which result when the assumption that the X_t are independently identically normally distributed has to be dropped. Approaches to process control with control charts under the assumption of correlated or non-normal quality data can for example be found in ALWAN/ROBERTS (1988) and MONTGOMERY (1991, p. 341ff).

Problem 4.4/6

a) Find the equation for the power functions given in figure 4.4/10.

b) Which formulas would define these power functions if the stochastic measurement error only occurs after the design of the mean chart? Draw their graphs analogous to figure 4.4/10.

b) Economic Design of SHEWHART Control Charts

We already pointed out that the design of a SHEWHART chart comprises the specification of the sample size, the control limits and the time interval between samples. Traditionally the control limits and sample size are chosen according to statistical criteria. They are determined so that the power curve of the underlying hypothesis test (4.34) has the desired shape. The interval between successive samples is rarely determined by analytical methods but rather intuitively based on the manufacturing speed, the expected time in which the process changes to an undesired state, the possible consequences of a process shift and production circumstances like breaks or shift changes. It is immediately obvious that this procedure can be very questionable, especially if one considers the economic consequences of control charting. There are costs for sampling, costs for following up on false

Costs in process monitoring with control charts

alarms, costs for intervention in the process and the internal and external costs related to nonconforming product units. Since all these costs are effected by the choice of the three control chart parameters it suggests itself to use an economic model for specifying these parameters.

After W. A. SHEWHART introduced the control chart in 1924 it took more than 25 years until the first approaches for determining the control chart parameters according to economic criteria appeared in statistical literature. The first who proposed such a procedure were the Americans L. A. AROIAN and H. LEVENE (AROIAN/LEVENE 1950). They noted that what matters is not the probability of a false alarm per sample but the frequency of false alarms, which also depends on the time interval between sampling. They assumed a process which operates in exactly two states, a desirable state and an undesireable state. Their aim was to minimize the number of product units produced in the undesirable state. In first approximation this number can be regarded as measure of costs connected with the production of nonconforming units. The new element in their approach was that instead of the false alarm probability they chose the average time between two false alarms as a side condition. Through this it was possible to determine the control limits in dependence of the admissible frequency of false alarms and the time interval between samples. What was not considered in this approach were the inspection costs.

First approaches to economic control chart design

Some time later WEILER (1952) proposed a model to minimize the average amount of inspection until discovery of a process shift of magnitude $\delta \cdot \sigma$ with the sample size as the only decision criterion. For example, in case of determining the control limits by using $\alpha = 0.01$ he obtained an optimal sample size of $n = 4.4\delta^2$. His approach totally neglects that the time interval between samples and the probability of detecting a process shift effect the average run length of the process in an undesired state and thus also the costs related to the production of units nonconforming.

The next progress was presented by PFANZAGL (1954). His model had – in reference to the ideas of AROIAN/LEVENE – a lower limit for the time until the occurrence of a blind alarm but also an upper limit for the average run length in an undesirable state. What was still not considered were the costs related to a false alarm, the costs related to defectives which arise while the production process is in an undesirable state and the frequency of shifts between the two process states.

More advanced models

A major breakthrough to a full consideration of all the previously mentioned factors came through the work of DUNCAN (1956), BARNARD (1959), BARISH/HAUSER (1963) and WEICHSELBERGER (1966). DUNCAN and WEICHSELBERGER investigated models with only one undesirable state whereas BARNARD as well as BARISH/HAUSER considered models with an arbitrary number of undesirable states. All these works have in common that they are searching for control strategies which aim at minimizing the average total costs per time unit of the respective production and control system. In the mean time many theoretical treatises on minmal cost process control have been written. An overview of works until 1980 is given by MONTGOMERY (1980), whereas VON COLLANI (1990) summarizes the approaches published after 1980. One of the few recent textbooks on quality assurance which treat minimal cost process control in detail is the one by MONTGOMERY (1991, p.413ff.)

Presentation of a simple model for an economic control chart

In the following we will show by means of the exemplarily chosen SHEWHART mean chart and by using a small and simple model how to determine economic control charts. As before we will assume that the quality characteristic of interest X is $no(\mu_t, \sigma_0^2)$-distributed with constant and known variance σ_0^2. Furthermore we will make the following assumptions concerning the technical and economical aspects of the process and its control:

A1: The process always operates in exactly one of two possible states "0" and "1". The state 0 with the property $\mu = \mu_0$ is the desired state, the state "1" with $\mu = \mu_1 > \mu_0$ the undesired state. The location parameters μ_0 and μ_1 are known.

A2: The shift from state "0" to state "1" occurs randomly after T time units. For the time in state "0" it holds that $T \sim ex(\lambda)$ with known parameter λ.

A3: The transition from state "0" to state "1" is irreversible, i.e., the process cannot leave state 1 by itself. Rather, a corrective action has to be taken in form of a repair including diagnosis of the disturbance and re-establishment of state "0". During such an intervention in the process there will be a standstill of fixed length d. The costs of the standstill including the repair are fixed and of amount U.

A4: The loss per time unit while the process is in state "0" is L_0 and L_1 in state "1" with $L_1 > L_0$. It further holds that $L_0 \leq U/d$.

A5: The costs per inspected sample (sampling and inspection costs) are a linear non-homogenous function of the sample size with A as fixed costs and B as costs per sampled unit.

A6: The evaluation of a sample will take Δ time units (Δ fixed) during which the production continues.

A7: The speed of the production process (production time per unit) is high enough to be negligible as an influential factor.

Comments on the model assumptions

With A1 we are making the basic assumption of an especially simple 2-state-model. It is much easier to explain the principal approaches to designing minimal cost control charts in the context of this simplified setup than using a more complex but also more realistic model. With A2 we are assuming that the time T the process remains in the desired state has an exponential distribution with known expectation

$$\Theta := E(T) = \frac{1}{\lambda}. \tag{4.186}$$

This is a common assumption for models in economic control charting. Under the assumption of a different lifetime distribution the analysis generally becomes more difficult. The requirement of $L_0 \leq U/d$ in A4 contains that the costs of a production standstill per time unit are higher than the costs related to producing conforming units (Note there are no costs for repairs and diagnosis during a standstill). If $L_0 \leq U/d$ should not be fullfilled it would be most advantageous to entirely stop the production, provided one aims at minimizing the costs and is not considering production.

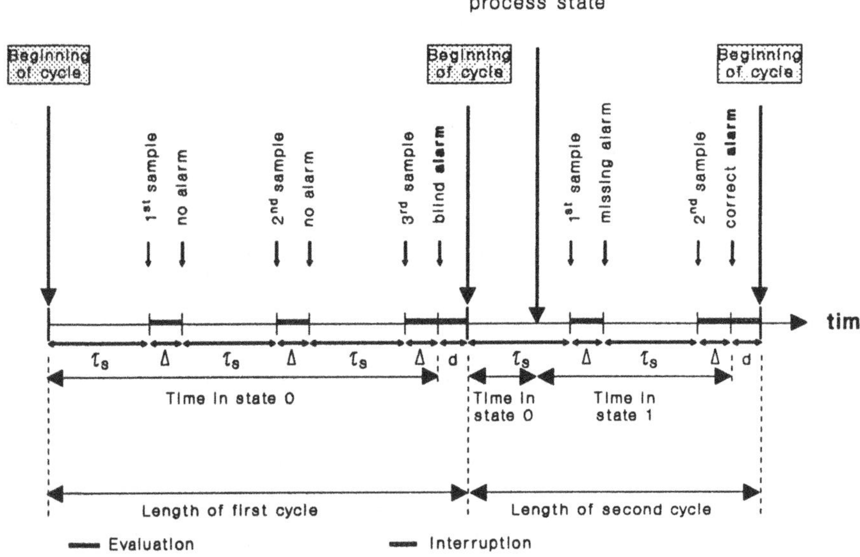

Figure 4.4/11: Renewal cycles when applying economic control charts

Production, monitoring and process adjustment with the help of a cost minimal mean chart with sampling interval τ_S can be seen as a series of independent **renewal cycles**. Each new cycle starts when the process switches back to production in the desired state "0". The production then goes on until the control chart indicates that the process has shifted to the undesirable state "1". This signals causes a process adjustment (readjustment to state "0") which concludes the present cycle. After its completion the following cycle starts. Figure 4.4/11 presents a sequence of such process cycles and their structure.

The length of the i-th renewal cycle is a random variable and so are the total costs related to the i-th cycle ($i = 1, 2, \ldots$). In this model the cycle length as well as the total costs per cycle are independently identically distributed. Because of this we can pick an arbitrary cycle for further analysis. Let the length of this cycle be denoted by Z and the related costs by K. Then the ratio K/Z can be interpreted as the **total costs per time unit**. The goal of economic process control models usually is to minimize the expectation $E(K/Z)$ of this cost variable. Since in our model $E(K/Z)$ with probability 1 is equal to

General formulation of the target function

$$k := \frac{E(K)}{E(Z)} \tag{4.187}$$

(see ROSS 1970) we will work with target function (4.187) and thus minimize the ratio of the average cost per cycle and the average cycle length.

When designing an economic SHEWHART mean chart one tries to specify the parameters of the control chart in such a way that the target variable (4.187) becomes minimal. The decision parameters are the specified constant sampling interval τ_S between two consecutive samples, the sample size n and – as $\mu_1 > \mu_0$ – an upper control limit UCL. The latter has the property $\mu_0 < UCL < \mu_1$. As before in the case of the onesided SHEWHART mean chart without cost parameters the control limit UCL is in general not specified directly but is determined from $Pr(\bar{X} \geq UCL | \mu = \mu_0) = \alpha$ through specifying the false alarm probability α. The test statistc $\bar{X}$ is $no(\mu; \sigma_0^2/n)$-distributed with $\mu = \mu_0$ in the desirable state "0" and $\mu = \mu_1$ in the undesirable state "1". From this approach one obtains after standardization the equation

$$\Phi\left(\frac{UCL - \mu_0}{\sigma_0} \cdot \sqrt{n}\right) = 1 - \alpha \tag{4.188}$$

which gives, for a specified sample size n, a one-to-one-mapping between UCL and α. Since this model only assumes one undesirable state μ_1 the probability of a type II error $\beta = Pr(\bar{X} < UCL | \mu = \mu_1)$ is also uniquely determined by

$$\Phi\left(\frac{UCL - \mu_1}{\sigma_0} \cdot \sqrt{n}\right) = \beta. \tag{4.189}$$

It can be seen from equations (4.188) and (4.189) that it doesn't make any difference whether one minimizes the target function (4.187) with respect to the triple (τ_S, UCL, n) or to the triple (τ_S, α, β). We will choose the latter alternative. Since the total cost K of a cycle can be divided into stochastic inspection costs I, stochastic losses L and fixed stillstand cost U the starting point for determining an economic SHEWHART mean chart is the target function

Target function for the determination of an economic SHEWHART mean chart

$$k_S = k_S(\tau_S, \alpha, \beta) = \frac{E(I) + E(L) + U}{E(Z)}. \tag{4.190}$$

The expectations $E(I), E(L)$ and $E(Z)$ are given by relatively complicated expressions which we will not derive in this text:

$$E(I) = (A + B \cdot n)\frac{1 - \beta \cdot \exp(-\lambda \cdot \tau_S)}{(1-\beta) \cdot [1 - (1-\alpha) \cdot \exp(-\lambda \cdot \tau_S)]} \tag{4.191 a}$$

$$E(L) = L_1\Delta - \frac{L_1 - L_0}{\lambda} + \frac{L_1\tau_S \dfrac{1 - \beta \cdot \exp(-\lambda \cdot \tau_S)}{1-\beta} + \alpha \dfrac{L_1 - L_0}{\lambda} \exp\left[-\lambda(\tau_S + \right.}{1 - (1-\alpha) \cdot \exp(-\lambda \cdot \tau_S)} \tag{4.191 b}$$

$$E(Z) = \Delta + d + \frac{1 - \beta \cdot \exp(-\lambda \cdot \tau_S)}{(1-\beta) \cdot [1 - (1-\alpha) \cdot \exp(-\lambda \cdot \tau_S)]} \cdot \tau_S. \tag{4.191 c}$$

The minima k_S^{min} of the target function (4.190) which are attained at $(\tau_S^{opt}, \alpha^{opt}, \beta^{opt})$ can be numerically determined by iterative procedures like that of Newton-Raphson. We will state without proof that k_S attains two minima (one local and one global), which may coincide for certain parameter constellations.

Alternatives to economic control charts (comparison strategies)

Before illustrating the determination of cost minimal control charts by means of an example we will introduce two alternative strategies for comparison. The first strategy is the **process control with full information**. It corresponds to a **decision under certainty** (see table 3.2/28). Under this strategy the company knows the process state at any time without having any additional cost. In this ideal situation the company can decide how long it wants to let the process continue in an undesirable state before scheduling a repair. This decision parameter is denoted by ε. With optimally fixed ε one gets the true process costs which cannot be beaten by any other strategy. The target function is given by the right side of (4.190) with $E(I) = 0$ because of the absence of sampling costs. The other two expectations in (4.190) are given by $E(L) = L_0 \cdot \Theta + L_1 \cdot \varepsilon$ and $E(Z) = \Theta + \varepsilon + d$ with $\Theta = 1/\lambda$ from (4.186) as the average time in the desirable state. After substituting these expectations in (4.190) we will denote the resulting target function by $k_F = k_F(\varepsilon)$:

$$k_F = k_F(\varepsilon) = \frac{E(L) + U}{E(Z)} = \frac{L_0 \cdot \Theta + L_1 \cdot \varepsilon + U}{\Theta + \varepsilon + d}. \tag{4.192}$$

After elementary transformations and using the notation

$$D := (L_1 - L_0) \cdot \Theta + L_1 \cdot d - U \qquad (4.193\text{ a})$$

one gets the more compact representation

Target function in the case of process control with full information

$$k_F = k_F(\varepsilon) = L_1 - \frac{D}{\Theta + \varepsilon + d}. \qquad (4.193\text{ b})$$

The term D determines the value of the cost minimum k_F^{min} and also the optimal value ε^{opt} leading to this cost minimum:

$$\begin{aligned} D > 0 &\Rightarrow k_F^{min} = k_F(0) = \frac{L_0 \cdot \Theta + U}{\Theta + d} \\ D = 0 &\Rightarrow k_F^{min} = k_F(\varepsilon) = L_1 \ (\varepsilon \text{ arbitrary}) \\ D < 0 &\Rightarrow k_F^{min} = \lim_{\varepsilon \to \infty} k_F(\varepsilon) = L_1. \end{aligned}$$

In the case of $D < 0$ one would let the process continue permanently once it has changed to the undesirable state.

The second alternative approach is called **blind stopping**. Here the process is controlled without knowing what its present state is and without getting partial information about the process through taking samples. The decision parameter is the time τ_B for which one lets the process run before stopping it for a period d to diagnose and – if necessary – readjust it for the cost U. The optimal strategy under this approach gives us the upper limit for all other strategies which involve costs for getting information about the present process state. If the optimal costs of a strategy with expenses for obtaining information are higher than those of the optimal blind stategy then one might as well drop such a strategy because of economic reasons.

When applying the blind stop strategy we again set $E(I) = 0$ in the target function (4.190) because as before there are no inspection costs. For the resulting target function $k_B = k_B(\tau_B)$ one can derive the representation

Target function for blind stopping

$$k_B = k_B(\tau_B) = \frac{L_1 \cdot \tau_B - \dfrac{L_1 - L_0}{\lambda}[1 - \exp(-\lambda \cdot \tau_B] + U}{\tau_B + d}. \qquad (4.194)$$

The optimal time interval τ_B^{opt} which leads to a cost minimum k_B^{min} can again be determined numerically by iterative procedures.

Example 4.4/11

The determination of the optimal values $(\tau_S^{opt}, \alpha^{opt}, \beta^{opt}), \varepsilon^{opt}$ or respectively τ_B^{opt} as well as the corresponding cost minima k_S^{min}, k_B^{min} and k_F^{min}

will now be illustrated by means of a numerical example. The optimal strategy in the three described procedures is not influenced by the absolute values of the cost and/or loss parameters L_0, L_1, U, A, B but only by their ratios. We will take L_0 as a reference value and without loss of generality give it the value $L_0 = 1$. The loss per time unit in the und sirable state is given by $L_1 = 5$, the cost of production standstill by $U = 3$, while the fixed inspection costs A and unit inspection costs B are given by $A = 0.01$ and $B = 0.001$. The distribution parameters σ_0 and μ_0 and respectively μ_1 of the normally distributed quality characteristic of interest do not need to be specified individually. It is sufficient to specify a value for the standardized process shift $\delta := (\mu_1 - \mu_0)/\sigma_0$. We will assume that the loss L_0 in the desirable state is due to the production of 1% nonconforming units with measurements above the tolerance limit G_u. Because of the proportionality of the cost related to nonconforming units (loss) and the fraction nonconforming it follows that in the undesirable state the fraction nonconforming has to be 5%. Substituting according to (3.138b) the values $\mu_1 = G_u - z_{0.99} \cdot \sigma_0$ and $\mu_0 = G_u - z_{0.95} \cdot \sigma_0$ into $\delta = (\mu_1 - \mu_0)/\sigma_0$ we get with the help of table 5.2/1 the value $\delta = z_{0.99} - z_{0.95} \approx 0.681$.

Finally we have to specifiy the technical parameters of the cost model, i.e., the length d of a standstill, the time Δ required for analysing a sample and the average time $\Theta = 1/\lambda$ the production remains in the desirable state (each measured in hours). We will set $d = 0.1$ and $\Delta = 0.05$, while varying the quantity Θ which represents the reliability of the process. In the following we will present for each of the three strategies how the optimal decision parameters and the corresponding minimal costs depend on the average time Θ in the desirable process state.

In the following table Θ runs from 10,000 to 0.625. The quantities d, Δ, Θ and ε are measured in the same time units as τ_B^{opt} and τ_S^{opt} (for example hours). Calculations for $\Theta < 0.625$ are unneccessary because then the factor D becomes negative and for $D < 0$ it is optimal to not control the process at all. Table 4.4/8 gives in columns 2 - 4 the values of the decision parameters of a cost minimal mean chart. Column 5 gives as an additional information the optimal sample size n^{opt}. These values are relatively high compared to the standard sample size $n = 5$. For a given Θ the columns 6 - 7 give the optimal values of the decision parameters ε and τ_B which lead to a cost minimum for the alternative strategies "process control with full information" and "blind stopping". It is remarkable that the optimal run lenght τ_B^{opt} does not decrease monotonously with Θ but again starts to increase from $\Theta = 0.8$ onwards. The same holds for τ_S^{opt}, whereby it always holds that $\tau_S^{opt} < \tau_B^{opt}$.

Θ	Optimal values of the decision parameters						Cost minima		
	τ_s^{opt}	α^{opt}	β^{opt}	n^{opt}	ε^{opt}	τ_B^{opt}	k_S^{min}	k_F^{min}	k_B^{min}
(1)	(2)	(3)	(4)	(5)	(6)	(7)	(8)	(9)	(10)
10,000	14.93	0.0020	0.0937	38	0	120.80	1.0075	1.0003	1.0480
1,000	4.73	0.0020	0.0935	38	0	34.87	1.0258	1.0029	1.1510
200	2.13	0.0020	0.0933	38	0	17.43	1.0661	1.0145	1.3338
100	1.51	0.0020	0.0930	38	0	12.45	1.1023	1.0290	1.4682
50	1.08	0.0020	0.0927	38	0	8.93	1.1619	1.0579	1.6543
20	0.69	0.0020	0.0920	38	0	5.82	1.3089	1.1443	2.0104
10	0.50	0.0022	0.0980	37	0	4.27	1.5178	1.2871	2.3910
5	0.37	0.0022	0.0964	37	0	3.20	1.8837	1.5686	2.8927
2	0.28	0.0025	0.0993	36	0	2.35	2.8062	2.3810	3.7635
1	0.28	0.0032	0.1061	34	0	2.16	4.0297	3.6364	4.5404
0.8	0.35	0.0038	0.1065	33	0	2.33	4.5277	4.2222	4.7835
0.667	0.76	0.0082	0.1265	27	0	3.00	4.9289	4.7826	4.9558
0.650	1.17	0.0160	0.1306	23	0	3.31	4.9721	4.8667	4.9754
0.625	∞	0	0	0	$\varepsilon \geq 0$	∞	5.0000	5.0000	5.0000

Table 4.4/8: Optimal values of the decision parameters and cost minima for different values of the reliability parameter Θ

Columns 8 - 10 of table 4.4/8 list the cost minima corresponding to the optimal decision parameters. Note that the true process costs k_F increase from about $k_F^{min} \approx L_0 = 1$ in the case of a very reliable process ($\Theta = 10,000$) to $k_F^{min} = L_1 = 5$ in the case of a very unreliable process. The same holds for the costs k_B^{min} which result under the strategy of "blind stopping". Please note that the minima k_B^{min} are always above k_F^{min}. (This is the price for not knowing the true process state!) Figure 4.4/12 graphically displays the columns 8 - 10 of the table. The table inserted into figure 4.4/12 contains the differences between the minimal costs of the two alternative strategies. This difference gives the amount of expense per time unit that one should be willing to spend in order to obtain information about the process state, for example through drawing samples. If the cost of information per time unit is more than this difference one should not "buy" the information. One can see that for very reliable (Θ large) processes as well as very unreliable processes (Θ small) there is only a small cost margin for obtaining information.

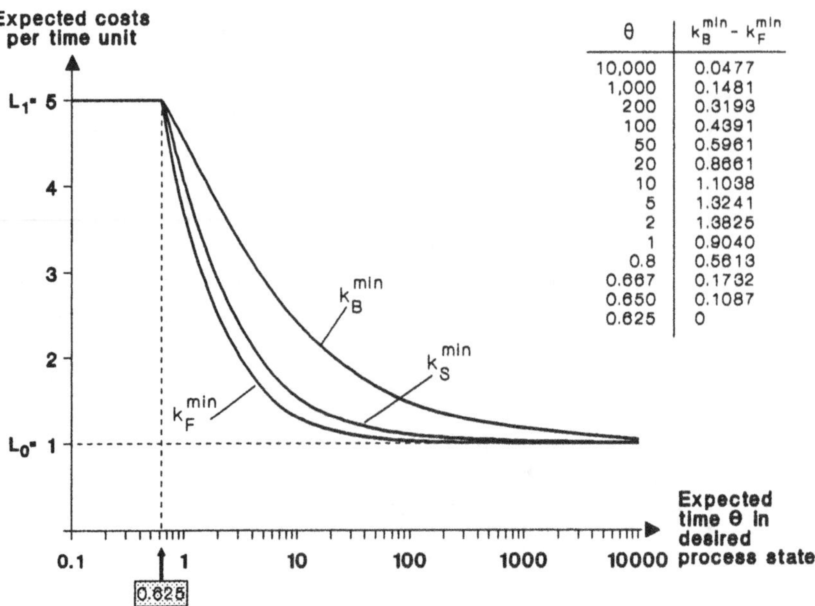

Θ	$k_B^{min} - k_F^{min}$
10,000	0.0477
1,000	0.1481
200	0.3193
100	0.4391
50	0.5961
20	0.8661
10	1.1038
5	1.3241
2	1.3825
1	0.9040
0.8	0.5613
0.667	0.1732
0.650	0.1087
0.625	0

Figure 4.4/12: Average costs per time unit for three different process control strategies as a function of the reliability parameter Θ

The main conclusion of this figure is that the costs related to the economic SHEWHART chart are always below those that result under the strategy of "blind stopping".

Problem 4.4/7

In table 4.4/8 we find that with $\Theta = 10$ and the technical and economic specifications of the example we get $\tau_B^{opt} = 4.27$ with $k_B^{min} = 2.3910$ for the optimal blind strategy. Suppose that $\Theta = 5$ but that the company is overestimating the reliability of the production plant and is working with the decision parameters resulting for $\Theta = 10$. What would be the cost of the blind stopping strategy in the long run? Comment on this effect of overestimating Θ.

4.5 Modified SHEWHART Charts for Variables

We will continue to discuss SHEWHART-type control charts for measurements, in other words, control charts for continuous random variables. As in section 4.4 we will confine ourselves to the most relevant case where the quality characteristic X is normally distributed. Similar to section 3.3, we will assume that there are specification limits for X which are usually determined during the design phase of a product. In section 4.5.1 we will show how to determine whether the production process is actually capable of maintaining the given specification limits. In section 4.5.2 we will then sketch the construction of control charts for the process location, which explicitly take into account the specification limits. In order to facilitate the comparison with the twosided control charts introduced in section 4.4.2, we will only discuss *twosided* control charts. In the interests of a succinct presentation, we shall omit the derivation of formulae for warning limits.

4.5.1 Process Capability Studies

When there are specification limits G_l and G_u for a quality characteristic X one should determine in the context of the prerun whether the process lacks the capability of maintaining the specifications even in a stable state (fairly constant level and spread). The degree of the **process capability** depends on the proportion of manufactured units whose quality characteristic X lies within the tolerance region $[G_l; G_u]$. In practice, the process capability is expressed in terms of a **process capability index**, a dimensionless measure for the capability of the process.

In order to illustrate the background of the most common process capability indices, we will first explain the causes of nonconformity with the specification limits and their meaning. Suppose that a process is stable, i.e., that it continuously generates product units with a $no(\mu; \sigma^2)$-distributed quality characteristic X. Then insufficient process capability is always due to at least one of the following two causes:

Reasons for lack of process capability in the case of twosided tolerance specification

- The process spread σ is too big compared to the length $G_u - G_l$ of the specified tolerance region.
- The process level μ lies too far from the centre $G_m := (G_l + G_u)/2$ of the tolerance interval.

Figure 4.5/1 shows the density function of a normally distributed quality characteristic over time for two manufacturing processes. Part a) of the figure describes a process which is initially not under statistical control (unstable distribution) but changes to a stable process. This is not a "capable" process because at any time it generates a non-negligible fraction

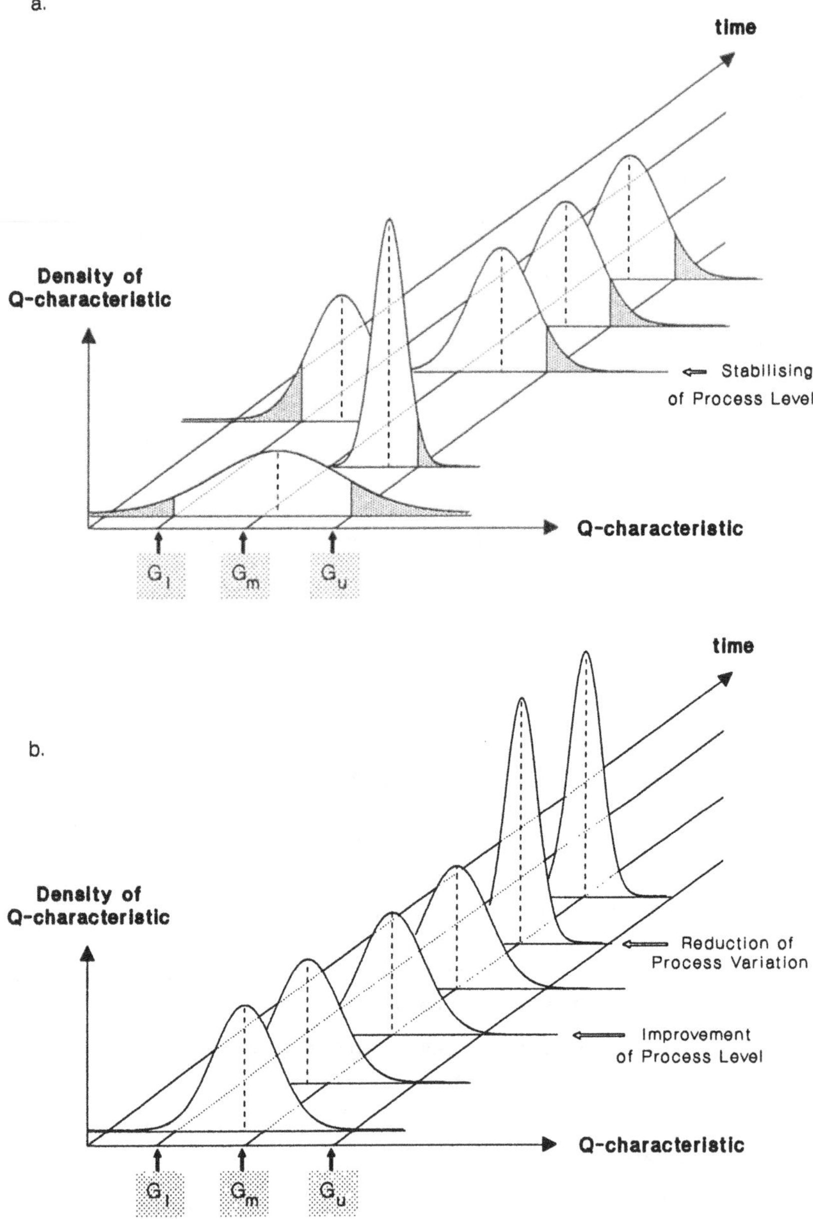

Figure 4.5/1: Illustration of process capability
a) incapable process
b) capable process

of nonconforming product units (see areas under the densities). Part b) of the figure displays a "capable" process. Here, the process capability even increases over time.

Measuring potential process capability (twosided specification)

In SQA literature several measures for the process capability have been suggested (see KANE 1986, CHAN/CHENG/SPIRING 1988 and BOYLES 1991, for example). The most common measure is the **C_p-index**[10] defined by

$$C_p := \frac{G_u - G_l}{6\sigma}. \tag{4.195}$$

The larger the C_p-value the larger is the specified tolerance range in comparison to the "natural process tolerance". In practice, the latter is taken to be the length 6σ of the interval $[\mu - 3\sigma; \mu + 3\sigma]$, which contains almost all – to be exact 99.73 % – realizations of a $no(\mu; \sigma^2)$-distributed quality characteristic. In quality assurance textbooks, one often finds the requirement $C_p > 4/3$. This implies that the standard deviation of a capable process should satisfy $G_u - G_l > 8\sigma$.

Since the C_p-index (4.195) does not depend on the process location, it can be seen as a measure for the process capability of an optimally centred process, i.e., a measure of the **potential process capability**. A high value for the C_p-index is not a sufficient condition for good process capability. Figure 4.5/4a will demonstrate this fact. There we chose $G_l = 96$ and $G_u = 104$. The figure shows the density functions of a $no(\mu; 1)$-distributed quality characteristic for $\mu_1 = 100$ and $\mu_2 = 102.8$. In both cases we have $C_p = 8/(6 \cdot 1) = 4/3$.

Measuring actual process capability (twosided specification)

The most common process capability index which takes into account process spread and process location in the case of twosided specification limits, is the **C_{pk}-index** defined by

$$C_{pk} := C_p(1 - k). \tag{4.196}$$

The factor

$$k := \frac{|G_m - \mu|}{\frac{1}{2} \cdot (G_u - G_l)} \tag{4.197}$$

is a dimensionless measure for the distance $|G_m - \mu|$ between the actual and the optimal process locations. It is a non-negative quantity, which takes on the value zero when $G_m = \mu$, and the value one at the ends of the tolerance region. The smaller its value, the better is the process situation.

The C_{pk}-index is a function of the two process parameters μ and σ. For a fixed value of $\sigma > 0$, the function $C_{pk} = C_{pk}(\mu)$ is symmetric with respect to $\mu = G_m$. At G_m it attains its maximum $C_{pk}(G_m) = C_p$ and takes on

[10] In this notation "C" stands for "capability" and "p" for "process".

the value zero at G_l and G_u. For $\mu \in [G_l; G_u]$, the function $C_{pk}(\mu)$ lies between 0 and C_p, outside this interval it is negative.

An alternative to the C_{pk}-index has been proposed by CHAN/CHENG/SPIRING (1988). They recommend the process capability index

$$C_{pm} := \frac{G_u - G_l}{6\sigma_m}, \tag{4.198 a}$$

where $\sigma_m^2 := E[(X - G_m)^2]$ denotes the process spread around G_m. It can be easily verified that between σ_m^2 and $\sigma^2 = E[(X - \mu)^2]$ there is the relationship

$$\sigma_m^2 = \sigma^2 + (\mu - G_m)^2.$$

Hence, one can rewrite the C_{pm}**-index** as

$$C_{pm} := \frac{G_u - G_l}{6\sqrt{\sigma^2 + (\mu - G_m)^2}} = \frac{C_p}{\sqrt{1 + \dfrac{(\mu - G_m)^2}{\sigma^2}}} \tag{4.198 b}$$

instead of (4.198a). From (4.198b) it can be seen directly that the C_{pm}-index depends on the parameters μ and σ. For a fixed $\sigma > 0$, the function $C_{pm} = C_{pm}(\mu)$ is also symmetric with respect to $\mu = G_m$ and has a maximal value of C_p at G_m. Contrary to the C_{pk}-index, the C_{pm}-index is bounded below by zero. The following 3-D graphs show the behaviour of the C_{pk}-index and the C_{pm}-index for varying process level μ and varying process spread σ. The tolerance limits are assumed to be $G_u = 8.5$ and $G_l = 5.5$.

The indices C_{pk} and C_{pm} are related through the unique, invertible relationship

$$C_{pk} = C_{pm}(1 - k)\sqrt{1 + \frac{(\mu - G_m)^2}{\sigma^2}}$$

which is obtained from (4.198b) after reorganization and multiplication by $(1 - k)$.

Esimating process capability indices

If the process parameters are not known exactly, but are only available in the form of estimates, then these are substituted into (4.195), (4.196) and (4.198). In this case, one gets estimates $\hat{C}_p$, $\hat{C}_{pk}$ and $\hat{C}_{pm}$ for the three process capability indices.

a.

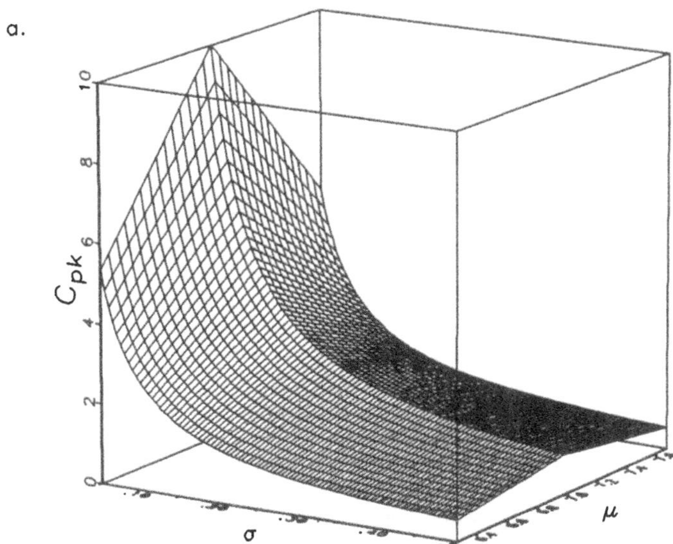

b.

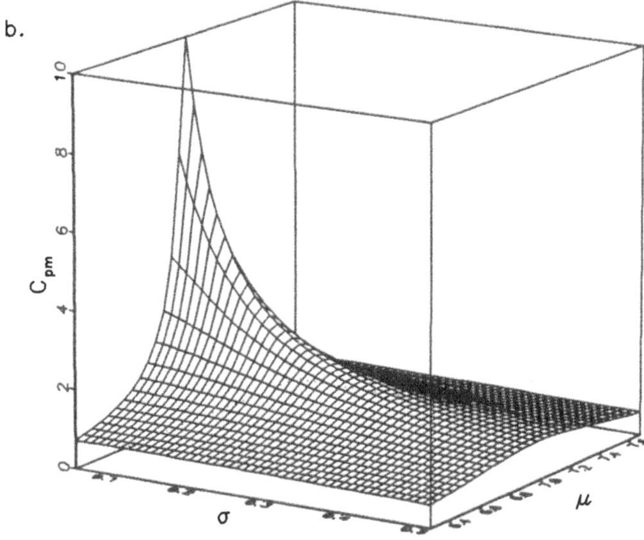

Figure 4.5/2: C_{pk}- and C_{pm}-index as a function of μ and σ in the case of $G_l = 5.5$ and $G_u = 8.5$

Remarks

1. In the case of *onesided* specification limits, the C_p-index is defined by $C_p^u := (G_u - \mu)/(3\sigma)$ or $C_p^l := (\mu - G_l)/(3\sigma)$, respectively, and thus also depends on the process level. It can be shown that the definition $C_p := \min(C_p^l; C_p^u)$ is equivalent to the definition in (4.196).
2. In the literature mentioned above one also finds generalizations of the process capability indices introduced here. They deal with the case when the target level μ_{opt} differs from the centre G_m of the specified tolerance region.
3. Another measure for the process capability is the fraction nonconforming $P = P(\mu; \sigma)$. For given specification limits G_l and G_u, we derived its form in (3.136). Compared to the indices C_{pk} and C_{pm} the fraction nonconforming has the advantage of being more illustrative and also of being bounded from above. Thus, it should actually be preferred over the indices C_{pk} and C_{pm}.
4. From the fraction nonconforming, as well as from the C_{pk}- or C_{pm}-values of an unsatisfactory process, without further information, it *cannot* be determined whether the insufficient process capability is due to a too large process spread or an insufficiently adjusted process level. However, this deduction is possible in connection with the C_p-value, because if the C_p-value is sufficiently large then the process spread cannot be the cause of an insufficient process capability.
5. In October 1992, the *Journal of Quality Technology* published a special issue exclusively dealing with process capability indices.

Example 4.5/1

Suppose, that the soft drinks manufacturer considered in example 4.4/1 has to comply with an order specifying a minimum of 5.5 [$g\ CO_2/liter$] and a maximum of 8.5 [$g\ CO_2/liter$]. What are the estimates for the indices C_p, C_{pk} and C_{pm} if we estimate the process parameters $\mu = \mu_0$ and $\sigma = \sigma_0$ by $\hat{\mu}_0 \approx 6.908$ and $\hat{\sigma}_0 \approx 0.2901$ as we did in examples 4.4/3-4?

Substituting the above estimates into (4.195), (4.196) and (4.198) gives

$$\hat{C}_p = \frac{G_u - G_l}{6\hat{\sigma}_0} = \frac{3}{1.7406} \approx 1.72$$

$$\hat{C}_{pk} = (1 - \hat{k}) \cdot \hat{C}_p \approx 0.94 \cdot 1.72 \approx 1.62$$

$$\hat{C}_{pm} = \frac{G_u - G_l}{6\sqrt{\hat{\sigma}_0^2 + (\hat{\mu}_0 - G_m)^2}} = \frac{3}{6\sqrt{0.2901^2 + (-0.092)^2}} \approx 1.64.$$

4.5.2 Control Charts for Monitoring the Process Level

a) Introductory Remarks

In the following, we will assume that we want to control a stream of product units with respect to a quality characterisitc X, and that at any time t this stream is at least approximately $no(\mu_t; \sigma_0^2)$-distributed. Thus, we are assuming that during production the standard deviation of X has a constant value $\sigma_t = \sigma_0$ where σ_0 denotes the target value for the process spread. We will further assume that there are given specification limits for X, critical values G_l and G_u specified by a law, a standard or by design, for example. A product unit will be considered to be **defective** or **nonconforming** if its measured value x lies either below G_l or above G_u, respectively, or – in the case of two specifications – outside the interval $[G_l; G_u]$ (see table 3.3/1). In the case of only one specification limit, G_l or G_u, one administers a *onesided* control chart, and in the case of two specification limits, a *twosided* control chart for the process location.

Assumption of a normally distributed quality characteristic with constant variance

We will denote SHEWHART-type control charts which explicitely take into account tolerance specifications as **modified SHEWHART charts**. Due to lack of space, we will limit ourselves to the case of twosided charts. The centre line CL of a modified SHEWHART chart is given by the midpoint G_m of the tolerance interval $[G_l; G_u]$.

The determination of the control limits differs from the standard approach described in (4.29) and figure 4.2/2. In order to illustrate the basic idea, we will first recall a few points already discussed in section 3.3. According to (3.136c) a product unit with quality characteristic X, which is randomly selected from the production stream, will be classified as nonconforming with probability[11]

$$P(\mu_t) = Pr(X \notin [G_l; G_u] | \mu_t) = \underbrace{\Phi\left(\frac{G_l - \mu_t}{\sigma_0}\right)}_{P_1(\mu_t)} + \underbrace{\Phi\left(\frac{\mu_t - G_u}{\sigma_0}\right)}_{P_2(\mu_t)}. \quad (4.199)$$

With (4.199) we now have a formula for the individual **fraction nonconforming**. If the variables $X = X_t$ are independently and identically normally distributed, then $P_t = P(\mu_t)$ gives the actual **process fraction nonconforming**. In any case, in the following we will consider the quantity P_t in (4.199) to be the momentary process fraction nonconforming. Under our assumption of a constant process variance, the value of P_t only depends on the expectation μ_t of the normal distribution. In figure 3.3/3, we gave an example demonstrating the functional relationship (4.199) between P_t and

Interpretation of P as the actual process fraction defective

[11] In (3.136c), one needs to add the time index t to μ and replace σ by σ_0.

μ_t. One can see there, or from (4.199), that $P(\mu_t)$ consists of two additive components $P_1(\mu_t)$ and $P_2(\mu_t)$, where $P_1(\mu_t) := P(X < G_l|\mu_t)$ represents the probability of falling below G_l, and $P_2(\mu_t) := P(X > G_u|\mu_t)$, the probability of exceeding G_u. According to (3.141a), the **minimal process fraction nonconforming** P^* is attained at the midpoint G_m of the interval $[G_l; G_u]$:

$$P^* = P(\mu^*) = 2\Phi\left(\frac{G_l - G_u}{2\sigma_0}\right) = 2 \cdot \left[1 - \Phi\left(\frac{G_u - G_l}{2\sigma_0}\right)\right] \qquad (4.200\text{ a})$$

$$\mu^* = G_m. \qquad (4.200\text{ b})$$

Equation (4.200a) implies that the minimal fraction nonconforming P^* is always bigger than zero and only depends, for a constant spread, on the length of the interval $G_u - G_l$ of the tolerance region. However, in the case of $G_u - G_l > 8\sigma$ the value of P^* is smaller than $2\Phi(-4) \approx 0.0001$.

For several values of the lenght $G_l - G_u$, the following table 4.5/1 lists the minimal fraction nonconforming P^* as well as the process fraction nonconforming that results when μ is shifted from μ^* by $\pm\sigma_0$ and $\pm 2\sigma_0$. Note that the latter four values of P^* only became zero after rounding.

$G_u - G_l$	$P^* = P(\mu^*)$	$P_t = P(\mu_t)$	
		$\mu_t = \mu^* \pm \sigma_0$	$\mu_t = \mu^* \pm 2\sigma_0$
$2\sigma_0$	0.3173	0.5228	0.8427
$3\sigma_0$	0.1336	0.3147	0.6917
$4\sigma_0$	0.0455	0.1600	0.5000
$5\sigma_0$	0.0124	0.0670	0.3085
$6\sigma_0$	0.0027	0.0228	0.1587
$7\sigma_0$	0.0005	0.0062	0.0668
$8\sigma_0$	0.0001	0.0014	0.0228
$9\sigma_0$	0.0000	0.0002	0.0062
$10\sigma_0$	0.0000	0.0000	0.0013
$11\sigma_0$	0.0000	0.0000	0.0002
$12\sigma_0$	0.0000	0.0000	0.0000

Table 4.5/1: Minimal process fraction nonconforming and changes in the fraction nonconforming when shifting the process mean

One can see from table 4.5/1 that for $G_u - G_l > 8\sigma_0$ the process mean μ can be shifted comparatively far away from $\mu^* = G_m$ without creating noticeable increases in the fraction nonconforming. Consequently, if a production process has a C_p-value of 4/3 or more – this is equivalent to the condition $G_u - G_l > 8\sigma_0$ – then it does not significantly affect the fraction nonconforming even if the process mean μ moves a fair bit away from G_m.

Assumption of $C_p > 4/3$

In the following we will assume that the C_p-value lies above 4/3. Compared to the process spread σ_0, the length $G_u - G_l$ of the tolerance interval is then sufficiently large to ensure that the density curve of X lies almost completely within the interval $[G_l; G_u]$ for $\mu_t = G_m$ (see figure 4.5/4a). From this it follows that, for $\mu_t > G_m$ and for $\mu_t < G_m$ the terms $P_1(\mu_t)$ and $P_2(\mu_t)$, respectively, can be neglected. Since the minimal process fraction nonconforming is almost zero for $C_p > 4/3$ we get by (4.199) and (4.200) that

$$P(\mu_t) = \begin{cases} P_1(\mu_t) = \Phi\left(\dfrac{G_l - \mu_t}{\sigma_0}\right) & \text{for } \mu_t < G_m \\ 0 & \text{for } \mu_t = G_m \\ P_2(\mu_t) = \Phi\left(\dfrac{\mu_t - G_u}{\sigma_0}\right) & \text{for } \mu_t > G_m. \end{cases} \tag{4.201}$$

Here, contrary to the case of onesided specification, we are not able to deduce the particular process mean μ_t from a given fraction nonconforming $P_t = P(\mu_t)$. By means of figure 3.3/3b, we can see that in the case of twosided specification, there exist, for each fraction nonconforming $P \neq P^*$, two process levels μ_t defined by $P(\mu_t) = P$. These two levels are symmetric with respect to the midpoint G_m of the tolerance interval.[12] Analogous to (3.138) we get

$$\mu(P_t) = \begin{cases} G_l + z_{1-P_t} \cdot \sigma_0 & \text{for } \mu_t \leq G_m{}^{13} \\ G_u - z_{1-P_t} \cdot \sigma_0 & \text{for } \mu_t > G_m. \end{cases} \tag{4.202}$$

Specifying the control limits of a twosided modified SHEWHART control chart for the process mean

When specifying the control limits of a modified SHEWHART control chart for the process mean one proceeds as follows: First, the process mean μ_t is allowed to vary around G_m and within the interval $[G_l; G_u]$ as long as the fraction nonconforming $P_t = P(\mu_t)$ does not exceed a specified threshold P^+. If this critical fraction nonconforming P^+ is reached one requires the probability of intervening into the process to have a given high value of G^+ (see figure 4.5/4). Instead of (4.29), we now have the approach

$$Pr[g(\mathbf{X}) \notin (LCL; UCL) | P^+] = G^+, \tag{4.203}$$

where $g(\mathbf{X})$ again denotes the test statistic of the control chart. In the interval $[G_l; G_u]$, there are two values $\mu_{\min}$ and $\mu_{\max}$ which are symmetric

[12] In figure 3.3/3b our assumption of $C_p > 4/3$ only has the effect that the curve of $P = P(\mu)$ is actually steeper than shown there. For the minimum (4.200a) it now holds that $P^* \approx 0$.

[13] Because of $P_1(G_m) = P_2(G_m)$, it is arbitrary whether the case $\mu_t = G_m$ is assigned to the upper or lower part of formula (4.202).

around $\mu^* = G_m$ and are defined by $P(\mu_{\min}) = P^+$ and $P(\mu_{\max}) = P^+$, respectively (see figure 3.3/3b). Hence, for calculating of the control limits, one can also, instead of (4.203) use one of the two equations

$$Pr[g(\mathbf{X}) \notin (LCL; UCL)|\mu_{\max}] = G^+ \quad (4.204\text{ a})$$

$$Pr[g(\mathbf{X}) \notin (LCL; UCL)|\mu_{\min}] = G^+. \quad (4.204\text{ b})$$

Under our assumption $C_p > 4/3$, it holds that

$$Pr[g(\mathbf{X}) \notin (LCL; UCL)|\mu_{\max}] \approx Pr[g(\mathbf{X}) \geq UCL|\mu_{\max}]$$

$$Pr[g(\mathbf{X}) \notin (LCL; UCL)|\mu_{\min}] \approx Pr[g(\mathbf{X}) \leq LCL|\mu_{\min}]$$

so that we can in good approximation use

$$Pr[g(\mathbf{X}) \geq UCL|\mu_{\max}] = G^+ \quad (4.205\text{ a})$$

$$Pr[g(\mathbf{X}) \leq LCL|\mu_{\min}] = G^+ \quad (4.205\text{ b})$$

instead of (4.204). As a result of (4.202) it holds for $\mu_{\max}$ and $\mu_{\min}$ that

$$\mu_{\max} = G_u - z_{1-P^+} \cdot \sigma_0 \quad (4.206\text{ a})$$

$$\mu_{\min} = G_l + z_{1-P^+} \cdot \sigma_0. \quad (4.206\text{ b})$$

For a chosen test statistic $g(\mathbf{X})$ the control limits in (4.205) have to lie within the tolerance interval $[G_l; G_u]$ on the one hand and, on the other hand, because of symmetry, they have to lie equally far away from G_u and G_l, respectively. Thus, they can always be written as [14]

$$UCL = G_u - k^C \cdot \sigma_0 \quad (4.207\text{ a})$$

$$LCL = G_l + k^C \cdot \sigma_0. \quad (4.207\text{ b})$$

Consequently, a twosided modified SHEWHART control chart has the basic structure given by figure 4.5/3.

If the standard deviation σ_0 is not known in the form of a nominal or empirical value $\sigma_0 = \sigma_N$ or $\sigma_0 = \sigma_E$, respectively, but is only available in the form of an estimate $\hat{\sigma}_0$, than the latter is substituted into (4.207). For estimating the process spread, one of the five alternatives listed in table 4.4/2 can be used. The different options to construct a modified SHEWHART chart for the process mean are summarized in table 4.5/2.

[14] Also see the remark at the end of this section.

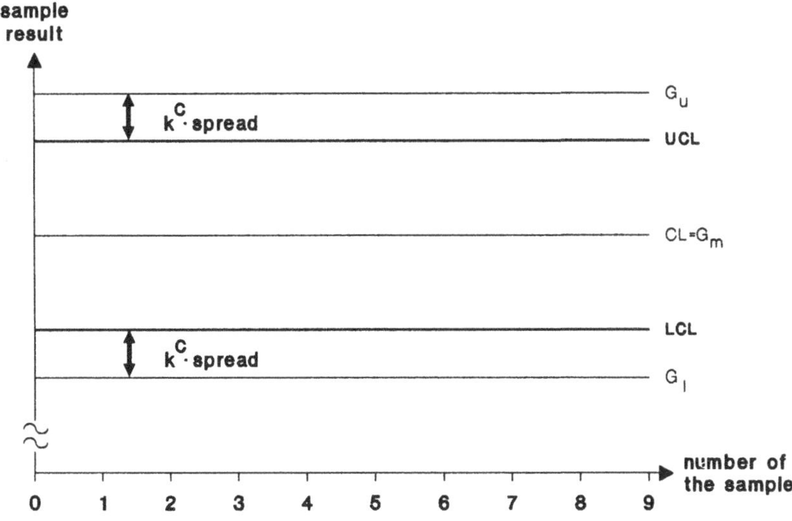

Figure 4.5/3: Structure of a twosided modified SHEWHART control chart for the process mean

<table>
<tr><th rowspan="2">Level CL of the centre line</th><th rowspan="2">Information about σ_0</th><th colspan="2">Levels of the limiting lines</th></tr>
<tr><th>LCL</th><th>UCL</th></tr>
<tr><td rowspan="7">$CL = G_m$</td><td>$\sigma_0 = \sigma_N$</td><td rowspan="2">$G_l + k^C \cdot \sigma_0$</td><td rowspan="2">$G_u - k^C \cdot \sigma_0$</td></tr>
<tr><td>$\sigma_0 = \sigma_E$</td></tr>
<tr><td>$\hat{\sigma}_0 = \dfrac{s_{m \cdot n}}{a_{m \cdot n}}$</td><td rowspan="5">$G_l + k^C \cdot \hat{\sigma}_0$</td><td rowspan="5">$G_u - k^C \cdot \hat{\sigma}_0$</td></tr>
<tr><td>$\hat{\sigma}_0 = \dfrac{\sqrt{\overline{s_m^2}}}{a_{m \cdot (n-1)+1}}$</td></tr>
<tr><td>$\hat{\sigma}_0 = \dfrac{\bar{s}_m}{a_n}$</td></tr>
<tr><td>$\hat{\sigma}_0 = \dfrac{\bar{r}_m}{d_n}$</td></tr>
<tr><td>$\hat{\sigma}_0 = \dfrac{\tilde{r}_m}{\tilde{d}_n}$</td></tr>
</table>

Table 4.5/2: Calculation of the control lines of a twosided modified SHEWHART control chart for the process mean

The magnitude of the coefficient k^C depends on the sample size and on the chosen test statistic $g(\mathbf{X})$ of the control chart. Whenever we want to emphasize the first relationship we write $k^C = k^C(n)$. The corresponding test statistic is sometimes indicated by an index, $k^C = k^C_{\bar{x}}(n)$.

To evaluate control charts of the type shown in figure 4.5/3, we can again look at their power functions. These specify the intervention probabilities depending on the process state. It can be seen from (4.201) - (4.202) that the process state is equally described by the process level $\mu = \mu_t$ as well as by the momentary process fraction nonconforming $P = P_t$. Similar to the way we distinguished between two OC functions $L_1(\mu)$ and $L_2(P)$ when evaluating sampling plans for variable acceptance control, we now have two types of power functions to assess control charts for measurements

Two power functions for modified SHEWHART control charts

$$G_1(\mu_t) := Pr[\text{ test statistic } \notin (LCL; UCL)|\mu_t] \tag{4.208}$$

$$G_2(P_t) := Pr[\text{ test statistic } \notin (LCL; UCL)|P_t]. \tag{4.209}$$

Under the assumption of $C_p > 4/3$ it makes no difference whether one uses $G_1(\mu_t)$ or $G_2(P_t)$. For $C_p > 4/3$, the function $G_1(\mu_t)$ has the representation

$$G_1(\mu_t) \approx \begin{cases} Pr(\text{ test statistic } \leq LCL|\mu_t) & \text{for} \quad \mu_t \leq G_m \\ Pr(\text{ test statistic } \geq UCL|\mu_t) & \text{for} \quad \mu_t > G_m. \end{cases} \tag{4.210}$$

Both power functions are linked by the relationship

$$G_2(P_t) = G_1\left(\mu(P_t)\right). \tag{4.211}$$

Remark

The formulae in (4.207) can easily be written in a form analogous to (4.112), i.e., the control limits can be expressed in the form $CL \pm c^C \cdot \sigma_0$ with $CL = G_m$. It is also easily verified that the relationship between the factors c^C and k^C is given by $c^C = (G_u - G_l)/(2\sigma_0) - k^C$. The choice of CL as a reference point has the instructional advantage of emphasizing the analogies between sections 4.4 and 4.5. Because the form (4.207) is more common in SQA literature we have chosen not to proceed in this way.

b) Mean Charts

We will now begin our presention of twosided modified SHEWHART charts with the **mean chart**. Its test statistic $\bar{X}_n$ is $no(\mu_t; \sigma_0^2/n)$-distributed. This implies that the determining equations for the control limits are, according to (4.205), given by

$$G^+ = 1 - Pr(\bar{X}_n < UCL|\mu_{\max}) = 1 - \Phi\left(\sqrt{n} \cdot \frac{UCL - \mu_{\max}}{\sigma_0}\right)$$

$$G^+ = Pr(\bar{X}_n \leq LCL|\mu_{\min}) = \Phi\left(\sqrt{n}\cdot\frac{LCL-\mu_{\min}}{\sigma_0}\right).$$

From this we can obtain (see figure 5.2/1)

$$\sqrt{n}\cdot\frac{UCL-\mu_{\max}}{\sigma_0} = z_{1-G^+} = -z_{G^+}$$

$$\sqrt{n}\cdot\frac{LCL-\mu_{\min}}{\sigma_0} = z_{G^+}.$$

Solving for UCL or LCL, respectively, yields

$$UCL = \mu_{\max} - z_{G^+}\cdot\frac{\sigma_0}{\sqrt{n}} \tag{4.212}$$

$$LCL = \mu_{\min} + z_{G^+}\cdot\frac{\sigma_0}{\sqrt{n}}. \tag{4.213}$$

Finally, we can substitute (4.206) and get

Control limits of the twosided modified mean chart for known σ_0

$$UCL = G_u - k_{\bar{x}}^C\cdot\sigma_0 \tag{4.214}$$

$$LCL = G_l + k_{\bar{x}}^C\cdot\sigma_0 \tag{4.215}$$

with

$$k_{\bar{x}}^C := z_{1-P^+} + \frac{z_{G^+}}{\sqrt{n}}. \tag{4.216}$$

If an estimate $\hat{\sigma}_0$ is used instead of σ_0 in the above formulae for the control limits, then the statement in (4.203) only holds approximately.

From (4.210) we can obtain the **power function with argument** μ

$$G_{1;\bar{x}}(\mu_t) = \begin{cases} Pr(\bar{X}_n \leq LCL|\mu_t) & \text{for} \quad \mu_t \leq G_m \\ Pr(\bar{X}_n \geq UCL|\mu_t) & \text{for} \quad \mu_t > G_m. \end{cases} \tag{4.217 a}$$

Since $\bar{X}_n \sim no(\mu_t; \sigma_0^2/n)$ we have

$$G_{1;\bar{x}}(\mu_t) = \begin{cases} \Phi\left(\sqrt{n}\cdot\frac{LCL-\mu_t}{\sigma_0}\right) & \text{for} \quad \mu_t \leq G_m \\ \\ 1-\Phi\left(\sqrt{n}\cdot\frac{UCL-\mu_t}{\sigma_0}\right) & \text{for} \quad \mu_t > G_m. \end{cases} \tag{4.217 b}$$

Power function of the twosided modified mean chart with argument μ

Substituting (4.214) – (4.215) gives the final result

$$G_{1;\bar{x}}(\mu_t) = \begin{cases} \Phi\left[\sqrt{n}\cdot\left(\dfrac{G_l-\mu_t}{\sigma_0}+k_{\bar{x}}^C\right)\right] & \text{for} \quad \mu_t \le G_m \\ 1-\Phi\left[\sqrt{n}\cdot\left(\dfrac{G_u-\mu_t}{\sigma_0}-k_{\bar{x}}^C\right)\right] & \text{for} \quad \mu_t > G_m. \end{cases} \tag{4.217 c}$$

The function $G_{1;\bar{x}}(\mu_t)$ is *symmetric* with respect to the midpoint $\mu^* = G_m$ of the tolerance interval. Consequently, any two process levels with the same distance from G_m have the same intervention probability. Since UCL and LCL are also symmetric with respect to the interval midpoint, it follows for every $\Delta_t \in \mathbb{R}$ that

$$G_{1;\bar{x}}(G_u-\Delta_t) = G_{1;\bar{x}}(G_l+\Delta_t) = 1-\Phi\left[\sqrt{n}\left(\frac{\Delta_t}{\sigma_0}-k_{\bar{x}}^C\right)\right]. \tag{4.218}$$

The **power function with argument P** is related to $G_{1;\bar{x}}(\mu_t)$ by (4.211). If we substitute the term $\mu(P_t) = G_l - z_{P_t}\cdot\sigma_0$ for μ_t in (4.217c) for $\mu_t \le G_m$, and the term $\mu(P_t) = G_u - z_{1-P_t}\cdot\sigma_0$ in the case of $\mu_t > G_m$, the result is

$$G_{2;\bar{x}}(P_t) = \begin{cases} \Phi\left[\sqrt{n}\cdot\left(z_{P_t}+k_{\bar{x}}^C\right)\right] & \text{for} \quad \mu_t \le G_m \\ 1-\Phi\left[\sqrt{n}\cdot\left(z_{1-P_t}-k_{\bar{x}}^C\right)\right] & \text{for} \quad \mu_t > G_m. \end{cases}$$

Power function of the twosided modified mean chart with argument P

By (2.51) and taking into account that $z_P = -z_{1-P}$, we get the representation

$$G_{2;\bar{x}}(P_t) = \Phi\left[\sqrt{n}\cdot\left(z_{P_t}+k_{\bar{x}}^C\right)\right] = 1-\Phi\left[\sqrt{n}\cdot\left(z_{1-P_t}-k_{\bar{x}}^C\right)\right]. \tag{4.219}$$

We will illustrate these relationships by means of a figure. Let us assume a $no(\mu_t;1)$-distributed quality characteristic and let [96;104] be the tolerance interval. The upper part of figure 4.5/4 shows the density of X when the process runs on the optimal level $\mu_t = \mu^* = G_m$ and for the case of reaching one of the two critical levels $\mu_{\min}$ or $\mu_{\max}$. According to (4.201), $\mu_t = \mu^* = G_m$ is related to the minimal fraction nonconforming $P(\mu^*) \approx 0$, and $\mu_{\min}$ or $\mu_{\max}$ to the specified critical fraction nonconforming P^+. The magnitude of the fraction nonconforming P^+ corresponds to the size of the shaded areas in the graph. In the lower part of the figure we can see the density of the test statistic $\bar{X}_n$ for $n = 4$ for the same two process states as above. The shaded area indicates the intervention probability G^+.

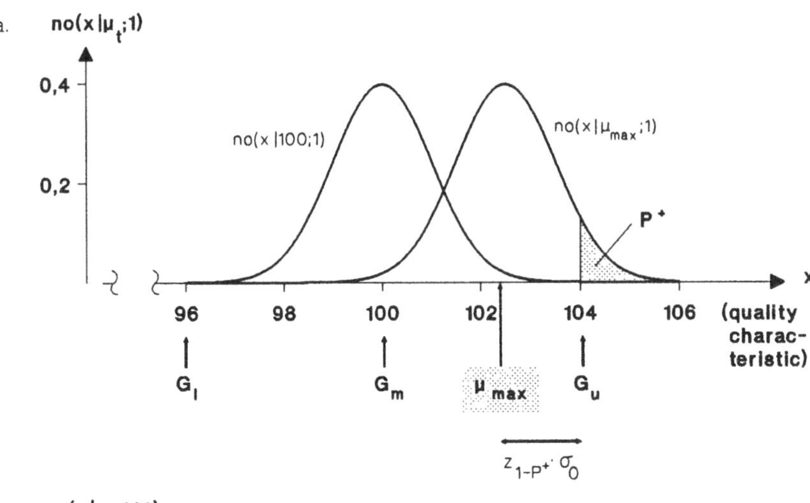

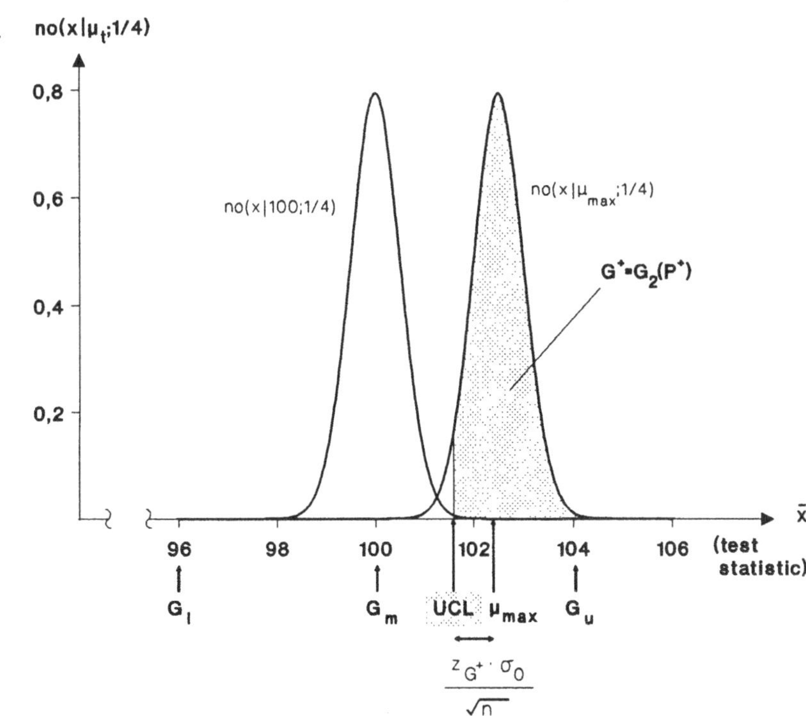

Figure 4.5/4: Determination of the control limits of a twosided modified SHEWHART mean chart

---

Example 4.5/2

Suppose the requirements for the soft drinks manufacturer in example 4.4/1 are now $G_l = 5.5$ and $G_u = 8.5$. What are the control limits of a modified mean chart with $n = 5$ for a fraction nonconformig of $P^+ = 0.02$ when the intervention probability is supposed to be $G^+ = 0.99$? We are asked to use the estimate $\hat{\sigma}_0 = \bar{s}_{15}/a_5 \approx 0.2901$ of example 4.4/2 for the determination of the control lines and the power function.

First we calculate the factor

$$k_{\bar{x}}^C = z_{0.98} + \frac{z_{0.99}}{\sqrt{5}} \approx 2.054 + \frac{2.326}{\sqrt{5}} \approx 3.0942$$

in (4.216) using table 5.2/1. The *control limits* can now be obtained from (4.214) - (4.215) by replacing σ_0 with $\hat{\sigma}_0$:

$$UCL = G_u - k_{\bar{x}}^C \cdot \hat{\sigma}_0 \approx 8.5 - 3.0942 \cdot 0.2901 \approx 7.60$$

$$LCL = G_l + k_{\bar{x}}^C \cdot \hat{\sigma}_0 \approx 5.5 + 3.0942 \cdot 0.2901 \approx 6.40.$$

The 15 means in column 5 of table 4.4/1 all lie within these limits.

According to (4.218), for the *power function* with argument μ of the modified $\bar{x}$ chart we get the approximate result

$$G_{1;\bar{x}}(G_u - \Delta_t) = G_{1;\bar{x}}(G_l + \Delta_t) \approx 1 - \Phi\left[\sqrt{5}\left(\frac{\Delta_t}{0.2901} - 3.0942\right)\right].$$

Table 4.5/3 lists various process levels $\mu_t = G_u - \Delta_t$ in column 2 and the corresponding process levels with the same fraction nonconforming $P_t = P(\mu_t)$ in column 3. The fractions nonconforming P_t are given in column 4 and the intervention probabilities in column 5. The process levels $\mu_{\max}$ and $\mu_{\min}$ at which the critical fraction nonconforming P^+ is reached are printed bold.

Δ_t	$\mu_t = G_u - \Delta_t$	$\mu_t = G_l + \Delta_t$	$P_t = P_t(\mu_t)$	$G_{1;\bar{x}}(\mu_t)$
(1)	(2)	(3)	(4)	(5)
0.40	8.10	5.90	0.0838	1.0000
0.45	8.05	5.95	0.0606	0.9997
0.50	8.00	6.00	0.0427	0.9989
0.55	7.95	6.05	0.0287	0.9963
0.596	**7.904**	**6.096**	0.0202	0.9900
0.60	7.90	6.10	0.0192	0.9800
0.65	7.85	6.15	0.0125	0.9719
0.70	7.80	6.20	0.0080	0.9357
0.75	7.75	6.25	0.0048	0.8729
0.80	7.70	6.30	0.0021	0.7734
0.85	7.65	6.35	0.0017	0.6443
0.90	7.60	6.40	0.0010	0.4920
0.95	7.55	6.45	0.0005	0.3446
1.00	7.50	6.50	0.0003	0.2148
1.50	7.00	7.00	0.0000	0.0000

Table 4.5/3: Calculating the values of the power function for a twosided modified mean chart

---

Problem 4.5/1

a) For $n = 5, G_l = 5.5$ and $G_u = 8.5$, find the levels of the control limits of the twosided modified mean chart, if the chart is required to intervene in the process with a probability of $G^+ = 0.95$ in the case of reaching the fraction nonconforming $P^+ = 0.01$. As in example 4.5/2, use the estimate $\hat{\sigma}_0 \approx 0.2901$ for the process spread.

b) What is the probability $G_{2;\bar{x}}(P_t)$ of intervening in the process, if the process is operating with a fraction nonconforming of 2% or 0.5%, respectively?

c) Median Charts

Instead of the $no(\mu_t; \sigma_0^2/n)$-distributed sample mean $\bar{X}_n$, we can also use the $no(\mu_t; c_n^2 \cdot \sigma_0^2/n)$-distributed sample median $\tilde{X}_n$ as a test statistic. The factors c_n are tabulated in table 5.3/1 for $n = 2, 3, \ldots, 20$. Since their values are bigger than one for $n > 2$, it follows that whenever the control chart works with a sample size of $n > 2$, the variance of $\tilde{X}_n$ is larger than that of $\bar{X}_n$. As a result, the interval $[LCL; UCL]$ will be wider.

The starting point for the determination of the control limits of the twosided modified median chart are again equations (4.205). Analogous to (4.214) - (4.216) we get from these that

Control limits of the twosided modified median chart for known σ_0

$$UCL = G_u - k^C_{\tilde{x}} \cdot \sigma_0 \tag{4.220}$$

$$LCL = G_l + k^C_{\tilde{x}} \cdot \sigma_0 \tag{4.221}$$

with

$$k^C_{\tilde{x}} := z_{1-P^+} + \frac{z_{G^+}}{\sqrt{n}} \cdot c_n. \tag{4.222}$$

The **power function with argument** μ of the median chart is now obtained from (4.217a) by replacing $\bar{X}_n$ by $\tilde{X}_n$. As $\tilde{X}_n \sim no(\mu_t; c_n^2 \cdot \sigma_0^2/n)$, it follows analogous to (4.217c) that

Power function of the twosided median chart with argument μ

$$G_{1;\tilde{x}}(\mu_t) = \begin{cases} \Phi\left[\frac{\sqrt{n}}{c_n} \cdot \left(\frac{G_l - \mu_t}{\sigma_0} + k^C_{\tilde{x}}\right)\right] & \text{for} \quad \mu_t \leq G_m \\ 1 - \Phi\left[\frac{\sqrt{n}}{c_n} \cdot \left(\frac{G_u - \mu_t}{\sigma_0} - k^C_{\tilde{x}}\right)\right] & \text{for} \quad \mu_t > G_m. \end{cases} \tag{4.223}$$

For the calculation of values of this function one can use the relationship

$$G_{1;\tilde{x}}(G_u - \Delta_t) = G_{1;\tilde{x}}(G_l + \Delta_t) = 1 - \Phi\left[\frac{\sqrt{n}}{c_n}\left(\frac{\Delta_t}{\sigma_0} - k^C_{\tilde{x}}\right)\right]. \tag{4.224}$$

Similar to (4.218), it is based on the symmetry of the power function with respect to $\mu^* = G_m$.

From (4.223) and under consideration of (4.211) we can derive the **power function with argument** P of a modified median chart:

Power function of a twosided modified median chart with argument P

$$G_{2;\tilde{x}}(P_t) = \Phi\left[\frac{\sqrt{n}}{c_n} \cdot \left(z_{P_t} + k^C_{\tilde{x}}\right)\right] = 1 - \Phi\left[\frac{\sqrt{n}}{c_n}\left(z_{1-P_t} - k^C_{\tilde{x}}\right)\right]. \tag{4.225}$$

d) Extreme Value Charts

Finally, we want to briefly discuss how to determine the control lines and the power function of the modified extreme value chart. Here, the control limits UCL and LCL are determined so that, when the process fraction defective reaches a given critical value P^+, *all* n components of the test statistic $\mathbf{X} = (X_1, \ldots, X_n)$ lie within the limits with probability G^+. Under this condition, the limits are given by

Control limits of the twosided modified extreme value chart for known σ_0

$$UCL = G_u - k^C_{\mathbf{X}} \cdot \sigma_0 \tag{4.226}$$

$$LCL = G_l + k^C_{\mathbf{X}} \cdot \sigma_0 \tag{4.227}$$

with

$$k_{\mathbf{X}}^{C} := z_{1-P^+} - z_{P_n} \qquad (4.228\text{ a})$$

$$P_n = P_n(G^+) := \sqrt[n]{1-G^+}. \qquad (4.228\text{ b})$$

The percentiles of order $P_n = P_n(G^+)$ of the standard normal distribution in (4.228a) are given in table 4.5/4 for several sample sizes n and probabilities G^+.

n	G^+			
	0.99	0.95	0.90	0.50
1	-2.326	-1.645	-1.282	0.000
2	-1.282	-0.760	-0.478	0.545
3	-0.787	-0.336	-0.090	0.819
4	-0.478	-0.068	0.157	0.998
5	-0.258	0.124	0.334	0.129
6	-0.090	0.271	0.471	1.231
7	0.045	0.390	0.582	1.315
8	0.157	0.489	0.674	1.385
9	0.252	0.573	0.753	1.446
10	0.334	0.647	0.821	1.499

Table 4.5/4: Percentiles of order $P_n = P_n(G^+)$ of the standard normal distribution

The **power function with argument** μ of the extreme value chart has the form

Power function of the twosided modified extreme value chart with argument μ

$$G_{1;\mathbf{X}}(\mu_t) = \begin{cases} 1 - \left[1 - \Phi\left(\dfrac{G_l - \mu_t}{\sigma_0} + k_{\mathbf{X}}^{C}\right)\right]^n & \text{for} \quad \mu_t \leq G_m \\ 1 - \left[\Phi\left(\dfrac{G_u - \mu_t}{\sigma_0} - k_{\mathbf{X}}^{C}\right)\right]^n & \text{for} \quad \mu_t > G_m. \end{cases} \qquad (4.229)$$

Its values can be calculated using the symmetry relationship

$$G_{1;\mathbf{X}}(G_u - \Delta_t) = G_{1;\mathbf{X}}(G_l + \Delta_t) = 1 - \left[\Phi\left(\frac{\Delta_t}{\sigma_0} - k_{\mathbf{X}}^{C}\right)\right]^n. \qquad (4.230)$$

From (4.229) and (4.211) we get the following representation for the **power function with argument** P:

Power function of the modified twosided extreme value chart with argument P

$$G_{2;\mathbf{X}}(P_t) = 1 - \left[\Phi\left(z_{1-P_t} - k_{\mathbf{X}}^{C}\right)\right]^n. \qquad (4.231)$$

Example 4.5/3

In example 4.5/2 we determined the control limits and the power function of a twosided modified mean chart for given specifications $G_l = 5.5$, $G_u = 8.5, n = 5$ and the intervention probability $G^+ = 0.99$ at $P^+ = 0.02$. With these specifications we will now determine the control limits and the power function of both a modified median and a modified extreme value chart. We will again use the estimate $\hat{\sigma}_0 \approx 0.2901$ for these charts.

From table 5.3/1 we get the factor

$$k_{\tilde{x}}^C := z_{0.98} + \frac{z_{0.99}}{\sqrt{5}} \cdot c_5 \approx 2.054 + \frac{2.326}{\sqrt{5}} \cdot 1.198 \approx 3.3002.$$

Thus, according to (4.220) - (4.221), the *control limits of the median chart* result to be

$$UCL = G_u - k_{\tilde{x}}^C \cdot \hat{\sigma}_0 \approx 8.5 - 3.3002 \cdot 0.2901 \approx 7.54$$

$$LCL = G_l + k_{\tilde{x}}^C \cdot \hat{\sigma}_0 \approx 5.5 + 3.3002 \cdot 0.2901 \approx 6.46.$$

Observe that none of the 15 medians in the prerun lies outside of these limits (see column 6 of table 4.4/1).

Determination of the *control limits of the extreme value chart* first requires to calculate the factor (4.228a). Using table 4.5/4 we find

$$k_{\mathbf{x}}^C = z_{0.98} - z_{P_5(0.99)} \approx 2.054 + 0.258 = 2.312.$$

By (4.226) - (4.227) it follows that

$$UCL = G_u - k_{\mathbf{x}}^C \cdot \hat{\sigma}_0 \approx 8.5 - 2.312 \cdot 0.2901 \approx 7.83$$

$$LCL = G_l + k_{\mathbf{x}}^C \cdot \hat{\sigma}_0 \approx 5.5 + 2.312 \cdot 0.2901 \approx 6.17.$$

Among the 15 samples of the prerun none of the observations is found to lie outside of these limits (see column 2 of table 4.4/1)

The *power functions with argument* μ for both control charts constructed above are, according to (4.229) and (4.230), respectively, given by

$$G_{1;\tilde{x}}(G_u - \Delta_t) = G_{1;\tilde{x}}(G_l + \Delta_t) \approx 1 - \Phi\left[\frac{\sqrt{5}}{1.198} \cdot \left(\frac{\Delta_t}{0.2901} - 3.3002\right)\right]$$

$$G_{1;\mathbf{x}}(G_u - \Delta_t) = G_{1;\mathbf{x}}(G_l + \Delta_t) \approx 1 - \left[\Phi\left(\frac{\Delta_t}{0.2901} - 2.312\right)\right]^5.$$

Table 4.5/5 lists process levels with equal fraction nonconforming in columns $2-3$, i.e., process levels $\mu_t = G_u - \Delta_t$ and $\mu_t = G_l + \Delta_t$, respectively. The corresponding proportions of nonconforming items $P_t = P_t(\mu_t)$ are given in column 4 and the intervention probabilities of the two charts, in columns $5-6$. In order to simplify the comparison we used the same arguments as in table 4.5/3.

Δ_t	$\mu_t = G_u - \Delta_t$	$\mu_t = G_l - \Delta_t$	$P_t = P(\mu_t)$	$G_1(\mu_t)$	
				median chart	extreme value chart
(1)	(2)	(3)	(4)	(5)	(6)
0.40	8.10	5.90	0.0838	0.9998	0.9998
0.45	8.05	5.95	0.0606	0.9995	0.9994
0.50	8.00	6.00	0.0427	0.9984	0.9984
0.55	7.95	6.05	0.0287	0.9956	0.9956
0.596	**7.904**	**6.096**	0.0202	0.9900	0.9900
0.60	7.90	6.10	0.0192	0.9893	0.9891
0.65	7.85	6.15	0.0125	0.9761	0.9765
0.70	7.80	6.20	0.0080	0.9515	0.9542
0.75	7.75	6.25	0.0048	0.9082	0.9180
0.80	7.70	6.30	0.0021	0.8438	0.8613
0.85	7.65	6.35	0.0017	0.7549	0.7893
0.90	7.60	6.40	0.0010	0.6443	0.7015
0.95	7.55	6.45	0.0005	0.5199	0.6025
1.00	7.50	6.50	0.0003	0.3936	0.4932
1.50	7.00	7.00	0.0000	0.0002	0.0105

Table 4.5/5: Calculation of selected values of the power function of a modified twosided median and an extreme value chart

---

e) Comparison of Mean, Median and Extreme Value Charts

A comparison of the three twosided modified SHEWHART control charts for the process level can again be made via their power functions. Let us first present a summary of the formulae which are used to calculate the values of the power functions with arguments μ and P, respectively:

$$G_{1;\bar{x}}(G_u - \Delta_t) = G_{1;\bar{x}}(G_l + \Delta_t) = 1 - \Phi\left[\sqrt{n}\cdot\left(\frac{\Delta_t}{\sigma_0} - k_{\bar{x}}^C\right)\right] \quad (4.232\text{ a})$$

$$G_{1;\tilde{x}}(G_u - \Delta_t) = G_{1;\tilde{x}}(G_l + \Delta_t) = 1 - \Phi\left[\frac{\sqrt{n}}{c_n}\left(\frac{\Delta_t}{\sigma_0} - k_{\tilde{x}}^C\right)\right] \quad (4.232\text{ b})$$

$$G_{1;\mathbf{x}}(G_u - \Delta_t) = G_{1;\mathbf{x}}(G_l + \Delta_t) = 1 - \left[\Phi\left(\frac{\Delta_t}{\sigma_0} - k_{\mathbf{x}}^C\right)\right]^n . \qquad (4.232\text{ c})$$

The corresponding power functions with argument P are:

$$G_{2;\bar{x}}(P_t) = \Phi\left[\sqrt{n}\cdot\left(z_{P_t} + k_{\bar{x}}^C\right)\right] = 1 - \Phi\left[\sqrt{n}\cdot\left(z_{1-P_t} - k_{\bar{x}}^C\right)\right] \qquad (4.233\text{ a})$$

$$G_{2;\tilde{x}}(P_t) = \Phi\left[\frac{\sqrt{n}}{c_n}\cdot\left(z_{P_t} + k_{\tilde{x}}^C\right)\right] = 1 - \Phi\left[\frac{\sqrt{n}}{c_n}\left(z_{1-P_t} - k_{\tilde{x}}^C\right)\right] \qquad (4.233\text{ b})$$

$$G_{2;\mathbf{x}}(P_t) = 1 - \left[\Phi\left(z_{1-P_t} - k_{\mathbf{x}}^C\right)\right]^n . \qquad (4.233\text{ c})$$

The three power functions with argument μ are all symmetric with respect to the midpoint G_m of the tolerance interval. According to design, they attain the specified value G^+ at the points $\mu_{\max}$ and $\mu_{\min}$ defined by $P(\mu_{\max}) = P(\mu_{\min}) = P^+$. The power of the modified mean chart is the steepest of the three (highest discriminatory power). The extreme value chart has the least steep power curve.

Figure 4.5/5 displays the power curves (4.232a-c) corresponding to the three charts for the case of $n = 5, G_l = 5.5, G_u = 8.5,\ P^+ = 0.02$ and $G^+ = 0.99$. Values of the functions are listed in tables 4.5/3 and 4.5/5 (column 5 and columns 5-6, respectively). For $\mu_t \in (\mu_{\max}; \mu_{\min})$, we have the inequality $P_t < P^+$ for the corresponding fractions nonconforming $P_t = P(\mu_t)$. Also, for all three charts the intervention probabilities lie below the value of G^+, with the smallest values being those of the mean chart. For $\mu_t \notin (\mu_{\min}; \mu_{\max})$, we have $P_t > P^+$ and the intervention probabilities of all charts lie above G^+, with the largest values corresponding to the mean chart.[15]

We can conclude from the discussion above that the $\bar{x}$ chart is more powerful than the $\tilde{x}$ and $\mathbf{x}$ charts. In the case of a shift in the process level, which causes the fraction nonconforming P_t to exceed the critical value P^+, it has the highest probability of a (desirable) intervention in the process. On the other hand, in the case of shifts which do not cause P_t to exceed P^+, it leads to an (undesired) intervention with the lowest probability. The extreme value chart is ranked last.

Remark

The *numerical* determination of the control lines and the power curves of classical and modified SHEWHART mean value, median and extreme value charts, presented in section 4.4.2 and 4.5.2 can be replaced by *graphical* methods. The necessary nomograms as well as a description of their application can be found in DGQ (1979).

[15]This statement can be verified using tables 4.5/3 and 4.5/5 (see the first four data rows); figure 4.5/5 is too "rough" for this purpose.

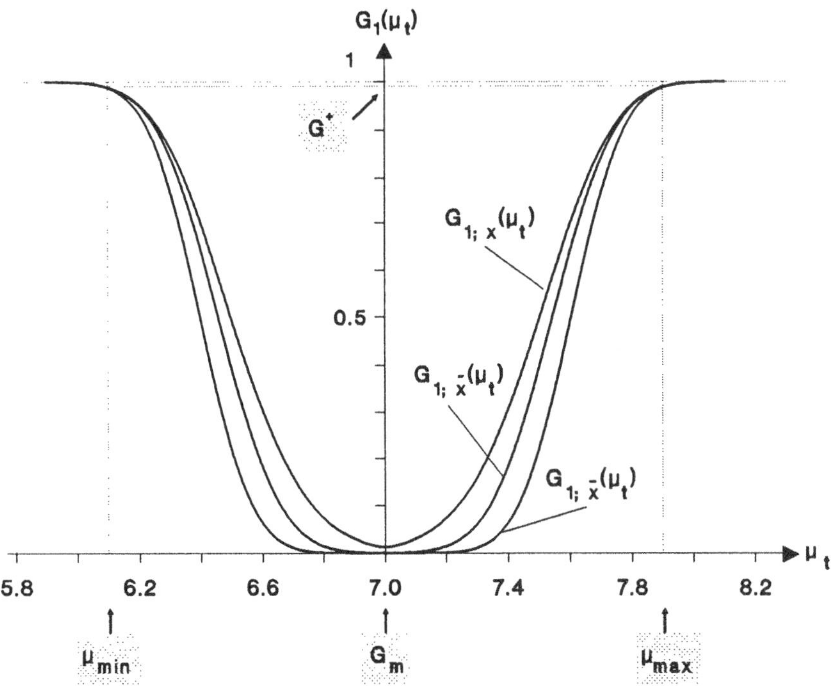

Figure 4.5/5: Power functions of the twosided modified mean, median and extreme value charts for $n = 5$

Problem 4.5/2

Solve problem 4.5/1 for the modified median and modified extreme value charts and compare the results.

4.6 Control Charts with Memory

So far we have introduced classical and modified SHEWHART control charts. These charts only use the present sample result for the decision on whether or not to intervene in the production process. For this reason they are also called **control charts without memory**. Actually, SHEWHART control charts are the standard control charts in SQA. For more than 30 years, however, there have been more sophisticated procedures for control charting which also consider previous sample results. Such **control charts with memory** can, under certain circumstances, be more sensitive towards disturbances, i.e., they can possibly detect an undesired shift in the process level or spread at an earlier stage and indicate the necessity for a corrective action. In the context of increasing demands on quality, this point is gaining more and more importance, because today it is often crucial to detect even small shifts quickly and accurately.

In section 4.6.1, we will first demonstrate how to provide a control chart with memory through an appropriate choice of a test statistic. We will present a general linear approach which includes the memoryless SHEWHART control chart as a special case. In sections 4.6.2 and 4.6.3 we will briefly discuss two special control charts with memory, the **CUSUM chart** and the **EWMA chart**, which are not yet widely used in Europe as well as in the US. We will restrict ourselves to the *twosided* CUSUM-$\bar{x}$ chart and EWMA-$\bar{x}$ chart and will compare them to the twosided SHEWHART-$\bar{x}$ chart. A more comprehensive presentation of control charts with memory is not possible due to lack of space. In particular, we do not deal with either CUSUM or EWMA charts for attributes nor with charts for monitoring process spread. We are, however, hoping that this brief introduction will spark the readers interest and thus contribute to a wider introduction of non-SHEWHART control charts in industrial practice.

4.6.1 Classification of Control Charts with Respect to their Memory

A control chart continually tests whether a production process is under statistical control, that is, whether the distribution parameters of the quality characteristic under scrutiny agree with a given target value. In the control charts previously introduced, the test statistic of this parameter test was always a function $\mathbf{g}(\mathbf{X})$ of the *present* sample vector $\mathbf{X} = (X_1, \ldots, X_n)$, for example, the sample mean or standard deviation of the most recent sample. However, this simple and transparent approach is not the only possible way of process control via control charts. There are good arguments in favour of also using the results of previous samples. A control chart which uses the outcomes of previous samples in addition to the present sample outcomes is called **control chart with memory**. If the test statistic of the control chart considers all the previous sample outcomes then we say that the control chart has a **memory of unlimited length**. If the test statistic only regards the k most recent sample data sets ($k > 1$) the corresponding control chart has a **memory of limited length**. In the case $k = 1$, i.e., if only the most recent sample result is considered, we get the **control chart without memory** which was already discussed in detail. Among control charts with memory we also distinguish between **control charts with uniform memory** and **control charts with nonuniform memory**. In the first case, all sample variables from the past have the same weight, and in the latter case they are weighted differently in the test statistic. Among the control charts with nonuniform memory, an important class is the **control charts with decreasing memory**. Here the weight of the previous sample results decreases as the distance to the most recent sampling time increases.

Types of memory

In the following, we want to illustrate these introductory remarks by specifying test statistics and discussing examples. In order to distinguish the sample variables originating from the different sampling points we will modify our previous notation by adding a time index j which takes value from 1 to t. The first sampling point is denoted by $j = 1$ and the most recent sampling point by $j = t$. The variables of all the samples drawn until time t are summarized in the sample vectors

$$\mathbf{X}_j := (X_{j1}, \ldots, X_{jn}) \qquad j = 1, \ldots, t.$$

For every j, the variables $X_{j1}, \ldots, X_{jn}$, summarized by $\mathbf{X}_j$, are applied to the same test statistic g(.). We only need to specify how to combine the functions $g(\mathbf{X}_1), \ldots, g(\mathbf{X}_t)$ to a scalar test statistic Y_t. One approach that has been suggested is the general linear approach

General linear approach defining the test statistic of a control chart with memory

$$Y_t = a_t + \sum_{j=1}^{t} b_j \cdot g(\mathbf{X}_j). \tag{4.234}$$

The following discussion will be based on this approach (see also LAI 1974). The memory type of a control chart operating with test statistic (4.234) depends on the choice of the coefficients $b_1, \ldots, b_t$. We will consider four special cases:

▷ Case 1: SHEWHART **chart**

The SHEWHART **chart** uses the test statistic

$$Y_t = g(\mathbf{X}_t), \tag{4.235}$$

which is obtained from (4.234) by setting

$$a_t := 0 \tag{4.236 a}$$

$$b_j := \begin{cases} 1 & j = t \\ 0 & j = 1, 2, \ldots, t-1. \end{cases} \tag{4.236 b}$$

If one chooses the function $g(\mathbf{X}_t)$ to be the sample mean $\bar{X}_{tn}$ of the sample drawn at time t, then one gets the previously discussed SHEWHART **mean chart** (SHEWHART-$\bar{x}$ chart). Since $b_1 = b_2 = \ldots = b_{t-1} = 0$ the SHEWHART chart is without memory.

▷ Case 2: **MOSUM chart**

The **MOSUM chart** works with the test statistic

$$Y_t = \frac{1}{k} \cdot \sum_{j=t-k+1}^{t} g(\mathbf{X}_j) \tag{4.237}$$

which results from (4.234) by setting

$$a_t := 0 \tag{4.238 a}$$

$$b_j := \begin{cases} 1/k & \text{for } j = t-k+1, \ldots, t-1, t \\ 0 & \text{else .} \end{cases} \tag{4.238 b}$$

The test statistic here is a moving average (MOSUM = **moving sum**) of the last k sample outcomes. If $g(\mathbf{X}_j)$ is chosen to be the mean $\bar{X}_{jn}$ in the j-th sample, we get the **MOSUM-mean chart** (MOSUM-$\bar{x}$ chart). The MOSUM chart has a finite and uniform memory over k sampling periods. It can only detect process shifts during these last k periods.

We will not present MOSUM charts in this text. They are discussed in BAUER/HACKL (1978,1980) and NELSON (1983), for example.

▷ Case 3: **EWMA chart**

The **EWMA chart** operates with the recursively defined test statistic

$$Y_t = (1-d) \cdot Y_{t-1} + d \cdot g(\mathbf{X}_t), \qquad 0 < d \leq 1, \tag{4.239}$$

where Y_0 is a given target value for the process level or spread. This test statistic is an exponentially weighted average (**EWMA** = exponentially **weighted moving average**) of all samples drawn until time t. Through reverse substitution we get

$$\begin{aligned} Y_t &= (1-d)\cdot[(1-d)\cdot Y_{t-2} + d\cdot g(\mathbf{X}_{t-1})] + d\cdot g(\mathbf{X}_t) \\ &= \ldots = (1-d)^t \cdot Y_0 + d\cdot \sum_{j=1}^{t}(1-d)^{t-j}\cdot g(\mathbf{X}_j). \end{aligned}$$

Thus, the test statistic of the EWMA chart results from (4.234) by setting

$$a_t := (1-d)^t \cdot Y_0 \tag{4.240 a}$$

$$b_j := d\cdot(1-d)^{t-j} \qquad \text{for } j = 1,2,\ldots,t. \tag{4.240 b}$$

The EWMA chart has a memory of unlimited length. Since all coefficients b_j are non-zero, starting from $j = 1$, the memory reaches back to $j = 1$ being defined as the beginning of the process or the time of the last intervention. The memory of an EWMA chart is nonuniform because the coefficients b_j are not constant. In fact, they form a decreasing geometric sequence. In the case of $d = 1$ the EWMA test statistic (4.239) is identical to the SHEWHART chart test statistic $Y_t = g(\mathbf{X_t})$. With $d = 0$ we would get a chart which does not learn from the sample results, i.e., it ignores even the most recent quality data. For this reason the choice of $d = 0$ is excluded. If the function $g(\mathbf{X}_t)$ in (4.239) is chosen to be the t-th sample mean $\bar{X}_{tn}$, then with $Y_0 = \mu_0$ (target value of the process level) we get the **EWMA-mean chart**. The special case of $n = 1$ leads to the **EWMA single value chart**.

EWMA charts are discussed in ROBERTS (1959), WORTHAM/HEINRICH (1972, 1973), ROBINSON/HO (1978), HUNTER (1986), CROWDER (1987a,b), LUCAS/SACCUCCI (1990), DOMANGUE/PATCH (1991) and GAN (1991a,b), for example.

▷ Case 4: **CUSUM chart**

The **CUSUM chart** works with the test statistic

$$Y_t = \sum_{j=1}^{t}[g(\mathbf{X}_j) - Y_0] = -t\cdot Y_0 + \sum_{j=1}^{t} g(\mathbf{X}_j), \tag{4.241}$$

where Y_0 is defined as in (4.239). Substituting

$$a_t = -t\cdot Y_0 \tag{4.242 a}$$

$$b_j = 1 \qquad \text{for} \quad j = 1,2,\ldots,t \tag{4.242 b}$$

in (4.234) yields the test statistic of the CUSUM chart. The test statistic (4.241) can be interpreted as the **cu**mulative **sum** of the deviations from the target value Y_0 where the cumulation procedure refers to all preceeding samples. Since the coefficients b_j are constant, the CUSUM chart has a uniform memory which, similar to the EWMA chart, goes back to $j = 1$. The test statistic of the **CUSUM mean chart** is given by (4.241) with $g(\mathbf{X}_j) = \bar{X}_{jn}$ and $Y_0 = \mu_0$. In the special case of $n = 1$, the CUSUM-mean chart becomes the **CUSUM single value chart**.

There is a wide selection of literature about the CUSUM chart. As a basic and introductory presentation we refer the reader to PAGE (1954, 1961), BARNARD (1959), JOHNSON/LEONE (1962a,b), WOODWARD/GOLDSMITH (1964), VAN DOBBEN DE BRUYN (1968), WETHERILL (1969) and BSI (1980a, 1980b, 1981, 1983).

The most important results of this section are summarized in table 4.6/1.

Type of chart	Characteristic	Example
Chart with memory of unlimited length	All sample vectors beginning from $j = 1$ are considered.	CUSUM chart EWMA chart
Chart with memory of limited length	Only the last k sample vectors are taken into account ($k > 1$).	MOSUM chart
Chart with uniform memory	The relevant sample vectors all have the same weight in the test statistic.	CUSUM chart MOSUM chart
Chart with nonuniform memory	The relevant sample vectors have different weights in the test statistic.	EWMA chart

Table 4.6.1: Two classifications for control charts with memory

4.6.2 CUSUM-Mean Charts

a) Introductory Remarks

We now want to illustrate how the test statistics of the SHEWHART-$\bar{x}$ chart and the CUSUM-$\bar{x}$ chart behave both when the process is undisturbed and when disturbances occur. This will very clearly show the basic differences between both charts. In all of the following derivations, we will assume that we are monitoring the level μ_t of a $no(\mu_t; \sigma_0^2)$-distributed quality characteristic X. The process variance σ_0^2 will be assumed to be constant. We have a given target value μ_0 for μ_t for which we want to early detect significant deviations above and below (*twosided* problem).

Assumption of a normally distributed quality characteristic with constant variance

In the SHEWHART-**mean chart** the test statistic is $Y_t = \bar{X}_{tn}$, i.e., the mean of a sample of size n taken at time t. The assumptions above imply that this statistic is $no(\mu_t; \sigma_0^2/n)$-distributed. In particular, it holds that

$$E(Y_t) = E(\bar{X}_{tn}) = \mu_t. \qquad (4.243\text{ a})$$

From this it follows that

Expectation of the test statistic of the classic $\bar{x}$ chart in the case of a constant process level μ

$$E(Y_t) \equiv \mu \quad \text{if } \mu_t \equiv \mu. \tag{4.243 b}$$

The values of the statistic $Y_t = \bar{X}_{tn}$ are, for a constant process level μ, spread around the line $y = \mu$ which is parallel to the time axis. For an undisturbed process, i.e., in the special case of $\mu = \mu_0$, the graph of the values of y_t – i.e., the line connecting the sequence of points (t, y_t) – is fluctuating around the line $y = \mu_0$.

In the **CUSUM-mean chart**, the deviations $\bar{X}_{jn} - \mu_0$ between the j-th sample average and the target value μ_0 are accumulated over all samples taken since the beginning of the process or since the time of the last intervention:

Test statistic of the CUSUM-$\bar{x}$ chart

$$Y_t = \sum_{j=1}^{t} (\bar{X}_{jn} - \mu_0). \tag{4.244}$$

Since $\bar{X}_{jn} \sim no(\mu_j, \sigma_0^2/n)$, the test statistic has the expectation

$$E(Y_t) = \sum_{j=1}^{t} \left[E(\bar{X}_{jn}) - \mu_0\right] = \sum_{j=1}^{t} (\mu_j - \mu_0). \tag{4.245 a}$$

In particular, from (4.244) it follows that

$$E(Y_t) = (\mu - \mu_0) \cdot t \qquad \text{if } \mu_t \equiv \mu. \tag{4.245 b}$$

Expectation of the test statistic of the CUSUM-$\bar{x}$ chart in the case of a constant process level μ

Thus, in the case of a constant process level μ, the expectation of the cumulated deviations $E(Y_t)$ is a linear function of t. The corresponding straight line has a slope $\mu - \mu_0$. If $\mu = \mu_0$, the graph of the values of Y_t is oscillating stochastically around the t-axis. If the test statistic (4.244) is drawn as a function of the sample number t, then, in the case of an undisturbed process, one gets a curve that is oscillating around the t-axis. If a shift of $\gamma := \mu - \mu_0$ starts to occur in the process level at time $t = t_0$, then, from time t_0 onwards, the curve will on the average follow a straight line with slope γ.

The following figure 4.6/1 illustrates this point. It shows how the test statistics of the two $\bar{x}$ charts behave on the average, if the process level μ_t agrees with the target value μ_0 until time t_0 and then is shifted by a fixed value $|\gamma|$ either upwards or downwards, from this point on.

We can see from figure 4.6.1b that even a minimal shift in the process level causes the CUSUM chart to depart more and more from the time axis. This explains why one evaluates the graph of a CUSUM chart by its slope. If the slope of the graph is too steep one will conclude that an intolerable

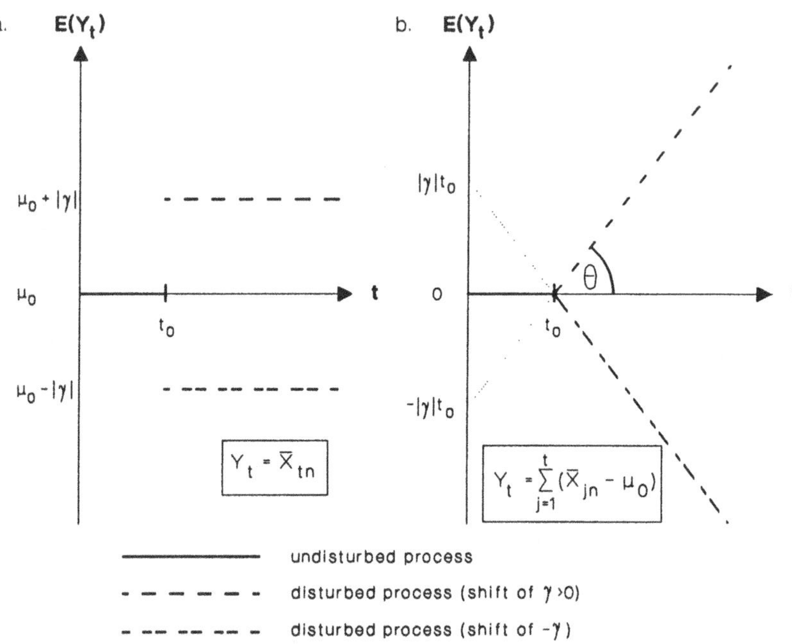

Figure 4.6.1: Expectation of the test statistic of a SHEWHART-$\bar{x}$ and CUSUM-$\bar{x}$ chart as a function of time
a) SHEWHART chart b) CUSUM chart

change in the process level has occurred and take corrective actions. In the SPC literature two procedures have been developed for evaluating a CUSUM graph:

Procedures for evaluating a CUSUM graph

- graphical evaluation by means of the so-called **V mask**, which is attributed to BARNARD (1959) and which is very easy to understand;
- the evaluation with a **tabular scheme**, due to PAGE (1954, 1961), which is more suitable where computer graphics facilities are lacking.

We will now explain these two procedures with the help of an "artificial" demonstration data set. The test theoretical background and the equivalence of the two procedures will be discussed thereafter.

b) Sensitivity of the CUSUM Chart towards Shifts in the Process Level and Procedures for Evaluation

The properties of the CUSUM-$\bar{x}$ chart, in comparison to the classical SHEWHART-$\bar{x}$ chart in particular, are best presented by applying the underlying monitoring schemes to a given data set. We will use such a common data set in order to investigate the behaviour of both these mean charts under shifts of the process level. In this context, we will also illustrate the evaluation of CUSUM graphs.

Comparing the CUSUM-$\bar{x}$ and the SHEWHART-$\bar{x}$ chart by means of simulated quality data

Let us assume that, at time t, the quality characteristic X under scrutiny is $no(\mu_t; \sigma_0^2)$-distributed. For the standard deviation of the process we are given the value $\sigma_0 = 20$ [mm], and the target value of the process level is given to be $\mu_0 = 100$ [mm]. At each of 30 time points, $t = 1, \ldots, 30$, samples of size $n = 5$ are generated by running a simulation – each time 5 realizations of the $no(100; 20^2)$-distributed random variable X.[16] These generated measurements are given in table 4.6/2 in column 2 and the corresponding sample means in column 3. According to (4.115), for $\alpha = 0.01$, the control limits of the SHEWHART-$\bar{x}$ chart result to be

$$\left.\begin{matrix} UCL \\ LCL \end{matrix}\right\} = \mu_0 \pm \frac{z_{0.995}}{\sqrt{5}} \cdot \sigma_0 \approx 100 \pm 1.152 \cdot 20 \approx \left\{\begin{matrix} 123.04 \\ 76.96. \end{matrix}\right. \tag{4.246}$$

The 30 sample averages in column 3 all lie within the control limits, as we would expect for an undisturbed process.

We will now consider two further process variants. In the first situation, the process level is disturbed at $t = 11$ by a shift $\gamma = -5$ [mm] from the target value $\mu_0 = 100$ to $\mu_t = 95$ [mm], where it remains until $t = 30$. In the second situation an upward shift occurs at $t = 16$. The level μ_t is increased from $\mu_0 = 100$ by $\gamma = +10$ to the value $\mu_t = 110$ and this shift again lasts until $t = 30$. If one expresses the mentioned shifts by using the standardised shift variable $\delta = (\mu - \mu_0)/\sigma_0 = \gamma/\sigma_0$ the described process disturbances are characterised by $\delta = -0.25$ and $\delta = 0.5$, respectively. The sample means corresponding to these two courses of the process are listed in colums 6 and 9 of table 4.6/2, respectively. The sample averages in column 6 are 5 [mm] lower than those in column 3 from $t = 11$ onwards, and those in column 9 are 10 [mm] higher than the corresponding values in column 3 from $t = 16$ onwards. All means are accentuated by bold-faced types as long as no process disturbance takes place. Please note that even after shift occurrence all means in columns 6 and 9 still lie within the control limits given by (4.246). This is clearly illustrated in figure 4.6/2, which displays the SHEWHART chart with the inspection results for the three different process courses.

Sensitivity of the SHEWHART chart towards the simulated shifts

[16] For this, we have used values z of a standard normally distributed random variable, since they are commonly generated by most pocket calculators. From these the realizations of a $no(\mu; \sigma^2)$-distributed random variable are obtained with the formula $x = \mu + z \cdot \sigma$ according to (2.48). The numbers x were then rounded to the nearest integer.

Time	Individual measurements					Sample statistics in an undisturbed process			Sample statistics in a disturbed process					
									Shift of $\delta_t = -0.25$ from $t = 11$ onwards			Shift of $\delta_t = +0.5$ from $t = 16$ onwards		
						$\bar{x}_{t5}$	$\bar{x}_{t5} - 100$	CUSUM	$\bar{x}_{t5}$	$\bar{x}_{t5} - 100$	CUSUM	$\bar{x}_{t5}$	$\bar{x}_{t5} - 100$	CUSUM
(1)	(2)					(3)	(4)	(5)	(6)	(7)	(8)	(9)	(10)	(11)
1	107	80	77	106	87	**91.4**	-8.6	-8.6	**91.4**	-8.6	-8.6	**91.4**	-8.6	-8.6
2	96	88	84	94	124	**97.2**	-2.8	-11.4	**97.2**	-2.8	-11.4	**97.2**	-2.8	-11.4
3	116	76	97	97	78	**92.8**	-7.2	-18.6	**92.8**	-7.2	-18.6	**92.8**	-7.2	-18.6
4	96	112	115	109	107	**107.8**	+7.8	-10.8	**107.8**	+7.8	-10.8	**107.8**	+7.8	-10.8
5	111	91	103	117	128	**110.0**	+10.0	-0.8	**110.0**	+10.0	-0.8	**110.0**	+10.0	-0.8
6	100	83	128	120	55	**97.2**	-2.8	-3.6	**97.2**	-2.8	-3.6	**97.2**	-2.8	-3.6
7	84	150	91	98	139	**112.4**	+12.4	+8.8	**112.4**	+12.4	+8.8	**112.4**	+12.4	+8.8
8	88	117	108	126	76	**103.0**	+3.0	+11.8	**103.0**	+3.0	+11.8	**103.0**	+3.0	+11.8
9	99	99	74	90	116	**95.6**	-4.4	+7.4	**95.6**	-4.4	+7.4	**95.6**	-4.4	+7.4
10	110	68	113	103	82	**95.2**	-4.8	+2.6	**95.2**	-4.8	+2.6	**95.2**	-4.8	+2.6
11	125	126	83	105	77	**103.2**	+3.2	+5.8	98.2	-1.8	+0.8	**103.2**	+3.2	+5.8
12	91	92	75	99	122	**95.8**	-4.2	+1.6	90.8	-9.2	-8.4	**95.8**	-4.2	+1.6
13	130	93	95	50	87	**91.0**	-9.0	-7.4	86.0	-14.0	-22.4	**91.0**	-9.0	-7.4
14	98	84	107	79	105	**94.6**	-5.4	-12.8	89.6	-10.4	-32.8	**94.6**	-5.4	-12.8
15	83	123	124	112	103	**109.0**	+9.0	-3.8	104.0	+4.0	-28.8	**109.0**	+9.0	-3.8
16	76	101	98	103	132	**102.0**	+2.0	-1.8	97.0	-3.0	-31.8	112.0	+12.0	+8.2
17	100	126	111	100	88	**105.0**	+5.0	+3.2	100.0	0.0	-31.8	115.0	+15.0	+23.2
18	120	99	106	121	102	**109.6**	+9.6	+12.8	104.6	+4.6	-27.2	119.6	+19.6	+42.8
19	93	80	107	107	146	**106.6**	+6.6	+19.4	101.6	+1.6	-25.6	116.6	+16.6	+59.4
20	99	115	91	69	89	**92.6**	-7.4	+12.0	87.6	-12.4	-38.0	102.6	+2.6	+62.0
21	74	126	116	95	92	**100.6**	+0.6	+12.6	95.6	-4.4	-42.4	110.6	+10.6	+72.6
22	91	100	86	66	93	**87.2**	-12.8	-0.2	82.2	-17.8	-60.2	97.2	-2.8	69.8
23	113	84	102	99	67	**93.9**	-7.0	-7.2	88.0	-12.0	-72.2	103.0	+3.0	+72.8
24	88	143	113	96	103	**108.6**	+8.6	+1.4	103.6	+3.6	-68.6	118.6	+18.6	+91.4
25	111	79	90	84	109	**94.6**	-5.4	-4.0	89.6	-10.4	-79.0	104.6	+4.6	+96.0
26	95	127	76	98	131	**105.4**	+5.4	+1.4	100.4	+0.4	-78.6	115.4	+15.4	+111.4
27	91	134	77	95	67	**92.8**	-7.2	-5.8	87.8	-12.2	-90.8	102.8	+2.8	+114.2
28	82	99	68	89	114	**90.4**	-9.6	-15.4	85.4	-14.6	-105.4	100.4	+0.4	+114.6
29	120	82	84	76	105	**93.4**	-6.6	-22.0	88.4	-11.6	-117.0	103.4	+3.4	+118.0
30	76	133	75	89	114	**97.4**	-2.6	-24.6	92.4	-7.6	-124.6	107.4	+7.4	+125.4

Table 4.6/2: Database for comparing the sensitivity of the SHEWHART-$\bar{x}$ and the CUSUM-$\bar{x}$ chart under shifts in the process level

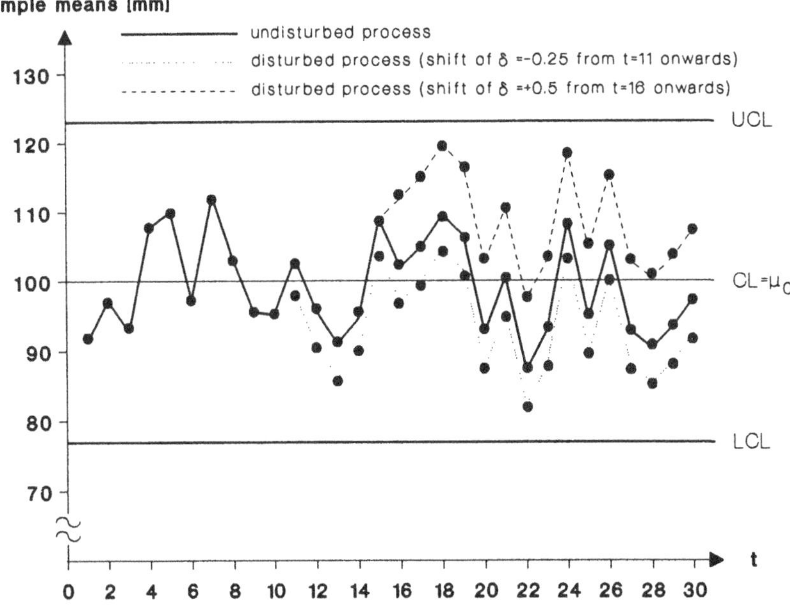

Figure 4.6/2: Sensitivity of the SHEWHART-$\bar{x}$ chart under shifts in the process level

We see from the example above that the SHEWHART-$\bar{x}$ chart did neither detect the shift of $\delta = -0.25$ nor the one of $\delta = +0.5$.

Sensitivity of the CUSUM chart towards the simulated shifts

How does the CUSUM-$\bar{x}$ chart behave in these three process situations? Table 4.6/2 also contains the CUSUM values calculated according to (4.245), i.e., the cumulated deviations $\bar{x}_{j5} - 100$ of the sample averages from the target value. Column 5 gives the CUSUM values for the undisturbed process. The two disturbed process variants are found in columns 8 and 11, respectively. Figure 4.6/3 shows how the cumulative sums develop. We can see that in the case of an undisturbed process the CUSUM values actually oscillate randomly around the t-axis. For the variants with negative and positive shifts the CUSUM values lie significantly higher and lower, respectively, than for the undisturbed process. They increasingly depart from the t-axis and seem to follow a linear trend.

The behaviour of the CUSUM values thus agrees with figure 4.6/1b. How can these CUSUM values be evaluated? When do we decide that the CUSUM values are decreasing or increasing too fast and conclude that an intolerable shift in the process level has occurred? We will now introduce the two procedures previously mentioned for the evaluation of CUSUM charts and illustrate them by means of our demonstration data set from table 4.6/2.

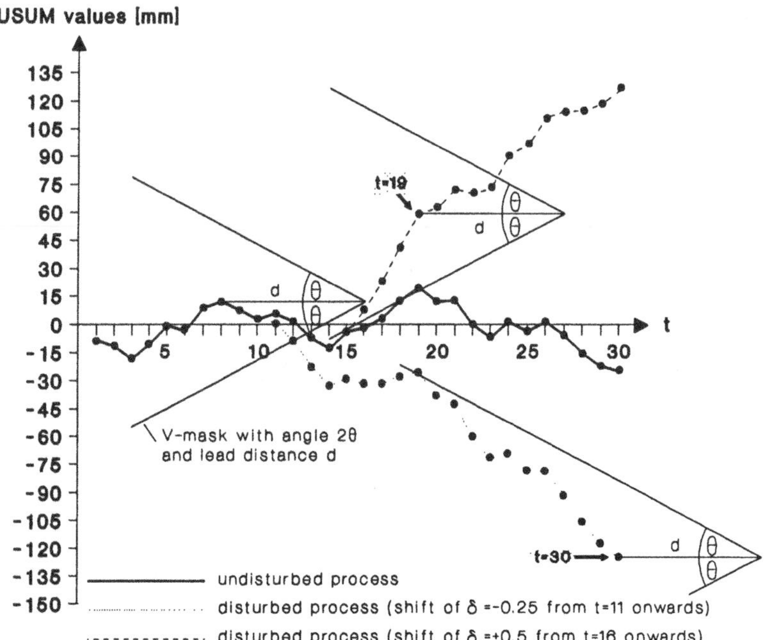

Figure 4.6/3: Sensitivity of the CUSUM-$\bar{x}$ chart under shifts in the process level (V-mask chart with $\Theta = 34.5$ and $d = 8$)

▷ Evaluation of a CUSUM chart with a V mask

By the term V mask we mean a template with a V-shaped cut-out. Its properties are defined by the lead distance d and the angle 2Θ:

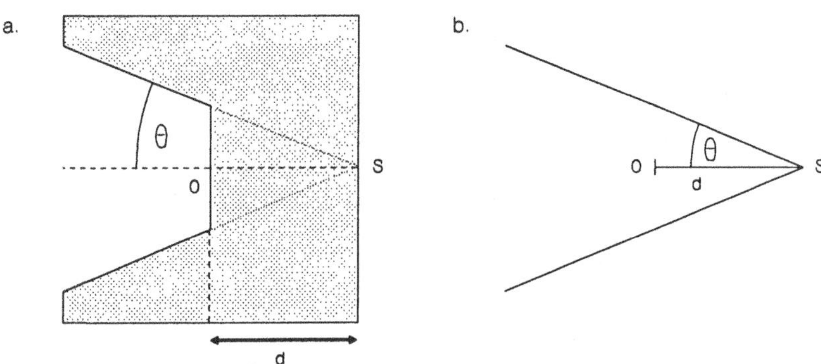

Figure 4.6/4: V mask with lead distance d and angle 2Θ
a) actual V mask b) simplified graphical representation

If a CUSUM graph is to be evaluated at time t with the help of a V mask, then one proceeds as follows:

V mask procedure

- One places the V mask as shown in figure 4.6.4 (with the opening to the left and with the line OS parallel to the t-axis).
- One moves the V mask so that the last point (t, y_t) of the CUSUM graph coincides with the point O of the V mask.

Now the following decision rule is applied:

- If the entire CUSUM graph, i.e., the line going through the point sequence $(1, y_1), \ldots, (t, y_t)$, lies within the V, then one will assume that the process level has not significantly departed from the target value μ_0 at time t. No corrective action is taken in this case.
- If the CUSUM line intersects one of the V mask borders, one considers this as evidence that at some point j $(1 \leq j \leq t)$ the process level has departed from the target value μ_0 to an extent requiring a corrective action. Depending on whether the upper or lower V mask arm was intersected, the process level has to be raised or lowered, respectively.

Illustration of the CUSUM evaluation with V mask using the demonstration data set

In figure 4.6/3 we used a V mask with angle $\Theta = 34.5^o$ and $d = 8$.[17] If this V mask is applied to the CUSUM graph corresponding to the undisturbed process from $t = 1$ to $t = 30$, one finds that no shift in the process level has occurred and thus no corrective action is indicated. For each of the thirty points, the sequence of points (j, y_j) to the left of this specific point lies within the V mask. In figure 4.6/3 the V mask is arbitrarily applied to the point $(8, y_8)$.

We will now consider the case where the process was disturbed by a shift of $\gamma = -5$ $(\delta = -0.25)$ starting at $t = 11$. It is very obvious that beginning at $t = 11$ the CUSUM graph is going downwards. If the same V mask is moved along the CUSUM graph, then the upper arm of the V mask is first intersected at $t = 30$. Thus, at $t = 30$, this CUSUM-$\bar{x}$ chart will cause a corrective action leading to an increase in the process level.

Let us now consider the case in figure 4.6/3 where the process is shifted by $\gamma = +10$ $(\delta = 0.5)$ from $t = 16$ onwards. If the V mask with $\Theta = 34.5^o$ and $d = 8$ is again moved along the CUSUM graph, then the lower arm of the mask is intersected at the point $(19, y_{19})$. Consequently, the CUSUM chart will cause a corrective action at $t = 19$ in this situation, which will result in lowering the process level.

In summary we want to state that in our example the CUSUM-$\bar{x}$ chart indicated both process disturbances whereas the SHEWHART-$\bar{x}$ chart did

---

[17] How the parameters of a V mask are specified will be discussed in section 4.6.2e.

not. In the situation with the larger shift the time until detection of the disturbance was shorter, as we would expect (3 time units for $\delta = 0.5$ compared to 19 time units for $\delta = -0.25$).

▷ Evaluation of a CUSUM chart using a tabular scheme

We will now describe the second procedure for evaluating CUSUM-$\bar{x}$ charts, that is the use of a **tabular CUSUM form**. This CUSUM scheme has – similar to the V mask – two positive parameters K and H. Instead of (4.244), in this procedure one looks at the two CUSUM variables defined by

$$S_t^+ := \sum_{j=1}^{t} (\bar{X}_{jn} - \mu_0 - K) \qquad (4.247\text{ a})$$

$$S_t^- := \sum_{j=1}^{t} (\bar{X}_{jn} - \mu_0 + K) \qquad (4.247\text{ b})$$

and tests whether their realizations s_t^+ and s_t^- have reached the limits of the decision interval $[-H, H]$. The reference value K is often chosen to be half the magnitude of the shift $\gamma = \mu - \mu_0$ which one is interested to quickly detect. The interval $[-H; H]$ normally corresponds to the interval $[LCL; UCL]$ in the SHEWHART control scheme. In particular, one proceeds as follows:

Procedure of the tabular CUSUM scheme

- As long as the conditions $\bar{X}_{jn} - \mu_0 - K \leq 0$ and $\bar{X}_{jn} - \mu_0 + K \geq 0$ are simultaneously satisfied, no values are entered into the chart.
- Beginning with $\bar{X}_{jn} - \mu_0 - K > 0$ one starts to form the sum S_t^+. This cumulative sum increases or decreases depending on the magnitude of each new term. If the sum reaches or falls below zero the summation stops. The same applies when S_t^+ reaches or exceeds the value H.
- Beginning with $\bar{X}_{jn} - \mu_0 + K < 0$ one forms the sum S_t^-. This sum also increases or decreases depending on each new term. If the sum reaches or exceeds zero the summation stops. The same applies if S_t^- reaches or falls below the value $-H$.
- After each time the accumulation of a sum stops, the accumulation of S_t^+ resumes whenever $\bar{X}_{jn} - \mu_0 - K > 0$ and, in the case of S_t^-, whenever $\bar{X}_{in} - \mu_0 + K < 0$.

During the entire procedure the following **decision rule** is used:

- As long as no values are entered into the chart or as long as the modified CUSUM values lie within the decision interval $[-H, H]$, one assumes that up to time t the process level has not significantly departed from the target value μ_0. No corrective action is taken.

- As soon as S_t^+ reaches the upper limit H or S_t^- reaches the lower limit $-H$, one assumes that at some time j $(j \leq t)$ the process level has deviated from the target level to an extent that makes it necessary to take a corrective action. Depending on whether this action is caused by S_t^+ or S_t^-, the process level will be raised or lowered, respectively.

The modified CUSUM values can be entered into a table or displayed graphically in a coordinate system as a function of t. The graphical approach has a similar structure as the SHEWHART control chart and is called **CUSUM status chart**. The control limits are again two parallel lines with an equal distance H to the centre line CL (here $CL = 0$).

Illustration of the CUSUM evaluation with the tabular scheme using the demonstration data set

We will illustrate the tabular CUSUM scheme again with the simulated demonstration data set of table 4.6/2. For these data and the three different process courses, we have calculated the values of the cumulative sums S_t^+ and S_t^- and listed them in columns 4, 6, 9, 11, 14 and 16 of table 4.6/3. For the parameters H and K we have chosen the values $K = 5.1473$ and $H = 41.1784$.[18] A horizontal line in a column of the table indicates a point where an accumulation starts and ends. For example, in the case of the undisturbed process variant, we can see that in column 6 the summation of S_t^- starts with $t = 1$ and ends with $t = 4$, then starts again with $t = 13$ and ends with $t = 15$. The formation of the sum S_t^+ (see column 4) for the case of the undisturbed process begins with $t = 4$ and ends with $t = 6$, then begins again immediately with $t = 7$ and ends with $t = 9$, and so on. The limits of the decision interval $[-H, H]$ are not reached until $t = 30$ for either S_t^- or S_t^+. The tabular CUSUM scheme thus until $t = 30$ does not lead to corrective actions, exactly as with the evaluation using the V mask in figure 4.6/3.

Let us now consider the process courses with negative shift $\delta = -0.25$ beginning at $t = 11$ and with positive shift $\delta = 0.5$ from $t = 16$ onwards. The limits of the decision interval are here reached at $t = 30$ and $t = 19$, respectively. The corresponding values $s_{30}^- < -H$ and $s_{19}^+ > H$ at the bottom of columns 11 and 14 in table 4.6/3 are emphasized through bold print. The intervention time points t agree with the values found with the V mask approach in figure 4.6/3. Figure 4.6/5 gives the graphical display of the tabular CUSUM scheme. In order to clarify the presentation we are presenting a separate graph for each of the three process courses.

[18] These values of K and H were determined in such a way that the tabular CUSUM procedure and the CUSUM V mask approach with $\Theta = 34.5°$ and $d = 8$ are equivalent.

Time	Sample statistics in an undisturbed process					Sample statistics in a disturbed process									
						Shift of $\delta_t = -0.25$ from $t = 11$ onwards					Shift of $\delta_t = +0.5$ from $t = 16$ onwards				
	$\bar{x}_{t5}$	$\bar{x}_{t5} - 100 - K$	s_t^+	$\bar{x}_{t5} - 100 + K$	s_t^-	$\bar{x}_{t5}$	$\bar{x}_{t5} - 100 - K$	s_t^+	$\bar{x}_{t5} - 100 + K$	s_t^-	$\bar{x}_{t5}$	$\bar{x}_{t5} - 100 - K$	s_t^+	$\bar{x}_{t5} - 100 + K$	s_t^-
(1)	(2)	(3)	(4)	(5)	(6)	(7)	(8)	(9)	(10)	(11)	(12)	(13)	(14)	(15)	(16)
1	91.4	-13.7473		-3.4527	-3.4527	91.4	-13.7473		-3.4527	-3.4527	91.4	-13.7473		-3.4527	-3.4527
2	97.2	-7.9473		2.3473	-1.1054	97.2	-7.9473		2.3473	-1.1054	97.2	-7.9473		2.3473	-1.1054
3	92.8	-12.3473		-2.0527	-3.1581	92.8	-12.3473		-2.0527	-3.1581	92.8	-12.3473		-2.0527	-3.1581
4	107.8	2.6527	2.6527	12.9473	9.7892	107.8	2.6527	-2.6527	12.9473	9.7892	107.8	2.6527	2.6527	12.9473	9.7892
5	110.0	4.8527	7.5054	15.1473		110.0	4.8527	7.5054	15.1473		110.0	4.8527	7.5054	15.1473	
6	97.2	-7.9473	-0.4419	2.3473		97.2	-7.9473	-0.4419	2.3473		97.2	-7.9473	-0.4419	2.3473	
7	112.4	7.2527	7.2527	17.5472		112.4	7.2527	7.2527	17.5472		112.4	7.2527	7.2527	17.5472	
8	103.0	-2.1473	5.1054	8.1473		103.0	-2.1473	5.1054	8.1473		103.0	-2.1473	5.1054	8.1473	
9	95.6	-9.5473	-4.4419	0.7473		95.6	-9.5473	-4.4419	0.7473		95.6	-9.5473	-4.4419	0.7473	
10	95.2	-9.9473		0.3473		95.2	-9.9473		0.3473		95.2	-9.9473		0.3473	
11	103.2	-1.9473		8.3473		98.2	-6.9473		3.3473		103.2	-1.9473		8.3473	
12	95.8	-9.3473		0.9473		90.8	-14.3473		-4.0527	-4.0527	95.8	-9.3473		0.9473	
13	91.0	-14.1473		-3.8527	-3.8527	86.0	-19.1473		-8.8527	-12.9054	91.0	-14.1473		-3.8527	-3.8527
14	94.6	-10.5473		-0.2527	-4.1054	89.6	-15.5473		-5.2527	-18.1581	94.6	-10.5473		-0.2527	-4.1054
15	109.0	3.8527	3.8527	14.1473	10.0419	104.0	-1.1473		9.1473	-9.0108	109.0	3.8527	3.8527	14.1473	10.0419
16	102.0	-3.1473	0.7054	7.1473		97.0	-8.1473		2.1473	-6.8635	112.0	6.8527	10.7054	17.1473	
17	105.0	-0.1473	0.5581	10.1473		100.0	-5.1473		5.1473	-1.7162	115.0	9.8527	20.5581	20.1473	
18	109.6	4.4527	5.0108	14.7473		104.6	-0.5473		9.7473	8.0311	119.6	14.4527	35.0108	24.7473	
19	106.6	1.4527	6.4627	11.7473		101.6	-3.5473		6.7473		116.6	11.4527	**46.4635**	21.7473	
20	92.6	-12.5473	-6.0838	-2.2527	-2.2527	87.6	-17.5473		7.2527	-7.2527					
21	100.6	-4.5473		5.7473	3.4946	95,6	-9.5473		0.7473	-6.5054					
22	87.2	-17.9473		-7.6527	-7.6527	82.2	-22.9473		-12.6527	-19.1581					
23	93.0	-12.1473		-1.8527	-9.5054	88.0	-17.1473		-6.8527	-26.0108					
24	108.6	3.4527	3.4527	13.7473	4.2419	103.6	-1.5473		8.7473	-17.2635					
25	94.6	-10.5473	-7.0946	-0.2527	-0.2527	89.6	-15.5473		-5.2527	-22.5162					
26	105.4	0.2527	0.2527	10.5473	10.2946	100.4	-4.7473		5.5473	-16.9689					
27	92.8	-12.3473	-12.0946	-2.0527	-2.0527	87.8	-17.3473		-7.0527	-24.0216					
28	90.4	-14.7473		-4.4527	-6.5101	85.4	-19.7473		-9.4527	-33.4743					
29	93.4	-11.7473		-1.4527	-7.9628	88.4	-16.7473		-6.4527	-39.9270					
30	97.4	-7.7473		2.5473	-5.4155	92.4	-12.7473		-2.4527	**-42.3797**					

Table 4.6/3: Tabular CUSUM-$\bar{x}$ scheme ($K = 5.1473$ and $H = 41.1784$)

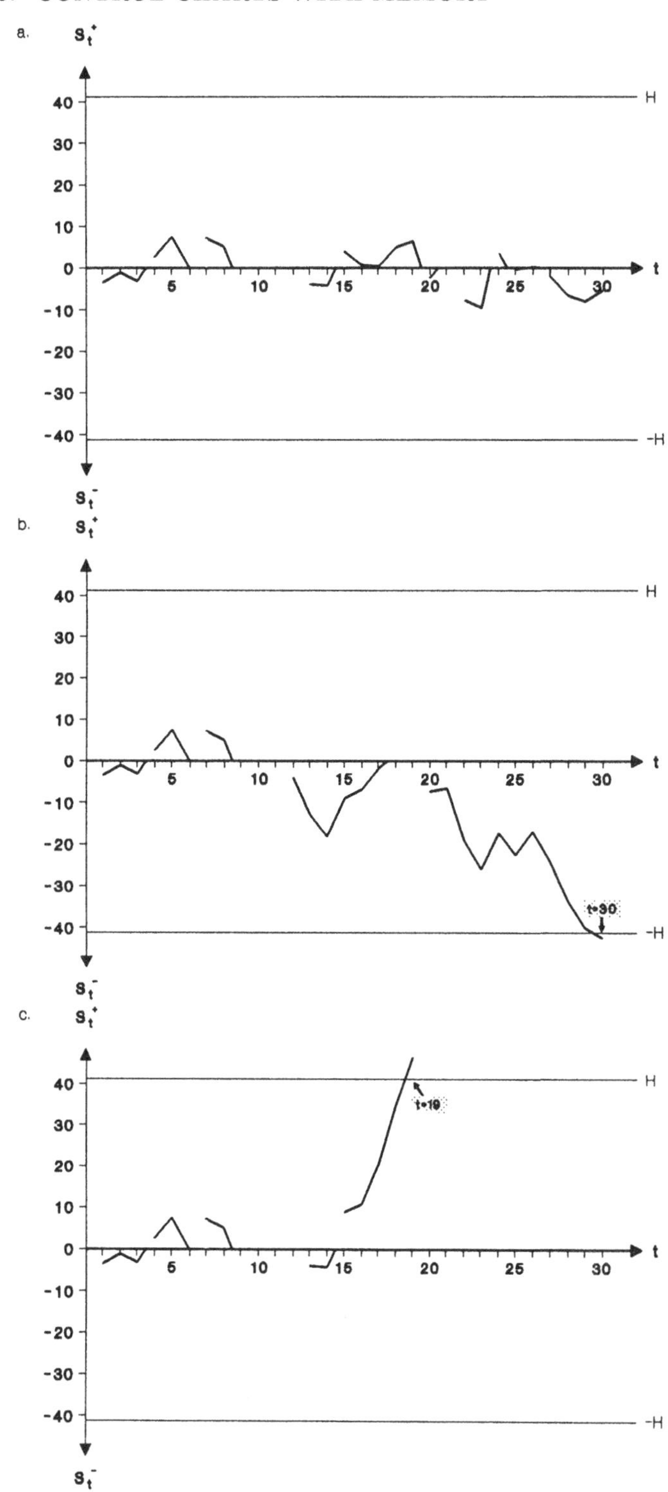

Figure 4.6/5: CUSUM-$\bar{x}$ chart ($K = 5.1473$ and $H = 41.1784$)
a) undisturbed process
b) disturbed process (shift of size $\delta = -0.25$ from $t = 11$ onwards)
c) disturbed process (shift of size $\delta = +0.5$ from $t = 16$ onwards)

Once an out-of-control situation has been observed at time t, the CUSUM chart allows, contrary to the SHEWHART chart, the chance of directly estimating the time j, of when the shift probably took place, as well as the amount and direction of the shift. The **estimate of the shift occurrence time** j can be subjectively taken to be the point where the graph apparently starts to significantly increase or decrease. A more objective estimate of j is given by the t-coordinate of the point where the CUSUM graph intersects an arm of the V mask. According to the latter method, in figure 4.6/3 we would estimate j to be 15 for the curve that is drifting upwards and to be 19 for the curve which is drifting downwards (true values: $j = 11$ and $j = 16$, respectively).

The **estimation of the out-of-control process level** μ or of the shift $\gamma = \mu - \mu_0$ is related to figure 4.6/1b. If one considers the upper line in this graph, then its slope γ for any $t > t_0 = j$ is given by

$$\gamma = \frac{E(Y_t) - E(Y_j)}{t - j}.$$

If one substitutes the two expectations in this equation by the observed CUSUM values y_t and y_j, then one gets an estimate $\hat{\gamma}$ of the shift $\gamma = \mu - \mu_0$ and, with $\hat{\mu} = \mu_0 + \hat{\gamma}$, an estimate for the new process level.
For the process course with shift $\gamma = -5$ in figure 4.6/3, we thus get

$$\hat{\gamma} = \frac{y_{30} - y_{19}}{30 - 19} = \frac{-124.6 - (-25.6)}{11} = -9; \qquad \hat{\mu} = 100 - 9 = 91.$$

For the course with $\gamma = +10$ the result is

$$\hat{\gamma} = \frac{y_{19} - y_{15}}{19 - 15} = \frac{59.4 - (-3.8)}{4} = 15.8; \qquad \hat{\mu} = 100 + 15.8 = 115.8.$$

Remark

For appropriately defined design parameters the CUSUM chart and the EWMA chart have the ability to detect small shifts. MITTAG (1991) found that this characteristic can be a disadvantage in the case of data with severe measurement errors. For example, if after the installation of a CUSUM chart a constant measurement error occurs at time t – e.g., after a new measuring device has been installed – then this error will appear as a shift (see figure 4.4/9). A SHEWHART chart would probably not react to this shift, but it is more likely that the CUSUM- or EWMA chart would give an alarm. Thus, the SHEWHART chart is less sensitive towards small disturbances of the process but more robust towards measurement errors.

c) Average Run Length (ARL)

For evaluating the performance of a CUSUM chart one usually recourses to the average run length because the power function of a control chart with memory cannot be represented in closed form. By **run length** we mean the random number of samples between two successive interventions. The **average run length** is the expectation of the run length. From figure 4.6/3, we know that the run length depends on how much the process deviates from the target value μ_0. It is convenient to measure the process shift not by $\gamma = \mu - \mu_0$ but by means of the dimensionless variable $\delta = (\mu - \mu_0)/\sigma_0$. The **ARL function** $ARL(\delta)$ specifies the relationship between the average run length and the process shift δ. It is obvious that $ARL(0)$ should be large and $ARL(\delta)$ small for large values of δ.

The derivation of the ARL function and the calculation of its values is rather complicated in the case of the CUSUM-$\bar{x}$ chart. It involves solving the so-called FREDHOLM integral equation which we do not want to discuss here. We refer the reader to JOHNSON/LEONE (1962) and KOTZ/JOHNSON (1982, vol. 2, p. 236f).

The first mentioned authors calculated the average run length of the CUSUM-$\bar{x}$ chart for various shifts δ and probabilities α of a false alarm and compared them to the average run length of the SHEWHART-$\bar{x}$ chart. Table 4.6/4 presents an excerpt of their results:

$\lvert\delta\rvert$	α				
	0.05	0.025	0.01	0.005	0.001
0.5	7.9*	13.9*	29.5*	52.7	209
	24.0	29.5	36.8	42.4	55.3
0.75	5.4*	8.8*	17.4	29.5	104
	10.6	13.1	16.4	18.8	24.6
1.00	3.8*	5.9*	10.8	17.4	54.6
	6.0	7.4	9.2	10.6	13.8
1.25	2.9*	4.0*	7.1	10.8	30.4
	3.8	4.7	5.9	6.8	8.8
2.00	2.4*	3.1*	4.9	7.1	17.9
	2.7	3.3	4.1	4.7	6.1

upper value: ARL of the CUSUM-$\bar{x}$ chart;
lower value: ARL of the SHEWHART-$\bar{x}$ chart

Table 4.6/4: ARL of the CUSUM-$\bar{x}$ chart and the SHEWHART-$\bar{x}$ chart (according to JOHNSON/LEONE 1962)

We can see that the ARL values of both charts increase as α and/or $|\delta|$ decrease. This is plausible and was to be expected. The cases where the CUSUM-ARL is lower than the SHEWHART-ARL are indicated in the table by an asterisk (*). At these points, with small shifts and not too small probabilities α, the CUSUM-$\bar{x}$ chart detects the shift in the process mean at an earlier stage. In the example illustrated in figures 4.6/2 and 4.6/3 we had $\delta = -0.25$ or $\delta = 0.5$ and $\alpha = 0.01$, and the CUSUM chart was the first to give alarm.[19] Consequently, it is especially recommended to apply the CUSUM chart in those situations where small shifts in the process are relevant and should be detected quickly.

d) Test-theoretical Background of CUSUM Charts

Running a CUSUM chart is equivalent to performing a **sequential LR test**, where in the case of a *onesided* CUSUM chart, the hypothesis test (4.34) has the form (2.157) or (2.162), respectively (test for positive or negative shift). In the case of a *twosided* CUSUM chart, according to (2.164) one tests the hypotheses

$$\begin{aligned} H_0 &: \mu_t = \mu_0 \\ H_1 &: \mu_t = \mu_0 \pm |\delta| \cdot \sigma_0. \end{aligned} \tag{4.248}$$

Applying the sequential LR test in the case of single observations

Suppose we have given probabilities α and β for committing type I and type II errors, respectively, when testing (4.248). In the case of the **CUSUM single value chart** the test is administered by taking a sample of size $n = 1$ from the production at time t, calculating the likelihood ratio LR_t according to (2.158) and testing whether it has the property $LR_t \leq A$, $LR_t \geq B$ or $LR_t \in (A; B)$, where[20]

$$A := \frac{\beta}{1 - \alpha/2} \tag{4.249 a}$$

$$B := \frac{1 - \beta}{\alpha/2}. \tag{4.249 b}$$

In section 2.3.3c we showed that this procedure is equivalent to testing whether the quasi-standard normally distributed variable

$$Z_t := \frac{1}{\sigma_0} \sum_{j=1}^{t} (X_j - \mu_0) \tag{4.250}$$

has a value z_t for which $|z_t| \leq a + ct$, $|z_t| \geq b + ct$ or $z_t \in I_t$ with the indifference interval

$$I_t := (a + ct; b + ct) \cup (-b - ct; -a - ct) \tag{4.251}$$

[19] Here we did not specify α explicitly; for this see example 4.6/1.

[20] Compared to (2.151) we need to replace α by $\alpha/2$ because H_0 is now tested against a twosided alternative.

Parameters of the indifference interval

defined by the parameters

$$a = \frac{\ln A}{|\delta|} = \frac{1}{|\delta|} \cdot \ln \frac{\beta}{1-\alpha/2} \qquad (4.252\text{ a})$$

$$b = \frac{\ln B}{|\delta|} = \frac{1}{|\delta|} \cdot \ln \frac{1-\beta}{\alpha/2} \qquad (4.252\text{ b})$$

$$c = \frac{|\delta|}{2}. \qquad (4.252\text{ c})$$

We accept H_0 in the first case and H_1 in the second case, whereas in the last case, we take a $(t+1)$-th sample and repeat the procedure.

How do we have to modify this procedure for the **CUSUM-$\bar{x}$ chart**? The preceeding presentation only changes marginally if one works with samples of arbitrary size n instead of samples of size $n = 1$ and uses the value z_t of the quasi-standardized CUSUM variable

Applying the sequential LR test when the sample mean is used as a test statistic

$$Z_t := \frac{1}{\sigma_0} \sum_{j=1}^{t} (\bar{X}_{jn} - \mu_0) \qquad (4.253)$$

instead of (4.250) for the decision to reject or accept the null hypothesis. The change is that the parameters a and b of the indifference interval have to be divided by n.

The variable Z_t differs from the usual CUSUM test statistic Y_t, introduced in (4.244), by a factor σ_0:

$$Y_t := \sum_{j=1}^{t} (\bar{X}_{jn} - \mu_0) = \sigma_0 \cdot Z_t. \qquad (4.254)$$

If one wants to work with the usual $no(0, t \cdot \sigma_0^2)$-distributed test statistic Y_t of the CUSUM-$\bar{x}$ chart for decision making, instead of using the $no(0, t \cdot 1)$-distributed variable Z_t, then the three parameters a, b and c have to be multiplied by σ_0. The parameters a, b and c of the indifference interval I_t are then defined as follows:[21]

$$a = \frac{\sigma_0}{n \cdot |\delta|} \cdot \ln \frac{\beta}{1-\alpha/2} = \frac{\sigma_0^2}{n \cdot |\gamma|} \cdot \ln \frac{\beta}{1-\alpha/2} \qquad (4.255\text{ a})$$

$$b = \frac{\sigma_0}{n \cdot |\delta|} \cdot \ln \frac{1-\beta}{\alpha/2} = \frac{\sigma_0^2}{n \cdot |\gamma|} \cdot \ln \frac{1-\beta}{\alpha/2} \qquad (4.255\text{ b})$$

[21] In order to not complicate the notation we are using the letters a, b and c for the parameters of the indifference interval regardless of the chosen test statistic.

$$c = \frac{\sigma_0 \cdot |\delta|}{2} = \frac{|\gamma|}{2}. \qquad (4.255\ c)$$

If $|y_t| \leq a + ct$ we accept H_0, for $|y_t| \geq b + ct$ we accept H_1, and in the case of $|y_t| \in I_t$ we draw an additional sample and repeat the decision procedure. If we display the limits of the indifference interval I_t for $t = 1, 2, \ldots$ in a coordinate system we get two point sequences which lie on straight lines with slope c and $-c$, respectively. The area within these lines is called the **continuation region** and has the shape of a V turned on its side. Its outer borders are the **rejection boundaries**. In practice however, one will never consider the hypothesis "H_0: the production is under statistical control" to be definitely confirmed and will continue to sample even if the test statistic falls into the acceptance region for H_0. Thus, in practice the standard approach is to make a decision about the process only if the test statistic falls into the rejection region of H_0, i.e., if $|y_t| \geq b + ct$.

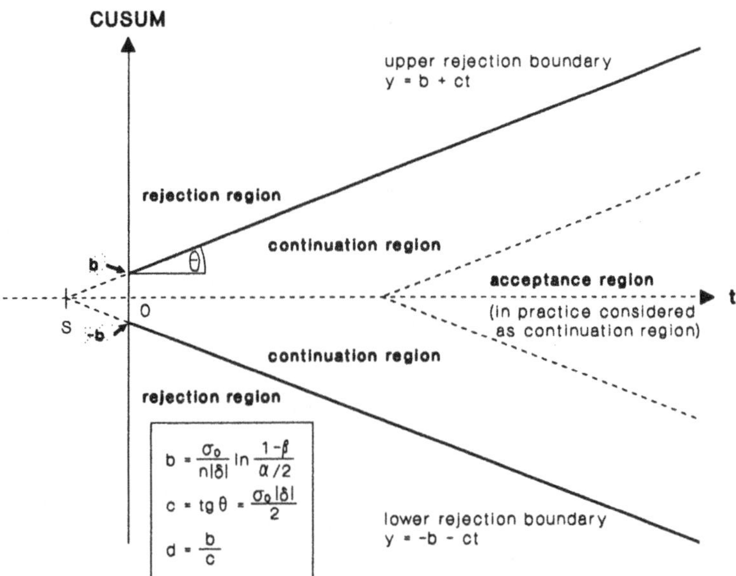

Figure 4.6/6: Running a CUSUM chart as application of a sequential LR test

Remarks

1. Hitherto, we have only introduced the twosided CUSUM-$\bar{x}$ chart. CUSUM charts for monitoring the process level can of course also be applied in an onesided approach. The administration of an *onesided* CUSUM chart is equivalent to performing a hypothesis test of type (4.248), if instead of $\pm$ we use only one of the signs in the formulation of the hypothesis H_1. When evaluating an onesided CUSUM-$\bar{x}$ chart with a V mask, one accordingly gets only "half a V" (upper or

lower part of figure 4.6/4). Its angle Θ is again determined by (4.258). The lead distance d is determined for a given α according to (4.257) where $\alpha/2$ is replaced by α. When evaluating the onesided CUSUM chart in tabular form one works with only one of the two test statistics S_t^+ and S_t^- from (4.247).

2. Due to lack of space we have neither discussed **CUSUM charts for monitoring the process spread** nor **CUSUM charts for count data.** Both these types of charts are possible with the V mask and in tabular form. We have also omitted modified CUSUM procedures aiming at improving the chart sensitivity at process start-up (**fast initial response CUSUM**) or at improving the ability to detect large shifts (**CUSUM schemes with parabolic V mask** or **combined** SHEWHART **CUSUM procedures**). We refer the interested reader to WADSWORTH/STEPHENS/GODFREY (1986, p.249ff), MONTGOMERY (1991, p.296ff) and RYAN (1989, p.162ff as well as p.193ff).

e) CUSUM-$\bar{x}$ Chart Design and Equivalence of V Mask and Tabular CUSUM Form

We already stressed that one usually evaluates the performance of a control chart with memory by means of the *ARL* criterion. The design procedure could also be based on given type I and type II error probabilities α and β, respectively. In the SPC literature one finds different *options* for designing a control chart with memory:

Approaches for designing a control chart with memory

- *Specifying the sample size n and the average run length ARL(0) for an undisturbed process*

  In the case of a CUSUM chart this approach implies that the chart parameters Θ and d (V mask CUSUM variant) or respectively K and H (tabular CUSUM scheme), are determined in such a way that the out-of control average run length ARL(δ) attains a minimum for a specified shift δ. This CUSUM design approach can be found in VAN DOBBEN DE BRUYN (1968), REYNOLDS (1975), KHAN (1978) and GAN (1991 b), for example.

- *Specifying the average run length ARL(0) for the undisturbed process as well as ARL(δ) for given shift δ*

  In the case of a CUSUM chart these specifications uniquely determine the parameters n, Θ and d or n, K and H. This design variant is discussed by KEMP (1961).

- *Specifying the sample size n as well as the probabilities α and β for the occurrence of false and neglected alarm, respectively*

  In the case of a CUSUM chart these specifications again uniquely determine the chart parameters. This CUSUM design approach goes back to JOHNSON/LEONE (1962).

When discussing the CUSUM chart design we will use the last mentioned approach, whereas the first described option will be illustrated in connection with the EWMA chart. Before dealing with the CUSUM chart design procedure we will point out that the V mask and the tabular CUSUM scheme are equivalent.

In order to illustrate the analogy between the tabular CUSUM scheme and the V mask procedure, we have extended the two rejection lines $y = b + ct$ and $y = -b - ct$ in figure 4.6/6 into the region of negative t-values until they intersect the t-axis. The rejection boundaries intersect the t-axis at $t = -b/c$. Thus, according to (4.255), the distance $d = b/c$ between the intersection point S and the origin satisfies the relationship

$$d = \frac{2}{n \cdot \delta^2} \cdot \ln \frac{1-\beta}{\alpha/2} = \frac{2\sigma_0^2}{n \cdot \gamma^2} \cdot \ln \frac{1-\beta}{\alpha/2}. \tag{4.256}$$

If we ignore β in this equation we get the very useful approximation

$$d \approx -\frac{2}{n \cdot \delta^2} \cdot \ln \frac{\alpha}{2} = -\frac{2\sigma_0^2}{n \cdot \gamma^2} \cdot \ln \frac{\alpha}{2}.^{22} \tag{4.257}$$

The procedure for testing the hypotheses (4.248) with test statistic (4.254) illustrated in figure 4.6/6 is also called a **forward sequential LR test**. The V mask CUSUM scheme is an equivalent sequential procedure which tests the same hypotheses (4.248) (see JOHNSON/LEONE 1962). Since the V in the V mask is pointing in the opposite direction, the V mask procedure is also called a **backward sequential LR test**. In the V mask CUSUM approach, one positions the V-shaped template at the most recent value y_t with a lead distance d. The V is open to the left and the point (t, y_t) is thus a moving origin. The boundaries of the V are the rejection lines in figure 4.6/6 and they form an angle of 2Θ. From this analogy we can deduce that, in the case of the CUSUM-$\bar{x}$ chart, the two parameters d and Θ of the V mask are determined by (4.256) and (4.257), respectively, and

$$\tan \Theta = \tfrac{1}{2} \cdot \sigma_0 \cdot |\delta|.$$

For the last equation, we can write equivalently that

$$\Theta = \arctan(\tfrac{1}{2} \cdot \sigma_0 \cdot |\delta|).$$

Determining the two parameters Θ and d of a V mask and introducing a scaling factor f

This determining equation for Θ can only be applied, however, in the special case when the scales of the horizontal t-axis and the vertical axis for the CUSUM values are chosen to be the same. In practice, one often works

[21] The value of d calculated according to (4.257) is always positive because $\ln(\alpha/2) < 0$.

with different measuring scales for t and y_t. Then one has to enlarge or reduce the angle Θ appropriately. Suppose that f units ($f > 0$) on the vertical axis correspond to one unit on the horizontal t-axis. Then Θ is determined according to the formula

$$\Theta = \arctan \frac{\sigma_0 \cdot |\delta|}{2f} = \arctan \frac{|\gamma|}{2f}. \tag{4.258}$$

In summary, we can say that the V mask parameters d and Θ of a CUSUM-$\bar{x}$ chart are determined according to the following instructions, provided that d is calculated by the approximation (4.257):

- First, specify the sample size n of the CUSUM-$\bar{x}$ chart, the scaling ratio f and a critical shift δ respectively $|\delta|$, as well as a corresponding probability α of a false alarm. The probability of a type II error (β) is neglected.

- With these specifications, and for a given process standard deviation σ_0, determine the lead distance d and the half angle Θ of the V mask by using (4.257) and (4.258).

Determining the tabular CUSUM scheme parameters K and H

The only thing that remains to be discussed is how to determine the parameters K and H of the tabular CUSUM scheme so that the evaluations of the CUSUM-$\bar{x}$ chart with the V mask and the tabular form are equivalent. Let us assume that we have determined a V mask with parameters d and Θ according to the above instructions. With the V mask there is no intervention as long as the change $|y_t - \mu_0|$ of the CUSUM graph from $t-1$ to t is smaller than $\tan\Theta$, i.e., as long as

$$|y_t - \mu_0| < \tan\Theta \quad \text{for } t = 1, 2, \ldots$$

With the tabular scheme no intervention is made unless

$$|y_t - \mu_0| < K \quad \text{for } t = 1, 2, \ldots.$$

Comparing these coefficients gives the condition $K = \tan\Theta$ for the equivalence of the two approaches. If we take the scaling factor f of the V mask into account we get

$$K = f \cdot \tan\Theta. \tag{4.259}$$

A similar simple relationship can be found for the parameters d and H of the two procedures. In order to derive this relationship we will now consider a process with CUSUM values which increase from $t = t_0$ onwards.

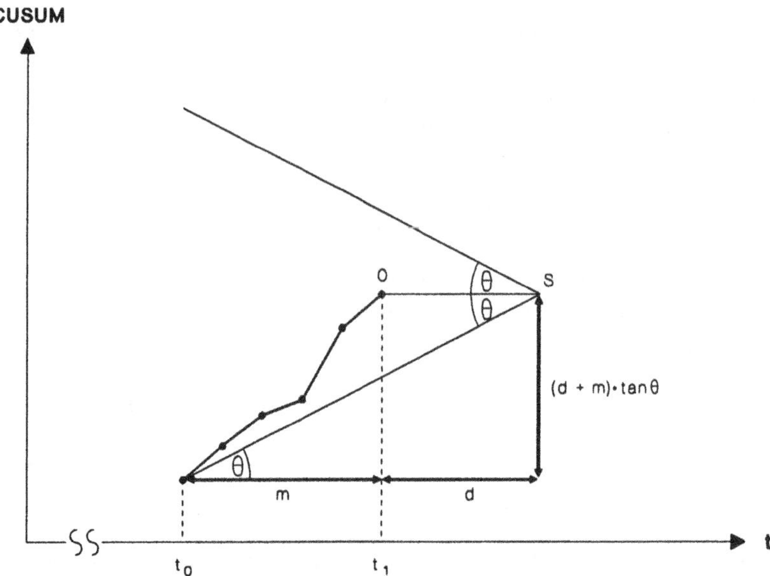

Figure 4.6/7: Equivalence of V mask and tabular CUSUM scheme

We can see from figure 4.6/7 that the CUSUM evaluation with the V mask leads to an intervention at time $t_1 = t_0 + m$ if the following holds:

$$\sum_{j=t_0}^{t_0+m} (y_j - \mu_0) \geq (d+m) \cdot \tan\Theta.$$

After elementary transformations, this inequality becomes

$$\sum_{j=t_0}^{t_0+m} (y_j - \mu_0 - \tan\Theta) \geq d \cdot \tan\Theta.$$

The tabular CUSUM scheme leads to an intervention at time $t_1 = t_0 + m$ if

$$\sum_{j=t_0}^{t_0+m} (y_j - \mu_0 - K) \geq H$$

is satisfied. A comparison of the coefficients yields $H = d \cdot \tan\Theta$ or, in the case of taking a scaling factor f into account,

$$H = d \cdot f \cdot \tan\Theta. \tag{4.260}$$

Example 4.6/1

When specifying the CUSUM-$\bar{x}$ chart with V mask in the illustrative example in section 4.6.2b we determined d and Θ in a slightly different way than had been previously outlined. Instead of specifying for a given sample size n a shift δ and a blind alarm probability α related to this shift, we specified the lead distance $d = 8$ of the V mask besides n and the probability α to ensure that d is a "round" number. We specified the value 0.01 for α because the control limits (4.246) of the SHEWHART chart were calculated with $\alpha = 0.01$.

Thus, we determined the V mask for the given values $\alpha = 0.01$ and $d = 8$ and calculated the critical shift γ, or $\delta = \gamma/\sigma_0$, for these specifications. The value of $|\gamma|$ is obtained by solving for $|\gamma| = \sqrt{\gamma^2}$ in (4.257) and setting $\sigma_0 = 20$, $n = 5$, $\alpha = 0.01$ and $d = 8$:

$$|\gamma| = \sqrt{-\frac{2\sigma_0^2}{nd}\ln\frac{\alpha}{2}} = \sqrt{-\frac{2\cdot 400}{5\cdot 8}\ln 0.005} \approx 10.2940.$$

It then follows for $|\delta| = |\gamma|/\sigma_0$ that

$$|\delta| = \frac{|\gamma|}{20} \approx \frac{10.2940}{20} = 0.5147.$$

In figure 4.6/3, every 7.5 units on the CUSUM axis correspond to one unit on the time axis, i.e., $f = 7.5$. With this value we get the following result for Θ:

$$\Theta = \arctan\frac{|\gamma|}{2f} = \arctan\frac{10.2940}{15} = \arctan 0.6863 \approx 34.5^o.$$

If we want to apply the tabular CUSUM scheme which is equivalent to the V mask then we need to determine the tabular form parameters according to (4.259) and (4.260). With $d = 8$, $\Theta = 34.5°$ and the scale factor $f = 7.5$ it results that

$$\begin{aligned} K &= 7.5\cdot\tan 34.5^o = 7.5\cdot 0.6863 \approx 5.1473 \\ H &= 8\cdot 7.5\cdot\tan 34.5^o \approx 41.1784 \end{aligned}$$

These are exactly the values that we used in figure 4.6/5.

Problem 4.6/1

a) Which factors influence the parameters Θ and d of a V mask and what is their influence?

b) Suppose a twosided CUSUM-$\bar{x}$ chart with sample size $n = 5$ is operated with a V mask. What are the values of the parameters Θ and d of the V mask if one wants to detect shifts of size $|\gamma| = 1$ and specifies $\alpha = 0.01$. Suppose that $\sigma_0 = 2$. The scaling of the chart is chosen so that 0.5 units on the CUSUM axis correspond to 1 unit on the time axis.

4.6.3 EWMA-Mean Charts

a) Introductory Remarks

We will now discuss the EWMA chart, first introduced by ROBERTS (1959), which represents a further alternative to the classical SHEWHART control chart. The EWMA chart is, similar to the CUSUM chart, very sensitive towards small disturbances but is easier to understand and simple to apply. Analogous to the CUSUM chart we will only discuss the *twosided* EWMA-$\bar{x}$ chart. We will assume that at any sampling time t the monitored quality characteristic is $no(\mu_t, \sigma_0^2)$-distributed. A target value for μ_t is given by μ_0.

Assuming a normally distributed quality characteristic with constant variance

The test statistic of the **EWMA-mean chart** is defined by the recursive relationship

Test statistic of the EWMA-$\bar{x}$ chart

$$Y_t = (1-d) \cdot Y_{t-1} + d \cdot \bar{X}_{tn}, \; 0 < d \leq 1, \tag{4.261}$$

where $\bar{X}_{tn}$ denotes the $no(\mu_t, \sigma_0^2/n)$-distributed mean of the t-th sample and d a design parameter which can be arbitrarily specified within a given range. Taking the starting value $Y_0 := \mu_0$ we get the equivalent representation

$$Y_t = (1-d)^t \cdot \mu_0 + d \cdot \sum_{j=1}^{t} (1-d)^{t-j} \cdot \bar{X}_{jn}. \tag{4.262}$$

If one puts the values $t,\ t-1, \ldots$ for j in (4.262) one can see that the most current mean has the weight d, the preceeding the weight $d \cdot (1-d)$ and so on. The weight factors $b_j = d \cdot (1-d)^{t-j}$ of the sample means form a geometric series over time[23]. The sum

$$d \cdot \sum_{j=1}^{t} (1-d)^{t-j} = d \cdot \sum_{j=0}^{t-1} (1-d)^j = d \cdot \left[\frac{1-(1-d)^t}{1-(1-d)} \right] = 1-(1-d)^t$$

[23] Because of this the EWMA chart is sometimes called **geometric moving average chart** or **GMA chart**.

of these factors converges to 1 as $t \to \infty$:

$$\lim_{t\to\infty} d \cdot \sum_{j=1}^{t} (1-d)^{t-j} = 1 - \lim_{t\to\infty} (1-d)^t = 1. \tag{4.263}$$

Effect of the design parameter d

When specifying the design parameter d one makes a decision on how much previous sample results influence the present decision. The larger d is chosen the smaller is the influence of the quality history. The more d approaches the value 1 the more the test statistic of the EWMA chart resembles the test statistic of the SHEWHART chart. If one sets $d = 1$ in (4.261) or the more general representation (4.239) then one actually gets the memoryless test statistic of the SHEWHART chart. The more the value of d approaches 0 – the value $d = 0$ was excluded in (4.261) and (4.239) because in this case the recursion (4.261) does not work – the more the weight factors resemble those of the CUSUM chart. Thus, with respect to the importance of previous sample results, the EWMA chart lies between the SHEWHART and the CUSUM chart and one can actually choose its position between those two charts (see problem 4.6/2).

Structure of an EWMA chart for monitoring the process location

The structure of an EWMA-$\bar{x}$ chart is in principle not different to that of a classical SHEWHART-$\bar{x}$ chart. The EWMA chart also has a centre line CL at the target level $CL = \mu_0$ which describes the path of the test statistic in the case of an undisturbed process. The control limits UCL and LCL are positioned at the levels $CL \pm k \cdot \sigma_{Y_t}$, where k denotes a suitable constant and σ_{Y_t} the standard deviation of the EWMA test statistic at time t:

$$\left.\begin{matrix} UCL \\ LCL \end{matrix}\right\} = CL \pm k \cdot \sigma_{Y_t} = \mu_0 \pm k \cdot \sigma_{Y_t}. \tag{4.264}$$

Taking into account that the sample averages are independently and identically $no(\mu_t; \sigma_0^2/n)$-distributed one can derive the following form for the variance of the variables (4.262):

Variance of the EWMA test statistic

$$\sigma_{Y_t}^2 = \frac{\sigma_0^2}{n} \cdot \left(\frac{d}{2-d}\right) \cdot \left[1 - (1-d)^{2t}\right]. \tag{4.265}$$

For $t \to \infty$ one gets the asymptotic variance σ_a^2 of the EWMA test statistic:

$$\sigma_a^2 := \lim_{t\to\infty} \sigma_{Y_t}^2 = \frac{\sigma_0^2}{n} \cdot \frac{d}{2-d}. \tag{4.266}$$

Different to the SHEWHART chart, the variance of the EWMA test statistic and thus the levels of the control limits depend on the time t of observation. However, the asymptotic values

Asymptotic control limits of a twosided EWMA chart

$$\left.\begin{matrix} UCL_a \\ LCL_a \end{matrix}\right\} = CL \pm k \cdot \sigma_a = \mu_0 \pm k \cdot \sigma_0 \cdot \sqrt{\frac{d}{n \cdot (2-d)}} \tag{4.267}$$

of the control limits are, in approximation, usually reached very quickly. I.e., after evaluation of a moderately large number of samples the EWMA test statistic has sufficiently "constructed" itself so that one can approximate its variance by (4.266) and its control limits by (4.267). The speed of convergence of (4.264) to (4.267) is influenced by the choice of the initial value Y_0 and also of the design parameter d, the so-called **smoothing constant** (see figure 4.6/8).

Problem 4.6/2

a) Calculate the relative weights $w_j := b_{t-j}/b_t$ of an EWMA chart with design parameter $d = 0.1; 0.15; 0.20; 0.25$ and 0.30 for $j = 1, 2, \ldots, 10$. Present the result in tabular form and comment.

b) In the case of $d = 0.30$ the inequality $w_j < 0.03$ for the weight of the j-th previous sample outcome holds for $j > 9$. This means that in the EWMA approach with $d = 0.3$ a sample outcome which lies back more than 9 time units has less than 3% weight in the present result. How large do we need to choose j in case of $d = 0.1$ in order to drop below this threshold of 3%?

b) Average Run Length (ARL) and Design of EWMA-$\bar{x}$ Charts

An EWMA chart is completely determined by the sample size n, the design parameter d which defines the weight of the quality history, and the factor k in (4.264). As with the CUSUM chart, in the case of the EWMA chart one has to think about how long one wants an undisturbed process to run before it is interrupted by a false alarm. One also has to determine a process shift $\delta = (\mu - \mu_0)/\sigma_0$ or respectively $|\delta|$ which one wants to be detected by the EWMA chart with certainty, i.e., with not too much delay. The performance of an EWMA chart is evaluated, as with all other control charts having a memory, by means of the **average run length (ARL)**. The derivation of the ARL function $ARL(\delta)$ is, similar to the case of the CUSUM chart, rather complicated; one again ends up with FREDHOLM-type integral equations. We will omit the presentation of these equations and refer to CROWDER (1987b,1989).

Constructing an EWMA chart

If one considers the sample size n to be a constant determined by the production circumstances then the design of an EWMA chart requires specification of exactly two parameters, i.e., d and k. We will confine to present an EWMA design procedure suggested by CROWDER (1989)[24]:

▷ Step 1: *Specifying ARL(0) and the critical shift* δ

We first specify the in-control average run length $ARL(0)$ and the standardized critical shift δ that we want to detect. Here, in the case of a twosided EWMA chart we will specify the absolute value $|\delta|$. The specification of $ARL(0)$, i.e., the expected time between two false alarms, can, for example, be based on economic considerations (cost of interrupting the process, cost of a false alarm). The choice of the critical shift δ which one wants to detect quickly depends on company specific economic factors as well as technical circumstances (cost of a corrective action, process capability).

▷ Step 2: *Optimally choosing the smoothing constant* d

The smoothing constant d is chosen so that the out-of-control average run length $ARL(\delta)$, i.e., the expected process run length after occurrence of the critical shift δ, attains a minimum. In order to enable professionals to solve this optimization problem CROWDER (1989, p. 158 - 159) has developed nomograms from which the value of d can be easily obtained.

▷ Step 3: *Determining the chart parameter* k

The specification of $ARL(0)$ from step 1 was not necessary for determining the smoothing constant d, but is now used for determining the remaining design parameter k. Among all possible EWMA charts with the parameters (d, k) and d from step 2 one will now choose the chart which satisfies the specification for $ARL(0)$. CROWDER (1989, p. 160-161) also gives nomograms for this step.

We remind the reader that CROWDER uses a shift variable that is defined differently from our form. His shift variable is a multiple of the standard deviation $\sigma_0/\sqrt{n}$ of the sample mean. Denoting CROWDER's shift variable by Δ, the relation between our shift variable δ and his form is given by $\Delta = \delta \cdot \sqrt{n}$.

Which types of errors are controlled?

The preceeding description shows that the design of an EWMA chart may take into account the probability of type I as well as type II errors. The same holds for the CUSUM chart but not for the classical SHEWHART-chart in which only the type I error is explicitly considered (see again figure 4.2/2). The type I error in the EWMA chart is controlled by specifying $ARL(0)$. This corresponds to specifying the probability of a false alarm $\alpha = 1/ARL(0)$ in a SHEWHART chart. In the EWMA chart as well as other control charts with memory the control of the type II error (neglected alarm) is achieved by specifying $ARL(\delta)$ with the given critical shift δ.

[24] Other EWMA design options were outlined in section 4.6.2e.

c) Sensitivity of the EWMA Chart towards Shifts in the Process Level

Comparing the EWMA-$\bar{x}$ and the SHEWHART-$\bar{x}$ chart by means of simulated data

In order to illustrate the EWMA chart performance and to demonstrate the flexibility of this chart we will again draw on the data set from column 2 of table 4.6/2. This data set contains 150 values of a $no(100, 20^2)$-distributed random variable which were obtained from 30 samples of size $n = 5$. We will consider all the sample averages which result for the undisturbed process as well as those that were obtained after occurrence of a standardized shift of magnitude $\delta = -0.25$ or $\delta = 0.5$ at time $t = 11$ or $t = 16$, respectively (columns 3, 6 and 9). For these three processes the following table 4.6/5 shows the behaviour of the test statistic (4.262) for two EWMA charts which are both based on an in-control value $ARL(0) = 100$ but differ with respect to their sensitivity against process disturbances. The first chart, EWMA-1, is – similar to the CUSUM chart in figure 4.6/3 and example 4.6/1 – designed for the critical shift $\delta = 0.5147$. From the first nomogram in CROWDER (1989, p.158) one can see that the parameter d which minimises the out-of-control average run length $ARL(0.5)$ has to be $d \approx 0.23$. Using the second nomogram in CROWDER (1989, p.159) one finds for the side condition $ARL(0) = 100$ that the parameter k has to be taken as $k \approx 2.4$. The second chart, EWMA-2, with $d = 0.57$ is designed to detect a larger process disturbance ($\delta = 1.0$). The second nomogram tells us that for the side condition $ARL(0) = 100$ the value for k is $k \approx 2.55$.

Figure 4.6/8 shows both EWMA charts as well as the behaviour of the test statistic for the three different process courses.[25] We can see in part a) of the graph that the EWMA-1 quickly detects the process disturbance in the case of the two process variants corresponding to the broken lines. The time between occurrence and detection of the disturbance is only 2 time units for the shift $\delta = 0.5$; in the case of the process with $\delta = -0.25$ it is 12 time units. The SHEWHART chart in figure 4.6/2 did not detect these shifts within the observation period, whereas the comparable CUSUM chart from figure 4.6/3 needed 3 time units in the case of $\delta = 0.5$ and 19 time units in the case of $\delta = -0.25$. If the production circumstances allow some variation in the process level or if the measuring instruments are not very precise then in order to avoid too frequent corrective actions one will specify a larger critical shift δ and choose the less sensitive chart EWMA-2. Figure 4.6/8b indicates that this chart needed 2 time units for detecting a shift of magnitude $\delta = 0.5$ whereas it did not signal the negative shift until $t = 30$.

[25] A comparison of figure 4.6/3 and 4.6/8 shows that the EWMA test statistic smoothes the sample means. This explains why transforming the original sample statistics into the EWMA variable is called **exponential smoothing**. The smaller the smoothing constant d is chosen the more of the original variation is filtered out.

Time	Individual measurements					Sample statistics in an undisturbed process			Sample statistics in a disturbed process					
									Shift of $\delta_t = -0.25$ from $t = 11$ onwards			Shift of $\delta_t = +0.5$ from $t = 16$ onwards		
						$\bar{x}_{t5}$	EWMA-1	EWMA-2	$\bar{x}_{t5}$	EWMA-1	EWMA-2	$\bar{x}_{t5}$	EWMA-1	EWMA-2
(1)	(2)					(3)	(4)	(5)	(6)	(7)	(8)	(9)	(10)	(11)
1	107	80	77	106	87	**91.4**	98.02	95.10	**91.4**	98.02	95.10	**91.4**	98.01	95.10
2	96	88	84	94	124	**97.2**	97.83	96.30	**97.2**	97.83	96.30	**97.2**	97.83	96.30
3	116	76	97	97	78	**92.8**	96.68	94.30	**92.8**	96.68	94.30	**92.8**	96.68	94.30
4	96	112	115	109	107	**107.8**	99.23	102.0	**107.8**	99.23	102.0	**107.8**	99.23	102.0
5	111	91	103	117	128	**110.0**	101.71	106.66	**110.0**	101.71	106.66	**110.0**	101.71	106.66
6	100	83	128	120	55	**97.2**	100.67	101.22	**97.2**	100.67	101.22	**97.2**	100.67	101.22
7	84	150	91	98	139	**112.4**	103.37	107.59	**112.4**	103.37	107.59	**112.4**	103.37	107.59
8	88	117	108	126	76	**103.0**	103.28	104.98	**103.0**	103.28	104.98	**103.0**	103.28	104.98
9	99	99	74	90	116	**95.6**	101.52	99.63	**95.6**	101.52	99.63	**95.6**	101.52	99.63
10	110	68	113	103	82	**95.2**	100.06	97.11	**95.2**	100.06	97.11	**95.2**	100.06	97.11
11	125	126	83	105	77	**103.2**	100.79	100.58	98.2	99.64	97.73	**103.2**	100.79	100.58
12	91	92	75	99	122	**95.8**	99.64	97.86	90.8	97.60	93.78	**95.8**	99.64	97.86
13	130	93	95	50	87	**91.0**	97.65	93.95	86.0	94.93	89.35	**91.0**	97.65	93.95
14	98	84	107	79	105	**94.6**	96.95	94.32	89.6	93.17	89.49	**94.6**	96.95	94.32
15	83	123	124	112	103	**109.0**	99.72	102.69	104.0	96.07	97.76	**109.0**	99.72	102.69
16	76	101	98	103	132	**102.0**	100.25	102.30	97.0	96.29	97.33	112.0	102.55	108.00
17	100	126	111	100	88	**105.0**	101.34	103.84	100.0	97.14	98.85	115.0	105.41	111.99
18	120	99	106	121	102	**109.6**	103.24	107.12	104.6	98.86	102.13	119.6	108.67	116.33
19	93	80	107	107	146	**106.6**	104.01	106.82	101.6	99.49	101.83	116.6	110.50	116.48
20	99	115	91	69	89	**92.6**	101.39	98.72	87.6	96.75	93.72	102.6	108.68	108.57
21	74	126	116	95	92	**100.6**	101.21	99.79	95.6	96.49	94.79	110.6	109.12	109.73
22	91	100	86	66	93	**87.2**	97.98	92.61	82.2	93.20	87.61	97.2	106.38	102.59
23	113	84	102	99	67	**93.9**	96.84	92.83	88.0	92.01	87.83	103.0	105.60	102.82
24	88	143	113	96	103	**108.6**	99.54	101.82	103.6	94.67	96.82	118.6	108.59	111.82
25	111	79	90	84	109	**94.6**	98.41	97.70	89.6	93.51	92.70	104.6	107.67	107.70
26	95	127	76	98	131	**105.4**	100.01	102.09	100.4	95.09	97.09	115.4	109.45	112.09
27	91	134	77	95	67	**92.8**	98.36	96.80	87.8	93.41	91.80	102.8	107.92	106.79
28	82	99	68	89	114	**90.4**	96.53	93.15	85.4	91.57	88.15	100.4	106.19	103.15
29	120	82	84	76	105	**93.4**	95.81	93.29	88.4	90.84	88.29	103.4	105.55	103.29
30	76	133	75	89	114	**97.4**	96.18	95.63	92.4	91.20	90.63	107.4	105.97	105.63

Table 4.6/5: Database for comparing the sensitivity of SHEWHART-$\bar{x}$ and and EWMA-$\bar{x}$ chart under shifts in the process level (EWMA-1: $d = 0.23; k = 2.4$; EWMA-2: $d = 0.57; k = 2.45$)

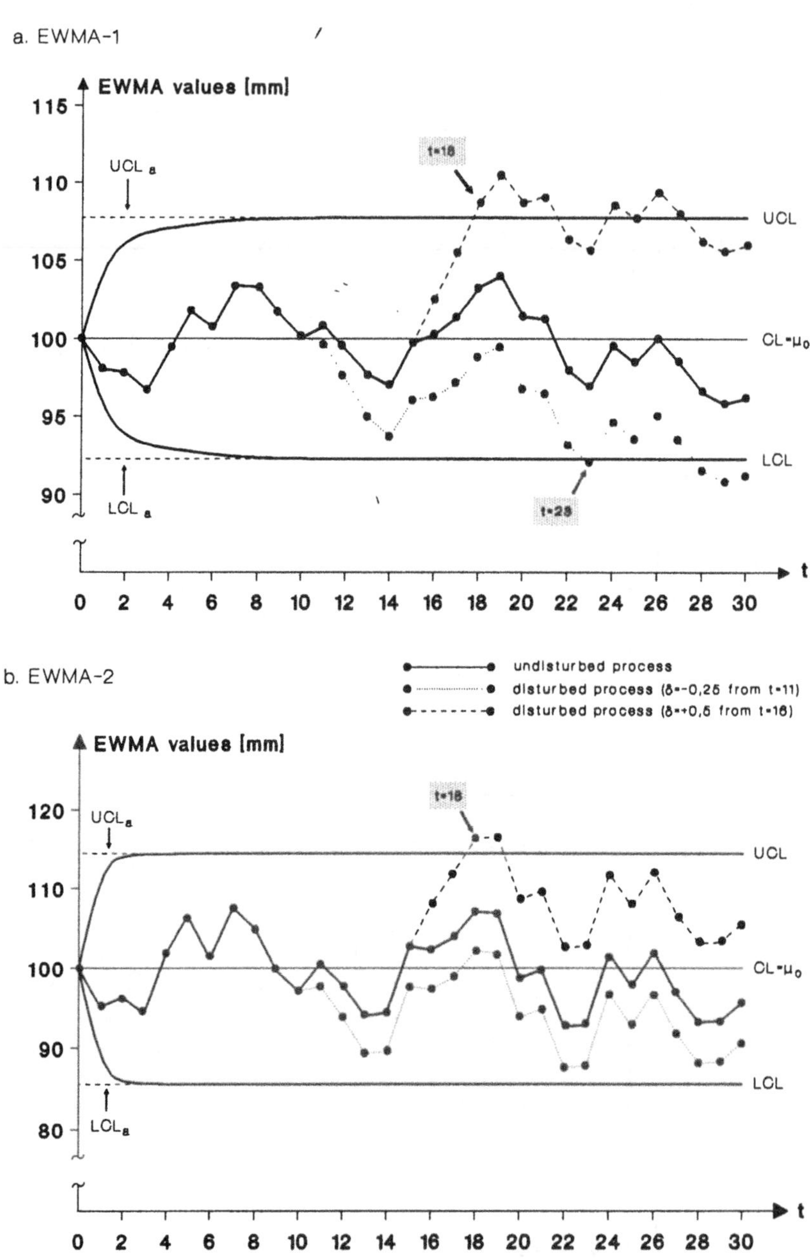

Figure 4.6/8: **Sensitivity of the EWMA chart with respect to shifts in the process level**
a) EWMA-1 with $d = 0.23$ and $k = 2.4$
b) EWMA-2 with $d = 0.57$ and $k = 2.55$

5 Statistical Tables

N	n	M	k	Hy(k | N;M;n)	hy(k | N;M;n)
20	9	6	0	0,011919	0,011919
20	9	6	1	0,119195	0,107276
20	9	6	2	0,425697	0,306502
20	9	6	3	0,783282	0,357585
20	9	6	4	0,962074	0,178793
20	9	6	5	0,997833	0,035759
20	9	6	6	1,000000	0,002167
20	9	9	5	0,905097	0,247559
20	9	9	6	0,987616	0,082520
20	9	9	7	0,999405	0,011789
20	9	9	8	0,999994	0,000589
20	9	9	9	1,000000	0,000006

N	n	M	k	Hy(k | N;M;n)	hy(k | N;M;n)
20	10	1	0	0,500000	
20	10	1	1	1,000000	
20	10	2	0	0,236842	
20	10	2	1	0,763158	
20	10	2	2	1,000000	
20	10	3	0	0,105263	
20	10	3	1	0,500000	
20	10	3	2	0,894737	
20	10	3	3	1,000000	
20	10	4	0	0,043344	0,043344
20	10	4	1	0,291022	0,247678
20	10	4	2	0,708978	0,417957
20	10	4	3	0,956656	0,247678
20	10	4	4	1,000000	0,043344
20	10	5	0	0,016254	0,016254
20	10	5	1	0,151703	0,135449
20	10	5	2	0,500000	0,348297
20	10	5	3	0,848297	0,348297
20	10	5	4	0,983746	0,135449
20	10	5	5	1,000000	0,016254
20	10	6	0	0,005418	0,005418
20	10	6	1	0,070433	0,065015
20	10	6	2	0,314242	0,243808
20	10	6	3	0,685759	0,371517
20	10	6	4	0,929567	0,243808
20	10	6	5	0,994582	0,065015
20	10	6	6	1,000000	0,005418
	10	7	4	0,825077	
	10	7	5	0,971362	
20	10	7	6	0,998452	
20	10	7	7	1,000000	
20	10	8	0	0,000357	
20	10	8	1	0,009883	
20	10	8	2	0,084901	
20	10	8	3	0,324958	
20	10	8	4	0,675042	
	10	8	5	0,915099	
	10	8	6	0,990117	
	10	8	7	0,999643	
		8	8		
20	10	9	5	0,815075	
20	10	9	6	0,965111	
20	10	9	7	0,997261	
20	10	9	8	0,999940	
20	10	9	9	1,000000	0,000060
20	10	10	0	0,000005	0,000005
20	10	10	1	0,000547	0,000541
20	10	10	2	0,011507	0,010960
20	10	10	3	0,089448	0,077941
20	10	10	4	0,328141	0,238693
20	10	10	5	0,671859	0,343718

In chapter 5 we have compiled all the statistical tables needed for working through this textbook. For the benefit of readers who use this book for self study purposes we have included at the beginning of each table a brief review of the corresponding theoretical background. In many cases the meaning of the tabulated values is illustrated by means of a graph. We are also giving examples for the application of the tables.

Figure on the title page of this chapter:
Excerpt of a table for the hypergeometric distribution
(Design: P. Becker, Centre for Correspondence Study Development at the FernUniversität Hagen, Germany)

5.1 Distribution Functions

5.1.1 Standard Normal Distribution

Every normally distributed random variable can be standardized with the help of the linear transformation (2.48). The cumulative **distribution function** of the standard normal distribution is according to (2.49) and (2.50) given by

$$\Phi(z) = \int_{-\infty}^{z} \phi(u)du = \frac{1}{\sqrt{2\pi}} \int_{-\infty}^{z} \exp\left(-\frac{u^2}{2}\right) du.$$

For a given z the value $\Phi(z)$ corresponds according to figure 2.1/5a to the shaded area below the **density function** $\phi(z)$:

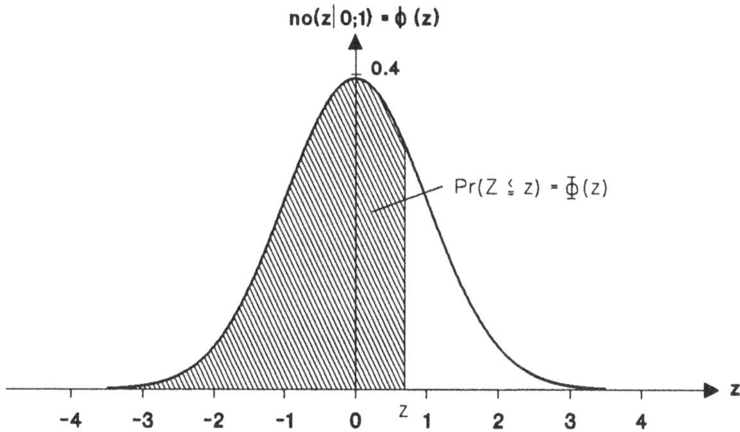

Figure 5.1/1: Interpreting the values of the standard normal distribution function as areas under a density

For the distribution function $No(x|\mu, \sigma^2)$ of a normally distributed random variable X with expectation μ and variance σ^2 it holds that

$$No(x|\mu;\sigma^2) = \Phi\left(\frac{x-\mu}{\sigma}\right).$$

Table 5.1/1 lists, for selected values z, the corresponding values $\Phi(z)$ rounded to six decimal points. Because of the symmetry relationship

$$\Phi(-z) = 1 - \Phi(z)$$

the function $\Phi(z)$ is only tabulated for $z \geq 0$.

Examples: $\Phi(-2.91) \approx 0.001807$; $No(11|5;2) = \Phi(3) \approx 0.998650$.

Table 5.1/1: Standard normal distribution

Values of the cumulative distribution function $\Phi(z)$ for $0 \leq z < 3.0$:

z	.00	.01	.02	.03	.04	.05	.06	.07	.08	.09
0.0	.500000	.503989	.507978	.511966	.515953	.519939	.523922	.527903	.531881	.535856
0.1	.539828	.543795	.547758	.551717	.555670	.559618	.563559	.567495	.571424	.575345
0.2	.579260	.583166	.587064	.590954	.594835	.598706	.602568	.606420	.610261	.614092
0.3	.617911	.621720	.625516	.629300	.633072	.636831	.640576	.644309	.648027	.651732
0.4	.655422	.659097	.662757	.666402	.670031	.673645	.677242	.680822	.684386	.687933
0.5	.691462	.694974	.698468	.701944	.705401	.708840	.712260	.715661	.719043	.722405
0.6	.725747	.729069	.732371	.735653	.738914	.742154	.745373	.748571	.751748	.754903
0.7	.758036	.761148	.764238	.767305	.770350	.773373	.776373	.779350	.782305	.785236
0.8	.788145	.791030	.793892	.796731	.799546	.802337	.805105	.807850	.810570	.813267
0.9	.815940	.818589	.821214	.823814	.826391	.828944	.831472	.833977	.836457	.838913
1.0	.841345	.843752	.846136	.848495	.850830	.853141	.855428	.857690	.859929	.862143
1.1	.864334	.866500	.868643	.870762	.872857	.874928	.876976	.879000	.881000	.882977
1.2	.884930	.886861	.888768	.890651	.892512	.894350	.896165	.897958	.899727	.901475
1.3	.903200	.904902	.906582	.908241	.909877	.911492	.913085	.914657	.916207	.917736
1.4	.919243	.920730	.922196	.923641	.925066	.926471	.927855	.929219	.930563	.931888
1.5	.933193	.934478	.935745	.936992	.938220	.939429	.940620	.941792	.942947	.944083
1.6	.945201	.946301	.947384	.948449	.949497	.950529	.951543	.952540	.953521	.954486
1.7	.955435	.956367	.957284	.958185	.959070	.959941	.960796	.961636	.962462	.963273
1.8	.964070	.964852	.965620	.966375	.967116	.967843	.968557	.969258	.969946	.970621
1.9	.971283	.971933	.972571	.973197	.973810	.974412	.975002	.975581	.976148	.976705
2.0	.977250	.977784	.978308	.978822	.979325	.979818	.980301	.980774	.981237	.981691
2.1	.982136	.982571	.982997	.983414	.983823	.984222	.984614	.984997	.985371	.985738
2.2	.986097	.986447	.986791	.987126	.987455	.987776	.988089	.988396	.988696	.988989
2.3	.989276	.989556	.989830	.990097	.990358	.990613	.990863	.991106	.991344	.991576
2.4	.991802	.992024	.992240	.992451	.992656	.992857	.993053	.993244	.993431	.993613
2.5	.993790	.993963	.994132	.994297	.994457	.994614	.994766	.994915	.995060	.995201
2.6	.995339	.995473	.995604	.995731	.995855	.995975	.996093	.996207	.996319	.996427
2.7	.996533	.996636	.996736	.996833	.996928	.997020	.997110	.997197	.997282	.997365
2.8	.997445	.997523	.997599	.997673	.997744	.997814	.997882	.997948	.998012	.998074
2.9	.998134	.998193	.998250	.998305	.998359	.998411	.998462	.998511	.998559	.998605

Values of the cumulative distribution function $\Phi(z)$ for $3.0 \leq z < 4.5$:

z	.00	.05	0.10	.15	.20	.25	.30	.35	.40	.45
3.0	.998650	.998856	.999032	.999184	.999313	.999423	.999517	.999596	.999663	.999720
3.5	.999767	.999807	.999841	.999869	.999892	.999912	.999928	.999941	.999952	.999961
4.0	.999968	.999974	.999979	.999983	.999987	.999989	.999991	.999993	.999995	.999996
4.5	.999997	.999997	.999998	.999998	.999999	.999999	.999999	.999999	1.000000	1.000000

5.1.2 Hypergeometric Distribution

For integer valued arguments $k \geq 0$ the **mass function** of the hypergeometric distribution is according to (2.80) and (2.84a) given by

$$hy(k|N;M;n) = hy(k|N;n;M) = \frac{\binom{M}{k}\binom{N-M}{n-k}}{\binom{N}{n}}.$$

This holds if $k \in [c_1, c_2]$ with $c_1 := max(0, n+M-N)$ and $c_2 := min(n, M)$. If $k \in (c_1, c_2)$ the function $hy(k|N, n, M)$ is zero. The following relationships from (2.85) are sometimes useful:

$$\begin{aligned} hy(k|N;M;n) &= hy(n-k|N;N-M;n) \\ &= hy(M-k|N;M;N-n) \\ &= hy(N-n-M+k|N;N-M;N-n). \end{aligned}$$

For the cumulative **distribution function** it holds for $k \in [c_1, c_2]$ according to (2.81) and (2.84b) that

$$Hy(k|N;M;n) = Hy(k|N;n;M) = \sum_{i=c_1}^{k} hy(i|N;M;n).$$

For $k < c_1$ the distribution function has the value zero, for $k > c_2$ the value one. As given in (2.86) it holds that

$$\begin{aligned} Hy(k|N;M;n) &= 1 - Hy(n-k-1|N;N-M;n) \\ &= 1 - Hy(M-k-1|N;M;N-n) \\ &= Hy(N-n-M+k|N;N-M;N-n). \end{aligned}$$

This chain of equalities makes it possible to only tabulate $Hy(k|N, M, n)$ for values with $0 \leq k \leq M \leq n \leq 0.5N$. The following table covers this range exemplarily for $N = 20$. The listed values of $Hy(k|N, M, n)$ and $hy(k|N, M, n)$ are rounded to six decimal points. For all considered combinations of n, M and N it holds that $k \in [c_1, c_2]$ with $c_1 = 0$.

Examples: $hy(0|20;8;7) \approx 0.010217$; $Hy(2|20;3;9) \approx 0.926316$.

Table 5.1/2: Hypergeometric cumulative distribution and mass function

N	n	M	k	$Hy(k\|N;M;n)$	$hy(k\|N;M;n)$
20	1	1	0	0.950000	0.950000
20	1	1	1	1.000000	0.050000
20	2	1	0	0.900000	0.900000
20	2	1	1	1.000000	0.100000
20	2	2	0	0.805263	0.805263
20	2	2	1	0.994737	0.189474
20	2	2	2	1.000000	0.005263
20	3	1	0	0.850000	0.850000
20	3	1	1	1.000000	0.150000
20	3	2	0	0.715789	0.715789
20	3	2	1	0.984211	0.268421
20	3	2	2	1.000000	0.015789
20	3	3	0	0.596491	0.596491
20	3	3	2	0.999123	0.044737
20	3	3	3	1.000000	0.000877
20	4	1	0	0.800000	0.800000
20	4	1	1	1.000000	0.200000
20	4	2	0	0.631579	0.631579
20	4	2	1	0.968421	0.336842
20	4	2	2	1.000000	0.031579
20	4	3	0	0.491228	0.491228
20	4	3	1	0.912281	0.421053
20	4	3	2	0.996491	0.084211
20	4	3	3	1.000000	0.003509
20	4	4	0	0.375645	0.375645
20	4	4	1	0.837977	0.462332
20	4	4	2	0.986584	0.148607
20	4	4	3	0.999793	0.013209
20	4	4	4	1.000000	0.000206
20	5	1	0	0.750000	0.750000
20	5	1	1	1.000000	0.250000
20	5	2	0	0.552632	0.552632
20	5	2	1	0.947368	0.394737
20	5	2	2	1.000000	0.052632
20	5	3	0	0.399123	0.399123
20	5	3	1	0.859649	0.460526
20	5	3	2	0.991228	0.131579
20	5	3	3	1.000000	0.008772
20	5	4	0	0.281734	0.281734
20	5	4	1	0.751290	0.469556
20	5	4	2	0.968008	0.216718
20	5	4	3	0.998968	0.030960
20	5	4	4	1.000000	0.001032
20	5	5	0	0.193692	0.193692
20	5	5	1	0.633901	0.440209
20	5	5	2	0.927374	0.293473
20	5	5	3	0.995098	0.067724
20	5	5	4	0.999935	0.004837
20	5	5	5	1.000000	0.000064
20	6	1	0	0.700000	0.700000
20	6	1	1	1.000000	0.300000
20	6	2	0	0.478947	0.478947
20	6	2	1	0.921053	0.442105
20	6	2	2	1.000000	0.078947
20	6	3	0	0.319298	0.319298
20	6	3	1	0.798246	0.478947
20	6	3	2	0.982456	0.184211
20	6	3	3	1.000000	0.017544
20	6	4	0	0.206605	0.206605
20	6	4	1	0.657379	0.450774
20	6	4	2	0.939112	0.281734
20	6	4	3	0.996904	0.057792
20	6	4	4	1.000000	0.003096
20	6	5	0	0.129128	0.129128
20	6	5	1	0.516512	0.387384
20	6	5	2	0.868679	0.352167
20	6	5	3	0.986068	0.117389
20	6	5	4	0.999613	0.013545
20	6	5	5	1.000000	0.000387
20	6	6	0	0.077477	0.077477
20	6	6	1	0.387384	0.309907
20	6	6	2	0.774768	0.387384
20	6	6	3	0.962590	0.187822
20	6	6	4	0.997807	0.035217
20	6	6	5	0.999974	0.002167
20	6	6	6	1.000000	0.000026
20	7	1	0	0.650000	0.650000
20	7	1	1	1.000000	0,350000
20	7	2	0	0.410526	0.410526
20	7	2	1	0.889474	0.478947
20	7	2	2	1.000000	0.110526
20	7	3	0	0.250877	0.250877
20	7	3	1	0.729825	0.478947
20	7	3	2	0.969298	0.239474
20	7	3	3	1.000000	0.030702
20	7	4	0	0.147575	0.147575
20	7	4	1	0.560784	0.413209
20	7	4	2	0.898865	0.338080
20	7	4	3	0.992776	0.093911
20	7	4	4	1.000000	0.007224

Table 5.1/2: Hypergeometric cumulative distribution and mass function (cont.)

N	n	M	k	$Hy(k\|N;M;n)$	$hy(k\|N;M;n)$
20	7	5	0	0.083011	0.083011
20	7	5	1	0.405831	0.322820
20	7	5	2	0.793215	0.387384
20	7	5	3	0.969298	0.176084
20	7	5	4	0.998645	0.029347
20	7	5	5	1.000000	0.001354
20	7	6	0	0.044272	0.044272
20	7	6	1	0.276703	0.232430
20	7	6	2	0.664087	0.387384
20	7	6	3	0.922343	0.258256
20	7	6	4	0.992776	0.070433
20	7	6	5	0.999819	0.007043
20	7	6	6	1.000000	0.000181
20	7	7	0	0.022136	0.022136
20	7	7	1	0.177090	0.154954
20	7	7	2	0.525735	0.348645
20	7	7	3	0.848555	0.322820
20	7	7	4	0.977683	0.129128
20	7	7	6	0.999987	0.001174
20	7	7	7	1.000000	0.000013
20	8	1	0	0.600000	0.600000
20	8	1	1	1.000000	0.400000
20	8	2	0	0.347368	0.347368
20	8	2	1	0.852632	0.505263
20	8	2	2	1.000000	0.147368
20	8	3	0	0.192982	0.192982
20	8	3	1	0.656140	0.463158
20	8	3	2	0.950877	0.294737
20	8	3	3	1.000000	0.049123
20	8	4	0	0.102167	0.102167
20	8	4	1	0.465428	0.363261
20	8	4	2	0.846852	0.381424
20	8	4	3	0.985552	0.138700
20	8	4	4	1.000000	0.014448
20	8	5	0	0.051084	0.051084
20	8	5	1	0.306502	0.255418
20	8	5	2	0.703818	0.397317
20	8	5	3	0.942208	0.238390
20	8	5	4	0.996388	0.054180
20	8	5	5	1.000000	0.003612
20	8	6	0	0.023839	0.023839
20	8	6	1	0.187307	0.163468
20	8	6	2	0.544892	0.357585
20	8	6	3	0.862745	0.317853
20	8	6	4	0.981940	0.119195
20	8	6	5	0.999278	0.017337
20	8	6	6	1.000000	0.000722

N	n	M	k	$Hy(k\|N;M;n)$	$hy(k\|N;M;n)$
20	8	7	0	0.010217	0.010217
20	8	7	1	0.105573	0.095356
20	8	7	2	0.391641	0.286068
20	8	7	3	0.749226	0.357585
20	8	7	4	0.947885	0.198658
20	8	7	6	0.999897	0.004334
20	8	7	7	1.000000	0.000103
20	8	8	0	0.003930	0.003930
20	8	8	1	0.054227	0.050298
20	8	8	2	0.259610	0.205382
20	8	8	3	0.611694	0.352084
20	8	8	4	0.886759	0.275066
20	8	8	5	0.984560	0.097801
20	8	8	6	0.999231	0.014670
20	8	8	7	0.999993	0.000762
20	8	8	8	1.000000	0.000007
20	9	1	0	0.550000	0.550000
20	9	1	1	1.000000	0.450000
20	9	2	0	0.289474	0.289474
20	9	2	1	0.810526	0.521053
20	9	2	2	1.000000	0.189474
20	9	3	0	0.144737	0.144737
20	9	3	1	0.578947	0.434211
20	9	3	2	0.926316	0.347368
20	9	3	3	1.000000	0.073684
20	9	4	0	0.068111	0.068111
20	9	4	1	0.374613	0.306502
20	9	4	2	0.783282	0.408669
20	9	4	3	0.973994	0.190172
20	9	4	4	1.000000	0.026006
20	9	5	0	0.029799	0.029799
20	9	5	1	0.221362	0.191563
20	9	5	2	0.604489	0.383127
20	9	5	3	0.902477	0.297988
20	9	5	4	0.991873	0.089396
20	9	5	5	1.000000	0.008127
20	9	6	0	0.011919	0.011919
20	9	6	1	0.119195	0.107276
20	9	6	2	0.425697	0.306502
20	9	6	3	0.783282	0.357585
20	9	6	4	0.962074	0.178793
20	9	6	5	0.997833	0.035759
20	9	6	6	1.000000	0.002167

Table 5.1/2: Hypergeometric cumulative distribution and mass function (cont.)

N	n	M	k	$Hy(k\|N;M;n)$	$hy(k\|N;M;n)$
20	9	7	0	0.004257	0.004257
20	9	7	1	0.057895	0.053638
20	9	7	2	0.272446	0.214551
20	9	7	3	0.630031	0.357585
20	9	7	4	0.898220	0.268189
20	9	7	5	0.987616	0.089396
20	9	7	6	0.999536	0.011919
20	9	7	7	1.000000	0.000464
20	9	8	0	0.001310	0.001310
20	9	8	1	0.024887	0.023577
20	9	8	2	0.156918	0.132031
20	9	8	3	0.464992	0.308073
20	9	8	4	0.795071	0.330079
20	9	8	5	0.960110	0.165039
20	9	8	6	0.996785	0.036675
20	9	8	7	0.999929	0.003144
20	9	8	8	1.000000	0.000071
20	9	9	0	0.000327	0.000327
20	9	9	1	0.009169	0.008841
20	9	9	2	0.079900	0.070731
20	9	9	3	0.310955	0.231055
20	9	9	4	0.657538	0.346583
20	9	9	5	0.905097	0.247559
20	9	9	6	0.987616	0.082520
20	9	9	7	0.999405	0.011789
20	9	9	8	0.999994	0.000589
20	9	9	9	1.000000	0.000006
20	10	1	0	0.500000	0.500000
20	10	1	1	1.000000	0.500000
20	10	2	0	0.236842	0.236842
20	10	2	1	0.763158	0.526316
20	10	2	2	1.000000	0.236842
20	10	3	0	0.105263	0.105263
20	10	3	1	0.500000	0.394737
20	10	3	2	0.894737	0.394737
20	10	3	3	1.000000	0.105263
20	10	4	0	0.043344	0.043344
20	10	4	1	0.291022	0.247678
20	10	4	2	0.708978	0.417957
20	10	4	3	0.956656	0.247678
20	10	4	4	1.000000	0.043344
20	10	5	0	0.016254	0.016254
20	10	5	1	0.151703	0.135449
20	10	5	2	0.500000	0.348297
20	10	5	3	0.848297	0.348297
20	10	5	4	0.983746	0.135449
20	10	5	5	1.000000	0.016254

N	n	M	k	$Hy(k\|N;M;n)$	$hy(k\|N;M;n)$
20	10	6	0	0.005418	0.005418
20	10	6	1	0.070433	0.065015
20	10	6	2	0.314242	0.243808
20	10	6	3	0.685759	0.371517
20	10	6	4	0.929567	0.243808
20	10	6	5	0.994582	0.065015
20	10	6	6	1.000000	0.005418
20	10	7	0	0.001548	0.001548
20	10	7	1	0.028638	0.027090
20	10	7	2	0.174923	0.146285
20	10	7	3	0.500000	0.325077
20	10	7	4	0.825077	0.325077
20	10	7	5	0.971362	0.146285
20	10	7	6	0.998452	0.027090
20	10	7	7	1.000000	0.001548
20	10	8	0	0.000357	0.000357
20	10	8	1	0.009883	0.009526
20	10	8	2	0.084901	0.075018
20	10	8	3	0.324958	0.240057
20	10	8	4	0.675042	0.350083
20	10	8	5	0.915099	0.240057
20	10	8	6	0.990117	0.075018
20	10	8	7	0.999643	0.009526
20	10	8	8	1.000000	0.000357
20	10	9	0	0.000060	0.000060
20	10	9	1	0.002739	0.002679
20	10	9	2	0.034889	0.032150
20	10	9	3	0.184925	0.150036
20	10	9	4	0.500000	0.315075
20	10	9	5	0.815075	0.315075
20	10	9	6	0.965111	0.150036
20	10	9	7	0.997261	0.032150
20	10	9	8	0.999940	0.002679
20	10	9	9	1.000000	0.000060
20	10	10	0	0.000005	0.000005
20	10	10	1	0.000547	0.000541
20	10	10	2	0.011507	0.010960
20	10	10	3	0.089448	0.077941
20	10	10	4	0.328141	0.238693
20	10	10	5	0.671859	0.343718
20	10	10	6	0.910552	0.238693
20	10	10	7	0.988493	0.077941
20	10	10	8	0.999453	0.010960
20	10	10	9	0.999995	0.000541
20	10	10	10	1.000000	0.000005

5.1.3 Binomial Distribution

For integer valued k with $0 \le k < n$ the cumulative **distribution function** of the binomial distribution is according to (2.93) of form

$$Bi(k|P;n) = \sum_{i=0}^{k} \binom{n}{i} P^i (1-P)^{n-i}.$$

The following table contains the values of $Bi(k|P,n)$ rounded to five decimal points for various choices of k and P and selected sample sizes in the range from 10 to 40. Due to the symmetry relationship

$$Bi(k|P;n) = 1 - Bi(n-k-1|1-P;n)$$

from (2.95d) it is sufficient to only tabulate values for the range $0 < P \le 0.5$.

Examples: $Bi(3|0.07;30) \approx 0.84502; Bi(25|0.07;40) \approx 1{-}0.80745 = 0.19255.$

Table 5.1/3: Cumulative binomial distribution function

$n = 10;\ \ 0.01 \le P \le 0.07$

$k \setminus P$	0.01	0.02	0.03	0.04	0.05	0.06	0.07
0	0.90438	0.81707	0.73742	0.66483	0.59874	0.53862	0.48398
1	0.99573	0.98382	0.96549	0.94185	0.91386	0.88241	0.84827
2	0.99989	0.99914	0.99724	0.99379	0.98850	0.98116	0.97166
3	1.00000	0.99997	0.99985	0.99956	0.99897	0.99797	0.99642
4	1.00000	1.00000	0.99999	0.99998	0.99994	0.99985	0.99969
5	1.00000	1.00000	1.00000	1.00000	1.00000	0.99999	0.99998
6	1.00000	1.00000	1.00000	1.00000	1.00000	1.00000	1.00000

$n = 10;\ \ 0.08 \le P \le 0.50$

$k \setminus P$	0.08	0.09	0.10	0.20	0.30	0.40	0.50
0	0.43439	0.38942	0.34868	0.10737	0.02825	0.00605	0.00098
1	0.81212	0.77455	0.73610	0.37581	0.14931	0.04636	0.01074
2	0.95992	0.94596	0.92981	0.67780	0.38278	0.16729	0.05469
3	0.99420	0.99117	0.98720	0.87913	0.64961	0.38228	0.17188
4	0.99941	0.99899	0.99837	0.96721	0.84973	0.63310	0.37695
5	0.99996	0.99992	0.99985	0.99363	0.95265	0.83376	0.62305
6	1.00000	1.00000	0.99999	0.99914	0.98941	0.94524	0.82813
7	1.00000	1.00000	1.00000	0.99992	0.99841	0.98771	0.94531
8	1.00000	1.00000	1.00000	1.00000	0.99986	0.99832	0.98926
9	1.00000	1.00000	1.00000	1.00000	0.99999	0.99990	0.99902
10	1.00000	1.00000	1.00000	1.00000	1.00000	1.00000	1.00000

Table 5.1/3: Cumulative binomial distribution function (cont.)

$n = 20;\ \ 0.01 \le P \le 0.07$

$k \setminus P$	0.01	0.02	0.03	0.04	0.05	0.06	0.07
0	0.81791	0.66761	0.54379	0.44200	0.35849	0.29011	0.23424
1	0.98314	0.94010	0.88016	0.81034	0.73584	0.66045	0.58686
2	0.99900	0.99293	0.97899	0.95614	0.92452	0.88503	0.83900
3	0.99996	0.99940	0.99733	0.99259	0.98410	0.97103	0.95287
4	1.00000	0.99996	0.99974	0.99904	0.99743	0.99437	0.98929
5	1.00000	1.00000	0.99998	0.99990	0.99967	0.99913	0.99807
6	1.00000	1.00000	1.00000	0.99999	0.99997	0.99989	0.99972
7	1.00000	1.00000	1.00000	1.00000	1.00000	0.99999	0.99997
8	1.00000	1.00000	1.00000	1.00000	1.00000	1.00000	1.00000

$n = 20;\ \ 0.08 \le P \le 0.50$

$k \setminus P$	0.08	0.09	0.10	0.20	0.30	0.40	0.50
0	0.18869	0.15164	0.12158	0.01153	0.00080	0.00004	0.00000
1	0.51686	0.45160	0.39175	0.06918	0.00764	0.00052	0.00002
2	0.78795	0.73343	0.67693	0.20608	0.03548	0.00361	0.00020
3	0.92938	0.90067	0.86705	0.41145	0.10709	0.01596	0.00129
4	0.98166	0.97096	0.95683	0.62965	0.23751	0.05095	0.00591
5	0.99620	0.99321	0.98875	0.80421	0.41637	0.12560	0.02069
6	0.99936	0.99871	0.99761	0.91331	0.60801	0.25001	0.05766
7	0.99991	0.99980	0.99958	0.96786	0.77227	0.41589	0.13159
8	0.99999	0.99997	0.99994	0.99002	0.88667	0.59560	0.25172
9	1.00000	1.00000	0.99999	0.99741	0.95204	0.75534	0.41190
10	1.00000	1.00000	1.00000	0.99944	0.98286	0.87248	0.58810
11	1.00000	1.00000	1.00000	0.99990	0.99486	0.94347	0.74828
12	1.00000	1.00000	1.00000	0.99998	0.99872	0.97897	0.86841
13	1.00000	1.00000	1.00000	1.00000	0.99974	0.99353	0.94234
14	1.00000	1.00000	1.00000	1.00000	0.99996	0.99839	0.97931
15	1.00000	1.00000	1.00000	1.00000	0.99999	0.99968	0.99409
16	1.00000	1.00000	1.00000	1.00000	1.00000	0.99995	0.99871
17	1.00000	1.00000	1.00000	1.00000	1.00000	0.99999	0.99980
18	1.00000	1.00000	1.00000	1.00000	1.00000	1.00000	0.99998
19	1.00000	1.00000	1.00000	1.00000	1.00000	1.00000	1.00000

Table 5.1/3: Cumulative binomial distribution function (cont.)

$n = 30;\ 0.01 \le P \le 0.07$

$k \setminus P$	0.01	0.02	0.03	0.04	0.05	0.06	0.07
0	0.73970	0.54548	0.40101	0.29386	0.21464	0.15626	0.11337
1	0.96385	0.87945	0.77308	0.66118	0.55354	0.45547	0.36936
2	0.99668	0.97828	0.93993	0.88310	0.81218	0.73240	0.64875
3	0.99978	0.99711	0.98810	0.96941	0.93923	0.89738	0.84502
4	0.99999	0.99970	0.99815	0.99368	0.98436	0.96846	0.94474
5	1.00000	0.99997	0.99977	0.99894	0.99672	0.99205	0.98377
6	1.00000	1.00000	0.99998	0.99985	0.99943	0.99833	0.99601
7	1.00000	1.00000	1.00000	0.99998	0.99992	0.99970	0.99917
8	1.00000	1.00000	1.00000	1.00000	0.99999	0.99995	0.99985
9	1.00000	1.00000	1.00000	1.00000	1.00000	0.99999	0.99998
10	1.00000	1.00000	1.00000	1.00000	1.00000	1.00000	1.00000

$n = 30;\ 0.08 \le P \le 0.50$

$k \setminus P$	0.08	0.09	0.10	0.20	0.30	0.40	0.50
0	0.08197	0.05905	0.04239	0.00124	0.00002	0.00000	0.00000
1	0.29579	0.23427	0.18370	0.01052	0.00031	0.00000	0.00000
2	0.56540	0.48553	0.41135	0.04418	0.00211	0.00005	0.00000
3	0.78421	0.71747	0.64744	0.12271	0.00932	0.00031	0.00000
4	0.91264	0.87231	0.82451	0.25523	0.03015	0.00151	0.00003
5	0.97071	0.95194	0.92681	0.42751	0.07659	0.00566	0.00016
6	0.99175	0.98475	0.97417	0.60697	0.15952	0.01718	0.00072
7	0.99803	0.99588	0.99222	0.76079	0.28138	0.04352	0.00261
8	0.99959	0.99904	0.99798	0.87135	0.43152	0.09401	0.00806
9	0.99993	0.99981	0.99955	0.93891	0.58881	0.17629	0.02139
10	0.99999	0.99997	0.99991	0.97438	0.73037	0.29147	0.04937
11	1.00000	0.99999	0.99998	0.99051	0.84068	0.43109	0.10024
12	1.00000	1.00000	1.00000	0.99689	0.91553	0.57847	0.18080
13	1.00000	1.00000	1.00000	0.99910	0.95995	0.71450	0.29233
14	1.00000	1.00000	1.00000	0.99977	0.98306	0.82463	0.42777
15	1.00000	1.00000	1.00000	0.99995	0.99363	0.90294	0.57223
16	1.00000	1.00000	1.00000	0.99999	0.99788	0.95189	0.70767
17	1.00000	1.00000	1.00000	1.00000	0.99937	0.97876	0.81920
18	1.00000	1.00000	1.00000	1.00000	0.99984	0.99170	0.89976
19	1.00000	1.00000	1.00000	1.00000	0.99996	0.99715	0.95063
20	1.00000	1.00000	1.00000	1.00000	0.99999	0.99914	0.97861
21	1.00000	1.00000	1.00000	1.00000	1.00000	0.99978	0.99194
22	1.00000	1.00000	1.00000	1.00000	1.00000	0.99995	0.99739
23	1.00000	1.00000	1.00000	1.00000	1.00000	0.99999	0.99928
24	1.00000	1.00000	1.00000	1.00000	1.00000	1.00000	0.99984
25	1.00000	1.00000	1.00000	1.00000	1.00000	1.00000	0.99997
26	1.00000	1.00000	1.00000	1.00000	1.00000	1.00000	1.00000

Table 5.1/3: Cumulative binomial distribution function (cont.)

$n = 40;\ 0.01 \leq P \leq 0.07$

$k \setminus P$	0.01	0.02	0.03	0.04	0.05	0.06	0.07
0	0.66897	0.44570	0.29571	0.19537	0.12851	0.08416	0.05487
1	0.93926	0.80954	0.66154	0.52098	0.39906	0.29904	0.22006
2	0.99250	0.95433	0.88217	0.78553	0.67674	0.56650	0.46252
3	0.99931	0.99176	0.96860	0.92516	0.86185	0.78274	0.69369
4	0.99995	0.99882	0.99333	0.97898	0.95197	0.91042	0.85463
5	1.00000	0.99986	0.99884	0.99512	0.98612	0.96909	0.94185
6	1.00000	0.99999	0.99983	0.99905	0.99661	0.99094	0.98015
7	1.00000	1.00000	0.99998	0.99984	0.99929	0.99772	0.99415
8	1.00000	1.00000	1.00000	0.99998	0.99987	0.99950	0.99850
9	1.00000	1.00000	1.00000	1.00000	0.99998	0.99990	0.99966
10	1.00000	1.00000	1.00000	1.00000	1.00000	0.99998	0.99993
11	1.00000	1.00000	1.00000	1.00000	1.00000	1.00000	0.99999
12	1.00000	1.00000	1.00000	1.00000	1.00000	1.00000	1.00000

$n = 40;\ 0.08 \leq P \leq 0.50$

$k \setminus P$	0.08	0.09	0.10	0.20	0.30	0.40	0.50
0	0.03561	0.02300	0.01478	0.00013	0.00000	0.00000	0.00000
1	0.15945	0.11397	0.08047	0.00146	0.00001	0.00000	0.00000
2	0.36945	0.28942	0.22281	0.00794	0.00010	0.00000	0.00000
3	0.60075	0.50921	0.42313	0.02846	0.00060	0.00000	0.00000
4	0.78679	0.71029	0.62902	0.07591	0.00256	0.00003	0.00000
5	0.90327	0.85347	0.79373	0.16133	0.00862	0.00014	0.00000
6	0.96236	0.93608	0.90048	0.28589	0.02376	0.00059	0.00000
7	0.98731	0.97576	0.95810	0.43715	0.05528	0.00205	0.00002
8	0.99626	0.99195	0.98450	0.59313	0.11101	0.00606	0.00009
9	0.99903	0.99764	0.99494	0.73178	0.19593	0.01557	0.00034
10	0.99978	0.99939	0.99853	0.83923	0.30874	0.03522	0.00111
11	0.99995	0.99986	0.99962	0.91249	0.44061	0.07095	0.00321
12	0.99999	0.99997	0.99991	0.95676	0.57718	0.12851	0.00829
13	1.00000	0.99999	0.99998	0.98059	0.70325	0.21116	0.01924
14	1.00000	1.00000	1.00000	0.99208	0.80745	0.31743	0.04035
15	1.00000	1.00000	1.00000	0.99706	0.88485	0.44022	0.07693
16	1.00000	1.00000	1.00000	0.99901	0.93669	0.56813	0.13409
17	1.00000	1.00000	1.00000	0.99970	0.96805	0.68852	0.21480
18	1.00000	1.00000	1.00000	0.99991	0.98522	0.79107	0.31791
19	1.00000	1.00000	1.00000	0.99998	0.99375	0.87023	0.43731
20	1.00000	1.00000	1.00000	0.99999	0.99758	0.92565	0.56269
21	1.00000	1.00000	1.00000	1.00000	0.99915	0.96083	0.68209
22	1.00000	1.00000	1.00000	1.00000	0.99973	0.98109	0.78520
23	1.00000	1.00000	1.00000	1.00000	0.99992	0.99166	0.86591
24	1.00000	1.00000	1.00000	1.00000	0.99998	0.99665	0.92307
25	1.00000	1.00000	1.00000	1.00000	0.99999	0.99878	0.95965
26	1.00000	1.00000	1.00000	1.00000	1.00000	0.99960	0.98076

5.1.4 Poisson Distribution

For integer valued arguments $k \geq 0$ the cumulative **distribution function** of the Poisson distribution is according to (2.17) given by

$$Po(k|\lambda) = \sum_{i=0}^{k} \frac{\lambda^i}{i!} e^{-\lambda}.$$

The following table lists the values of $Po(k|\lambda)$ rounded to five decimal points for selected Poisson intensities λ and several k.

Example: $Po(2|0.35) \approx 0.99449$.

Table 5.1/4: Cumulative Poisson distribution function

$0.01 \leq \lambda \leq 0.10$

$k \setminus \lambda$	0.01	0.02	0.03	0.04	0.05	0.06	0.07	0.08	0.09	0.1
0	0.99005	0.98020	0.97045	0.96079	0.95123	0.94176	0.93239	0.92312	0.91393	0.90484
1	0.99995	0.99980	0.99956	0.99922	0.99879	0.99827	0.99766	0.99697	0.99618	0.99532
2	1.00000	1.00000	1.00000	0.99999	0.99998	0.99997	0.99995	0.99992	0.99989	0.99985
3	1.00000	1.00000	1.00000	1.00000	1.00000	1.00000	1.00000	1.00000	1.00000	1.00000

$0.15 \leq \lambda \leq 0.60$

$k \setminus \lambda$	0.15	0.20	0.25	0.30	0.35	0.40	0.45	0.50	0.55	0.60
0	0.86071	0.81873	0.77880	0.74082	0.70469	0.67032	0.63763	0.60653	0.57695	0.54881
1	0.98981	0.98248	0.97350	0.96306	0.95133	0.93845	0.92456	0.90980	0.89427	0.87810
2	0.99950	0.99885	0.99784	0.99640	0.99449	0.99207	0.98912	0.98561	0.98154	0.97688
3	0.99998	0.99994	0.99987	0.99973	0.99953	0.99922	0.99880	0.99825	0.99753	0.99664
4	1.00000	1.00000	0.99999	0.99998	0.99997	0.99994	0.99989	0.99983	0.99973	0.99961
5	1.00000	1.00000	1.00000	1.00000	1.00000	1.00000	0.99999	0.99999	0.99998	0.99996
6	1.00000	1.00000	1.00000	1.00000	1.00000	1.00000	1.00000	1.00000	1.00000	1.00000

$0.65 \leq \lambda \leq 1.00$

$k \setminus \lambda$	0.65	0.70	0.75	0.80	0.85	0.90	0.95	1.00
0	0.52205	0.49659	0.47237	0.44933	0.42741	0.40657	0.38674	0.36788
1	0.86138	0.84420	0.82664	0.80879	0.79072	0.77248	0.75414	0.73576
2	0.97166	0.96586	0.95949	0.95258	0.94512	0.93714	0.92866	0.91970
3	0.99555	0.99425	0.99271	0.99092	0.98887	0.98654	0.98393	0.98101
4	0.99944	0.99921	0.99894	0.99859	0.99817	0.99766	0.99705	0.99634
5	0.99994	0.99991	0.99987	0.99982	0.99975	0.99966	0.99954	0.99941
6	0.99999	0.99999	0.99999	0.99998	0.99997	0.99996	0.99994	0.99992
7	1.00000	1.00000	1.00000	1.00000	1.00000	1.00000	0.99999	0.99999
8	1.00000	1.00000	1.00000	1.00000	1.00000	1.00000	1.00000	1.00000

Table 5.1/4: Cumulative Poisson distribution function (cont.)

$1.1 \leq \lambda \leq 2.0$

$k \setminus \lambda$	1.1	1.2	1.3	1.4	1.5	1.6	1.7	1.8	1.9	2.0
0	0.33287	0.30119	0.27253	0.24660	0.22313	0.20190	0.18268	0.16530	0.14957	0.13534
1	0.69903	0.66263	0.62682	0.59183	0.55783	0.52493	0.49325	0.46284	0.43375	0.40601
2	0.90042	0.87949	0.85711	0.83350	0.80885	0.78336	0.75722	0.73062	0.70372	0.67668
3	0.97426	0.96623	0.95690	0.94627	0.93436	0.92119	0.90681	0.89129	0.87470	0.85712
4	0.99456	0.99225	0.98934	0.98575	0.98142	0.97632	0.97039	0.96359	0.95592	0.94735
5	0.99903	0.99850	0.99777	0.99680	0.99554	0.99396	0.99200	0.98962	0.98678	0.98344
6	0.99985	0.99975	0.99960	0.99938	0.99907	0.99866	0.99812	0.99743	0.99655	0.99547
7	0.99998	0.99996	0.99994	0.99989	0.99983	0.99974	0.99961	0.99944	0.99921	0.99890
8	1.00000	1.00000	0.99999	0.99998	0.99997	0.99995	0.99993	0.99989	0.99984	0.99976
9	1.00000	1.00000	1.00000	1.00000	1.00000	0.99999	0.99999	0.99998	0.99997	0.99995
10	1.00000	1.00000	1.00000	1.00000	1.00000	1.00000	1.00000	1.00000	0.99999	0.99999
11	1.00000	1.00000	1.00000	1.00000	1.00000	1.00000	1.00000	1.00000	1.00000	1.00000

$2.1 \leq \lambda \leq 3.0$

$k \setminus \lambda$	2.1	2.2	2.3	2.4	2.5	2.6	2.7	2.8	2.9	3.0
0	0.12246	0.11080	0.10026	0.09072	0.08208	0.07427	0.06721	0.06081	0.05502	0.04979
1	0.37961	0.35457	0.33085	0.30844	0.28730	0.26738	0.24866	0.23108	0.21459	0.19915
2	0.64963	0.62271	0.59604	0.56971	0.54381	0.51843	0.49362	0.46945	0.44596	0.42319
3	0.83864	0.81935	0.79935	0.77872	0.75758	0.73600	0.71409	0.69194	0.66962	0.64723
4	0.93787	0.92750	0.91625	0.90413	0.89118	0.87742	0.86291	0.84768	0.83178	0.81526
5	0.97955	0.97509	0.97002	0.96433	0.95798	0.95096	0.94327	0.93489	0.92583	0.91608
6	0.99414	0.99254	0.99064	0.98841	0.98581	0.98283	0.97943	0.97559	0.97128	0.96649
7	0.99851	0.99802	0.99741	0.99666	0.99575	0.99467	0.99338	0.99187	0.99012	0.98810
8	0.99966	0.99953	0.99936	0.99914	0.99886	0.99851	0.99809	0.99757	0.99694	0.99620
9	0.99993	0.99990	0.99986	0.99980	0.99972	0.99962	0.99950	0.99934	0.99914	0.99890
10	0.99999	0.99998	0.99997	0.99996	0.99994	0.99991	0.99988	0.99984	0.99978	0.99971
11	1.00000	1.00000	0.99999	0.99999	0.99999	0.99998	0.99997	0.99996	0.99995	0.99993
12	1.00000	1.00000	1.00000	1.00000	1.00000	1.00000	0.99999	0.99999	0.99999	0.99998
13	1.00000	1.00000	1.00000	1.00000	1.00000	1.00000	1.00000	1.00000	1.00000	1.00000

$3.1 \leq \lambda \leq 4.0$

$k \setminus \lambda$	3.1	3.2	3.3	3.4	3.5	3.6	3.7	3.8	3.9	4.0
0	0.04505	0.04076	0.03688	0.03337	0.03020	0.02732	0.02472	0.02237	0.02024	0.01832
1	0.18470	0.17120	0.15860	0.14684	0.13589	0.12569	0.11620	0.10738	0.09919	0.09158
2	0.40116	0.37990	0.35943	0.33974	0.32085	0.30275	0.28543	0.26890	0.25313	0.23810
3	0.62484	0.60252	0.58034	0.55836	0.53663	0.51522	0.49415	0.47348	0.45325	0.43347
4	0.79819	0.78061	0.76259	0.74418	0.72544	0.70644	0.68722	0.66784	0.64837	0.62884
5	0.90567	0.89459	0.88288	0.87054	0.85761	0.84412	0.83009	0.81556	0.80056	0.78513
6	0.96120	0.95538	0.94903	0.94215	0.93471	0.92673	0.91819	0.90911	0.89948	0.88933
7	0.98579	0.98317	0.98022	0.97693	0.97326	0.96921	0.96476	0.95989	0.95460	0.94887
8	0.99532	0.99429	0.99309	0.99171	0.99013	0.98833	0.98630	0.98402	0.98147	0.97864
9	0.99860	0.99824	0.99781	0.99729	0.99669	0.99598	0.99515	0.99420	0.99311	0.99187
10	0.99962	0.99950	0.99936	0.99919	0.99898	0.99873	0.99843	0.99807	0.99765	0.99716
11	0.99990	0.99987	0.99983	0.99978	0.99971	0.99963	0.99953	0.99941	0.99926	0.99908
12	0.99998	0.99997	0.99996	0.99994	0.99992	0.99990	0.99987	0.99983	0.99978	0.99973
13	1.00000	0.99999	0.99999	0.99999	0.99998	0.99997	0.99997	0.99996	0.99994	0.99992
14	1.00000	1.00000	1.00000	1.00000	1.00000	0.99999	0.99999	0.99999	0.99999	0.99998

Table 5.1/4: Cumulative Poisson distribution function (cont.)

$4.2 \leq \lambda \leq 6.0$

$k \setminus \lambda$	4.2	4.4	4.6	4.8	5.0	5.2	5.4	5.6	5.8	6.0
0	0.01500	0.01228	0.01005	0.00823	0.00674	0.00552	0.00452	0.00370	0.00303	0.00248
1	0.07798	0.06630	0.05629	0.04773	0.04043	0.03420	0.02891	0.02441	0.02059	0.01735
2	0.21024	0.18514	0.16264	0.14254	0.12465	0.10879	0.09476	0.08239	0.07151	0.06197
3	0.39540	0.35945	0.32571	0.29423	0.26503	0.23807	0.21329	0.19062	0.16996	0.15120
4	0.58983	0.55118	0.51323	0.47626	0.44049	0.40613	0.37331	0.34215	0.31272	0.28506
5	0.75314	0.71991	0.68576	0.65101	0.61596	0.58091	0.54613	0.51186	0.47831	0.44568
6	0.86746	0.84365	0.81803	0.79080	0.76218	0.73239	0.70167	0.67026	0.63839	0.60630
7	0.93606	0.92142	0.90495	0.88667	0.86663	0.84492	0.82166	0.79698	0.77103	0.74398
8	0.97207	0.96420	0.95493	0.94418	0.93191	0.91806	0.90265	0.88568	0.86719	0.84724
9	0.98887	0.98511	0.98047	0.97486	0.96817	0.96033	0.95125	0.94087	0.92916	0.91608
10	0.99593	0.99431	0.99222	0.98958	0.98630	0.98230	0.97749	0.97178	0.96510	0.95738
11	0.99863	0.99799	0.99714	0.99601	0.99455	0.99269	0.99037	0.98751	0.98405	0.97991
12	0.99957	0.99934	0.99902	0.99858	0.99798	0.99719	0.99617	0.99486	0.99321	0.99117
13	0.99987	0.99980	0.99969	0.99953	0.99930	0.99899	0.99857	0.99802	0.99730	0.99637
14	0.99997	0.99994	0.99991	0.99985	0.99977	0.99966	0.99950	0.99928	0.99899	0.99860
15	0.99999	0.99998	0.99997	0.99996	0.99993	0.99989	0.99984	0.99976	0.99964	0.99949
16	1.00000	1.00000	0.99999	0.99999	0.99998	0.99997	0.99995	0.99992	0.99988	0.99983
17	1.00000	1.00000	1.00000	1.00000	0.99999	0.99999	0.99999	0.99998	0.99996	0.99994
18	1.00000	1.00000	1.00000	1.00000	1.00000	1.00000	1.00000	0.99999	0.99999	0.99998
19	1.00000	1.00000	1.00000	1.00000	1.00000	1.00000	1.00000	1.00000	1.00000	0.99999

$6.5 \leq \lambda \leq 11.0$

$k \setminus \lambda$	6.5	7.0	7.5	8.0	8.5	9.0	9.5	10.0	10.5	11
0	0.00150	0.00091	0.00055	0.00034	0.00020	0.00012	0.00007	0.00005	0.00003	0.00002
1	0.01128	0.00730	0.00470	0.00302	0.00193	0.00123	0.00079	0.00050	0.00032	0.00020
2	0.04304	0.02964	0.02026	0.01375	0.00928	0.00623	0.00416	0.00277	0.00183	0.00121
3	0.11185	0.08177	0.05915	0.04238	0.03011	0.02123	0.01486	0.01034	0.00715	0.00492
4	0.22367	0.17299	0.13206	0.09963	0.07436	0.05496	0.04026	0.02925	0.02109	0.01510
5	0.36904	0.30071	0.24144	0.19124	0.14960	0.11569	0.08853	0.06709	0.05038	0.03752
6	0.52652	0.44971	0.37815	0.31337	0.25618	0.20678	0.16495	0.13014	0.10163	0.07861
7	0.67276	0.59871	0.52464	0.45296	0.38560	0.32390	0.26866	0.22022	0.17851	0.14319
8	0.79157	0.72909	0.66197	0.59255	0.52311	0.45565	0.39182	0.33282	0.27941	0.23199
9	0.87738	0.83050	0.77641	0.71662	0.65297	0.58741	0.52183	0.45793	0.39713	0.34051
10	0.93316	0.90148	0.86224	0.81589	0.76336	0.70599	0.64533	0.58304	0.52074	0.45989
11	0.96612	0.94665	0.92076	0.88808	0.84866	0.80301	0.75199	0.69678	0.63873	0.57927
12	0.98397	0.97300	0.95733	0.93620	0.90908	0.87577	0.83643	0.79156	0.74196	0.68870
13	0.99290	0.98719	0.97844	0.96582	0.94859	0.92615	0.89814	0.86446	0.82535	0.78129
14	0.99704	0.99428	0.98974	0.98274	0.97257	0.95853	0.94001	0.91654	0.88789	0.85404
15	0.99884	0.99759	0.99539	0.99177	0.98617	0.97796	0.96653	0.95126	0.93167	0.90740
16	0.99957	0.99904	0.99804	0.99628	0.99339	0.98889	0.98227	0.97296	0.96039	0.94408
17	0.99985	0.99964	0.99921	0.99841	0.99700	0.99468	0.99107	0.98572	0.97814	0.96781
18	0.99995	0.99987	0.99970	0.99935	0.99870	0.99757	0.99572	0.99281	0.98849	0.98231
19	0.99998	0.99996	0.99989	0.99975	0.99947	0.99894	0.99804	0.99655	0.99421	0.99071
20	1.00000	0.99999	0.99996	0.99991	0.99979	0.99956	0.99914	0.99841	0.99721	0.99533
21	1.00000	1.00000	0.99999	0.99997	0.99992	0.99983	0.99964	0.99930	0.99871	0.99775
22	1.00000	1.00000	1.00000	0.99999	0.99997	0.99993	0.99985	0.99970	0.99943	0.99896
23	1.00000	1.00000	1.00000	1.00000	0.99999	0.99998	0.99994	0.99988	0.99976	0.99954
24	1.00000	1.00000	1.00000	1.00000	1.00000	0.99999	0.99998	0.99995	0.99990	0.99980

Table 5.1/4: Cumulative Poisson distribution function (cont.)

$11.5 \leq \lambda \leq 16.0$

$k \setminus \lambda$	11.5	12.0	12.5	13.0	13.5	14.0	14.5	15.0	15.5	16.0
0	0.00001	0.00001	0.00000	0.00000	0.00000	0.00000	0.00000	0.00000	0.00000	0.00000
1	0.00013	0.00008	0.00005	0.00003	0.00002	0.00001	0.00001	0.00000	0.00000	0.00000
2	0.00080	0.00052	0.00034	0.00022	0.00014	0.00009	0.00006	0.00004	0.00003	0.00002
3	0.00336	0.00229	0.00155	0.00105	0.00071	0.00047	0.00032	0.00021	0.00014	0.00009
4	0.01075	0.00760	0.00535	0.00374	0.00260	0.00181	0.00125	0.00086	0.00059	0.00040
5	0.02773	0.02034	0.01482	0.01073	0.00773	0.00553	0.00394	0.00279	0.00197	0.00138
6	0.06027	0.04582	0.03457	0.02589	0.01925	0.01423	0.01045	0.00763	0.00554	0.00401
7	0.11373	0.08950	0.06983	0.05403	0.04148	0.03162	0.02394	0.01800	0.01346	0.01000
8	0.19059	0.15503	0.12492	0.09976	0.07900	0.06206	0.04838	0.03745	0.02879	0.02199
9	0.28879	0.24239	0.20143	0.16581	0.13526	0.10940	0.08776	0.06985	0.05519	0.04330
10	0.40173	0.34723	0.29707	0.25168	0.21123	0.17568	0.14486	0.11846	0.09612	0.07740
11	0.51980	0.46160	0.40576	0.35316	0.30445	0.26004	0.22013	0.18475	0.15378	0.12699
12	0.63295	0.57597	0.51898	0.46310	0.40933	0.35846	0.31108	0.26761	0.22827	0.19312
13	0.73304	0.68154	0.62784	0.57304	0.51825	0.46445	0.41253	0.36322	0.31708	0.27451
14	0.81526	0.77202	0.72503	0.67513	0.62327	0.57044	0.51760	0.46565	0.41541	0.36753
15	0.87829	0.84442	0.80603	0.76361	0.71779	0.66936	0.61916	0.56809	0.51701	0.46674
16	0.92360	0.89871	0.86931	0.83549	0.79755	0.75592	0.71121	0.66412	0.61544	0.56596
17	0.95425	0.93703	0.91584	0.89046	0.86088	0.82720	0.78972	0.74886	0.70518	0.65934
18	0.97383	0.96258	0.94815	0.93017	0.90838	0.88264	0.85296	0.81947	0.78246	0.74235
19	0.98568	0.97872	0.96941	0.95733	0.94213	0.92350	0.90122	0.87522	0.84551	0.81225
20	0.99250	0.98840	0.98269	0.97499	0.96491	0.95209	0.93622	0.91703	0.89437	0.86817
21	0.99623	0.99393	0.99060	0.98592	0.97955	0.97116	0.96038	0.94689	0.93043	0.91077
22	0.99818	0.99695	0.99509	0.99238	0.98854	0.98329	0.97630	0.96726	0.95584	0.94176
23	0.99915	0.99853	0.99754	0.99603	0.99382	0.99067	0.98634	0.98054	0.97296	0.96331
24	0.99962	0.99931	0.99881	0.99801	0.99678	0.99498	0.99241	0.98884	0.98402	0.97768
25	0.99984	0.99969	0.99944	0.99903	0.99838	0.99739	0.99592	0.99382	0.99087	0.98688
26	0.99993	0.99987	0.99975	0.99955	0.99922	0.99869	0.99789	0.99669	0.99496	0.99254
27	0.99997	0.99994	0.99989	0.99980	0.99963	0.99936	0.99894	0.99828	0.99731	0.99589
28	0.99999	0.99998	0.99995	0.99991	0.99983	0.99970	0.99948	0.99914	0.99861	0.99781
29	1.00000	0.99999	0.99998	0.99996	0.99993	0.99986	0.99976	0.99958	0.99930	0.99887
30	1.00000	1.00000	0.99999	0.99998	0.99997	0.99994	0.99989	0.99980	0.99966	0.99943
31	1.00000	1.00000	1.00000	0.99999	0.99999	0.99997	0.99995	0.99991	0.99984	0.99972
32	1.00000	1.00000	1.00000	1.00000	0.99999	0.99999	0.99998	0.99996	0.99993	0.99987
33	1.00000	1.00000	1.00000	1.00000	1.00000	1.00000	0.99999	0.99998	0.99997	0.99994
34	1.00000	1.00000	1.00000	1.00000	1.00000	1.00000	1.00000	0.99999	0.99999	0.99997
35	1.00000	1.00000	1.00000	1.00000	1.00000	1.00000	1.00000	1.00000	0.99999	0.99999
36	1.00000	1.00000	1.00000	1.00000	1.00000	1.00000	1.00000	1.00000	1.00000	0.99999
37	1.00000	1.00000	1.00000	1.00000	1.00000	1.00000	1.00000	1.00000	1.00000	1.00000

5.2 Percentile Functions

5.2.1 Percentiles of the Standard Normal Distribution

The cumulative **distribution function** of the standard normal distribution has according to (2.49) and (2.50) the form

$$\Phi(z) = \frac{1}{\sqrt{2\pi}} \int\limits_{-\infty}^{z} \exp\left(-\frac{u^2}{2}\right) du.$$

Its inverse function

$$z = \Phi^{-1}(y)$$

is defined on the interval [0,1] and is called the **percentile function** of the standard normal distribution. The values $z_\omega = \Phi^{-1}(\omega)$ of this function are the **percentiles** or the **percentage points** of the standard normal distribution. One can determine them approximately with the help of the graph of the cumulative distribution function $\Phi(z)$, because with $\Phi^{-1}(\omega) = z_\omega$ it obviously holds that $\Phi(z_\omega) = \omega$:

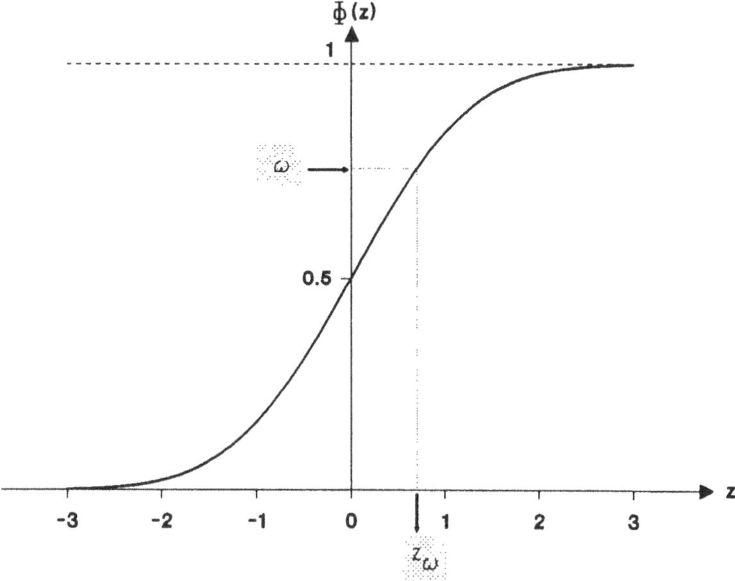

Figure 5.2/1: Determining the percentiles of the standard normal distribution

Since the graphical procedure is not very exact the following table lists for various ω the corresponding percentiles rounded to three decimal points. Due to the relationship

$$z_{1-\omega} = -z_\omega$$

from (2.55) it would be sufficient to tabulate for values $\omega \geq 0.5$. In order to simplify the use of this in SQA frequently used table we have also listed the percentiles z_ω with $0 \leq \omega < 0.5$.

Examples: $z_{0.25} \approx -0.674$; $z_{0.995} \approx 2.576$

Table 5.2/1: Percentiles of the standard normal distribution

$0.00 \leq \omega \leq 0.99$

ω	.00	.01	.02	.03	.04	.05	.06	.07	.08	.09
0.0	$-\infty$	-2.327	-2.054	-1,881	-1.751	-1.645	-1.555	-1.476	-1.405	-1.341
0.1	-1.282	-1.227	-1.175	-1.126	-1.080	-1.036	-0.994	-0.954	-0.915	-0.878
0.2	-0.841	-0.806	-0.772	-0.739	-0.706	-0.674	-0.643	-0.612	-0.582	-0.553
0.3	-0.524	-0.495	-0.467	-0.439	-0.412	-0.385	-0.358	-0.331	-0.305	-0.279
0.4	-0.253	-0.227	-0.202	-0.176	-0.151	-0.125	-0.100	-0.075	-0.050	-0.025
0.5	0.000	0.025	0.050	0.075	0.100	0.125	0.151	0.176	0.202	0.227
0.6	0.253	0.279	0.305	0.331	0.358	0.385	0.412	0.439	0.467	0.495
0.7	0.524	0.553	0.582	0.612	0.643	0.674	0.706	0.739	0.772	0.806
0.8	0.841	0.878	0.915	0.954	0.994	1.036	1.080	1.126	1.175	1.227
0.9	1.282	1.341	1.405	1.476	1.555	1.645	1.751	1.881	2.054	2.326

$0.970 \leq \omega \leq 0.999$

ω	.000	.001	.002	.003	.004	.005	.006	.007	.008	.009
0.97	1.881	1.896	1.911	1.927	1.943	1.960	1.977	1.995	2.014	2.034
0.98	2.054	2.075	2.097	2.120	2.144	2.170	2.197	2.226	2.257	2.290
0.99	2.326	2.366	2.409	2.457	2.512	2.576	2.652	2.748	2.878	3.090

$0.9990 \leq \omega \leq 0.9999$

ω	.0000	.0001	.0002	.0003	.0004	.0005	.0006	.0007	.0008	.0009
0.999	3.090	3.121	3.156	3.195	3.239	3.291	3.353	3.432	3.540	3.719

5.2.2 Percentiles of the t Distribution

The cumulative **distribution function** of the central t distribution with ν degrees of freedom is according to (2.104) given by

$$F_t(x|\nu) = \frac{\Gamma\left(\frac{\nu+1}{2}\right)}{\Gamma\left(\frac{1}{2}\right)\Gamma\left(\frac{\nu}{2}\right)\sqrt{\nu}} \cdot \int\limits_{-\infty}^{x} \left(1 + \frac{u^2}{\nu}\right)^{-(\nu+1)/2} du.$$

Its inverse function

$$t_\nu = F_t^{-1}(y|\nu)$$

is defined on the interval [0,1] and is called the **percentile function** of the central t distribution with ν degrees of freedom. The values $t_{\nu;\omega} = F_t^{-1}(\omega|\nu)$ are the **percentiles** or **percentage points** of this distribution. From $F_t^{-1}(\omega|\nu) = t_{\nu;\omega}$ it follows that $F_t(t_{\nu;\omega}|\nu) = \omega$. Thus the percentiles can be determined graphically. We are illustrating this procedure exemplarily for the t distributions with respectively $\nu = 5$ and $\nu = 50$ degrees of freedom:

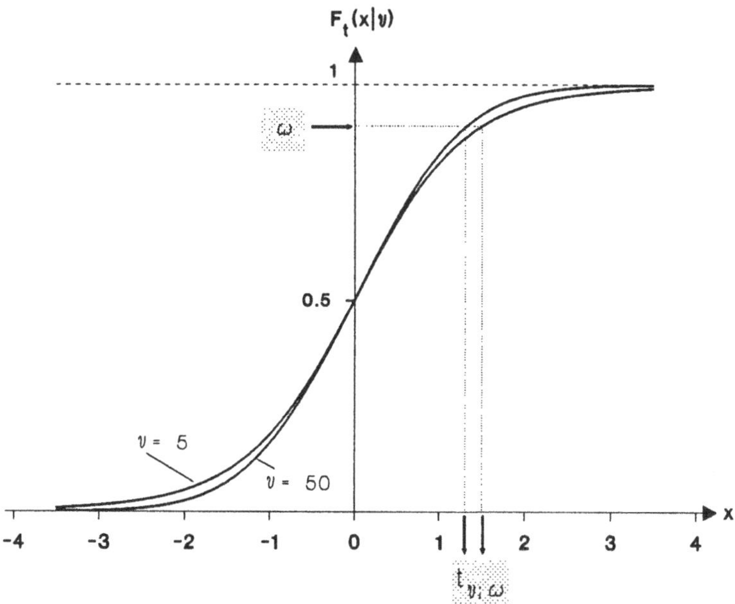

Figure 5.2/2: Determining the percentiles of two t distributions

For $\nu \to \infty$ the function $F_t(x|\nu)$ converges to the distribution function of the standard normal distribution. According to (2.106c) the difference between these two functions is for say $\nu > 30$ not very significant and thus the percentiles $t_{\nu;\omega}$ agree for $\nu > 30$ approximately with the percentiles z_ω of the standard normal distribution:

$$t_{\nu:\omega} \approx z_\omega \qquad (\nu > 30).$$

In table 5.2/2 the percentiles $t_{\nu;\omega}$, rounded to four decimal points, are listed for various ν and ω. Because of the relationship

$$t_{\nu:1-\omega} = -t_{\nu:\omega}$$

it is sufficient to tabulate t percentiles for values $(\nu;\omega)$ with $\omega \geq 0.5$.

Examples: $t_{22;0.99} \approx 2.5083$; $t_{15;0.01} = -t_{15;0.99} \approx 2.6025$.

Table 5.2/2: Percentiles of the t distribution

$\nu \setminus \omega$	0.75	0.90	0.95	0.975	0.99	0.995
1	1.0000	3.0777	6.3138	12.7062	31.8207	63.6574
2	0.8165	1.8856	2.9200	4.3072	6.9646	9.9248
3	0.7649	1.6377	2.3534	3.1824	4.5407	5.8409
4	0.7407	1.5332	2.1318	2.7764	3.7469	4.6041
5	0.7267	1.4759	2.0150	2.5706	3.3649	4.0322
6	0.7167	1.4398	1.9432	2.4469	3.1427	3.7044
7	0.7111	1.4149	1.8946	2.3646	2.9980	3.4995
8	0.7064	1.3968	1.8595	2.3060	2.8965	3.3554
9	0.7027	1.3839	1.8331	2.2622	2.8214	3.2498
10	0.6998	1.3722	1.8125	2.2281	2.7638	3.1693
11	0.6974	1.3634	1.7959	2.2010	2.7181	3.1058
12	0.6955	1.3562	1.7832	2.1788	2.6810	3.0545
13	0.6938	1.3502	1.7709	2.1604	2.6503	3.0123
14	0.6924	1.3450	1.7613	2.1448	2.6245	2.9768
15	0.6912	1.3406	1.7531	2.1315	2.6025	2.9467
16	0.6901	1.3368	1.7459	2.1199	2.5835	2.9208
17	0.6892	1.3334	1.7396	2.1098	2.5669	2.8982
18	0.6884	1.3304	1.7341	2.1009	2.5524	2.8784
19	0.6876	1.3277	1.7291	2.0930	2.5395	2.8609
20	0.6870	1.3253	1.7247	2.0860	2.5280	2.8453
21	0.6864	1.3232	1.7207	2.0796	2.5177	2.8314
22	0.6858	1.3212	1.7171	2.0739	2.5083	2.8188
23	0.6853	1.3195	1.7139	2.0687	2.4999	2.8073
24	0.6848	1.3178	1.7109	2.0639	2.4922	2.7969
25	0.6844	1.3163	1.7081	2.0595	2.4851	2.7874
26	0.6840	1.3150	1.7056	2.0555	2.4786	2.7787
27	0.6837	1.3137	1.7033	2.0518	2.4727	2.7707
28	0.6834	1.3125	1.7011	2.0484	2.4671	2.7633
29	0.6830	1.3114	1.6991	2.0452	2.4620	2.7564
30	0.6828	1.3104	1.6973	2.0423	2.4573	2.7500

Table 5.2/2: Percentiles of the t distribution (cont.)

$\nu \setminus \omega$	0.75	0.90	0.95	0.975	0.99	0.995
32	0.6822	1.3086	1.6939	2.0369	2.4487	2.7385
34	0.6818	1.3070	1.6909	2.0322	2.4411	2.7284
36	0.6814	1.3055	1.6883	2.0281	2.4345	2.7195
38	0.6810	1.3042	1.6860	2.0244	2.4286	2.7116
40	0.6807	1.3031	1.6839	2.0211	2.4233	2.7045
42	0.6804	1.3020	1.6820	2.0181	2.4185	2.6981
44	0.6801	1.3011	1.6802	2.0154	2.4141	2.6923
46	0.6799	1.3002	1.6787	2.0129	2.4102	2.6870
48	0.6796	1.2994	1.6772	2.0106	2.4066	2.6822
50	0.6794	1.2987	1.6759	2.0086	2.4033	2.6778
55	0.6790	1.2971	1.6730	2.0040	2.3961	2.6682
60	0.6786	1.2958	1.6706	2.0003	2.3901	2.6603
65	0.6783	1.2947	1.6686	1.9971	2.3851	2.6536
70	0.6780	1.2938	1.6669	1.9944	2.3808	2.6479
75	0.6778	1.2929	1.6654	1.9921	2.3771	2.6430
80	0.6776	1.2922	1.6641	1.9901	2.3739	2.6387
85	0.6774	1.2916	1.6630	1.9883	2.3710	2.6349
90	0.6772	1.2910	1.6620	1.9867	2.3685	2.6316
95	0.6771	1.2905	1.6611	1.9853	2.3662	2.6286
100	0.6770	1.2901	1.6602	1.9840	2.3642	2.6259
110	0.6767	1.2893	1.6588	1.9818	2.3607	2.6213
120	0.6765	1.2886	1.6577	1.9799	2.3578	2.6174
130	0.6764	1.2881	1.6567	1.9784	2.3554	2.6142
140	0.6762	1.2876	1.6578	1.9771	2.3533	2.6114
150	0.6761	1.2872	1.6551	1.9759	2.3515	2.6090
200	0.6757	1.2858	1.6525	1.9719	2.3451	2.6006
300	0.6753	1.2844	1.6499	1.9679	2.3388	2.5923
400	0.6751	1.2837	1.6487	1.9659	2.3357	2.5882
500	0.6750	1.2832	1.6479	1.9647	2.3338	2.5857
1000	0.6747	1.2824	1.6464	1.9623	2.3301	2.5808
∞	0.6745	1.2816	1.6449	1.9600	2.3263	2.5758

5.2.3 Percentiles of the F distribution

The cumulative **distribution function** of the central F distribution with ν_1 and ν_2 degrees of freedom has for $x \geq 0$ according to (2.115) and (2.114) the form

$$Fi(x|\nu_1;\nu_2) = \frac{\Gamma\left(\frac{\nu_1+\nu_2}{2}\right)\cdot\left(\frac{\nu_1}{\nu_2}\right)^{\nu_1/2}}{\Gamma\left(\frac{\nu_1}{2}\right)\cdot\Gamma\left(\frac{\nu_2}{2}\right)}\int\limits_0^x \frac{u^{(\nu_1-2)/2}}{\left(1+\frac{\nu_1}{\nu_2}\cdot u\right)^{(\nu_1+\nu_2)/2}}du.$$

For $x < 0$ it takes on the value zero. Its inverse function

$$F_{\nu_1;\nu_2} := Fi^{-1}(y|\nu_1;\nu_2)$$

defined on the interval [0,1] is the **percentile function** of the F distribution with ν_1 and ν_2 degrees of freedom. The values $F_{\nu_1;\nu_2;\omega} = Fi^{-1}(\omega|\nu_1,\nu_2)$ of this function are the **percentiles** or **percentage points** of this distribution. For the percentile $F_{\nu_1;\nu_2;\omega}$ it holds that $Fi(F_{\nu_1;\nu_2;\omega}|\nu_1;\nu_2) = \omega$.

Table 5.2/3 lists the percentiles $F_{\nu_1;\nu_2;\omega}$ rounded to two decimal points for various degrees of freedom ν_1 and ν_2 as well as selected values of ω. Because of the symmetry relationship

$$F_{\nu_1;\nu_2;\omega} = \frac{1}{F_{\nu_2;\nu_1;1-\omega}}$$

it is sufficient to tabulate for $\omega \geq 0.5$.

Examples: $F_{5;10;0.95} \approx 3.33$; $\quad F_{7;15;0.1} = \dfrac{1}{F_{15;7;0.9}} \approx 0.38.$

Table 5.2/3: Percentiles of the F distribution

$\omega = 0.5$

$\nu_2 \setminus \nu_1$	1	2	3	4	5	7	10	15	20	30	50	100	200	500	∞
1	1.00	1.50	1.71	1.82	1.89	1.98	2.04	2.09	2.12	2.15	2.17	2.18	2.19	2.19	2.20
2	0.67	1.00	1.13	1.21	1.25	1.30	1.35	1.38	1.39	1.41	1.42	1.43	1.44	1.44	1.44
3	0.59	0.88	1.00	1.06	1.10	1.15	1.18	1.21	1.23	1.24	1.25	1.26	1.26	1.27	1.27
4	0.55	0.83	0.94	1.00	1.04	1.08	1.11	1.14	1.15	1.16	1.18	1.18	1.19	1.19	1.19
5	0.53	0.80	0.91	0.96	1.00	1.04	1.07	1.10	1.11	1.12	1.13	1.14	1.15	1.15	1.15
7	0.51	0.77	0.87	0.93	0.96	1.00	1.03	1.05	1.07	1.08	1.09	1.10	1.10	1.10	1.10
10	0.49	0.74	0.85	0.90	0.93	0.97	1.00	1.02	1.03	1.05	1.06	1.06	1.07	1.07	1.07
15	0.48	0.73	0.83	0.88	0.91	0.95	0.98	1.00	1.01	1.02	1.03	1.04	1.04	1.04	1.05
20	0.47	0.72	0.82	0.87	0.90	0.94	0.97	0.99	1.00	1.01	1.02	1.03	1.03	1.03	1.03
30	0.47	0.71	0.81	0.86	0.89	0.93	0.96	0.98	0.99	1.00	1.01	1.02	1.02	1.02	1.02
50	0.46	0.70	0.80	0.85	0.88	0.92	0.95	0.97	0.98	0.99	1.00	1.01	1.01	1.01	1.01
100	0.46	0.70	0.79	0.84	0.88	0.91	0.94	0.96	0.97	0.98	0.99	1.00	1.00	1.01	1.01
200	0.46	0.70	0.79	0.84	0.87	0.91	0.94	0.96	0.97	0.98	0.99	1.00	1.00	1.00	1.00
500	0.46	0.69	0.79	0.84	0.87	0.91	0.93	0.96	0.97	0.98	0.99	0.99	1.00	1.00	1.00
∞	0.46	0.69	0.79	0.84	0.87	0.91	0.93	0.96	0.97	0.98	0.99	0.99	1.00	1.00	1.00

$\omega = 0.9$

$\nu_2 \setminus \nu_1$	1	2	3	4	5	7	10	15	20	30	50	100	200	500	∞
1[1]	3.99	4.95	5.36	5.58	5.72	5.89	6.02	6.12	6.17	6.23	6.27	6.31	6.32	6.33	6.33
2	8.53	9.00	9.16	9.24	9.29	9.35	9.39	9.42	9.44	9.46	9.47	9.48	9.49	9.49	9.49
3	5.54	5.46	5.39	5.34	5.31	5.27	5.23	5.20	5.18	5.17	5.15	5.14	5.14	5.14	5.14
4	4.54	4.32	4.19	4.11	4.05	3.98	3.92	3.87	3.84	3.82	3.80	3.78	3.77	3.76	3.76
5	4.06	3.78	3.62	3.52	3.45	3.37	3.30	3.24	3.21	3.17	3.15	3.13	3.12	3.11	3.11
7	3.59	3.26	3.07	2.96	2.88	2.78	2.70	2.63	2.59	2.56	2.52	2.50	2.48	2.48	2.47
10	3.28	2.92	2.73	2.61	2.52	2.41	2.32	2.24	2.20	2.16	2.12	2.09	2.07	2.06	2.06
15	3.07	2.70	2.49	2.36	2.27	2.16	2.06	1.97	1.92	1.87	1.83	1.79	1.77	1.76	1.76
20	2.97	2.59	2.38	2.25	2.16	2.04	1.94	1.84	1.79	1.74	1.69	1.65	1.63	1.62	1.61
30	2.88	2.49	2.28	2.14	2.05	1.93	1.82	1.72	1.67	1.61	1.55	1.51	1.48	1.47	1.46
50	2.81	2.41	2.20	2.06	1.97	1.84	1.73	1.63	1.57	1.50	1.44	1.39	1.36	1.34	1.33
100	2.76	2.36	2.14	2.00	1.91	1.78	1.66	1.56	1.49	1.42	1.35	1.29	1.26	1.23	1.21
200	2.73	2.33	2.11	1.97	1.88	1.75	1.63	1.52	1.46	1.38	1.31	1.24	1.20	1.17	1.14
500	2.71	2.31	2.09	1.96	1.86	1.73	1.61	1.50	1.44	1.36	1.28	1.21	1.16	1.12	1.09
∞	2.71	2.30	2.08	1.95	1.85	1.72	1.60	1.49	1.42	1.34	1.26	1.18	1.13	1.08	1.00

[1] The numbers in this line ($\nu_2 = 1$) need to be multiplied by 10.

Table 5.2/3: Percentiles of the F distribution (cont.)

$\omega = 0.95$

$\nu_2 \setminus \nu_1$	1	2	3	4	5	7	10	15	20	30	50	100	200	500	∞
1	161	200	216	225	230	237	242	246	248	250	252	253	254	254	254
2	18.5	19.0	19.2	19.2	19.3	19.4	19.4	19.4	19.4	19.5	19.5	19.5	19.5	19.5	19.5
3	10.1	9.55	9.28	9.12	9.01	8.89	8.79	8.70	8.66	8.62	8.58	8.55	8.54	8.53	8.53
4	7.71	6.94	6.59	6.39	6.26	6.09	5.96	5.86	5.80	5.75	5.70	5.66	5.65	5.64	5.63
5	6.61	5.79	5.41	5.19	5.05	4.88	4.74	4.62	4.56	4.50	4.44	4.41	4.39	4.37	4.37
7	5.59	4.74	4.35	4.12	3.97	3.79	3.64	3.51	3.44	3.38	3.32	3.27	3.25	3.24	3.23
10	4.96	4.10	3.71	3.48	3.33	3.14	2.98	2.85	2.77	2.70	2.64	2.59	2.56	2.55	2.54
15	4.54	3.68	3.29	3.06	2.90	2.71	2.54	2.40	2.33	2.25	2.18	2.12	2.10	2.08	2.07
20	4.35	3.49	3.10	2.87	2.71	2.51	2.35	2.20	2.12	2.04	1.97	1.91	1.88	1.86	1.84
30	4.17	3.32	2.92	2.69	2.53	2.33	2.16	2.01	1.93	1.84	1.76	1.70	1.66	1.64	1.62
50	4.03	3.18	2.79	2.56	2.40	2.20	2.03	1.87	1.78	1.69	1.60	1.52	1.48	1.46	1.44
100	3.94	3.09	2.70	2.46	2.31	2.10	1.93	1.77	1.68	1.57	1.48	1.39	1.34	1.31	1.28
200	3.89	3.04	2.65	2.42	2.26	2.06	1.88	1.72	1.62	1.52	1.41	1.32	1.26	1.22	1.19
500	3.86	3.01	2.62	2.39	2.23	2.03	1.85	1.69	1.59	1.48	1.38	1.28	1.21	1.16	1.11
∞	3.84	3.00	2.60	2.37	2.21	2.01	1.83	1.67	1.57	1.46	1.35	1.24	1.17	1.11	1.00

$\omega = 0.975$

$\nu_2 \setminus \nu_1$	1	2	3	4	5	7	10	15	20	30	50	100	200	500	∞
1	648	800	864	900	922	948	969	985	993	1001	1008	1013	1016	1017	1018
2	38.5	39.0	39.2	39.2	39.3	39.4	39.4	39.4	39.4	39.5	39.5	39.5	39.5	39.5	39.5
3	17.4	16.0	15.4	15.1	14.9	14.6	14.4	14.3	14.2	14.1	14.0	14.0	13.9	13.9	13.9
4	12.2	10.6	9.98	9.60	9.36	9.07	8.84	8.66	8.56	8.46	8.38	8.32	8.29	8.27	8.26
5	10.0	8.43	7.76	7.39	7.15	6.85	6.62	6.43	6.33	6.23	6.14	6.08	6.05	6.03	6.02
7	8.07	6.54	5.89	5.52	5.29	4.99	4.76	4.57	4.47	4.36	4.28	4.21	4.18	4.16	4.14
10	6.94	5.46	4.83	4.47	4.24	3.95	3.72	3.52	3.42	3.31	3.22	3.15	3.12	3.09	3.08
15	6.20	4.77	4.15	3.80	3.58	3.29	3.06	2.86	2.76	2.64	2.55	2.47	2.44	2.41	2.40
20	5.87	4.46	3.86	3.51	3.29	3.01	2.77	2.57	2.46	2.35	2.25	2.17	2.13	2.10	2.09
30	5.57	4.18	3.59	3.25	3.03	2.75	2.51	2.31	2.20	2.07	1.97	1.88	1.84	1.81	1.79
50	5.34	3.97	3.39	3.05	2.83	2.55	2.32	2.11	1.99	1.87	1.75	1.66	1.60	1.57	1.55
100	5.18	3.83	3.25	2.92	2.70	2.42	2.18	1.97	1.85	1.71	1.59	1.48	1.42	1.38	1.35
200	5.10	3.76	3.18	2.85	2.63	2.35	2.11	1.90	1.78	1.64	1.51	1.39	1.32	1.27	1.23
500	5.05	3.72	3.14	2.81	2.59	2.31	2.07	1.86	1.74	1.60	1.46	1.34	1.25	1.19	1.14
∞	5.02	3.69	3.12	2.79	2.57	2.29	2.05	1.83	1.71	1.57	1.43	1.30	1.21	1.13	1.00

Table 5.2/3: Percentiles of the F distribution (cont.)

$\omega = 0.99$

$\nu_2 \setminus \nu_1$	1	2	3	4	5	7	10	15	20	30	50	100	200	500	∞
1[2]	405	500	540	563	576	593	606	616	621	626	630	633	635	636	637
2	98.5	99.0	99.2	99.2	99.3	99.4	99.4	99.4	99.4	99.5	99.5	99.5	99.5	99.5	99.5
3	34.1	30.8	29.5	28.7	28.2	27.7	27.2	26.9	26.7	26.5	26.4	26.2	26.2	26.1	26.1
4	21.2	18.0	16.7	16.0	15.5	15.0	14.5	14.2	14.0	13.8	13.7	13.6	13.5	13.5	13.5
5	16.3	13.3	12.1	11.4	11.0	10.5	10.1	9.72	9.55	9.38	9.24	9.13	9.08	9.04	9.02
7	12.2	9.55	8.45	7.85	7.46	6.99	6.62	6.31	6.16	5.99	5.86	5.75	5.70	5.67	5.65
10	10.0	7.56	6.55	5.99	5.64	5.20	4.85	4.56	4.41	4.25	4.12	4.01	3.96	3.93	3.91
15	8.68	6.36	5.42	4.89	4.56	4.14	3.81	3.52	3.37	3.21	3.08	2.98	2.92	2.89	2.87
20	8.09	5.85	4.94	4.43	4.10	3.70	3.37	3.09	2.94	2.78	2.64	2.54	2.48	2.44	2.42
30	7.56	5.39	4.51	4.02	3.70	3.30	2.98	2.70	2.55	2.39	2.24	2.13	2.07	2.03	2.01
50	7.17	5.06	4.20	3.72	3.41	3.02	2.70	2.42	2.27	2.10	1.95	1.82	1.76	1.71	1.68
100	6.89	4.82	3.98	3.51	3.21	2.82	2.50	2.22	2.07	1.89	1.74	1.60	1.52	1.47	1.43
200	6.76	4.71	3.88	3.41	3.11	2.73	2.41	2.13	1.97	1.79	1.63	1.48	1.39	1.33	1.28
500	6.69	4.65	3.82	3.36	3.05	2.68	2.36	2.07	1.92	1.74	1.56	1.41	1.31	1.23	1.16
∞	6.63	4.61	3.78	3.32	3.02	2.64	2.32	2.04	1.88	1.70	1.52	1.36	1.25	1.15	1.00

$\omega = 0.995$

$\nu_2 \setminus \nu_1$	1	2	3	4	5	7	10	15	20	30	50	100	200	500	∞
1[3]	162	200	216	225	231	237	242	246	248	250	252	253	254	254	255
2	198	199	199	199	199	199	199	199	199	199	199	199	199	200	200
3	55.6	49.8	47.5	46.2	45.4	44.4	43.7	43.1	42.8	42.5	42.2	42.0	41.9	41.9	41.8
4	31.3	26.3	24.3	23.2	22.5	21.6	21.0	20.4	20.2	19.9	19.7	19.5	19.4	19.4	19.3
5	22.8	18.3	16.5	15.6	14.9	14.2	13.6	13.1	12.9	12.7	12.5	12.3	12.2	12.2	12.1
7	16.2	12.4	10.9	10.0	9.52	8.89	8.38	7.97	7.75	7.53	7.35	7.22	7.15	7.10	7.08
10	12.8	9.43	8.08	7.34	6.87	6.30	5.85	5.47	5.27	5.07	4.90	4.77	4.71	4.67	4.64
15	10.8	7.70	6.48	5.80	5.37	4.85	4.42	4.07	3.88	3.69	3.52	3.39	3.33	3.29	3.26
20	9.94	6.99	5.82	5.17	4.76	4.26	3.85	3.50	3.32	3.12	2.96	2.83	2.76	2.72	2.69
30	9.18	6.35	5.24	4.62	4.23	3.74	3.34	3.01	2.82	2.63	2.46	2.32	2.25	2.21	2.18
50	8.62	5.90	4.83	4.23	3.85	3.38	2.99	2.65	2.47	2.27	2.10	1.95	1.87	1.82	1.79
100	8.24	5.59	4.54	3.96	3.59	3.13	2.74	2.41	2.23	2.02	1.84	1.68	1.59	1.53	1.49
200	8.05	5.44	4.41	3.84	3.47	3.01	2.63	2.30	2.11	1.91	1.71	1.54	1.44	1.37	1.31
500	7.95	5.36	4.33	3.76	3.40	2.94	2.56	2.23	2.04	1.84	1.64	1.46	1.35	1.26	1.18
∞	7.88	5.30	4.28	3.72	3.35	2.90	2.52	2.19	2.00	1.79	1.59	1.40	1.28	1.17	1.00

[2] The numbers in this line ($\nu_2 = 1$) need to be multiplied by 10.
[3] The numbers in this line ($\nu_2 = 1$) need to be multiplied by 100.

5.2.4 Percentiles of the χ^2 distribution

The central χ^2 distribution with ν degrees of freedom has according to (2.108b) the cumulative **distribution function**

$$Ch(x|\nu) = \frac{1}{2^{\nu/2}\Gamma\left(\frac{\nu}{2}\right)} \int_0^x u^{(\nu-2)/2} e^{-u/2} du.$$

The inverse function

$$\chi_\nu^2 := Ch^{-1}(y|\nu)$$

which is defined on the interval [0,1] is the **percentile function** of the central χ^2 distribution with ν degrees of freedom. The values $\chi^2_{\nu;\omega}$ of this function are the **percentiles** or **percentage points** of this distribution. Since $Ch^{-1}(\omega|\nu) = \chi^2_{\nu;\omega}$ it holds that $Ch(\chi^2_{\nu;\omega}|\nu) = \omega$. Thus, in analogy to figure 5.2/2, for a given ν the percentiles $\chi^2_{\nu;\omega}$ can be determined with the help of the graph of $Ch(x|\nu)$.

For $\nu \to \infty$ the function $Ch(x|\nu)$ converges to $No(x|\nu, 2\nu)$. Since for $\nu > 100$ the difference between these two functions is neglegible the percentiles $\chi^2_{\nu;\omega}$ agree for $\nu > 100$ approximately to those of a normal distribution with expectation $\mu = \nu$ and variance $\sigma^2 = 2\nu$. Because of (2.56) we thus get the approximation

$$\chi^2_{\nu;\omega} \approx \nu + z_\omega \cdot \sqrt{2\nu} \qquad (\nu > 100),$$

where z_ω denotes again the percentile of the standard normal distribution.

In table 5.2/4 the percentiles $\chi^2_{\nu;\omega}$ rounded to three decimals are listed for various degrees of freedom ν and selected ω.

Examples: $\chi^2_{32;0.95} \approx 46.194$; $\chi^2_{150;0.90} \approx 172.58$[4]

Table 5.2/4: Percentiles of the χ^2 distribution

$\nu \setminus \omega$	0.005	0.010	0.025	0.050	0.100	0.250	0.750	0.900	0.950	0.975	0.990	0.995
1	0.000	0.000	0.001	0.004	0.016	0.102	1.323	2.706	3.841	5.024	6.635	7.879
2	0.010	0.020	0.051	0.103	0.211	0.575	2.773	4.605	5.991	7.378	9.210	10.597
3	0.072	0.115	0.216	0.352	0.584	1.213	4.108	6.251	7.815	9.348	11.345	12.838
4	0.207	0.297	0.484	0.711	1.064	1.923	5.385	7.779	9.488	11.143	13.277	14.860
5	0.412	0.554	0.831	1.145	1.610	2.675	6.626	9.236	11.071	12.833	15.086	16.750
6	0.676	0.872	1.237	1.635	2.204	3.455	7.841	10.645	12.592	14.449	16.812	18.548
7	0.989	1.239	1.690	2.167	2.833	4.255	9.037	12.017	14.067	16.013	18.475	20.278
8	1.344	1.646	2.180	2.733	3.490	5.071	10.219	13.362	15.507	17.535	20.090	21.955
9	1.735	2.088	2.700	3.325	4.168	5.899	11.389	14.684	16.919	19.023	21.666	23.589
10	2.156	2.558	3.247	3.940	4.865	6.737	12.549	15.987	18.307	20.483	23.209	25.188

[4] With the above approximation we would get $\chi^2_{150;0.9} = 150 + z_{0.9} \cdot \sqrt{300} \approx 172.21$.

Table 5.2/4: Percentiles of the χ^2 distribution (cont.)

$\nu \setminus \omega$	0.005	0.010	0.025	0.050	0.100	0.250	0.750	0.900	0.950	0.975	0.990	0.995
11	2.603	3.053	3.816	4.575	5.578	7.584	13.701	17.275	19.675	21.920	24.725	26.757
12	3.074	3.571	4.404	5.226	6.304	8.438	14.845	18.549	21.026	23.337	26.217	28.299
13	3.565	4.107	5.009	5.892	7.041	9.299	15.984	19.812	22.362	24.736	27.688	29.819
14	4.075	4.660	5.629	6.571	7.790	10.165	17.117	21.064	23.685	26.119	29.141	31.319
15	4.601	5.229	6.262	7.261	8.547	11.037	18.245	22.307	24.996	27.488	30.578	32.801
16	5.142	5.812	6.908	7.962	9.312	11.912	19.369	23.542	26.296	28.845	32.000	34.267
17	5.697	6.408	7.564	8.672	10.085	12.792	20.489	24.769	27.587	30.191	33.408	35.718
18	6.265	7.015	8.231	9.390	10.865	13.675	21.605	25.989	28.869	31.526	34.805	37.156
19	6.844	7.633	8.907	10.117	11.651	14.562	22.718	27.204	30.144	32.852	36.191	38.582
20	7.434	8.260	9.591	10.851	12.443	15.452	23.828	28.412	31.410	34.169	37.567	39.997
21	8.034	8.897	10.283	11.591	13.240	16.344	24.935	29.615	32.671	35.479	38.932	41.401
22	8.643	9.543	10.982	12.338	14.042	17.240	26.039	30.813	33.924	36.781	40.289	42.796
23	9.260	10.196	11.689	13.090	14.848	18.137	27.141	32.007	35.173	38.076	41.638	44.181
24	9.886	10.856	12.401	13.848	15.659	19.037	28.241	33.196	36.415	39.364	42.980	45.559
25	10.520	11.524	13.120	14.611	16.473	19.939	29.339	34.382	37.652	40.646	44.314	46.928
26	11.160	12.198	13.844	15.379	17.292	20.843	30.435	35.563	38.885	41.923	45.642	48.290
27	11.808	12.879	14.573	16.151	18.114	21.749	31.528	36.741	40.113	43.194	46.963	49.645
28	12.461	13.565	15.308	16.928	18.939	22.657	32.621	37.916	41.337	44.461	48.278	50.993
29	13.121	14.256	16.047	17.708	19.768	23.567	33.711	39.087	42.557	45.722	49.588	52.336
30	13.787	14.953	16.791	18.493	20.599	24.478	34.800	40.256	43.773	46.979	50.892	53.672
32	15.134	16.362	18.291	20.072	22.271	26.304	36.973	42.585	46.194	49.480	53.485	56.328
34	16.501	17.789	19.806	21.664	23.952	28.136	39.141	44.903	48.602	51.966	56.061	58.964
36	17.887	19.233	21.336	23.269	25.643	29.973	41.304	47.212	50.998	54.437	58.619	61.581
38	19.289	20.691	22.878	24.884	27.343	31.815	43.462	49.513	53.384	56.896	61.162	64.181
40	20.707	22.164	24.433	26.509	29.051	33.660	45.616	51.805	55.758	59.342	63.691	66.766
42	22.138	23.650	25.999	28.144	30.765	35.510	47.766	54.090	58.124	61.777	66.206	69.336
44	23.584	25.148	27.575	29.787	32.487	37.363	49.913	56.368	60.481	64.202	68.709	71.893
46	25.041	26.657	29.160	31.439	34.215	39.220	52.056	58.641	62.830	66.616	71.201	74.437
48	26.511	28.177	30.755	33.098	35.949	41.079	54.196	60.907	65.171	69.023	73.683	76.969
50	27.991	29.707	32.357	34.764	37.689	42.942	56.334	63.167	67.505	71.420	76.154	79.490
60	35.534	37.485	40.482	43.188	46.459	52.294	66.981	74.397	79.082	83.297	88.380	91.952
70	43.275	45.442	48.758	51.739	55.329	61.698	77.577	85.527	90.531	95.023	100.43	104.22
80	51.172	53.540	57.153	60.391	64.278	71.144	88.130	96.578	101.88	106.63	112.33	116.32
90	59.196	61.754	65.647	69.126	73.291	80.625	98.650	107.57	113.15	118.14	124.12	128.30
100	67.328	70.065	74.222	77.930	82.358	90.133	109.14	118.50	124.34	129.56	135.81	140.17
110	75.550	78.458	82.867	86.792	91.471	99.666	119.61	129.39	135.48	140.92	147.41	151.95
120	83.852	86.923	91.573	95.705	100.62	109.22	130.06	140.23	146.57	152.21	158.95	163.65
130	92.223	95.451	100.33	104.66	109.81	118.79	140.48	151.05	157.61	163.45	170.42	175.28
140	100.66	104.03	109.14	113.66	119.03	128.38	150.89	161.83	168.61	174.65	181.84	186.85
150	109.14	112.67	117.99	122.69	128.28	137.98	161.29	172.58	179.58	185.80	193.21	198.36
200	152.24	156.43	162.73	168.28	174.84	186.17	213.10	226.02	233.99	241.06	249.45	255.26
300	240.66	245.97	253.91	260.88	269.07	283.14	316.14	331.79	341.40	349.87	359.91	366.84
400	330.90	337.16	346.48	354.64	364.21	380.58	418.70	436.65	447.63	457.31	468.72	476.61
500	422.30	429.39	439.94	449.15	459.93	478.32	520.95	540.93	553.13	563.85	576.49	585.21
1000	888.56	898.91	914.26	927.59	943.13	969.48	1029.8	1057.7	1074.7	1089.5	1107.0	1119.0

5.2.5 Percentiles of a Special Gamma Distribution

The cumulative distribution function of the gamma distribution is given by (2.35b). If we consider the special case $b = 1$ then for $x \geq 0$ the cumulative **distribution function** is of form

$$Ga(x|1;\delta) = \frac{1}{\Gamma(\delta)} \cdot \int_0^x u^{\delta-1} e^{-u} du$$

with $\delta > 0$. Its inverse function

$$g_\delta = Ga^{-1}(y|1;\delta)$$

which is defined on the interval [0,1] is called the **percentile function** of the gamma distribution with $b = 1$. The values $g_{\delta;\omega} = Ga^{-1}(\omega|1;\delta)$ are the **percentiles** or **percentage points** of this distribution. With $Ga^{-1}(\omega|1;\delta) = g_{\delta;\omega}$ it holds that $Ga(g_{\delta;\omega}|1;\delta) = \omega$. Thus for a given δ the percentiles $g_{\delta;\omega}$ can, in analogy to figure 5.2/2, be determined with the help of the graph of $Ga(x|1;\delta)$.

For integer valued δ it holds that

$$g_{\delta;\omega} = \tfrac{1}{2}\chi^2_{2\delta;\omega}.$$

Table 5.2/5 lists the percentiles $g_{\delta;\omega}$ rounded to three decimals for selected values of δ and ω.

Example: $g_{6;0.05} \approx 2.613$ [5]

[5]From table 5.2/4 we would get $g_{6;0.05} = \frac{1}{2}\chi^2_{12;0.05} \approx 2.613$.

Table 5.2/5: Percentiles of a special gamma distribution

$\delta \setminus \omega$	.005	.010	.025	.050	.100	.200	.500	.800	.900	.950	.975	.990	.995
1.0	.0050	.0101	.0253	.0513	.1054	.2231	.6931	1.609	2.303	2.996	3.689	4.605	5.298
1.2	.0132	.0236	.0513	.0931	.1719	.3280	.8879	1.900	2.641	3.373	4.097	5.049	5.765
1.4	.0268	.0443	.0868	.1459	.2497	.4425	1.084	2.182	2.967	3.733	4.486	5.469	6.206
1.6	.0464	.0723	.1311	.2081	.3367	.5643	1.282	2.458	3.282	4.079	4.859	5.872	6.628
1.8	.0702	.1072	.1831	.2783	.4311	.6920	1.480	2.728	3.589	4.416	5.220	6.261	7.035
2.0	.1035	.1486	.2422	.3554	.5318	.8244	1.678	2.994	3.890	4.744	5.572	6.638	7.430
2.2	.1406	.1959	.3075	.4385	.6378	.9607	1.877	3.257	4.185	5.065	5.915	7.006	7.815
2.4	.1829	.2488	.3783	.5268	.7484	1.100	2.076	3.516	4.475	5.380	6.251	7.366	8.190
2.6	.2301	.3067	.4541	.6198	.8629	1.243	2.275	3.773	4.761	5.689	6.580	7.719	8.558
2.8	.2818	.3693	.5344	.7169	.9809	1.388	2.475	4.027	5.043	5.995	6.905	8.065	8.919
3.0	.3379	.4360	.6187	.8177	1.102	1.535	2.674	4.279	5.322	6.296	7.225	8.406	9.274
3.2	.3978	.5068	.7067	.9218	1.226	1.684	2.874	4.529	5.599	6.593	7.540	8.742	9.623
3.4	.4615	.5811	.7981	1.029	1.352	1.835	3.073	4.778	5.873	6.888	7.852	9.073	9.968
3.6	.5286	.6588	.8925	1.139	1.481	1.988	3.273	5.025	6.144	7.179	8.160	9.401	10.31
3.8	.5989	.7396	.9899	1.251	1.612	2.142	3.472	5.271	6.413	7.467	8.465	9.725	10.64
4.0	.6722	.8232	1.090	1.366	1.745	2.297	3.672	5.515	6.681	7.754	8.767	10.05	10.98
4.2	.7483	.9096	1.192	1.483	1.879	2.453	3.872	5.758	6.946	8.038	9.067	10.36	11.31
4.4	.8271	.9986	1.297	1.602	2.015	2.611	4.072	6.000	7.210	8.319	9.364	10.68	11.63
4.6	.9084	1.090	1.404	1.723	2.153	2.769	4.271	6.242	7.473	8.599	9.658	10.99	11.96
4.8	.9921	1.183	1.513	1.846	2.292	2.929	4.471	6.482	7.734	8.877	9.951	11.30	12.28
5.0	1.078	1.279	1.623	1.970	2.433	3.090	4.671	6.721	7.994	9.154	10.24	11.60	12.59
6.0	1.537	1.785	2.202	2.613	3.152	3.904	5.670	7.906	9.275	10.51	11.67	13.11	14.15
7.0	2.037	2.330	2.814	3.285	3.895	4.734	6.670	9.075	10.53	11.84	13.06	14.57	15.66
8.0	2.571	2.906	3.454	3.981	4.656	5.576	7.669	10.23	11.77	13.15	14.42	16.00	17.13
9.0	3.132	3.507	4.115	4.695	5.432	6.428	8.669	11.38	12.99	14.43	15.76	17.40	18.58
10.0	3.717	4.130	4.795	5.425	6.221	7.289	9.669	12.52	14.21	15.71	17.08	18.78	20.00
11.0	4.321	4.771	5.491	6.169	7.021	8.157	10.67	13.65	15.41	16.96	18.39	20.14	21.40
12.0	4.943	5.428	6.201	6.924	7.829	9.031	11.67	14.78	16.60	18.21	19.68	21.49	22.78
13.0	5.580	6.099	6.922	7.690	8.646	9.910	12.67	15.90	17.78	19.44	20.96	22.82	24.14
14.0	6.231	6.782	7.654	8.464	9.470	10.79	13.67	17.01	18.96	20.67	22.23	24.14	25.50
15.0	6.893	7.477	8.395	9.246	10.30	11.68	14.67	18.13	20.13	21.89	23.49	25.45	26.84
16.0	7.567	8.181	9.145	10.04	11.14	12.57	15.67	19.23	21.29	23.10	24.74	26.74	28.16
17.0	8.251	8.895	9.903	10.83	11.98	13.47	16.67	20.34	22.45	24.30	25.98	28.03	29.48
18.0	8.943	9.616	10.67	11.63	12.82	14.37	17.67	21.44	23.61	25.50	27.22	29.31	30.79
19.0	9.644	10.35	11.44	12.44	13.67	15.27	18.67	22.54	24.76	26.69	28.45	30.58	32.09
20.0	10.35	11.08	12.22	13.25	14.53	16.17	19.67	23.63	25.90	27.88	29.67	31.85	33.38
25.0	14.00	14.85	16.18	17.38	18.84	20.72	24.67	29.08	31.58	33.75	35.71	38.08	39.74
30.0	17.77	18.74	20.24	21.59	23.23	25.32	29.67	34.49	37.20	39.54	41.65	44.19	45.98
35.0	21.64	22.72	24.38	25.87	27.66	29.95	34.67	39.86	42.76	45.27	47.51	50.21	52.11
40.0	25.59	26.77	28.58	30.20	32.14	34.60	39.67	45.20	48.29	50.94	53.31	56.16	58.16
45.0	29.60	30.88	32.82	34.56	36.65	39.28	44.67	50.53	53.78	56.57	59.07	62.06	64.15
50.0	33.66	35.03	37.11	38.96	41.18	43.97	49.67	55.83	59.25	62.17	64.78	67.90	70.08

5.3 Special Tables

5.3.1 Special Factors

The following table contains conversion factors which are needed to calculate unbiased estimators (and their variances) for the mean and the standard deviation of normally distributed populations.

We are considering a production process which generates product units with a $no(\mu;\sigma^2)$-distributed quality characteristic X. Suppose that for the **estimation of the process level** μ and the process standard deviation σ one takes m samples $X_{i1},\ldots,X_{in}$ of constant size n. The distribution parameter μ can then be estimated unbiasedly by the mean $\bar{\tilde{X}}_m$ of the individual sample medians $\tilde{X}_{1n},\ldots,\tilde{X}_{mn}$. The variance of this estimator is

$$V(\bar{\tilde{X}}_m) = \frac{\sigma^2}{m\cdot n}\cdot c_n^2.$$

For the **estimation of the process standard deviation** σ one can for example use the mean $\bar{S}_m$ of the m sample standard deviations $S_{1n},\ldots,S_{mn}$. After dividing $\bar{S}_m$ by the term a_n, previously introduced in (2.74), we get the unbiased estimate $\hat{\sigma} := \bar{S}_m/a_n$. Its variance is according to (4.103) given by

$$V\left(\frac{\bar{S}_m}{a_n}\right) = \left(\frac{b_n}{a_n}\right)^2\cdot\frac{\sigma^2}{m}$$

where $b_n := \sqrt{1-a_n^2}$. The process standard deviation can also be estimated by the mean $\bar{R}_m$ or the median $\tilde{R}_m$ of the sample ranges $R_{1n},\ldots,R_{mn}$, i.e., by $\hat{\sigma} := \bar{R}_m/d_n$ or $\hat{\sigma} := \tilde{R}_m/\tilde{d}_m$, respectively. As stated in (4.106) or (4.107) the variances of these estimators are

$$V\left(\frac{\bar{R}_m}{d_n}\right) = \left(\frac{e_n}{d_n}\right)^2\cdot\frac{\sigma^2}{m};\qquad V\left(\frac{\tilde{R}_m}{\tilde{d}_n}\right) = \frac{\sigma^2}{4m\cdot\tilde{e}_n^2}.$$

The constants $c_\nu, a_\nu, b_\nu, b_\nu/a_\nu, d_\nu, e_\nu, e_\nu/d_\nu$ as well as $\tilde{d}_\nu$ and $\tilde{e}_\nu$ are listed in the following table for $\nu = 2,3,\ldots,20$. For larger values of ν one can use the approximations

$$c_\nu \approx \sqrt{\pi/2} \approx 1.253$$

$$a_\nu \approx 1 - \frac{1}{4(\nu-1)};\qquad b_\nu = \sqrt{1-a_\nu^2} \approx \frac{1}{\sqrt{2(\nu-1)}}.$$

We also have the asymptotic results

$$\lim_{\nu \to \infty} c_\nu = \sqrt{\pi/2} \approx 1.253$$

$$\lim_{\nu \to \infty} a_\nu = 1; \qquad \lim_{\nu \to \infty} b_\nu = 0.$$

Example

We want to estimate σ by using the corrected mean of the m sample ranges, i.e., by $\hat{\sigma} = \bar{R}_m / d_n$. The sample ranges are obtained from samples of size $n = 15$. The result is

$$\hat{\sigma} = \frac{\bar{R}_m}{d_{15}} \approx \frac{\bar{R}_m}{3.472}; \qquad V\left(\frac{\bar{R}_m}{d_{15}}\right) = \left(\frac{e_{15}}{d_{15}}\right)^2 \cdot \frac{\sigma^2}{m} \approx 0.217^2 \cdot \frac{\sigma^2}{m}.$$

Table 5.3/1: Special factors

ν	c_ν	a_ν	b_ν	b_ν/a_ν	d_ν	e_ν	e_ν/d_ν	$\tilde{d}_\nu$	$\tilde{e}_\nu$
(1)	(2)	(3)	(4)	(5)	(6)	(7)	(8)	(9)	(10)
2	1.000	0.798	0.603	0.756	1.128	0.853	0.756	0.954	0.450
3	1.160	0.886	0.463	0.523	1.693	0.888	0.525	1.588	0.435
4	1.092	0.921	0.389	0.422	2.059	0.880	0.427	1.978	0.445
5	1.198	0.940	0.341	0.363	2.326	0.864	0.371	2.257	0.457
6	1.136	0.952	0.308	0.324	2.534	0.848	0.335	2.472	0.468
7	1.214	0.959	0.282	0.294	2.704	0.833	0.308	2.645	0.477
8	1.159	0.965	0.262	0.272	2.847	0.820	0.288	2.791	0.487
9	1.223	0.969	0.246	0.254	2.970	0.808	0.272	2.915	0.495
10	1.175	0.973	0.232	0.238	3.078	0.797	0.259	3.024	0.503
11	1.229	0.975	0.221	0.227	3.173	0.787	0.248	3.121	0.509
12	1.190	0.978	0.211	0.216	3.258	0.778	0.239	3.207	0.515
13	1.233	0.979	0.202	0.206	3.336	0.770	0.231	3.285	0.521
14	1.195	0.981	0.194	0.198	3.407	0.762	0.224	3.356	0.527
15	1.237	0.982	0.187	0.190	3.472	0.755	0.217	3.422	0.532
16	1.202	0.983	0.181	0.184	3.532	0.749	0.212	3.382	
17	1.238	0.985	0.175	0.178	3.588	0.743	0.207	3.538	
18	1.207	0.985	0.170	0.173	3.640	0.738	0.203	3.591	
19	1.239	0.986	0.165	0.167	3.689	0.733	0.199	3.640	
20	1.212	0.987	0.161	0.163	3.735	0.729	0.195	3.686	
∞	1.253	1	0	0	-	-	-	-	

5.3.2 Percentiles of the Standardized Sample Range

The following table lists selected percentiles of the standardized sample range based on a sample from a normally distributed population. Suppose that we have a $no(\mu;\sigma^2)$-distributed polulation. The **sample range** in a sample of size n is according to (2.70) given by

$$R_n := X_{<n;n>} - X_{<1;n>}$$

where $X_{<n;n>}$ denotes the biggest and $X_{<1;n>}$ the smallest component of the sample vector (2.63). The range R_n is a random variable. The same holds for the **standardized sample range**

$$R_n^* := \frac{R_n}{\sigma}.$$

In table 5.3/2 we have tabulated the **percentiles** or **percentage points** $r_{n;\omega}^*$ of the variable R_n^* for various sample sizes n and probabilities ω. Let $F(r_n^*) := P(R_n^* \leq r_n^*)$ denote the cumulative distribution function of R_n^*. Then it holds that

$$F(r_{n;\omega}^*) = Pr(R_n^* \leq r_{n;\omega}^*) = \omega.$$

As in figure 5.2/2 the percentiles $r_{n;\omega}^*$ can also be determined graphically.

Example: It holds that $r_{5;0.95}^* \approx 3.86$, i.e. the cumulative distribution function of R_5^* reaches the value 0.95 at r_5^*.

Table 5.3/2: Percentiles of the sample range

ω	.001	.005	.01	.025	.05	.10	.30	.50	.70	.90	0.95	0.975	0.99	0.995	0.999
2	0.00	0.01	0.02	0.04	0.09	0.18	0.54	0.95	1.47	2.33	2.77	3.17	3.64	3.97	4.65
3	0.06	0.13	0.19	0.30	0.43	0.62	1.14	1.59	2.09	2.90	3.31	3.68	4.12	4.42	5.06
4	0.20	0.34	0.43	0.59	0.76	0.98	1.53	1.98	2.47	3.24	3.63	3.98	4.40	4.69	5.31
5	0.37	0.55	0.67	0.85	1.03	1.26	1.82	2.26	2.73	3.48	3.86	4.20	4.60	4.89	5.48
6	0.53	0.75	0.87	1.07	1.25	1.49	2.04	2.47	2.94	3.66	4.03	4.36	4.76	5.03	5.62
7	0.69	0.92	1.05	1.25	1.44	1.68	2.22	2.65	3.10	3.81	4.17	4.49	4.88	5.15	5.73
8	0.83	1.08	1.20	1.41	1.60	1.84	2.38	2.79	3.24	3.93	4.29	4.60	4.99	5.25	5.82
9	0.97	1.21	1.34	1.55	1.74	1.97	2.51	2.92	3.35	4.04	4.39	4.70	5.08	5.34	5.90
10	1.08	1.33	1.47	1.67	1.86	2.09	2.62	3.02	3.46	4.13	4.47	4.78	5.16	5.42	5.97
11	1.19	1.45	1.58	1.78	1.97	2.20	2.72	3.12	3.55	4.21	4.55	4.86	5.23	5.49	6.04
12	1.29	1.55	1.68	1.88	2.07	2.30	2.82	3.21	3.63	4.28	4.62	4.92	4.29	5.55	6.09
13	1.39	1.64	1.77	1.98	2.16	2.39	2.90	3.28	3.70	4.35	4.68	4.99	5.35	5.60	6.14
14	1.47	1.72	1.86	2.06	2.24	2.47	2.97	3.36	3.77	4.41	4.74	5.04	5.40	5.65	6.19
15	1.55	1.80	1.93	2.14	2.32	2.54	3.04	3.43	3.83	4.47	4.80	5.09	5.45	5.70	6.23
16	1.62	1.88	2.01	2.21	2.39	2.61	3.11	3.48	3.89	4.52	4.85	5.14	5.49	5.74	6.27
17	1.69	1.94	2.07	2.27	2.45	2.67	3.17	3.54	3.94	4.57	4.89	5.18	5.54	5.78	6.31
18	1.76	2.01	2.14	2.34	2.52	2.73	3.22	3.59	3.99	4.61	4.91	5.22	5.57	5.82	6.35
19	1.82	2.07	2.20	2.39	2.57	2.79	3.27	3.64	4.03	4.65	4.97	5.26	5.61	5.86	6.38
20	1.88	2.13	2.25	2.45	2.63	2.84	3.32	3.69	4.08	4.69	5.01	5.30	5.65	5.89	6.41

6 Solutions to Exercises

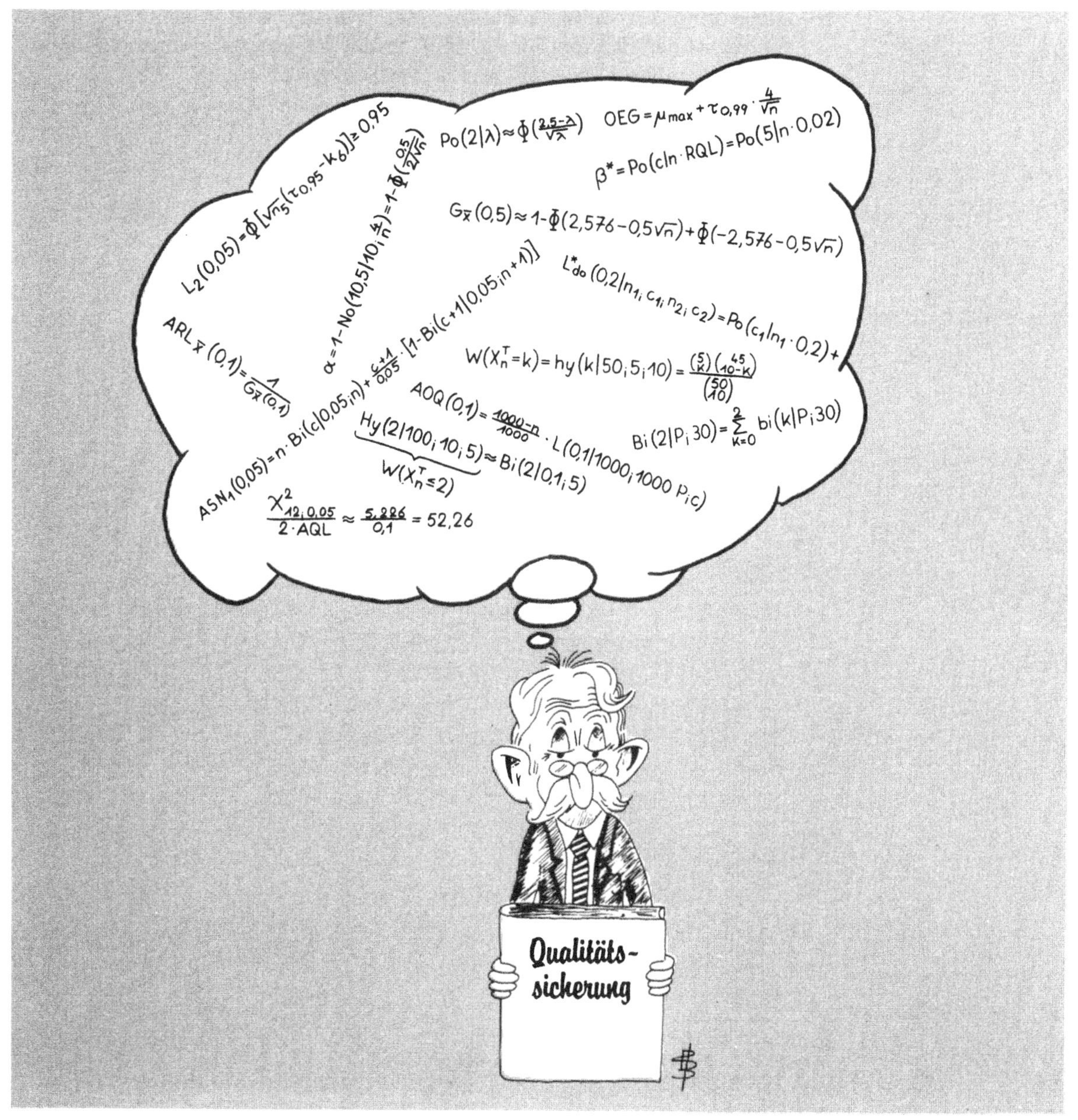

Since this text is intended to be a self-instructional introduction to quality assurance, chapters 2 – 4 contain a variety of problems for enhancing and monitoring the readers understanding of the material presented. Chapter 6 presents detailed solutions to these problems. Graphical illustrations and summary tables have been used as much as possible.

Figure on the title page of this chapter:
A reader of this text while working on the problems
(Design: P. Becker, Centre for Correspondence Study Development at the FernUniversität Hagen)

6.1 Solutions for Chapter 2

Problem 2.1/1

Nominal:	color reproduction of a photographic film (true, blue tint, red tint)
Cardinal:	Surface quality of a work piece (very rough = 1, rough = 2, smooth = 3)
Interval scale:	temperature in ° Celsius or ° Fahrenheit
Proportional scale:	temperature in ° Kelvin
Absolute scale:	number of knots per 1000 m of yarn
Continuous:	dimensions of a work piece
Discrete:	number of switching times of a relais until breakdown

Problem 2.1/2

a) $$P(A_1) = 0.85;\quad P(A_2) = 0.07;\quad P(A_3) = 0.03;\quad P(A_4) = 0.05;$$

A_2^* and A_3^* are statistically dependent since $P(A_2^* \cap A_3^*) \neq P(A_2^*) \cdot P(A_3^*)$.

$$P(A_2^*|A_3^*) = \frac{P(A_2^* \cap A_3^*)}{P(A_3^*)} = \frac{0.05}{0.08} = \frac{5}{8};\quad P(A_3^*|A_2^*) = \frac{P(A_2^* \cap A_3^*)}{P(A_2^*)} = \frac{0.05}{0.12} = \frac{5}{12}.$$

b) Seven different classes B_1 – B_7 have to be formed. These classes constitute mutually exclusive outcomes of a new quality characteristic:

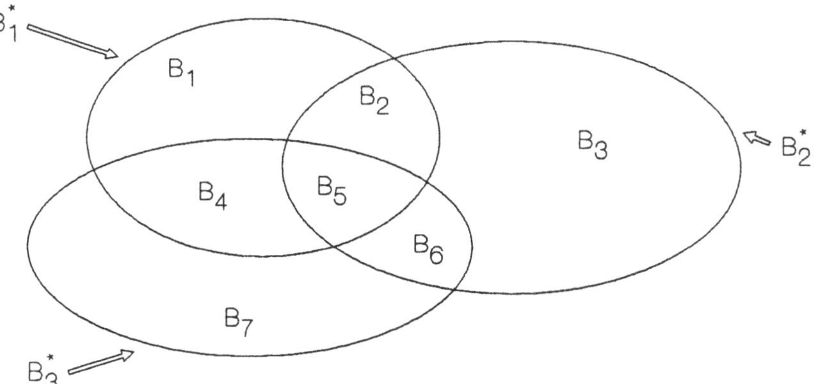

Figure 6.1/1: Venn diagram for seven mutually exclusive outcomes of a quality characteristic

$B_1 := B_1^* \setminus [(B_1^* \cap B_2^*) \cup (B_1^* \cap B_3^*)]$	(only B_1^*)
$B_2 := (B_1^* \cap B_2^*) \setminus (B_1^* \cap B_2^* \cap B_3^*)$	(B_1^* and B_2^* without B_3^*)
$B_3 := B_2^* \setminus [(B_1^* \cap B_2^*) \cup (B_2^* \cap B_3^*)]$	(only B_2^*)
$B_4 := (B_1^* \cap B_3^*) \setminus (B_1^* \cap B_2^* \cap B_3^*)$	(B_1^* and B_3^* without B_2^*)
$B_5 := B_1^* \cap B_2^* \cap B_3^*$	(B_1^* and B_2^* and B_3^*)
$B_6 := (B_2^* \cap B_3^*) \setminus (B_1^* \cap B_2^* \cap B_3^*)$	(B_2^* and B_3^* without B_1^*)
$B_7 := B_3^* \setminus [(B_1^* \cap B_3^*) \cup (B_2^* \cap B_3^*)]$	(only B_3^*)

c) Quality characteristic:
The surface quality of window glass, characterized by the number of air bubbles and visible scratches. A piece of glass can be perfect, have only bubbles or only scratches, or have both scratches and bubbles.

Problem 2.1/3

a) Mass function:

$$Pr(X = x) = \begin{cases} \frac{1}{36} & \text{if } x = 2 \quad \text{or } x = 12 \\ \frac{2}{36} & \text{if } x = 3 \quad \text{or } x = 11 \\ \frac{3}{36} & \text{if } x = 4 \quad \text{or } x = 10 \\ \frac{4}{36} & \text{if } x = 5 \quad \text{or } x = 9 \\ \frac{5}{36} & \text{if } x = 6 \quad \text{or } x = 8 \\ \frac{6}{36} & \text{if } x = 7 \end{cases}$$

Distribution function:

$$F(x) = Pr(X \leq x) = \begin{cases} 0 & \text{for } x < 2 \\ \frac{1}{36} \cdot [1 + 2 + \ldots + (i-1)] & \text{for } i \leq x < i+1; i = 2, \ldots, 7 \\ \frac{21}{36} + \frac{1}{36} \cdot [5 + 4 + \ldots + (13 - i)] & \text{for } i \leq x < i+1; i = 8, \ldots, 11 \\ 1 & \text{for } x \geq 12 \end{cases}$$

Expectation: $\mu = 7$
Variance and standard deviation: $\sigma^2 = 35/6 \approx 5.8333$; $\sigma \approx 2.4152$
Mode and median: $x_M = x_{0.5} = 7$; skewness: $a_3 = 0$.

b) We have a uniform distribution with $a = 0$, $b = 1$ and $L = 9$:

$$un(x \mid 0;1;9) = \begin{cases} 0.1 & \text{for } x = 0, 1, \ldots, 9 \\ 0 & \text{else} \end{cases}$$

$$Un(x \mid 0;1;9) = \begin{cases} 0 & \text{for } x < 0 \\ 0.1 \cdot (k+1) & \text{for } k \le x < k+1 \quad (k = 0, \ldots, 8) \\ 1 & \text{for } x \ge 9 \end{cases}$$

$$Un^{-1}(y \mid 0;1;9) = \begin{cases} 0 & \text{for } 0 < y \le 0.1 \\ 1 & \text{for } 0.1 < y \le 0.2 \\ \vdots & \qquad \vdots \\ 9 & \text{for } 0.9 < y \le 1 \end{cases}$$

Expectation: $\mu = 4.5$
Variance and standard deviation: $\sigma^2 = 8.25$; $\sigma \approx 2.8723$
Mode: not defined; median: $x_{0.5} = 4$; skewness: $a_3 = 0$.

Problem 2.1/4

a)
$$be(x \mid 0.15) = \begin{cases} 0.85 & \text{for } x = 0 \\ 0.15 & \text{for } x = 1 \\ 0 & \text{else} \end{cases}$$

$$Be(x \mid 0.15) = \begin{cases} 0 & \text{for } x < 0 \\ 0.85 & \text{for } 0 \le x < 1 \\ 1 & \text{for } x \ge 1 \end{cases}$$

$$Be^{-1}(0.5 \mid 0.15) = 0$$

Expectation: $\mu = P = 0.15$
Variance: $\sigma^2 = PQ = 0.15 \cdot 0.85 = 0.1275$
Mode: $x_M = 0$.

See next page for the graphs of the mass function and the distribution function.

b) Differentiate the function $\sigma^2 = P(1 - P)$ with respect to P and set the result to zero:

$$\frac{d[P(1-P)]}{dP} = 1 - 2P = 0.$$

Thus σ^2 attains its maximum $\sigma^2 = 0.25$ at $P = 0.5$.

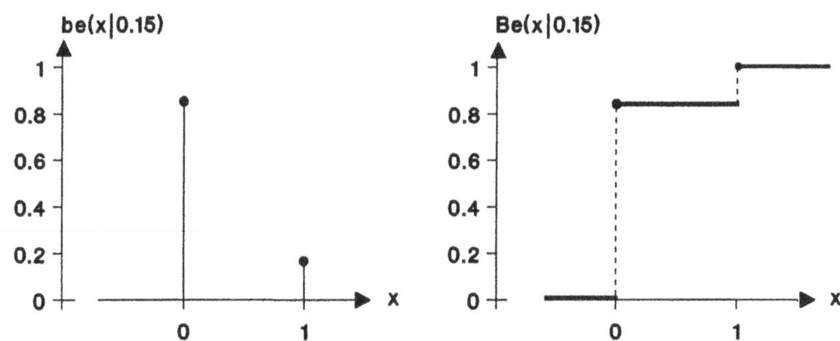

Figure 6.1/2: Mass and distribution function of the Bernoulli distribution with $P = 0.15$

c) $$E[(X-\mu)^3] = (0-P)^3 \cdot (1-P) + (1-P)^3 P = P(1-P) \cdot (1-2P)$$

$$a_3 = \frac{P(1-P)(1-2P)}{\sqrt{[P(1-P)]^3}} \begin{cases} > 0 & \text{for } 0 < P < 0.5 \\ = 0 & \text{for } P = 0.5 \\ < 0 & \text{for } 0.5 < P < 1. \end{cases}$$

Problem 2.1/5

a) The number of impurities per 5 dm^2 of area is Poisson distributed with $\lambda = 1$. Because of the reproductivity of the Poisson distribution, for the number X of impurities per 50 dm^2 disc it holds that $X \sim po(10)$.

b)
$$\begin{aligned} P(\text{first grade}) &= Pr(X \le 10) = Po(10 \mid 10) = 0.58304 \\ P(\text{second grade}) &= Pr(10 < X \le 15) = Po(15 \mid 10) - Po(10 \mid 10) \\ &= 0.95126 - 0.58304 = 0.36822 \\ P(\text{scrap}) &= Pr(X > 15) = 1 - Po(15 \mid 10) = 1 - 0.95126 = 0.04874. \end{aligned}$$

c)
$$\begin{aligned} po\left(0 \mid \tfrac{1}{3}\right) &= \frac{\left(\frac{1}{3}\right)^0}{0!} \cdot e^{-1/3} = 0.71653 & Po\left(0 \mid \tfrac{1}{3}\right) &= 0.71653 \\ po\left(1 \mid \tfrac{1}{3}\right) &= \tfrac{1}{3} \cdot po\left(0 \mid \tfrac{1}{3}\right) = 0.23884 & Po\left(1 \mid \tfrac{1}{3}\right) &= 0.95537 \\ po\left(2 \mid \tfrac{1}{3}\right) &= \tfrac{1}{6} \cdot po\left(1 \mid \tfrac{1}{3}\right) = 0.03981 & Po\left(2 \mid \tfrac{1}{3}\right) &= 0.99518 \\ po\left(3 \mid \tfrac{1}{3}\right) &= \tfrac{1}{9} \cdot po\left(2 \mid \tfrac{1}{3}\right) = 0.00442 & Po\left(3 \mid \tfrac{1}{3}\right) &= 0.99960 \\ po\left(4 \mid \tfrac{1}{3}\right) &= \tfrac{1}{12} \cdot po\left(3 \mid \tfrac{1}{3}\right) = 0.00037 & Po\left(4 \mid \tfrac{1}{3}\right) &= 0.99997. \end{aligned}$$

The values $Po(x|1/3)$, $x = 0, 1, 2, \ldots$ lie between the values $Po(x|0.3)$ and $Po(x|0.35)$ which can be found in table 5.1/4.

$$Pr(1 \le X \le 3) = Po\left(3 \mid \tfrac{1}{3}\right) - Po\left(0 \mid \tfrac{1}{3}\right) = 0.99960 - 0.71653 = 0.28307.$$

Problem 2.1/6

a) $$c = \frac{1}{b-a}.$$

b) $$\mu = \frac{1}{b-a}\int_a^b x\,dx = \frac{b^2-a^2}{2(b-a)} = \frac{a+b}{2}.$$

c) $$\begin{aligned} E(|X-\mu|) &= \frac{1}{b-a}\left[\int_a^\mu (\mu-x)dx + \int_\mu^b (x-\mu)dx\right] \\ &= \frac{1}{b-a}\left[\frac{\mu^2}{2} - a\left(\mu - \frac{a}{2}\right) + b\left(\frac{b}{2}-\mu\right) + \frac{\mu^2}{2}\right] \\ &= \frac{1}{b-a}\left[\left(\frac{a+b}{2}\right)^2 - a\cdot\frac{b}{2} + b\cdot\left(-\frac{a}{2}\right)\right] \\ &= \frac{b-a}{4}. \end{aligned}$$

d) $x_{0.95} = a + (b-a)\cdot 0.95$; $x_{0.05} = a + (b-a)\cdot 0.05$; $x_{0.95} - x_{0.05} = (b-a)\cdot 0.9$.

e) $$re(x \mid c; d) = \begin{cases} 1/(2d) & \text{for } c-d \le x \le c+d \\ 0 & \text{else} \end{cases}$$

$$Re(x \mid c; d) = \begin{cases} 0 & \text{for } x < c-d \\ (x+d-c)/(2d) & \text{for } c-d \le x \le c+d \\ 1 & \text{for } x > c+d \end{cases}$$

$$Re^{-1}(c; d) = 2dy - d + c; \quad 0 \le y \le 1$$

$$\mu = c; \quad \sigma^2 = \frac{d^2}{3}.$$

f) $$re(x|0;1) = \begin{cases} 1 & \text{for } 0 \le x \le 1 \\ 0 & \text{else} \end{cases}$$

$$Re(x|0;1) = \begin{cases} 0 & \text{for } x < 0 \\ x & \text{for } 0 \le x \le 1 \\ 1 & \text{for } x > 1 \end{cases}$$

$$Re^{-1}(y|0;1) = y \quad \text{for } 0 \le y \le 1$$

$$\mu = 0.5; \quad \sigma^2 = 1/12.$$

Problem 2.1/7

a) $$\mu = \frac{1}{\lambda} = 0.5; \;\; \sigma^2 = \frac{1}{\lambda^2} = 0.25$$

$$Pr(X < 1) = Ex(1|2) = 1 - e^{-2} \approx 0.8647$$

$$Pr(X > 2) = 1 - Ex(2|2) = 1 - (1 - e^{-4}) \approx 0.0183.$$

$$Pr(0.5 < X < 1.5) = Ex(1.5|2) - Ex(0.5|2) = (1 - e^{-3}) - (1 - e^{-1}) \approx 0.3181$$

$$Pr(\mu - 3\sigma < X < \mu + 3\sigma) = Pr(-1 < X < 2) = Ex(2|2) = 1 - e^{-4} \approx 0.9817$$

$$x_{0.5} = -\frac{\ln\ 0.5}{2} \approx 0.3466 \qquad x_{0.975} = -\frac{\ln\ 0.025}{2} \approx 1.8444$$

$$x_{0.025} = -\frac{\ln\ 0.975}{2} \approx 0.0127 \quad x_{0.975} - x_{0.025} \approx 1.8317$$

b) $$Ex\left(\frac{1}{\lambda}|\lambda\right) = 1 - e^{-1} \approx 0.6321, \text{ i.e. } x_{0.6321} = \frac{1}{\lambda} = \mu.$$

Hence, in the case of the exponential distribution the expectation and the percentile of order 0.6321 are identical.

c) Since $\mu = 1/\lambda = 2000$, we have $\lambda = 0.0005$ and thus

$$Pr(X < 250) = Ex(250|0.0005) = 1 - e^{-0.125} \approx 0.1175.$$

Problem 2.1/8

$$Pr(X \geq 10) = 1 - No(10|2; 25) = 1 - \Phi\left(\tfrac{10-2}{5}\right) = 1 - \Phi(1.6) = 0.054799$$

$$Pr(-3 \leq X \leq 7) = \Phi\left(\tfrac{7-2}{5}\right) - \Phi\left(\tfrac{-3-2}{5}\right) = \Phi(1) - [1 - \Phi(1)] \approx 0.682690$$

$$Pr(X \leq -13) = \Phi\left(\tfrac{-13-2}{5}\right) = 1 - \Phi(3) \approx 0.001350.$$

Problem 2.1/9

a) As μ increases (decreases) the density curve is shifted to the right (left).

b) As σ^2 increases (decreases) the density curve becomes less steep (steeper).

Problem 2.1/10

a) $$P(1001) = Pr(X \notin [998.5; 1001.5] | \mu) = Pr(X < 998.5 | \mu) + Pr(X > 1001.5 | \mu)$$

With result (2.52) and table 5.1/1 it follows that

$$P(1001) \quad = \Phi\left(\frac{998.5 - 1001}{0.5}\right) + \left[1 - \Phi\left(\frac{1001.5 - 1001}{0.5}\right)\right] = 0.158655.$$

Thus about 15.87% of the filled packages are nonconforming to specifications ("scrap").

b) $$P(\mu) \quad = \Phi\left(\frac{998.5 - \mu}{0.5}\right) + \left[1 - \Phi\left(\frac{1001.5 - \mu}{0.5}\right)\right]$$

$$= \Phi\left(\frac{998.5 - \mu}{0.5}\right) + \Phi\left(\frac{\mu - 1001.5}{0.5}\right)$$

The function is symmetric with respect to $\mu = 1000$, i.e., $P(1000 + \Delta) = P(1000 - \Delta)$:

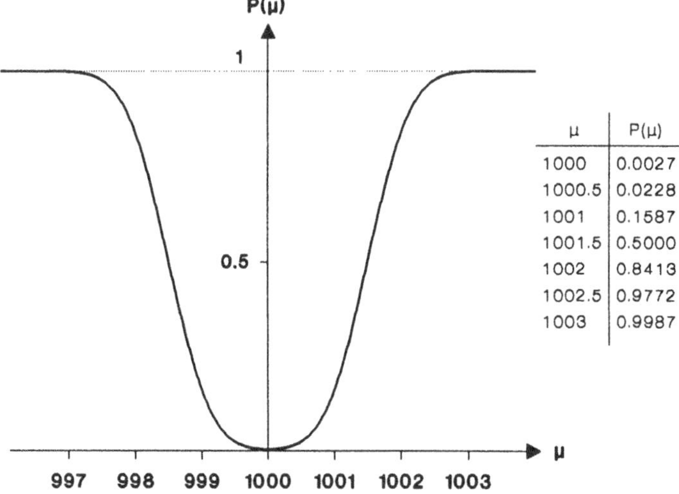

μ	P(μ)
1000	0.0027
1000.5	0.0228
1001	0.1587
1001.5	0.5000
1002	0.8413
1002.5	0.9772
1003	0.9987

Figure 6.1/3: Fraction nonconforming of a normally distributed quality characteristic as a function of μ

c) From the previous graph we can see that $P(\mu)$ attains its minimum at $\mu = 1000$. With $\mu = 1000$ it holds that $X \sim no(1000; 0.5^2)$ and the fraction nonconforming $P = P(1000)$ has the value 0.27 %:

$$P = \Phi\left(\frac{998.5 - 1000}{0.5}\right) + \Phi\left(\frac{1000 - 1001.5}{0.5}\right) = 2[1 - \Phi(3)] = 0.0027.$$

This result can also be seen from the tabulated values to the right of the graph. Formally, the value $\mu = 1000$ with minimum fraction nonconforming can be obtained by differentiating the function $P(\mu)$, which is given in the solution of part b, and setting the result to zero. Since the first derivative of (2.50) is given by (2.49) it follows for $dP/d\mu$ that:

$$\frac{dP(\mu)}{d\mu} = \phi\left(\frac{998.5-\mu}{0.5}\right) - \phi\left(\frac{1001.5-\mu}{0.5}\right)$$

$$= \frac{1}{\sqrt{2}}\left[\exp\left\{-\frac{(998.5-\mu)^2}{2\cdot 0.5^2}\right\} - \exp\left\{-\frac{(1001.5-\mu)^2}{2\cdot 0.5^2}\right\}\right].$$

The term in the square brackets is obviously zero only for $\mu = 1000\ g$. With the help of the second derivative of the function $P(\mu)$, it is easily verified that $P(\mu)$ attains a minimum at this point.

d) $$P(\sigma) = \Phi\left(\frac{998.5-1000}{\sigma}\right) - \Phi\left(\frac{1000-1001.5}{\sigma}\right) = 2[1-\Phi\left(\frac{1.5}{\sigma}\right)].$$

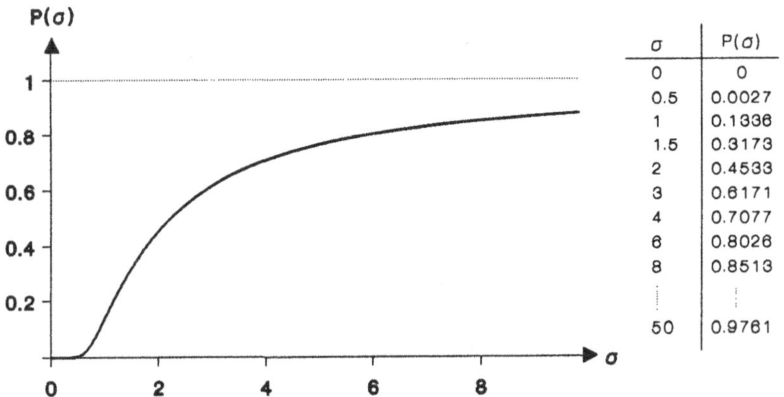

σ	P(σ)
0	0
0.5	0.0027
1	0.1336
1.5	0.3173
2	0.4533
3	0.6171
4	0.7077
6	0.8026
8	0.8513
⋮	⋮
50	0.9761

Figure 6.1/4: Fraction nonconforming of a normally distributed quality characteristic as a function of σ

e) $$P(\mu = 1000.5) = P(\mu = 999.5) = 0.0228;\ P(\sigma = 1) = 0.1336.$$

Consequently an increase of 0.5 g in σ is more dangerous.

Problem 2.1/11

a)

Thickness X_1 of the first outer glass layer:	$X_1 \sim no(3; 0.04)$
Thickness X_2 of the first adhesive layer:	$X_2 \sim no(0.1; 0.01)$
Thickness X_3 of the middle glass layer:	$X_3 \sim no(6; 0.09)$
Thickness X_4 of the second adhesive layer:	$X_4 \sim no(0.1; 0.01)$
Thickness X_5 of the second outer glass layer:	$X_5 \sim no(3; 0.04)$
Thickness Y of the bullet-proof glass:	$Y \sim no(12.2; 0.19)$

b) Twosided 99 %-variation interval in *mm*:

$$12.2 - 2.576 \cdot \sqrt{0.19} \leq Y \leq 12.2 + 2.576 \cdot \sqrt{0.19}, \text{ i.e., } 11.08 \leq Y \leq 13.32.$$

Onesided 99 %-variation intervals in *mm*:

$$Y \geq 12.2 - 2.326 \cdot \sqrt{0.19} = 11.19$$

$$Y \leq 12.2 + 2.326 \cdot \sqrt{0.19} = 13.21.$$

Problem 2.1/12

$$P(\text{first grade}) = Po(10|10) \approx \Phi\left(\tfrac{10.5-10}{\sqrt{10}}\right) = \Phi(0.16) = 0.563559$$

$$P(\text{second grade}) = Po(15|10) - Po(10|10) \approx \Phi\left(\tfrac{15.5-10}{\sqrt{10}}\right) - \Phi\left(\tfrac{10.5-10}{\sqrt{10}}\right)$$

$$\approx \Phi(1.74) - \Phi(0.16) = 0.395511$$

$$P(\text{scrap}) = 1 - Po(15|10) \approx 1 - \Phi\left(\tfrac{15.5-10}{\sqrt{10}}\right) \approx 1 - \Phi(1.74) = 0.040930.$$

Problem 2.1/13

With $\mu_i \equiv \mu$ and $\sigma_i^2 \equiv \sigma^2$, the random variable Y_n has the form

$$Y_n = \frac{\sum X_i - n\mu}{\sqrt{n\sigma^2}} = \frac{\bar{X}_n - \mu}{\sqrt{V(\bar{X}_n)}}; \quad \bar{X}_n := \frac{1}{n}\sum X_i; \quad V(\bar{X}_n) = \frac{\sigma^2}{n}$$

(summation from $i = 1, \ldots, n$). The term $V(\bar{X}_n)$ denotes the variance of the mean $\bar{X}_n$. The variable Y_n can be interpreted to be the standardized form of $\bar{X}_n$. According to the LINDEBERG-FELLER theorem it is approximately normally distributed for sufficiently large n.

Problem 2.2/1

a) Uniform distribution: a, b, L — Rectangular distribution: a, b

Bernoulli distribution: P — Exponential distribution: λ

Poisson distribution: λ — Normal distribution: μ, σ^2.

b) $$P = Pr(X < 99.8) + Pr(X > 100.2) = \Phi\left(\tfrac{99.8-\mu}{\sigma}\right) + \left[1 - \Phi\left(\tfrac{100.2-\mu}{\sigma}\right)\right] \leq 0.05.$$

Control of this quality standard:

$$\mu = 100; \sigma = 0.1 \quad \Rightarrow \quad P = \Phi(-2) + [1 - \Phi(2)] = 0.0455 \leq 0.05$$
$$\mu = 100; \sigma = 0.2 \quad \Rightarrow \quad P = \Phi(-1) + [1 - \Phi(1)] = 0.3173 > 0.05$$
$$\mu = 99.9; \sigma = 0.1 \quad \Rightarrow \quad P = \Phi(-1) + [1 - \Phi(3)] = 0.1600 > 0.05.$$

The standard $P \leq 0.05$ is fulfilled only in the first case.

Problem 2.2/2

a) The range of X is divided into ten equally distant intervals:

$I_0 := [0; 0.1),\ I_1 := [0.1; 0.2), ..., \ I_9 := [0.9; 1).$

If one arbitrarily considers an interval I_n $(0 \leq n \leq 9)$, then a realization of X lies in this interval with probability 0.1: $Pr(X \in I_n) = 0.1$. Therefore, one can define Y as follows:

$$Y := \begin{cases} 0 & \text{if } X \in I_0 \\ 1 & \text{if } X \in I_1 \\ \vdots & \vdots \quad \vdots \\ 9 & \text{if } X \in I_9. \end{cases}$$

b) *Case 1: Numbered lot*

If one considers only random numbers Z with $000 \leq Z \leq 299$:

$$S_i := 852 + Z_i; \qquad i = 1, ..., 10.$$

If one considers all random numbers Z with $000 \leq Z \leq 899$:

$$S_i := \begin{cases} 852 + Z_i & \text{if } 000 \leq Z_i \leq 299 \\ 852 + (Z_i - 300) & \text{if } 300 \leq Z_i \leq 599 \\ 852 + (Z_i - 600) & \text{if } 600 \leq Z_i \leq 899. \end{cases} \quad i = 1, ..., 10.$$

Both selection algorithms ensure that each serial number has the same probability of being selected.

Case 2: Random selection from a box

The selection is made with the help of three-digit random numbers Z. The first digit of Z gives the level in the box, where only the numbers 1 to 6 are drawn. (If the first digit of Z is not $1, 2, \ldots, 5$ or 6 then this particular Z is not considered.) The second digit of Z gives the row number on the selected level, for example the digits 1 or 2 indicate selection from row 1, the digits 3 or 4 indicate selection from row 2, ..., and the digits 9 or 0 indicate selection from row 5. The third digit says which column of the selected level is chosen.

Case 3: Systematic selection with randomized start

Since $N/n = 30$, each 30th unit is selected, and the starting number is determined by a random number between 1 and 30.

Problem 2.2/3

a) There are $2^3 = 8$ different possible realizations (x_1, x_2, x_3). Their corresponding probabilities of occurrence are calculated as follows:

$$\begin{aligned} Pr(0;0;0) &= 0.95^3 = 0.857375 \\ Pr(0;0;1) &= Pr(0;1;0) = Pr(1;0;0) = 0.05 \cdot 0.95^2 = 0.045125 \\ Pr(0;1;1) &= Pr(1;0;1) = Pr(1;1;0) = 0.05^2 \cdot 0.95 = 0.002375 \\ Pr(1;1;1) &= 0.05^3 = 0.000125. \end{aligned}$$

b)
$$\begin{aligned} Pr(0;0;0) &= \tfrac{95}{100} \cdot \tfrac{94}{99} \cdot \tfrac{93}{98} \approx 0.855999 \\ Pr(0;0;1) &= Pr(0;1;0) = Pr(1;0;0) = \tfrac{5}{100} \cdot \tfrac{95}{99} \cdot \tfrac{94}{98} \approx 0.046021 \\ Pr(0;1;1) &= Pr(1;0;1) = Pr(1;1;0) = \tfrac{5}{100} \cdot \tfrac{4}{99} \cdot \tfrac{95}{98} \approx 0.001958 \\ Pr(1;1;1) &= \tfrac{5}{100} \cdot \tfrac{4}{99} \cdot \tfrac{3}{98} \approx 0.000062. \end{aligned}$$

c) The distribution of a sample vector depends on:

- the distribution of the lot from which the sample is drawn,
- the sample size,
- the sampling procedure (single or multiple sampling, drawing with or without replacement, drawing with equal or unequal selection probability).

Problem 2.2/4

Distribution	Parameter to be estimated	Estimator
Bernoulli distribution	P	$\hat{P} := \bar{X}_n$
Poisson distribution	λ	$\hat{\lambda} := \bar{X}_n$
Rectangular distribution	a, b	$\hat{a} := X_{<1;n>}$ $\hat{b} := X_{<n;n>}$
Normal distribution	μ, σ^2	$\hat{\mu} := \bar{X}_n$ or $\hat{\mu} := \tilde{X}_n$ $\hat{\sigma}^2 := S_n^2$

Table 6.1/1: Distribution parameters and their estimators

Problem 2.2/5

In the following, the summation is from $i = 1, \dots, n$:

a) $$E(\hat{\mu}_{1;n}) = \frac{1}{n-1}\sum E(X_i) = \frac{n}{n-1}\cdot\mu \neq \mu;$$

$$E(\hat{\mu}_{2;n}) = \frac{1}{n}\sum [E(X_i) - 0.5] = \frac{1}{n}\cdot n\cdot(\mu - 0.5) = \mu - 0.5.$$

Only $\hat{\mu}_{1;n}$ is asymptotically unbiased.

b) Analogous to (2.77a) it holds that:

$$V(\hat{\mu}_{1;n}) = \frac{1}{(n-1)^2}\sum V(X_i) = \frac{n}{(n-1)^2}\cdot\sigma^2$$

$$V(\hat{\mu}_{2;n}) = \frac{1}{n^2}\sum V(X_i - 0.5) = \frac{1}{n^2}\sum V(X_i) = \frac{\sigma^2}{n}.$$

c) If h is linear, i.e., if $h(\theta) = a + b\theta$, because of the linearity of the expectation operator and the assumed unbiasedness of the estimator $\hat{\theta}_n$ it holds that:

$$E\left[h(\hat{\theta}_n)\right] = a + bE(\hat{\theta}_n) = a + b\theta = h(\theta).$$

d) Since $V(\bar{X}_n) < V(\tilde{X}_n)$, the estimator $\bar{X}_n$ is more efficient (see also (2.77a)). A measure of the efficiency of $\bar{X}_n$ compared to $\tilde{X}_n$ is given by the ratio

$$w = \frac{V(\tilde{X}_n)}{V(\bar{X}_n)} = \frac{\pi}{2} \approx 1.5708.$$

When working with $\tilde{X}_n$, one needs a 57.08% larger sample size than with $\bar{X}_n$ in order to ensure that both estimators have the same variance.

Problem 2.2/6

a) With $\lambda = 0.01$, according to (2.33a) and (2.33b), the exponential distribution has the expectation $\mu = 100$ and the variance $\sigma^2 = 100^2$. According to (2.77a) it follows that $V(\bar{X}_{100}) = 100$. The twosided variation interval of level 0.99 is then given by [100–25.76; 100+25.76], i.e., by [74.24;125.76] since $z_{0.995} = 2.576$ (see table 2.1/2).

b) The twosided confidence interval with confidence level 0.99 is [109–25.76;109+25.76]. As we expected (with probability of 0.99) this interval contains the point $\mu = 100$.

Problem 2.2/7

a) The equality of $hy(k|N;M;n)$ and $hy(k|N;n;M)$ can be shown using (2.80) and writing out the binomial coefficients:

$$hy(k|N;M;n) = \frac{\binom{M}{k}\binom{N-M}{n-k}}{\binom{N}{n}} = \frac{M!(N-M)!n!(N-n)!}{k!(M-k)!(n-k)!(N-M-n+k)!N!}$$

$$hy(k|N;n;M) = \frac{\binom{n}{k}\binom{N-n}{M-k}}{\binom{N}{n}} = \frac{n!(N-n)!M!(N-M)!}{k!(n-k)!(M-k)!(N-n-M+k)!N!}$$

b) Each of the four values in the interior of table 2.2/3 has to be non-negative.

From the simultaneous non-negativity of k and $N-n-M+k$, i.e., from combining the inequalities $k \geq 0$ and $k \geq n+M-N$, it follows that $k \geq \max(0; n+M-N) =: c_1$.

From the simultaneous non-negativity of $n-k$ and $M-k$, i.e., from combining the inequalities $k \leq n$ and $k \leq M$, it follows that $k \leq \min(n; M) =: c_2$.

c) With (2.84) - (2.86) and table 5.1/2 it can be verified that:

$$\begin{aligned} hy(6|20;7;16) &= hy(6|20;16;7) = hy(7-6|20;20-16;7) = hy(1|20;4;7) \approx 0.413209 \\ Hy(6|20;7;16) &= Hy(6|20;16;7) = 1 - Hy(7-6-1|20;20-16;7) \\ &= 1 - Hy(0|20;4;7) \approx 0.852425. \end{aligned}$$

Problem 2.2/8

a) The random variable X_n^T is hy(50;5;10)-distributed. Since the boundaries c_1 and c_2 in (2.80) are given by

$$c_1 = \max(0; 10+5-50) = 0; \qquad c_2 = \min(10;5) = 5$$

it holds for $k = 0, 1, \ldots, 5$ that

$$Pr(X_n^T = k) = hy(k|50;5;10) = \frac{\binom{5}{k}\binom{45}{10-k}}{\binom{50}{10}}.$$

Since the range of the table does not cover $N = 50$, we need to calculate $Pr(X = 0)$ using the definiton of the binomial coefficient

$$\binom{n}{k} := \frac{n(n-1)(n-2)\dots(n-k+1)}{1\cdot 2\cdot 3\cdot\ldots\cdot k} = \frac{n!}{k!(n-k)!}; \qquad \binom{n}{0} := 1.$$

We thus get

$$hy(0|50;5;10) = \frac{\binom{45}{10}}{\binom{50}{10}} = \frac{45!}{10!35!}\cdot\frac{10!40!}{50!} = \frac{36\cdot 37\cdot 38\cdot 39\cdot 40}{46\cdot 47\cdot 48\cdot 49\cdot 50} \approx 0.310563.$$

The other probabilities are obtained according to (2.83a):

$$hy(1|50;5;10) = \frac{(5-0)\cdot(10-0)}{(0+1)\cdot(50-5-10+0+1)}\cdot hy(0|50;5;10) \approx 0.431336$$

$$hy(2|50;5;10) = \frac{(5-1)\cdot(10-1)}{(1+1)\cdot(50-5-10+1+1)}\cdot hy(1|50;5;10) \approx 0.209839$$

$$hy(3|50;5;10) = \frac{(5-2)\cdot(10-2)}{(2+1)\cdot(50-5-10+2+1)}\cdot hy(2|50;5;10) \approx 0.044177$$

$$hy(4|50;5;10) = \frac{(5-3)\cdot(10-3)}{(3+1)\cdot(50-5-10+3+1)}\cdot hy(3|50;5;10) \approx 0.003965$$

$$hy(5|50;5;10) = \frac{(5-4)\cdot(10-4)}{(4+1)\cdot(50-5-10+4+1)}\cdot hy(4|50;5;10) \approx 0.000119.$$

The mode is found to be $k_M = 1$. The expectation and variance are calculated using (2.90):

$$\mu = n\cdot\frac{M}{N} = 10\cdot\frac{5}{50} = 1; \qquad \sigma^2 = n\cdot\frac{M}{N}\cdot\frac{N-M}{N}\cdot\frac{N-n}{N-1} \approx 0.7347.$$

b) The random variable X has a negative hypergeometric distribution with $N = 50$, $M = 5$ and $c = 3$. Since all the given sample sizes lie in the range between $c = 3$ and $N-M+c = 48$, it first follows by (2.88a) that:

$$nh(25|50;5;3) = \frac{\binom{5}{2}\binom{45}{22}}{\binom{50}{24}} \cdot \frac{5-3+1}{50-25+1} \approx 0.039079.$$

For calculating $nh(25|50;5;3)$ we can again use the definition of the binomial coefficient. The remaining probabilities $Pr(X=k) = nh(k|50;5;3)$ are then calculated using (2.91):

$$nh(26|50;5;3) = \frac{25 \cdot (50-5+3-25)}{(25-3+1)\cdot(50-25)} \cdot nh(25|50;5;3) \approx 0.039079$$

$$nh(27|50;5;3) = \frac{26 \cdot (50-5+3-26)}{(26-3+1)\cdot(50-26)} \cdot nh(26|50;5;3) \approx 0.038808$$

$$nh(24|50;5;3) = \frac{(25-3)\cdot(50-25+1)}{(25-1)\cdot(50-5+3-25+1)} \cdot nh(25|50;5;3) \approx 0.038808$$

$$nh(23|50;5;3) = \frac{(24-3)\cdot(50-24+1)}{(24-1)\cdot(50-5+3-24+1)} \cdot nh(24|50;5;3) \approx 0.038268.$$

The expectation and variance are finally obtained from (2.90):

$$\mu = c \cdot \frac{N+1}{M+1} = 3 \cdot \frac{51}{6} = 25.5;$$

$$\sigma^2 = c \cdot \frac{(N+1)(N-N)(M+1-c)}{(M+1)^2(M+2)} = 3 \cdot \frac{51 \cdot 45 \cdot 3}{6^2 \cdot 7} \approx 81.9643.$$

Problem 2.2/9

a) The expectations are equal: $\mu = \underbrace{\lambda}_{\mu_P} = \underbrace{nP}_{\mu_H,\,\mu_B}.$

Since $0 < Q := 1-P < 1$ and $N > n \geq 1$ it holds for the variances that:

$$\underbrace{nP}_{\sigma_P^2} > \underbrace{nPQ}_{\sigma_B^2} \geq \underbrace{nPQ\frac{N-n}{N-1}}_{\sigma_H^2} \quad \text{(equality for } n=1\text{)}.$$

(The indices "P", "H" and "B" indicate which of the three distributions is meant.)

b)
$$Pr(X_n^T = 2) = hy(2|100;10;5) = \frac{\binom{10}{2}\binom{90}{3}}{\binom{100}{5}} \approx 0.07022$$

$$\begin{aligned} Pr(X_n^T \le 2) &= Hy(2|100;10;5)^{1)} \\ &= hy(0|100;10;5) + hy(1|100;10;5) + hy(2|100;10;5) \\ &\approx 0.58375 + 0.33939 + 0.07022 \\ &= 0.99336. \end{aligned}$$

Since $n = 5$, the conditions for the application of the approximations (2.87a-c) are not completely satisfied. If one uses them nevertheless, one gets the following results:

Binomial approximation

$$hy(2|100;10;5) \approx bi(2|0.1;5) = \binom{5}{2} \cdot 0.1^2 \cdot 0.9^3 = 0.07290$$

$$\begin{aligned} Hy(2|100;10;5) &\approx Bi(2|0.1;5)^{2)} \\ &= bi(0|0.1;5) + bi(1|0.1;5) + bi(2|0.1;5) \\ &\approx 0.59049 + 0.32805 + 0.07290 \\ &= 0.99144. \end{aligned}$$

Poisson approximation

$$\begin{aligned} hy(2|100;10;5) &\approx po(1|0.5) \approx 0.0758 \\ Hy(2|100;10;5) &\approx Po(1|0.5) \approx 0.9856. \end{aligned}$$

Normal approximation with continuity correction

Using table 5.1/1, one can verify that

$$\begin{aligned} hy(2|100;10;5) &\approx \Phi\left(\frac{2+0.5-5\cdot 0.1}{\sqrt{5\cdot 0.1\cdot 0.9\cdot \frac{95}{99}}}\right) - \Phi\left(\frac{2-0.5-5\cdot 0.1}{\sqrt{5\cdot 0.1\cdot 0.9\cdot \frac{95}{99}}}\right) \\ &\approx \Phi(3.04) - \Phi(1.52) \\ &\approx 0.9988 - 0.9357 \\ &= 0.0631. \end{aligned}$$

$$Hy(2|100;10;5) \approx \Phi\left(\frac{2+0.5-5\cdot 0.1}{\sqrt{5\cdot 0.1\cdot 0.9\cdot \frac{95}{99}}}\right) = \Phi(3.04) \approx 0.9988.$$

With respect to the relative error, $Hy(2|100;10;5)$ is better approximated than is $hy(2|100;10;5$

[1]This value is not tabulated in table 5.1/2. It can be determined using (2.81), (2.80) and (2.83a).
[2]This value is not tabulated in table 5.1/3. It can be determined using (2.92) and (2.93).

c) According to table 5.1/3 we get

$$bi(6|0.7;10) = bi(4|0.3;10) = Bi(4|0.3;10) - Bi(3|0.3;10) \approx 0.20012$$

$$Bi(6|0.7;10) = 1 - Bi(3|0.3;10) \approx 1 - 0.64961 = 0.35039.$$

Problem 2.2/10

a) Now, the random variable X_n^T is bi(0.1;10)-distributed. With (2.92), (2.93) and table 5.1/3, one can verify that

$$bi(0|0.1;10) = Bi(0|0.1;n) \approx 0.34868.$$

The other values of the density function are determined using (2.95a):

$$\begin{aligned}
bi(1|0.1;10) &= \frac{10}{1 \cdot 9} \cdot bi(0|0.1;10) \approx 0.38742 \\
bi(2|0.1;10) &= \frac{9}{2 \cdot 9} \cdot bi(1|0.1;10) \approx 0.19371 \\
bi(3|0.1;10) &= \frac{8}{3 \cdot 9} \cdot bi(2|0.1;10) \approx 0.05739 \\
bi(4|0.1;10) &= \frac{7}{4 \cdot 9} \cdot bi(3|0.1;10) \approx 0.01117 \\
bi(5|0.1;10) &= \frac{6}{5 \cdot 9} \cdot bi(4|0.1;10) \approx 0.00148.
\end{aligned}$$

The mode is $k_M = 1$. The expectation and variance are calculated using (2.94):

$$\mu = nP = 10 \cdot 0.1 = 1; \qquad \sigma^2 = nPQ = 10 \cdot 0.1 \cdot 0.9 = 0.9.$$

b) The discrete random variable X is $nb(0.1;3)$-distributed. By (2.98a) it follows that

$$nb(25|0.1;3) = \binom{24}{2} \cdot 0.1^3 \cdot 0.9^{22} = \frac{24 \cdot 23}{2} \cdot 0.1^3 \cdot 0.9^{22} \approx 0.027180.$$

The other probabilities $Pr(X = k) = nb(k|0.1;3)$ are calculated using (2.101):

$$nb(26|0.1;3) = \frac{25 \cdot 0.9}{25 - 3 + 1} \cdot nb(25|0.1;3) \approx 0.026589$$

$$nb(27|0.1;3) = \frac{26 \cdot 0.9}{26 - 3 + 1} \cdot nb(26|0.1;3) \approx 0.025924$$

$$nb(24|0.1;3) = \frac{25 - 3}{(25 - 1) \cdot 0.9} \cdot nb(25|0.1;3) \approx 0.027683$$

$$nb(23|0.1;3) = \frac{24 - 3}{(24 - 1) \cdot 0.9} \cdot nb(24|0.1;3) \approx 0.028084.$$

The expectation and variance are calculated according to (2.100):

$$\mu = \frac{c}{P} = \frac{3}{0.1} = 30; \qquad \sigma^2 = \frac{cQ}{P^2} = \frac{3 \cdot 0.9}{0.1^2} = 270.$$

Problem 2.2/11

The desired interval is obtained from (2.78) by substituting $\mu = 1000$ for θ, $t_{3;0.995}$ for $z_{1-\alpha/2}$ and $s_4/2$ for $\sqrt{V(\hat{\theta}_n)}$. With $s_4 = 0.286$ and $t_{3;0.995} = 5.8409$ (see table 5.2/2), it follows that approximately 99% of all values of $\bar{X}_4$ lie in the interval [999.165;100.835].

Problem 2.2/12

a) Rewriting the probability statement in example 2.2/11 with $n = 10$ and $1 - \alpha = 0.95$ gives the following result for $Y_{10} = S^2_{10}/\sigma^2 - 1$:

$$Pr\left(\frac{\chi^2_{9;0.025}}{9} - 1 \leq Y_{10} \leq \frac{\chi^2_{9;0.975}}{9} - 1\right) = 1 - \alpha.$$

According to table 5.2/4 we have

$$\chi^2_{9;0.025} \approx 2.700; \qquad \chi^2_{9;0.975} \approx 19.023.$$

The relative estimation error Y_{10} lies with probability 0.95 in the interval $[-0.7; 1.11]$, which is the twosided variation interval of level 0.95 for Y_{10}. If Y_{10} lies within this interval then the unknown variance is, at the worst, underestimated by 70% or overestimated by 110%.

b) From (2.112b) with $k = 7$ and $P = Po(k|\lambda) = 0.01$ it follows that $\lambda = 16$. Consequently, we have $Po(7|16) = 0.01$.

c)
$$\begin{aligned} po(k|\lambda) &= Po(k|\lambda) - Po(k-1|\lambda) \\ &= 1 - Ch[2\lambda|2(k+1)] - \{1 - Ch[2\lambda|2k]\} \;\; = Ch[2\lambda|2k] - Ch[2\lambda|2(k+1)]. \end{aligned}$$

Problem 2.2/13

a) With (2.118a) we get

$$Bi(4|0.25;10) = 1 - Fi(0.4|10;12) \approx 0.9219$$

and thus

$$Fi(0.4|10;12) \approx 1 - 0.9219 = 0.0781; \quad F_{10;12;0.0781} \approx 0.4.$$

b) With (2.117b) and table 5.2/3 it follows that

$$F_{5;7;0.05} = \frac{1}{F_{5;7;0.95}} = \frac{1}{4.88} = 0.2049.$$

c)
$$bi(k|P;n) = Bi(k|P;n) - Bi(k-1|P;n)$$
$$= Fi\left[\frac{n-k+1}{k}\frac{P}{1-P} \mid 2k; 2(n-k+1)\right] - Fi\left[\frac{n-k}{k+1}\frac{P}{1-P} \mid 2(k+1); 2(n-k)\right].$$

Problem 2.3/1

There are six possible ways to specify two of the four quantities n, K, α, β.

Case 1: With $n = 16$ and $K = 10$ it follows from (2.120a,b) and table 5.1/1 that

$$\alpha = 1 - \Phi\left(\frac{10.7 - 10}{2/\sqrt{16}}\right) = 1 - \Phi(1.4) \approx 0.080757$$

$$\beta = \Phi\left(\frac{10.7 - 11}{2/\sqrt{16}}\right) = \Phi(-0.6) = 1 - \Phi(0.6) \approx 0.274253.$$

Case 2: With $n = 16$ and $\alpha = 0.10$ we find with the help of table 5.2/1 that

$$\Phi\left(\frac{K - 10}{2/\sqrt{16}}\right) = 0.90; \qquad z_{0.90} \approx 1.282 = \frac{K - 10}{2/\sqrt{16}}$$

and consequently that $K \approx 10.64$. Thus we get

$$\beta \approx \Phi\left(\frac{10.64 - 11}{2/\sqrt{16}}\right) = \Phi(-0.72) = 1 - \Phi(0.72) \approx 0.235763.$$

Case 3: With $n = 16$ and $\beta = 0.05$ it follows that

$$\Phi\left(\frac{K-11}{2/\sqrt{16}}\right) = 0.05; \qquad z_{0.05} \approx -1.645 = \frac{K-11}{2/\sqrt{16}}$$

and hence that $K \approx 10.18$. As a result it holds that

$$\alpha \approx 1 - \Phi\left(\frac{10.18-10}{2/\sqrt{16}}\right) = 1 - \Phi(0.36) \approx 0.359423.$$

Case 4: With $K = 10.7$ and $\alpha = 0.10$ we get the result

$$\Phi\left(\frac{10.7-10}{2/\sqrt{n}}\right) = 0.90; \qquad z_{0.90} \approx 1.282 = \frac{10.7-10}{2/\sqrt{n}}$$

and hence that $n \approx 13.42$. We round the value of n to the next largest integer regardless of the value of the first decimal, i.e., to $n = 14$ in this example. Proceeding this way we ensure that the error probability lies below the specified threshold.[3] For β we find

$$\beta \approx \Phi\left(\frac{10.7-11}{2/\sqrt{14}}\right) = \Phi(-0.56) = 1 - \Phi(0.56) \approx 0.287740.$$

Case 5: Specifying $K = 10.7$ and $\beta = 0.05$ we can verify that

$$\Phi\left(\frac{10.7-11}{2/\sqrt{n}}\right) = 0.05; \qquad z_{0.05} \approx -1.645 = \frac{10.7-11}{2/\sqrt{n}}$$

and thus that $n \approx 120.27$, i.e. $n = 121$ after rounding.[4] The result for α is

$$\alpha = 1 - \Phi\left(\frac{10.7-10}{2/\sqrt{121}}\right) = 1 - \Phi(3.85) \approx 0.000059.$$

Case 6: If we specify $\alpha = 0.10$ and $\beta = 0.05$ then we get

$$\Phi\left(\frac{K-10}{2/\sqrt{n}}\right) = 0.90; \qquad z_{0.90} \approx 1.282 = \frac{K-10}{2/\sqrt{n}}$$

[3]For $n = 14$ (case 4) the effective error probability α can be calculated by using $K = 10.7$ and (2.120a). The result is found to be $\alpha = 0.09508$. This value is only slightly lower than the specified value.

[4]For $n = 121$ (case 5) we get, according to (2.120b), that β has the effective value $\beta \approx 0.049471$.

$$\Phi\left(\frac{K-11}{2/\sqrt{n}}\right) = 0.05; \qquad z_{0.05} \approx -1.645 = \frac{K-11}{2/\sqrt{n}}$$

and consequently that

$$K \approx 10 + \frac{1.282 \cdot 2}{\sqrt{n}}; \qquad K \approx 11 + \frac{1.645 \cdot 2}{\sqrt{n}}.$$

Combining these two relationships yields $n \approx 34.27$, i.e. $n = 35$ after rounding.[5] Substituting this value into one of the two expressions for K gives $K \approx 10.44$.

Problem 2.3/2

a) $\alpha = Pr(\bar{X}_n < K|\mu = 10) = \Phi\left(\frac{K-10}{2/\sqrt{n}}\right)$; $\beta = Pr(\bar{X}_n \geq K|\mu = 11) = 1 - \Phi\left(\frac{K-11}{2/\sqrt{n}}\right)$.

b)

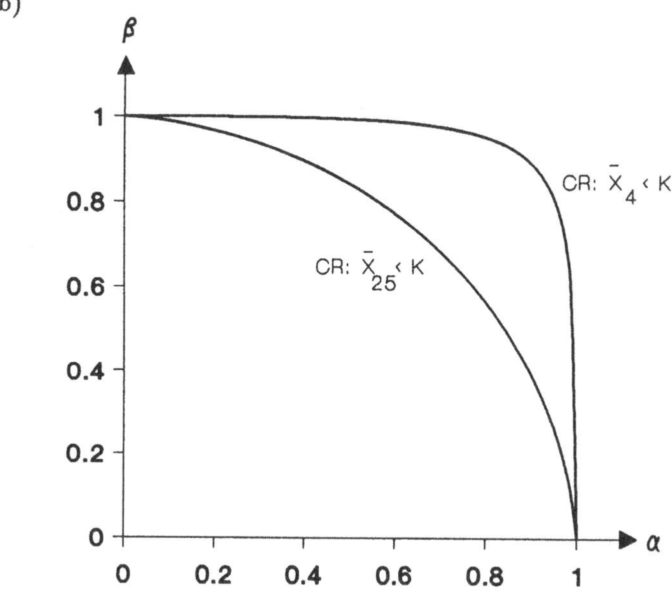

Figure 6.1/5: Trade-off functions of α and β for two tests

[5] For $n = 35$ (case 6) the effective error probabilities are $\alpha \approx 0.096800$ and $\beta \approx 0.048457$.

Problem 2.3/3

a) Instead of (2.102) we would use (2.103), i.e., $T_n = \sqrt{n}(\bar{X}_n - \mu)/S_n$. For $\mu = \mu_0$ this sample statistic is no longer standard normally distributed, but has a t distribution with $n-1$ degrees of freedom. In (2.125) the percentile z_P of the standard normal distribution has to be replaced by the percentile $t_{n-1;P}$ of the t distribution with $n-1$ degrees of freedom:

$$CR = (-\infty; t_{24;0.995}) \cup (t_{24;0.995}; \infty) \approx (-\infty; -2.7969) \cup (2.7969; \infty).$$

b) The alternative hypothesis is $H_1 : \mu < \mu_0$. Now $H_0 : \mu = \mu_0$ has to be rejected if the realization of $Y_n = \sqrt{n}(\bar{X}_n - \mu)/\sigma$ is smaller than $-z_{1-\alpha}$. Instead of (2.125) we thus get

$$CR = (-\infty; -z_{1-\alpha}).$$

In particular, with $\alpha = 0.01$ it follows that

$$CR \approx (-\infty; -2.32635).$$

The value $y_{25} = -2.4$ of the test statistic Y_{25} lies in the rejection region. This means that we have significant statistical evidence to conclude that H_0 is not true.

We want to note that neither the procedure nor the result of the above hypothesis test changes if the null hypothesis is chosen to be $H_0 : \mu \geq \mu_0$, i.e., if one tests $H_0 : \mu \geq \mu_0$ against $H_1 : \mu < \mu_0$. The distribution of the test statistic Y_{25} would then be determined on the boundary of the range of H_0, which is $\mu = \mu_0$, as before.

c) For the test of (2.123) the rejection region of H_0 is, according to (2.56), given by

$$CR = \left(-\infty; \mu_0 - z_{1-\frac{\alpha}{2}} \cdot \frac{\sigma}{\sqrt{n}}\right) \cup \left(\mu_0 + z_{1-\frac{\alpha}{2}} \cdot \frac{\sigma}{\sqrt{n}}; \infty\right).$$

Problem 2.3/4

Since we want to investigate whether the expectation still has the value $\lambda = 12$, we need to test $H_0 : \lambda = 12$ against $H_1 : \lambda \neq 12$. The test statistic is the number X of stand-stills per month, and under H_0 it holds that $X \sim po(12)$. Since $\alpha = 0.05$ and $H_1 : \lambda \neq 12$ the rejection region CR contains all very small and all very large realizations of X. To be more exact, it contains roughly the 2.5% smallest and largest values (not exactly 2.5% each since X is a discrete random variable). Using table 5.1/4 we can verify that

$$\sum_{k=0}^{5} po(k|12) = Po(5|12) \approx 0.02034 < \frac{\alpha}{2} = 0.025$$

$$\sum_{k=20}^{\infty} po(k|12) = 1 - Po(19|12) \approx 0.02128 < \frac{\alpha}{2} = 0.025$$

and thus that

$$CR = \{0, 1, \ldots, 5\} \cup \{20, 21, \ldots\}.$$

Since 20 stand-stills were observed, H_0 is to be rejected. Consequently, one can no longer assume that $E(X)$ still has the value $\lambda = 12$.

Problem 2.3/5

a) Under H_0 the sample mean $\bar{X}_n$ has a normal distribution with expectation $E(\bar{X}_n) = \mu_0 = 1600$ and variance $V(\bar{X}_n) = 120^2/25$. Instead of $\bar{X}_n$, it is more convenient to use the test statistic $Y_n = \sqrt{n}(\bar{X}_n - \mu)/\sigma$ which has a standard normal distribution under H_0. According to (2.125) the rejection region is given by

$$CR_1 = (-\infty; -z_{0.975}) \cup (z_{0.975}; \infty) \approx (-\infty; -1.96) \cup (1.96; \infty).$$

Since the value of the test statistic Y_{25} is

$$y_{25} = \frac{1560 - 1600}{120} \cdot \sqrt{25} = -1.\bar{6}$$

which does not fall into the rejection region CR_1, one cannot reject H_0 in this case. Of course, the same result is obtained if the test statistic $\bar{X}_{25}$ is used instead of Y_{25}. In this case one would calculate (see problem 2.3/3c)

$$CR_2 = (-\infty; -1552.96) \cup (1647.04; \infty).$$

The realization $\bar{x}_{25} = 1560$ does not lie in CR_2.

b) According to (2.134b), the probability of a type II error is for all $\mu \neq 1600$ given by the value of the OC function

$$\begin{aligned} L(\mu) &= Pr(\bar{X}_n \in \overline{CR}|\mu) \\ &= W(1552.96 \leq \bar{X}_n \leq 1647.04|\mu) \\ &= W\left(\frac{1552.96 - \mu}{\sigma/\sqrt{n}} \leq Y_n \leq \frac{1647.04 - \mu}{\sigma/\sqrt{n}}\right) \end{aligned}$$

where $Y_n := \sqrt{n}(\bar{X}_n - \mu)/\sigma$ has a standard normal distribution. With $\sigma = 120$ and $n = 25$ it follows that

$$L(\mu) = \Phi\left(\frac{1647.04-\mu}{24}\right) - \Phi\left(\frac{1552.96-\mu}{24}\right).$$

For $\mu = 1620$ and $\mu = 1570$, respectively, we get using table 5.1/1 that

$$L(1620) = \Phi(1.12\bar{6}) - [1 - \Phi(2.799\bar{3})] \approx 0.8700 - 0.0026 = 0.8674.$$

$$L(1570) = \Phi(3.21) - [1 - \Phi(0.71)] \approx 0.9993 - 0.2389 = 0.7604.$$

Problem 2.3/6

a) The test statistic $g(\mathbf{X}) = X_n^T$ is $bi(P;3)$-distributed with unknown parameter P. We further have that $CR = \{2;3\}$. It follows from (2.130) that

$$G(P) = \sum_{i=2}^{3} bi(k|P;3) = \binom{3}{2}P^2(1-P) + \binom{3}{3}P^3 = P^2(3-2P).$$

An equivalent solution is that $G(P) = 1 - Bi(1|P;3)$. For L(P) it follows that

$$L(P) = 1 - G(P) = 1 - P^2(3-2P) = Bi(1|P;3).$$

b) The qualitative description of the power curve is given in figure 2.3/4. Because of the monotonicity of $G(P)$, the probability of a type I error is bounded above by $G(0.5) = 0.5$. The probability of a type II error is at most $L(0.5) = 0.5$.

c) In the case of drawing without replacement, $g(\mathbf{X}) = X_n^T$ has a hypergeometric distribution with $n = 3$, $N = 10$ and unknown parameter $M = 10P$. According to (2.130) with $CR = \{2;3\}$ and the result (2.80), it follows for the power function that

$$\begin{aligned} G(P) &= \sum_{k=2}^{3} hy(k|10;10P;3) \\ &= \frac{\binom{10P}{2}\binom{10-10P}{1}}{\binom{10}{3}} + \frac{\binom{10}{3}\binom{10-10P}{0}}{\binom{10}{3}} \\ &= \frac{1}{36}\cdot P(10P-1)(14-10P). \end{aligned}$$

An equivalent solution is $G(P) = 1 - Hy(1|10;10P;3)$.

Problem 2.3/7

a) The test statistic $g(\mathbf{X}) = X_n^T/n = \Pi$ approximately has a normal distribution with expectation $\mu = P$ and variance $\sigma^2 = P(1-P)/n$. Since the null hypothesis is of the form $H_0 : P \geq 0.6$, only small values of Π give evidence against H_0. Thus the rejection region is of the form $CR : \Pi < p$. We have to determine n and the endpoint p of the rejection region. The two determining equations are:

$$G(0.5) = \Phi\left(\frac{p-0.5}{\sqrt{0.5^2}}\sqrt{n}\right) = 0.9; \quad G(0.64) = \Phi\left(\frac{p-0.64}{\sqrt{0.64\cdot 0.36}}\sqrt{n}\right) = 0.001.$$

From these equations we get using table 5.2/1

$$\frac{p-0.5}{0.5}\sqrt{n} = z_{0.9} \approx 1.282; \quad \frac{p-0.64}{\sqrt{0.64\cdot 0.36}}\sqrt{n} = z_{0.001} \approx -3.09023.$$

The solution of this system of equations is determined to be $p = 0.5422$ and $n = 231$. Hence, the rejection region is given by $CR : \Pi < 0.5422$.

b) The significance level α is obtained as the value of the power function $G(P)$ at $P = 0.6$:

$$\alpha = G(0.6) = \Phi\left(\frac{0.5422-0.6}{\sqrt{0.6\cdot 0.4}}\sqrt{231}\right) = \Phi(-1.79) = 1-\Phi(1.79) \approx 0.0367.$$

Problem 2.3/8

a) On the next page we again present the graph of the OC function of $L(P) := L_1(P) = Bi(10|P;30)$ of figure 2.3/5 and indicate the procedure of reading the values by dotted lines. We can see that $P_{0.1} \approx 0.47$, $P_{0.5} \approx 0.35$ and $P_{0.975} = 0.2 - \epsilon$ with small $\epsilon > 0$.

b) Because of (2.136) the determining equations of the three OC percentiles are

$$\begin{aligned} Bi(10|P_{0.1};30) &= 0.1 \\ Bi(10|P_{0.5};30) &= 0.5 \\ Bi(10|P_{0.975};30) &= 0.975. \end{aligned}$$

Since table 5.1/3 does not contain the exact values (see for $n = 30$ the row with $k = 10$), it is not possible to exactly determine the OC percentiles. However, one can see that $P_{0.975}$ is smaller than 0.2 and that for the IQL it holds that $0.3 < P_{0.5} < 0.4$. With equations (3.38) and (3.39) we will learn a way to exactly determine the desired OC percentiles. Note that the resulting exact values are $P_{0.1} \approx 0.4665$, $P_{0.5} \approx 0.3526$ and $P_{0.975} \approx 0.1993$.

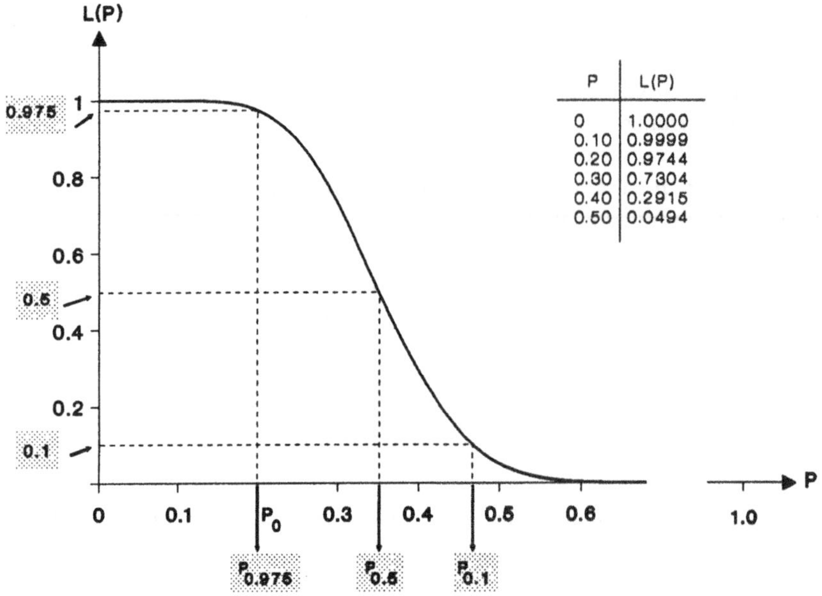

Figure 6.1/6: OC function of a test $H_0 : P \leq P_0$ against $H_1 : P > P_0$ with $n = 30$

Problem 2.3/9

With the given values it follows that

$$LQ_{20} = \frac{0.06^4 \cdot 0.94^{16}}{0.02^4 \cdot 0.98^{16}} \approx \frac{4.8156 \cdot 10^{-6}}{1.1581 \cdot 10^{-7}} \approx 41.58.$$

The result means that the sample drawn under $H_1 : P = RQL = 0.06$ has a probability which is 41.58 times higher than under $H_0 : P = AQL = 0.02$.

6.2 Solutions for Chapter 3

Problem 3.2/1

a) The prior distribution is

$$\pi(M) = un(M|0;1;N) = \begin{cases} \dfrac{1}{N+1} & \text{for } M = 0, 1, ..., N. \\ 0 & \text{else.} \end{cases}$$

The variable X_n^T has an equidistant uniform distribution; see (2.4).

b) According to (2.7) and (2.8), the expectation and variance of this uniform distribution are given by

$$\mu_N = \frac{N}{2}; \quad \sigma_N^2 = \frac{N(N+2)}{12}.$$

For μ_N^* in (3.6) it follows for all $N > 1$ that

$$\mu_N^* = \frac{N}{2}\left(1 - \frac{1}{2}\right) = \frac{3N}{12} < \sigma_N^2.$$

This shows that the decision procedure given in figure 3.2/1 is adequate.

Problem 3.2/2

According to (3.7) it holds that

$$L(P|25;2;0) = Hy(0|25;25P;2) = \frac{\binom{25P}{0}\binom{25(1-P)}{2}}{\binom{25}{2}} = \frac{\binom{25(1-P)}{2}}{\binom{25}{2}}.$$

Since $N = 25$ is not tabulated in table 5.1/2 the calculation is made using the definition of the binomial coefficient (see the solution for problem 2.2/8). The result is

$$L(P|25;2;0) = \frac{[25(1-P)]!}{2![25(1-P)-2]!} \cdot \frac{2! \cdot 23!}{25!} = \frac{25}{24} \cdot (1-P) \cdot \left(\frac{24}{25} - P\right).$$

Using this formula we get the following table for $P \in \{0, 1/25, 2/25, \ldots, 1\}$:

P	$L(P\|25;2;0)$	P	$L(P\|25;2;0)$
0	1.0000	0.52	0.2200
0.04	0.9200	0.56	0.1833
0.08	0.8433	0.60	0.1500
0.12	0.7700	0.64	0.1200
0.16	0.7000	0.68	0.0933
0.20	0.6333	0.72	0.0700
0.24	0.5700	0.76	0.0500
0.28	0.5100	0.80	0.0333
0.32	0.4533	0.84	0.0200
0.36	0.4000	0.88	0.0100
0.40	0.3500	0.92	0.0033
0.44	0.3033	0.96	0.0000
0.48	0.2600	1	0.0000

Table 6.2/1: Values of the hypergeometric OC function for the single-sampling plan (25;2;0)

Problem 3.2/3

a) $$L(0.45|20;n;2) = Hy(2|20;9;n) = Hy(2|20;n;9).$$

This chain of equalities follows from (3.7a) and (2.84b). With table 5.1/2 one can verify:

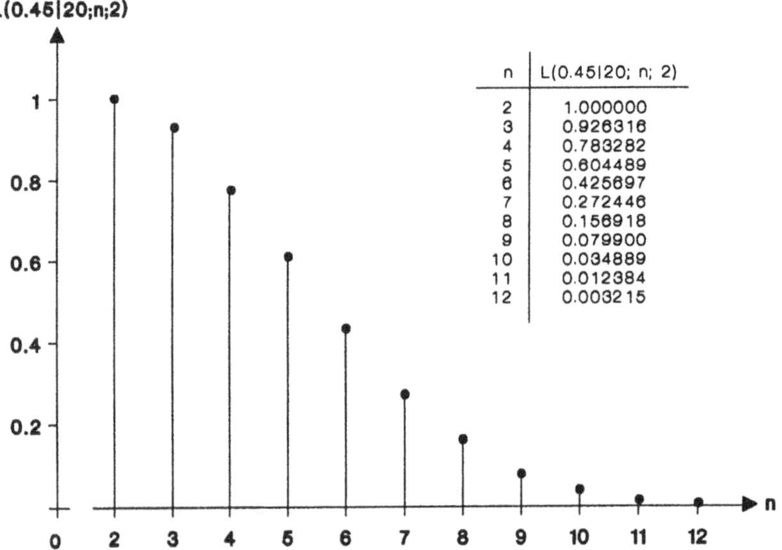

n	L(0.45|20; n; 2)
2	1.000000
3	0.926316
4	0.783282
5	0.604489
6	0.425697
7	0.272446
8	0.156918
9	0.079900
10	0.034889
11	0.012384
12	0.003215

Figure 6.2/1: Acceptance probabilities for a lot with $P = 0.45$ for inspection with various plans $(20;n;2)$

The results are compatible with the conclusions from figure 3.2/5. Accordingly, the function $L(P|N;n;c)$ decreases as the sample size increases when P, N and c are fixed.

b) $$L(0.4|20;5;c) = Hy(c|20;8;5) = Hy(c|20;5;8).$$

By using table 5.1/2 one gets the following figure:

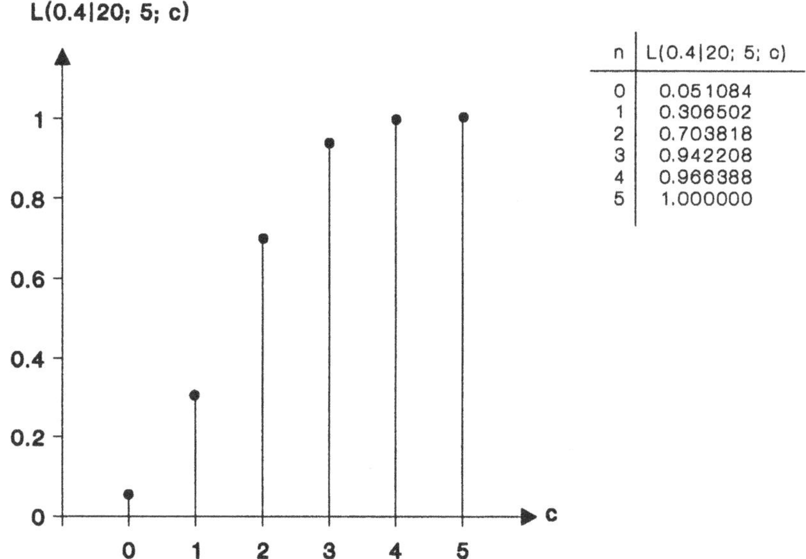

Figure 6.2/2: Acceptance probabilities for a lot with $P = 0.4$ for inspection with various plans $(20;5;c)$

The trend in the graph is compatible with the conclusions from figure 3.2/6: $L(P|N;n;c)$ increases as the acceptance number c increases when P, N and n are constant.

Problem 3.2/4

According to (3.9) and (3.8b), it holds that

$$L(P|25;2;0) \approx L(P|2;0) = \binom{2}{0} P^0(1-P)^2 = (1-P)^2.$$

For $P \in \{0, 1/25, 2/25, \ldots, 1\}$ we get the following table:

P	$L(P\|2;0)$	P	$L(P\|2;0)$
0	1.0000	0.52	0.2304
0.04	0.9216	0.56	0.1936
0.08	0.8464	0.60	0.1600
0.12	0.7744	0.64	0.1296
0.16	0.7056	0.68	0.1024
0.20	0.6400	0.72	0.0784
0.24	0.5776	0.76	0.0576
0.28	0.5184	0.80	0.0400
0.32	0.4624	0.84	0.0256
0.36	0.4096	0.88	0.0144
0.40	0.3600	0.92	0.0064
0.44	0.3136	0.96	0.0016
0.48	0.2704	1	0.0000

Table 6.2/2: Binomial approximation of values of the hypergeometric OC function for the plan (25;2;0)

A comparison with table 6.2/1 verifies that $L(P|25;2;0) < L(P|2;0)$ for all considered values of P with $0 < P < 1$. The differences are, however, relatively small (see also the solution for problem 3.2/6 and in addition figure 6.2/3).

Problem 3.2/5

According to (3.14b) and (3.15b), it holds that

$$L(P|25;2;0) \approx L^*(P|2;0); \qquad L(P|2;0) \approx L^*(P|2;0).$$

According to (3.16), the values of $L(P|25;2;0)$ as well as of $L(P|2;0)$ are approximated by

$$L^*(P|2;0) = Po(0|2P) = \frac{(2 \cdot P)^0}{0!} e^{-2P} = e^{-2P}.$$

For $P \in \{0, 1/25, 2/25, \dots, 1\}$ we get table 6.2/3.

A comparison with tables 6.2/1-2 verifies that, for all considered P with $0 < P < 1$, it holds that

$$L(P|25;2;0) < L(P|2;0) < L^*(P|2;0).$$

We want to note that, different to the other two functions, at the point $P = 1$ the function $L^*(P|2;0)$ is larger than zero.

P	$L^*(P\|2;0)$	P	$L^*(P\|2;0)$
0	1.0000	0.52	0.3535
0.04	0.9231	0.56	0.3262
0.08	0.8521	0.60	0.3012
0.12	0.7866	0.64	0.2780
0.16	0.7261	0.68	0.2567
0.20	0.6703	0.72	0.2369
0.24	0.6188	0.76	0.2187
0.28	0.5712	0.80	0.2019
0.32	0.5273	0.84	0.1864
0.36	0.4868	0.88	0.1720
0.40	0.4493	0.92	0.1588
0.44	0.4148	0.96	0.1466
0.48	0.3829	1	0.1353

Table 6.2/3: Poisson approximation of values of the hypergeometric and binomial OC function for the plan (25;2;0)

Problem 3.2/6

a) For the hypergeometric OC function

$$L(P|50;8;0) = Hy(0|50;50P;8) = \frac{\binom{50(1-P)}{8}}{\binom{50}{8}}$$

and its approximations

$$L(P|8;0) = Bi(0|P;8) = (1-P)^8; \quad L^*(P|8;0) = Po(0|8P) = e^{-8P}$$

we get the following table:

P	$L(P\|50;8;0)$	$L(P\|8;0)$	$L^*(P\|8;0)$
0	1.0000	1.0000	1.0000
0.02	0.8400	0.8508	0.8521
0.04	0.7029	0.7214	0.7261
0.06	0.5857	0.6069	0.6188
0.08	0.4860	0.5132	0.5273
0.10	0.4015	0.4305	0.4493
0.12	0.3301	0.3596	0.3829
0.14	0.2701	0.2992	0.3263
0.16	0.2198	0.2479	0.2780
0.18	0.1780	0.2044	0.2369
0.20	0.1432	0.1678	0.2019
0.22	0.1146	0.1370	0.1720
0.24	0.0911	0.1113	0.1466
0.26	0.0719	0.0899	0.1249
0.28	0.0564	0.0722	0.1065
0.30	0.0438	0.0576	0.0907

Table 6.2/4: Values of the hypergeometric, binomial and Poisson OC function for the plan (50;8;0)

We can again see that, for all considered P with $0 < P < 1$, it holds that

$$L(P|50;8;0) < L(P|8;0) < L^*(P|8;0).$$

b) The following figure contains the graph of the OC functions $L(P|50;8;0)$, $L(P|8;0)$ and $L^*(P|8;0)$. In order to improve the readability of the graph, the curves are drawn continuously, although strictly speaking, they are only defined for $P = M/50$, with $M = 0, 1, \ldots, 50$:

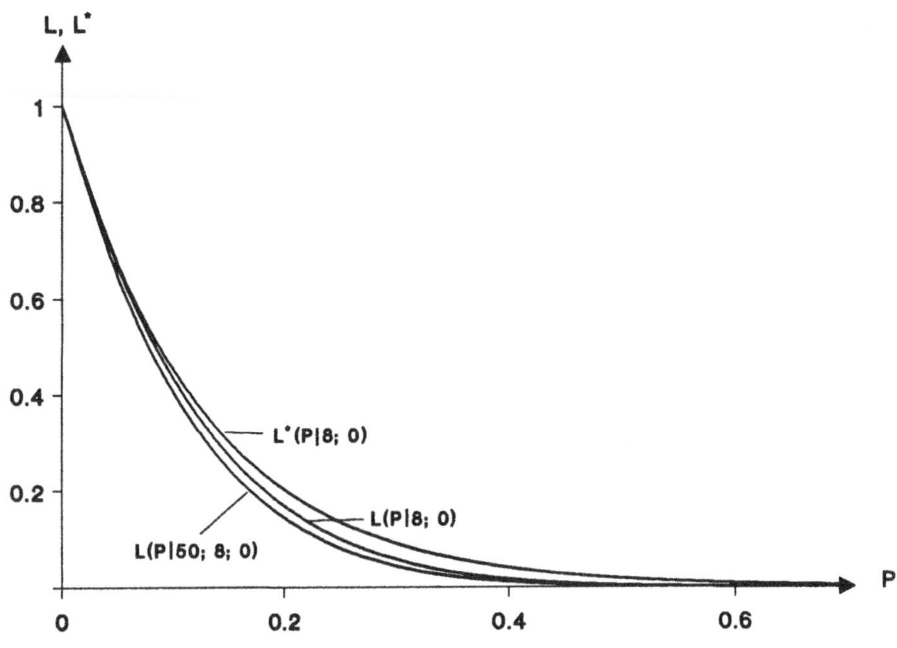

Figure 6.2/3: Hypergeometric, binomial and Poisson OC curve for the plan $(50;8;0)$

Problem 3.2/7

a) According to (3.16) we have that $L^*(P|100;3) = Po(3|100 \cdot P)$. For the specified values of P one can obtain the following values from table 5.1/4:

$$L^*(0.01|100;3) = Po(3|1) \approx 0.98101$$
$$L^*(0.05|100;3) = Po(3|5) \approx 0.26503$$
$$L^*(0.10|100;3) = Po(3|10) \approx 0.01034$$
$$L^*(0.15|100;3) = Po(3|15) \approx 0.00021.$$

b) According to (3.16) we have that $L^*(0.01|n;2) = Po(2|n \cdot 0.01)$. For the specified values of n one can obtain the following values from table 5.1/4:

$$L^*(0.01|50;2) = Po(2|0.5) \approx 0.98561 \qquad L^*(0.01|150;2) = Po(2|1.5) \approx 0.80885$$
$$L^*(0.01|100;2) = Po(2|1.0) \approx 0.91970 \qquad L^*(0.01|200;2) = Po(2|2.0) \approx 0.67668.$$

c) According to (3.16) we have that $L^*(0.01|100;c) = Po(c|1)$. For the specified values of c one can obtain the following values from table 5.1/4:

$$L^*(0.01|100;0) = Po(0|1) \approx 0.36788 \qquad L^*(0.01|100;2) = Po(2|1) \approx 0.91970$$
$$L^*(0.01|100;1) = Po(1|1) \approx 0.73576 \qquad L^*(0.01|100;3) = Po(3|1) \approx 0.98101.$$

Problem 3.2/8

a) The percentiles are calculated according to (3.35b) with $P_\omega^P = 0.01 \cdot g_{4;1-\omega}$, where the term $g_{4;1-\omega}$ is given in table 5.2/5. After rounding to four decimal places the results are:

ω	0.999	0.99	0.95	0.50	0.10	0.01
P_ω^P	0.0043	0.0082	0.0137	0.0365	0.0668	0.1005

Table 6.2/5: Poisson OC percentiles for a single-sampling plan (N;100;3)

b) With the exact formula (3.38b) and table 5.2/3 we get the following results:

– $n = 20, c = 1:$ $\quad P_{0.95}^B = \dfrac{2}{2 + 19 \cdot F_{38;4;0.95}} \approx \dfrac{2}{2 + 19 \cdot 5.72} \approx 0.0181$

– $n = 60, c = 3:$ $\quad P_{0.95}^B = \dfrac{4}{4 + 57 \cdot F_{114;8;0.95}} \approx \dfrac{4}{4 + 57 \cdot 2.97} \approx 0.0231$

– $n = 300, c = 15:$ $\quad P_{0.95}^B = \dfrac{16}{16 + 285 \cdot F_{570;32;0.95}} \approx \dfrac{16}{16 + 285 \cdot 1.61} \approx 0.0337.$

c) Application of (3.39a) and table 5.2/5 yields the following approximations:

– $n = 20, c = 1:$ $\quad P_{0.95}^B \approx \dfrac{g_{2;0.05}}{20} \approx \dfrac{0.3554}{20} = 0.0177$

– $n = 60, c = 3:$ $\quad P_{0.95}^B \approx \dfrac{g_{4;0.05}}{60} \approx \dfrac{1.366}{60} = 0.0228$

– $n = 300, c = 15:$ $\quad P_{0.95}^B \approx \dfrac{g_{16;0.05}}{300} \approx \dfrac{10.04}{300} = 0.0335.$

The approximation (3.39b) is more exact and gives (rounded to four decimal places):

- $n = 20, c = 1: \quad P^B_{0.95} \approx \dfrac{0.3554}{20 + 0.5 \cdot (0.3554 - 1)} \approx 0.0181$
- $n = 60, c = 3: \quad P^B_{0.95} \approx \dfrac{1.366}{60 + 0.5 \cdot (1.366 - 3)} \approx 0.0231$
- $n = 300, c = 15: \quad P^B_{0.95} \approx \dfrac{10.04}{300 + 0.5 \cdot (10.04 - 15)} \approx 0.0337.$

Problem 3.2/9

a) With the exact formula (3.35b) and table 5.2/5, we get the Poisson OC percentiles

$$P^P_{0.1} \approx \frac{g_{3;0.9}}{8} \approx \frac{5.322}{8} \approx 0.6653$$

$$P^P_{0.5} \approx \frac{g_{3;0.5}}{8} \approx \frac{2.674}{8} = 0.3343$$

$$P^P_{0.95} \approx \frac{g_{3;0.05}}{8} \approx \frac{0.8177}{8} = 0.1022.$$

The IQL approximation (3.37) yields

$$P^P_{0.5} \approx \frac{1}{8} \cdot \left(2 + \frac{2}{3}\right) = \frac{1}{3} \approx 0.3333.$$

b) According to (3.39a), the binomial OC percentiles P^B_ω can be approximated by the values P^P_ω. With the more exact approximation (3.39b) one gets

$$P^B_{0.1} \approx \frac{5.322}{8 + 0.5 \cdot (5.322 - 2)} \approx 0.5509$$

$$P^B_{0.5} \approx \frac{2.674}{8 + 0.5 \cdot (2.674 - 2)} \approx 0.3207$$

$$P^B_{0.95} \approx \frac{0.8177}{8 + 0.5 \cdot (0.8177 - 2)} \approx 0.1104.$$

One can use (3.38) and table 5.2/3 to determine the IQL value with an exact formula:

$$P^B_{0.5} = \frac{3}{3 + 6 \cdot F_{12;6;0.5}} \approx \frac{3}{3 + 6 \cdot 1.06} \approx 0.3205.$$

We can see that the approximation (3.39b) is actually better than the approximation (3.39a) which gives the result 0.3343. The very simple approximation formula (3.40) yields an approximation that is almost as good:

$$P^B_{0.5} \approx \frac{2 + \frac{2}{3}}{8 + \frac{1}{3}} = \frac{8}{25} = 0.32.$$

c) According to (3.41c) the hypergeometric OC percentiles are given by

$$P^H_{0.1} \approx \frac{5.322 \cdot (100-8+1)+2\cdot(8-1)}{50\cdot(16+5.322-2)} \approx 0.5268$$

$$P^H_{0.5} \approx \frac{2.674 \cdot (100-8+1)+2\cdot(8-1)}{50\cdot(16+2.674-2)} \approx 0.3151$$

$$P^H_{0.95} \approx \frac{0.8177 \cdot (100-8+1)+2\cdot(8-1)}{50\cdot(16+0.8177-2)} \approx 0.1215.$$

A less exact approximation of the *IQL* value $P^H_{0.5}$ is given by $P^P_{0.5} \approx 0.3343$ (see above). With approximation formula (3.42) we get:

$$P^H_{0.5} \approx \frac{\left(2+\frac{2}{3}\right)-\frac{8}{150}}{\left(8+\frac{1}{3}\right)-\frac{16}{150}} \approx 0.3177.$$

Problem 3.2/10

a) With $n = 8$, $c = 2$ and $P^P_{0.5} \approx \frac{1}{3}$, it follows by (3.31) and $Po(2|\frac{8}{3}) \approx 0.5018$ that

$$\varepsilon\left(\frac{1}{3}\right) \approx -\frac{8}{3\cdot 0.5018\cdot 2}\cdot\left(\frac{8}{3}\right)^2\cdot e^{-\frac{8}{3}} \approx -1.3129.$$

The approximation formula (3.32) gives

$$\varepsilon\left(P^P_{0.5}\right) \approx -\sqrt{\frac{2}{\pi}}\cdot 2.73 \approx -1.3183.$$

The latter result says that an increase of 1% in the fraction nonconforming $P^P_{0.5}$, i.e., a change from $P = 1/3$ to $P = 1.01/3$ decreases the probability of accepting the lot by 1.32%.

b) Instead of (3.31), in the binomial case we get, according to (3.8a), (3.22) and (2.146):

$$\varepsilon(P) = -\frac{P}{Bi(c|P;n)}\cdot\frac{n!}{c!(n-c-1)!}\cdot P^c(1-P)^{n-c-1}.$$

Since $Bi(2|0.32;8) \approx 0.5013$, with $P^B_{0.5} \approx 0.32$ we get the result

$$\varepsilon(0.32) = -\frac{0.32}{0.5013}\cdot\frac{8!}{2!5!}\cdot 0.32^2 0.68^5 \approx -1.5966.$$

Problem 3.2/11

a) If the *RQL* and *AQL* values are supposed to lie close together, then the OC curve has to be steep (see figure 3.2/10). How the sampling plan parameters N, n and c need to be modified to achieve a steeper OC curve, and thus better discriminatory power, is indicated at the end of section 3.2.1b. There we explained, for example, that an increase in n or a decrease in c (with the remaining conditions fixed) improves the discriminatory power of the plan.

b) Since $c = 0$, the three OC functions $L(P|N;n;c)$, $L(P|n;c)$ and $L^*(P|n;c)$ are convex, for all $0 < P < 1$, and (3.27) holds. Consequently, we have $P_\omega^H < P_\omega^B < P_\omega^P$. If one draws the three curves the resulting graph is similar to figure 3.2/4, where the Poisson curve was the upper curve and the hypergeometric curve the lower curve. Using the graphical method (see figure 6.1/6) to determine the percentile of order ω, for an arbitrary ω with $0 < \omega < 1$, shows that $P_\omega^H < P_\omega^B < P_\omega^P$ holds.

Problem 3.2/12

a) The *AOQL* values are again indicated by an asterisk (*):

P	$L(P\|.)$	$AOQ(P)$ values for the combinations:								
		S_1/L_1	S_1/L_2	S_1/L_3	S_2/L_1	S_2/L_2	S_2/L_3	S_3/L_1	S_3/L_2	S_3/L_3
(1)	(2)	(3)	(4)	(5)	(6)	(7)	(8)	(9)	(10)	(11)
0	1	0	0	0	0	0	0	0	0	0
0.02	0.8400	0.02	0.0169	0.0168	0.0164	0.0142	0.0142	0.0163	0.0142	0.0141
0.04	0.7029	0.04	0.0285	0.0281	0.0317	0.0240	0.0238	0.0315	0.0239	0.0236
0.06	0.5857	0.06	0.0360	0.0350	0.0460	0.0304	0.0298	0.0453	0.0301	0.0295
0.08	0.4860	0.08	0.0405	0.0389	0.0588	0.0342	0.0331	0.0575	0.0338	0.0327
0.10	0.4015	0.10	0.0427	0.0402*	0.0701	0.0361	0.0343*	0.0678	0.0355	0.0337*
0.12	0.3301	0.12	0.0431*	0.0396	0.0796	0.0364*	0.0339	0.0761	0.0357*	0.0333
0.14	0.2701	0.14	0.0421	0.0378	0.0871	0.0356	0.0325	0.0821	0.0347	0.0318
0.16	0.2198	0.16	0.0402	0.0352	0.0926	0.0340	0.0303	0.0857	0.0330	0.0295
0.18	0.1780	0.18	0.0376	0.0320	0.0959	0.0318	0.0277	0.0870*	0.0307	0.0269
0.20	0.1432	0.20	0.0348	0.0287	0.0971*	0.0293	0.0249	0.0860	0.0282	0.0241
0.22	0.1146	0.22	0.0313	0.0252	0.0958	0.0264	0.0220	0.0826	0.0253	0.0212
0.24	0.0911	0.24	0.0280	0.0219	0.0927	0.0236	0.0191	0.0776	0.0225	0.0184
0.26	0.0719	0.26	0.0246	0.0187	0.0878	0.0208	0.0164	0.0712	0.0197	0.0157
0.28	0.0564	0.28	0.0215	0.0158	0.0816	0.0181	0.0139	0.0640	0.0170	0.0133
0.30	0.0438	0.30	0.0184	0.0131	0.0742	0.0155	0.0116	0.0561	0.0145	0.0110

Table 6.2/6: *AOQ* values of the single-sampling plan (50;8;0) for different combinations of sample and remaining lot disposition

b) According to table 6.2/6 (see column 11) the function $AOQ(P)$ for the case of S_3/L_3 attains its maximum at the point $P_M = 0.1$, and it holds that

$$AOQL = AOQ(0.1) = 0.0337.$$

Using (3.52) and table 3.2/6 we would get the approximations $P_M = 1.00/8 = 0.125$ and

$$AOQL = 0.368 \cdot \left(\frac{1}{8} - \frac{1}{50}\right) \approx 0.0386.$$

Problem 3.2/13

According to table 3.2/5 for the combination S_3/L_3, the AOQ function of the plans $(50; 8; c)$ with $c = 2$ and $c = 0$, respectively, is given by

$$AOQ(P) = \frac{50-8}{50} \cdot P \cdot L(P|50; 8; c).$$

It holds for all $P \in (0; 1)$ that $L(P|50; 8; 2) > L(P|50; 8; 0)$; see figure 3.2/6. Consequently, the AOQ curve for $c = 2$ has to lie above the AOQ curve for $c = 0$. This can be seen immediately: In the case of the "more strict" inspection ($c = 0$) a smaller number of defective items slip through the inspection. Using tables 3.2/7 and 6.2/6 (column 11 in both cases), we get the following graph:

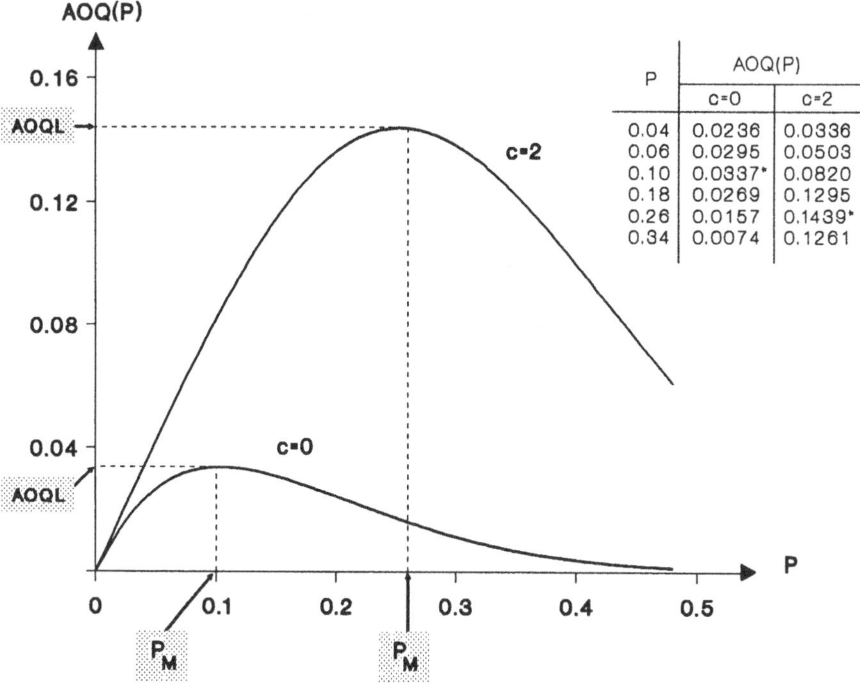

Figure 6.2/4: AOQ curve for the single-sampling plans (50;8;2) and (50;8;0)

Problem 3.2/14

If we substitute $N = 50$ and $n = 8$ into table 3.2/8 we get the following results by using $L(P) = L(P|50;8;0)$ and the fact that $L(0.1) = 0.4015$ and $AFI(0.1) = ATI(0.1)/50$

disposition combination	$ATI(0.1)$	$AFI(0.1)$
$S_1/L_1, S_2/L_1$	8	0.1600
$S_1/L_2, S_2/L_2$	33.1370	0.6627
$S_1/L_3, S_2/L_3$	35.9300	0.7186
S_3/L_1	8.8889	0.1778
S_3/L_2	34.0259	0.6806
S_3/L_3	36.8189	0.7364

Table 6.2/7: ATI and AFI values for the sampling plan (50;8;0) at $P = 0.1$ and for different combinations of sample and remaining lot disposition

Problem 3.2/15

a) With $N = 50$, $n = 8$, $c = 0$ and (3.58a-b) we get

$$ASN_1(P) = 8 \cdot F(0|8) + \frac{1}{P}\,[1 - F(1|9)]$$

$$ASN_2(P) = \frac{8}{1-P} \cdot F(0|9) + \frac{1}{P}\,[1 - F(1|9)]\,.$$

With $P = 0.1$ and (3.58c) it follows that:

	hypergeometric case	binomial case	Poisson case
$ASN_1(0.1)$	5.3733	5.6953	5.8698
$ASN_2(0.1)$	5.3053	5.6953	5.8891

Table 6.2/8: ASN values for the sampling plan (50;8;0) at $P = 0.1$

b) According to (3.58c), in the binomial case we have that $F(c|n) = Bi(c|P;n)$. This implies that the two equations presented above become

$$ASN_1(P) = 8 \cdot Bi(0|P;8) + \frac{1}{P}\,[1 - Bi(1|P;9)]$$

$$ASN_2(P) = \frac{8}{1-P} \cdot Bi(0|P;9) + \frac{1}{P}\,[1 - Bi(1|P;9)]\,.$$

Because of $Bi(0|P;9) = (1-P)^9$ it follows that $ASN_1(P) = ASN_2(P)$.

Problem 3.2/16

We only need to replace "repeat until $i = n$" by

- "repeat until $(i = n$ or $Z = c + 1)$" in the case of semi-curtailed inspection and
- "repeat until $(i = n$ or $Z = c + 1$ or $i - Z = n - c)$" in the case of fully curtailed inspection.

Problem 3.2/17

In the Poisson case, the plan with $n = 47$ and $c = 5$ is an admissible plan because it satisfies the specifications (3.65) or the equivalent conditions (3.67). It is admissible for the binomial case if it satisfies (3.64) or (3.66), respectively. With $n = 47$ and $c = 5$ the inequalities in (3.66) become

$$AQL \leq \frac{6}{6 + (47 - 5) \cdot F_{84;12;0.95}} \approx \frac{6}{6 + 42 \cdot 2.36} = 0.0571$$

$$RQL \geq \frac{6 \cdot F_{12;84;0.90}}{47 - 5 + 6 \cdot F_{12;84;0.90}} \approx \frac{6 \cdot 1.63}{42 + 6 \cdot 1.63} = 0.1889.$$

This can be verified using table 5.2/3. Because $AQL = 0.05$ and $RQL = 0.2$ these inequalities are actually satisfied. Consequently this plan is also admissible under the binomial approximation. However, it does not minimize the sample size. In the binomial case, the plan with the minimum amount of inspection is given by $n = 38$ and $c = 4$, as was shown in example 3.2/12.

Problem 3.2/18

a)

$$\left.\begin{array}{lll} c = 0: & q_1(0) \approx \dfrac{5.991}{0.2} & = 29.96 \\ & q_2(0) \approx \dfrac{0.103}{0.04} & = 2.58 \end{array}\right\} \Rightarrow q_1(0) > q_2(0)$$

$$\vdots \qquad \vdots \qquad \vdots$$

$$\left.\begin{array}{lll} c = 3: & q_1(3) \approx \dfrac{15.507}{0.2} & = 77.54 \\ & q_2(3) \approx \dfrac{2.733}{0.04} & = 68.33 \end{array}\right\} \Rightarrow q_1(3) > q_2(3)$$

$$\left.\begin{array}{lll} c = 4: & q_1(4) \approx \dfrac{18.307}{0.2} & = 91.5 \\ & q_2(4) \approx \dfrac{3.940}{0.04} & = 98.5 \end{array}\right\} \Rightarrow q_1(4) < q_2(4)$$

Thus we get $c = 4$ and $n = 92$.

b) Each integer valued n with $n \in [q_1(4); q_2(4)]$ is a sample size of an admissible plan. These are the values $92, 93, \ldots, 98$. The effective risks α^* and β^* with $c = 4$ and the above sample sizes are calculated by $\alpha^* = 1 - Po(4 \cdot 0.02)$ and $\beta^* = Po(4|n \cdot 0.10)$ and result to be:

n	α^*	β^*
92	0.0394	0.0486
93	0.0409	0.0456
94	0.0425	0.0429
95	0.0444	0.0403
96	0.0453	0.0378
97	0.0474	0.0355
98	0.0491	0.0333

Table 6.2/9: Effective risks for different admissible sample sizes

Problem 3.2/19

a)
$$\phi_1 = \arcsin\sqrt{0.05} \approx 0.226; \qquad \phi_2 = \arcsin\sqrt{0.20} \approx 0.464$$
$$z_{0.95} \approx 1.645; \qquad z_{0.90} \approx 1.282.$$

With these values we get

$$n \approx \frac{1}{4} \cdot \left(\frac{1.645 + 1.282}{0.464 - 2.226}\right)^2 - \frac{1}{4 \cdot 0.226 \cdot 0.464} \approx 35.428,$$

i.e., one chooses $n = 36$. Because of

$$\phi^* = \frac{1}{2} \cdot (0.226 + 0.464) \cdot \left(1 - \frac{1}{8 \cdot 36 \cdot 0.226 \cdot 0.464}\right) + \frac{1.645 + 1.282}{4 \cdot \sqrt{36}} \approx 0.456$$

we get for the sample size $n = 36$

$$c \approx 36 \cdot \sin^2 0.456 - 0.5 \approx 36 \cdot 0.193 - 0.5 \approx 6.455,$$

i.e. $c = 7$.

b) The plan in the binomial case with $n = 36$ and $c = 7$ is admissible if and only if it fulfills the conditions (3.64), i.e. if it satisfies $L(0.05|36;7) \geq 0.95$ and $L(0.2|36;7) \leq 0.1$. The calculation yields $L(0.05|36;7) \approx 0.9997$ and $L(0.2|36;7) \approx 0.5660$. Thus the effective consumer risk $\beta^* \approx 0.5660$ is significantly too high; the plan is not admissible.

Problem 3.2/20

According to (3.69a) the acceptance number is calculated as

$$c \approx \frac{\pi}{2} \cdot 1^2 - 0.73 \approx 0.8408,$$

i.e., one chooses $c = 1$. For n it follows by (3.69b) that

$$n \approx \frac{1+\frac{2}{3}}{0.05} = \frac{100}{3},$$

i.e., one draws a sample of size $n = 34$.

Problem 3.2/21

a) The condition "repeat until $i = n_1$" needs to be replaced by

- repeat until ($i = n_1$ or $Z = d_1$) in case of semi-curtailed inspection,
- repeat until ($i = n_1$ or $Z = d_1$ or $i - Z = n_1 - c_1$) in case of fully curtailed inspection.

In addition the condition "repeat until $i = n_1 + n_2$" needs to be replaced by

- repeat until ($i = n_1 + n_2$ or $Z = c_2 + 1$) in case of semi-curtailed inspection,
- repeat until ($i = n_1 + n_2$ or $Z = c_2 + 1$ or $i - Z = n_1 + n_2 - c_2$) in case of fully curtailed inspection.

b)

Sampling procedure	Criterion for stopping inspection	Number of sampled units	
		for accepted lots	for rejected lots
double-sampling without curtailment	–	random variable (RV) with the realizations n_1 and $n_1 + n_2$	
double semicurtailed sampling	Discovery of the d_1-th nonconforming or $(c_2 + 1)$-th conforming sample unit	RV with the realizations n_1 and $n_1 + n_2$	RV with realizations in $[d_1; n_1]$ and $[n_1 + c_2 - d_1 + 2; n_1 + n_2]$

Table 6.2/10: Uncurtailed and semi-curtailed double-sampling by attributes

Problem 3.2/22

The following results were taken from table 5.1/4 and rounded to three decimals:

$$\begin{aligned}
Pr_a^1(0.06) &= Po(1|50 \cdot 0.06) = Po(1|3) \approx 0.199 \\
Pr_r^1(0.06) &= 1 - Po(4|50 \cdot 0.06) = 1 - Po(4|3) \approx 0.185 \\
Pr_a^2(0.06) &= \sum_{j=2}^{4} po(j|50 \cdot 0.06) \cdot Po(7 - j|100 \cdot 0.06) \\
&= po(2|3) \cdot Po(5|6) + po(3|3) \cdot Po(4|6) + po(4|3) \cdot Po(3|6) \\
&\approx 0.224 \cdot 0.446 + 0.224 \cdot 0.285 + 0.168 \cdot 0.151 \\
&\approx 0.189 \\
Pr_r^2(0.06) &= 1 - Pr_a^1(0.06) - Pr_r^1(0.06) - Pr_a^2(0.06) \approx 0.427 \\
Pr_s(0.06) &= Pr_a^2(0.06) - Pr_r^2(0.06) \approx 0.616 \\
L_{do}^*(0.06) &= Pr_a^1(0.06) + Pr_a^2(0.06) = 0.199 + 0.189 \approx 0.388.
\end{aligned}$$

Problem 3.2/23

For the probabilities $Pr_a^1(0.15)$ and $Pr_r^1(0.15)$ we get the following results from table 5.1/2 (under $n = 5$, $M = 3$ and rounded to three decimals):

$$Pr_a^1(0.15) = Hy(0|20;3;5) \approx 0.399$$

$$Pr_r^1(0.15) = 1 - Hy(1|20;3;5) \approx 1 - 0.860 = 0.140.$$

For $Pr_a^2(0.15)$ it can be verified with (3.73) that

$$\begin{aligned} Pr_a^2(0.15) &= \sum_{j=1}^{1} hy(j|20;3;5) \cdot Hy(2-j|15;3-j;5) \\ &\approx 0.461 \cdot \left[\frac{\binom{2}{0}\binom{13}{5}}{\binom{15}{5}} + \frac{\binom{2}{1}\binom{13}{4}}{\binom{15}{5}} \right] \\ &= 4.461 \cdot (0.4286 + 0.4762) \\ &\approx 0.417. \end{aligned}$$

For $Pr_r^2(0.06), Pr_s(0.06)$ and $L_{do}(0.06)$ it then follows that

$$Pr_r^2(0.15) = 1 - Pr_a^1(0.15) - Pr_r^1(0.15) - Pr_a^2(0.15) \approx 0.044$$

$$Pr_s(0.15) = Pr_a^2(0.15) - Pr_r^2(0.15) \approx 0.417 + 0.044 = 0.461$$

$$L_{do}(0.15) = Pr_a^1(0.15) + Pr_a^2(0.15) = 0.399 + 0.417 \approx 0.816.$$

Problem 3.2/24

a) According to the solution of problem 3.2/23 we have in the hypergeometric case the result $Pr_s(0.15) \approx 0.461$ and thus

$$ASN_{do}(0.15) = n_1 + n_2 \cdot Pr_s(0.15) \approx 5 + 5 \cdot 0.461 = 7.305.$$

b) According to the solution of problem 3.2/22 we have in the Poisson case that $Pr_s(0.06) \approx 0.616$ and thus

$$ASN_{do}(0.06) = n_1 + n_2 \cdot Pr_s(0.06) \approx 50 + 100 \cdot 0.616 = 111.6.$$

In the case of semi-curtailed inspection this value becomes smaller. This can be verified with table 5.1/4 and (2.16):

$$\begin{aligned} ASN_{do}^{(1)}(0.06) &= n_1 + \sum_{j=2}^{4} po(j|n_1 \cdot 0.06) \cdot \left[\frac{8-j}{0.06} + n_2 \cdot Po(7-j|n_2 \cdot 0.06) \right. \\ &\quad \left. - \frac{8-j}{0.06} \cdot Po(8-j|(n_2+1) \cdot 0.06)\right] \\ &\approx 50 + \left[0.2240 \cdot \left(\tfrac{6}{0.06} + 100 \cdot 0.4457 - \tfrac{6}{0.06} \cdot 0.5967\right)\right. \\ &\quad +0.2240 \cdot \left(\tfrac{5}{0.06} + 100 \cdot 0.2851 - \tfrac{5}{0.06} \cdot 0.4391\right) \\ &\quad \left. +0.1680 \cdot \left(\tfrac{4}{0.06} + 100 \cdot 0.1512 - \tfrac{4}{0.06} \cdot 0.2771\right) \right] \\ &\approx 96.5. \end{aligned}$$

Problem 3.2/25

Because of (3.85) we only need to show that $E(Y_2) = A(P) + (1-P) \cdot N$. For the average number Y_2 of those units that are accepted during the first and second inspection stages we get in the case of S_2/L_2 in analogy to (3.48) the result

$$Y_2 = \begin{cases} N - n_1 P & \text{if } \; X_{n_1}^T \le c_1 \\ N - (n_1 + n_2)P & \text{if } \; X_{n_1}^T \in (c_1, d_1) \text{ and } X_{n_1+n_2}^T \le c_2 \\ N - NP & \text{else.} \end{cases}$$

The chain of equalities (3.49) corresponds now to

$$\begin{aligned} E(Y_2) &= (N - n_1 P) \cdot Pr_a^1(P) + [N - (n_1+n_2)P] \cdot Pr_a^2(P) + (N - NP) \cdot [1 - L_{do}(P)] \\ &= (N - n_1 P) \cdot L_{do}(P) - n_2 P \cdot Pr_a^2 + (N - NP) \cdot [1 - L_{do}(P)] \\ &= P \cdot [(N - n_1) \cdot L_{do}(P) - n_2 \cdot Pr_a^2(P)] + (1-P)N \\ &= A(P) + (1-P)N. \end{aligned}$$

Problem 3.2/26

For the average number Y_3 of units that need to be inspected in a double-sampling plan for a lot with fraction nonconforming P we get in case of S_3/L_3 in analogy to (3.55) the result

$$Y_3 = \begin{cases} \dfrac{n_1}{1-P} & \text{if } \; X_{n_1}^T \le c_1 \\ \dfrac{n_1+n_2}{1-P} & \text{if } \; X_{n_1}^T \in (c_1, d_1) \text{ and } X_{n_1+n_2}^T \le c_2 \\ \dfrac{N}{1-P} & \text{else.} \end{cases}$$

For the average amount of inspection $ATI_{do}(P) = E(Y_3)$ we get from $A(P)$ in (3.85) that

$$\begin{aligned} ATI_{do}(P) &= \frac{n_1}{1-P} \cdot Pr_a^1(P) + \frac{n_1+n_2}{1-P} \cdot Pr_a^2(P) + \frac{N}{1-P} \cdot [1 - L_{do}(P)] \\ &= \frac{1}{1-P} \{N - N \cdot L_{do}(P) + n_1[L_{do}(P) - Pr_a^2(P)] + (n_1+n_2) \cdot Pr_a^2(P)\} \\ &= \frac{1}{1-P} \{N - [(N-n_1) \cdot L_{do}(P) - n_2 Pr_a^2(P)]\} \\ &= \frac{1}{1-P} \left[N - \frac{A(P)}{P}\right]. \end{aligned}$$

Problem 3.2/27

In the formulas of tables 3.2/15-16 one only needs to substitute, besides N and P, $A(P)$ and $ASN_{do}(P)$. With the given probabilities $Pr_a^2(P), Pr_s(P)$ and $L_{do}(P)$ one gets with the help of (3.85) and (3.80) the results

$$A(P_1) = 49.194; \; A(P_2) = 16.452; \quad ASN_{do}(P_1) = 88.1; \; ASN_{do}(P_2) = 101.1.$$

Substituting these results into tables 3.2/15-16 we get the following table for $P_1 = 0.027$ (number in brackets for $P_2 = 0.085$):

	AOQ_{do}			ATI_{do}		
	L_1	L_2	L_3	L_1	L_2	L_3
S_1	0.027 (0.085)	0.0258 (0.0094)	0.0257 (0.0087)	88.1 (101.1)	178 (1806.4)	180.5 (1964.8)
S_2	0.0258 (0.0575)	0.0247 (0.0089)	0.0246 (0.0083)			
S_3	0.0258 (0.0558)	0.0246 (0.0089)	0.0246 (0.0082)	90.5 (110.4)	180.5 (1815.8)	182.9 (1974.2)

Table 6.2/11: AOQ and ATI values of the double-sampling plan (2000;50;1;5;100;7) for two quality levels

Problem 3.2/28

With the specifications for AQL, RQL, α and β we get the following results with the help of table 5.2/4 (see also example 3.2/12):

$$\left.\begin{aligned} c = 0: \quad q_1(0) &= \frac{\chi^2_{2;0.90}}{2 \cdot RQL} \approx \frac{4.605}{0.114} = 40.39 \\ q_2(0) &= \frac{\chi^2_{2;0.10}}{2 \cdot AQL} \approx \frac{0.211}{0.0232} = 9.09 \end{aligned}\right\} \Rightarrow q_1(0) > q_2(0)$$

$$\left.\begin{aligned} c=1: \quad q_1(1) &= \frac{\chi^2_{4;0.90}}{2\cdot RQL} \approx \frac{7.779}{0.114} = 68.24 \\ q_2(1) &= \frac{\chi^2_{4;0.10}}{2\cdot AQL} \approx \frac{1.064}{0.0232} = 45.86 \end{aligned}\right\} \Rightarrow q_1(1) > q_2(1)$$

$$\left.\begin{aligned} c=2: \quad q_1(2) &= \frac{\chi^2_{6;0.90}}{2\cdot RQL} \approx \frac{10.645}{0.114} = 93.38 \\ q_2(2) &= \frac{\chi^2_{6;0.10}}{2\cdot AQL} \approx \frac{2.204}{0.0232} = 95.00 \end{aligned}\right\} \Rightarrow q_1(2) < q_2(2).$$

Hence , we have $c = 2$, $n = 94$ and

$$w_{do} = \frac{ASNL_{do}}{n} = \frac{76.70}{94} \approx 0.816.$$

Problem 3.2/29

a)

$$\begin{aligned} Pr_a^1(0.02) &= Bi(0|0.02;20) \approx 0.6676 \\ Pr_a^2(0.02) &= [bi(1|0.02;20)\cdot Bi(1|0.02;20) + bi(2|0.02;20)\cdot Bi(0|0.02;20)] \\ &\approx 0.2725\cdot 0.9401 + 0.0528\cdot 0.6676 \\ &\approx 0.2914 \\ Pr_a^3(0.02) &\approx bi(1|0.02;20)\cdot bi(2|0.02;20)\cdot Bi(0|0.02;20)\cdot 2 \\ &\approx 0.2725\cdot 0.0528\cdot 0.6676\cdot 2 \\ &\approx 0.0192 \\ L_3(0.02) &= Pr_a^1(0.02) + Pr_a^2(0.02) + Pr_a^3(0.02) \approx 0.9782. \end{aligned}$$

b)

$$\begin{aligned} ASN_3(0.02) &= 20 + 20\cdot[bi(1|0.02;20) + bi(2|0.02;20)] \\ &\quad +20\cdot bi(1|0.02;20)\cdot bi(2|0.02;20)\cdot 2 \\ &\approx 20 + 20\cdot(0.2725 + 0.0528) + 20\cdot 0.2725\cdot 0.0582\cdot 2 \\ &\approx 27.08. \end{aligned}$$

Problem 3.2/30

a) The path intersects the rejection line $k = 2.4 + 0.05n$ already after the inspection of $n = 3$ units if all three sample units are nonconforming. It intersects the acceptance line $k = -1.8 + 0.05n$ at $n = 36$, provided no nonconforming unit is found up to that point.

b) The slope c is given by (3.93c). We can immediately see that c only depends on the values AQL and RQL. A closer analysis shows that on the one hand c depends on the distance between AQL and RQL. On the other hand that for a given length of the interval $[AQL; RQL]$ it also depends on its location within the interval [0;1]. The closer AQL and RQL lie together, the smaller becomes c. If AQL and RQL are shifted to the right, towards larger values, while the distance between them remains constant, then c increases.

c) For the distance $b - a$ on the vertical axis between the two lines we get from (3.93a,b) and (3.94) that

$$b - a = \frac{\ln\left(\frac{1-\beta}{\alpha}\right) - \ln\left(\frac{\beta}{1-\alpha}\right)}{\ln\left[\frac{RQL(1-AQL)}{AQL(1-RQL)}\right]}.$$

The term $b-a$ thus only depends on AQL, RQL, α and β. In order to analyse this in more detail we will first keep the values AQL and RQL constant. The bigger the values of α and β the smaller becomes $b - a$. Generally this leads to an earlier decision about the lot. If one of the error probabilities is kept constant and one increases the other, then $b - a$ also decreases. We will now keep the values of α and β constant. The closer AQL and RQL lie together, the larger is the distance $b - a$. In general, this increases the time needed for a final decision. If AQL and RQL are shifted to the right while the distance between them remains constant then $b - a$ becomes smaller.

Problem 3.2/31

a) The desired inspection plan is uniquely determined if one knows the quantities a^*, b^* and c^* which determine the indifference interval

$$I_n^* = (a^* + c^*n; b^* + c^*n).$$

For $\alpha = 0.01, \beta = 0.05$, $\lambda_0 = 2$ and $\lambda_1 = 5$ the above quantities result to be

$$a^* = \frac{\ln A}{\ln\left(\frac{\lambda_1}{\lambda_0}\right)} = \frac{\ln\beta - \ln(1-\alpha)}{\ln\lambda_1 - \ln\lambda_0} \approx -\frac{2.985682}{0.916291} \approx -3.2584$$

$$b^* = \frac{\ln B}{\ln\left(\frac{\lambda_1}{\lambda_0}\right)} = \frac{\ln(1-\beta) - \ln\alpha}{\ln\lambda_1 - \ln\lambda_0} \approx \frac{4.553877}{0.916291} \approx 4.9699$$

$$c^* = \frac{\lambda_1 - \lambda_0}{\ln\left(\frac{\lambda_1}{\lambda_0}\right)} = \frac{\lambda_1 - \lambda_0}{\ln\lambda_1 - \ln\lambda_0} \approx \frac{3}{0.916291} \approx 3.2741.$$

One continues to inspect until the value k^* of the the cumulative count X_n^{*T} of nonconforming sample units lies outside of the interval I_n^*.

b) For $n = 5$ we have $I_n^* = (13.1121; 21.3404)$. Since the observed value $k^* = 10$ is smaller than the lower boundary of the interval the lot is accepted (see again figure 3.2/23).

Problem 3.2/32

a)
$$A = \frac{\beta}{1-\alpha} = \frac{0.1}{0.9} = \frac{1}{9}; \quad B = \frac{1-\beta}{\alpha} = \frac{0.9}{0.1} = 9$$
$$\frac{1-AQL}{1-RQL} = \frac{0.9884}{0.9430} \approx 1.048; \quad \frac{RQL(1-AQL)}{AQL(1-RQL)} = \frac{0.057 \cdot 0.9884}{0.0116 \cdot 0.943} \approx 5.150$$
$$a \approx \frac{\ln 1 - \ln 9}{\ln 5.150} \approx -1.3405; \quad b \approx \frac{\ln 9}{\ln 5.150} \approx 1.3405; \quad c \approx \frac{\ln 1.048}{\ln 5.150} \approx 0.0287.$$

b)

h	$P = \psi(h)$	$L_s(P)$	$ASN_s(P)$
-1.0	**0.0570**	**0.1000**	37.89
-0.5	0.0415	0.2500	52.36
-0.3	0.0361	0.3409	57.64
-0.1	0.0310	0.4453	63.76
0.0	0.0287	0.5000	64.46
0.1	0.0265	0.5547	66.66
0.3	**0.0224**	0.6591	**67.71**
0.5	0.0187	0.7500	67.03
1.0	**0.0116**	**0.9000**	62.71

Table 6.2/12: Values of the OC and ASN functions of a sequential-sampling plan (binomial case)

We can see that the OC curve goes through the points (0.0116;0.9) and (0.0570;0.1). The ASN function attains a maximum $ASNL_s \approx 67.71$ roughly at $P_M = 0.0224$.

c) The single-sampling plan works with $n = 94$, whereas the double- and sequential-sampling plans work with the maximum average sample numbers $ASNL_{do} \approx 76.70$ or $ASNL_s \approx 67.71$, respectively. Hence, the sequential-sampling plan is the most efficient. In comparison to the single-sampling plan its efficiency (3.103) results to be

$$w_s = \frac{67.71}{94} \approx 0.720.$$

This tells us that the sequential plan reduces the amount of inspection on the average by at least 28.0%. The double-sampling plan achieves because of

$$w_{do} = \frac{76.70}{94} \approx 0.816$$

a reduction of at least 18.4% in the amount of inspection.

Problem 3.2/33

a)

h	$\lambda = \psi(h)$	$L_s(\lambda)$	$ASN_s(\lambda)$
0.2	6.59	0.0053	1.48
0.4	5.00	0.0500	2.64
0.6	4.18	0.1770	3.87
0.8	3.65	0.3853	4.75
1.0	3.27	0.6040	4.95
1.2	2.98	0.7670	4.64
2.0	2.27	0.9713	3.01
2.5	2.00	0.9900	2.49

Table 6.2/13: Values of the OC and ASN function of a sequential-sampling plan (Poisson case)

It can be verified that the OC curve goes through (2;0.99) and (5;0.05). The ASN curve attains a maximum $ASNL_s \approx 4.95$ at $\lambda_M \approx c^*$.

b) The equivalent single-sampling plan is determined in analogy to figure 3.2/16. The specifications are now $\lambda_0 = 2, \lambda_1 = 5, \alpha = 0.01$ and $\beta = 0.05$. We get

$$c = 0: \quad \left.\begin{aligned} q_1(0) &= \frac{\chi^2_{2;0.05}}{2 \cdot \lambda_1} \approx \frac{5.991}{10} = 0.5991 \\ q_2(0) &= \frac{\chi^2_{2;0.01}}{2 \cdot \lambda_0} \approx \frac{0.020}{4} = 0.005 \end{aligned}\right\} \Rightarrow q_1(0) > q_2(0)$$

$$\vdots \qquad \vdots \qquad \vdots$$

$$c = 19: \quad \left.\begin{aligned} q_1(19) &= \frac{\chi^2_{40;0.95}}{2 \cdot \lambda_1} \approx \frac{55.758}{10} = 5.5758 \\ q_2(19) &= \frac{\chi^2_{40;0.01}}{2 \cdot \lambda_0} \approx \frac{22.164}{4} = 5.541 \end{aligned}\right\} \Rightarrow q_1(19) > q_2(19)$$

$$c = 20: \quad \left.\begin{aligned} q_1(20) &= \frac{\chi^2_{42;0.95}}{2 \cdot \lambda_1} \approx \frac{58.124}{10} = 5.8124 \\ q_2(20) &= \frac{\chi^2_{42;0.01}}{2 \cdot \lambda_0} \approx \frac{23.650}{4} = 5.9125 \end{aligned}\right\} \Rightarrow q_1(20) < q_2(20)$$

$$\vdots \qquad \vdots \qquad \vdots$$

$$c = 23: \quad \left.\begin{aligned} q_1(23) &= \frac{\chi^2_{48;0.95}}{2 \cdot \lambda_1} \approx \frac{65.171}{10} = 6.5171 \\ q_2(23) &= \frac{\chi^2_{48;0.01}}{2 \cdot \lambda_0} \approx \frac{28.177}{4} = 7.04425 \end{aligned}\right\} \Rightarrow q_1(23) < q_2(23).$$

The loop in figure 3.2/16 cannot yet be terminated at $c = 20$, inspite of $q_1(20) < q_2(20)$, because the interval $[q_1(20); q_2(20)]$ does not contain an integer. This is only the case for $c = 23$.

The result is $c = 23$ and $n = 7$. In this obtained single-sampling plan one would thus inspect 7 tubes from each lot of $N = 1000$ tubes. If the total number X_7^{*T} of the observed defects in the lamination of the 7 tubes does not exceed the value 23 then the lot is accepted. We want to note that this plan has an effective producer's risk of $\alpha^* = 0.0093$ (instead of $\alpha = 0.01$) and an effective consumer's risk of $\beta^* = 0.0207$ (instead of $\beta = 0.05$).

c) The sequential plan is more efficient than the single-sampling plan. With $ASNL_s \approx 4.95$ and $n = 7$ the efficiency (3.103) results to be

$$w_s = \frac{4.95}{7} \approx 0.707.$$

Problem 3.2/34

a) For the producer's risk $\alpha = 1 - L^*(AQL|n; c)$ we get from table 5.1/4 with $AQL = 0.01$ the result

$$\alpha = 1 - L^*(0.01|200; 5) = 1 - Po(5|200 \cdot 0.01) \approx 0.01656.$$

b) For the consumer's risk $\beta = L^*(RQL|n; c)$ it similarily holds that

$$\beta = L^*(0.02|200; 5) = Po(5|200 \cdot 0.02) \approx 0.78513$$

$$\beta = L^*(0.03|200; 5) = Po(5|200 \cdot 0.03) \approx 0.44568$$

$$\beta = L^*(0.04|200; 5) = Po(5|200 \cdot 0.04) \approx 0.19124$$

$$\beta = L^*(0.05|200; 5) = Po(5|200 \cdot 0.05) \approx 0.06709.$$

Problem 3.2/35

a) No particular action is taken: according to figure 3.2/28 one only leaves the normal inspection level after two of five consecutive lots have been rejected.

b) No particular action is taken: according to figure 3.2/28 the tightened inspection has already been terminated after 5 consecutive good lots, and consequently by now one is again on normal inspection. On this level one can – as explained above – after rejection of only one lot not yet go back to tightened inspection.

c) One switches to normal inspection.

Problem 3.2/36

The desired probabilities are all calculated according to (3.77a):

a)
$$\begin{aligned} & L_{do}(0.04|200;20;1;4;20;4) \\ &= Hy(1|200;8;20) + \sum_{j=2}^{3} hy(j|200;8;20) \cdot Hy(4-j|180;8-j;20) \\ &\approx 0.8155 + (0.1497 \cdot 0.9803 + 0.0308 \cdot 0.9995) \\ &\approx 0.9930 \end{aligned}$$

b)
$$\begin{aligned} & L_{do}(0.04|200;20;0;3;20;3) \\ &= Hy(0|200;8;20) + \sum_{j=2}^{3} hy(j|200;8;20) \cdot Hy(3-j|180;8-j;20) \\ &\approx 0.4236 + (0.3918 \cdot 0.9690 + 0.1497 \cdot 0.8659) \\ &\approx 0.9329. \end{aligned}$$

Problem 3.2/37

a) With $N = 1000$ and $AQL = 0.04$ (4% nonconforming) the ISO 2859 specifies according to table 3.2/23 the single-sampling plan (1000;80;7). The probability of accepting a lot with $N = 1000$ and $P = 0.04$ is then given by

$$L(0.04|1000;80;7) = Hy(7|1000;1000 \cdot 0.04;80) \approx 0.9890.$$

The latter value cannot be found in table 5.1/2. However, since the lot size N only has a marginal influence on the shape of the OC curve (see figure 3.2/4) we get a good approximation by replacing $L(0.04|1000;80;7)$ by the value $L(0.04|850;80;7) \approx 0.9897$ which is listed in table 3.2/25.

b) With $N = 500$ and the same AQL one finds that table 3.2/23 specifies the sampling plan (500;50;5). The probability of accepting two lots with $N = 500$ and $P = 0.04$ is given by

$$L^2(0.04|500;50;5) = [Hy(5|500;500 \cdot 0.04;40)]^2 \approx 0.9904^2 \approx 0.9809.$$

Table 5.1/2 has a limited range, but one can use table 3.2/25 to get the result

$$L^2(0.04|500;50;5) \approx L^2(0.04|400;50;5) \approx 0.9915^2 \approx 0.9831.$$

The partition of the lots with $N = 1000$ into two equally sized lots is thus a slight disadvantage for the producer.

Problem 3.2/38

a) The desired probability is given by $L^5(P)$. We get

$$\begin{aligned} L^5(0.04) &\approx 0.8740^5 \approx 0.5100 \\ L^5(0.0725) &= 0.5^5 = 0.03125 \\ L^5(0.125) &\approx 0.0982^5 \approx 9.13 \cdot 10^{-6}. \end{aligned}$$

b) The desired probability has the value $[1 - L(P)]^{10}$:

$$\begin{aligned} [1 - L(0.04)]^{10} &\approx 0.1260^{10} \approx 1.01 \cdot 10^{-9} \\ [1 - L(0.0725)]^{10} &= 0.5^{10} \approx 9.77 \cdot 10^{-4} \\ [1 - L(0.125)]^{10} &\approx 0.9118^{10} \approx 0.3557. \end{aligned}$$

Problem 3.2/39

With (3.8a) and table 5.1/3 we get the following result for the binomial OC function at $P = 0.05$:

$$L(0.05) = Bi(1|0.05; 20) \approx 0.73584.$$

If we substitute this value as well as $i = 4$ and $f = 0.25$ into (3.107) – (3.109), then it follows that

$$L_{Sk}(0.05) = \frac{(1 - 0.25) \cdot 0.73584^4 + 0.25 \cdot 0.73584}{(1 - 0.25) \cdot 0.73584^4 + 0.25} \approx 0.85945$$

$$AFI_{Sk}(0.05) = \frac{0.25}{(1 - 0.25) \cdot 0.73584^4 \cdot 0.25} \approx 0.5320$$

$$ASN_{Sk}(0.05) \approx 0.5320 \cdot 20 = 10.64.$$

Problem 3.2/40

The mass function $P(X_{10}^T = k)$ of the test statistic X_{10}^T is given by (2.92), if one substitutes $n = 10$. For $P = 0.1$ it follows that

$$\begin{aligned} Pr\left(X_n^T = 0\right) &= bi(0|P; 10) = \binom{10}{0} \cdot 0.1^0 \cdot 0.9^{10} \approx 0.3487 \\ Pr\left(X_n^T = 1\right) &= bi(1|P; 10) = \binom{10}{1} \cdot 0.1^1 \cdot 0.9^9 \approx 0.3874. \end{aligned}$$

Substituting these values and $i = 2$ into (3.110) yields

$$L_{Ch}(0.1) \approx 0.3487 + 0.3874 \cdot 0.3487^2 \approx 0.3958.$$

Then it holds according to (3.111) that

$$AOQ_{Ch}(0.1) \approx 0.1 \cdot 0.3958 = 0.03958.$$

Problem 3.2/41

a) If attribute sampling is performed by inspection personnel then human error is a possible cause of misclassification. This could be for example insufficient training, tiredness, lack of concentration or inadequate use of one's judgement.
In the case of automized attribute inspection it can also come to misclassifications, for example due to insufficient calibration of the measuring instrument.

b) If attribute sampling is performed by inspection personnel, then the for each inspector the probability of misclassification can vary over time; the performance curve of human beings over the period of a day or a week is not constant. In addition the probabilities vary from one inspector to the other (different performance curves).
In the case of automized inspection there can be changes in the probability of misclassification for example through wear and tear in the instruments.

c) The functions $L(P)$ and $L^e(P)$ are identical, if the true and the empirical fraction nonconforming in the lot are equal. With $\Pi = P$ we get the following result from (3.115) through solving for P and setting the result equal to P_I:

$$P_I = \frac{\varepsilon}{\varepsilon + \phi}.$$

In the case of $\varepsilon = 0.1$ and $\phi = 0.2$ we get that $P_I \approx 0.33$, whereas for $\varepsilon = 0.2$ and $\phi = 0.2$ the result is $P_I = 0.50$. These values can also be read from figure 3.2/30.

Problem 3.2/42

a) The empirical fraction nonconforming is according to (3.115) given by

$$\Pi = \begin{cases} 0.8P + 0.2 & \text{if } \varepsilon = 0.2; \quad \phi = 0 \\ 0.8P & \text{if } \varepsilon = 0; \quad \phi = 0.2 \\ 0.7P + 0.1 & \text{if } \varepsilon = 0.1; \quad \phi = 0.2 \\ 0.6P + 0.2 & \text{if } \varepsilon = 0.2; \quad \phi = 0.2. \end{cases}$$

Because of (3.117b) it follows that the empirical OC function has the form

$$L^e(P) = \begin{cases} L(0.8P + 0.2) & \text{if } \varepsilon = 0.2; \quad \phi = 0 \\ L(0.8P) & \text{if } \varepsilon = 0; \quad \phi = 0.2 \\ L(0.7P + 0.1) & \text{if } \varepsilon = 0.1; \quad \phi = 0.2 \\ L(0.6P + 0.2) & \text{if } \varepsilon = 0.2; \quad \phi = 0.2. \end{cases}$$

In figure 3.2/29-30 these four functions were denoted by $L_1^e(P)$ to $L_4^e(P)$.

b) At the point $P = 0.15$ one can find $L_1^e(P)$ to $L_4^e(P)$ by using $L(P) = Bi(P|30;10)$ and table 5.1/3 obtaining the results 0.6451, 0.9995, 0.9697 and respectively 0.7695. For the true value of the OC function we would get $L(0.15) \approx 0.9971$.

Problem 3.2/43

a) We first define the quantities

$$a^* := \max(a_1; a_1 + a_2); \qquad r^* := \max(r_1; r_1 + r_2)$$
$$a^{**} := (a_1 + a_2) - (r_1 + r_2); \quad r^{**} := r_1 - a_1.$$

With this notation both target functions lead under the minimax rule to acceptance of the lot, if and only if $a^* < r^*$ and $a^{**} < r^{**}$ and both lead to rejection, if and only if $a^* > r^*$ and $a^{**} > r^{**}$.

b) We have $v_a(P) = -10 + 50P$ and $v_r(P) = 30 - 20P$. The graphs of these functions and the corresponding regret functions are given in figure 3.2/38. Best with respect to the loss function is the one of the two actions, for which the maximal value of the expected loss, i.e. the maximum of $E[v_a(P)]$ and $E[v_r(P)]$, has the smallest value in the interval [0;1]. For (3.131) we get

$$E[v_a(P)] = \int_0^1 2 \cdot (-10 + 50p) \cdot (1 - p)dp = \tfrac{20}{3}$$
$$E[v_r(P)] = \int_0^1 2 \cdot (30 - 20p) \cdot (1 - p)dp = \tfrac{70}{3}.$$

Because of $E[v_a(P)] < E[v_r(P)]$ lot acceptance is the best decision under this loss function.

c) According to (3.127) we have $P_0 = 4/7$. If one uses the regret functions

$$\rho_a(P) = \begin{cases} 0 & \text{for } 0 \le P \le \frac{4}{7} \\ 70\left(P - \frac{4}{7}\right) & \text{for } \frac{4}{7} < P \le 1 \end{cases}$$

$$\rho_r(P) = \begin{cases} 70\left(\frac{4}{7} - P\right) & \text{for } 0 \le P \le \frac{4}{7} \\ 0 & \text{for } \frac{4}{7} < P \le 1 \end{cases}$$

then (3.132) becomes

$$E[\rho_a(P)] = \int_{4/7}^{1} 70 \cdot \left(p - \tfrac{4}{7}\right) \cdot 2 \cdot (1 - p) \cdot dp \approx 1.8367$$
$$E[\rho_r(P)] = \int_{0}^{4/7} 70 \cdot \left(\tfrac{4}{7} - p\right) \cdot 2 \cdot (1 - p) \cdot dp \approx 18.5034.$$

Because of $E[\rho_a(P)] < E[\rho_r(P)]$ acceptance is also the optimal decision under the regret function.

d) The prior information for P gives a continuous uniform distribution with density

$$\pi(P) = \begin{cases} 5 & \text{for } P \in [0.5; 0.7] \\ 0 & \text{else.} \end{cases}$$

As a result one gets the average losses

$$E[v_a(P)] = \int_{0.5}^{0.7} 5 \cdot (-10 + 50p)dp = 20$$

$$E[v_r(P)] = \int_{0.5}^{0.7} 5 \cdot (30 - 20p)dp = 18,$$

so that rejection is the optimal decision. The average regret is found to be

$$E[\rho_a(P)] = \int_{4/7}^{0.7} 70 \cdot (p - \tfrac{4}{7}) \cdot 5 \cdot dp \approx 2.8929$$

$$E[\rho_r(P)] = \int_{0.5}^{4/7} 70 \cdot (\tfrac{4}{7} - p) \cdot 5 \cdot dp \approx 0.8929,$$

i.e. rejection is here also optimal.

Problem 3.3/1

a) For $\sigma = 1$ it holds for the fraction nonconforming $P(\mu)$ according to (3.136b) that

$$P(\mu) = \Phi(\mu - 5) = 1 - \Phi(5 - \mu).$$

Using this equation one can calculate the corresponding fraction nonconforming $P = P(\mu)$ for a given μ. In the other direction one can because of (3.138b) with the help of

$$\mu(P) = 5 + z_P = 5 - z_{1-P}$$

for a given P uniquely deduce a value μ with $P(\mu) = P$.

The graph of $P(\mu) = \Phi(\mu - 5)$ is obtained from the graph of $P(\mu) = \Phi(5 - \mu)$ presented in figure 3.3/2b through reflection on the vertical $\mu = 5$ (parallel to the P-axis):

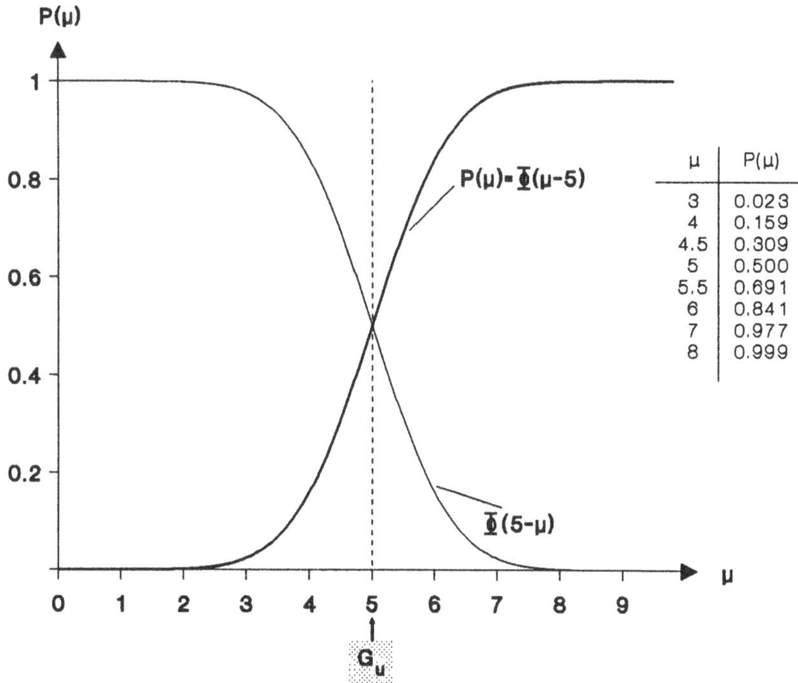

μ	P(μ)
3	0.023
4	0.159
4.5	0.309
5	0.500
5.5	0.691
6	0.841
7	0.977
8	0.999

Figure 6.2/5: Fraction nonconforming P as a function of μ in the case of given upper specification limit G_u

b) The desired values of $P(\mu) = \Phi(\mu - 5)$ are tabulated to the right of figure 6.2/5.

Problem 3.3/2

a) According to (3.41b) the minimal fraction nonconforming is reached at $\mu^* = (12+6)/2 = 9$ and has by (3.41a) the value

$$P^* = P(9) = 2\Phi(-1.5) \approx 2 \cdot 0.0668 = 0.1336.$$

b) The side condition $P_1(\mu) = P_2(\mu) = 0.1$ can not be satisfied because $P_1(\mu)$ and $P_2(\mu)$ only agree at the point $\mu = \mu^* = 9$ (see also figure 3.3/3a). But at this point we have $P_1(9) = P_2(9) = \Phi(-1.5) \approx 0.0668$.

c) According to (3.142) we have two expectations $\mu_{1,2} = 9 \pm d$ with $P(\mu_{1,2}) = 0.2$. Because of the side condition $P_1(\mu) = 0.05$ and $P_1(\mu) < P(\mu)/2$ the solution can only be $\mu_1 = 9 + d$. From (3.136c) and $G_l = 6$ it follows that (also see figure 5.2/1)

$$P_1(9+d) = \Phi\left(\frac{-3-d}{2}\right) = 0.05; \quad z_{0.05} = \frac{-3-d}{2}.$$

According to table 5.2/1 we have $z_{0.05} = -1.645$ and thus

$$d = -2 \cdot z_{0.05} - 3 \approx 0.29.$$

With $\mu_1 = 9.29$ it consequently holds that $P(\mu_1) = 0.2$ and $P_1(\mu_1) = 0.05$

d) Again we first have two values $\mu_{1,2} = 9 \pm d$ with $P(\mu_{1,2}) = 0.2$. Because of $P_1(\mu) = 0.12 > P(\mu)/2$ only $\mu_2 = 9 - d$ can be considered. It follows by (3.136c) that

$$P_2(9-d) = \Phi\left(\frac{-3+d}{2}\right) = 0.12; \quad z_{0.12} = \frac{-3+d}{2}.$$

With $z_{0.12} \approx -1.175$ we get the result

$$d = 2 \cdot z_{0.12} + 3 \approx 0.65.$$

Hence for $\mu_2 = 8.35$ we have $P(\mu_2) = 0.2$ and $P_1(\mu_2) = 0.12$. Without the side condition $P_1(\mu) = 0.12$, $\mu_1 = 9.65$ also were, besides $\mu_2 = 8.35$, a solution of $P(\mu) = 0.2$.

Problem 3.3/3

	$\bar{X}_{10}$	Z_{10}	Q_{10}	$\hat{P}_{10}$
Realization of the test statistic	$\bar{x}_{10} = 10.9$	$z_{10} = 10.9 - 2 \cdot 0.5$ $= 9.9$	$q_{10} = \frac{10.9-10}{0.5}$ $= 1.8$	$\hat{p}_{10} = 1 - \Phi(q_{10} \cdot \sqrt{10/9})$ ≈ 0.0294
lot rejection if and only if	$\bar{x} < 10 + 2 \cdot 0.5$ $= 11$	$z_{10} < 10 = G_l$	$q_{10} < 2 = k$	$\hat{p}_{10} > 1 - \Phi(2 \cdot \sqrt{10/9})$ ≈ 0.0174
Decision	rejection	rejection	rejection	rejection

Table 6.2/14: Test statistics and alternative procedures for sampling by variables with the plan (10;2) in the case of a specified lower limit and known variance

Problem 3.3/4

By (3.150) and (3.151) and the strict monotonicity of the distribution function $\Phi(z)$ (see figure 5.2/1) and abbreviating $r_n := \sqrt{n/(n-1)}$ we get the following equivalent statements:

$$\begin{aligned}
\hat{P} \le M_n \quad &\Leftrightarrow 1 - \Phi(Q_n \cdot r_n) \le 1 - \Phi(k \cdot r_n) \\
&\Leftrightarrow \Phi(Q_n \cdot r_n) \ge \Phi(k \cdot r_n) \\
&\Leftrightarrow Q_n \cdot \ge k \cdot r_n \\
&\Leftrightarrow Q_n \ge k.
\end{aligned}$$

Problem 3.3/5

a) An increase in the sample size n leads as before in the case of sampling by attributes (see figure 3.2/5) to an improvement in the discriminatory power, i.e. the absolute value of the slope at the turning point of the OC curve increases.

b) An increase of k has the same effect as a decrease in the acceptance number c in sampling by attributes (see figure 3.2/6) and thus also leads to an increase in the discriminatory power of the inspection procedure.

Problem 3.3/6

a) One only needs to reverse the inequalities in (3.143).

b) The OC function is according to table 3.3/3 given by $L_1(\mu) = \Phi[5 \cdot (4.8 - \mu)]$. The graph of this function is obtained from the graph of the OC-function $L_1(\mu) = \Phi[5 \cdot (\mu - 5.2)]$ in figure 3.3/5b through reflection on the vertical line $\mu = 5$:

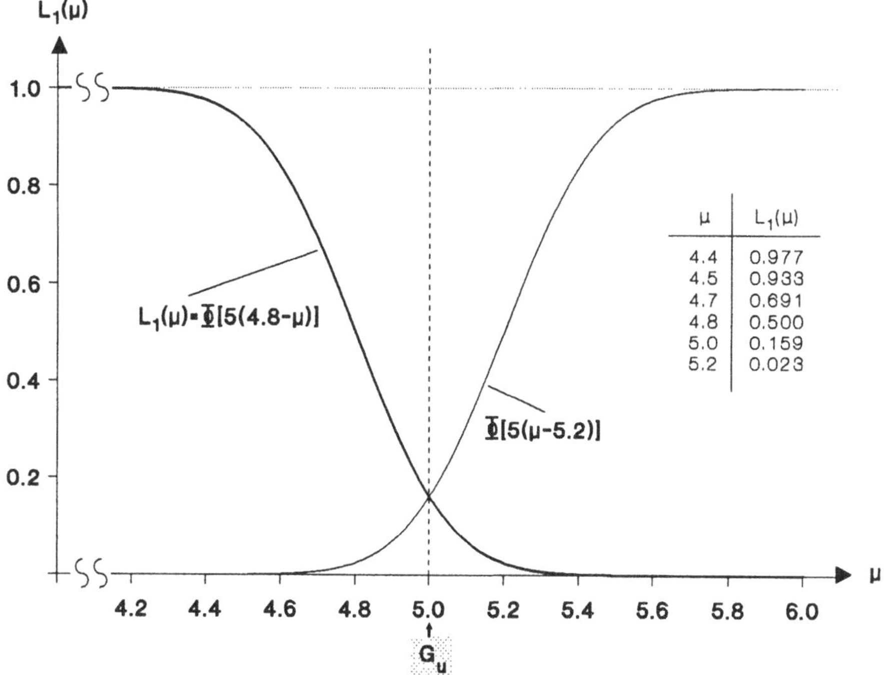

μ	$L_1(\mu)$
4.4	0.977
4.5	0.933
4.7	0.691
4.8	0.500
5.0	0.159
5.2	0.023

Figure 6.2/6: OC function $L_1(\mu)$ for the sampling plan (25;0.2) in case of a specified upper limit G_u

Problem 3.3/7

a) Setting $\omega = 0.5$ for the OC percentiles in table 3.3/3 it follows because of $z_{0.5} = 0$ that

- in the case of a specified lower limit G_l: $\mu_{0.5} = G_l + k\sigma$
- in the case of a specified upper limit G_u: $\mu_{0.5} = G_u - k\sigma$.

b) In a similar way one gets form (3.155b) with $\omega = 0.5$ the IQL formula $P_{0.5} = \Phi(-k)$

Problem 3.3/8

a) Substituting $n = 10$, $k = 2$ as well as $G_l = 10$ and $\sigma = 0.5$ in (3.152) yields

$$L_1(\mu) = \Phi\left[\sqrt{10}\left(\frac{\mu - 10}{0.5} - 2\right)\right] = \Phi\left[2\sqrt{10}\ (\mu - 11)\right].$$

With the help of table 5.1/1 it can be verified that

$$\begin{aligned} L_1(10.8) &= \Phi(-0.4 \cdot \sqrt{10}) \approx \Phi(-1.26) \approx 0.1038 \\ L_1(11) &= \Phi(0) = 0.5 \\ L_1(11.2) &= \Phi(0.4 \cdot \sqrt{10}) \approx \Phi(1.26) \approx 0.8962. \end{aligned}$$

b) The percentiles of $L_1(\mu)$ are calculated according to (3.155a):

$$\mu_\omega = 10 + \left(\frac{z_\omega}{\sqrt{10}} + 2\right) \cdot 0.5.$$

From table 5.2/1 one gets

$$\begin{aligned} \mu_{0.05} &= 10 + (-0.52 + 2) \cdot 0.5 \approx 10.74 \\ \mu_{0.5} &= 10 + (0 + 2) \cdot 0.5 = 11 \\ \mu_{0.95} &= 10 + (0.52 + 2) \cdot 0.5 \approx 11.26. \end{aligned}$$

c) In analogy to part a) it follows from (3.153b) that

$$L_2(P) = L_1(10 + z_{1-P} \cdot 0.5) = \Phi[\sqrt{10}\ (z_{1-P} - 2)]$$

and thus

$$\begin{aligned} L_2(0.05) &= \Phi[\sqrt{10}\ (1.645 - 2)] &\approx& \ \Phi(-1.12) &\approx& \ 0.1314 \\ L_2(0.1) &= \Phi[\sqrt{10}\ (1.282 - 2)] &\approx& \ \Phi(-2.27) &\approx& \ 0.0116 \\ L_2(0.15) &= \Phi[\sqrt{10}\ (1.036 - 2)] &\approx& \ \Phi(-3.05) &\approx& \ 0.0011. \end{aligned}$$

d) According to (3.155b) the percentiles of $L_2(P)$ are given by

$$P_\omega = \Phi\left(\frac{z_{1-\omega}}{\sqrt{10}} - 2\right).$$

In particular it follows from table 5.1/1 that

$$\begin{aligned} P_{0.05} &= \Phi(0.52-2) &\approx 0.0694\\ P_{0.5} &= \Phi(0-2) &\approx 0.0228\\ P_{0.95} &= \Phi(-0.52-2) &\approx 0.0059. \end{aligned}$$

Problem 3.3/9

a) We are using the abbreviation $c := \sqrt{1+k^2/2}$. For the percentiles μ_ω of the approximate OC function $L_1(\mu)$ we can according to (3.169) write

$$\mu_\omega \approx G_l + \left(\frac{c \cdot z_\omega}{\sqrt{n}} + k\right) \cdot \sigma.$$

b) Substituting μ_ω into (3.136a) gives the percentiles of the approximate OC function (3.170):

$$P_\omega = \Phi\left(\frac{G_l - \mu_\omega}{\sigma}\right) = \Phi\left(-\frac{c \cdot z_\omega}{\sqrt{n}} - k\right) = \Phi\left(\frac{c \cdot z_{1-\omega}}{\sqrt{n}} - k\right).$$

Problem 3.3/10

a) With $n = 10$ and $k = 2$ we get from (3.170) that

$$L_2(P) = \Phi\left[\sqrt{\frac{10}{3}} \cdot (z_{1-P} - 2\right].$$

It follows from table 5.2/1 that

$$\begin{aligned} L_2(0.05) &\approx \Phi[1.826 \cdot (1.645-2)] &\approx \Phi(-0.65) &\approx 0.2578\\ L_2(0.10) &\approx \Phi[1.826 \cdot (1.282-2)] &\approx \Phi(-1.31) &\approx 0.0951\\ L_2(0.15) &\approx \Phi[1.826 \cdot (1.036-2)] &\approx \Phi(-1.76) &\approx 0.0392. \end{aligned}$$

b) The percentiles of $L_2(P)$ are calculated according to

$$P_\omega = \Phi\left(\frac{c \cdot z_{1-\omega}}{\sqrt{10}} - k\right)$$

with $c := \sqrt{1 + k^2/2}$ (see solution to problem 3.3/9b). This implies $c = \sqrt{3}$ and

$$P_{0.05} \approx \Phi\left(\frac{\sqrt{3} \cdot 1.645}{\sqrt{10}} - 2\right) \approx \Phi(-1.10) \approx 0.1357$$

$$P_{0.5} = \Phi(0 - 2) \approx 0.0228$$

$$P_{0.95} \approx \Phi\left(-\frac{\sqrt{3} \cdot 1.645}{\sqrt{10}} - 2\right) \approx \Phi(-2.90) \approx 0.0019.$$

c) The OC curves of numerically identical sampling plans are in the case of known variance steeper (greater discriminatory power).

6.3 Solutions for Chapter 4

Problem 4.1/1

a) Let V denote the length of a screening period. Then the realization $i+1$ occurs if and only if the first inspected unit is nonconforming and the following i units are conforming. The realization $i+2$ occurs if and only if either the first two units are nonconforming and the following i units are good or the first unit is good, the second nonconforming and the next i are all conforming. Based on this idea and using the notation $Q := 1-P$, one can write the probabilities of occurrence in the following way:

$$Pr(V = i+1) = PQ^i; \qquad Pr(V = i+2) = P^2Q^i + PQi+1 = PQ^i.$$

b) Let $Y = X \cdot k$ denote the lenght of a $f \cdot 100\%$ inspection period. Since the random variable X has a negative binomial distribution with the parameters P and $c = 1$ (geometric distribution), it follows according to (2.98a) that:

$$\begin{aligned} Pr(Y = k) &= Pr(X = 1) &= nb(0|P;1) &= P \\ Pr(Y = 2k) &= Pr(X = 2) &= nb(1|P;1) &= PQ \\ Pr(Y = 3k) &= Pr(X = 3) &= nb(2|P;1) &= PQ^2. \end{aligned}$$

Problem 4.1/2

a) With $i = 100$ and $AOQL = 0.01$ it follows according to (4.15b) that

$$k \approx 1 + 1.01 \cdot e^{2.01} \approx 8.54.$$

In a similar way one determines with $i = 200$ and $AOQL = 0.01$ the value

$$k \approx 1 + 2.01 \cdot e^{3.01} \approx 41.78.$$

In the first case we choose the plan parameter to be $k = 8$, in the second case $k = 41$.

b) For the specification $P^* = 0.05$ one first calculates k according to (4.16) and obtains the result $k \approx 21.74$. For this $k \approx 21.74$ or respectively $f = 1/k \approx 0.046$ one can then read the value $i = 160$ from the ISO-AOQL curve in figure 4.1/7.

c) The performance measures are given in the table below. According to (4.21) the last column contains the obtained values $AOQ^*(P|i;k)$ of the average outgoing quality in the case of not replacing observed nonconforming product units:

$(i;k)$	P	$u(P)$	$v(P)$	$z(P)$	$ATI(P)$	$AFI(P)$	$L(P)$	$AOQ(P)$	$AOQ^*(P)$
$i = 100;$	0.01	173.2	800.0	973.2	273.2	0.2807	0.8220	0.0072	0.0072
$k = 8$	0.02	327.0	400.0	727.0	377.0	0.5186	0.5502	0.0096	0.0097
	0.03	667.6	266.7	934.3	701.0	0.7503	0.2854	0.0075	0.0077
	0.04	1456.9	200.0	1656.9	1481.9	0.8944	0.1207	0.0042	0.0044
	0.05	3358.0	160.0	3518.0	3378.0	0.9602	0.0455	0.0020	0.0021
$i = 200;$	0.01	646.4	4100.0	4746.4	746.6	0.1573	0.8638	0.0084	0.0084
$k = 41$	0.02	2792.9	2050.0	4842.9	2842.8	0.5870	0.4233	0.0083	0.0084
	0.03	14707.8	1366.6	16074.5	14741.9	0.9171	0.0850	0.0025	0.0026
	0.04	87815.2	1025.0	88840.2	87836.3	0.9887	0.0115	0.0005	0.0005
	0.05	570550.0	820.0	571370.0	570570.0	0.9986	0.0014	0.0001	0.0001
$i = 160;$	0.01	399.3	2100.0	2499.3	499.4	0.1998	0.8402	0.0080	0.0080
$k = 21$	0.02	1271.1	1050.0	2267.1	1276.1	0.5589	0.4632	0.0088	0.0089
	0.03	4325.8	700.0	5025.8	4359.4	0.8674	0.1393	0.0040	0.0041
	0.04	17136.0	525.0	17661.0	17161.2	0.9717	0.0297	0.0011	0.0012
	0.05	73305.2	420.0	73725.2	73327.1	0.9946	0.0057	0.0003	0.0003

Table 6.3/1: Performance measures of three *CSP*-1

d)

i	k	$AOQL$	$UAOQL_1$	$UAOQL_1^*$	$UAOQL_2$	$UAOQL_3$	λ_M
100	8	0.01	0.0648	0.0654	0.8750	0.0544	21
200	41	0.01	0.1660	0.1667	0.9756	0.1231	85
160	21	0.01	0.1105	0.1111	0.9524	0.0869	50

Table 6.3/2: *AOQL* and *UAOQL* of three *CSP*-1

Problem 4.1/3

a) After drawing three blocks of samples of size $k = 4$, one found the first nonconforming sample unit, as described in figure 4.1/1. One continues to take samples of size $k = 4$. Since the fourth sample already contains a second nonconforming unit, one switches to screening mode after the fourth sample. This inspection intensity is applied until $i = 8$ consecutive good units are observed.

b) With a *CSP*-3 one will after the first three samples submit the following four sample units to screening. Since this will lead to the discovery of a second nonconforming unit, the screening will be continued until i consecutive good units occur. In this case the inspection proceeds exactly as described in figure 4.1/1.

Problem 4.1/4

If one sets $m = i$ in (4.23a) and (4.23b) then one can get the following result after some transformations in the denominator:

$$AOQ(P|i;k;i) = \frac{(k-1)PQ^i(2-Q^i)}{1+Q^i(k-1)(2-Q^i)}; \quad AOQ^*(P|i;k;i) = \frac{AOQ(P|i;k;i)}{Q+AOQ(P|i;k;i)}.$$

Problem 4.1/5

a) For the CSP-2 the values of $AOQ(0.02|100;20;m)$ are calculated according to (4.23a), for the CSP-3 according to (4.24a):

m	CSP-2	CSP-3
20	0.017567	0.017285
50	0.016857	0.016675
100	0.016495	0.016356
150	0.016387	0.016260

Table 6.3/3: Average outgoing quality of a CSP-2 and CSP-3 for $P = 0.02$ (inspection without replacement of nonconforming units)

One can see that for increasing m the average outgoing quality of both plans decreases.

b) For $m \to \infty$ it holds that $Q^m \to 0$. Consequently one gets for the CSP-2 according to (4.23a) that

$$\lim_{m\to\infty} AOQ(P|i;k;m) = \frac{2(k-1)PQ^i}{(1-Q^i)+2Q^i} = \frac{(k-1)PQ^i}{0.5+(k-0.5)Q^i}$$

and for the CSP-3 according to (4.24a) that

$$\begin{aligned}\lim_{m\to\infty} AOQ(P|i;k;m) &= \frac{(k-1)PQ^i(1+Q^4)}{(1-Q^i)+kQ^i(1+Q^4)+4PQ^i} \\ &= \frac{(k-1)PQ^i(1+Q^4)}{1+Q^i[k(1+Q^4)+4P-1]}.\end{aligned}$$

In the case of a CSP-2 $m \to \infty$ means that once one switches to the $f \cdot 100\%$ inspection period, one will never leave this mode. In the case of a CSP-3 one will only terminate this inspection intensity if, after observing one nonconforming unit, a second nonconforming unit is found within the next four units.

Problem 4.1/6

a) Solving (4.28) for M^* gives

$$M^* = \frac{AOQL \cdot f \cdot N}{1-f} = \frac{0.018 \cdot 0.1 \cdot 1000}{1-0.1} = 2.$$

b) By (4.26) and (4.27) it follows that

$$\begin{aligned} AFI(0.02) &= 1 - \frac{2 \cdot 0.9}{0.02 \cdot 0.1 \cdot 1000} + \frac{0.9}{0.02 \cdot 0.1 \cdot 1000} \sum_{i=0}^{1} 1 \cdot \binom{100}{i} 0.02^i \cdot 0.98^{100-i} \\ &\approx 0.2815 \end{aligned}$$

$$AOQ(0.02) = 0.018 \cdot \left[1 - \frac{1}{2} \sum_{i=0}^{1} (2-i) \binom{100}{i} 0.02^i \cdot 0.98^{100-i}\right] \approx 0.0132.$$

Problem 4.1/7

In acceptance sampling by attributes there are three different inspection levels as described in figure 3.2/27. In this respect there is an analogy to the twolevel *CSP*, in the sense that, besides screening, there are two additional inspection intensities, i.e. a total of three inspection intensities f_0, f_1, f_2 $(1 = f_0 < f_1 < f_2)$. Screening in a *CSP* corresponds to tightened inspection in figure 3.2/27 and inspection with the sampling fraction f_1 and f_2 corresponds to normal or reduced inspection.

Problem 4.2/1

a) A false alarm (intervening in the undisturbed process) happens if the sample result lies on or beyond the control limit, while the process is still in a desirable state (type I error; see also table 2.3/1). A neglected alarm (not intervening in the disturbed process) happens if the sample outcome lies within the control limits while the process is in an undesirable state (type II error).

b) A false warning is given if the sample outcome falls on a warning limit or between warning and control limits while the process is operating in a desirable state. A neglected warning means that the sample result lies within the warning limits while the process is in an undesirable state.

c) If the control limits (warning limits) are the boundaries of the 99% (95%) variation interval then the probability of a false alarm is 1% (of a false warning 4%).

Problem 4.3/1

a) In the case of the control chart of example 4.3/1 a warning is given if and only if the $po(\lambda_t)$-distributed test statistic X satisfies the condition $UWL \leq X < UCL$. Since here we have $UWL = 14$ and $UCL = 16$ this is the case for $x = 14$ and $x = 15$. For the warning probability we thus get

$$H(\lambda_t) = po(14|\lambda_t) + po(15|\lambda_t).$$

b) In the case of $\lambda_t \geq 9$ we can also use the normal approximation (2.60a) and get

$$\begin{aligned} H(\lambda_t) &= \left[\Phi\left(\frac{14.5 - \lambda_t}{\sqrt{\lambda_t}}\right) - \Phi\left(\frac{13.5 - \lambda_t}{\sqrt{\lambda_t}}\right)\right] + \left[\Phi\left(\frac{15.5 - \lambda_t}{\sqrt{\lambda_t}}\right) - \Phi\left(\frac{14.5 - \lambda_t}{\sqrt{\lambda_t}}\right)\right] \\ &= \Phi\left(\frac{15.5 - \lambda_t}{\sqrt{\lambda_t}}\right) - \Phi\left(\frac{13.5 - \lambda_t}{\sqrt{\lambda_t}}\right). \end{aligned}$$

c)

λ_t	2	4	6	8	10	12	14	16	18
$H(\lambda_t)$	0	0.0001	0.0031	0.0260	0.0868	0.1629	0.2049	0.1922	0.1441

Table 6.3/4: Warning probabilities in the case of a onesided x chart for the number of nonconformities per product unit

Problem 4.3/2

The UCL is again obtained from (4.44) with $\alpha = 0.01$ and $\lambda_0 = 8$ by substituting $n = 3$. Because of $n\lambda_0 \geq 9$ one can also obtain the UCL according to (4.47), i.e.

$$UCL \approx 24 + z_{0.99} \cdot \sqrt{24} + 0.5 \approx 24 + 2.326 \cdot 4.899 + 0.5 \approx 35.895.$$

For the determination of the UWL one can use the same formula with $\alpha = 0.05$:

$$UWL \approx 24 + z_{0.95} \cdot \sqrt{24} + 0.5 \approx 24 + 1.645 \cdot 4.899 + 0.5 \approx 32.559.$$

Since the results need to be rounded to the next largest integer we get $UCL = 36$ and $UWL = 33$.

Problem 4.3/3

a) Substituting $n = 1$, $\lambda_0 = 8$ and $\alpha = 0.01$ in (4.52) it follows that

$$Po(UCL - 2|8) < 0.995 \leq Po(UCL - 1|8)$$

$$Po(LCL|8) \leq 0.005 < Po(LCL + 1|8).$$

With table 5.1/4 it can be verified that this chain of inequalities is satisfied for $UCL = 17$ and $LCL = 1$.

If one substitutes the terms UCL and LCL in (4.52) by UWL and LWL then it follows with $n = 1, \lambda_0 = 8$ and $\alpha = 0.05$

$$Po(UWL - 2|8) < 0.975 \leq Po(UWL - 1|8)$$

$$Po(LWL|8) \leq 0.025 < Po(LWL + 1|8).$$

From this one gets $UWL = 15$ and $LWL = 2$.

b) In the case of the first procedure variant the power function is given by (4.55):

$$G_1(\lambda_t) = 1 - Po(16|\lambda_t) = Po(1|\lambda_t).$$

In the case of the second variant the power function is determined according to (4.48):

$$G_2(\lambda_t) = 1 - Po(16|\lambda_t).$$

c) For $\lambda_t \leq 16$ the following values were determined with the help of table 5.1/4:

λ_t	2	4	6	8	10	12	14	16	18
$G_1(\lambda_t)$	0.4060	0.0916	0.0176	0.0067	0.0275	0.1308	0.2441	0.4340	0.6368
$G_2(\lambda_t)$	0.0000	0.0000	0.0002	0.0037	0.0270	0.1307	0.2441	0.4340	0.6368

Table 6.3/5: Intervention probabilities for a twosided x chart for the number of nonconformities per product unit

Problem 4.3/4

For the randomized test one uses the following decision rule:

- If the test statistic $X = X_1^{*T}$ satisfies the condition $X \geq 17$ or $X \leq 1$ one always intervenes.
- In the case of $2 < X < 16$ one does not intervene.
- In the case of $X = 2$ and $X = 16$ one intervenes in the process with probability α' or respectively α''. The determining equations for these probabilities are

$$\alpha' \cdot Pr(X = 2|\lambda_t = \lambda_0) = a/2 - Pr(X \leq 1); \quad \alpha'' \cdot Pr(X = 16|\lambda_t = \lambda_0) = a/2 - Pr(X \leq 17).$$

If $\lambda_t = \lambda_0 = 8$ it holds that $X \sim po(8)$, so that with $\alpha = 0.01$ these equations can be written as

$$\alpha' \cdot po(2|8) = 0.005 - Po(1|8); \quad \alpha'' \cdot po(16|8) = 0.005 - [1 - Po(16|8)].$$

From figure 4.3/1 one can read the values

$$po(2|8) = 0.0108; \quad Po(1|8) = 0.0030; \quad po(16|8) = 0.0045; \quad Po(16|8) = 0.9963$$

and thus get the results

$$\alpha' = \frac{0.005 - 0.003}{0.0108} \approx 0.1852; \quad \alpha'' = \frac{0.005 - 0.0037}{0.0045} \approx 0.2889.$$

Problem 4.3/5

a) The control limits of the twosided x chart are according to (4.69) obtained with the help of

$$Bi(UCL-2|0.07;100) < 0.995 \leq Bi(UCL-1|0.07;100)$$

$$Bi(LCL|0.07;100) \leq 0.005 < Bi(LCL+1|0.07;100).$$

It follows from table 5.1/3 that $UCL = 15$ and $LCL = 0$. For the warning limits we get for $\alpha = 0.05$ in the same way the values $UWL = 13$ and $LWL = 1$.

The limits of the p chart are $UCL^r = 0.15$, $LCL^r = 0$, $UWL^r = 0.13$ and $LWL^r = 0.01$.

b) The power function of the two charts is according to (4.71) given by

$$G(P_t) = 1 - Bi(14|P_t;100) + Bi(0|P_t;100).$$

Because of $X_n^T \sim bi(P_t;n)$ the effective warning probability is

$$\begin{aligned} H(P_t) &= Pr(LCL < X_n^T \leq LWL|P_t) + Pr(UWL \leq X_n^T < UCL|P_t) \\ &= Pr(X_n^T = 1|P_t) + Pr(13 \leq X_n^T < 15|P_t) \\ &= bi(1|P_t;100) + Bi(14|P_t;100) - Bi(12|P_t;100). \end{aligned}$$

c) The effective intervention probability for $P_t = P_0 = 0.07$ is given by

$$\begin{aligned} G(0.07) &= 1 - Bi(14|0.07;100) + Bi(0|0.07;100) \\ &\approx 1 - 0.99591 + 0.00071 \\ &= 0.00480. \end{aligned}$$

For the effective warning probability in the case of $P_t = 0.07$ one gets

$$\begin{aligned} H(0.07) &= bi(1|0.07;100) + Bi(14|0.07;100) - Bi(12|0.07;100) \\ &\approx 0.00530 + 0.99591 - 0.97759 \\ &= 0.02362. \end{aligned}$$

We can see that for $P_t = 0.07$ the effective intervention and warning probabilities lie considerably below the nominal values of 0.01 and 0.04, respectively.

d) With the help of table 5.1/3 we get the following table for $G(P_t)$ rounding to four decimals:

P_t	0.01	0.02	0.03	0.04	0.05	0.06	0.07	0.08	0.09	0.10	0.20
$G(P_t)$	0.3660	0.1326	0.0476	0.0169	0.0061	0.0030	0.0048	0.0135	0.0342	0.0726	0.9196

Table 6.3/6: Intervention probabilities of a twosided x chart for the number of nonconforming sample units

Problem 4.4/1

i	prerun data x_{ij}	$\sum_{j=1}^{5} x_{ij}$	$\sum_{j=1}^{5} x_{ij}^2$	$\bar{x}_{i5}$	$\tilde{x}_{i5}$	s_{i5}^2	s_{i5}	r_{i5}
(1)	(2)	(3)	(4)	(5)	(6)	(7)	(8)	(9)
1	235; 235; 230; 232; 226	1158	268250	231.6	232	14.3	3.78	9
2	238; 234; 229; 231; 240	1172	274802	234.4	234	21.3	4.62	11
3	235; 239; 234; 230; 236	1174	275698	234.8	235	10.7	3.27	9
4	234; 233; 235; 227; 226	1155	266875	231.0	233	17.5	4.18	9
5	238; 236; 230; 235; 231	1170	273826	234.0	235	11.5	3.39	8
6	230; 231; 229; 237; 235	1162	270096	232.4	231	11.8	3.44	8
7	237; 239; 231; 233; 240	1180	278540	236.0	237	15.0	3.87	9
8	231; 240; 232; 231; 228	1162	270130	232.4	231	20.3	4.51	12
9	231; 230; 232; 237; 238	1168	272898	233.6	232	13.3	3.65	8
10	230; 235; 228; 233; 240	1166	271998	233.2	233	21.7	4.66	12
	sum	11667	2723113	2333.4	2333	157.4	39.37	95

Table 6.3/7: Measurements and evaluation of a prerun (tensile strenght of wire)

In order to perform the BARTLETT test with $\alpha = 0.05$ one first calculates

$$\overline{s_{10}^2} = \frac{1}{10} \cdot \sum_{i=1}^{10} s_{i5}^2 = \frac{1}{10} \cdot 157.4 = 15.74; \quad \ln \overline{s_{10}^2} \approx 2.7562; \quad \sum_{i=1}^{10} \ln s_{i5}^2 \approx 27.2456.$$

For the test statistic (4.91) it follows that

$$\chi^2 = \frac{480}{131} \cdot (10 \cdot 2.7562 - 27.2456) \approx 1.1539.$$

Because of $1.1593 < \chi^2_{9;0.95} = 29.141$ one cannot reject the hypothesis of a time constant variance. In order to perform the F-test with $\alpha = 0.05$ one starts calculating

$$Q_1 = 5 \cdot \left(\sum_{i=1}^{10} \bar{x}_{i5}^2 - 10 \cdot \bar{\bar{x}}_{50}^2 \right) = 5 \cdot (544496.68 - 10 \cdot 233.34^2) \approx 105.62$$

$$Q_2 = 4 \cdot \sum_{i=1}^{10} s_{i5}^2 = 4 \cdot 157.4 = 629.6.$$

After substituting the results into (4.94) one gets

$$F = \frac{105.62/9}{629.6/40} \approx 0.7456.$$

Since $0.7456 < F_{9;40;0.95} = 2.12$ the hypothesis of a time constant process level cannot be rejected.

Problem 4.4/2

With columns 5 - 6 of table 6.3/7 one gets the following estimates for μ_0:

$$\hat{\mu}_0 = \bar{\bar{x}}_{10} = \tfrac{1}{10} \cdot \sum_{i=1}^{10} \bar{x}_{i5} = \tfrac{1}{10} \cdot 2333.4 = 233.34 \qquad \text{(see column 5)}$$
$$\hat{\mu}_0 = \tilde{\tilde{x}}_{10} = \tfrac{1}{2} \cdot (\tilde{x}_{<5;10>} + \tilde{x}_{<6;10>}) = \tfrac{1}{2} \cdot (233 + 233) = 233 \qquad \text{(see column 6)}$$
$$\hat{\mu}_0 = \bar{\tilde{x}}_{10} = \tfrac{1}{10} \cdot \sum_{i=1}^{10} \tilde{x}_{i5} = \tfrac{1}{10} \cdot 2333 = 233.3 \qquad \text{(see column 6)}$$
$$\hat{\mu}_0 = \tilde{\bar{x}}_{10} = \tfrac{1}{2} \cdot (\bar{x}_{<5;10>} + \bar{x}_{<6;10>}) = \tfrac{1}{2} \cdot (233.2 + 233.6) = 233.4 \qquad \text{(see column 5).}$$

In order to calculate the estimates of σ_0 one needs among others columns 7 - 9 of table 6.3/7. Because of $Q_1 \approx 105.62$ and $Q_2 = 629.6$ it follows that

$$s_{50} = \sqrt{s_{50}^2} \approx \sqrt{\tfrac{105.62+629.6}{49}} \approx \sqrt{15.0045} \approx 3.8735$$
$$\bar{s}_{10} = \tfrac{1}{10} \cdot 39.37 = 3.9370 \qquad \text{(see column 8)}$$
$$\bar{r}_{10} = \tfrac{1}{10} \cdot 95 = 9.5 \qquad \text{(see column 9)}$$
$$\tilde{r}_{10} = \tfrac{1}{2} \cdot (r_{<5;10>} + r_{<6;10>}) = \tfrac{1}{2}(9 + 9) = 9 \qquad \text{(see column 9)}$$
$$\sqrt{\overline{s_{10}^2}} = \sqrt{\tfrac{1}{10} \cdot 157.4} = \sqrt{15.74} \qquad \text{(see column 7).}$$

After including the correction factors the following results are obtained by using table 5.3/1:

$$\hat{\sigma}_0 = \frac{s_{50}}{a_{50}} \approx \frac{3.8735}{0.9949} \approx 3.8934$$

$$\hat{\sigma}_0 = \frac{\bar{s}_{10}}{a_5} = \frac{3.9370}{0.940} \approx 4.1883$$

$$\hat{\sigma}_0 = \frac{\bar{r}_{10}}{d_5} = \frac{9.5}{2.326} \approx 4.0843$$

$$\hat{\sigma}_0 = \frac{\tilde{r}_{10}}{\tilde{d}_5} = \frac{9}{2.257} \approx 3.9876$$

$$\hat{\sigma}_0 = \frac{\sqrt{\overline{s^2_{10}}}}{a_{41}} = \frac{\sqrt{15.74}}{0.9938} \approx 3.9921.$$

Problem 4.4/3

In problem 4.4/2 we calculated

$$\hat{\mu}_0 = \tilde{\bar{x}}_{10} = 233; \quad \hat{\sigma}_0 = \bar{r}_{10}/d_5 \approx 4.0843.$$

Control limits of the *mean chart* according to (4.115):

$$\left.\begin{array}{l} UCL \\ LCL \end{array}\right\} = \hat{\mu}_0 \pm \frac{z_{0.995}}{\sqrt{5}} \cdot \hat{\sigma}_0 \approx 233 \pm 1.152 \cdot 4.0843 \approx \left\{\begin{array}{l} 237.71 \\ 228.29. \end{array}\right.$$

Control limits of the *median chart* according to (4.124) with $c_5 = 1.198$:

$$\left.\begin{array}{l} UCL \\ LCL \end{array}\right\} = \hat{\mu}_0 \pm \frac{z_{0.995} \cdot c_5}{\sqrt{5}} \cdot \hat{\sigma}_0 \approx 233 \pm 1.380 \cdot 4.0843 \approx \left\{\begin{array}{l} 238.64 \\ 227.36. \end{array}\right.$$

Control limits of the *extreme value chart* according to (4.131) with $P_5(0.01) \approx 0.9990$ (see example 4.4/5):

$$\left.\begin{array}{l} UCL \\ LCL \end{array}\right\} = \hat{\mu}_0 \pm z_{P_5(0.01)} \cdot \hat{\sigma}_0 \approx 233 \pm 3.09 \cdot 4.0843 \approx \left\{\begin{array}{l} 245.62 \\ 222.38. \end{array}\right.$$

The warning limits are determined in the same manner. One only needs to replace $z_{0.995}$ and $z_{P_5(0.01)}$ by $z_{0.975}$ and $z_{P_5(0.05)}$.

Problem 4.4/4

If one uses for the level M of the center line the estimation

$$\hat{\sigma}_0 = \frac{\bar{r}_{10}}{d_5} = \frac{9.5}{2.326} \approx 4.08$$

which was obtained in problem 4.4/2 then the limits of the s *chart* are for $n = 5$ found according to (4.148) - (4.149) and table 5.2/4:

$$\begin{aligned} UCL &= \frac{1}{2} \cdot \sqrt{\chi^2_{4;0.99}} \cdot \hat{\sigma}_0 &&\approx 1.822 \cdot 4.08 &&\approx 7.43 \\ UWL &= \frac{1}{2} \cdot \sqrt{\chi^2_{4;0.95}} \cdot \hat{\sigma}_0 &&\approx 1.540 \cdot 4.08 &&\approx 6.28. \end{aligned}$$

All standard deviations s_{i5} of the prerun lie below the warning limits (see column 8 in table 6.3/7).

The limits of the r *chart* calculated according to (4.158) - (4.159) lie significantly higher than those of the s chart:

$$\begin{aligned} UCL &= r^*_{5;0.99} \cdot \hat{\sigma}_0 &&\approx 4.60 \cdot 4.08 &&\approx 18.77 \\ UWL &= r^*_{5;0.95} \cdot \hat{\sigma}_0 &&\approx 3.86 \cdot 4.08 &&\approx 15.75. \end{aligned}$$

The ranges r_{i5} of the prerun (column 9 of table 6.3/7) all lie below the warning limit.

Problem 4.4/5

If one substitutes $n = 5, \delta_t = 1.5$ and $\varepsilon_t = 1.3064$ in (4.167b) then with $z_{0.995} \approx 2.576$ and $\chi^2_{4;0.99} \approx 13.277$ one gets:

$$\begin{aligned} G^*_{\bar{x};s}(1.5; 1.3064) &\approx 1 - [\Phi(2.576 - 1.5 \cdot \sqrt{5}) - \Phi(-2.576 - 1.5 \cdot \sqrt{5})] \cdot Ch\left(\frac{13.277}{1.3064^2}|4\right) \\ &\approx 1 - [\Phi(-0.778) - \Phi(-5.930)] \cdot Ch(7.779|4) \\ &\approx 1 - 0.2183 \cdot 0.90 \\ &\approx 0.8035. \end{aligned}$$

If the same values for n, σ_t and ε_t are substituted into (4.173) then one gets

$$\begin{aligned} G^{**}_{\bar{x}}(1.5; 1.3064) &\approx 1 - \left[\Phi\left(\frac{-1.5 + 2.8782}{1.3064}\right) - \Phi\left(\frac{-1.5 - 2.8782}{1.3064}\right)\right]^5 \\ &\approx 1 - [\Phi(1.055) - \Phi(-3.351)]^5 \\ &\approx 1 - [0.8543 - 0.0004]^5 \\ &\approx 0.5460. \end{aligned}$$

Hence in this situation the $\bar{x}$-s chart is better; it has a significantly higher intervention probability.

Problem 4.4/6

a) The power curves shown in figure 4.4/10 can be obtained through (4.183) by setting $n = 5$ and, successively, $r^2 = 0, r^2 = 0.25$ and $r^2 = 1$.

b) In the case of a stochastic measurement error occurring only after the design of the chart, the power functions are calculated according to (4.185) with $n = 5$ and the same three values for r^2. Drawing their graphs results in figure 6.3/1:

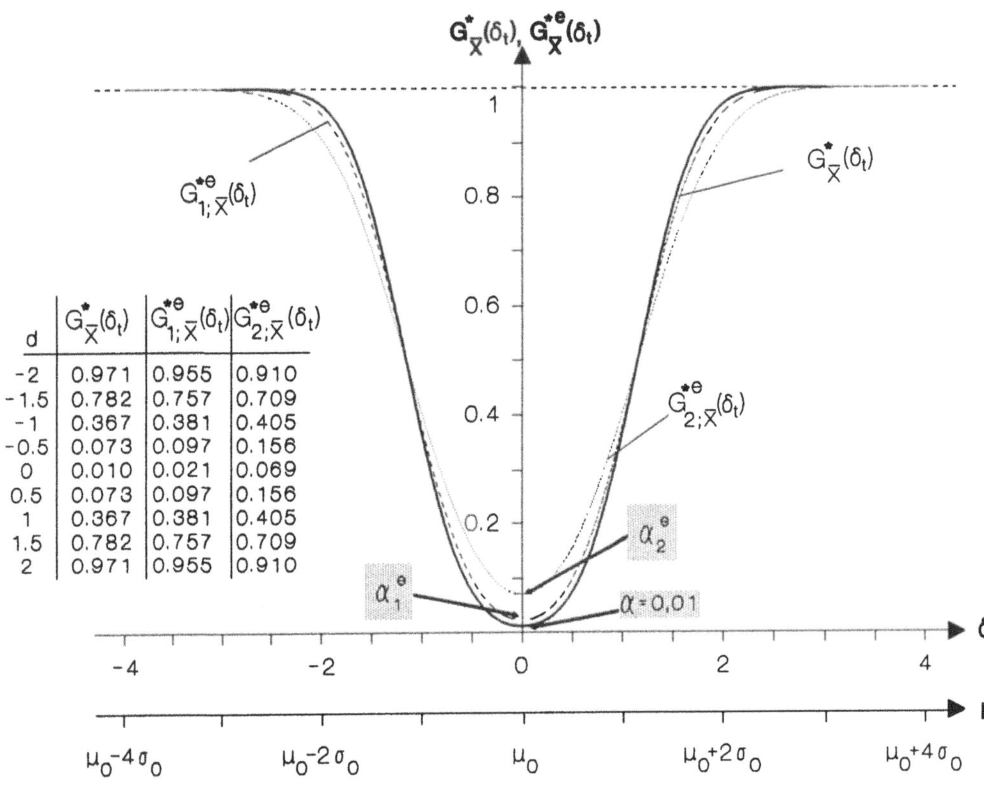

d	$G^*_{\bar{X}}(\delta_t)$	$G^{*e}_{1;\bar{X}}(\delta_t)$	$G^{*e}_{2;\bar{X}}(\delta_t)$
-2	0.971	0.955	0.910
-1.5	0.782	0.757	0.709
-1	0.367	0.381	0.405
-0.5	0.073	0.097	0.156
0	0.010	0.021	0.069
0.5	0.073	0.097	0.156
1	0.367	0.381	0.405
1.5	0.782	0.757	0.709
2	0.971	0.955	0.910

Figure 6.3/1: True and empirical power curves in the case of stochastic measurement errors and different degrees r^2 of error contamination ($G^{*e}_{1;\bar{x}} : r^2 = 0.25$; $G^{*e}_{2;\bar{x}} : r^2 = 1$); Source: MITTAG 1991

Problem 4.4/7

The coefficients required are $L_0 = 1; L_1 = 5; U = 3; A = 0.01; B = 0.001; d = 0.1$ and $\Delta = 0.05$. Using $\tau_B^{opt} = \tau_B = 4.27$ for $\Theta = 5$, i.e., $\lambda = 0.2$, by (4.194) gives

$$\begin{aligned} k_B &= \frac{L_1 \cdot \tau_B - \frac{L_1 - L_0}{\lambda}\left[1 - \exp(-\lambda \cdot \tau_B)\right] + U}{\tau_B + d} \\ &= \frac{5 \cdot 4.27 - \frac{4}{0.2}\left[1 - \exp(-0.2 \cdot 4.27)\right] + 3}{4.27 + 0.1} \\ &\approx 2.9438 \end{aligned}$$

If $\Theta = 5$ had been known and the corresponding optimal policy with $\tau_B^{opt} = 3.20$ been adopted (compare column 7 of table 4.4/8), the cost would have been only $k_B^{min} = 2.8927$, i.e., overestimating Θ by 100% results in a suboptimal solution with cost being just 1.8% higher.

Problem 4.5/1

a) With (4.216) and table 5.2/1 we get

$$k_{\bar{x}}^C := z_{0.99} + \frac{z_{0.95}}{\sqrt{5}} \approx 2.326 + \frac{1.645}{\sqrt{5}} \approx 3.0617$$

and according to (4.214)-(4.215) it holds that

$$UCL = G_u - k_{\bar{x}}^C \cdot \hat{\sigma}_0 \approx 8.5 - 3.0617 \cdot 0.2901 \approx 7.61$$

$$LCL = G_l + k_{\bar{x}}^C \cdot \hat{\sigma}_0 \approx 5.5 - 3.0617 \cdot 0.2901 \approx 6.39.$$

b) If one substitutes into (4.219) the value $k_{\bar{x}}^C$ from above and $n = 5$ as well as $P = 0.02$ or respectively $P = 0.005$ then the result is

$$G_{2;\bar{x}}(0.02) = 1 - \Phi\left[\sqrt{5}\,(z_{0.98} - 3.0617)\right] \approx 1 - \Phi(-2.25) = \Phi(2.25) = 0.9878$$

$$G_{2;\bar{x}}(0.005) = 1 - \Phi\left[\sqrt{5}\,(z_{0.995} - 3.0617)\right] \approx 1 - \Phi(-1.09) = \Phi(1.09) = 0.8621.$$

Problem 4.5/2

a) By (4.222) and table 5.3/1 it follows that

$$k_{\tilde{x}}^C := z_{0.99} + \frac{z_{0.95}}{\sqrt{5}} \cdot c_5 \approx 2.326 + \frac{1.645}{\sqrt{5}} \cdot 1.198 \approx 3.2073.$$

The control limits of the *median chart* are according to (4.220) - (4.221) given by

$$UCL = G_u - k_{\tilde{x}}^C \cdot \hat{\sigma}_0 \approx 8.5 - 3.2073 \cdot 0.2901 \approx 7.57$$

$$LCL = G_l + k_{\tilde{x}}^C \cdot \hat{\sigma}_0 \approx 5.5 - 3.2073 \cdot 0.2901 \approx 6.43.$$

For the factor k_x^C from (4.228a) it follows from table 4.5/3 that

$$k_x^C := z_{0.99} - z_{P_5(0.95)} \approx 2.326 - 0.124 \approx 2.202.$$

The control limits of the *extreme value chart* are according to (4.226)-(4.227) of form

$$UCL = G_u - k_x^C \cdot \hat{\sigma}_0 \approx 8.5 - 2.202 \cdot 0.2901 \approx 7.86$$

$$LCL = G_l + k_x^C \cdot \hat{\sigma}_0 \approx 5.5 - 2.202 \cdot 0.2901 \approx 6.14.$$

A comparison with the control limits $UCL = 7.61$ and $LCL = 6.39$ of the $\bar{x}$ chart from problem 4.5/1a shows that the limits of the $\bar{x}$ chart and $\tilde{x}$ chart hardly differ from each other, whereas those of the **x** chart lie significantly further away from the midpoint $G_m = 7$ of the tolerance range.

b) By (4.225) we get the following values for the power function of the median chart:

$$G_{2;\tilde{x}}(0.02) = 1 - \Phi\left[\frac{\sqrt{5}}{1.198}(z_{0.98} - 3.2073)\right] \approx 1 - \Phi(-2.15) = 0.9842$$

$$G_{2;\tilde{x}}(0.005) = 1 - \Phi\left[\frac{\sqrt{5}}{1.198}(z_{0.995} - 3.2073)\right] \approx 1 - \Phi(-1.18) = 0.8810.$$

For the *power function of the extreme value chart* we get according to (4.231) the values

$$G_{2;x}(0.02) = 1 - [\Phi(z_{0.98} - 2.202)]^5 \approx 1 - [\Phi(-0.148)]^5 \approx 1 - 0.4412^5 \approx 0.9833$$

$$G_{2;x}(0.005) = 1 - [\Phi(z_{0.995} - 2.202)]^5 \approx 1 - [\Phi(-0.374)]^5 \approx 1 - 0.6458^5 \approx 0.8877.$$

Problem 4.6/1

a) One can see from (4.258) that the angle θ and thus the opening of the V-mask is only influenced by the scale factor f and the magnitude $\gamma = \mu - \mu_0$ that one wants to detect. The larger $|\gamma|$ and/or the larger f the smaller is the angle θ.

The lead distance d depends according to (4.256) on the value of the process spread σ_0^2 (which is assumed to be constant), the sample size n, the critical shift γ and the two error probabilities α and β. The larger n and $|\gamma|$ and/or α the smaller becomes the lead distance d, or respectively the smaller σ_0 and/or β the smaller the lead distance d. If one uses the approximation (4.257) for the calculation of the lead distance, than β is no longer an influential factor for d.

b) If one substitutes $n = 5$, $\alpha = 0.01, \sigma_0 = 2, \gamma = 1$ and $f = 0.5$ into (4.257) and (4.258) then one gets

$$\theta = arctg\frac{1}{2 \cdot 0.5} = 45°; \quad d \approx -\frac{2 \cdot 2^2}{5 \cdot 1^1} \ln 0.005 \approx 8.5.$$

Problem 4.6/2

a) Because of (4.240b), the relative weights are all calculated according to

$$w_j = \frac{b_{t-j}}{b_t} = \frac{d \cdot (1-d)^j}{d} = (1-d)^j.$$

With $j = 1, 2, \ldots, 10$ and the given values for d, the following table is obtained.[6]

j	$d = 0.1$	$d = 0.15$	$d = 0.20$	$d = 0.25$	$d = 0.30$
1	0.9000	0.8500	0.8000	0.7500	0.7000
2	0.8100	0.7250	0.6400	0.5625	0.4900
3	0.7290	0.6141	0.5120	0.4219	0.3430
4	0.6561	0.5220	0.4096	0.3164	0.2401
5	0.5905	0.4437	0.3277	0.2373	0.1681
6	0.5314	0.3771	0.2621	0.1780	0.1176
7	0.4783	0.3206	0.2097	0.1335	0.0824
8	0.4305	0.2725	0.1678	0.1001	0.0576
9	0.3874	0.2316	0.1342	0.0751	0.0404
10	0.3487	0.1969	0.1074	0.0563	0.0282

Table 6.3/8: Relative weights of recent sample outcomes for different EWMA charts

The table clearly shows that, with an EWMA chart, the weight of a sample outcome lying back j time units (j fixed) decreases as d increases.

b) Starting from $w_j = 0.9^j < 0.03$, taking logarithms (base 10) gives $j \cdot \log 0.9 < \log 0.03$ and finally, noting that $\log 0.9 < 0$

$$j > \frac{\log 0.03}{\log 0.9} = \frac{\log 3 - 2}{\log 9 - 1} \approx 33.25.$$

Thus, in this case j has to take on the value $j = 34$.

[6] The results are rounded to four decimal places.

7 Index Lists

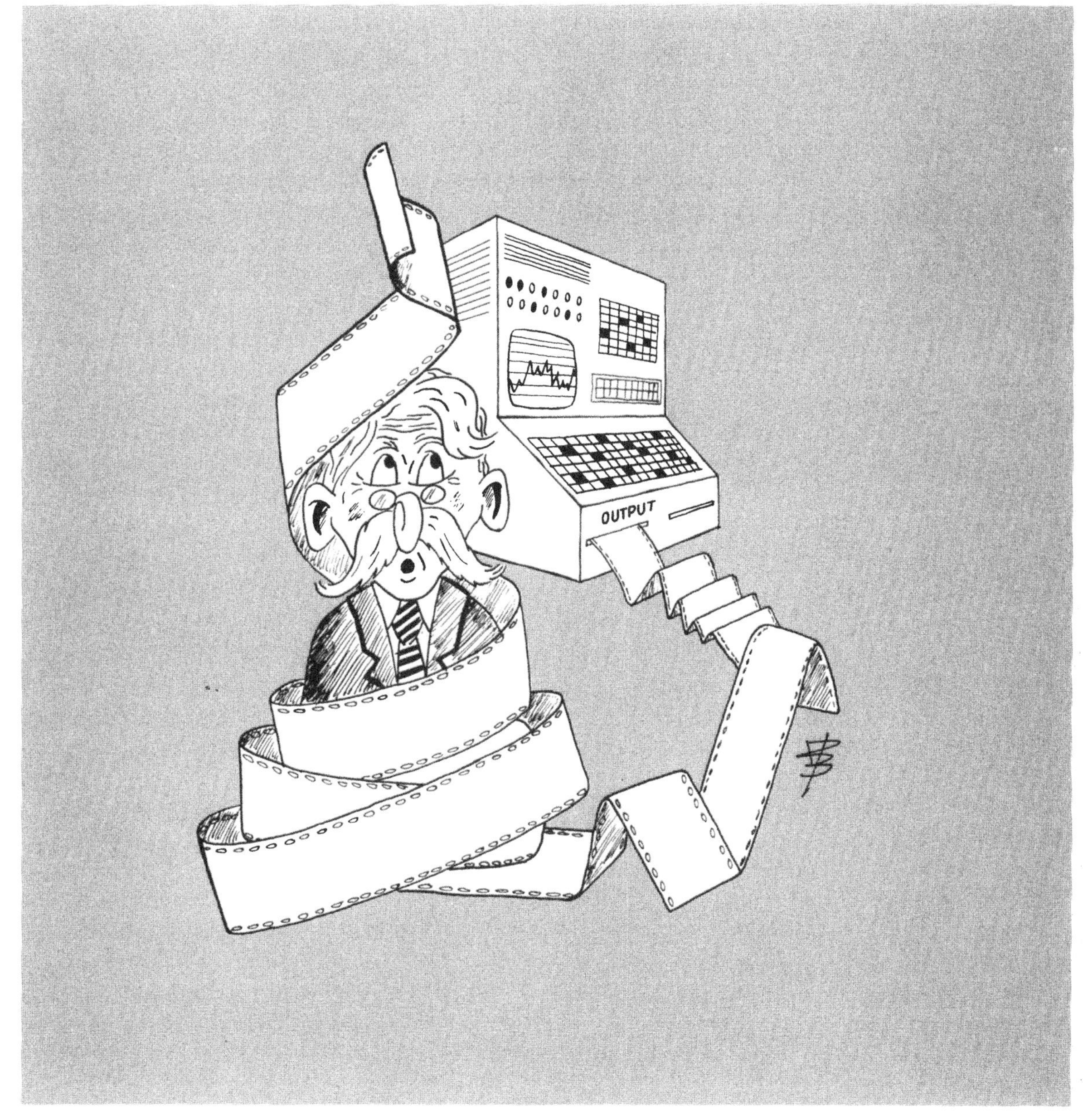

In order to give the book a clear and simple structure, we have gathered all the indices into a separate chapter. This chapter contains an annotated list of references useful for self-study purposes, a comprehensive bibliography, a list of abbreviations and mathematical symbols, an author index and a detailed subject index.

Figure on the title page of this chapter:
A reader of this text while organising the various index lists. (Design: P. Becker, Centre for Correspondence Study Development at the FernUniversität Hagen)

7.1 Bibliography

All the bibliographical references in this text are listed in the complete bibliography of section 7.1.2. However, this list is only useful if one knows the name of the author and is only looking for the detailed biliographical data. If one first needs an introduction then an annotated reference list is far more useful. Because of this we have first compiled a list of selected references with a brief commentary for each entry.

7.1.1 Annotated Reference List of Selected Journals, Textbooks and Reference Books

If you have a deeper interest in Quality Assurance, we recommend reading the specific journals and periodicals. In the following we are presenting a brief selection of these: Journals and Abstracts

Brochures of the Deutsche Gesellschaft für Qualität (DGQ, German Society for Quality)

Brochures, written by trade professionals for professionals. They present monographs of the different areas of quality control. The most important DGQ-Brochures are listed in the Bibliography (see under DGQ).

Journal of Quality Technology

Leading scientific journal in the area of statistical quality assurance. This quarterly journal of the AMERICAN SOCIETY FOR QUALITY CONTROL (ASQC) primarily presents new theoretical results and their relevance for industrial practice.

Qualität und Zuverlässigkeit

This monthly periodical, published by the Deutsche Gesellschaft für Qualität, is very applied. Its focus are recent trends in the technological development of quality assurance and it mainly omits the presentation of the mathematical-statistical theory.

Quality and Reliability Engineering International

Recent journal for engineers with emphasis on the areas of life testing and experimental design. The published articles usually refer to concrete problems in the production of Hi-Tech products.

Quality Progress

Application oriented monthly journal of the ASQC. In design and purpose it is comparable to the journal *Qualität und Zuverlässigkeit* but also contains introductory articles about the theoretical background of quality assurance.

Quality

Applied monthly journal of the EUROPEAN ORGANIZATION FOR QUALITY (EOQ).

Technometrics

Quarterly journal of the AMERICAN STATISTICAL ASSOCIATION (ASA), which writes about the development and application of statistical methods in science and engineering. The area of statistical quality assurance is not the main subject of this journal, but occasionally one finds interesting theoretical articles about SQA.

The American Statistician

Quarterly journal with a high didactical standard. Similar to the journal *Technometrics* it covers QA topics only occasionally, but the articles are not as condensed as it is costum in other journals.

Total Quality Management

A scientific journal which comes out three times per year, starting from 1990. It is based on the quality assurance philosophy of DEMING and has the goal of promoting the issue of quality in industrial applications in a general way.

For readers who are looking for recent scientific publications in a special area of statistical quality assurance we want to especially mention the three following indices and abstracts services:

Quality Control and Applied Statistics

Monthly abstract service published by the EXECUTIVE SCIENCE INSTITUTE, Whippany, New Jersey (USA).

Statistical Theory and Methods Abstracts

Quarterly abstract service published by the INTERNATIONAL STATISTICAL INSTITUTE.

The Current Index to Statistics

Annual index of all new publications (journals, periodicals and books) in the area of statistics, ordered by author and subject. It is published by the INSTITUTE OF MATHEMATICAL STATISTICS and the ASA.

Handbooks and Encyclopedias

We cannot present a complete list of all books and encyclopedias that are related to statistical quality assurance. We only mention:

KOTZ, S. / JOHNSON, N.L. (Editors; since 1982)

Encyclopedia of Statistical Sciences. 9 volumes plus supplementary volume. Wiley, New York.

In this excellent encyclopedia one also finds topics of SQA, for example under the subjects 'control charts', 'quality control' or 'acceptance sampling'.

KRISHNAIAH, P.R. / RAO, C.R. (Editors; since 1988)

Handbook of Statistics, Volume 7: Quality Control and Reliability. North-Holland, Amsterdam.

The 14 volumes of this series are each dedicated to recent research results in various areas of statistics. The emphasis of volume 7 is on the area of 'life distributions anf reliability theory'.

MASING, W. (Editor, 1988)

Handbuch der Qualitätssicherung. 2nd ed., Hanser Verlag, München, 975 p.

A handbook of quality assurance designed for professionals like quality engineers.

MESSERSCHMIDT-BÖLKOW-BLOHM GMBH (Editor, 1984)

Qualitätsbegriffe (Definitionen und Erläuterungen). German, English and French; 2nd ed.; MBB, Ottobrunn, 298 p.

A Handbook of Quality Terminology (definitions and explanations). It covers all areas of QA and reliability theory and lists terms and brief definitions. Generally more suitable for a professional than a student.

WADSWORTH, H.M. (Editor, 1989)

Handbook of Statistical Methods for Engineers and Scientists. McGraw-Hill, New York.

In 20 chapters this handbook covers the most important topics of technical statistics, e.g. graphical approaches to quality assurance, process control with control charts or multivariate methods.

For finding terms related to the area of quality assurance we also recommend the sources ANSI/ASQC (1978), DGQ (1987b) and EOQ (1976).

We want to mention the following handbooks of statistical formulae and tables:

Handbooks of Tables and Formulae

ABRAMOVITZ, M. / STEGUN, I.A. (Editors, 1972)

Handbook of Mathematical Functions. 9th ed., Dover Publications, New York, 1045 p.

GRAF, U. / HENNING, H.J. / STANGE, K. / WILRICH, P.-TH. (1987)

Formeln und Tabellen in der angewandten mathematischen Statistik. 3rd ed., Springer, Berlin/Heidelberg, 529 p.

KOKOSKA, S. / NEVISON, C. (1989)

Statistical Tables and Formulae. Springer, New York, 88 p.

ODEH, R.E. / OWEN, D.B. / BIRNBAUM, Z.W. / FISHER, L. (1977)

Pocket Book of Statistical Tables. Marcel Dekker, New York, 166 p.

RINNE, H. (1988)

Statistische Formelsammlung. 3rd ed., Harri Deutsch, Frankfurt/Thun, 159 p.

Textbooks

We recommend the following selection of titles for supplementing and deepening the study of this textbook:

BANKS, J. (1989)

Principles of Quality Control. Wiley, New York, 634 p.

Very general, didactically well written textbook that contains many exercises (exercises without solutions).

BESTERFIELD, D.H. (1990)

Quality Control: A Practical Approach. 3rd ed., Prentice-Hall, Englewood Cliffs, New Jersey, 440 p.

Elementary, clearly arranged textbook. The choice of topics is more on the conventional side.

GRANT, E.L. / LEAVENWORTH, R.S. (1988)

Statistical Quality Control. 6th ed., McGraw-Hill, New York, 714 p.

Didactically nicely written textbook for professionals which also contains many exercises (without solutions). The choice of topics is more on the conventional side.

MESSINA, W.S. (1987)

Statistical Quality Control for Manufacturing Managers. Wiley, New York, 331 p.

Concise introductory textbook which also covers the issue of quality management.

MONTGOMERY, D.C. (1991)

Introduction to Statistical Quality Control. 2nd ed. Wiley, New York, 752 p.

A modern SQA textbook which only requires a moderate background in statistics and emphasises applications. It also contains a chapter on minimising cost in process control and on foundations of experimental design.

RYAN, T.P. (1989)

Statistical Methods for Quality Improvement. Wiley, New York, 446 p.

A modern textbook that gives a good overview of the present trends in quality assurance. The book also covers multivariate process control as well as the foundations of experimental design.

SCHILLING, E.G. (1982)

Acceptance Sampling in Quality Control. Marcel Dekker, New York, 775 p.

Applied textbook which supplements and deepens the topics in chapter 3 of this text.

UHLMANN, W. (1982)

Statistische Qualitätskontrolle. 2nd revised ed., Teubner Verlag, Stuttgart, 292 p.

A very theoretical textbook in statistical quality control which is not easy to read, but has a mathematically very exact presentation. The industrial-technical field of quality assurance is not covered.

VOGT, H. (1988)

Methoden der Statistischen Qualitätskontrolle. Teubner Verlag, Stuttgart, 295 p.

An also very theoretical text which almost has the character of lecture notes more than a textbook. Minimal cost inspection procedures are treated very elaborately.

WADSWORTH, H.M. / STEPHENS, K.S. / GODFREY, A.B. (1986)

Modern Methods for Quality Control and Improvement. Wiley, New York, 690 p.

Very applied textbook. Besides the classical topics of SQA it also covers issues of experimental design, the foundations of reliability theory and the business management aspects of quality assurance.

An annotated list of textbooks in SQA can also be found in VARDEMAN/CORNELL (1987).

7.1.2 Complete Bibliography

ABRAHAM, B. (1977)

Control Charts and Measurement Error. *Annual Technical Conference Transactions of the American Society for Quality Control* 31, 370-374.

ABRAMOWITZ, M. / STEGUN, I.A. (eds., 1972)

Handbook of Mathematical Functions. 9th ed., Dover Publications, New York.

ALBRECHT, L. / GULDE, H. / MCLEAN, A. / THOMPSON, P. (1955)

Continuous sampling at Minneapolis-Honeywell. *Industrial Quality Control* 12, 4-9.

ALT, F.B. / SMITH, N.D. (1988)

Multivariate Process Control. In: P.R. KRISHNAIAH/C.R. RAO (eds.), Handbook of Statistics, Vol. 7: *Quality Control and Reliability*, North-Holland, Amsterdam.

ALWAN, L.C. / ROBERTS, H.V (1988)

Time-Series Modeling for Statistical Process Control. *Journal of Business and Economic Statistics* 6, 87-95.

ANSCOMBE, F.J. (1949)

Tables of Sequential Inspection Schemes to Control Fraction Defective. *Journal of the Royal Statistical Society* A112, 180-206.

ANSCOMBE, F.J. / GODWIN, H.J. / PLACKETT, R.L. (1947)

Methods of Deferred Sentencing in Testing the Fraction Defective of a Continuous Output. *Supplement to the Journal of the Royal Statistical Society* 9, 198-217.

ANSI / ASQC A1 (1978)

Definitions, Symbols, Formulas and Tables for Control Charts. American Society for Quality Control, Milwaukee, USA.

ANSI / ASQC A2 (1978)

Terms, Symbols and Definitions for Acceptance Sampling. American Society for Quality Control, Milwaukee, USA.

ANSI / ASQC A3 (1978)

Quality Systems Terminology. American Society for Quality Control, Milwaukee, USA.

AROIAN, L.A. / LEVENE, H. (1950)

The Effectiveness of Quality Control Charts. *Journal of the American Statistical Association* 45, 520-529.

BAMBERG, G. / BAUR, F. (1989)
Statistik. 6th ed., Oldenbourg Verlag, München/Wien.

BAMBERG, G./COENENBERG, A.G. (1985)
Betriebswirtschaftliche Entscheidungslehre. 4th ed., Vahlen Verlag, München.

BANKS, J. (1989)
Principles of Quality Control. Wiley, New York.

BANZHOF, R.A. / BRUGGER, R.M. (1970)
Review of Standards and Specifications: MIL-STD 1235 (ORD), Single and Multilevel Continuous Sampling Prodedures and Tables for Inspection by Attributes. *Journal of Quality Technology* 2, 41-53.

BARISH, N.N. / HAUSER, N. (1963)
Economic Design for Control Decisions. *Journal of Industrial Engineering*, 125-134.

BARNARD, G.A. (1959)
Control Charts and Stochastic Processes. *Journal of the Royal Statistical Society* B21, 239-271.

BAUER, L. (1987)
Inspektionsfehler in der attributiven Qualitätskontrolle. Physica-Verlag, Heidelberg.

BAUER, P. / HACKL, P. (1978)
The Use of MOSUMs for Quality Control. *Technometrics* 20, 431-436.

BAUER, P. / HACKL, P. (1980)
An Extension of the MOSUM Technique for Quality Control. *Technometrics* 22, 1-7.

BEAINY, I. / CASE, K.E. (1981)
A Wide Variety of AOQ and ATI Performance Measures with and without Inspection Error. *Journal of Quality Technology* 13, 1-9.

BEICHELT, F. / FRANKEN, P. (1984)
Zuverlässigkeit und Instandhaltung – Mathematische Methoden. Hanser Verlag, München.

BENDELL, T. / DISNEY, J. / PRIDMORE, W.A. (eds., 1989)
Taguchi Methods: Applications in World Industry. IFS Publications and Springer Verlag, Berlin/Heidelberg.

BENNETT, C.A. (1954)
Effect of Measurement Error on Chemical Process Control. *Industrial Quality Control* 10, 17-20.

BESTERFIELD, D.H. (1990)
Quality Control: A Practical Approach. 3rd ed., Prentice-Hall, Englewood Cliffs/ New Jersey.

BLACKWELL, M.T.R. (1977)
The Effects of Short Production Runs on CSP-1. *Technometrics* 19, 249-263.

BOWKER, A.H. (1956)
Continuous Sampling Plans. *Proceedings of the Third Berkeley Symposium on Mathematical Statistics and Probability,* Vol. 5 (ed.: J. NEYMAN), Berkeley/Los Angeles, 75-85.

BOX, G.E.P. / HUNTER, W.G. / HUNTER, J.S. (1978)
Statistics for Experimenters. Wiley, New York.

BOYLES, R.A. (1991)
The Taguchi Capability Index. *Journal of Quality Technology* 23, 17-26.

BSI (1980a)
Data Analysis and Quality Control Using Cusum Techniques. Part 1: Introduction to Cusum Charting. British Standards Institution (BS 5703), London.

BSI (1980b)
Data Analysis and Quality Control Using Cusum Techniques. Part 2: Decision Rules and Statistical Tests for Cusum Charts and Tabulations. British Standards Institution (BS 5703), London.

BSI (1981)
Data Analysis and Quality Control Using Cusum Techniques. Part 3: Cusum Methods for Process/Quality Control by Measurement. British Standards Institution (BS 5703), London.

BSI (1983)
Data Analysis and Quality Control Using Cusum Techniques. Part 4: Cusums for Counted/Attribute Data. British Standards Institution (BS 5703), London.

CASE, K.E. / BENNETT, G.K. / SCHMIDT, J.W. (1973)
The Dodge CSP-1 Continuous Sampling Plan under Inspection Error. *AIIE Transactions* 5, 193-202.

CHAN, L.K. / CHENG, S.W. / SPIRING, F.A. (1988)
A New Measure of Process Capability: Cpm. *Journal of Quality Technology* 20, 162-175.

COLLANI, E. VON (1974)
Zur Wahl eines mehrstufigen Stichprobenplans. *Metrika* 21, 175-196.

COLLANI, E. VON (1984)
Optimale Wareneingangskontrolle. Teubner Verlag, Stuttgart.

COLLANI, E. VON (1989)
The Economic Design of Control Charts. Teubner Verlag, Stuttgart.

COLLANI, E. VON (1990)
Wirtschaftliche Qualitätskontrolle – Eine Übersicht über einige neuere Ergebnisse. *OR-Spektrum* 12, 1-23.

CROWDER, S.V. (1987a)
Average Run Lengths of Exponentially Weighted Moving Average Control Charts. *Journal of Quality Technology* 19, 161-164.

CROWDER, S.V. (1987b)
A Simple Method for Studying Run Length Distributions of Exponentially Weighted Moving Average Charts. *Technometrics* 19, 401-407.

CROWDER, S.V. (1989)
Design of Exponentially Weighted Moving Average Schemes. *Journal of Quality Technology* 21, 155-162.

D

DEHNAD, K. (ed., 1989)
Quality Control, Robust Design and the Taguchi Method. Wadsworth & Brooks, Pacific Grove.

DEMING, W.E. (1967)
Walter A. Shewhart. 1891-1967. *The American Statistician* 21, 35-40.

DEMING, W.E. (1982)
Quality, Productivity and Competitive Position. MIT Centre for Advanced Engineering Study, Cambridge, Massachusetts (USA).

DERMAN, C. / JOHNS, M.V. / LIEBERMAN, G.J. (1959)
Continuous Sampling Procedures without Control. *Annals of Mathematical Statistical* 30, 1175-1191.

DERMAN, C. / LITTAUER, S.B. / SOLOMON, H. (1957)

Tightened-Multi-Level Continuous Sampling Plans. *Annals of Mathematical Statistics* 28, 395-404.

DGQ (ed., 1979)

Qualitätsregelkarten. 3rd ed., Beuth Verlag, Berlin.

DGQ (ed., 1980)

Stichprobenpläne für quantitative Merkmale (Variablenstichprobenpläne). Beuth Verlag, Berlin.

DGQ (ed., 1984a)

Methoden zur Ermittlung geeigneter AQL-Werte, 3rd ed., Beuth Verlag, Berlin.

DGQ (ed., 1984b)

Qualitätszirkel. Beuth Verlag, Berlin.

DGQ (ed., 1985)

Qualitätskosten: Rahmenempfehlungen zu ihrer Definition, Erfassung, Beurteilung. 5th ed., Beuth Verlag, Berlin.

DGQ (ed., 1986a)

Stichprobenprüfung anhand qualitativer Merkmale (Verfahren und Tabellen nach DIN 40080). 9th ed., Beuth Verlag, Berlin.

DGQ (ed., 1986b)

Qualität und Haftung: Die Verantwortung des Herstellers für sein Produkt. 3rd ed., Beuth Verlag, Berlin.

DGQ (ed., 1987a)

Rechnerunterstützung in der Qualitätssicherung (CAQ). Beuth Verlag, Berlin.

DGQ (ed., 1987b)

Begriffe im Bereich Qualitätssicherung. 4th ed., Beuth Verlag, Berlin.

DGQ (ed., 1987c)

Einführung in die Zuverlässigkeitssicherung. Beuth Verlag, Berlin.

DGQ (ed., 1988)

Stichprobenprüfung für kontinuierliche Fertigung anhand qualitativer Merkmale. 2nd ed., Beuth Verlag, Berlin.

DIN 40080 .

Verfahren und Tabellen für Stichprobenprüfung anhand qualitativer Merkmale (Attributenprüfung). Beuth Verlag, Berlin.

DODGE, H.F. (1943)

A Sampling Plan for Continuous Production. *Annals of Mathematical Statistics* 14, 264-279.

DODGE, H.F. (1955a)

Chain Sampling Inspection Plan. *Industrial Quality Control* 11, 10-13.

DODGE, H.F. (1955b)

Skip-Lot Sampling Plan. *Industrial Quality Control* 11, 3-5.

DODGE, H.F. (1973)

Notes on the Evaluation of Acceptance Sampling Plans. American Society of Quality Control, Milwaukee, USA.

DODGE, H.F. / PERRY, R.L. (1971)

A System of Skip-Lot Plans for Lot by Lot Inspection. *American Society for Quality Control, Technical Conference Transactions,* 469-477.

DODGE, H.F. / ROMIG, H.G. (1959)

Sampling Inspection Tables: Single and Double Sampling. 2nd ed., Wiley, New York.

DODGE, H.F / TORREY, M.N. (1951)

Additional Continuous Sampling Inspection Plans. *Industrial Quality Control* 7, 7-12.

DOMANGUE, R. / PATCH, S.C. (1991)

Some Omnibus Exponentially Weighted Moving Average Statistical Process Monitoring Schemes. *Technometrics* 33, 299-313.

DUNCAN, A.J. (1956)

The Economic Design of $\bar{x}$-Charts Used to Maintain Current Control of a Process. *Journal of the American Statistical Association* 51, 228-242.

ELFVING, A. (1962/63)

The AOQL of Multi-Level Continuous Sampling Plans. *Zeitschrift für Wahrscheinlichkeitstheorie und verwandte Gebiete* 1, 70-81.

ENDRES, A. (1969)

The Computation of the Unrestricted AOQL when Defective Material is Removed but not Replaced. *Journal of the American Statistical Association* 64, 665-668.

EOQ (ed.,1976)

Internationales Wörterbuch der Qualitätssteuerung. Glossary of Terms used in Quality Control. 5th ed., Bern.

F

FREUND, R.A. (1985)

Definitions and Basic Quality Concepts. *Journal of Quality Technology* 17, 50-56.

G

GAN, F.F. (1991a)

EWMA Control Chart under Linear Drift. *Journal of Statistical Computing and Simulation* 38, 181-200.

GAN, F.F. (1991b)

An Optimal Design of CUSUM Quality Control Charts. *Journal of Quality Technology* 23, 279-286.

GEIGER, W. (1973)

Bedeutung des AQL-Wertes des ABC-STD 105. *Qualität und Zuverlässigkeit* 18, 289-293.

GIRSHICK, M.A. (1954)

A Sequential Inspection Plan for Quality Control. Applied Mathematics and Statistics Laboratory. Technical Report No. 16, Stanford University, Stanford/California.

GRAF,U. / HENNING, H.J. / STANGE, K. / WILRICH, P.-TH. (1987)

Formeln und Tabellen der angewandten mathematischen Statistik. 3rd ed., Springer Verlag, Berlin/Heidelberg.

GRANT, E.L. / LEAVENWORTH, R.S. (1988)

Statistical Quality Control. 6th ed., McGraw-Hill, New York.

GUENTHER, W.C. (1969)

Use of the Binomial, Hypergeometric and Poisson Tables to Obtain Sampling Plans. *Journal of Quality Technology* 1, 105-109.

GUENTHER, W.C. (1977)

Sampling Inspection in Statistical Quality Control. Griffin, London.

H

HAILEY, W.A. (1980)
Minimum Sample Size Single Sampling Plans: A Computerized Approach. *Journal of Quality Technology* 12, 230-235.

HALD, A. (1981)
Statistical Theory of Sampling Inspection by Attributes. Academic Press, London.

HAMAKER, H.C. (1950)
The Theory of Sampling Inspection Plans. *Philips Technical Review* 11, 260-270.

HAMAKER, H.C. / TAUDIN CHABOT, J.J.M. / WILLEMZE, F.G. (1950)
The Practical Application of Sampling Inspection Plans and Tables. *Philips Technical Review* 11, 362-370.

HÄRTLER, G. (1983)
Statistische Methoden für die Zuverlässigkeitsanalyse. VEB Verlag Technik, Berlin.

HARTUNG, J. (1987)
Statistik. 7th ed., Oldenbourg Verlag, München/Wien.

HILL, I.D. / HORSNELL, G. / WARNER, B.T. (1959)
Deferred Sentencing Schemes. *Applied Statistics* 8, 76-91.

HUNTER, J.S. (1986)
The Exponentially Weighted Moving Average. *Journal of Quality Technology* 18, 203-210.

IRESON, W.G. / BIEDENBENDER, R. (1958)
Multi-Level Continuous Sampling Procedures and Tables for Inspection by Attributes. *Industrial Quality Control* 15, 10-15.

J

JOHNSON, N.L. / KOTZ, S. (1970)
Continuous Univariate Distributions, Vol. 2, Houghton Mifflin, Boston.

JOHNSON, N.L. / LEONE, F.C. (1962a)
Cumulative Sum Control Charts. Mathematical Principles Applied to their Construction and Use, Part I. *Industrial Quality Control* 18, 15-21.

JOHNSON, N.L. / LEONE, F.C. (1962b)
Cumulative Sum Control Charts. Mathematical Principles Applied to their Construction and Use, Part II. *Industrial Quality Control* 19, 29-36.

KALBFLEISCH, J.D. / PRENTICE, R.L. (1980)
The Statistical Analysis of Failure Time Data. Wiley, New York.

KANAZUKA, T. (1986)
The Effect of Measurement Error on the Power of $\bar{X}$-R Charts. *Journal of Quality Technology* 18, 91-95.

KANE, V.E. (1986)
Process Capability Indices. *Journal of Quality Technology* 18, 41-52.

KEATS, J.B. / HUBELE, N.F. (1989)
Statistical Process Control in Automated Manufacturing. Marcel Dekker, New York/Basel.

KEMP, K.W. (1961)
The Average Run Length of the Cumulative Sum Chart when a V-Mask is Used. *Journal of the Royal Statistical Society* B 23, 149-153.

KHAN, R.A. (1978)
Wald's Approximation to the Average Run Length in Cusum Procedures. *ISPI* 2, 63-77.

KIRSTEIN, H. (1984)
Die sich ändernde Rolle der Qualitätssicherung in der Großserie. *Qualität und Zuverlässigkeit* 29, 2-6.

KOKOSKA, S. / NEVISON, N.C. (1989)
Statistical Tables and Formulae. Springer Verlag, New York.

KOTZ, S. / JOHNSON, N.L. (eds.; since 1982)
Encyclopedia of Statistical Sciences. 9 volumes plus Supplement, Wiley, New York.

KRISHNAIAH, P.R. / RAO, C.R. (eds., 1988)
Handbook of Statistics. Vol. 7: *Quality Control and Reliability*, North-Holland, Amsterdam.

KUNITZ, H. (1985)
Neue Aspekte der Lebensdaueranalyse. Dissertation, Hagen.

L

LAI, T.L. (1974)
Control Charts Based on Weightened Sums. *Annals of Statistics* 2, 134-147.

LIEBERMAN, G.J. (1953)
A Note on Dodge's Continuous Inspection Plan. *Annals of Mathematical Statistics* 24, 480-484.

LIEBERMAN, G.J. / RESNIKOFF, G.J. (1955)
Sampling Plans for Inspection by Variables. *Journal of the American Statistical Association* 50, 457-516.

LIEBERMAN, G.J. / SOLOMON, H. (1955)
Multi-Level Continuous Sampling Plans. *Annals of Mathematical Statistics* 24, 686-704.

LOWRY, C.A. / WOODALL, W.H. / CHAMP, C.W. / RIGDON, S.E. (1992)
A Multivariate Exponentially Weighted Moving Average Control Chart. *Technometrics* 34, 46-53.

LUCAS, J.M. / SACCUCCI, M.S. (1990)
Exponentially Weighted Moving Average Control Schemes: Properties and Enhancements. *Technometrics* 1, 1-12.

LUDWIG, R. (1974)
Bestimmung kostenoptimaler Parameter für den kontinuierlichen Stichprobenplan von Dodge. *Metrika* 21, 83-126.

MÄDER, U. (1986)
Kostenoptimale Prüfpläne für ein quantitatives Merkmal. *Metrika* 33, 143-163.

MASING, W. (ed., 1988)
Handbuch der Qualitätssicherung. 2nd ed., Hanser Verlag, München/Wien.

MASON, R.L. / GUNST, R.F. / HESS, J.L. (1989)
Statistical Design and Analysis of Experiments. Wiley, New York.

MESSINA, W.S. (1987)
Statistical Quality Control for Manufacturing Managers. Wiley, New York.

MILLER, R.G. (1981)
Survival Analysis. Wiley, New York.

MITTAG, H.-J. (1991)
Auswirkungen von Mefehlern auf die Eingriffskennlinie von Qualitätsregelkarten des SHEWHART-Typs. *Diskussionspapier No. 167 des Fachbereichs Wirtschaftswissenschaften der FernUniversität,* Hagen.

MITTAG, H.-J. / STEMANN, D. (1993a)

Auswirkungen stochastischer Meßfehler auf die Eingriffskennlinie von SHEWHART-Qualitätsregelkarten zur Überwachung der Fertigungsstreuung. *Diskussionspapier No. 203 des Fachbereichs Wirtschaftswissenschaften der FernUniversität,* Hagen.

MITTAG, H.J. (1993b, in prep.)

Qualitätsregelkarten. Hanser Verlag, München/Wien.

MIZUNO, S. (1961)

Problems of Measurement Errors in Process Control. Bulletin of the International Statistical Institute 38, 405-415.

MONTGOMERY, D.C. (1980)

The Economic Design of Control Charts: A Review and Literature Survey. *Journal of Quality Control* 12, 75-87.

MONTGOMERY, D.C. (1991)

Introduction to Statistical Quality Control. 2nd ed., Wiley, New York.

MONTGOMERY, D.C. / MASTRANGELO, C.M. (1991)

Some Statistical Process Control Methods for Autocorrelated Data. *Journal of Quality Technology* 23, 179-193.

MOOD, A.M. (1943)

On the Dependence of Sampling Inspection Plans upon Population Distributions. *Annals of Mathematical Statistics* 14, 415-425.

MOOD, A.M. / GRAYBILL, F.A. / BOES, D.C. (1983)

Introduction to the Theory of Statistics. 3rd ed., McGraw-Hill, Tokio.

MURPHY, R.B. (1959)

Stopping Rules with CSP-1 Sampling Inspection Plans in Continuous Production. *Industrial Quality Control* 16, 10-16.

NELSON, L.S. (1983)

The Deceptiveness of Moving Averages. *Journal of Quality Technology* 15, 99-100.

NELSON, W. (1982)

Applied Life Data Analysis. Wiley, New York.

NEYMAN, J. / PEARSON, E.S. (1928)

On the Use and Interpretation of Certain Test Criteria for Purposes of Statistical Inference. *Biometrica* 20A, 263-294.

O

O'Connor, P.D.T. (1985)
Practical Reliability Engineering. 2nd ed., Wiley, New York.

Odeh, R.E. / Owen, D.B. (1980)
Attribute Sampling Plans, Tables of Tests and Confidence Limits for Proportions. Marcel Dekker, New York.

Odeh, R.E. / Owen, D.B. / Birnbaum, Z.W. / Fisher, L. (1977)
Pocket Book of Statistical Tables. Marcel Dekker, New York.

Olmstead, P.S. (1956)
Walter Andrew Shewhart. *Industrial Quality Control* 12, 5 ff.

Padberg, K.H. / Wilrich, P.-Th. (1981)
Die Auswertung von Daten und ihre Abhängigkeit von der Merkmalsart. *Qualität und Zuverlässigkeit* 26, 180 ff.

Page, E.S. (1954)
Continuous Inspection Schemes. *Biometrica* 41, 100-115.

Page, E.S. (1961)
Cumulative Sum Charts. *Technometrics* 3, 1-9.

Parasuraman, A. / Zeithaml, V.A. / Berry, L.L. (1985)
A Conceptual Model of Service Quality and its Implications for Future Research. *Journal of Marketing* 49, 41-50.

Peach, P. / Littauer, S.B. (1946)
A Note on Sampling Inspection. *Annals of Mathematical Statistics* 17, 81-84.

Perry, R.L. (1970)
A System of Skip-Lot Sampling Plans for Lot Inspection, Ph. D. Dissertation, Rutgers – The State University, New Brunswick/New Jersey (USA).

Perry, R.L. (1973a)
Skip-Lot Sampling Plans. *Journal of Quality Technology* 5, 123-130.

Perry, R.L. (1973b)
Two-Level Skip-Lot Sampling Plans Operating Characteristic Properties. *Journal of Quality Technology* 5, 160-166.

Pfanzagl, J. (1954)

Das zeitliche Moment bei der Fertigungsüberwachung. *Statistische Viertelsjahresschrift* 7, 145-149.

Pignatiello, J.J. / Runger, G.C. (1980)

Comparisons of Multivariate CUSUM Charts. *Journal of Quality Technology* 22, 173-186.

R

Rendtel, U. / Lenz, H.-J. (1990)

Adaptive Bayes'sche Stichprobensysteme für die Gut-Schlecht-Prüfung. Physica-Verlag, Heidelberg.

Resnikoff, G.J. (1960)

Minimum Average Fraction Inspected for a Continuous Sampling Plan. *Journal of Industrial Engineering* 11, 208-209.

Reynolds, M.R. (1975)

Approximations to the Average Run Length in Cumulative Sum Control Charts. *Technometrics* 17, 65-71.

Rinne, H. (1979)

Lebensdauerprüfpläne. *Qualität und Zuverlässigkeit* 24, 89-93.

Rinne, H. (1981)

Cost Minimal Process Control. In: H.-J. Lenz / G.B. Wetherill / P.-Th. Wilrich (eds.), *Frontiers in Quality Control*, Vol. 1, Physica-Verlag, Würzburg/ Wien, 227-235.

Rinne, H. (1988)

Statistische Formelsammlung. 3rd ed., Harri Deutsch, Frankfurt/Thun.

Roberts, S.W. (1959)

Control Chart Tests Based on Geometric Moving Averages. *Technometrics* 1, 239-250.

Robinson, P.B. / Ho, T.Y. (1978)

Average Run Lengths of Geometric Moving Average Charts by Numerical Methods. *Technometrics* 20, 85-93.

Ross, J. (1988)

Taguchi Techniques for Quality Engineering. Quality Press, Milwaukee.

ROSS, S.M. (1970)

Applied Probability Models with Optimization Applications. Holden-Day Inc., San Francisco.

ROSSOW, E. (1971)

Zur effektiven Operationscharakteristik bei Attributenprüfung nach ABC 105. *Qualität und Zuverlässigkeit* 16, 121-124 and 152-155.

RYAN, T.P. (1989)

Statistical Methods for Quality Improvement. Wiley, New York.

SACKROWITZ, H. (1975)

A Note on Unrestricted AOQL's. *Journal of Quality Technology* 7, 77-80.

SCHAAFSMA, A.H. / WILLEMZE, F.G. (1973)

Moderne Qualitätskontrolle. 7th ed., Deutsche Philips GmbH, Hamburg.

SCHEER, A.-W. (1988)

CIM: Computer Integrated Manufacturing. Springer Verlag, Heidelberg/Wien.

SCHILLING, E.G. (1982)

Acceptance Sampling in Quality Control. Marcel Dekker, New York/Basel.

SCHILLING, E.G. / SHEESLEY, J.H. (1978)

The Performance of MIL-STD-105 D under the Switching Rules. *Journal of Quality Technology* 10, 76-83 und 104-124.

SCHINDOWSKI, E. / SCHÜTZ, O. (1965)

Statistische Qualitätskontrolle. 3rd ed., VEB Verlag Technik, Berlin.

SCHNEEWEISS, H. (1967)

Entscheidungskriterien bei Risiko. Springer Verlag, Berlin/Heidelberg.

SCHNEEWEISS, H. / MITTAG, H.-J. (1986)

Lineare Modelle mit fehlerbehafteten Daten. Physica-Verlag, Heidelberg/Wien.

SCHRÖDER, J. (1985)

Kostenoptimale Variablenprüfpläne für normalverteilte Merkmale mit zweiseitigen Toleranzgrenzen. Diskussionspapier No. 20 des Fachbereichs Wirtschafts- und Organisationswissenschaften der Bundeswehrhochschule, Hamburg.

SHEESLEY, J.H. (1977)
A Computer Programm to Evaluate Direct Continuous Sampling Plans. *Journal of Quality Technology* 7, 43-45.

SHEWHART, W.A. (1931)
Economic Control of Quality of Manufactured Product. Van Nostrand, New York.

SOUNDARARAJAN, V. (1978)
Procedures and Tables for Construction and Selection of Chain Sampling Plans (ChSP-1). *Journal of Quality Technology* 10, 56-60 and 99-103.

STANGE, K. (1964)
Die Berechnung wirtschaftlicher Pläne für die messende Prüfung. *Metrika* 8, 48-82.

STANGE, K. (1975)
Kontrollkarten für meßbare Merkmale. Springer Verlag, Berlin/Heidelberg/New York.

STANGE, K. (1977)
Bayes-Verfahren. Springer Verlag, Berlin/Heidelberg/New York.

STEPHENS, K.S. (1979)
How to Perform Continuous Sampling (CSP). The ASQC Basic Reference in Quality Control: Statistical Techniques 2, ASQC, Milwaukee, USA.

STEPHENS, K.S. (1981)
CSP-1 for Consumer Protection. *Journal of Quality Technology* 13, 249-253.

STEPHENS, K.S. / DODGE, H.F. (1974)
An Application of Markov Chains for the Evaluation of the Operating Characteristics of Chain Sampling Inspection Plans. *IAQR Journal* 1, 131-138.

STEPHENS, K.S. / DODGE, H.F. (1976a)
Comparison of Chain Sampling Plans with Single and Double Sampling Plans. *Journal of Quality Technology* 8, 24-33.

STEPHENS, K.S. / DODGE, H.F. (1976b)
Two-Stage Chain Sampling Inspection Plans with Different Sample Sizes in the Two Stages. *Journal of Quality Technology* 8, 207-224.

TAGUCHI, G. / WU, Y. (1979)
Introduction to Off-line Quality Control. Central Japan Quality Control Association, Nagoya/Japan.

UHLMANN, W. (1969)
Kostenoptimale Prüfpläne. Physica-Verlag, Würzburg/Wien.

UHLMANN, W. (1982)
Statistische Qualitätskontrolle. 2nd ed., Teubner Verlag, Stuttgart.

U.S. GOVERNMENT PRINTING OFFICE (ed., 1958)
Inspection and Quality Control Handbook (Interim) H 106, Washington DC.

U.S. GOVERNMENT PRINTING OFFICE (ed., 1959)
Inspection and Quality Control Handbook (Interim) H 107, Washington DC.

U.S. GOVERNMENT PRINTING OFFICE (ed., 1974)
Military Standard 1235A, Washington DC.

U.S. GOVERNMENT PRINTING OFFICE (ed., 1982)
Military Standard 1235B, Washington DC.

VAN DOBBEN DE BRUYN, C.S. (1968)
Cumulative Sum Tests: Theory and Practice. Griffin, London.

VARDEMAN, S. / CORNELL, J.A. (1987)
A Partial Inventory of Statistical Literature on Quality and Productivity through 1985. *Journal of Quality Technology* 19, 90-97.

VOGT, H. (1986)
Application of the Minimax-Regret Principle to Continuous Sampling. *Statistische Hefte* 27, 279-296.

VOGT, H. (1988)
Methoden der statistischen Qualitätskontrolle. Teubner Verlag, Stuttgart.

WADSWORTH, H.M. (ed., 1989)
Handbook of Statistical Methods for Engineers and Scientists. McGraw-Hill, New York.

WADSWORTH, H.M. / STEPHENS, K.S. / GODFREY, A.B. (1986)
Quality Control. Wiley, New York.

WALD, A. (1947)
Sequential Analysis. Wiley, New York.

WALD, A. / WOLFOWITZ, J. (1945)

Sampling Inspection Plans for Continuous Production which Insure a Prescribed Limit on the Outgoing Quality. *Annals of Mathematical Statistics* 16, 30-49.

WEICHSELBERGER, K. (1966)

Probleme der statistischen Qualitätskontrolle. *Der Wirtschaftsingenieur in der Praxis*, 26-40.

WEILER, H. (1952)

On the Economical Sample Size for Controlling the Mean of a Population. *Annals of Mathematical Statistics* 23, 247-254.

WETHERILL, G.B. (1969)

Sampling Inspection and Quality Control. Methuen, London.

WETHERILL, G.B. (1977)

Sampling Inspection and Quality Control. 2nd ed., Chapman and Hall, London.

WHITE, L.S. (1965)

Markovian Decision Models for the Evaluation of a Large Class of Continuous Sampling Inspection Plans. *Annals of Mathematical Statistics* 36, 1408-1420.

WOODWARD, R.H. / GOLDSMITH, P.L. (1964)

Cumulative Sum Techniques. Oliver and Boyd (ICI-Monograph No. 3), London/Edinburgh.

WORTHAM, A.W. / HEINRICH, G.F. (1972)

Control Charts Using Exponential Smoothing Techniques. In: Annual Conference Transactions ASQC, Milwaukee/Wiscounsin (USA), 451-458.

WORTHAM, A.W. / HEINRICH, G.F. (1973)

A Computer Program for Plotting Exponentially Smoothed Average Control Charts. *Journal of Quality Technology* 5, 84-90.

WORTHAM, A.W. / MOGG, J.W. (1970)

A Technical Note on Average Outgoing Quality. *Journal of Quality Technology* 2, 30-31.

7.2 Abbreviations, Symbols and Index Registers

7.2.1 Abbreviations and Mathematical Symbols

Due to lack of space we only list those abbreviations, symbols and notations that are frequently used in chapters 1 – 6.

Abbreviations in quality assurance

AFI	average fraction inspected
AOQ	average outgoing quality
AOQL	average outgoing quality limit
AQL	acceptable quality level
ARL	average run length
ASN	average sample number
ATI	average total inspection
CA ...	computer aided ...
CIM	computer integrated manufacturing
CSP	continuous sampling plan
CUSUM	cumulative sum
EWMA	exponentially weighted moving average
IQL	indifferent quality level
MIL-STD	Military Standard
OC function	operating characteristic function
CC	control chart
QA	quality assurance
RQL	rejectable quality level
SQA	statistical quality assurance
SPC	statistical process control

Logical symbols and equivalence relations

$a = b$; $a \neq b$	a and b are equal respectively not equal
$a := b$, $b =: a$	a and b are defined to be equal
$a \approx b$	a and b are approximately equal
$a > b$, $b < a$	a is larger than b
$a \geq b$, $b \leq a$	a is larger or equal to b
$a \in M$; $a \notin M$	a is an element of M; a is not an element of M
$A \Rightarrow B$, $B \Leftarrow A$	A implies B
$A \Leftrightarrow B$	A and B are equivalent

Notation in analysis and algebra

$f(.);\ f^{-1}(.)$	general notation for function and inverse function
$\lim_{x \to a} f(x)$	limit of the function $f(x)$ as $x \to a$
$\Delta x/\Delta y;\ dx/dy$	quotient of differences and differentials
$\sum_{i=1}^{n} a_i$	sum of the terms $a_1, a_2, \ldots, a_n$
n!	product of the natural numbers $1 \cdot 2 \cdot 3 \ldots \cdot n$ (read: n-factorial)
$\binom{n}{k} = \frac{n!}{k!(n-k)!}$	binomial coefficient
$\mathbf{X} = (X_1, \ldots, X_n)$	vector with the components $X_1, \ldots, X_n$

Symbols and notations in statistics

$X \sim \ldots$	the random variable X is distributed according to ...
$X \sim bi(P;n)$	X has a binomial distribution with parameteres P and n
$X \sim po(\lambda)$	X has a Poisson dsitribution with parameter λ
$X \sim no(\mu;\sigma^2)$	X has a normal distribution with parameters μ and σ^2
$X \sim \chi^2(\nu)$	X has a central χ^2 distribution with ν degrees of freedom
$Pr(A)$	occurrence probability of the event A
$f(x)$	mass or density function of X
$F(x) = P(X \leq x)$	distribution function of X
$\mu = E(X)$	expectation of X
$\sigma^2 = V(X),\quad \sigma = \sqrt{\sigma^2}$	variance and standard deviation of X
z_ω	percentile of the standard normal distribution
$\chi^2_{\nu,\omega}$	percentile of a $\chi^2(\nu)$-distributed random variable
$F_{\nu_1;\nu_2;\omega}$	percentile of a $F(\nu_1;\nu_2)$-distributed random variable
$t_{\nu;\omega}$	percentile of a $t(\nu)$-distributed random variable
$P_\omega;\ \lambda_\omega$	OC percentiles

Special functions

e^x, $\exp x$	exponential function
$\ln x$	natural logarithm
$\Gamma(x)$	gamma function
$[x]$	Gaussian bracket function
$\|x\|$	absolute value function
$bi(.\|P;n);\ Bi(.\|P;n)$	mass and distribution function of the binomial distribution
$po(.\|\lambda);\ Po(.\|\lambda)$	mass and distribution function of the Poisson disstribution
$no(.\|\mu;\sigma^2);\ No(.\|\mu;\sigma^2)$	density and distribution function of the normal distribution
$\phi(.);\ \Phi(.)$	density and distribution function of the standard normal distribution
$\Phi^{-1}(.)$	percentile function of the standard normal distribution

$L(.)$; $G(.)$	OC function; power function
$L(P\|N;n;c)$	hypergeometric OC function
$L(P\|n;c)$	binomial OC function
$L^*(P\|n;c)$	Poisson OC function

Greek alphabet

A	α	Alpha	I	ι	Iota	P	ρ	Rho
B	β	Beta	K	κ	Kappa	Σ	σ	Sigma
Γ	γ	Gamma	Λ	λ	Lambda	T	τ	Tau
Δ	δ	Delta	M	μ	Mu	Υ	υ	Upsilon
E	ϵ	Epsilon	N	ν	Nu	Φ	ϕ	Phi
Z	ζ	Zeta	Ξ	ξ	Xi	X	χ	Chi
H	η	Eta	O	o	Omicron	Ψ	ψ	Psi
Θ	θ	Theta	Π	π	Pi	Ω	ω	Omega

7.2.2 Author Index

7.2.3 Subject Index

In order to ease the use of this text as a handbook we have designed the index very carefully. For example the term "average outgoing quality" can be found under "outgoing quality" and also under "average outgoing quality". A remark like "see also (s.a.) under AOQ function" means that one should look under "AOQ function" if one desires more detailed information as for example "AOQ functions in single sampling for attributes".

D

Q

For Product Safety Concerns and Information please contact our EU representative GPSR@taylorandfrancis.com Taylor & Francis Verlag GmbH, Kaufingerstraße 24, 80331 München, Germany

Printed and bound by CPI Group (UK) Ltd, Croydon, CR0 4YY
08/05/2025
01864431-0001